STRATEGIC ASIA 2002–03

STRATEGIC ASIA 2002–03

ASIAN AFTERSHOCKS

Edited by
Richard J. Ellings and Aaron L. Friedberg
with Michael Wills

With contributions from
Thomas J. Christensen, Stephen P. Cohen, Nicholas N. Eberstadt,
Robert W. Hefner, Eric Heginbotham, Martha Brill Olcott,
Richard J. Samuels, Sheldon W. Simon, and William C. Wohlforth

 The National Bureau of Asian Research
Seattle, Washington

THE NATIONAL BUREAU OF ASIAN RESEARCH

Published in the United States of America by

The National Bureau of Asian Research
4518 University Way NE, Suite 300
Seattle, Washington 98105
http://www.nbr.org

Preparation of this publication was supported in part by the U.S. Department of Energy under Grant No. DE-FG03-02SF22499. The views expressed in these papers are those of the authors, and do not necessarily reflect the views of the Department of Energy.

The National Bureau of Asian Research (NBR) makes no warranties or representations regarding the accuracy of any map in this volume. Depicted boundaries are meant as guidelines only and do not represent the views of NBR, the authors and editors, or NBR's funders.

Publisher's Cataloging-in-Publication Data
Strategic Asia, 2002–03: Asian Aftershocks / edited by Richard J. Ellings and Aaron L. Friedberg with Michael Wills

ISBN 0-9713938-2-6
Publisher's Cataloging-in-Publication Data available.

Design and publishing services by The National Bureau of Asian Research
Cover design by Todd Duren at Firefly Graphics

Printed in Canada

CONTENTS

PREFACE

Strategic Asia 2002–03: Asian Aftershocks is the second in a series of annual volumes from NBR's Strategic Asia Program. These integrated sets of studies aim to provide the most authoritative information and analysis possible on strategic issues affecting U.S. interests in Asia. A groundbreaking companion website makes this book and accompanying executive summary available online and contains an unprecedented wealth of essential data, ranging from demographic, trade, and financial statistics to measures of nations' economic performance and military capabilities. Consequently, there is now a single place to go for strategic analysis or data on the Asia Pacific region.

The National Bureau of Asian Research developed this program to fulfill three goals: 1) to provide the best possible understanding of the current strategic environment in Asia; 2) to look forward five years, and in some cases beyond, to contemplate the region's future; and 3) to establish a record of data and assessment that will assist those interested in understanding changes taking place in the Asian strategic landscape. In essence, the aim of the Strategic Asia Program is to help policymakers, strategists, and scholars comprehend this critical region.

The first volume, *Strategic Asia 2001–02: Power and Purpose*, provided a baseline assessment of the balance of power in Strategic Asia that covered economic performance, military capabilities, technological sophistication, political stability, and social cohesion. In addition to these ingredients of power, it assessed the politics, perceptions, and strategies of the most powerful Asian countries—China, Japan, Korea, Russia, and India. *Power and Purpose* analyzed emerging patterns of interaction among major powers, within and across sub-regions in Strategic Asia, and, in cases when it made sense, beyond the region to other parts of the world. Each of the volume's studies looked forward to discover where underlying trajectories, possible discontinuities, and grand strategies of the major Asian powers might lead them and the region as a whole.

Starting from this baseline assessment, the studies that make up *Strategic Asia 2002–03: Asian Aftershocks* examine how the September 11 terrorist attacks on the United States and their aftermath have changed the distribution of power in the region, caused key states to alter their perceptions and policies, and set in motion new patterns of strategic interaction. The volume explains the recent and ongoing evolution of U.S. policy toward the region, and the impact of new U.S. policy on regional actors' calculations. It also addresses the characteristics of Islam in Asia and the extent to which, and under what conditions, radical Islam is likely to be a significant political force and threat in Strategic Asia's future.

Advisors and Research Directors

The Strategic Asia Program is advised by an executive committee made up of many of the nation's leading specialists in Asian affairs and international relations. Nine members of the committee direct parts of the program and have served this year as authors or editors (shown in italics below), while others have advised the program and reviewed the studies. Former Chairman of the Joint Chiefs of Staff, General (Ret.) John Shalikashvili, serves as the program's Senior Advisor.

- *Thomas Christensen, Massachusetts Institute of Technology (Research Director for China)*
- *Stephen Cohen, Brookings Institution (Research Director for South Asia)*
- *Nicholas Eberstadt, American Enterprise Institute (Research Director for Korea)*
- *Richard Ellings, The National Bureau of Asian Research (Program Director)*
- Herbert Ellison, University of Washington
- Francine Frankel, University of Pennsylvania
- *Aaron Friedberg, Princeton University (Research Director)*
- James Fuller, Pacific Northwest National Laboratory
- (Michael Green, on leave while on the National Security Council)
- General (Ret.) Mark Hamilton, University of Alaska

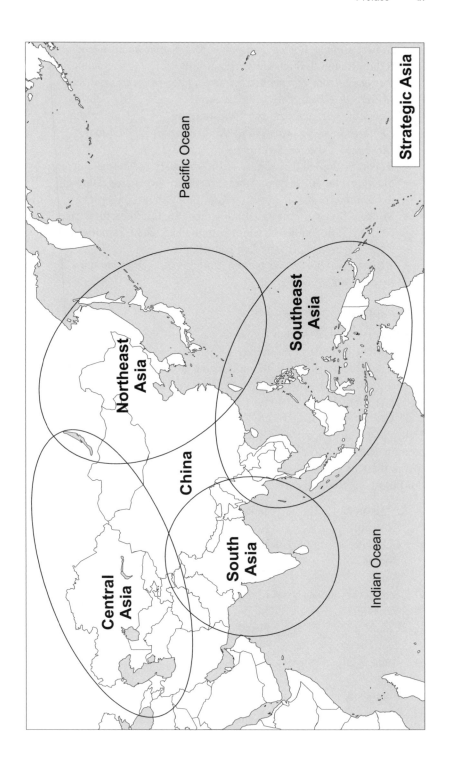

Strategic Asia

- *Robert Hefner, Boston University (Islam and Asian Security)*
- Rajan Menon, Lehigh University
- *Martha Olcott, Carnegie Endowment for International Peace (Research Director for Central Asia)*
- Kenneth Pyle, University of Washington
- *Richard Samuels, Massachusetts Institute of Technology (Research Director for Japan)*
- Robert Scalapino, University of California-Berkeley
- *Sheldon Simon, Arizona State University (Research Director for Southeast Asia)*
- Michael Swaine, Carnegie Endowment for International Peace
- (Ashley Tellis, on leave while with the U.S. State Department)
- Enders Wimbush, Booz Allen Hamilton
- *William Wohlforth, Dartmouth College (Research Director for Russia)*

Geographical Coverage

The Strategic Asia Program considers as "Asia" the entire eastern half of the Eurasian landmass and the arc of offshore islands in the western Pacific. This vast expanse can be pictured as an area centered on China and consisting of four distinct sub-regions arrayed clockwise around it: Northeast Asia (including the Russian Far East, the Korean Peninsula, and Japan), Central Asia (Kazakhstan, Kyrgyzstan, Tajikistan, Turkmenistan, and Uzbekistan), Southeast Asia (including both its mainland and maritime components), and South Asia (including India and Pakistan, and bordered to the west by Afghanistan). Strategic Asia is thus defined as including the following countries and territories:

Afghanistan	Japan	Philippines
Australia	Kazakhstan	Russia
Bangladesh	Kyrgyzstan	Singapore
Bhutan	Laos	South Korea
Brunei	Macao	Sri Lanka
Burma (Myanmar)	Malaysia	Taiwan
Cambodia	Mongolia	Tajikistan
China	Nepal	Thailand
East Timor	New Zealand	Turkmenistan
Hong Kong	North Korea	Uzbekistan
India	Pakistan	Vietnam
Indonesia	Papua New Guinea	

The program also collects data on the United States and Canada.

Organization of the Report

Strategic Asia 2002–03: Asian Aftershocks begins with a brief introduction that summarizes the main themes in this year's report and draws attention to key findings. Following this are Aaron Friedberg's assessment of U.S. strategy toward Asia in light of the war against terrorism, and seven area or regional studies: China, Japan, Korea, Russia, Central Asia, South Asia, and Southeast Asia. *Asian Aftershocks* finishes with a special study on Islam and Asian security, and provides a statistical appendix of tables and figures based on the data available on the Strategic Asia website.

Executive Summary

In addition to their presentation in this book, key findings from *Strategic Asia 2002–03: Asian Aftershocks* are available in a separate executive summary. This concise document, organized along the same lines as the full report and including relevant tables and figures, captures key developments in the region and highlights their implications for policymakers. The executive summary is available on the Strategic Asia website and in printed form upon request from The National Bureau of Asian Research.

Strategic Asia Website and Database—http://strategicasia.nbr.org

The Strategic Asia website is designed for the non-specialist and specialist alike. The site enables users to download all Strategic Asia publications. It features a fully interactive—and freely accessible—database that allows users to download or dynamically link to data sets. This database, which is being developed and updated constantly, contains over 300 "indicators" for each country or territory in the region for each year since 1990. The indicators are divided into 12 broad thematic areas:

National economy
Foreign trade
Foreign investment and assistance
Government spending
Population
Energy and environment
Information infrastructure
Conventional military forces
Nuclear, biological, and chemical forces
Force projection
Politics
International relations

The Strategic Asia database leverages extensible markup language (XML) and was built in .NET, Microsoft's next generation XML platform. XML is the emerging *lingua franca* for sharing data among diverse applications on diverse platforms. Leading applications such as Microsoft Office XP and Microsoft SQL Server support XML, as does the latest version of the statistical analysis tool SPSS.

Presenting data in an XML format allows users—individuals, organizations, businesses, and other websites—to dynamically link to all or part of the Strategic Asia Program's data set. For example, a user can embed a data set from the Strategic Asia website in an Excel spreadsheet on his/her local computer and thus always have access to the most current data. The user also has access to metadata—information about data, such as the original source and the date that particular piece of information was last updated. As XML becomes a universal standard for dynamic data integration, NBR will be able to seamlessly incorporate data from primary sources and channel it quickly to end users.

In addition to offering complete, dynamic access to the program's data sets, the Strategic Asia website provides selected charts and graphs on topics addressed in the annual reports. A future goal of the program is to integrate sophisticated data visualization tools and analysis tools that will enable users to explore and analyze data in a dynamic, graphically enhanced, and user-friendly environment.

Attribution

Readers of Strategic Asia reports and visitors to the Strategic Asia website may use data, charts, graphs, and quotes from these sources without requesting permission from The National Bureau of Asian Research on the condition that they cite NBR *and* the appropriate primary source in any published work. No report, chapter, separate study, or extensive text (or any other substantial part of the Strategic Asia Program's products) may be reproduced without the written permission of The National Bureau of Asian Research. To request permission please write to the Managing Editor at The National Bureau of Asian Research, 4518 University Way NE, Suite 300, Seattle, WA 98105, or at nbr@nbr.org.

Acknowledgements

After receiving a detailed briefing and a "virtual tour" of a prototype of the Strategic Asia database, General John Shalikashvili turned to NBR's IT gurus Karolos Karnikis and Erick Thompson to express his deeply felt admiration. He then said, and we paraphrase, "If any data contained in the website is flawed this entire effort has been worthless." This was one of those moments in the development of the program that will remain etched in our minds—and we knew that he was right. General Shalikashvili, who serves as Strategic Asia's congenial Senior Advisor and most articulate champion, has urged us all along to sustain the highest and clearest standards possible in the presentation as well as the substance of our products. If we are succeeding at all it is in no small measure due to his wise and experienced stewardship.

We have also benefited enormously from the advice of distinguished members of the executive committee (listed above), Don Emmerson, and Jack Gill, among others, many of whom wrote studies or critiqued early drafts, and to all of whom we owe a debt of gratitude for their counsel.

A prestigious group of sponsors has made the Strategic Asia Program possible. Supporters this year include the Henry M. Jackson Foundation, Lynde and Harry Bradley Foundation, U.S. Department of Energy, AOL/Time-Warner, Bank of America, Boeing Company, and Microsoft Corporation. NBR Vice President Brigitte Allen, whose initiative and persistence are reminders of her Dutch commercial heritage, coordinated this successful fundraising effort.

The Strategic Asia team owes deep appreciation to these funders and to many people who have assisted at various stages. At the Department of Energy we wish to thank Linton Brooks, Stephen Black, Scott Davis, and Trisha Dedik; from the Pacific Northwest National Laboratory Jim Fuller and Mark Leek; and from the U.S. Pacific Command Dennis Blair, Thomas Case, Cos Spofford, William Hicks, Michael Finnegan, William Comley, Leif Rosenberger, Mark Harstad, and Tricia Kiyoshi. Richard Cronin has helped at several junctures, and he and his colleague from the Congressional Research Service, Mark Manyin, participated in a planning meeting this past winter. Prosser Gifford and his staff at the Library of Congress graciously hosted that meeting.

As explained in last year's report, Program Codirector Michael Wills manages the effort day-to-day, wearing more caps at one time than the most traveled utility infielder ever donned in a career. In addition to assisting in recruiting the authors, organizing the planning meeting, scheduling the entire year of the program, and coordinating felicitously with everyone, Michael serves as managing editor. He is responsible for the production of the book and executive summary, and critiques all, and copyedits many, of the chapters. Erica Johnson copyedited the remaining chapters again this year, and worked with Todd Duren to develop and refine the cover design. The authors (and editors) are deeply indebted to both of them. We would also like to extend our sincere thanks to Carrie Jones and Neil Beck who edited this year's executive summary.

NBR Vice President of Information Management and Technology Karolos Karnikis oversees the Strategic Asia database, a Herculean effort that has been possible only in the past year and a half due to much creative thinking, hard work, and a technology breakthrough. Karolos teamed with Senior Programmer Erick Thompson to design the database, and Erick built and continues to develop it.

As people managers extraordinaire, Michael and Karolos inspired the talented young scholars who do the unheralded work that goes into the program. This year these remarkable graduate students and post-graduates have included senior interns Jocelyn Roberts and Loren Runyon, who helped develop the database over the past 18 months, plus the following: Jonathan Acuff, Julie Bennion, Jonathan Carver, Michael Hatada, Yoonie Kim, and Emily Nicklett. All have been involved in one or more aspects of research assistance, copyediting, proofreading, layout, and indexing.

Finally, we wish to thank those just slightly behind the scenes in administrative and other supportive roles, and who assist in some cases on a daily basis. They include NBR's Katie Yocom especially (endlessly helping with travel arrangements and book sales), and Richard Alfieri, Monic Hsiung, Nikita Kovrigin, Rian Jensen, and Tracy Timmons-Gray. We hope that it is clear how little credit the program and research directors can claim for any value the Strategic Asia Program may possess.

Richard J. Ellings
Aaron L. Friedberg
August 2002

STRATEGIC ASIA

OVERVIEW

INTRODUCTION

Richard J. Ellings and
Aaron L. Friedberg

The September 11 terrorist attacks against the World Trade Center and the Pentagon constituted a strategic event of seismic proportions. The most devastating terrorist attacks the world had ever seen (and the most damaging assault on the American homeland since British soldiers torched the White House and Capitol Building in August 1814) reverberated through the presidency and Congress as well as the public consciousness. The September 11 attacks caused a sense of vulnerability in the world's sole superpower not felt since the Cuban missile crisis, and the analogy most recalled in the media and by politicians was the Japanese attack on Pearl Harbor on December 7, 1941. Commentators and analysts soon began to speak of a new era, one in which everything seemed to have changed—diplomatic priorities, the economy, and threat assessments (including the possibility of attacks by weapons of mass destruction)[1]— as the Bush administration declared war on international terrorism.

Consequently, the "tectonic plates" of Strategic Asia began to shift.[2] The United States and Russia redefined their bilateral relationship, with

Richard Ellings is President of The National Bureau of Asian Research and Director of the Strategic Asia Program. Aaron Friedberg is Professor of Politics and International Affairs and Director of the Center for International Studies Program at Princeton University, and Research Director of the Strategic Asia Program. The authors thank Jonathon Acuff, Michael Hatada, Yoonie Kim, and Loren Runyon for their assistance in preparing this introduction.

important repercussions for integrating Russia into Europe, development of a U.S. national missile defense (NMD) system, and close collaboration in the war on terrorism. To a far greater extent than ever before, the United States became deeply engaged across South Asia—working with both India and Pakistan simultaneously—and within several months Washington opened a second front against Islamist terrorist groups in Southeast Asia. Conspicuously, the events of September 11 jolted, but did not cause any significant strategic movement among, the major powers located in Northeast Asia. Japan sought to help in the war on terrorism within the narrow confines of its political constraints, while China did little more than tolerate America's new presence on its western border.

Among the most visible effects of the war on terrorism was a significant increase in direct U.S. military engagement in Asia. In the weeks following the attacks, Washington pulled together a loose international coalition of states willing to support its efforts to destroy the Al Qaeda network in Afghanistan. By the time the primary military campaign concluded in December 2001, with the collapse of the Taliban regime, U.S. military personnel were stationed in Afghanistan and Pakistan, and in Kyrgyzstan and Uzbekistan in Central Asia—the first ever U.S. military presence in that region. These forces were supported by two aircraft carrier battle groups in the Arabian Sea.[3] By January 2002, U.S. troops had also been deployed to the Philippines—10 years after the closure of U.S. military bases there—to assist Manila in its campaign against the Abu Sayyaf group.

Developments in the months following the September 11 attacks reaffirmed tenets expressed in these pages one year ago: America has enormous and growing stakes in Asia and Asia increasingly functions as a zone of strategic interaction, with countries across the region acutely sensitive to each other's power and perceived intentions. How this zone evolves is of great importance to the United States. The increasing concentration and yet differing rates of growth of national economic and military capabilities in Asia, the region's demographic dominance, and its long-standing history of rivalries and grievances all suggest that the most significant challenges to peace and security in the coming century are likely to arise in Strategic Asia.[4] Moreover, the cultural divide exploited by Al Qaeda terrorists extends from the Middle East through South Asia and across Southeast Asia to the largest Muslim country of all, Indonesia.

America's Stakes in Asia

As the world's preponderant power, the United States alone is capable of intervening throughout Strategic Asia, and Washington has a strong vested interest in doing so when its security is threatened. America had major strategic and commercial interests in Asia before September 11, none of which has diminished since the war on terrorism was launched.

From the Spanish-American War through the Cold War, the United States has understood that its security depends upon preventing any hostile foreign power or coalition from dominating the Asia-Pacific. America's alliances in the region and its military presence, directed from the Pacific Command in Hawaii and, now also, from the Central Command in Florida, have provided a stable security structure for the region in recent decades. Of the Pacific Command's 300,000 personnel, almost one-third is forward-deployed in permanent bases in Japan and South Korea.[5] Mutual defense treaties with Tokyo and Seoul (plus unofficial agreements with Taipei) underpin the U.S. security presence in Northeast Asia. In Southeast Asia, the United States has security treaties with Australia, the Philippines, and Thailand, and now has the just-noted deployments in the Philippines, as well as agreements to use facilities there and in Thailand and Singapore. For Operation Enduring Freedom, 8,000 U.S. personnel were deployed in Afghanistan (augmented by 8,000 personnel from coalition allies); in August 2002 more than 7,000 remained, along with smaller numbers of troops stationed in Pakistan, Kyrgyzstan, and Uzbekistan. In sum, the U.S. security interests and military presence in Strategic Asia were significant before September 11 and have broadened significantly since.

Asia is, of course, also increasingly important to the U.S. economy, and U.S. growth is a major driver of many Asian economies. Asia is the most important trading region for the United States, having exceeded even North America, but its economic importance is not limited to trade alone. During the extraordinary growth of the mid- to late-1990s, U.S. equity investors shifted their focus increasingly to Asian markets and, over time, the stock of American investment in the region expanded dramatically.

The 1980s and 1990s witnessed a dramatic shift in the U.S. trade relationship with Asia and Europe. Although some economists now place the two continents on parity with each other in terms of their importance for the United States, Asia lags somewhat behind Europe as a market for U.S. goods and services. U.S. exports to Asia rose from about $135 billion in 1990 to $238 billion in 2000, while exports to Western Europe increased from almost $228 billion to $397 billion during the same period.[6] Asia's importance as a provider of inexpensive, high-quality products to U.S. consumers, however, is far greater than Europe's. In 2000, the U.S. trade deficit with Western Europe as a whole was about $64 billion. The U.S deficit with Japan *alone* was $82 billion, and total value of U.S. imports from Asia was nearly *three times* that of imports from Western Europe.[7] Total trade volume between the United States and Asia more than doubled in the last decade, rising from almost $196 billion in 1990 to more than $431 billion in 2000, and these figures do not take into account the mammoth imports of oil that are shipped from the Persian Gulf through the Strait of Malacca across the Pacific.

In addition, U.S. investors increasingly focused on Asia. From 1987 to 1997, U.S. investors doubled the proportion of equity they placed in foreign stocks, particularly in Asian markets, although the flow of private bank and portfolio investment to Asia slowed significantly as a result of the 1997–98 financial crisis. Even as rates of equity investment declined, however, Asia enjoyed a surge in foreign direct investment (FDI) from the United States and elsewhere in the 1990s. From 1993 onward there was an extraordinary increase in FDI in developing and transitional economies, and four Asian states are among the top ten developing countries receiving the largest share of FDI. From 1993 to 1997, China alone averaged more than 30 percent of all FDI in developing economies.[8] The International Monetary Fund recorded $29 billion in FDI in Asia in 1990, which ballooned to $154 billion in 2000, outstripping FDI in the European Union.[9]

Major Challenges Ahead

Underlying trends in economic performance, political development, and military strength across Asia in the past decade document clearly that of the four major Asian powers, China and India—the two most populous countries in the world—are rising, while Russia and Japan are both in relative decline. Consequently, there is a process of realignment underway across Strategic Asia.[10] Last year's *Strategic Asia* report noted several trends influencing the perceptions and policies of the regional powers, including the modernization of their armed forces and their acquisition of more powerful weapons systems (including WMD), the rise of militant Muslim groups, increasing demand for energy, and the dependence of more Asian states on oil imports from the Persian Gulf.[11] The September 11 terrorist attacks and subsequent events shook all the major powers (and the weaker ones as well), bringing new challenges to light and reaffirming existing concerns.

Foremost among these, of course, is the threat of international terrorism made manifest in its most acute and immediate form by the existence of the Al Qaeda network. Although Al Qaeda's infrastructure in Afghanistan was largely destroyed during the U.S.-led campaign, intelligence agencies have been tracking the movement of Al Qaeda operatives into neighboring countries in South and Central Asia, as well as further afield to places such as Indonesia. The United States is keen to ensure that Al Qaeda not reestablish a base of operations elsewhere, and U.S. deployments indicate that Southeast Asia is a major concern in this regard. The influence of radical Muslim organizations and militant groups is also a concern for many regimes in Asia—from China and the Philippines, where such groups are engaged in separatist campaigns, to Indonesia and Pakistan, where large Muslim populations, in some cases restive as a result of social dislocation, political conditions, and economic hardship, are seen as a potential breeding grounds for terrorists. Although the extent of the connections between these militant Muslim groups and Al Qaeda is not clear, there is no doubt that dealing with the threat they pose will demand substantial commitments by intelligence agencies, police forces, and in some cases militaries in the years ahead.

A second, and related, challenge is that Al Qaeda and other terrorist groups seek WMD for use against targets in the United States or against U.S. targets in Asia. The anthrax scare shortly after September 11 exemplified the havoc even small-scale attacks can bring. As a result of both direct state actions and lax controls, Strategic Asia is a potential source of proliferation of materials or expertise that could be employed in the production of WMD. The region is also one of the most likely trans-shipment points for the movement of WMD or related components. The threat of potential acquisition and use of WMD by terrorist groups is not the only, or even necessarily primary, WMD problem in the region, of course. Many states in Strategic Asia are involved in disputes where there is a substantial risk of conflict and where at least one party (if not both) has WMD capabilities (see "fourth concern" below).

A third concern is ensuring that economic growth continues in the United States and across the region. Japan has undergone more than a decade of weak economic performance. China, despite accession to the World Trade Organization in December 2001, faces major challenges to sustain its economic growth. The ASEAN states, despite some successes, are still struggling to recover from the 1997–98 financial crisis and implement the structural reforms required for long-term growth. All of these challenges have been compounded by the possibility that, in part because of the continuing threat of terrorism, the costs of waging war against it, and the looming prospect of further conflict in the Middle East, the U.S. economy may not revert quickly to its previous upward trajectory.[12]

A fourth concern is that none of the potential flashpoints for major conflict in Asia—in Northeast Asia between China and Taiwan and between North and South Korea, and in South Asia between India and Pakistan—have seen a reduction in tension since September 11. In the latter case, to the contrary, the South Asian neighbors engaged in a dangerous military buildup and game of nuclear brinkmanship in the first half of 2002, prompting a frantic expenditure of diplomatic energies in an effort to avoid war. While temporarily reduced, the threat has not disappeared and could emerge again in an even more menacing form. Northeast Asia also has seen tensions and potentially destabilizing incidents—the sinking of a suspected North Korean naval vessel by the Japanese coast guard in Chinese waters in December 2001 and the deaths of four South Korean sailors in a clash with two North Korean patrol craft in July 2002. As Thomas Christensen argues in this volume, although an examination of cross-Strait relations reveals increasing economic interdependence between China and Taiwan, the concurrent buildup of military forces suggests that in the medium term Beijing may consider using coercion or even force against the island.

September 11—Asian Aftershocks

Almost one year after the September 11 attacks on the United States, what has been the impact on Strategic Asia? To what extent have governments aligned themselves with Washington and cooperated in the U.S. war on terrorism? What have been the motivations for these responses? How have perceptions and strategies changed in the past year? What new challenges are likely to emerge in the years ahead?

Beginning to address these questions, Aaron Friedberg in chapter two assesses U.S. foreign policy toward Asia and Russia and considers how September 11 has altered Washington's view of the strategic importance of Asia. He finds that, while they have not fundamentally altered the course of U.S. policy in Asia, recent events have led to a broadening of the scope of U.S. engagement across the region, and an overall strengthening in U.S. relations with most of its strategic partners, friends, and allies. At the same time, however, recent events have also served to intensify tensions and suspicions between the United States and those countries that it regards as actual or potential strategic competitors.

The United States has sought, in most cases successfully, to strengthen existing relationships with partners such as Australia, India, Japan, and Taiwan (relations with South Korea, by contrast, have become somewhat strained). Closer relations have also developed between the United States and Russia, culminating in a successful summit in May 2002. At the other extreme, the Bush administration signaled its mistrust of North Korea, linking it in a January 2002 speech with Iran and Iraq in an "axis of evil." The most complex relationship, of course, has been that with Beijing, in which Washington has continued a policy of engagement while at the same time increasing its efforts to contain and counterbalance the growth of Chinese power through the maintenance and expansion of the U.S. military presence in Asia.

The shock of September 11 and the subsequent U.S. war on terrorism have constituted a major blow to China's security strategies. In chapter three, Thomas Christensen argues that while Beijing's initial response was cautious and reserved, some analysts saw potential for increased cooperation between China and the United States, although Beijing was surprised to find its purported partner Moscow quickly siding with Washington. One year after September 11, China finds itself in a much more challenging strategic environment—with increased U.S. influence and military presence in Central and South Asia, a more active Japanese military, and closer Russian alignment with the West.

Coping with this new environment will fall to a new generation of Chinese leaders, emerging in the transfer of political power and authority from Jiang Zemin to Hu Jintao. To ensure a smooth transition, Beijing will likely seek to maintain peaceful international relations in the short term. But if economic reforms and possible political liberalization lead to social unrest, Hu will need to establish his regime's nationalist identity—probably by emphasizing the Taiwan issue. Christensen argues that in early 2001 Beijing was highly confident cross-Strait economic trends and political directions in Taiwan were tending toward eventual reunification. This optimism was deflated after Taiwan's December 2001 legislative elections, in which pro-independence parties fared unexpectedly well. Many analysts in Beijing now perceive Taipei to be pursuing "creeping independence."

Failure to reunite Taiwan with the mainland would seriously undermine the Chinese Communist Party's legitimacy and could lead the regime to consider taking coercive or violent actions. At the same time, a conflict over Taiwan would risk alienating China from its three largest trade and investment partners: Taiwan itself, the United States, and Japan. China's economy, despite impressive growth, faces daunting challenges in the form of rising unemployment, significant non-performing loans, difficult economic reforms, and international competition, and could ill afford such a shock.

In chapter four, Eric Heginbotham and Richard Samuels examine Japan's comprehensive security doctrine, which places equal weight on economic and military concerns, and assess the extent to which Japan's security policy changed after September 11. They argue that the U.S.-Japan alliance still allows Tokyo to adopt a "mercantile realist" approach to foreign policy, deferring most responsibilities for national security to the United States while concentrating on economic and technological development. This has resulted in Japan attempting a "dual hedge" approach in which it seeks to balance its security obligations and the pursuit of its economic interests.

Heginbotham and Samuels point out that the dual hedge approach to some extent has undermined Japan's international credibility, most recently in the months following the terrorist attacks. Washington looked favorably upon Japan for its deployment of naval ships in support of the U.S.-led campaign in Afghanistan, although the value of this contribution was actually quite limited. At the same time, Koizumi Junichiro's proposal that Japan host a peace conference for post-Taliban Afghanistan backfired, likely due to his seeking a more prominent, non-military role in the counter-terrorism coalition. Britain, France, and Germany bristled at the suggestion, noting that their military contributions to the campaign were far greater. The post-conflict conference for a political settlement was eventually held in Bonn; a subsequent conference on economic reconstruction took place in Tokyo. Heginbotham and Samuels conclude by arguing that the notion that Tokyo substantially changed its security policy in response to September 11 is unwarranted. They note that, even as it depends upon the United States for its security, Japan continues to exhibit a tendency of relying upon other nations, including those that the United States has classified as security threats, to ensure its economic interests.

In chapter five, Nicholas Eberstadt notes that the security situation on the Korean Peninsula has been marked by relative calm for several years, and that this did not immediately change in the aftermath of the September 11 attacks. Nevertheless, he argues, this calm is inherently fragile and beneath the surface major forces are gathering that could potentially destabilize the security balance on the peninsula.

Foremost among these is the continued woeful economic performance of North Korea that, unless reversed by aggressive expansion of the new policies adopted in the summer of 2002, will lead inexorably to systemic failure, with potentially catastrophic consequences. Alongside this is Pyongyang's WMD development program that continues to undermine deterrence in the peninsula. Finally, Eberstadt argues that there are a number of problems in the U.S. security alliance with South Korea, which, if left unattended, could undermine public support for the arrangement. Addressing the last of these concerns, Eberstadt suggests it is incumbent on both U.S. and South Korean policymakers to elucidate to their respective electorates the rationale for the alliance—the common security objectives of the partnership and the continued threats it was designed to overcome.

Achieving this goal has been complicated by the growing distance between Washington and Seoul over the relationship, stemming partly from differing attitudes about the efficacy of the "sunshine policy" and partly from the changed security environment in Northeast Asia. Since September 11, however, there has been a notable improvement in U.S. relations with all of the major powers surrounding the Korean Peninsula—Japan, Russia, and, to a lesser extent, China—combined with an apparent increase in tension in relations with the two Koreas. This resulted from Seoul's tepid response and limited contribution to the war on terrorism, and the inclusion of Pyongyang, already designated a state sponsor of terrorism by the State Department, in George W. Bush's "axis of evil." In sum, September 11 has strained U.S. relations with South Korea, although the depth and duration of the damage done remain to be seen.

One of the most significant shifts in the post-September 11 strategic environment has been in U.S.-Russia relations. In chapter six, William Wohlforth describes this shift and the new direction in which Vladimir Putin has chosen to steer Russia. Wohlforth argues that Russia's declining power was increasingly insufficient to defend all of its national interests and great power prerogatives, still less to counter U.S. primacy. In attempting to achieve these goals, Moscow found itself stretched beyond its means and thus repeatedly humiliated; other countries, meanwhile, were happy to let Russia pay the economic and political consequences of challenging the United States. Putin recognized that Russia's decline in power had to be followed by a decline in status, and Moscow was forced to choose which of its national interests were to be pursued and which could be discarded.

Despite opposition from domestic conservatives, prior to September 11 Putin's government was already moving toward adopting a new, pragmatic course of imperial retrenchment, focused on modernization and economic recovery, and firmly aligning Russia with Europe, where much-needed trade and investment prospects lie. The attacks on the United States offered Putin the opportunity to accelerate this course to place Russia firmly with the West—supportive of the U.S. war in Afghanistan, acquiescent to NATO enlargement, and resigned to the U.S. withdrawal from the Anti-Ballistic Missile Treaty. In essence, Russia under Putin has moved to accept its diminished status as a junior partner to the West, a European power with territories in Asia. This new realism, Wohlforth suggests, means that, in the short term, Russia will not partner with any Asian powers to confront the United States, nor will it seek confrontation with any Asian state. Nevertheless, a weakened Russia, but one empowered with a clear purpose that is within its means to accomplish, is likely to be much more effective in the coming years than it was in the last decade. Wohlforth concludes by noting that Putin's political and economic reforms, if successful and sustained, will pave the way for Russia's return to the rank of a great power later this century.

Although Russia's retrenchment and more realistic policies might lead to improved ties with the United States as well as Europe, it has left a security void in Central Asia. In chapter seven, Martha Olcott describes the continuing security threats to stability in this region, which, although much improved following the destruction of the Taliban regime and Al Qaeda infrastructure in neighboring Afghanistan, is still far from secure.

Olcott argues that the five Central Asian states essentially "got it wrong" during their first decade of independence, failing to implement economic and structural reforms, suppressing political opposition, and refusing to build institutions that could encourage long-term political and economic development. Shortcomings in Russian and western policies toward the region were also at least partly to blame. One of the effects of these failures has been to drive political opponents in each state to extremes, providing fertile breeding ground for radical groups. Although weakened following the U.S. campaign in Afghanistan, two of these groups, the Islamic Movement of Uzbekistan and the Hizb-ut-Tahrir, continue to pose a threat to regional stability. Many of Central Asia's governments also face challenges from pro-democracy movements.

Olcott posits that the groundbreaking U.S. military presence in Central Asia provides a second chance for Central Asia to "get it right." With increased inflows of development and military assistance, the region's leaders may soon have some of the resources required to begin addressing the challenges they face, although whether they have the political will to make these changes remains an open question. Nevertheless, she argues, the Bush administration's reluctance to engage in nation-building and the possibility that security concerns will override other considerations may require Washington to make difficult choices in Central Asia. For example, the choice between backing repressive regimes or supporting extremist opposition groups is likely to "reinforce the U.S. desire to make its presence in the region as temporary as possible."

In chapter eight, Stephen Cohen examines the two crises gripping South Asia, the conflict in Afghanistan and the escalation of tensions between India and Pakistan. The United States has a played a key role in both since September 11. In Afghanistan, the U.S.-led coalition quickly routed the Taliban, and a new interim government was tasked with rebuilding the country. Afghanistan's stability is still threatened by rival warlords and pockets of Taliban resistance, and the possibility of spillover into other parts of Central and South Asia continues to be a concern. While leading the charge in Afghanistan, the United States simultaneously sought to reduce Indo-Pakistani tensions. Nevertheless, these escalated in the first half of 2002, as a series of terrorist attacks, including one against the Indian parliament, brought the two countries to the brink of war. While the standoff has been at least temporarily abated, Cohen notes that, given the strategies and perceptions of both countries' armed forces, even a limited conflict now has the potential to escalate into devastating nuclear exchange.

Despite near war between India and Pakistan, U.S. relations with both New Delhi and Islamabad have improved in the past year. Prior to September 11, India had been seen as a rising power, with increasingly close relations with the United States, while Pakistan was widely viewed as a failed state, suffering from economic lassitude, political instability, and sanctions imposed after its 1998 nuclear weapons tests. September 11 marked a dramatic reversal in Pakistan's fortunes. Central to altered U.S. priorities in the region, Pervez Musharraf quickly pledged support for the U.S. campaign in Afghanistan (although in so doing he turned his back on powerful Islamist groups operating in Pakistan, creating a potential threat to his political survival), receiving much-needed economic assistance in return. New Delhi was surprised at the sudden improvement in U.S.-Pakistani relations, but benefited from closer U.S. involvement with Islamabad as Washington came to share India's concerns about terrorism in the region.

Cohen concludes by noting that even if the current crisis over Kashmir is contained, the deep causes of the conflict will continue and, absent outside intervention and a lasting political solution, will likely lead to renewed violence.

After South Asia, Southeast Asia has seen the most obvious increase in U.S. engagement since September 11. In chapter nine, Sheldon Simon focuses on how the core ASEAN countries' responses to the war on terrorism have affected regional security cooperation. While Indonesia, Malaysia, the Philippines, Singapore, and Thailand all condemned the attacks, their reactions to the prospect of U.S. action against terrorist cells in Southeast Asia varied. Hampered by mutual suspicions, trans-border disputes, and the ASEAN norm of noninterference (which effectively prevents serious discussion of the most pressing regional issues), counter-terrorist cooperation in Southeast Asia has had mixed results.

In Indonesia, Megawati Sukarnoputri's initial response was cautious. Weakened by persistent economic and political instability, and with hundreds of far-flung islands and thousands of miles of porous borders, Indonesia is an ideal hiding place for terrorist groups. Jakarta has been at best moderately cooperative in the global counter-terrorism effort, however, as it has been concerned that overt support for the United States might arouse unrest among its large Muslim population. Thailand was similarly cautious in its initial response to the U.S. war on terrorism, although Bangkok eventually did assist the United States by permitting the use of its military bases. Although Malaysia warned the United States against targeting Islam in general, Mahathir Mohamad successfully used the focus on Muslim extremism to discredit his domestic political opposition; Malaysia and Singapore, moreover, have been cooperative in the counter-terrorism network. No Southeast Asian country, however, has been as enthusiastic in support for the war on terrorism as the Philippines. Despite significant political and popular opposition, Gloria Macapagal-Arroyo seized the opportunity to win much-needed U.S. economic aid and military support against Muslim rebels operating in the south of her country.

Although at this point none of the Muslim extremist groups operating in Southeast Asia appears to be operationally linked to the Al Qaeda network, there do seem to be some financial linkages. Poor socio-economic conditions, moreover, have prompted many desperate youths to join radical Islamic schools. Simon concludes by noting that terrorism will continue to flourish in Southeast Asia until the region's underlying social, political, and economic problems are resolved.

In chapter ten, Robert Hefner provides a comparative assessment of Muslim politics across Asia. Beginning with an overview of the social and political history of Islam in the region and a discussion of the varied political impact of the Islamic resurgence of the 1980s and 1990s, Hefner assesses the ways in which developments since September 11 have impacted state and society in Muslim Asia. He focuses especially on the transnational linkages within and among Central, South, and Southeast Asia. In his survey, he highlights one major effect—the rise of the radical fringe at the expense of the moderate center in Muslim politics in Asia.

Following the collapse of the Taliban in Afghanistan, Hefner asserts that the likelihood of a similar radical Muslim regime achieving power elsewhere in Muslim Asia is remote. He does, however, identify several areas where crises and grievances have the potential to cause unrest, such as:

- Uzbekistan in Central Asia, where the authoritarian regime of Islam Karimov has boosted support for the Islamic Movement of Uzbekistan;
- Xinjiang in northwestern China, where Chinese migration has altered the demographic balance and led to deep resentment;
- Mindanao in the southern Philippines, where the political and economic marginalization of the indigenous Muslim population has led to several armed opposition groups;
- Indonesia, where the post-Suharto transition has led to bitter ethnic and sectarian conflict and seen disaffected members of the former political elite sponsor radical Muslim groups; and
- Kashmir, where long-running ethnic and sectarian tensions converge with the rival claims of nuclear powers India and Pakistan to create a situation of truly volatile proportions.

Hefner concludes that Muslim extremists have been able to take advantage of globalizing trends, thereby introducing a destabilizing element into Muslim politics and society in Asia. Although the threat is real, responding to it requires dsitnguishing between the small numbers of radicals and ordinary Muslims seeking redress on perceived social and economic injustices. He argues that effective long-term policy will seek to contain extremism, while acknowledging and effectively addressing the Muslim majority's aspirations for social and economic advancement.

Endnotes

[1] See, for example, William J. Perry, "Preparing for the Next Attack," *Foreign Affairs,* vol. 80, no. 6 (November–December 2001), pp. 31–45.

[2] Strategic Asia is defined as the entire eastern half of the Eurasian landmass and the arc of offshore islands in the western Pacific. See the preface to this volume and Aaron L. Friedberg, "Introduction," in Richard J. Ellings and Aaron L. Friedberg, eds., *Strategic Asia 2001–02: Power and Purpose,* Seattle, Wash: The National Bureau of Asian Research, 2001.

[3] For a detailed assessment of the Afghanistan campaign, see Michael E. O'Hanlon, "A Flawed Masterpiece," *Foreign Affairs,* vol. 81, no. 3 (May–June 2002), pp. 47–63, and especially pp. 49–55.

[4] Friedberg, "Introduction," in Ellings and Friedberg, eds., *Strategic Asia 2001–02,* pp. 4–7.

[5] U.S. Pacific Command <www.pacom.mil/about/pacom.htm>.

[6] IMF data (*Direction of Trade Statistics*) from NBR's Strategic Asia database, <http://strategicasia.nbr.org>; and U.S. Bureau of Economic Analysis, "Table 10: U.S. International Transactions—Western Europe, Exports of Goods and Services," <www.bea.doc.gov/bea/international/bp_web/simple.cfm>.

[7] U.S. Bureau of Economic Analysis, *U.S. International Transactions,* April 2002, p. 58, <www.usbea.gov>.

[8] Howard J. Schatz and Anthony J. Venables, "The Geography of International Investment," *World Bank Policy Research Paper,* no. 2338 (May 2000), p. 4.

[9] IMF data (*International Financial Statistics*) from NBR's Strategic Asia database, <http://strategicasia.nbr.org>, and Eurostat, "International Trade," *Eurostat Yearbook 2002,* p. 3, <http://europa.eu.int/comm/eurostat/public/datashop/print-product/en?catalogue=eurostat&product=yearbook02-en&file=free.htm>. Future investment in Asia at this level is less certain, however. The World Bank and Deloitte & Touche recently found that of the top 23 countries slated for future investment by multinational corporations, only four are in Asia. World Bank/Multilateral Investment Guarantee Agency and Deloitte & Touche, *Foreign Direct Investment Survey,* January 2002, <www.worldbank.org>.

[10] Friedberg, "Introduction," in Ellings and Friedberg, eds., *Strategic Asia 2001–02,* pp. 16–23.

[11] Friedberg, "Introduction," Ellings and Friedberg, eds., *Strategic Asia 2001–02,* pp. 6–7.

[12] IMF economists estimated the direct economic cost of the attacks (i.e., structural property and equipment losses plus insurance losses) at more than $21 billion, with substantial indirect costs including higher operating costs, maintenance of larger inventories, higher risk premiums, and less confidence in globalization. International Monetary Fund, *World Economic Outlook: The Global Economy after September 11,* December 2001, pp. 16–18, <www.imf.org/external/pubs/ft/weo/2001/03/index.htm>. Subsequent revelations of fraudulent corporate accounting are hindering U.S. economic recovery. For an assessment of this, see David Wessel, "Troubled Stock Market Threatens to Take Economy Down with It," *Wall Street Journal,* July 25, 2002; for an alternate view, see Alan S. Blinder, "Stocks Are Only Part of the Story," *The New York Times,* July 21, 2002.

UNITED STATES

Aaron L. Friedberg

The history of U.S. involvement in Asia has been punctuated by a sequence of memorable dates and dramatic developments: Admiral George Dewey's destruction of the Spanish Fleet in Manila Bay on May 1, 1898, the Japanese attack on Pearl Harbor on December 7, 1941, and the North Korean invasion of the South on June 25, 1950. Each of these events was followed by a major, largely unplanned, expansion in the tangible manifestations of U.S. power in Asia and, somewhat more gradually and subtly, by an eventual broadening in the conception of American interests and responsibilities in the region.

The recent terror attacks on the United States were the work of shadowy groups intent on killing large numbers of American civilians rather than conventional acts of war by traditional nation-states. Whether this will lessen their ultimate impact on the conduct of U.S. foreign policy or make it more dramatic remains to be seen. Nevertheless, while it is too early to say with certainty, it may well be the case that September 11, 2001, will turn out to have been yet another turning point in America's career as an Asian power. Although they took place on the East Coast of the United States, the events of that day had an impact that quickly reverberated back

Aaron Friedberg is Professor of Politics and International Affairs and Director of the Center of International Studies at Princeton University. The author wishes to thank Richard Ellings, Mark Hamilton, and Michael Wills for their comments and suggestions, and Jocelyn Roberts, Loren Runyon, and Neil Beck for their invaluable research assistance.

to Afghanistan, and then radiated outward across all of Strategic Asia. Today the United States finds itself engaged militarily, diplomatically, and economically in Afghanistan, Central Asia, and South Asia in ways that would have seemed fanciful if they had been described only one year before. The crisis has contributed to what appears to be a transformation in the U.S. relationship with Russia and, to varying degrees, it has had a significant impact on America's dealings with China, Japan, India, Pakistan, North and South Korea, Taiwan, the Philippines, Indonesia, and Malaysia, among others. Nor is this a story whose ending is yet certain. The aftereffects of the attacks on New York and Washington are still being felt, and there may be further shocks to come.

The purpose of this chapter to is to offer a preliminary assessment of the implications of September 11 for America's position in, and strategy toward, Asia. It will begin with a review of the changes in U.S. Asia policy introduced by the George W. Bush administration during its first nine months in office. After a brief description of the U.S. response to the terrorist attacks as it has unfolded to date, it will then examine the wider implications. These can be summarized under three headings: September 11 has caused the United States to *broaden* its presence in and engagement with key parts of Strategic Asia; it has tended to *strengthen* America's relationships with its primary strategic partners, both formal allies and quasi-allied democracies; and the crisis has served to *intensify* the competitive aspects of U.S. relations with those countries that it has long regarded with suspicion, especially North Korea and China. Each of these features of the recent changes in the U.S. posture in Asia carries with it both risks and opportunities, which will be discussed in the closing section.

Early Innovations of the Bush Administration

One of the distinctive characteristics of American democracy is the extent to which it encourages members of both major parties to emphasize their differences to gain office but then, once they are in power, tends to force them to converge and compromise in order to govern. The changes that occur when control of the executive branch shifts from one party to the other are therefore usually less dramatic than the debates that precede them or the rhetorical flourishes with which they are described. This is especially so in the areas of foreign and defense policy, where, at least in recent decades, the elites of both parties have generally shared certain basic beliefs about the value of American alliances, the virtues of free trade, the importance of continuing U.S. engagement in the world, and so on. Real change in these areas is possible, but it is likely to come in comparatively small increments.

Figure 2.1. Importance of Asia to U.S. Trade

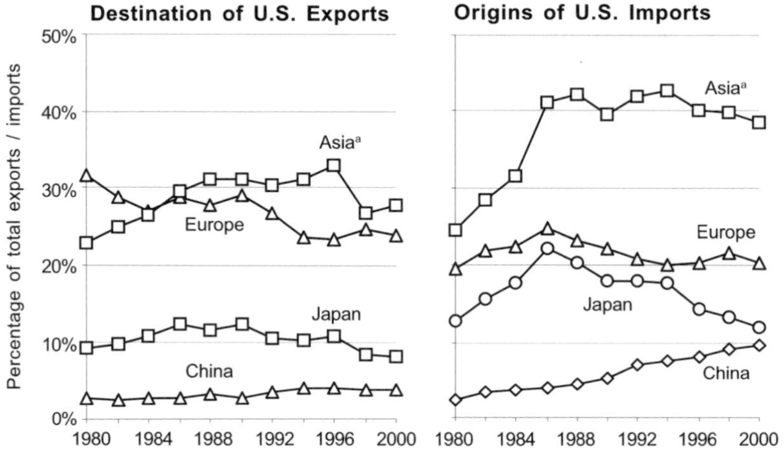

Source: International Monetary Fund, *Direction of Trade Statistics Yearbook*, Washington, DC: International Monetary Fund, various editions. Note: a) Asia including China and Japan.

Thus it was, in January 2001, that the Republican Party, led by George W. Bush, and returning to the White House for the first time in eight years, began to shift the direction of U.S. policy toward Asia. The changes that the new administration introduced during its first months in office were more marginal than monumental, but they were nevertheless important. As will be discussed more fully below, the administration (or, more precisely, parts of the Department of Defense) began to discuss the possibility that a greater fraction of U.S. defense and intelligence efforts should be devoted to Asia, as compared to other parts of the world. These suggestions did not amount to a proposal for revolutionizing American strategy by (for example) withdrawing from Europe in order to focus on Asia. But they did point toward possible long-term shifts in, among other things, the distribution, role, and design of the U.S. armed forces.

Within Asia itself, the new administration also began a process of strategic recalibration. Like their predecessors, the Bush team recognized the desirability of maintaining access to Asian markets for American companies and investors, and they continued to express hope that trade and economic development would promote the spread of democracy to places where it had not yet taken hold. Like their predecessors, they also believed in the necessity of maintaining an Asian balance of power favorable to U.S. interests. Between these objectives, however, the Bush team tended to place greater emphasis on the latter, and it initiated a series of steps designed to bolster U.S. military capabilities in Asia and to strengthen alliances and other security ties with an assortment of regional democracies.

Here again, the changes proposed were not radical. The new administration did not seek to isolate and contain China, nor did it wish to provoke a war with North Korea. But it was willing to take a tougher stance toward both countries than the Clinton administration and to emphasize the ideological divide that continued to separate these countries from the United States and its democratic friends and allies.

A Turn Toward Asia?

Because America's power is so overwhelming and its influence so ubiquitous, no U.S. president can afford to say openly that he regards certain regions of the world as irrelevant, and he must even be careful in suggesting that he thinks some areas may be more important than others. To do this would be to risk, at best, accusations of neglect and, at worst, the possibility that by pulling back, or appearing to pull back, the United States might lose influence or encourage aggression.

Although in their public statements President Bush and his top advisors observed the usual protocol in such matters, there were intriguing indications during their first months in office that they might be inclined to devote comparatively greater attention and, in the long run, more resources to Asia. In February 2001, within weeks of being sworn into office, Secretary of Defense Donald Rumsfeld ordered a wide-ranging review of existing policies. The initial step in this process was a study of the United States' overall strategic posture prepared by the Pentagon's Office of Net Assessment and its director Andrew Marshall. This study was not made public, but according to press reports later in the spring it "cast the Pacific as the most important region for military planners." Because of the rapid economic growth and military modernization of many Asian countries the region seemed to be becoming a major new center of power and potential conflict. In order to maintain its preponderant position in the vast Asia-Pacific region the United States might have to increase the range and striking power of its forces, while at the same time reducing its reliance on increasingly vulnerable regional bases.[1]

A subsequent unclassified study sponsored by the Office of Net Assessment laid out the possible organizational implications of shifting away from a "highly Euro-centric" approach and devoting more attention to Asia. According to the report's authors: "Long-term trends—political, economic, and military—indicate that the primary security challenges the United States will face in the first decades of the 21st century will come from Asia." Meeting these challenges would require shifts in command structures, career paths, and patterns of language training in order to focus more attention and build more expertise on Asian security issues. Above all it would demand that the Pentagon's top leaders develop a conscious and careful strategy to "guide the necessary shift in regional focus."[2]

Albeit in somewhat more muted language, the Defense Department's major high-level strategic planning document, the so-called Quadrennial Defense Review (QDR), also hinted at the possible need for a long-term change in emphasis toward Asia and away from Europe. Noting that both Europe and the Western Hemisphere were "largely at peace," the report emphasized the possibility of threats arising in the Middle East and, above all, Asia. Apparently echoing the reasoning of the Marshall review, the QDR pointed out that Asia "in particular... is gradually emerging as a region susceptible to large-scale military competition." Without attempting to spell out all of the possible implications, it noted further that the region was characterized by vast distances, comparatively few U.S. bases, and "a volatile mix of rising and declining regional powers."[3]

The QDR was largely complete before the September 11 terrorist attacks and it was published several weeks after they occurred. Its suggestion of the need for a gradual turn toward Asia therefore went largely unnoticed. With top defense officials focused on fighting a war in Afghanistan, and on preparing for possible future acts of terrorism, discussion of long-term geopolitical trends appears also to have been curtailed, at least for the time being. But the possibility of a major shift in the U.S. strategic posture has now been introduced and, if the authors of the Marshall review and the QDR are right in their reading of the underlying trends, it seems certain at some point to reemerge.

Strategy: Friends and Foes

Whatever their beliefs about the relative importance of Asia, in their first few months in office Bush administration officials began to lay down the outlines of a distinct and reasonably coherent approach to the region. This approach had three central themes: a clear emphasis on maintaining a favorable Asian balance of power, a strong preference for cooperating with other democracies, and a decided inclination toward wariness in dealing with non-democratic regimes. The new administration did not seek conflict with these states, but it did aim to strengthen the position from which it approached them, to constrain and counterbalance their efforts to exert regional influence, and to be better prepared to deal with any confrontations that might eventually arise.

As has already been suggested, this approach involved a recalibration or rebalancing of the various elements of U.S. policy toward Asia. During the 1990s American scholars and politicians had debated the comparative virtues of the alternative strategies of "engagement" versus "containment" for dealing with Asia and, in particular, for coping with China. In reality, however, from at least the middle of the decade, the United States had been pursuing a hybrid strategy that combined elements of both. On the one hand, official policy during the Clinton years encouraged economic transactions, cultural and scientific links, and political dialogue at all levels, in the hopes that these connections would promote understanding, a convergence of interests and, in the long run, domestic reforms. At the same time, however, the U.S. government remained committed to maintaining its alliances and forward-based forces in Asia and it began to focus, with increasing intensity and seriousness, on the possibility that it might have to engage in military competitions, and perhaps even armed conflicts, with regional powers. The Bush administration did not propose to abandon this mix, but it did set out to change its composition, strengthening the containment elements of the formula without abandoning engagement. In so doing, it also took steps to draw a clearer ideological distinction between the United States and the other Asian democracies, on the one hand, and those countries still governed by non-democratic regimes (or regimes of dubious democratic legitimacy), on the other.

Japan, Australia and South Korea—Key Allies

The Bush team came into office convinced both that Japan was the key to the U.S. position in Asia and that the bilateral relationship between Washington and Tokyo was badly in need of repair. As the wealthiest and most powerful democracy in the region, Japan was "the keystone of... U.S. involvement in Asia" and the U.S.-Japan alliance was "central to America's global security strategy."[4] During the early Clinton years the relationship had been strained by disputes over market access and other trade issues. Efforts in the mid-1990s to increase defense and intelligence cooperation had been beneficial but had not gone far enough. In his second term in office President Clinton had sometimes seemed to regard China as more important to U.S. interests in Asia than Japan, at one point in 1998 traveling to Beijing without stopping in either Tokyo or Seoul. Meanwhile, since the early 1990s, the Japanese economy had lapsed into a prolonged recession that was eating into the nation's confidence and perhaps reducing its willingness and ability in the long-term to play an active role in ensuring the stability and security of Asia.

In deliberate contrast to the Clinton administration, the Bush team adopted a more hands-off approach regarding Japan's economic difficulties and its prospects for reform. On the security side of the ledger, however, the U.S. government made clear that it looked favorably on the efforts of Prime Minister Koizumi Junichiro to seek a loosening of constitutional restrictions on the deployment and use of the Japanese Self-Defense Forces (SDF).[5] Washington also pressed ahead with plans to pursue cooperative development of a theater ballistic missile defense system that could be used to counter weapons launched from North Korea, and potentially from China as well.[6]

While it clearly saw Japan as the centerpiece of the U.S. position in Asia, the new administration was also intent on strengthening relations with other key democratic allies. Despite differences with Seoul over how best to deal with North Korea, President Bush and his advisors were anxious to preserve and, if possible, to reinforce the existing U.S.-ROK alliance. Close ties to Seoul were seen as necessary to deter aggression by the Democratic People's Republic of Korea (DPRK), but also, in the longer run, to reduce the chance of any unfavorable shift in Korea's orientation. Especially if the two halves of the country were eventually rejoined it would be important to keep a unified Korea firmly in the American camp, and to discourage it from turning against Japan or leaning toward China. The best way to limit such dangers was to maintain a strong, healthy alliance.

The long and warm U.S. relationship with Australia also received considerable early attention. Prior to the 2000 elections, Bush advisor Richard Armitage had bluntly reminded listeners in Canberra that the U.S.-Australian alliance committed both sides to send their "sons and daughters" to fight and die if either party came under attack.[7] Armitage's comments caused a stir because they came in the context of a discussion of a possible confrontation across the Taiwan Strait between the United States and China. This flap quickly blew over, however, and following Bush's election (and the appointment of Armitage as Deputy Secretary of State), defense planners went back to the business of looking for ways to expand the already considerable military ties between the two countries. Among the options reportedly under consideration was a plan to use the north Australian port city of Darwin as "a staging post for future U.S. rapid deployment force operation in a 'flexible logistic network' for Asia."[8]

In addition to bolstering the separate, bilateral elements in the traditional "hub and spokes" relationship between the United States and its formal Asian allies, prior to September 11 the Bush administration also indicated an interest in trying to build some kind of new multilateral mechanism for security cooperation. Referring to the United States, Australia, and Japan, Armitage said at one point "we are all democracies, we're all concerned with the fate of Asia and it seems to me a perfectly reasonable proposition that we ought to get together and talk."[9] Some observers suggested that South Korea too might be included in an informal security grouping of Asian democracies.[10]

Taiwan and India—Quasi-allies

Moving beyond the sphere of existing, formal alliances, the Bush team also set about to strengthen U.S. strategic ties to other Asian democracies. Of these the most important were Taiwan and India.

The president and his advisors were convinced from the outset that their predecessors' approach to Taiwan had been flawed both morally and strategically. Especially since the political reforms of the early and mid-1990s, the island had blossomed into what future national security advisor Condoleezza Rice described during the campaign as "a model of democratic and market-oriented development."[11] Even more than in the past, when it had been governed by an authoritarian one-party regime, Taiwan seemed worthy of U.S. support. Although the new administration made clear that it intended to continue to adhere to a "one-China" policy and would not back any formal moves toward Taiwanese independence, it also made no secret about where its sympathies lay.

Ideological and moral considerations aside, the Bush team was convinced that a strong show of U.S. support for Taiwan was a strategic necessity. With China's capabilities growing rapidly, there was a danger that the military balance between Taiwan and the mainland would eventually begin to shift sharply in favor of the latter. Such a change, or even the *perception* that it had occurred, might encourage Beijing to believe it could someday use force to achieve its goal of unification. In order to prevent such a dangerous move, the United States would need to do more to bolster Taiwan's own military capabilities. Washington would also need to take steps to signal clearly its intention to intervene if the People's Republic of China (PRC) initiated the use of force. Bush and his advisors were inclined to believe that, while it had taken steps in the right direction, the Clinton administration had been too wary in approving arms sales to Taipei, too eager to reassure Beijing, and overly concerned about the need to discourage advocates of Taiwanese independence. The real problem was how best to bolster deterrence across the Taiwan Strait. The answer, in the view of the Bush team, was through a heightened display of firmness and resolve.

As in its dealings with Taiwan, the new administration did not launch off in entirely new directions as regards India, but it did accelerate trends that had been set in motion in the latter part of the 1990s. In March 2000, President Clinton had paid a visit to New Delhi and had begun to repair some of the damage to bilateral relations that had been caused by the 1998 Indian nuclear tests and the subsequent imposition of sanctions by the United States. President Bush came into office with the clear intention of going further and transforming the U.S.-Indian relationship into a major element in the overall American position in Asia.[12]

Here, as in so much else, the motivations were both ideological and geopolitical. In the words of the new U.S. Ambassador to India, Robert Blackwill, the two nations were "vibrant democracies" with a "shared heritage of pluralist federalism, born in a struggle against colonialism," and with a "profound common interest in seeing democracy flourish worldwide." India and America were thus natural friends, and while no one in Washington or New Delhi was willing to use the term, they were at least potential strategic partners.[13] While taking pains to emphasize that such actions were not "directed against any third party," U.S. officials nevertheless declared their desire to explore various forms of cooperation on strategic matters and to build a "new bilateral military relationship."[14] Such a connection would be useful in combating terrorism and ensuring flows of energy from the Persian Gulf. It would also make it easier for both parties to coordinate their efforts to counterbalance China's growing power.

Russia—Neither Friend nor Foe

India was an established democracy with an array of interests that seemed increasingly to coincide with those of the United States. Russia, on the other hand, was a polity of dubious ideological coloration and uncertain future intentions. The new administration therefore approached it with considerable wariness and suspicion. During the campaign, Bush and his surrogates had criticized the Democrats for linking the United States too closely to the fate of ailing Russian President Boris Yeltsin and to his faltering efforts at political and economic reform. They also expressed skepticism about whether Yeltsin's successor, Vladimir Putin, was genuinely committed to democracy, and they voiced disapproval of his vigorous prosecution of the ongoing war in Chechnya. In the past, they suggested, the United States had been too solicitous of Russia's bruised national ego and not sufficiently realistic or hard-nosed about the implications of its greatly weakened power position. As Colin Powell put it during his confirmation hearings, Russia could "gain enormous benefits from its relationship with us and with the West in general" but only if it did "what it needs to do," in other words to "get on with reform." This was something that could "only be done by the Russian people."[15]

The new administration was not disinterested in the outcome of the process of Russia's domestic reform, but it did not see the United States as having a major role to play in shaping how it would unfold. Henceforth, U.S. policy would concentrate on attempting to influence Russia's military posture and its external behavior. If President Bush were to proceed toward his declared goals of deploying national missile defenses and reducing nuclear arsenals, the best way forward appeared to be through some kind of negotiated agreements with Moscow.[16] Meanwhile, Russia's continuing arms sales to China and Iran, among other countries, and its lax controls over transfers of nuclear materials and technology, posed continuing threats to U.S. interests in Asia and the Middle East. Russia's links to China, in particular, were a source of special concern because they seemed to be contributing to a more rapid shift in the cross-Strait military balance than would otherwise have been possible. Bush and his advisors do not appear to have had a clear initial strategy for dealing with these aspects of Russian behavior, but they seem generally to have believed that they should adopt a firm stance in their dealings with Moscow.

China—"Strategic Competitor"

In contrast to Russia, China had not even begun to attempt the painful transition from communism to liberal democracy. And, where Russia's power was waning, the PRC's seemed to be fast increasing. These two factors together put China in an entirely separate category and helped to make it the central object of the administration's concern in Asia.

During the campaign, George W. Bush had labeled China "a competitor, not a strategic partner," but also made clear from the outset of his presidency that there were limits to how hard a line he intended take in dealing with the PRC. As compared to some in his party who argued that the United States should use its considerable economic leverage to weaken Beijing or to try to force changes in its policies, Bush made clear that he favored the fullest possible integration of China into the global economy. Bush supported China's entry into the World Trade Organization (WTO), arguing that freer trade would lead to more economic freedom. "Economic freedom," he reasoned, "creates habits of liberty. And habits of liberty create expectations of democracy.... Trade freely with China, and time is on our side."[17]

Here, despite their criticisms of the Clinton administration as soft and wooly-headed on China, Bush and his advisors were clearly embracing a central tenet of the policy of engagement. Like its predecessors the new administration also intended to combine engagement with aspects of what can only be described as a policy of containment: maintaining U.S. alliances and forward-based forces in Asia and providing political and material support to Taiwan. The primary differences, albeit significant ones, would be matters of degree. Under Bush, the United States would seek to broaden and deepen its alliance and quasi-alliance relationships in Asia, step up its support for Taiwan, and move forward with efforts to strengthen its capacity to project military power into the western Pacific.

All the various elements in this new blend of policies were clearly visible in the administration's handling of the so-called EP-3 incident in April

2001. While they could certainly have done so, the Bush team decided not to use the downing of the U.S. plane and the subsequent detention of its crew to mobilize public support for a much tougher approach to China.[18] The president permitted conciliatory language to be used to obtain release of the plane's crew and, once the immediate crisis had passed, did not move to impose economic sanctions in retaliation for Chinese behavior or alter his stance on the PRC's entry into the WTO.[19] Moreover, in the aftermath of the crisis, the president and his advisors backed away from describing China as a "strategic competitor" taking the position, as Colin Powell put it, that no single "label… term… word… or cliché" could capture the complexities of the U.S.-China relationship.[20]

At the same time, however, the spy plane incident was followed within a matter of weeks by Bush's comment that the United States would do "whatever it took to help Taiwan to defend herself" in the event of an attack by the mainland.[21] This was the strongest high-level statement of its kind to date and it was accompanied by White House approval of the largest arms sales package for Taiwan since 1992.[22] The Defense Department also suspended military-to-military contacts with the PRC pending a review of the policies governing such meetings.

Less public, but no less significant than these developments, were ongoing efforts in the Pentagon to focus more attention on long-term planning for possible military contingencies involving China. In addition to its general comments about the strategic importance of Asia, the September 2001 QDR came very close to identifying China by name as a future rival and potential enemy of the United States. The QDR's authors noted that "the possibility exists that a military competitor with a formidable resource base will emerge in Asia" and they asserted that the United States had an "enduring national interest" in "precluding hostile domination of critical areas." In listing these areas the Pentagon planners named not only Europe, the Middle East, Northeast Asia, and Southwest Asia but also, for the first time "the East Asian littoral," which they defined as "the region stretching from south of Japan through Australia and into the Bay of Bengal."[23] An effort to prevent hostile domination of this area seemed certain to involve the United States in opposing any significant expansion of Chinese influence into the South China Sea, as well as any attempted takeover of Taiwan.

North Korea—Enemy

If China was a potential long-term threat and a state that might yet undergo a process of political liberalization and reform, North Korea was a more immediate, albeit lesser danger. It was also a country whose government was, in every sense, beyond the pale. The Bush administration came into office believing that the Pyongyang regime was not only abhorrent but incapable of reform. They were convinced, therefore, that President Clinton's efforts to engage and transform the North, in conjunction with South Korean President Kim Dae Jung's so-called "sunshine policy," were not only morally objectionable but strategically misguided.

Soon after assuming power, President Bush ordered a full review of policy toward North Korea. This review focused in particular on the terms of the Agreed Framework, under which the United States, South Korea, and Japan were providing assistance to the North in return for a pledge to forgo further development of nuclear weapons. Some officials worried that outside aid was not only helping to keep Kim Jong Il in power, but, through the transfer of supposedly controlled, civilian nuclear reactors, that it might actually be helping him acquire weapons of mass destruction (WMD). Existing arrangements also did nothing to address the threat posed by the North's massive conventional forces or its ballistic missiles and, in any event, they amounted to a reward for international blackmail.[24]

After a period of internal debate, and some public tension between Washington and Seoul, the administration announced that it was prepared to enter into discussions with the North. But it insisted that these be broadened to include conventional and ballistic missile issues and it made clear its intention, as one observer put it, to "distrust and verify."[25] When the North refused to resume negotiations, the White House did not appear overly concerned and, in any case, it declined to make any concessions, rhetorical or substantive, to lure the DPRK back to the table.

September 11: Impact and Response

It is difficult to overstate the impact of the events of September 11 on the president and his top advisors. The audacity and terrible efficiency of the attacks themselves, the sheer magnitude of the devastation and human loss, and the knowledge that further casualties had probably been narrowly averted by the premature crash of one of the hijacked aircraft all contributed to an overwhelming sense of shock and horror.

The attacks on New York and Washington were a surprise, of course, but they were not entirely unexpected. Counter-terrorism experts had been warning for several years of the possibility of strikes on U.S. soil and, during the spring and summer of 2001, there had been an increased flow of reports suggesting that preparations for some kind of major operation, somewhere in the world, might be underway. While no one in the U.S. government appears to have had a clear sense of what was to come, the events of September 11 were thus preceded by a period of heightened awareness and official anxiety. When the blow finally fell, the fact that it had been anticipated can only have served to heighten its psychological impact.[26]

As terrible as they were, the September attacks also appeared to be merely an opening salvo, an augury of other and potentially much worse things yet to come. The appearance of anthrax-laden letters in the U.S. mail system drove home the point that future terrorist actions might involve the use of weapons of mass destruction. According to subsequent reports in October 2001, the White House also had what it regarded as credible warnings that terrorists might attempt to detonate a 10-kiloton nuclear device inside New York City.[27]

All of these factors combined to convince administration officials that their response would have to be not only swift and decisive, but also exceptionally broad. From the beginning, the aim of U.S. policy would be not simply to retaliate for the September 11 attacks, but to preempt future strikes by destroying the worldwide terrorist networks that sought to carry them out. In addition, as President Bush warned on September 20, the United States would "pursue nations that provide aid or safe haven to terrorism.... From this day forward, any nation that continues to harbor or support terrorism will be regarded by the United States as a hostile regime."[28]

A full discussion of the U.S. reaction to the events of September 11 is beyond the scope of this chapter. For our purposes it will be sufficient to note the broad outlines of U.S. policy, before turning to an analysis of its wider impact on Strategic Asia.

The first phase of the American response began within hours of the attacks themselves. Having concluded quickly and without evident difficulty who was responsible, the administration began to mobilize diplomatic support and military resources for operations against Osama bin Laden, his Al Qaeda organization, and, if necessary, the Taliban regime that permitted them sanctuary inside Afghanistan. These operations commenced with air strikes on October 7 followed, within two weeks, by the introduction of small special forces units on the ground. Over the next three months, U.S., British, and Australian troops, supported by massive U.S. airpower, helped opposition Afghan forces to defeat and overthrow the Taliban regime, kill or capture Al Qaeda fighters, and drive those remaining either into the eastern mountains or across the border into Pakistan. Although sporadic fighting continued into the early spring of 2002, large-scale operations in Afghanistan were effectively finished by the end of 2001.

The second phase of the U.S. response overlapped to a degree with the first and it seemed likely to continue, in one form or another, for an indefinite period of time. The September attacks triggered a major expansion of cooperation between the U.S. intelligence and domestic security services and their counterparts in Europe, Asia and around the world. Information obtained from captured documents and prisoners further fueled these efforts. In addition, fearing that remnants of Al Qaeda might seek to establish a new base of operations outside Afghanistan, and eager to strike at other cells of fighters and sympathizers, the United States initiated a series of widely dispersed, small-scale military operations. By the spring of 2002, U.S. forces were on the ground in the Philippines, Georgia, and Yemen. All of these operations were conducted with the knowledge, consent, and support of the governments involved and were billed primarily as training missions designed to assist local police and military forces in tracking down terrorist units operating in remote, uncontrolled areas. U.S. officials left open the possibility that more such operations might be conducted as needed, perhaps including some in countries like Somalia that might have to be carried out against the wishes of the local authorities.[29]

The beginning of a possible third phase in the U.S. war on terrorism was signaled in the State of the Union address at the end of January 2002. In his remarks President Bush sought to shift the focus of attention from Afghanistan, where military operations were winding down, to other state sponsors of terrorism, especially those that might also be seeking to acquire WMD. Casting aside diplomatic niceties, Bush described North Korea, Iran, and Iraq, together with "their terrorist allies," as constituting "an axis of evil." These states could provide WMD to terrorist groups "giving them the means to match their hatred" or use such weapons themselves to "attack our allies or attempt to blackmail the United States." In either case, the president warned, "the price of indifference would be catastrophic."[30]

Bush's speech was followed, in the spring of 2002, by a flurry of activity apparently aimed at preparing the ground for a future attack on Iraq. Any chance of a sudden U.S. strike disappeared with the dramatic worsening of the Israeli-Palestinian conflict. These events distracted the U.S. government and forced it to devote more attention to Middle East diplomacy, if only to try to preserve the possibility of support from friendly Arab regimes for a future move against Iraq.[31] But there were ample indications that the Bush administration still intended to proceed in this direction. The question, according to one account of Vice President Dick Cheney's remarks to a group of Senate Republicans, was "no longer if the U.S. would attack Iraq…. The only question was when."[32]

Reverberations and Aftershocks

The events of September 11 and the American response to them had effects all across Strategic Asia. From the point of view of U.S. interests and strategy these can be divided into three categories.

First, and perhaps most obviously, the unfolding of events gave rise to a striking expansion in America's presence in, and involvement with, countries and entire sub-regions of Strategic Asia where its attention had not previously been focused and where its role had generally been somewhat peripheral. This effect was especially evident in South and Central Asia, but it was also visible in parts of Southeast Asia.

Although the impact varied from country to country, as a general rule the American response tended to strengthen previously existing relationships with its primary strategic partners in Asia, both formal allies and quasi-allied democracies. In addition, in one of the more dramatic geopolitical shifts associated with the crisis, the United States found itself coming into much closer alignment than ever before with Russia.

Not all of the strategic effects of September 11 were positive, however. In part because of the way in which the United States responded to the crisis, its relations with North Korea became even tenser than they had been before. More subtle, and perhaps more significant, was an intensification in the "contradictions" between the United States and China. Instead of providing an occasion for a marked increase in U.S.-PRC cooperation, as some observers had hoped, the playing out of the crisis may actually turn out in the long run to have amplified the competitive aspects of their relationship.

Broadening

If Osama bin Laden had continued to make his headquarters in the Sudan, as he had done prior to 1996, the geopolitical impact of September 11 would have been much different, and much less wide ranging, than it actually was.[33] The fact that bin Laden took shelter in the remote mountains of Afghanistan, and used them as the base from which to plan and carry out his operations, did a great deal to shape the subsequent course of events.

In order to bring sufficient force to bear to destroy Al Qaeda's sanctuaries and topple its Taliban protectors, the United States was compelled to seek access to bases, facilities, and airspace in countries adjoining Afghanistan. The requirements of military strategy drove a stunning reversal in policy toward Pakistan, from which the United States had grown increasingly estranged since the 1980s. The need for access also gave rise to a sudden warming in the hitherto rather tentative and remote relationship between Washington and at least three of the five Central Asian states.

Within months of the September attacks, the United States went from having no presence or influence in Afghanistan to a situation in which it had thousands of troops on the ground and was playing the dominant role in shaping that country's political future. To the north, the United States was expanding runways, building barracks and stationing forces at bases in Uzbekistan and Kyrgyzstan, and discussing the possibility of similar arrangements in Tajikistan. American financial support for the governments of all of these countries, whether in the form of direct aid or landing fees, had also been markedly increased.[34]

Meanwhile, to the south, Washington had lifted the sanctions it imposed on Pakistan in the wake of its 1998 nuclear tests and 1999 military coup. U.S. planes were regularly flying through Pakistani airspace and U.S. forces were launching attacks from bases on its soil against targets inside Afghanistan. U.S. and Pakistani diplomats and intelligence officials were engaged in close, if wary, consultations, and Washington was providing Islamabad with substantial quantities of aid and help in obtaining relief from its staggering international debt burden. In sum, by the beginning of 2002 relations between the United States and Pakistan were closer than at any time since the withdrawal of Soviet forces from Afghanistan almost 15 years before.[35]

Concerns about Al Qaeda cells and about the possible wider threat of Islamist terrorism also led the United States to devote considerably more attention and resources to Southeast Asia. Despite continuing sensitivity in the Philippines to any appearance of American imperialism, strategic cooperation between the two countries increased markedly after September 11. In addition to welcoming small numbers of U.S. troops back onto its territory to assist in anti-terror operations, the Philippine government offered to let the U.S. military once again use the facilities at Subic Bay and Clark Air Base from which it had been evicted in 1992.[36]

Elsewhere in the region, Washington continued its close cooperation with Singapore and moved to repair relations with Malaysia, a country it had long viewed as authoritarian and anti-American but that one U.S. official now described as a "beacon of stability."[37] In May 2002, President Bush invited Prime Minister Mahathir Mohamad to Washington to thank him for his cooperation in the war on terror.[38] Meanwhile, the U.S. pledged to increase financial aid to Indonesia and moved cautiously toward restoring at least some of its ties to the Indonesian military and security services. These connections had been strong during the Cold War, but were cut back, and then suspended altogether in 1999, because of concerns about human rights abuses.[39] Finally, during a visit to Vietnam in February 2002, Admiral Dennis Blair, then commander-in-chief of U.S. forces in the Pacific, hinted that to support its participation in the ongoing anti-terror campaign, the U.S. Navy might be interested in gaining permission to dock at Cam Ranh Bay.[40] Although nothing immediate came from this suggestion, it was clear that, in other ways, the war on terrorism had already produced a substantial broadening in the scope of American engagement in Southeast, as well as South and Central Asia.

Strengthening

The course of events following September 11 tended, for the most part, to solidify America's relationships with its major Asian allies, as well as strengthening ties to its quasi-allied democratic strategic partners and also to Russia.

In contrast to its performance during the 1990–91 Gulf War, when it had only offered, somewhat belatedly, to help pay the bills, the Japanese government moved quickly to provide concrete, material assistance to the United States. In October 2001 the Diet passed a special bill authorizing the Japanese SDF to participate, albeit only in non-combat roles, in U.S.-led counter-terror operations. This marked a loosening of constitutional restrictions on the use of the armed forces for any purpose other than the direct defense of Japan. It therefore constituted movement in the direction long favored by high-ranking members of the Bush administration.[41]

Passage of the bill was followed by the dispatch of a small flotilla of support and intelligence gathering vessels to the Indian Ocean. Although there were indications that some in the U.S. government would have preferred even more dramatic steps, including use of the most sophisticated, Aegis-equipped destroyers, these actions constituted the largest, longest, and most far-flung deployment of Japanese naval vessels to a war zone since 1945.[42] Japan's actions were generally seen in Washington as marking a meaningful advance in bilateral security cooperation and they were warmly welcomed as such by American officials.[43]

The Afghan campaign marked another chapter in the long history of joint U.S.-Australian military operations and a strong indication that this tradition of close cooperation would continue into the post-Cold War era. Canberra quickly announced that it regarded the attacks on New York and Washington as events sufficient to trigger its bilateral defense treaty with the United States.[44] The Australian government offered to assist in whatever way it could and it subsequently sent special forces units to fight alongside their U.S. and British counterparts. As if in response to Richard Armitage's earlier admonition, an Australian solider was the first non-American combatant to die in Afghanistan.[45]

September 11 stimulated and accelerated the trend, already evident, toward a much closer strategic alignment between India and the United States. For fear of disrupting its fragile but critical new relationship with Pakistan, Washington declined to make use of Indian bases to conduct operations inside Afghanistan. To compensate, and also to discourage any independent Indian military action, U.S. officials went to considerable lengths to make clear that they understood and shared New Delhi's concerns about Islamist terrorism. Especially after the suicide attacks on India's parliament in December 2001, Washington put great pressure on Pakistan to crack down on terrorist organizations based within its borders and it also entered into close and continuing consultations with New Delhi on terrorism and a range of other issues.[46]

At the same time as he waived sanctions on Pakistan, President Bush also lifted those that had been applied to India. This action cleared the way for greatly expanded contacts on matters that extended well beyond the immediate crisis. In December the high-level U.S.-India Defense Policy Group held its first meeting since the Indian nuclear tests. Six months later the group met again, giving clear evidence, in the words of the official joint statement describing the event, that both sides wished "to accomplish something significant" and "to accelerate the pace of U.S.-India defense cooperation." Among other steps, the two nations agreed to combined naval patrols in the Strait of Malacca, a joint special forces airborne exercise (the first such event in almost 40 years), consultation on ballistic missile defense issues, a reopening of defense trade (beginning with the sale of a U.S. radar system), and "resumption of technical cooperation in defense research, development and production."[47] Some of these things might have come to pass eventually absent September 11, but there can be no question that they occurred far more rapidly because of it.

The U.S.-Taiwan relationship was not affected in any obvious or direct way by the attacks on Washington and New York. As we have seen, the Bush administration had decided as early as the spring of 2001 that an increase in rhetorical and material support for Taiwan was necessary in order to strengthen deterrence. The steps that it took subsequently reflected this judgment and do not appear to have been influenced by the unfolding of events in South and Central Asia.

Nevertheless, the sudden onset of the crisis may have served to deepen the administration's determination to support those it regarded as friends and to stand firm in the face of threats of force. Oblique suggestions from Beijing that the United States might need to soften its stance on Taiwan if it wanted China's help in fighting terrorism, and some nervousness in Taipei that Washington might actually be considering doing so, seem only to have stiffened the administration's resolve. While it does not appear to have done anything more than originally intended to bolster Taiwan, the administration also declined to do anything less.

As the war in Afghanistan reached its climax and then subsided, the U.S. government pushed ahead with efforts to find a manufacturer for the eight diesel submarines that it had promised to sell Taiwan in April 2001. In keeping with a desire to improve Taiwan's defense "software," its capacity for strategic planning, joint operations, and possible coordination with U.S. forces, the Bush administration also permitted the Taiwanese defense minister to make a quasi-official visit to the United States in March 2002. While the president himself did not repeat his public pledge to do "whatever it takes" to defend Taiwan, Deputy Defense Secretary Paul Wolfowitz used this formulation in a closed-door session of the U.S.-Taiwan Business Council at which the visiting defense minister was present. Wolfowitz's remarks soon found their way into the public domain. Another, unrelated leak, this time of an internal administration review of nuclear policy, seemed strongly to suggest that, under some circumstances, the United States might consider using nuclear weapons to defend Taiwan. None of this was entirely new, and none of it was directly related to the war on terrorism, but it was consistent with the sense of resolve that the administration had clearly been trying to convey since September 11.[48]

With the possible exception of the U.S.-Pakistani connection, the bilateral relationship that underwent the greatest change in the aftermath of the attacks was that between the United States and Russia.[49] Thanks in large part to President Putin's apparent decision to use the crisis to seek an opening to the West, U.S.-Russian relations shifted sharply toward enhanced cooperation. If before September 11 the Bush administration had not been sure quite how to regard Russia, the events that followed appeared to leave very little doubt; Putin's Russia was not yet an ally, or even a quasi-ally, but it was certainly a friend and no longer a foe.

Putin's symbolic success in being the first foreign leader to reach President Bush by telephone while he was still airborne and returning to Washington on the day of the terror attacks was followed by more concrete steps designed to ease the way for a U.S. military campaign in Afghanistan. While he might conceivably have sought to discourage the former Soviet Central Asian republics from cooperating, or perhaps attempted to extract some American concessions in return for his help, Putin instead offered his wholehearted support and urged Russia's smaller neighbors to do likewise. Drawing on their own extensive contacts and unfortunate experience in Afghanistan, the Russians provided the United States with what one U.S. officer later described as "very valuable information." They also gave some direct military assistance to the anti-Taliban Northern Alliance forces.[50]

Except for its stance on Moscow's ongoing war against Chechen separatists, where it seems to have muted its public criticisms, the Bush administration did not repay Putin with any tangible concessions on outstanding strategic issues. Indeed, to the contrary, and to the surprise of some observers, the White House announced in December 2001 that it intended to withdraw from the 1972 Anti-Ballistic Missile (ABM) Treaty as it had previously suggested it might, despite the fact that no understanding on missile defense issues had yet been reached with Moscow. Far from derailing the budding relationship, this event was followed by a period of intensified negotiations that resulted eventually in an agreement codifying major cuts in the strategic offensive forces of both sides. This understanding conformed more closely to America's wishes than it did to Russia's. In May 2002 President Bush traveled to Moscow to sign the treaty, and also to convey an invitation to Russia to participate more closely than ever before in the deliberations of NATO.[51] Thanks in part to the aftermath of September 11, relations between the United States and Russia were warmer than at any time since the end of World War II.

The U.S.-ROK alliance is the one instance in which an existing American friendship in Asia appears to have been strained rather than strengthened by the war on terrorism. As has been previously discussed, Washington's evident disapproval of South Korean president Kim Dae Jung's "sunshine policy" had already introduced a measure of discord into the relationship before the September crisis. While Seoul's formal response to the attacks on the United States was supportive, its substantive contributions were quite limited, certainly when compared to those of America's other major Asian alliance partners.[52]

President Bush's subsequent mention of North Korea in his January 2002 "axis of evil" speech served to heighten the sense of divergence and tension between Washington and Seoul. From the perspective of Kim Dae Jung's government, the United States was once again exposing it to domestic criticism by calling into question its preferred, conciliatory approach to dealing with the North.[53] In pursuing its campaign against state sponsors of terrorism and WMD development, the United States also appeared to be willing to risk confrontation and perhaps even war, despite the preferences of its most directly affected ally. The Bush administration, on the other hand, believed strongly in the necessity of stepping up pressure on the North. It was not about to allow itself to be deflected, especially by a South Korean leader whose strategic acumen it questioned and who, in any case, had less than a year remaining on his term of office.

The differences between Washington and Seoul were narrowed, to a degree, when President Bush visited South Korea in February 2002 and offered assurances that he had no intention of attacking the North.[54] But the Bush-Kim summit was accompanied by violent protests by left-wing groups and it was followed by a marked increase in anti-American sentiment among portions of the South Korean public.[55] How deep and long-lasting these shifts turn out to be, and whether they will do permanent damage to the foundations of the U.S.-ROK alliance, remain to be seen.

Intensifying

September 11 did not cause the Bush administration to alter its fundamental assessment of Pyongyang. Afterward, as before, the president and his advisors regarded the Kim Il Sung regime as illegitimate, untrustworthy, and dangerous. What did change, however, was the administration's assessment of the urgent need to deal with the problem of WMD proliferation. The attacks on New York and Washington demonstrated clearly that there were individuals and groups in the world intent on killing Americans in large numbers. If they could get their hands on more efficient and lethal weapons than hijacked commercial airlines there seemed little reason to doubt that such people would use them.

The Pyongyang regime had a long history of attempting to build WMD, and an established track record as a developer and exporter of ballistic missiles and other military systems. By isolating and applying pressure to North Korea (along with Iran and Iraq), the Bush administration hoped, among other things, to constrict one of the possible avenues through which highly destructive weapons might find their way into the hands of groups like Al Qaeda. In pursuit of this goal Washington was willing to risk the disapproval of its allies, as well as a further cooling of its already frosty relationship with the DPRK. Drawing on the experience of the early Reagan years, some in the administration may well have concluded that a worsening of relations, and a demonstrated willingness to endure the criticism that went with it, was a necessary prelude to any progress in dealing with the North.

The impact of September 11 on U.S. relations with China was more mixed and complex than was the case with North Korea but, on balance, the net effect appears also to have been to intensify the competitive aspects of the relationship between the two Pacific powers. In the aftermath of the attacks there were suggestions from both U.S. and Chinese observers that cooperation against the shared threat of terrorism could provide the basis for a dramatic improvement in bilateral relations.[56] Despite having been rebuffed in their initial efforts to extract concessions in return for their backing, the Chinese leaders did ultimately provide the United States with some modest measures of support. Although it offered various words of caution along the way, Beijing chose not to oppose publicly the U.S. use of force in Afghanistan. The Chinese government also reportedly reassured the Pakistanis about their own decision to accede to American demands and it agreed to share intelligence information on terrorist threats with the United States. While U.S. policymakers certainly welcomed these gestures, they appear also to have seen them as somewhat tentative and grudging, motivated by fairly narrow Chinese conceptions of their own national interests, and, in the end, not of decisive importance. As viewed from Washington, the most vigorous aspect of Beijing's response appeared to be a stepped-up campaign against domestic opposition groups, especially those in western China that it accused of violent separatism and links to Al Qaeda.[57]

In part because of its skeptical assessment of Beijing's contributions and motives, and also because of its general desire to appear tough and unwavering at a time of crisis, the Bush administration did not deviate from the general lines of its pre-September policies toward China. Indeed, in most respects, the course of events seems to have reinforced its basic instincts and inclinations. The strengthening of the U.S. strategic relationship with Taiwan, and the decision to withdraw from the ABM treaty, despite longstanding Chinese objections on both counts, have already been mentioned. Whatever their feelings about China's contributions to the war on terror, U.S. officials also did not mute their criticisms of what they saw as Beijing's continuing violations of human rights. To the contrary, at both of his post-attack summit meetings with Chinese leaders, President Bush went out of his way to emphasize the importance of religious and political freedom, at one point warning President Jiang Zemin against using the war on terrorism as "an excuse to persecute minorities."[58]

Before September 11 the U.S. government had shown no inclination to compromise with China in disputes over proliferation; afterward, U.S. determination to deal forcefully with this issue was, if anything, even stronger. Shortly before the crisis began, Washington had imposed new sanctions on Chinese companies that it accused of transferring ballistic missile technology to Iran and Pakistan. Despite subsequent rumors that it might strike some kind of deal that would allow these to be lifted in time for the first Bush-Jiang summit, the administration refused to give any ground and the restrictions remained in place.[59] Several months later, in the spring of 2002, the United States imposed still more sanctions on China, alleging that it was continuing to assist Iran in its efforts to develop WMD.[60]

In addition to these fairly direct and obvious consequences, the unfolding of the war on terrorism also had other, less visible effects on the tenor of Sino-American relations. Put simply, the broadening and strengthening of the U.S. position in Asia appears to have induced in many Chinese observers a heightened sense of insecurity. All along China's interior, land frontier, from Russia, through Central Asia to South and parts of continental Southeast Asia, the United States seemed to have made significant strategic gains in the months after September 11. Beijing's careful courtship of Moscow (which had culminated, as recently as July 2001, in the signing of a bilateral "friendship and cooperation" treaty) now seemed in danger of being undone by Russia's newfound ardor for the United States. The Shanghai Cooperation Organization (SCO), Beijing's preferred instrument for exerting influence in Central Asia, had been pushed to the sidelines by U.S. intervention and risked being reduced to irrelevance. The emerging entente between India and the United States had clearly been given a major boost by events. Even Pakistan, China's long-time ally in South Asia, and its principal means for exerting a restraining influence on India, had shifted toward the United States. All of these developments contributed to a feeling, expressed in various unofficial and quasi-official quarters in China, that the United States was taking advantage of events to advance toward its allegedly long-held goal of encircling the PRC.[61]

To the east, off China's Pacific coast, stepped-up U.S. support for Taiwan, the reappearance of U.S. troops in the Philippines, and indications of improving relations between the U.S. government and its counterparts in Indonesia and Malaysia, did nothing to discourage such speculations. Perhaps most disturbing from the Chinese perspective was the fact that Tokyo too appeared to be using the war on terror to justify expanding its military reach and geopolitical assertiveness. Chinese commentators warned that the new Japanese anti-terrorism law and the dispatch of Japanese ships to the Indian Ocean were "precedent-breaking" events that could threaten the stability of Asia.[62] The subsequent pursuit and sinking of an alleged North Korean spy boat by Japanese Coast Guard vessels at the end of 2001 was interpreted as providing more evidence of Tokyo's true character and likely future behavior.[63] Only on the Korean peninsula, where heightened tensions between the United States and the DPRK promised to increase Beijing's importance as an interlocutor, and divergences between the U.S. and the ROK offered some hope of expanded influence, did China's position appear marginally stronger after September 11 than it had before.

Looking Ahead: Risks and Opportunities

Every aspect of the recent changes in the American posture in Strategic Asia carries with it both risks and opportunities. The closing review that follows will pay particular attention to the dangers that the United States may face as it moves forward with its war on terrorism.

Broadening

As the scope of its engagement increases, the United States may have new opportunities to exert influence in places where it previously had little.

Washington's expanded relationships with the governments of Pakistan, Afghanistan, and the Central Asian states may increase the chances that it will be able to encourage them to undertake actions designed not only to combat terrorism but to build functioning democratic institutions. The widening or reopening of security ties with the Philippines and Indonesia may also make it easier for the United States to assist those struggling democracies in dealing with serious internal threats to their stability. Success in these endeavors would help to reduce the global threat of terrorism by denying safe havens to groups like Al Qaeda. It would also support the overarching American goal of promoting stability across Strategic Asia by building a network of nations that are tied together by common values and similar institutions.

But there are dangers too in the course on which the United States is presently embarked. As during the Cold War, the urgent need to combat an immediate threat may lead Washington into murky moral waters, shackling it to non-democratic regimes that it might otherwise have preferred to keep at arms length. In the process, the United States may actually help autocratic rulers to extend their grip on power, while at the same time stimulating anti-American and anti-western sentiments among their populations and perhaps even strengthening support for the very terrorist organizations that it hopes to see destroyed.

As in the past, the United States may also find it difficult to turn away from its new friends and to limit its commitments to their security and survival. This could lead to a dispersal of effort and resources and to quagmires of various kinds. A protracted war in Afghanistan, in which Taliban and Al Qaeda remnants and various warlords join forces to oppose the newly created Kabul government, is a far from implausible scenario. If it develops it could compel the Bush administration, against its better judgment, to engage in a full-scale exercise in nation-building, helping its Afghan allies to create functioning governmental institutions and committing U.S. forces to a traditional counter-insurgency campaign. A greatly expanded U.S. military effort in the Philippines does not appear imminent, at this point, but neither is it unthinkable.

Its rejuvenated relationship with Pakistan means that Washington now has leverage where it previously had none, but it also has new and potentially burdensome interests and obligations. For at least as long as the United States continues to conduct anti-terror operations in Afghanistan, and to make use of bases inside Pakistan, it will have to be intensely concerned with the fate of the present government in Islamabad. The unfolding of events since September 11 may well have heightened the risks to General Pervez Musharraf's survival; it has certainly increased awareness in the United States of the potential dangers to its interests if Pakistan should fall into chaos or under the control of a radical Islamist regime.

Having re-engaged with Pakistan, the United States is now extremely unlikely to disengage, unless it is somehow forced to do so. Whatever its other implications, this fact will surely complicate U.S. efforts to build a new strategic relationship with India and it has placed the United States squarely at the center of efforts to achieve a lasting political settlement between India and Pakistan. If these efforts succeed, among other benefits, the United States will find its position in South Asia, and in Strategic Asia more generally, to be greatly strengthened. If they fail, however, it could find itself caught in the middle of, and perhaps forced to take sides in, a horrifically destructive conflict. If there was ever a chance that the United States could choose to stand aside from events on the sub-continent, that option seems now to have disappeared.

Strengthening

The apparent strengthening of America's relationships with most of the other Asian democracies, and the dramatic improvement in its relations with Russia, should bode well for its ability to shape events and deal with possible future threats. Here too, however, there are risks.

The new friendships that the United States is forging with India and Russia could turn out to be quite fragile. While the heat of the current crisis has clearly accelerated the formation of these ties it could also render them brittle. Despite all the enthusiasm being expressed on both sides, it is not yet clear to what extent the long-term interests and strategic visions of Washington and New Delhi will truly converge. And, even in the short run, there is a danger that the two may yet be driven apart by differences over how to deal with Pakistan and the problem of Kashmir.

Similarly with Russia, the rapid progress and substantial forward momentum that have been achieved since September 11 may not be easy to sustain. The liquidation of long-standing disputes over old issues such as nuclear arms control and NATO enlargement should clear the way for dealing with new ones, including integrating Russia more fully into the global economy, and persuading it to cut back on its arms sales to Iran and China, among others. There are substantial opportunities for both sides, but also real possibilities of disappointment and disillusionment. If Putin does not gain clear benefits from his turn to the West, he will be attacked and perhaps replaced by other leaders less favorably disposed toward cooperation. By the same token, if Russia continues to support states that the United States accuses of sponsoring terrorism and promoting proliferation, the relationship between the two powers will quickly cool.

Relations between Washington and Taipei are probably closer now than at any time since "de-recognition" in 1979. Provided that the Taiwanese government does not try to take advantage of this fact to push hard for a more independent status, there is no reason why the new level of contact and cooperation cannot be sustained. In the spring of 2002, however, Bush administration spokesmen made a point of saying publicly that, despite all the recent increases in its support for Taiwan, the United States does not favor Taiwanese independence and continues to adhere to the "one-China policy."[64] These remarks did not indicate any change in the basic American stance, and they were probably aimed as much at reassuring Beijing as at dampening expectations in Taipei. But they also served as a reminder that the enhanced U.S.-Taiwanese relationship still has strict limits and may be subject to future tensions.

As regards its formal Asian alliances, the picture for the United States is already somewhat mixed. Ties with South Korea have been strained by recent events, though this could turn out to be a passing phase and perhaps a prelude to improved communication and coordination. With Japan, some analysts argue that Tokyo's new assertiveness, and the apparent progress that has been made toward a more equal and mature strategic partnership are illusory.[65] Japan's response to the current crisis may be impressive when compared to its own past behavior but, by almost any other standard, it is still strikingly limited and cautious. Instead of moving closer to Washington, as most U.S. observers prefer to believe, it may be that Tokyo is actually edging away, marginally improving its own capacity for independent action while at the same time putting some subtle distance between its own policies and those of the United States.

Whatever has happened to date, the next steps in the war on terrorism could impose a serious strain on America's friendships in Asia. A decision to use force against any of the states in the "axis of evil" would likely prove highly controversial with one or more of the countries that are presently aligning themselves with U.S. policy. Indeed, barring another catastrophic terrorist attack, or compelling evidence linking Saddam Hussein to September 11, it is difficult to imagine a substantial U.S. follow-on military action that would win as much support as the war in Afghanistan. The cohesiveness of the anti-terror coalition may already have passed its peak. While it is unlikely that any of America's allies would seek directly to block its actions, they might well choose to express their displeasure in various ways. Badly handled, differences with India and Russia over how to deal with Iran, or with Japan and Australia over Iraq, or with Japan and South Korea over North Korea, could damage U.S. bilateral relationships and weaken America's overall position in Strategic Asia.

Intensifying

Conventional wisdom to the contrary notwithstanding, the visible heightening of tensions in interstate relations is not always a harmful or dangerous thing. The willingness of the United States to endure periods of strain in its dealings with potentially hostile states can send strong signals of resolve, thereby contributing to the deterrence of actual conflict. Standing firm, even in the face of protests and threats, may help to induce others to change their bargaining positions, clearing the way for negotiated settlements on terms more favorable to the United States.

The intensification of "contradictions" can also, however, set in motion processes that are difficult fully to anticipate or control and whose end results can sometimes be harmful. Identifying the North Korean regime as a part of the "axis of evil" may put it on notice and make it eager to cut deals with the United States. But it is also possible that stepping up the pressure on Pyongyang will only cause it to redouble and accelerate its efforts to acquire WMD as the last hope of deterring a U.S. attack.

Without fully intending to do so, the United States may have fed Beijing's inclination toward paranoia by escalating its support for Taiwan while at the same time expanding its activities across all of Strategic Asia. Important aspects of this expansion were the unplanned result of September 11, but that does not mean that they will be seen as any less threatening to the PRC's long-term ambitions and interests. One way or another, Chinese strategists will be looking for opportunities to respond to, and if possible to blunt or offset, recent U.S. initiatives. When they do, it is likely that their American counterparts will see their actions as aimed at containing or undermining U.S. influence in Asia.

In extreme cases it is possible that instead of enhancing deterrence an intensification of competition and tension may end up by weakening it. If one party becomes convinced that the other is embarked on a course of action that threatens its vital interests and even its survival, it may decide to use force to forestall what it believes would otherwise be certain disaster. Thus, if it feels its back is to the wall, it is conceivable that North Korea could lash out against the South. There is also a danger that Beijing might resort to violence to prevent Taiwan from slipping further toward independence, even at the risk of provoking a war with the United States.

While the probability of these contingencies does not appear especially great at this point, the chances of conflict could increase if relations between the United States and North Korea, on the one hand, or China on the other, were to spiral sharply downward. The risks could be at a peak if, after a period of heightened tension, the United States finds itself preoccupied with events elsewhere, whether responding to another devastating terrorist strike on its own territory or prosecuting a war against a state sponsor of terrorism in the Middle East. It is a measure of how much has changed in the past year that these scenarios seem far more plausible now than they did before September 11, 2001.

Endnotes

1 Michael R. Gordon, "Pentagon Review Puts Emphasis on Long-Range Arms in Pacific," *The New York Times*, May 17, 2001. For more on this report and its emphasis on Asia, see also Thomas E. Ricks, "Pentagon Study May Bring Big Shake-Up: Unconventional Defense Thinker Conducting Review," *Washington Post*, February 9, 2001; and William Safire, "Octogenarian Futurist," *The New York Times*, April 16, 2001.

2 "Focusing the Department of Defense on Asia," project for the Office of the Secretary of Defense, Director for Net Assessment, Washington, DC: DFI International, September 30, 2001.

3 Department of Defense, *Quadrennial Defense Review Report*, Washington, DC: Department of Defense, September 30, 2001, pp. 4–5.

4 These are the words of the so-called "Armitage Report." The report was issued by a bipartisan group of experts on the eve of the 2000 presidential election. It bore the name of Richard Armitage, who subsequently was appointed Colin Powell's chief deputy at the State Department. See "The United States and Japan: Advancing Toward a Mature Partnership," October 11, 2000, <www.ndu.edu/ndu/sr_japan.html>.

5 Kenneth Lieberthal, "The United States and Asia in 2001: Changing Agendas," *Asian Survey*, vol. 42, no. 1 (January/February 2002), p. 3.

6 See Michael Swaine, Rachel Swanger, Takashi Kawakami, *Japan and Ballistic Missile Defense*, Santa Monica, Calif.: RAND, 2001, p. 23, <www.rand.org/publications/mr/mr1374/mr1374.ch2.pdf>.

7 "Australia 'Must Commit Troops in Taiwan War'," *Agence France-Presse*, August 19, 2001.

8 William Tow and Rod Lyon, "Everyone Loses in Ill-Timed 'JANZUS' Talks," *The Age*, August 2, 2001.

9 "U.S.-Australia-Japan Security Talks Backed," *Japan Times*, August 18, 2001.

10 Doug Bandow, "Reviewing Allies Down Under," *Washington Times*, August 25, 2001.

11 Condoleezza P. Rice, "Promoting the National Interest," *Foreign Affairs*, vol. 79, no. 1 (January/February 2000), p. 56.

12 See the discussion of India in "Speech by Governor George W. Bush on Foreign Policy," Ronald Reagan Presidential Library, Washington, DC. November 19, 1999, <www.foreignpolicy2000.org/library/index.html>.

13 Robert D. Blackwill, "The Future of US-India Relations," remarks to the Indo-American Chamber of Commerce and Indo-American Society, Bombay, India, September 6, 2001, <www.state.gov/pa/sa/rls/rm/4850pf.html>.

14 Ibid.

15 "Confirmation Hearing by Colin L. Powell," Washington, DC, January 17, 2001,

<www.state.gov/secreatry/rm/2001/443.htm>.

[16] For indications of early administration thinking on these issues see "Secretary of Defense Donald H. Rumsfeld Interview with PBS Newshour," transcript of interview with Ray Suarez, *PBS Newshour*, August 16, 2001, <www.defenselink.mil/news/aug2001/t08172001_t816pbst.html>.

[17] See "Speech by Governor George W. Bush on Foreign Policy," <www.foreign policy2000.org/library/index.html>.

[18] According to one survey, 74 percent of the American public would have supported the imposition of trade sanctions against China at the time of the crisis. Richard Morin and Claudia Deane, "Public Rallies around Bush over China Standoff," *Washington Post*, April 7, 2001.

[19] For an account of the crisis and its resolution, see "A Tale of 'Two Very Sorries' Redux," *Far Eastern Economic Review*, March 21, 2002.

[20] Quoted in Catharin Dalpino and Bates Gill, eds., *Brookings Northeast Asia Survey 2001–02*, Washington, DC: Brookings, 2002, p. 36.

[21] "Bush vows whatever it takes to defend Taiwan," CNN.com, April 25, 2001.

[22] Steven Mufson and Dana Milbank, "Taiwan to Get Variety of Arms," *Washington Post*, April 24, 2001.

[23] *Quadrennial Defense Review Report*, pp. 2–3.

[24] See David Sanger, "Korean to Visit Bush, but They Could Be at Odds," *The New York Times*, March 7, 2001.

[25] Michael H. Armacost, "Where Are We Today: A Geopolitical Overview," remarks to the Fourth Symposium on Korea and the Search for Peace in Northeast Asia, <www.brook.edu/views/speeches/armacost/20011118.htm>. For the findings of the administration's review, see Charles L. Pritchard, "U.S. Policy toward the Democratic People's Republic of Korea," testimony before the Subcommittee on East Asia and the Pacific, House Committee on International Relations, July 26, 2001, <www.state.gov/p/eap/rls/rm/2001/4304pf.htm>.

[26] Regarding early warning signals of an impending attack received during the spring and summer of 2001, see Michael Elliott, "How the U.S. Missed the Clues," *Time*, May 18, 2002.

[27] Massimo Calabresi and Romesh Ratnesar, "Can We Stop the Next Attack?" *Time*, March 3, 2002.

[28] President George W. Bush, "Address to a Joint Session of Congress and the American People," September 20, 2001, <www.whitehouse.gov/news/releases/2001/09/20010920-8.html>.

[29] For an overview see "U.S. expanding war on terrorism," CNN.com, March 6, 2002. Regarding the start of U.S. operations in Yemen, see "Yemeni tribes: Attack would be a 'strategic mistake'," CNN.com, May 17, 2002. Regarding the possibility of covert anti-terrorist operations in Somalia, see "U.S. officials visit Somalia," CNN.com, December 11, 2001. See also remarks by Deputy Assistant Secretary of Defense for African Affairs Michael Westphal, April 2, 2002, <www.defenselink.mil/news/apr2002/t04022002_t0402dasdaa.html>.

[30] President George W. Bush, "The President's State of the Union Address," January 29, 2002, <www.whitehouse.gov/news/releases/2002/01/20020129-11.html>.

[31] See John Donnelley and Anthony Ahadid, "U.S. Officials Say Easing Mideast Tensions Key to Support on Iraq," *Boston Globe*, March 15, 2002; Jeanne

Cummings, "Cheney Trip Forces Change in U.S. Plan—Arab Refusal to Back Iraq Move Means U.S. Must Focus on Mideast," *Wall Street Journal*, March 18, 2002; and James Gerstenzang, "Cheney Finds Israeli Issue Trumps Iraq," *Los Angeles Times*, March 18, 2002.

[32] "We're taking him out," CNN.com, May 6, 2002.

[33] On bin Laden's expulsion from the Sudan and subsequent arrival in Afghanistan, see Yossef Bodansky, *Bin Laden: The Man Who Declared War on America*, New York: Forum, 2001, p. 186.

[34] On these developments see Eric Schmitt and James Dao, "U.S. Is Building Up its Military Bases in Afghan Region," *The New York Times*, January 9, 2002; Bruce Pannier, "Tajikistan, Kyrgyzstan Balancing Relations with West, Russia," *Eurasia Insight*, January 28, 2002, <www.eurasianet.org/departments/insight/articles/pp12081.shtml>; Vernon Loeb, "Footprints in Steppes of Central Asia," *Washington Post*, February 9, 2002; Sally Buzbee, "United States Expanded Influence Likely to Remain in Central Asia," *Associated Press*, March 12, 2002, <www.globalsecurity.org/news/2002/020312-attack01.htm>; and Ahmed Rashid, "Trouble Ahead," *Far Eastern Economic Review*, May 9, 2002. See also chapter seven by Martha Olcott in this volume.

[35] These developments are discussed in Stephen Cohen's chapter in this volume.

[36] See Sheldon Simon, "Mixed Reactions in Southeast Asia to the U.S. War on Terrorism," *Comparative Connections*, vol. 3, no. 4, (January 2002), <www.csis.org/pacfor/cc/0104qus_asean.html>.

[37] Assistant Secretary of State for East Asian and Pacific Affairs James Kelly, quoted in Kim Chew Lee, "ASEAN Back in Spotlight as Big Players Come A-Wooing," *PacNet Newsletter*, no. 19, May 10, 2002, Pacific Forum/CSIS.

[38] Sonya Ross, "Malaysia Asks for U.S. Patience," *Washington Post*, May 14, 2002.

[39] There had already been some movement in this direction prior to September 11. See Jane Perlez, "U.S. to Renew Relationship with Military in Indonesia," *The New York Times*, August 12, 2001; and David E. Sanger and Thom Shanker, "U.S. Rules Out Training Indonesia Army, But Will Aid its Anti-terror Policy," *The New York Times*, March 22, 2002.

[40] Murray Hiebert with Susan Lawrence, "Hands Across the Ocean," *Far Eastern Economic Review*, March 14, 2002.

[41] See Kathryn Tolbert and Doug Struck, "Japan Expands Military Role to Support US," *Washington Post*, October 19, 2001.

[42] See "Japanese War Effort Sets Sail," CNN.com, November 25, 2001, <http://taiwansecurity.org/news/2001/cnn-112501.htm>; John Miller, "Japan Crosses the Rubicon," *Asia-Pacific Security Studies*, vol. 1, no. 1 (January 2002), <www.apcss.org/publications/japan%20crosses%20the%20robicon.pdf>; and "U.S. Eyes Japan Aid in Iraq Attack," *Asahi Shimbun*, April 22, 2002.

[43] See President George W. Bush, "Remarks by the President to the Diet," February 18, 2002, <www.whitehouse.gov/news/releases/2002/02/20020218-2.html>. For a more skeptical assessment of Japan's actions see the chapter by Eric Heginbotham and Richard Samuels in this volume.

[44] See statement by Peter Reith, Australian Minister for Defence, "ADF Support to the United States," September 18, 2001, <www.defence.gov.au/media/

index.html>.

[45] Regarding Australia's role see Department of Defense, "International Contributions to the War Against Terrorism," May 22, 2002, <www.defenselink.mil/news/may2002/d20020523cu.pdf>.

[46] These developments are discussed in Stephen Cohen's chapter in this volume. For a useful overview of events in the months before and immediately after September 11, see Satu P. Limaye, "U.S.-India Relations: Visible to the Naked Eye," *Comparative Connections*, vol. 3, no. 4 (January 2002), <www.csis.org/pacfor/cc/0104qoa.html>.

[47] See Department of Defense, "Joint Statement on U.S.-India Defense Policy Group Meeting," May 23, 2002, <www.defenselink.mil/news/may2002/b05232002_bt267-02.html>. Regarding the joint exercise, see "India-U.S. War Games Amid Standoff," CNN.com, May 16, 2002.

[48] For more on these issues see Aaron L. Friedberg, "11 September and the Future of Sino-American Relations," *Survival*, vol. 44, no. 1 (Spring 2002), pp. 33–50. See also Bill Gertz, "White House Backs Strong Defense of Taiwan," *Washington Times*, April 11, 2002; and John Pomfret, "In Fact and in Tone, U.S. Expresses New Fondness for Taiwan," *Washington Post*, April 30, 2002.

[49] Russia's "turn" toward the West is discussed at length in William Wohlforth's chapter in this volume.

[50] Air Force Brigadier General John W. Rosa, deputy director for operations of the Joint Staff. Quoted in Walter Pincus, "Anti-Terror War Binds U.S., Russian Militaries," *Washington Post*, May 3, 2002. The wider context of Putin's policies is discussed in William Wohlforth's contribution to this volume. For background, see also Oksana Antonenko, "Putin's Gamble," *Survival*, vol. 43, no. 4 (Winter 2001), pp. 49–60.

[51] See Dana Milbank and Sharon LaFraniere, "U.S., Russia Agree to Arms Pact," *Washington Post*, May 14, 2002; James Carney, "Our New Best Friend?" *Time*, May 19, 2002; and Peter Slevin, "Bush to Seek Cooperation but Press Issues," *Washington Post*, May 21, 2002.

[52] On South Korea's contributions, which consisted of sending a few transport aircraft and some money for Afghan reconstruction, see Oknim Chung, "U.S.-ROK Relations in the Aftermath of the September 11 Terrorist Attacks," *Asia Perspectives*, vol. 4, no. 2 (Spring 2002), p. 13. There have been reports that the U.S. approached the ROK about the possibility of sending combat troops to Afghanistan but was rebuffed, see "South Korea Rejects U.S. Calls for Combat Troops to Afghanistan," *Agence France-Presse*, May 28, 2002, <www.nautilus.org/napsnet/dr/index.html#item4>. For an analysis of the impact of September 11 on U.S.-ROK relations see the chapter by Nicholas Eberstadt in this volume.

[53] Choe Sang-hun, "Bush's 'Axis of Evil' Remark Impacts on South Korean Presidential Campaign," *Associated Press*, February 2, 2002, <www.nautilus.org/napsnet/dr/0202/feb19.html#item2>.

[54] Elisabeth Bumiller, "North Korea Safe from U.S. Attack, Bush Says in Seoul," *The New York Times*, February 20, 2002.

[55] Paul Eckert, "Tough Security, Protests as Bush Visits South Korea," *Reuters*, February 20, 2002. Regarding changes in public opinion, see Donald G. Gross,

"U.S.-South Korean Relations: Riding the Roller-Coaster," *Comparative Connections*, vol. 4, no. 1 (April 2002), p. 41. Gross notes that this shift appears to have been due to discomfort with U.S. policies, but it may also have been driven in part by controversies surrounding the Winter Olympics.

[56] See, for example, Jia Qingguo, "US-China Relations After 11 September: Time for a Change," *PacNet Newsletter* no. 50, December 14, 2001, Pacific Forum/ CSIS; and Richard Holbrooke, "A Defining Moment with China," *Washington Post*, January 2, 2002.

[57] These issues are discussed at greater length in Friedberg, "11 September and the Future of Sino-American Relations," See also the chapter by Thomas Christensen in this volume.

[58] David E. Sanger, "Bush Meets China's Leader and Emphasizes Need to Fight Terrorism Together," *The New York Times*, October 19, 2001.

[59] Craig S. Smith, "Frustrating US, China Balks at Pact to Stem Missile Sales," *The New York Times*, October 19, 2001; and Jeremy Page, "U.S., China to Lock Horns on Missile Proliferation," *Reuters*, November 23, 2001, <www.nautilus. org/napsnet/dr/0111/nov26.html>.

[60] "U.S. to Impose Sanctions on China, Others Over Iran," *Reuters*, May 8, 2002, <www.nautilus.org/napsnet/wir2002/0510.html#item20/may08html>.

[61] See for example, "US Military Presence in Central Asia Aimed at China, Not bin Laden," Foreign Broadcast Information Service (FBIS) translation of an article by Yi Yangsheng in *Kuang Chiao Ching* (Hong Kong), October 16, 2001, CPP 20011016000087; and "Liaowan Views Geopolitical Changes in Central Asia," FBIS translation of an article by Chen Qimin in *Beijing Liaowan*, January 2, 2001, CPP 20020130000083. Other examples of this kind of thinking are cited by Thomas Christensen in his contribution to this volume.

[62] See "Chinese Expert Voices Concerns over Japan Passing Anti-Terrorism Bills," FBIS translation of an article by Tang Hui and Zhang Xinhua in *Beijing Renmin Wan*, November 2, 2001, CPP20011102000049.

[63] See "PRC: Japan's Sinking of Ship Not 'Justifiable Defense'" FBIS translation of an article by Sheng Xin in *Beijing Jiefangjun Bao*, December 31, 2001, CPP 20011231000070.

[64] See the remarks by Deputy Secretary of Defense Paul Wolfowitz at the National Press Club, May 15, 2002, <www.defenselink.mil/news/may2002/ t05162002_t0515npc.html>.

[65] See the chapter by Eric Heginbotham and Richard Samuels in this volume.

STRATEGIC ASIA

REGIONAL STUDIES

CHINA

Thomas J. Christensen

S eptember 11 provided a significant opportunity for the reduction of
tensions and an increase in cooperation between the People's Republic of China (PRC) and the United States. The nature and source of the
attack on the United States provided the basic foundation for that cooperation. Both the PRC and the United States are threatened by militant
Islamism, albeit in different ways and in different places. China also has
had economic and related domestic security reasons to worry about U.S.
woes following September 11, so there was no vengeful glee expressed in
high circles in Beijing. On the contrary, Beijing took several steps diplomatically, financially, and in the intelligence realm to assist the U.S. counter-
terrorism effort. Although it would be wrong to exaggerate the importance
of those steps to the campaign, the spirit behind them is quite meaningful,
at least for the near term.

How long the spirit of cooperation will continue is an open question.
Beijing will be quite nervous about Washington's extension of the war to
sovereign states other than Afghanistan. Moreover, the September 2001
attacks occurred at a time when Beijing was extremely confident about its
long-term ability to produce desirable results in relations across the Taiwan Strait. That optimism about China's increasing leverage over the is-

Thomas Christensen is Professor of Political Science and a member of the Security Studies Program at the Massachusetts Institute of Technology. He is grateful
to Richard Ellings, Aaron Friedberg, Michael Swaine, and Michael Wills for very
helpful comments. He also thanks Michael Glosny for expert research assistance.

land reduced the initial sensitivity to many regional aspects of the U.S. war on terror. Since the December legislative elections in Taiwan, in which President Chen's traditionally pro-independence Democratic Progressive Party (DPP) fared surprisingly well, that optimism in Beijing has decreased markedly. These revived concerns will likely be magnified by the prospect of a sustained U.S. presence in Central Asia and South Asia, a more active Japanese military, President Bush's emphasis on the U.S. defense commitment to Taiwan, and the U.S. development of missile defense programs. As in the past, concerns over Taiwan will intensify Chinese sensitivities over broader U.S. foreign policy: in this case the details of the U.S. war on terror. On the reverse side of the equation, the war on terror will increase U.S. sensitivities over issues such as Chinese transfers of weapons and military technologies to the Middle East, the Persian Gulf, and South Asia.

This chapter will review the major motivations behind China's security strategy. It will discuss why China initially responded moderately and cooperatively after September 11 to the U.S. war on terror, even as it became clear that the war effort carried implications for U.S. foreign policy and the foreign policies of China's neighbors that Beijing would have sharply criticized under more normal conditions. Although many factors contributed to China's cooperation after September 11, one important factor that has not received sufficient attention in the media and scholarly literature is Beijing elites' extreme and arguably excessive confidence about trends in cross-Strait relations at the time of the attack. That optimism was based on economic trends across the Strait and perceived political trends in Taiwan, but has dissipated since the fall of 2001, especially since Taiwan's December 2001 Legislative Yuan elections. Not surprisingly, the more sober attitude about Taiwan and U.S. relations with Taiwan has led to more criticism of U.S. security policy generally, including aspects of the war on terror. The concluding sections of the paper will speculate about how regional economic, military, and political trends might affect China's security strategy in the remainder of this decade, discussing what events might derail China's current approach to Taiwan, the United States, and the region, and what factors could continue to strengthen China's hand.

During the political transition from Jiang Zemin's generation to Hu Jintao's in late 2002, we should expect Beijing to avoid belligerent behavior that will harm relations with the United States. But Hu and his colleagues nevertheless will need to protect their nationalist credentials, as did their predecessors. In fact, with the economic dislocations and international and domestic controversies that are likely to follow China's recent accession to the World Trade Organization (WTO), the new leadership might need to protect those credentials even more jealously than their predecessors. This will hold doubly true if they begin to promote political reform, as some expect. A liberalizing political process, while healthy in the long-term, might make Chinese Communist Party (CCP) leaders, more, not less sensitive to perceived failures on Taiwan policy over the next five to ten years. On the other hand, continued economic growth is also essential to domestic stability in China. Conflict over Taiwan would risk alienating China's relationship with its three biggest trade and investment partners: Taiwan itself, the United States, and Japan. Beijing might face very tough decisions in the second half of this decade. For Taiwan, the United States, and their friends and allies, this means deterrence of the PRC will be quite possible, but also potentially quite complicated.

Beijing's Strategic Priorities

Last year's chapter in this report outlined a plausible ranking of the CCP's strategic priorities; these remain unchanged even with the substantial impact of September 11 on Strategic Asia, and understanding them is essential to understanding Beijing's specific reactions and responses:

1) Regime security: protecting the CCP from popular overthrow, from internal divisions, and from foreign and domestic infiltration.
2) Preserving territorial integrity: preventing the breakup of a large, ethnically diverse nation, including especially the prevention of Taiwan's permanent separation from the mainland, preventing Tibetan independence, and quelling Muslim uprisings in Xinjiang.
3) Gaining international prestige, power, and respect: increasing China's "comprehensive national power" (*zonghe guoli*), which involves not only military but economic and political power.[1] This includes the acquisition of high-profile weapons systems, space programs and other technology initiatives, and the hosting of international events such as the Olympic Games.

There is little or no evidence that China's goal or expectation for the next two or three decades is to dominate East Asia militarily, but China need not do that in order to gain a much more powerful voice in world politics and more deference in the region. Rather, China needs to be an indispensable engine of regional economic growth, to maintain military superiority over most regional actors, to close the conventional military gap with Russia and Japan, to develop the economic and military capability to coerce Taiwan into accommodation with the mainland, and to deter the United States from taking effective action against China's core interests. These international goals alone will pose daunting challenges for

Beijing, but they are far more attainable than regional domination or peer competitor status with the United States.

It is not simply a critique of the CCP to state that domestic issues, especially regime stability, are at the top of China's national security priorities. Foreign policy elites in Beijing often refer to the domestic reasons that Beijing must stand firm on the Taiwan issue—to prevent a nationalist humiliation of the CCP and to prevent a domino effect in other potentially independence-minded areas of the PRC, including Xinjiang and Tibet.[2] Adding credibility to their claims is the total bankruptcy of communist social and economic ideals in the PRC, even within the CCP. Whereas many outside China speculate about the rise of nationalism in Beijing, it might be more accurate to say that nationalism appears taller than before because other buildings in the Maoist ideological skyline regarding class warfare and third-world solidarity have all collapsed.

The building of comprehensive national power—economic, military, and political—does matter to the regime for its own sake and for reasons of domestic legitimacy but is primarily intended to build national prestige and international respect. For domestic and international reasons, Beijing clearly seeks more than just material power. On a few important occasions, most notably the signing of the Comprehensive Test-Ban Treaty (CTBT) in 1996, China has sacrificed real material power—the speed of its nuclear weapons development program—in order to avoid being labeled an international pariah state outside the norms of international society.[3]

Understanding the PRC's Response to September 11[4]

The September 11 attacks and the U.S. response to them affected just about everything in international security politics. China's foreign relations were certainly no exception. The initial signals out of Beijing suggested to some observers that Chinese elites might offer only limited and very conditional support for a U.S. counter-terrorism campaign. Foreign Ministry spokespeople, for example, emphasized the need for UN approval of any U.S. military response.[5] But one week after the attacks, the PRC already seemed much more forthcoming and cooperative. By all accounts, the visit of Foreign Minister Tang Jiaxuan to Washington in late September was a great success from the U.S. perspective, and China seemed willing to help in the U.S.-led effort against terrorism, at least as it applied to the destruction of Al Qaeda and the Taliban regime in Afghanistan. Secretary of State Colin Powell emphasized that there was no quid pro quo with Beijing in return for its cooperation on terrorism.[6] And during his trip to Shanghai for the APEC summit, President Bush emphasized that President Jiang's support for the United States had been immediate and forthright.[7] The details of Chinese cooperation in the war on terrorism are understandably classified, but public statements and off-the-record comments of knowledgeable government officials and well-connected former officials suggest that China has been relatively forthcoming in assisting the United States through diplomacy, crackdowns on terrorist financial networks, and, to a more limited degree, intelligence sharing.[8]

In particular, China's diplomatic contributions were more significant to both China and the United States than is generally recognized in the western media. Sustained Pakistani cooperation was essential to the war effort in Afghanistan and only seems a sure thing in hindsight. As mutual rivals of India in South Asia, Pakistan and China are each other's most important allies. For the three decades prior to September 11, China had the most influence with Pakistan, particularly on security issues. China offered early political and even limited financial support for Pakistani President Pervez Musharraf as he aligned himself with the U.S. war effort. In the fall of 2001, many feared Musharraf could face an overthrow or a coup for supporting a foreign assault on an Islamic nation.[9] To the degree that this danger was real, Chinese backing at this critical juncture likely had important implications for Musharraf's ability to maintain sufficient domestic political support for his controversial decision to assist Washington.

Beijing also supported a UN Resolution condemning the September 11 attacks and justifying a vigorous international response to them. Early UN backing was an important legitimating tool for the U.S. war on Al Qaeda and the Taliban. As a Security Council member with a long tradition of active opposition to great power interference in the internal affairs of weaker states, China's support on this score was appreciated in Washington. This is especially true given Beijing's vigorous opposition to NATO's 1999 war in Yugoslavia, which was never presented to the United Nations for approval.

Finally, at a minimum we can say that China did not actively oppose U.S. basing in the Central Asian states. This is an important concession, as the Chinese Foreign Ministry had worked hard since the mid-1990s to forge closer relations with the former Soviet republics in Central Asia. China's leading role in the group of six nations now called the Shanghai Cooperation Organization (SCO) has been a source of some pride for Beijing. The goals of the organization were to build security confidence along their shared borders, fight terrorism, and promote economic cooperation. To watch Beijing's influence in the region being outstripped by the United States practically overnight could not have been easy for many in the CCP, especially since the SCO was designed in part to combat terrorism. Despite this, Beijing did not oppose the insertion of U.S. forces into SCO member nations north of Afghanistan.

Reasons to Expect PRC Cooperation

China has its own reasons to cooperate in U.S. efforts to bring down Osama bin Laden's Al Qaeda organization. Since Beijing's security policy starts with issues of regime security and protection of national integrity, the CCP places some importance on its struggle against militant Muslim separatists in its northwest Xinjiang region. The PRC has suffered terrorist attacks of its own, both in Xinjiang and in Beijing. Some militant members of the so-called East Turkestan Independence Movement in Xinjiang have apparently been trained and supported by radical Islamists in Afghanistan, including Al Qaeda.[10] In typical fashion, Beijing's public claims likely exaggerate the number of Xinjiang's Uighurs trained by Al Qaeda. One report claims that Osama bin Laden's organization trained 1,000 Uighur terrorists from China.[11] This seems unlikely simply because of resource limitations and the relatively low priority that attacks on the PRC must hold for Al Qaeda in comparison to other higher-value targets such as Russian forces in Chechnya, U.S. forces in the Persian Gulf and Middle East, Indian forces in Kashmir, and Arab and Central Asian regimes opposing Al Qaeda and the Taliban. Beijing also has predictably used September 11 as an occasion to increase pressure, arrests, and executions aimed at all "separatists" in Xinjiang. It is not at all clear that these detainees are directly linked to international or domestic terrorism.[12] In fact, soon after September 11 Beijing tried to lump with the terrorists other groups that might pose a threat to regime stability, including the Falun Gong movement, a group that can hardly be equated with hijackers and suicide bombers.[13]

Chinese elites also saw September 11 as an opportunity to patch up relations with the United States. Following the April 2001 EP-3 incident, China seemed eager to avoid further short-term damage in its relationship with the Bush administration. This was particularly true in the period leading up to President George W. Bush's visit to Shanghai for the October 2001 APEC summit.[14]

There were some significant blemishes on the summit. President Bush and President Jiang did not seem to have the personal chemistry that Bush appears to have with Russian President Vladimir Putin. It is also true that the Bush-Putin meeting in Shanghai was given higher prominence in the press than the Bush-Jiang meeting. While it appeared that Bush and Putin were nearing an accord on important strategic issues, the U.S. president failed to achieve his major concrete objective in Shanghai, an agreement with Beijing to curtail missile technology proliferation.[15]

Despite these shortcomings, there were reasons to consider the summit a success from both countries' perspective. The fact that President Bush traveled to China at all in a time of national emergency was a major accomplishment for Beijing. In addition, Shanghai provided a showcase to the world for China's accomplishments since 1978. Beijing's willingness to allow a heavy focus on terrorism at such an economic summit was doubtless appreciated in Washington. At a minimum, the Bush administration's intense focus on the war must have signaled to Beijing that the burdens and distractions of the war on terror would make conflict with China over Taiwan even more costly to Washington than it otherwise would be. The war on terror might then provide some restraint in U.S. policy toward cross-Strait relations even if it does not provide concessions on Taiwan.

Another reason for PRC cooperation with the United States in the anti-terror campaign is less widely discussed. China would have to be greatly concerned about the economic impact on the United States of a failed campaign against terror. The annual growth of Chinese exports had already dropped from nearly 28 percent in 2000 to about seven percent in the months before September 11.[16] Few things are as essential to CCP regime security as healthy U.S. and global economies as sources of export markets and capital investment. Exports have been critical to China's growth and job creation (and therefore to CCP regime stability[17]), and the United States has long been the biggest single market for Chinese exports, its relative importance increasing over time in the 1990s to constitute nearly one-third of China's export market by the end of the decade.[18] Given the dangers that U.S. or global recession poses to the CCP, Beijing will try to avoid additional security headaches for itself and the United States. Connections between economics and security and between the international terrorist threat and the world economy have been noted at high levels in Beijing. For example, in December 2001 Foreign Minister Tang Jiaxuan placed central importance on the slowdown in the U.S. and world economies as factors that threaten global stability and progress. He also stated his opinion that the terror attacks and their aftermath have created a major obstacle to U.S. economic recovery.[19]

Another factor driving China's cooperation with the United States in the anti-terror campaign is that China wants to be a respected great power. Chinese nationalism is often equated with shrill condemnation of U.S. "hegemonism" and the creation of coercive military capacity. But there are other, softer sides to Chinese nationalism. China is eager not to be excluded from any global coalition that includes all of the other great powers in the world. Since Russia was cooperating actively with the United States as the latter prepared for an assault on Afghanistan, China had little choice but to maintain a similar posture. China would be isolated in the world community if it were to refuse U.S. appeals for cooperation. Such isolation and loss of face would have both international and domestic repercussions for CCP efforts to portray the PRC as a responsible and respected international actor. On the other hand, if Russia and U.S. allies were to become more critical of future phases of the war on terror (for example, a U.S. invasion of Iraq), then this should provide China more leeway to oppose U.S. efforts without high costs to its international prestige.

A few months after the attacks one Chinese intellectual stated that liberal-minded younger Chinese believe Moscow had outsmarted Beijing. Putin allegedly did so by sensing the changing winds after September 11 more quickly than CCP elites and by adopting a more proactive and imaginative role for Russia than Jiang Zemin did for China. The scholar believes that, on the one hand, domestic legitimacy problems prevented too harsh a reaction to U.S. military activity in Central Asia because the CCP does not like to be seen as standing alone on the international stage. On the other hand, the same domestic concerns rendered the CCP elites too conservative to make China a more influential and prominent player in the campaign, especially in the days just after September 11.[20] There may be some truth to this. If one looks at the testimony to Congress of Assistant Secretary of State Elizabeth Jones in mid-December, the Bush administration emphasized the cooperative and influential role of Russia in Central Asia, whereas China is apparently only mentioned as an afterthought. This lack of public recognition must be particularly irksome to Beijing given China's efforts since the mid-1990s to build influence in Central Asia through the SCO.[21] And, for reasons discussed below, American "promises" to stay engaged in Central Asia after the war in Afghanistan are being taken more as threats to project U.S. power there by many thinkers in Beijing.[22]

That being said, the increased U.S. influence in South and Central Asia carries some real benefits for Beijing along with costs. To the degree that the SCO was designed to contain the threat of domestic and cross-border terrorism in Central Asia, the introduction of massive U.S. resources into the region for precisely that purpose cannot be seen in a purely negative light in Beijing. Moreover, China's security relationship with Pakistan is, to a large degree, designed to prevent the Indian domination of South Asia that might follow from a large-scale, Indo-Pakistani conflict over Kashmir. However jealous Beijing might be about the speedy growth of Washington's influence in Islamabad, the new importance of Pakistan to the United States necessitates a degree of U.S. attention to the region that might help prevent such a large-scale conflict from breaking out in the first place. Moreover, the importance of Islamabad to U.S. grand strategy will offset to some degree the quickly improving security relationship between Washington and New Delhi, a trend which actually began prior to September 11, and which has been viewed with some concern in Beijing.

The Importance of Cross-Strait Relations

One final factor that helps explain China's continuing cooperation with the counter-terrorism campaign is the optimistic view that many in Beijing had of trends in cross-Strait relations in the months leading up to the December 2001 Taiwanese legislative elections. When China is confident about Taiwan, it is much less alarmist about potential U.S. encirclement. Those otherwise potentially troubling factors for Beijing elites were plentiful in the weeks after September 11, including improved U.S.-Indian ties, improved U.S.-Pakistani ties, the unprecedented acceptance of rear-area support roles for the Japanese navy in the Indian Ocean, the close cooperation between Russia and the United States, and the deployment of U.S. forces in Central Asia. Without the degree of confidence that China had on the Taiwan issue, Beijing might have viewed the policies of the United States and its allies with much greater concern following September 11.

In January 2001 interviews, interlocutors in Beijing expressed confidence that a combination of three factors would prevent Taiwanese independence and lead Taiwan to accept the "one China principle," China's prerequisites for negotiations. Those factors were: 1) the political weakness of President Chen Shui-bian; 2) the weakness of the Taiwanese economy in comparison to the growing mainland economy; and 3) Taiwan's growing economic dependence on the mainland, manifested not only in tens of billions of dollars in trade and investment, but also in hundreds of thousands of Taiwanese citizens setting up residence on the mainland. These factors, Beijing analysts believed, would lead to the further weakening of the DPP, the moderation of Taipei's stance on cross-Strait relations, and the return to negotiations on the mainland's terms.

There was very solid economic data to support this reasoning. Beijing has done an admirable job of maintaining high growth rates while controlling inflation and increasing foreign exchange reserves.[23] Even in the years since the 1997–98 Asian financial crisis, according to official statistics, China's GDP grew between seven and eight percent.[24]

Thomas Rawski and others have called into question these rosy official statistics for China's economy, particularly for years like 1998 and 1999, when China's economic growth clearly slowed. Rawski believes that China's economy might have actually shrunk in that period and that China's overall growth rate for the period since 1997 might be as low as one-third of the official statistics.[25] Citing key trade indicators, Nicholas Lardy counters Rawski's analysis, claiming that the official Chinese statistics are probably much closer to reality than Rawski allows.[26]

Even if we were to accept Rawski's pessimistic view of the Chinese economy, we would have to recognize not only that China was a strong

Figure 3.1. China's Real GDP Growth

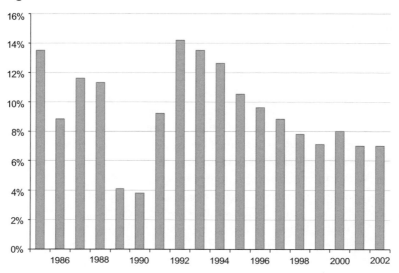

Source: National Bureau of Statistics, *China Statistical Yearbook 2000,* Beijing: China Statistics Press, 2000, p. 55; data for 2001 and the 2002 forecast are from the Economist Intelligence Unit, *China: Country Report*, April 2002.

performer compared to most regional economies following the Asian financial crisis but that it was a much stronger economic performer than Taiwan in 2001, President Chen's first full year in office. Taiwan's GNP dropped about two percent and unemployment reached record levels of over five percent as industrial output on the island dropped 10 to 15 percent. Trade, which makes up the majority of Taiwan's GNP, was off sharply. And all of this occurred while the government ran pump-priming deficits, banks kept interest rates low, and the Taiwan dollar depreciated on world markets.[27] The reasoning on the mainland in 2001 was that President Chen's long-term political prospects would be hurt by these economic trends.

What is more important for our purposes is that Taiwan's economy was becoming increasingly dependent on the fast-growing mainland. By 2001 the stock of Taiwanese investment in the mainland had increased to anywhere from $60 to $100 billion and some reports suggested that investment rates had increased sharply, by 25 percent, in the first three quarters of 2001 leading up to the December Legislative Yuan elections. By even the most conservative indicator (officially approved overseas investment), about 40 percent of Taiwan's accumulated investment abroad is now on the mainland.[28] Moreover, Taiwanese companies are no longer investing in just light plastics and footwear production, but increasingly in more value-added, high-tech manufacturing such as plants producing semiconductors and memory chips. The investment flow seemed immune to politics as business leaders previously averse to investment on the mainland broke their personal prohibition on mainland investments. Despite protests from traditional members of the DPP's popular base, President Chen's government approved the move of eight-inch silicon wafer production plants to the mainland.[29] China was attractive for a range of reasons, including intentional and politically driven policies of favoritism toward Taiwanese investors on the mainland and the drying up of traditional, alternative targets for Taiwanese investment in Southeast Asia following the Asian financial crisis.[30]

Like investment, trade across the Taiwan Strait is difficult to measure with assurance, but most estimates place cross-Strait trade at about \$35 to \$40 billion per year, with Taiwan enjoying a significant surplus.[31] The mainland market absorbs over 20 percent of Taiwanese exports.[32] Along with trade and investment flows go people, and an estimated 300,000 Taiwanese residents live at least part of the time in the Shanghai area alone. Underscoring the importance of Taiwan's growing economic stake in the mainland, in August 2001 President Chen took the advice of an independent committee he had formed and pushed for the lifting of various investment limits and trade regulations on cross-Strait economic interaction.[33]

For all of these economic reasons CCP analysts in 2001 felt very confident that long-term political trends toward Taiwan's independence could be kept in check and eventually reversed. Feeding this confidence were visitors to the mainland from opposition parties competing with Chen's DPP who stated to CCP elites that public opinion in Taiwan was turning away from Chen and toward accommodation with the mainland. As will be discussed below, the December 2001 election results seemed to upset this optimistic scenario for cross-Strait rapprochement. Before the election, however, in the first months of the war on terror, confidence was high that time was on the mainland's side and that non-military methods could bring Taiwan back into the fold down the road.

Potential Roadblocks to Long-Term PRC Cooperation with the United States

Chinese cooperation with the United States during the campaign in Afghanistan might not lead to longer-term U.S.-PRC cooperation in a broader anti-terror campaign. Beijing's cooperation with the United States will be severely tested in a campaign targeting other sovereign states and subnational actors around the globe who harbor, finance, arm, and provide intelligence for terrorist cells. There is also a real danger of significant fallout in U.S.-China relations if the cooperative framework breaks down during a longer campaign. The tone of President Bush's October speech to a joint session of Congress reflected the strong emotions in the United States about the importance of success in a broader struggle. In such an atmosphere even PRC fence-sitting (e.g., the Gulf War), let alone PRC support for U.S. enemies (e.g., the Kosovo operation), would be much more damaging to U.S.-China relations than it has been in the past. Unfortunately, for the reasons offered below, cooperation will likely not be easy to maintain. One key factor in China's attitudes about the implications of U.S. strategy for China will be Beijing's optimism or pessimism on trends in cross-Straits relations and the prospect of peaceful settlement on Beijing's terms.[34]

Beijing's Response to the December 2001 Taiwan Elections: Pessimism and Realism

Not-for-attribution interviews with civilian and military experts on the mainland in January 2001 and January 2002 about trends in cross-Strait relations and U.S. security policy toward China and Taiwan revealed degrees of optimism and pessimism. These varied among individuals and institutions, with the military consistently more pessimistic than the civilians. In 2002, however, there was a great deal more pessimism and concern about these issues in both civilian and military circles than in the previous year.

In the wake of the December 2001 Taiwanese legislative elections, CCP civilian and military experts had the following mix of attitudes.[35] On the negative side, there was a marked renewal of pessimism about trends in cross-Strait relations, particularly among military scholars. Although civilians and military officers alike continued to view growing economic interdependence across the Strait as a factor in Beijing's favor, the renewed pessimism resulted in a greater emphasis on the need for mainland military strength as a check on trends that would eventually lead to Taiwanese independence. Almost all interlocutors viewed China's military build-up across the Strait as a necessary component of a PRC effort to bring Taiwan to the table on Beijing's terms. Military and civilian analysts alike roundly rejected U.S. scholars' suggestions that the PRC should reduce forces in the Nanjing Military District in order to build confidence in Taipei and Washington.

On the positive side, there was clearly growing realism and sophistication about Taiwanese politics and recognition of the need to engage the DPP over the longer term. Taiwan experts in Beijing seemed more sobered than shocked by the DPP's strong showing in the legislative elections. Judging by their shift from high degrees of optimism in January 2001 to a mix of relative pessimism and much more cautious optimism in January 2002, the elections indeed had a big impact on their analysis.[36]

Despite all the negative economic trends in Taiwan and positive economic trends in cross-Strait relations outlined above, the elections provided a major boost to the DPP and a shattering blow to the more unification-oriented Kuomintang (KMT).[37] The DPP gained 17 seats in the election, for a total of 87 of the 225 seats in the legislature. In addition, the newly formed party of former president and KMT-exile Lee Teng-hui, the Taiwan Solidarity Union, won 13 seats. From Beijing's perspective, pro-independence forces now occupy 100 seats, and trend lines suggest that a majority is not out of the question in the future. Also negative from Beijing's perspective was the defeat of the KMT. KMT members had apparently been fueling Beijing's confidence about trends in Taiwanese politics by visiting the mainland and promising better cross-Straits relations once they had improved their position vis-à-vis the DPP. The KMT in fact dropped from 123 seats in 1998 to 68 seats in 2001. A final piece of bad news for Beijing was the devastating results for the New Party, the only party to explicitly advocate reunification, which held on to only one seat.[38]

The outcome was not all bad from Beijing's perspective, however. On the positive side, the new, relatively accommodationist People's First Party under former KMT member James Soong won an impressive 46 seats. The percentages of popular votes held by the independence-minded "green parties" and the more unification-minded "blue parties" remained about the same as in previous years, with both groups holding around 40 percent of the popular vote.[39] Yet, even this outcome could not be particularly satisfying in Beijing. According to the optimistic theory prevalent on the mainland earlier in 2001, economic trends before the elections should have hurt the green parties and helped the blue parties. According to Chinese interlocutors, this trend was supposed to make Taiwan more willing to return to the alleged "1992 consensus" in which, according to Beijing, both sides accepted that there is one China but agreed to disagree on what that meant. Eventually, growing economic interdependence was also supposed to lead to Taiwan's acceptance of the "one country, two systems" formula. It is fairly clear, however, that despite the most desirable conditions imaginable for these predictions no such trend emerged.[40]

In January 2002, the PRC's Taiwan watchers often seemed unwilling to recognize that they had misread the electoral trends the previous year. However, most were willing to admit that they had not expected the KMT to perform so poorly. They also admitted that it seemed quite likely that President Chen would win a second term, which would mean that the CCP would have to open better and more direct channels of communication with the DPP instead of relying on contacts with the opposition parties.[41] This belief was reflected in a key policy speech by Vice Premier Qian Qichen on

January 24, in which Qian argued that the majority of the DPP members were not independence activists and that only the minority of "splittists" in the party would continue to be shunned by Beijing. Qian called for more contacts with the alleged moderates in the DPP as long as the contacts were with people at an "appropriate" level in the party, presumably excluding top officials in Taipei.[42]

In addition to the election results themselves, Beijing elites were concerned about the subsequent policy initiatives of President Chen's government, which they saw as part of a "creeping independence" campaign. Those policies included: adding the word "Taiwan" to the cover of the ROC passport; the removal of the Chinese map from the Government Information Office seal in Taipei; and the reshuffling of top military officers to the advantage of native Taiwanese officers.[43] There was general concern about the local identity project (*bentuhua*) being pushed in schools, in government-sponsored cultural events, and on signs and symbols in Taiwan. Analysts in the PRC believe that, while an outright declaration of independence is still not likely in the foreseeable future, Chen's confidence is already manifesting itself in policies that are detrimental to the prospect of cross-Strait unification talks on Beijing's terms. One oft-repeated concern is that if Chen were to win a second term in 2004, Taipei might push provocative diplomatic initiatives prior to the 2008 Olympics under the theory that China would not dare retaliate with military force and thereby spoil the international environment for hosting the Games. Another concern in Beijing is that Taiwan might try to use its new membership in the WTO not just for the resolution of trade and investment problems, but for political purposes as well.[44]

Levels of pessimism about the dangers of eventual independence, however, apparently have not reached the level of early 2000, when there were severe doubts that peace could be maintained across the Taiwan Strait over the long term, and when China published its provocative *Taiwan White Paper*, suggesting growing impatience with current trends in cross-Strait relations and warning Taiwan about the danger of indefinite stalling over negotiations. In 2002, increasing pessimism was tempered by a recognition of increasing mainland economic leverage over Taiwan.[45]

Since interdependence is viewed as a factor favoring the mainland, we can better understand why Qian Qichen sent out moderate feelers to Taipei on January 24, 2002. In that message, he suggested that economic issues, such as the "three links" (trade, postal, and transportation), could be discussed by non-political actors, such as business elites. He also opened the door to more public engagement of DPP members by high-ranking CCP members, even if he did not accept the restoration of high-level cross-Strait governmental dialogue along the lines of the 1993 Singapore Talks. Beijing's pre-conditions for such dialogue remain the same: Taipei's acceptance of the 1992 consensus and some public recognition of a "one China principle." Those pre-conditions have been rejected by high-level officials in Taipei, who want dialogue to resume without pre-conditions.[46]

Other moderating influences in Beijing include the perception that, although he "would like to pursue independence," President Chen is a "practical politician" and therefore is less likely to take rash actions. The basis of comparison is former president Lee Teng-hui. Beijing elites consider Lee to be more risk acceptant and more wedded to Taiwanese independence than Chen.[47] In their minds, the key question for the future is this: as a practical politician committed to independence in an economy increasingly dependent on the mainland, will Chen try to improve political relations across the Strait and abandon his independence desires, or will he abandon economic practicality to try to pursue Taiwan sovereignty, with potentially disastrous consequences for cross-Strait relations? In 2001 many CCP experts stated with confidence that Chen would choose the former, but in 2002 there was much more uncertainty on this score.[48]

Among the most sensitive issues in Beijing is U.S. relations with Taiwan, particularly sales of weapons that can create peace-time linkages between the two militaries through interoperability. Future sea-based theater missile defense systems or F-16 data links were seen as creating real-time cooperation between U.S. and Taiwanese forces that could be seen as a renewed alliance. Several CCP analysts emphasized that U.S. and Taiwanese cooperation on "software" was seen as detrimental, even more so than many aspects of cooperation on military hardware.[49]

Beijing elites also express concern about the transit diplomacy of key Taiwanese leaders through the United States. One well-placed military officer posited that a visit by President Chen to Washington would very likely trigger a military response from the mainland that would exceed in scope the PLA exercises of March 1996.[50] If this actually represents elite thinking, his logic demonstrates the potential danger of excessive pessimism in Beijing about trends in cross-Straits relations, especially when that pessimism is combined with a belief in the efficacy of the military instrument in reshaping those trends.

U.S.-China Relations in 2002–03: The End of the Anti-Terror Honeymoon?

The apparent deepening of U.S. defense ties with Taiwan, especially after the February 2002 summit, has provided a catalyst for broader PRC concerns about U.S. activities in the region. Perhaps the most controversial event was the invitation to Taiwanese Defense Minister, Tang Yao-ming, to visit Florida for a mid-March defense industry meeting attended by Deputy Secretary of Defense Paul Wolfowitz and Assistant Secretary of State for East Asia James Kelly. Official and unofficial protests from Beijing branded this a violation of the 1979 U.S.-PRC normalization agreement.[51] This followed the Bush administration's consistent statements of commitment to Taiwan's defense since April 2001 (that the United States would "do whatever it takes" to help Taiwan) and a robust arms sales package including a promise to transfer eight diesel submarines to the island. Finally, the Department of Defense's *Nuclear Posture Review*, leaked to the press in March 2002, sparked a backlash in China because it specified a future Taiwan scenario as one in which nuclear weapons might be useful.[52]

Of course, there are many forces at work in determining Beijing's attitudes about U.S. security strategy. Attitudes about Taiwan constitute just one of those forces, albeit an important one. It is difficult to prove conclusively, but there does appear to be a direct relationship between PRC confidence levels on Taiwan and its attitudes about the role of the United States and its allies in the region. In the fall of 2001, when Beijing was confident that cross-Strait relations were moving in a positive direction, China provided fairly consistent support for the U.S. war on terror. In 2002, CCP elites grew more concerned about domestic political trends on Taiwan and trends in the U.S.-Taiwanese relationship. The former factor is more important than the latter because Beijing analysts recognize that, if Taiwan were willing to accommodate the mainland, there is nothing that any U.S. military or political commitment to Taiwan could do to dissuade the island from doing so. But when Taipei resists pressure from the mainland, Beijing elites view U.S. support for Taiwan as particularly important and particularly frustrating. When Beijing grows concerned about Taiwan and U.S.-Taiwanese relations, other aspects of U.S. foreign policy are viewed with increasing suspicion. Since Taiwan's legislative elections and the visit to the United States of its minister of defense, Beijing has grown more critical of U.S. and allied activities in the region and the potential for expansion of the anti-terror campaign to "axis of evil" states like Iraq, North Korea, and Iran.

Various aspects of the war on terror are of concern to Chinese security analysts: increased security ties with both India and Pakistan; the prospect of long-term U.S. military basing in Central Asia; and an invigorated Japanese military role in the U.S.-Japan alliance, including naval deployments in the Indian Ocean. These concerns were only catalyzed by President Bush's statements during his February 2002 trip to China regarding his adherence to the Taiwan Relations Act, and his avoidance of explicit public reference to the three joint communiqués signed with the PRC by

Presidents Nixon, Carter, and Reagan.[53] Under these circumstances any anti-terrorist or pre-summit honeymoon quickly ended. In fact, while President Bush was still on his return trip from China, the *PLA Daily* criticized recent U.S. security initiatives with India as potentially destabilizing in South Asia.[54] Such critiques were muted in the kiss-and-makeup period that generally precedes summits. By June the attacks were more direct. China's official media blasted President Bush's June 1 graduation speech at West Point, which discussed the need for preemptive U.S. strikes against terrorists and the regimes that support them. One prominent CCP newspaper stated that "the Bush Administration is now displaying not only a lack of the kind of discretion a global power should demonstrate but also its unwise ambition to abuse its power in its push for hegemony."[55]

The press on the mainland and in Hong Kong has published a fairly steady flow of implicit and explicit criticisms of aspects of the U.S. war on terror both as it applies to the region and to Central Asia and the Persian Gulf. The United States and Japan have been singled out in multiple articles for opportunistically exploiting September 11 to increase their military power projection capabilities in areas surrounding China. The underlying theme of these articles is that Tokyo planned to break out of the constraints of its constitution and the United States planned to increase its presence in Central Asia and Southeast Asia before September 11. The terrorist attacks, the argument runs, provided a pretext for the United States and its friends and allies to carry out their geostrategic plans, which are aimed as much at gaining hegemony and countering China as they are at countering terrorism.[56] Such "America threat" theories in China are not new, but seem to gain in prominence whenever there is a downturn in U.S.-China relations (such as the NATO bombing of the PRC embassy in Belgrade in 1999). At those tense times in U.S.-China relations, it appears that the pacifying effects of economic integration around the globe and across the Taiwan Strait are not emphasized nearly as consistently nor nearly as enthusiastically in the public or private statements of CCP elites.

Arms Control, Proliferation, and the Danger to U.S.-China Relations

In addition to the possibility that PRC frustration over Taiwan will eventually precipitate a use of coercive force by Beijing sometime later this decade, there is a serious, short-term danger to bilateral relations. When Beijing is frustrated about U.S. arms sales to Taiwan or other aspects of U.S. foreign policy, it has often implicitly used arms sales and technical cooperation with countries of concern to the United States as a tit-for-tat response. It is not at all clear that Chinese elites understand how much more dangerous this would be to bilateral relations after September 11, given the changed mood in the United States and the sharply increased possibility that the United States might take military action against countries like Iraq or Iran—some of the traditional Chinese end-users.[57]

After the U.S.-Taiwan defense meeting in Florida, and at a time when Chinese criticism of U.S. foreign policy in the war on terror was on the rise in Beijing, President Jiang and Prime Minister Zhu Rongji both made high-profile visits to the Middle East and Persian Gulf. Jiang visited two countries of concern to the United States, Iran and Libya. In Tehran he expressed concerns about "random expansion" of the war on terror.[58] Whether or not weapons transfers were discussed on this trip, such high-level visits must raise already high concerns in Washington about cooperation between Chinese defense firms and the militaries of these nations. According to news reports, the U.S. government is currently preparing sanctions against particular Chinese firms for transferring WMD-related technology and/or missile technology to Iran in particular.[59] Chinese proliferation of missile-related technologies to Pakistan, Iran, and "several other countries" was a focus of concern in Director of Central Intelligence George Tenet's testimony to a Senate Select Committee on Intelligence on February 6, 2002.[60] According to the Chinese press, proliferation was also a major topic of discussion between Vice President Dick Cheney and Vice President Hu during the latter's trip to Washington in May 2002.[61]

Long-Term Trends Across the Strait and the Pacific

The Continuing PLA Military Build-Up and the Likely U.S. and Taiwanese Response

China is in the early phases of a truly significant military build-up. China's official defense budget increased by 18 percent in real terms in each of the last two years and by about 12 percent the previous year. Previous nominal increases have been largely offset by inflation, but inflation has been near or even below zero for the past three years.[62]

Despite growing social welfare bills and deficit spending, Beijing might be able to sustain substantial defense increases for quite a while, and almost certainly plans to continue them through 2005, the last year of the tenth five-year plan. As discussed in last year's report, China's government absorbs a small percentage of GNP compared to governments in the West and to CCP governments before the reform period. In fact, some analysts have speculated that the government's share of GNP had fallen to 12 percent (or lower) in the 1990s. Moreover, the central government received only about half of that amount, leaving little for social welfare,

Figure 3.2. Official Chinese Military Spending

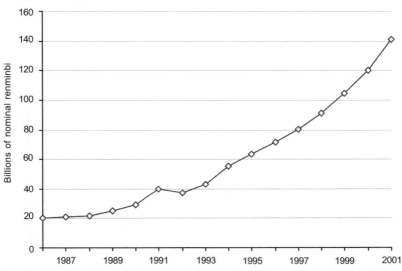

Source: International Institute for Strategic Studies, *The Military Balance*, London: Oxford University Press, various editions.

regional redistribution, and military spending.[63] From anecdotal reports it would appear that Zhu Rongji successfully turned those trend-lines around in his last few years in office and that the Chinese state is now able to absorb a somewhat higher percentage of GNP as a result of crackdowns on corruption and the creation of a more efficient tax collection bureaucracy. One recent Hong Kong article claims that the PRC should be able to reach the reported CCP goal of raising the state's share of GNP to 25 percent in the coming years. The author argues that this would have big implications for the Chinese military budget and domestic stability but little impact on China's economic growth, as demonstrated by the generally higher percentage of GNP absorbed by government in some rich western countries. Moreover, he argues, since a strong hand against Taiwan is considered essential to domestic stability in China and, therefore, long-term growth, Chinese elites do not now see a stark trade-off between defense spending and long-term growth, whereas they clearly did in the 1980s and most of the 1990s.[64]

As part of this military build-up, China is acquiring precisely the types of weapons it would need in a coercion campaign against Taiwan. Moreover, based on published reports and off-the-record comments by government experts in both Washington and Beijing, the People's Liberation Army (PLA) is training in more serious ways for actual combat in Taiwan scenarios. At the time of writing (summer 2002), the PLA is reported to be embarking on a six-month exercise opposite Taiwan involving some 100,000 troops. This follows large-scale exercises off Dongshan Island in the summer of 2001. Like those in 1995 and 1996, these exercises are almost certainly seen in Beijing as having deterrent value in Taiwan, but unlike earlier exercises they appear also to have much more practical implications for war-fighting in the future.[65]

Western analysts of the Chinese military often overemphasize the importance of overall relative military power and whether or not China is catching up with the United States or its allies. This misses the growth in China's coercive power against Taiwan and its supporters, even as the PLA fails to improve its ability to invade Taiwan or to fight successfully in a toe-to-toe war against the U.S.-Japan alliance, for example.[66] Although developing these capabilities may be difficult for China, it is a much lower threshold of success than would be creating the conditions for direct occupation of Taiwan or military defeat of Taiwan's international supporters.

Deterrence requirements for Taiwan and its supporters are particularly high because rather than simply maintaining a military balance across the Taiwan Strait, Taiwan, the United States, and Japan ideally would be able to demonstrate the ability to limit their costs in a cross-Strait conflict. This is particularly true when one considers that Chinese strategic analysts often emphasize that Taiwan's political resolve would be weak under attack. Moreover, some believe that the United States may take a long time to respond effectively, particularly if it is tied down elsewhere or if it loses the support of local allies like Japan. Finally, although expectations of U.S. intervention are high after Washington responded forcefully to the March 1996 exercises, at least some Chinese analysts seem to believe that the United States is too casualty averse to stay engaged with China for a protracted conflict over Taiwan.[67]

China's future ability to coerce Taiwan through a blockade, information warfare, strikes with accurate ballistic and cruise missiles, or special operations will depend heavily on continued access to Russian technology and expertise. So will its ability to deter, slow, alter, or end the deployment of U.S. forces to the Taiwan area. China's best submarines, fighter aircraft, surface ships, anti-ship cruise missiles, land attack cruise missiles, terminal guidance systems for ballistic missiles, and surface-to-air missiles are all dependent in whole or in part on Russian military production or expertise.[68] Much attention has been paid in the United States and elsewhere to the Chinese reaction to U.S. deployments in Central Asia and the changing military relationships between the United States, Japan, and India. However, perhaps the most troublesome aspect of the war on terror for Beijing is the budding relationship between the Bush administration and the Putin government. This has been symbolized not only by cooperation in Central Asia but also by Russia's muted reaction to the U.S. withdrawal from the ABM Treaty and Russia's effective entry into NATO as a "junior partner" in May 2002. If that relationship were to develop into a more robust one, perhaps the United States could pressure or persuade Russia to halt sales of weapons like supersonic anti-ship cruise missiles, which might endanger U.S. and Taiwanese forces in the future. This would be a heavy blow to China's efforts to coerce Taiwan and to modernize China's fighting forces.[69]

U.S. arms transfers to Taiwan, as they come on line, will also limit PRC coercive capacity against the island. The media has focused on the U.S. promise to transfer eight diesel submarines to Taiwan, equipment that the United States has not produced in decades and that other countries do not appear eager to supply at the expense of their relations with Beijing. But there are less dramatic aspects of the Bush administration's arms package that might provide more important defensive capabilities to Taiwan than the submarines. These include mine-clearing helicopters and P-3 Orion aircraft that can hunt for submarines and attack surface combatants, such as the PLA Navy's Russian-made Sovremenny destroyers.

That said, the challenges for Taiwan are real and are growing. In the standard wisdom about military affairs, defense generally has the advantage over offense. This is particularly true for islands because water is so difficult to cross under fire. But this wisdom is built on the assumption that the attacker is set on conquest of the defender's territory. If the attacker's goal is, rather, coercion and the raising of costs to the defender, offense generally has the advantage over defense, particularly if the defender in question is as dependent on international economic links as is Taiwan. In this sense, Taiwan and its supporters will require a very high level of sustainable local military superiority in order to ensure deterrence, and it is not at all clear that they will be able to do so for the next two decades. This is especially true if they become complacent about the challenges they face by referring to the clear overall superiority of U.S. forces to the PLA or the difficulty for the PLA of invading and occupying Taiwan, neither of which will change anytime soon.

Economic Trends Across the Taiwan Strait

Of course, as optimistic Chinese analysts eagerly point out, the mainland has much more than military sticks to influence Taiwan—it has economic leverage in the form of carrots for Taiwanese cooperation and sticks for Taiwanese transgressions. One of the questions everyone wants to ask

Table 3.1. Selected Relevant Military Systems for PRC Cross-Strait Coercive Strategies

China	Taiwan
Strategic Missiles	**Missile Defense**
Offensive Systems	Anti-Ballistic Missile Systems
300–500 SRBMs (M-9 and M-11)	Lower tier: a number of Patriot-
Likely to grow by 50 per year.	variant systems, including PAC-2+,
50–60 IRBMs (DF-21A)	likely to grow in next decade.
Reports of DF-31 attaining	Interest in obtaining PAC-3 capability.
operational status.	Inclusion in future upper tier
Land attack cruise missiles (LACMs)	systems: unknown.
Will be acquired soon in	
unknown numbers.	Anti-Cruise Missile Systems
	Kidd-class DDGs (SM-2 SAMs, due
	to arrive in 2005).
	Several Patriot-variant systems,
	including PAC-2+.
Air Force	**Air Force**
Tactical Air Power	Tactical Air Power
80–120 fourth-generation fighters	210 fourth-generation fighters (F-16,
(Su-30, Su-27); rapid increases	Mirage 2000-5).
possible contingent on continued	Small but unknown quantities of
Russian support.	AMRAAMs (BVR).
Small but unknown numbers of	Reports of sales of small quantities
AA-12 (beyond visual range).	of HARMs.
200 J-8s, to be followed with the	325 third-generation fighters (IDF,
J-10 (currently in prototype).	F-5E).
Hundreds of older J-6/J-7.	
	Airbases
SAMs	Infrastructure hardening still needed.
About 20 SA-10 variant SAM	
systems (each with several	SAMs
launchers).	Substantial number of tactical
Numerous indigenously produced	systems.
systems.	
	Force Multipliers
Force Multipliers	4 E-2C Hawkeye AWACS, capable
Perhaps 2–4 A-50E (Russian AWACS	of controlling 40 intercepts and
variant) in the future; significantly	monitoring 2,000 targets at range
less capable than U.S. systems.	of 300+ nautical miles; up to 4
3–4 patrol/reconnaisance planes	more may be purchased
(TU-154M, Y-8); may have some	Also seeking long-range early
limited early warning capabilities.	warning radar.

Navy	Navy
Surface Fleet	Surface Fleet
2 modern, Sovremenny-class destroyers; at least 2 more should be imported soon.	22 modern frigates (Perry, La Fayette, Knox).
60 other surface warfare ships with severe vulnerabilities to air and submarine attacks.	10 older warships (improved Gearing).
	4 Kidd-class destroyers to arrive in about 2005.
Submarine Fleet	Submarine Fleet
4 quality kilo-class (2 standard export variant, 2 enhanced); reportedly interested in importing 8 more from Russia.	4 SSKs (2 WWII-era, more-modern Dutch model).
5 nuclear submarines of questionable reliability (Han); may be supplemented by 2 newer submarines later in the decade.	8 newer SSKs could arrive around 2010, depending on U.S. ability to procure.
2–4 indigenous relatively modern Song-class submarines.	Key Anti-Submarine Warfare Assets (other than surface fleet)
40–60 older, noisier SSKs (Ming, Romeo).	20–30 S-2T patrol aircraft; soon to be supplemented with 12 P-3 Orions.
Anti-Ship Cruise Missiles	Counter-Mine Capabilities
Some advanced systems deployed.	4 relatively modern minehunter ships.
More capable systems likely under purchase contract with Russia or currently under development with Russian support.	Modern minesweeping helicopters (MH-53E); to be imported.
	8 older minesweeper ships.
Mine Warfare Assets	
Some evidence of advanced mines.	
Large inventory of backward mines.	

Sources: International Institute for Strategic Studies, *The Military Balance, 2001–2002*, New York: Oxford University Press, 2001; A. D. Baker III, *Combat Fleets of the World, 2000–2001: Their Ships, Aircraft, and Systems*, Annapolis, Calif.: Naval Institute Press, 2000; Paul Jackson, *et al*, eds., *Jane's All the World's Aircraft, 2001–2002*, Alexandria, Va.: Jane's Information Group, 2001; Tony Cullen and Christopher Foss, eds., *Jane's Land Based Air Defence, 2001–2002*, Alexandria, Va.: Jane's Information Group, 2001; Duncan Lennox, *Jane's Strategic Weapon Systems, 2001–2002*, Alexandria, Va.: Jane's Information Group, 2001; Mark A. Stokes, *China's Strategic Modernization: Implications for the United States*, Carlisle, Pa.: Strategic Studies Institute, U.S. Army War College, 1999. On future transfer of Kilo submarines and anti-ship cruise missiles, see "Report on Functions, Armament of Russian-Made 'Kilo'-Class Sumbarines," *Sing Tao Jih Pao*, Hong Kong, June 10, 2002, in *FBIS* (CPP20020910000043).

Chen Shui-bian is whether or not he believes "Shanghai fever" or "mainland fever" in Taiwan's business community will end, reducing the fast pace of growth in trade and investment relationships with the mainland.[70] The question arises from a concern about the impact of Taiwan's economic "hollowing out" and dependence on the mainland on Chen's efforts to preserve Taiwan's de facto independence. Chen, who seemingly always exudes confidence, claims that such a fever cannot last indefinitely. But, despite early signs that 2002 would see the fever break, the most recent available data shows, if anything, a slight increase in trade and investment across the Taiwan Strait through the spring of 2002.[71]

There are some hopeful signs about the Taiwanese economy more generally, however. Forecasters predict a reversal of last year's recession and growth of between two and four percent, particularly in the second half of 2002. The forecast is partially based on a prediction of recovery in the global computer industry, in which Taiwan's semiconductor sector is a leading player.[72] We should expect cooperation between Taiwan and the mainland to increase in this sector, so Taiwan's growth might actually increase Beijing's leverage over the island. Other factors signaling a recovery in Taiwan are a slight drop in the unemployment rate in the early months of 2002 and a sharp increase in foreign investment on the island.[73]

That said, Beijing's growing economic leverage still may not produce results in Taiwanese politics that suit Beijing's long-term interests. As we saw in the legislative elections, Taiwanese citizens supported the DPP fairly widely, despite a weak economy and poor cross-Strait relations. One likely reason for DPP success was the party's ability to blame the KMT majority in the legislature for the slow economy.[74] If the economy turns around in 2002, this might provide more ammunition for the DPP in its attack on the KMT. KMT leader and former prime minister Lien Chan recently attacked Chen and the DPP for mishandling cross-Strait relations by advocating "creeping independence." Lien even blamed U.S. support for encouraging Chen in this effort. Such rhetoric might suggest a joint campaign in 2004 by the KMT and the People's First Party.[75] The problem is that such rhetoric will likely appear to most Taiwanese as too soft on the mainland. As long as Chen does not spark a war in the process, there is little evidence that what Beijing and, now, the KMT label as "creeping independence" is unpopular in Taiwan.[76]

China's and Taiwan's accession to the WTO should encourage further links across the Taiwan Strait. In fact, trade increased nearly 13 percent in the first two months of 2002.[77] To the degree that interdependence is a source of peace, this should be welcomed. But WTO membership also poses some problems. First, some in Beijing worry that Taiwan's inclusion in the WTO will whet Taipei's appetite for inclusion in other international organizations, like the World Health Organization. In other words, Taiwan will use its entrance into the WTO as a launch pad to gain the status of a normal sovereign state on the international stage. They also worry that Taiwan will try to use the WTO for political purposes, despite warnings from the international community to both sides that the institution is for managing economic issues only.[78] Another source of potential conflict might be the exposure of Taiwan's agricultural sector to increased competition. If Taiwan were to open up this sector precipitously it could lead to widespread resentment against the mainland. If it does not, it will likely be in violation of WTO rules. However, it is somewhat doubtful that Beijing would file formal complaints against Taiwan in an international organization like the WTO and, in the process, raise Taiwan's profile as a legitimate international actor.[79]

Challenges for China's Economy

As stated earlier, domestic security is Beijing's primary policy focus. Economic growth and globalization influence the CCP's ability to provide employment and avoid criticism on nationalist grounds, so the most important questions for foreign analysts of China to answer are those relating to the future health and stability of mainland China's political economy, which will have implications for PRC security policy. A slowdown in the Chinese economy might reduce China's considerable and growing economic leverage over Taiwan and regional actors such as Japan and the ASEAN states.[80] That leverage is important in Beijing's efforts to isolate Taiwan diplomatically and, in the case of Japan, to discourage active cooperation with any future U.S. intervention on Taiwan's behalf. Economic growth also supplies funds for growing military budgets at home and weapons purchases abroad.

CCP economic leaders did a remarkable job in the mid-1990s of encouraging growth without sparking inflation, but there are still huge challenges. As discussed in greater detail in last year's *Strategic Asia* report, financial reform and the freeing of the Chinese banking system from the heavy burden of loans to inefficient state-owned enterprises (SOEs) is central to the smooth growth of the Chinese economy and to the maintenance of social stability. According to one recent report, SOEs still employ 55 percent of urban workers even as they produce a much smaller percentage of urban output.[81] On the one hand, a precipitous cut-off of funds to SOEs could have dire social consequences. On the other hand, the relationship between the state banks and the SOEs must be broken not simply to wean the SOEs off their addiction to public funds (in the form of soft loans), but to allow banks to play the role that they play in more efficient economies, as providers of loans to the more profitable and valuable sectors of the economy.[82] This is particularly true for China, where the banks have been by far the biggest domestic source of capital for Chinese economic growth. But the vast majority of bank loans—as much as 80 percent—has gone to inefficient SOEs.[83]

Non-performing loans (NPLs) in the banking system are estimated officially at approximately 25 percent of all outstanding loans, or about 25 percent of GDP (and are as perhaps as high as 40–50 percent of GNP in reality). Such high levels of NPLs are comparable to what was seen among China's financially troubled neighbors in East Asia before the 1997–98 financial crisis.[84] Corruption scandals of truly impressive scope have hampered recent efforts to marketize sections of the banking industry, such as the Bank of China, through the floating of shares in international stock markets. Such efforts are important, in part, because in the middle of this decade China is committed to begin opening up its commercial banking sector to international competition as part of its WTO obligations.[85]

So far, the practice of banks loaning primarily to SOEs has continued despite the following changes in CCP policies and China's economic conditions: financial reforms that have allegedly ended political pressure on the banks to loan to SOEs; the reduction of SOE production as a percentage of GNP; the state's encouragement of the banks to make loans purely on the basis of the profitability of borrowers; the encouragement of foreigners to purchase ownership shares in SOEs; and the creation of asset management companies (AMCs) to buy shares of heavily indebted SOEs in debt-equity swaps.[86] Recently the CCP has even experimented with the direct sale of NPLs to foreign bankers, such as Morgan Stanley. It remains to be seen if this formula can overcome the basic problem: the Chinese state is both lender and borrower. As such it has political and economic incentives to avoid low valuations of assets in debt-equity swaps with foreigners, even if those assets, from a market perspective, are fairly priced at those low levels.[87]

Despite these challenges, there are also some very positive signs for the Chinese economy. Although FDI fell off from 1997 to 1999, partially because of the drying up of capital from overseas Chinese in Southeast Asia, it has picked up again since 2000.[88] FDI rose sharply in 2001 to $46.8 billion.[89] Despite a slowdown in export growth from 21 percent to 8 percent from 2000 to 2001, foreign exchange reserves have apparently grown to $208 billion, allowing a larger macroeconomic cushion to help failing banks ride out the uncertainties of reform.[90] Private Chinese companies of sufficient size and profitability are now allowed to list on the Chinese do-

mestic stock market and thereby are able to find a source of capital outside the state banking sector and foreign investors.[91] These trends foster
the most hopeful indicator for China's sustained economic growth, the
privatization of the economy.[92] Another sign of hope is continued bank
liquidity. Despite their huge unrecoverable debt burdens, to date state banks
remain highly liquid, which in banking is more than half of the battle.[93]

WTO, Unemployment, and Social Welfare Concerns

The WTO poses huge challenges for the CCP as several sectors of the
economy, including SOEs and agriculture, will come under increased pressure from international competition and the Chinese economy will come
under increased international scrutiny.[94] Traditional subsidies and protec-
tions for these two sectors will begin to run up against WTO guidelines.[95]
The CCP has been holding seminars at the local level to drive home to
local cadres the significance of China's impending entrance into the organization. Two CCP reports point quite frankly to the danger of significant
social unrest and dislocation in the rural and urban sectors of the Chinese
economy and the likely energizing of various opposition movements and
secret societies as a result.[96] A recent report of the influential Chinese
Academy of Social Sciences already places urban unemployment in China
at above seven percent, the experts' red line for securing social stability.
The authors expect that these figures will worsen with China's accession
to the WTO.[97] Recent media reports from China suggest severe problems
with worker protest in rust-belt areas of the northeast and a breakdown of
local government accountability as local officials join with mobsters to
extract wealth.[98] Meanwhile, these local officials often provide little protection against violent crime or local clan clashes. In such an atmosphere
of local state illegitimacy, WTO-related protests are probably viewed as
particularly dangerous in Beijing because such unrest will have nationalist
overtones that will erode the CCP's legitimacy as defender of China's national sovereignty and pride against foreign incursions. Buying off pro-
testors is expensive and cracking down on them is unpopular at home and
abroad, threatening not only domestic cohesion but China's ability to
maintain robust FDI and export markets.

One potential solution to these problems is continued pump-priming
of the Chinese economy to produce jobs in infrastructure. There is a fiscal
problem here, however, as Beijing is beginning to run consistent, large-
scale budget deficits. While tax collection has apparently improved, so have
the burdens on the state for social spending and redistribution, particularly to the poorer western parts of the country.[99] In this sense, China's
increasing defense budgets are all the more impressive because even if

the overall economy will not be hurt by increased spending on defense, the fiscal opportunity costs of such increases are great. One might consider the growth in the PLA budget since 1999 to be all the more ominous from Taiwan's perspective because of what it says about CCP priorities.

Will Succession Politics, Political Reform, or Economic Interdependence Solve the Taiwan Issue?

Succession Politics and the Prospects for Reform

Beijing's financial and fiscal woes and the challenges posed by WTO compliance underscore the problems facing the generation of leaders preparing to succeed Jiang Zemin in the fall of 2002 as they craft policies toward Taiwan. Those successors, such as Hu Jintao (who is slated to be the next president) and Wen Jiabao (slated to be the next premier), are considered cautious, pragmatic, and relatively non-ideological, but given the dilemmas Beijing faces, it is not clear what pragmatism counsels. On the one hand, the potential for slowdowns in the overall economy and painful adjustments because of WTO accession pose domestic stability problems for the regime in and of themselves. Job creation and nationalism are the two last pillars of CCP legitimacy, given the bankruptcy of Marxism-Leninism-Mao Zedong Thought both inside and outside the Party. If the economy is weak and people are losing jobs in the decrepit state-run economy, this may be the worst time to create more economic damage by increasing tensions with Taiwan, the United States, and Japan. On the other hand, the CCP might feel particularly sensitive on critical issues such as Taiwan at a time when its legitimacy as a producer of new jobs is called into question. This is doubly true if protests over economic hardship take on nationalist and xenophobic overtones, as they often have throughout world history.

It is unclear as of this writing what type of leaders Jiang's successors will prove to be and what degree of authority Jiang Zemin will continue to exercise after the 16th Party Congress. The heir apparent Hu Jintao is a mystery to the outside world.[100] The predicted replacement for Zhu Rongji, Wen Jiabao, is considered to be much less fiery and much more of a consensus builder than his predecessor.[101] This might be the right type of personality switch at the right time. Zhu forced through WTO accession against significant bureaucratic resistance. That required a strong personality, a maverick leader. Wen needs to implement the decision and work with local officials who will be charged with enforcement of the international agreement—work that might require more diplomacy.

Regardless of who takes over top positions in the fall of 2002 at the 16th Party Congress, and regardless of whether or not Jiang retains significant power, CCP leaders will all face the same legitimacy problems, economic problems, and trade-offs in how they deal with issues such as Taiwan. And to the degree that the new leaders are bolder and more imaginative once in office than their reputations currently suggest, these problems will still not go away quickly. The CCP has been careful to include the traditionally domestically oriented Hu Jintao in several major international events, including trips to Europe and the United States. Hu also sat beside Qian Qichen during the latter's January 24 speech on Taiwan policy. Hu's resume is thin on foreign affairs, however, and he will almost certainly be careful not to appear too weak on Taiwan. When queried publicly about Taiwan during his first trip to Washington in early May 2002, Hu belied his reputation as someone who handles questions without notes by reading stiffly a pre-prepared and lengthy four-point statement on Taiwan policy. Although his language was quite moderate and far from vitriolic, there was little sense of new flexibility or new ideas.[102]

There is at least some reason, however, to anticipate some bold changes in Chinese politics. As president of the Central Party School, Hu Jintao has surrounded himself with what can fairly be called "new thinkers" in foreign policy and domestic politics.[103] Whether or not he has the intellectual inclination or the political space to implement their ideas is an open question. For our purposes, however, even if limited democratization follows his succession, as some speculate it might, this might not contribute to short-term cross-Strait stability and might even exacerbate tensions. Democratic peace theory applies poorly at best to struggles considered by one belligerent to be a civil war, and sophisticated versions of the theory argue that the process of democratization, however desirable its outcomes, is often fraught with dangers of hypernationalism, foreign scapegoating, and conflict. This is particularly true in those democratizing states with poorly developed civil societies and news media, such as China. Such states lack healthy outlets for popular grievances. They also lack a marketplace for ideas where views can be debated and counter-arguments brought to bear. This gives elites and opposition parties a strong incentive to manipulate populist, nationalist themes and to adopt tough international policies as an electoral strategy.[104]

Economic Interdependence and Peace

Even if the prospect of political reform on the mainland does not solve the Taiwan problem, perhaps economic integration and globalization will. There is a degree of confidence among many analysts in the West that economic interdependence will prevent conflict in the Taiwan Strait by restraining Taiwan's diplomacy and by making military assault by China too economically costly.[105] Some Chinese academics and government advisors believe that the United States could not sustain military protection of Taiwan, nor a sanctions regime against China, partially because business interests would lobby the U.S. government to sue for peace.[106] Some foreign observers point out that China currently has an $80 billion trade surplus with the United States and that the risk of a downturn in Sino-American relations to Chinese jobs and economic well-being is so great that its military options are limited, even in the face of tough U.S. policies, such as the Bush administration's recent arms sales package to Taiwan.[107]

The general theory that interdependence will prevent war between states is one that has often come under attack in the international relations literature. But wherever one stands on that debate might not matter in the case of cross-Strait relations, because the theories were not designed to handle issues of unification or regional independence following civil wars. In such cases, states' legitimacy and identity are wrapped up in the struggle in ways that they rarely are in interstate conflicts. For example, words that might seem stabilizing in an international context seem provocative in the case of cross-Strait relations. President Chen claims that economic and cultural contacts and integration should precede political integration. But the unusual Chinese term he uses for "integration" (*tonghe*) sounds to mainland elite ears like European integration. European-style integration on the surface might seem a pacifying analogy, but it is not, because it presupposes independent, sovereign nation-states before the integration process begins, a status Beijing is unwilling to grant Taipei.[108]

This major conceptual problem aside, interdependence is a two-way street in the best of circumstances. Each side can underestimate the other's resolve on a particular issue either because it overestimates the deterrent effect of putting the economic relationship at risk for the target or because it underestimates the counterpart's willingness or ability to use its own economic leverage.[109] Such attitudes on both sides of the Pacific and both sides of the Taiwan Strait are potentially dangerous if any leaders fail to recognize that there is more to politics than just economics. In China, for example, this can take the form of underestimating U.S. resolve in support of Taiwan. In the United States, it can take the form of complacency about growing PLA coercive power and growing CCP concern about political trends in Taiwan and in U.S.-Taiwan relations. In Taiwan, it can take the form of misperceptions about exactly where the CCP's redlines are and what Taipei needs to avoid in order to prevent conflict.

Conclusion

The September 11 attacks and the war on terror that followed them provided an occasion for the United States and the PRC to find common ground and patch up relations soured by the EP-3 incident earlier in the year. Cooperation in the war on Al Qaeda and the Taliban was notable and surprising to many skeptics, but there were several domestic and international reasons for Beijing's cooperation with that aspect of the war. Whether that cooperation is sustainable is a key question. There is little doubt that Beijing will be increasingly nervous about aspects of U.S. Asian strategy—including a sustained presence in Central Asia, a more active Japan, a closer relationship with India, and more cooperation with Russia. More nerve-wracking still would be an expansion of the war on terror to sovereign states in the current "axis of evil." But Beijing's reactions to the war on terror will likely be catalyzed or muted by the state of cross-Strait relations and Beijing's perceptions of U.S. policy toward both sides of the Strait.

On September 11, 2001, Beijing was sanguine about the PRC's long-term ability to gain accommodation from Taiwan without the overt use of force. That optimism has been reduced somewhat by subsequent events in Taiwan and the United States. Although it is too soon to know at the time of this writing, Beijing might be reassured by recent statements by top Bush administration officials. According to Chinese press reports, Vice President Cheney assured Hu Jintao that the United States was not supportive of Taiwanese independence, and this message has been reiterated by Deputy Secretary of Defense Paul Wolfowitz and others who are considered particularly strong in their backing of Taiwan.[110] If these statements were believed in Beijing, they might go a long way toward reducing the costs associated with the Bush administration's upgraded commitment to Taiwan's security. Such assurances might prove increasingly important, as there will almost certainly be an arms race of sorts in the Taiwan Strait between mainland coercive weapons and doctrine and the capabilities of Taipei, Washington, and Tokyo to defeat PRC tactics at limited cost. However unusual the form they take, arms races do not cause wars in the absence of political tensions. If Beijing can be convinced that the military superiority of the United States and its regional friends will not be used now or in the future for the purpose of promoting and protecting a legally independent Taiwan, then that superiority should not provoke war, but only deter it. If weapons sales to Taiwan do not appear to be encouraging Taiwanese independence, then the PRC will find them less provocative and might feel less inclined to proliferate weapons to countries of concern to the United States. Finally, if war with the United States over Taiwan seems less likely, Beijing should be marginally less resis   . prosecution of war in other parts of the globe, such as Iraq.

For China's new generation of leaders, what migₙₜ ₚ vide the key to war or peace with Taiwan and the United States is Beijing's assessment of political trends in Taiwan and trends in U.S.-Taiwan relations and in U.S. security policy more generally. Those key perceptions will form in a domestic political context in the PRC that will help determine whether Beijing's pessimism will lead to belligerence. Regime security is still of primary importance to the CCP, and Taiwan is among the few key issues that could undermine it catastrophically. The CCP often appears paranoid in cracking down on apparently apolitical groups like the Falun Gong or locking away unarmed democracy advocates from elite universities. But even if it is paranoid, that does not mean that it does not face real problems in maintaining stability. Any student of the trends of history knows that a party with "communist" as a middle name will likely have a very hard time as the twenty-first century progresses. This is doubly true when the same party is encouraging marketization of the economy and opening to the global economy at previously unimaginable levels. One need not be a Marxist or Maoist to believe in dialectics and contradictions, and it is fairly obvious that the CCP is sowing the seeds of its own destruction. Whether this will happen gradually and peacefully or in violent fits and starts is among the most important international security questions in the world today.

Cross-Strait and trans-Pacific economic trends might very well be part of the solution to this security problem. They are unlikely on their own to solve them, unfortunately. In a strategic situation in which actors with different political goals can easily overplay their hands, issues such as the impending Beijing Olympics in 2008 or accession to the WTO by Taiwan and the mainland can be forces for either stability or instability. Political reform on the mainland is desirable for intrinsic, moral reasons and because it should make long-term U.S.-China relations much more stable. But political liberalization might not solve many problems in cross-Strait relations in the short run, and might even exacerbate them by placing a premium on nationalism in Chinese politics in the early phases of democratization. As it progresses, however, political reform in China might remove one key issue from the U.S. security agenda: intervention in a cross-Strait conflict. Conflict across the Taiwan Strait between two local democracies is imaginable. Much less imaginable would be military conflict between the United States and a future democratic China over whether or not Taiwan's democracy should be folded into a larger Chinese nation. Even if a future administration wanted to intervene in such a conflict for strategic reasons, it would be very difficult to explain and justify to the public and Congress.

Endnotes

1 See, for example, Huang Shuofeng, *Zonghe guoli xin lun* (A new theory on comprehensive national power), Beijing: Zhongguo Shehui Kexue Chubanshe, September 1999.

2 Author interviews in Beijing 1993–2002.

3 Opinions differ on how much computer simulation and foreign intelligence efforts might reduce the costs of signing the CTBT to China's nuclear weapons program, but there seems to be a consensus that the costs were real. See Alastair Iain Johnston and Paul Evans, "China's Engagement of Multilateral Institutions," in Johnston and Robert S. Ross, *Engaging China: The Management of an Emerging Power*, London: Routledge, 1999; and Alistair Johnston, *Social State*, unpublished book manuscript, forthcoming from Princeton University Press.

4 The following two sections of this chapter borrow from my contributions to the *China Leadership Monitor*, a Stanford University online forum that can be accessed at <www.chinaleadershipmonitor.org/contributors.html>.

5 Initial statements on September 12 predicating any actions on UN approval, for example, seemed to suggest that China might attempt to be an obstacle to U.S. freedom of action. See Jeremy Page, "China Offers to Join Global War on Terrorism," *Reuters*, September 13, 2001 <http://taiwansecurityresearch.org/reu/2001/reuters-091301.htm>. For an almost cautionary initial official statement, see "AFP: Senior PRC Military Official Urges Restraint in Reaction to US Attacks," *Agence France-Presse* (Hong Kong), September 12, 2001 in FBIS, September 12, 2001, CPP200109120000066.

6 Charles Snyder, "Powell Assures Taipei There's No Deal With China," *Taipei Times*, September 23, 2001.

7 For a recap of the summit, see Michael Vatikiotis, et al., "Terror Throws Us Together, For Now," *Far Eastern Economic Review*, November 1, 2001.

8 Off-the-record discussions in October and November with current and former U.S. officials. As one well-connected interlocutor put it, there are four ways that China could have helped the United States: diplomatically, intelligence gathering and sharing, through financial tracking and controls, and militarily. He suggested that China has been almost surprisingly forthcoming on the first three, but not on the fourth, although no one expected or requested any direct military involvement by China in Afghanistan. The former commander in chief of the U.S. Pacific Command, Admiral Dennis Blair, expressed dissatisfaction with the level of specificity in Chinese intelligence about regional terrorist networks. See United States Pacific Command Transcript, Admiral Dennis C. Blair, Press Roundtable, Hong Kong, April 18, 2002 at <www.usinfo.state.gov>.

9 On October 1, 2001 a *Xinhua* report stated that Jiang Zemin had pledged 10 million renminbi to President Musharraf during a phone conversation.

10 Phillip P. Pan and John Pomfret, "Bin Laden's Chinese Connection," *Washington Post*, November 10, 2001; "Chinese FM Tang Eyes Afghan War, Terrorism, Ties with U.S., Japan, Vatican, Italy," *La Stampa* (Turin), FBIS 11/24/01 (EUP 200011126000152).

11 "Unveiling the Terrorist Nature of 'East Tujue' Elements," *People's Daily*, November 16, 2001.

[12] Elisabeth Rosenthal, "U.N. Official Fears China Uses Terror War as Front for Abuses," *The New York Times*, November 10, 2001.

[13] Vivien Pik-kwan Chan, "Falun Gong a Terrorist Operation, says Beijing," *South China Morning Post*, December 14, 2001.

[14] Perhaps the most startling example of this new spirit of cooperation can be found in a truly rosy *PLA Daily* article from October 18, 2001; see Ren Xiangqun, "Zhongmei guanxi jiankang fazhan de xin dongli: Zhong Mei shounaohui de zhongyao yiyi he yingxiang," (The new impetus in the healthy development of Sino-American relations: The important meaning and influence of the Sino-American summit), <www.pladaily.com.cn>.

[15] Craig Smith, "Jovial Bush and Jiang Mask Lack of Progress," *International Herald Tribune*, October 22, 2001; and Phillip P. Pan and Mike Allen, "U.S., China Agree on Little But Need to Fight Terrorism," *Washington Post*, October 20, 2001.

[16] "PRC Experts View Impact on US Terror Attacks on US Economy," *China Daily*, September 18, 2001, in FBIS 09/19/01 (CPP20010919000012).

[17] Thomas J. Christensen, "China," in Richard J. Ellings and Aaron L. Friedberg, eds., *Strategic Asia 2001–02: Power and Purpose*, Seattle, Wash.: The National Bureau of Asian Research, 2001.

[18] From 1989 to 1998, the percentage of overall Chinese exports absorbed by the United States jumped from nearly 18 percent to just over 30 percent. For an excellent analysis of these official Chinese statistics, see Phillip C. Saunders, "Supping with a Long Spoon: Dependence and Interdependence in Sino-American Relations," *The China Journal*, no. 43 (January 2000), pp. 55–82.

[19] "PRC Foreign Minister Tang Interviewed by RMRB on World Situation," *Beijing Renmin Ribao*, December 17, 2001, in FBIS (CPP20011217000111); see also "Central Bank Reveals '9/11 Incident' Impact on PRC Economy," *Beijing Renmin Ribao*, October 30, 2001, in FBIS 10/30/01 (CPP20011030000077).

[20] Interview with Chinese scholar in the United States, November 2001.

[21] See "US pledges not to abandon Central Asia after Afghan war," *Almaty Interfax* (Kazakhstan), December 19, 2001, FBIS (CEP20011219000233).

[22] For an unusually vitriolic article on this score from a PLA-connected Hong Kong magazine, see "Bush Acts with Hidden Motives in Central Asia: U.S. Military Presence in Central Asia Aimed at China, Not Bin-Laden," *Hong Kong Kuang Chiao Ching*, October 16, 2001, no. 349, pp. 20–22, in FBIS 10/16/01 (CPP 2001110160000087).

[23] William H. Overholt, "China's Economic Squeeze," *Orbis*, Winter 2000, pp. 13–33, at p. 14.

[24] Peter Wonacott, "Economic Growth of 8.1% Beats Forecasts for the Quarter," *Asian Wall Street Journal*, Weekly Edition, April 23–29, 2001.

[25] Thomas G. Rawski, "What is Happening to China's GDP Statistics," *China Economic Review*, vol. 12 (2001), pp. 347–54.

[26] Nicholas R. Lardy, "China's Economy After the WTO," paper presented at the 31st Sino-American Conference on Contemporary China, National Chengchi University, Taipei, June 2–4, 2002.

[27] Hsu Yu-chun, "Taiwan Economist on Mainland Investments, Economic Recovery, Other Economic Issues," *Taipei Chung-chi Jih-Pao*, March 7, 2002 in FBIS

03/07/02 (CPP20002050700037); and "WSJ Sees Feasibility of U.S.-Taiwan Free Trade Pact," *Taipei Central News Agency*, May 23, 2002, in FBIS 05/23/02 (CPP20020523000003).

[28] Department of Economic Affairs, Mainland Affairs Council, Executive Yuan, Taiwan ROC, January 2000, <www.mac.gov.tw>; Ing-wen Tsai, "A New Era in Cross-Straits Relations? Taiwan and China in the WTO," *Heritage Lectures*, no. 726 (January 14, 2002).

[29] The percentage figures come from "Taiwan's Approved Outward Investment: Cumulative till 2000" Investment Commission, Ministry of Economic Affairs, Taiwan ROC, <www.mac.gov.tw>. For the move of semiconductor plants to the mainland, see Maubo Chang, "Industrialists Laud Government's Decision on 8-inch Wafer Foundries," *Taipei Central News Agency*, March 9, 2002, FBIS 03/09/02 (CPP20020309000091); Maureen Pao, "Tied to China's Dragon," *Far Eastern Economic Review*, September 6, 2001; Bruce Gilley and Maureen Pao, "China-Taiwan: Defences Weaken," *Far Eastern Economic Review*, October 4, 2001; "Central News Agency: Taiwan's Exports to M'land as Ratio of Total Exports Hits New High," *Tapiei Central News Agency*, November 27, 2001, FBIS 11/27/01 (CPP20011127000069). For an article that questions how important this is to Taiwan's chip industries, see Terho Uimonen, "Who Needs China," *Far Eastern Economic Review*, April 18, 2002.

[30] For the intentional policy of luring Taiwan investment through preferential policies, see Tian Qunjian, "Sweet Deals and Sour Tastes: The Political Economy of Economic Interactions Across the Taiwan Strait," unpublished doctoral dissertation, Department of Government, Cornell University, August 2000. For the drying up of investment in Southeast Asia, which formerly rivaled mainland China as a Taiwan investment target, see "West Versus South: Taiwan Investors Do Have a Choice," *Sinorama*, vol. 26, no. 12 (December 2001), pp. 6–32. Taiwan was hardly alone in investing on the mainland, as Beijing enjoyed record contracted FDI of $48 billion in 2001, the second largest total in the world and a testimony to the fact that many in the business world are not as skeptical about China's economic prospects as is Thomas Rawski.

[31] John Tkacik, "Taiwan Dependence: Trade and Investment Dimensions of Cross-Strait Politics," in Julian Weiss, ed., *Tiger's Roar: Asia's Recovery and Its Impact*, New York, M. E. Sharpe, 2002.

[32] "WSJ Sees Feasibility of U.S.-Taiwan Free Trade Pact," *Taipei Central News Agency*.

[33] Pao, "Tied to China's Dragon," *Far Eastern Economic Review*; Gilley and Pao, "China-Taiwan: Defences Weaken" *Far Eastern Economic Review*; and "Taiwan's Exports to M'land as Ratio of Total Exports Hits New High," *Taipei Central News Agency*.

[34] For PRC rejection of the axis of evil formula, see Liu Jianfei, "Meiguo you zengjia 'xie'e zhouxin' chengyuan," (United States increases the membership of the "axis of evil"), *Jiefangjun Bao*, May 20, 2002, <www.pladaily. com.cn>.

[35] The author traveled with an entourage from Harvard University's Fairbank Center in both January 2001 and January 2002.

[36] For media coverage of concern on the mainland about the elections, see Sherman Wu et al., "Mainland Chinese Scholars See Change After Taiwan Elections,"

Taipei Central News Agency, December 1, 2001.

[37] For a relatively frank assessment of electoral trends in Taiwan and the concern they are causing in high-level circles in Beijing see Zhu Xianlong, "Possible Outbreak of Cross-Strait War in 2005," *Kuang Chiao Ching* (Hong Kong), no. 356 (May 2002), pp. 16–18, in FBIS 05/17/02 (CPP20020517000075).

[38] Interviews in Beijing in January 2002. For a published interview that makes some of the same points, see the comments of Zhou Jianming, a leading Shanghai think-tank expert, in "Tenacity and Fragility Co-exist in Sino-US Relations— Scholars Comment on Bush's Visit to China and Sino-US Cooperation," *Ta Kung Pao* (Hong Kong), February 24, 2002, in FBIS (CCP20020225000027).

[39] Myra Lu, "Voters Give Ruling Party Legislative Advantage," *Taipei Journal*, December 7, 2001, pp. 1–2.

[40] Instead a headline in the official *Taipei Journal* announced loudly "Voters reject 'one country, two systems' formula," December 7, 2001, p. 2. PRC and ROC government sources cite wildly different poll results for popular support of the "one country, two systems" formula on Taiwan. Some mainland sources brag that support has increased sharply to anywhere from 35 to 50 percent in 2002 from less than 15 percent in 2000. A recent Mainland Affairs Council survey places support for the formula at only 9.2 percent and as dropping sharply since 2000. Neutral sources state that the overwhelming majority of Taiwanese citizens consistently support maintenance of the status quo in cross-Strait relations and would oppose either a near-term declaration of independence or near-term unification. This last claim seems the most credible, especially given the election results in December 2001. Even if we were to accept the PRC's polling reports, we would still find no support for the CCP's common claim that only a small minority of pro-independence activists stand in the way of peaceful unification. For an example of the PRC's optimistic view of public opinion trends on Taiwan, see Lau Nai-kueng, "Chen Shui-bian's Independence Moves May Cause Reunification Showdown in 2008," *South China Morning Post*, February 4, 2002, in FBIS (CPP20020204000064). For the MAC poll, see Lin Miao-jung, "Taiwan Survey Shows Little Support for "One Country, Two Systems," *Taipei Times*, February 23, 2002, in FBIS (CPP 20020225 000135). For MAC reporting on public opinion trends on this question over the past decade, see <www.mac.gov.tw/english/pos/9105/9104e_8.gif>.

[41] Interviews, Beijing, January 2002.

[42] For coverage of the Qian Qichen speech, see "Quge Taidu, Qian huanying Minjin Dang fang Dalu," (Excepting Taiwan Independence [Supporters], Qian Invites the DPP to Visit the Mainland,) *Zhongguo Shibao*, January 25, 2002.

[43] Interviews, Beijing, January 2002. On military changes and the passport issue, see "Chen Shuibian jizhe duo junquan," (Chen Shui-bian pressing to seize military control), *Huanqiu Shibao*, January 17, 2002; David Lague, "Goodbye to the Mainland," *Far Eastern Economic Review*, February, 7, 2002; and "Tenacity and Fragility Co-exist in Sino-US Relations—Scholars Comment on Bush's Visit to China and Sino-US Cooperation."

[44] Interviews, Beijing, January 2002. National security experts on Taiwan recognized that the Olympics would not necessarily restrain Beijing from using force. Germany in 1936, Mexico in 1968, and the Soviet Union in 1980 were all used

as examples of the limited influence that the Olympics has on state belligerence. For concern about the potential for a Taiwan Olympics gambit, see Zhu, "Possible Outbreak of Cross-Strait War in 2005," *Kuang Chiao Ching*.

[45] Taiwan's investment on the mainland, by some estimates, increased 30 percent in 2001. See "WSJ Sees Feasibility…," *Taiwan Central News Agency*; "'China fever' Cooling: MOEA," *Liberty Times* February 22, 2002; see also Flor Wang, "Poll Says Mainland Investment Fever Among Taiwan Businessmen Declining," *Taiwan Central News Agency*, March 4, 2002, in FBIS 03/04/02 (CPP 20020304000150). Because of sharp increases in April, Taiwan investments on the mainland are up one percent for the first four months of 2002. See "Taiwan Investment in Mainland China up 1% January-April Period," *Taiwan Central News Agency*, May 20, 2002. One civilian analyst emphasized that Taiwan had no choice but to rely on the mainland economically and that the phenomenon of the Taiwanese and Japanese miracles was dependent on a closed mainland. Interview with Chinese intelligence analyst, Beijing, January 2001. One civilian official emphasized that, because of economic trends, time was still on China's side. He went so far as to suggest that political reform on the mainland would make it more attractive over time. Interviews, Beijing, January 2002.

[46] Interviews with officials and scholars in Taipei, late January 2002. The increased realism about Taiwanese politics among mainland interlocutors went past a simple recognition that the CCP had to be willing to engage the DPP. Civilian experts also emphasized that better regional targeting of Taiwan was necessary on the mainland. Recognizing the strong pull of the DPP and Taiwanese independence in the south, analysts emphasized that more had to be done to create positive incentives and increased economic leverage over cities like Kaohsiung by creating better links to mainland cities such as Xiamen. There was a general sense that the mainland was going to be flexible in dealing with local and central Taiwan authorities to deepen such economic and people-to-people contacts.

[47] Interviews, Beijing, January 2002. On a particularly optimistic note, one high ranking Foreign Ministry official stated something to the effect that individuals come and go but the mountains and rivers stay the same (paraphrased). This seemed to be a statement of diplomatic confidence that China's hand, including both economic and military cards, remained fundamentally strong.

[48] Interviews, Beijing, January 2001 and January 2002; also see Zhu, "Possible Outbreak of Cross-Strait War in 2005," *Kuang Chiao Ching*.

[49] Interviews with PLA officers, Beijing, January 2002. The term "software cooperation" seemed to be a reference to U.S. Department of Defense initiatives with Taiwan started under the Clinton administration. For published statements along the same lines, see "Jiefang Junbao: Defense Experts Warn on US-Taiwan Military Cooperation," *Jiefangjun Bao*, May 20, 2002, in FBIS 05/21/02 (CPP 20020521000003). One civilian analyst with good ties to military research institutes in Beijing expressed frustration about the United States' failure to reward the PRC for its allegedly beneficent, non-confrontational posture toward Taiwan over the past two years. As he put it, "China has tried to act like a good boy, but is still being punished (*chengfa*) by the United States."

[50] Interview with PLA officer, Beijing, January 2002. The officer stated that such an operation would not necessarily be a military strike against "Taiwan island"

itself and would likely be quite different than the March 1996 exercises but, he emphasized, it would be of greater scope. He stated that the 1996 exercises were successful as an "inoculation" against independence, but from time to time a "booster shot" may be needed. For subsequent confirmation that such a visit was being considered by some in Congress and by the ROC Foreign Ministry, see Carol Giacomo, "U.S. Mulls Inviting Taiwan Leader to Washington," *Reuters*, May 7, 2002; and Ella Lu, "ROC Foreign Ministry Hopes President Can Make Official Visit to U.S.," *Taiwan Central News Agency*, May 8, 2002.

[51] For official CCP reaction, see "China Summons U.S. Ambassador to Make Representations," *Xinhua*, March 16, 2002; "U.S.-Taiwan Secret Talks on Arms-Sales: Analysis," *People's Daily*, March 18, 2002, FBIS (CPP20020118000088); and "Where Lies the Mistake of Bush's Policy Toward Taiwan," *People's Daily*, April 28, 2002. For press reports of Chinese reactions to the visit of ROC Minister of Defense Tang Yao-ming, see Murray Hiebert and Susan V. Lawrence, "Taiwan: Crossing the Red Lines," *Far Eastern Economic Review*, April 4, 2002; and Willy Lo-lap Lam, "China's Army to Prepare for Military Struggle," March 13, 2002, CNN.com.

[52] On the Department of Defense's 2002 *Nuclear Posture Review*, see William Arkin, "Secret Plan Outlines the Unthinkable," *Los Angeles Times*, May 11, 2002. For Chinese reactions, see "China Summons U.S. Ambassador to Make Representations," *Xinhua*, March 16, 2002; "Where Lies the Mistake of Bush's Policy Toward Taiwan," *People's Daily*; "U.S.-Taiwan Secret Talks on Arms-Sales: Analysis," *People's Daily*; and John Pomfret, "U.S.-China Relations Appear Headed for Shaky Ground," *Washington Post Foreign Service*, March 19, 2002.

[53] For PRC reaction to President Bush's mention of the Taiwan Relations Act, see "Where Lies the Mistake of Bush's Policy Toward Taiwan," *People's Daily*; and "Shih Yin-hung Says Bush's Beijing Visit Mixed with Success and Failure," *Taipei Chung-Kuo Shih-Pao*, February 25, 2002, in FBIS (CPP20020225 000043). For President Bush's pubic statements, see "Full Text of Bush's Remarks—Opening Speech and Question and Answers," <www.1.chinadaily.com.cn /news/2002-02-22/57699.html>.

[54] See, for example, Ding Zengyi, "Yin-Mei junshi hezuo yin ren guanzhu" (U.S.-India military cooperation draws people's attention), *Jiefangjun Bao*, February 24, 2002. For more criticism of improved U.S.-India ties, see Zhang Guoping, "39 nian lai shouci juxing hezuo junshi yanxi, Meiyin fazhan junshi guanxi ge you suo tu" (The first joint military exercise in 39 years, in the development of U.S.-India military relations, each [side] has its own scheme), *Jiefangjun Bao*, May 13, 2002. Qian Feng "India Wants to Be the International Maritime Police of the Malacca Strait," *Beijing Renmin Wang*, April 20, 2002, in FBIS (CPP200020420000026). See also "Where Lies the Mistake of Bush's Policy Toward Taiwan," *People's Daily*. For an interesting analysis of the summit, see Susan Lawrence, "It Takes More to Make a Revolution," *Far Eastern Economic Review*, February 14, 2002. For a pessimistic view of U.S.-China relations after September 11 see Aaron Friedberg, "11 September and the Future of Sino-American Relations," *Survival*, vol. 44, no. 1 (Spring 2002), pp. 33–50.

[55] See "Chinese Newspaper Slams Bush First-Strike Policy," *Reuters*, June 12, 2002, citing a June 12 article in the official *China Daily*.

56 For Chinese press reactions to U.S. basing in Central Asia, see Ding Zhihong, "Meiguo 'zhanche' you jiasule" (The American 'war chariot' again picks up speed), *Jiefangjun Bao*, January 29, 2002; Ding Gang "Meijun jinle Zhongya bu xiang zou" (The United States entered Central Asia and doesn't want to leave), *Huanqiu Shiabao*, January 14, 2002; Gao Qiufu, "U.S. Wishful Thinking on its Military Presence in Central Asia and Real Purpose," *Beijing Liaowang*, April 29, 2002, in FBIS (CPP20020506000066); He Chong, "The United States Emphasizes the Purposes of the Long-term Stationing of Troops in Central Asia," *Tongxun She* (Hong Kong), January 9, 2002, in FBIS (CPP20020109 000124); and Shih Chun-yu, "United States Wants Long-term Military Deployment to Control Central Asia," *Ta Kung Pao* (Hong Kong), January 11, 2002, in FBIS (CPP20020111000037). A May report from Kazakhstan details official concern about U.S. presence in that country by the PRC Foreign Ministry, see "China Summons Kazakhstani Foreign Minister over US Bases," *Almaty Kazakh Commercial TV*, May 2, 2002, in FBIS 05/02/02 (CEP20020502 0000119). For descriptions of U.S.-Japanese activities during the war on terror, see "Two MSDF ships set sail for Indian Ocean," *Kyodo News*, February 12, 2002; and "MSDF to extend anti-terror tour," *Yomiuri Shimbun*, May 10, 2002. For Chinese reactions, see "9-11 cheng guanjian zhuanzhe Riben junshi xingdong huoyue wei wushinian zhi zui" (September 11 was the most critical turning point in 50 years for the invigoration of Japanese military activity), *Nanfang Dushi Bao*, April 16, 2002; and "Riben jin jun Dongnan Ya qitu he zai" (For what purpose is Japan planning to militarily enter Southeast Asia), *Canwang Xinwen Zhoukan*, May 3, 2002; and "Chinese Expert Voices Concerns Over Japan Passing Anti-Terrorism Bills," *Beijing Renmin Wang*, November 1, 2001, in FBIS 11/02//01 (CPP20011102000049). For PRC criticism of U.S. policy toward North Korea, see Yan Guoqun "Sunshine Policy is Shining Again," *Jiefangjun Bao*, April 11, 2002, in FBIS (CPP20020411000088).

57 Discussion with military scholars in Beijing, January 2002.

58 For coverage of both Zhu Rongji's and Jiang Zemin's April trips see the PRC Foreign Ministry website, <www.fmprc.gov.cn/eng>. The quotation in Tehran comes from one such document, "President Jiang Zemin Met With Iranian Leaders," <www.fmprc.gov.cn/eng/29173.html>.

59 See *Reuters*, "U.S. to Impose Sanctions on China, Others Over Iran," *The New York Times*, May 8, 2002.

60 For the unclassified transcript, see Office of International Information Programs, Department of State, <http://usinfo.state.gov>.

61 Hu Jintao yu Meiguo fuzongtong Qieni juxing huitan" (Hu Jintao and U.S. Vice President Cheney hold talks), *Jiefangjun Bao*, May, 3, 2002.

62 See Erik Eckholm, "China is Increasing Its Budget for Military Spending by 17.6%," *The New York Times*, March 7, 2002; Thomas J. Christensen, "Tracking China's Security Relations: Causes for Optimism and Pessimism," in *China Leadership Monitor*, no. 1 (Winter 2001), <www.chinaleadershipmonitor.org>.

63 Christensen, "China," in Ellings and Friedberg, eds., *Strategic Asia 2001–02: Power and Purpose*.

64 See Yu Li, "What Will Be the Appropriate Amount of Military Expenditures for China?" *Kuang Chiao Ching* (Hong Kong), no. 35616 (May 16, 2002), pp.

20–23, in FBIS 05/17/02 (CPP2002051700076). This article claims that the Chinese state is able to absorb 17 percent of GNP. If this were true, this would demonstrate that Zhu Rongji's drive for greater accumulation since the mid-1990s has already borne fruit.

[65] Discussion with CCP experts and U.S. government experts; see also Zeng Shuwang "PLA To Conduct Another Exercise in the East Sea," report by *Wen Wei Po* reporter Zeng Shuwang from the *Beijing News Center, Agence France-Presse*, May 17, 2002, in FBIS, 05/17/02 (CPP200205170000290).

[66] For further development of these themes, see Thomas J. Christensen, "Posing Problems Without Catching Up: China's Rise and Challenges for U.S. Security Policy," *International Security*, vol. 25, no. 4 (Spring 2001), pp. 5–40. See also "PRC Military Journal Examines Conventional Deterrence," *Beijing Junshi Kexue*, September 30, 2001, in FBIS 11/06/01 (CPP20011106 000255).

[67] As one PLA major general stated recently in a published interview: "Once we decide to use force against Taiwan, we definitely will consider an intervention by the United States. The United States likes vain glory; if one of its aircraft carriers should be attacked and destroyed, people in the United States would begin to complain and quarrel loudly, and the U.S. president would find the going harder and harder." See Xu Bodong, "Peace Will Prevail Only When the Two Sides of the Taiwan Strait Are Reunified—an Interview with Major General Huang Bin, Noted Military Strategist on the Mainland," *Ta Kung Pao* (Hong Kong), May 13, 2002, in FBIS 05/13/02 (CPP2002051300000481). For a general analysis of U.S. forces' psychological vulnerability, see Liu Dewei, "Di si zhong zhanzheng, de leng sikao—cong Meijun 'Haiwan Zhanzheng zonghe zheng' shouqi" (A cold analysis of the fourth kind of war based on the U.S. military's "Gulf War syndrome), *Jiefangjun Bao*, May 22, 2002.

[68] China has also received important technology from Israel. See David Lague, "Buying Some Major Muscle," *Far Eastern Economic Review*, January 24, 2002.

[69] For more on the burgeoning U.S.-Russia relationship, see William Wohlforth's chapter in this volume.

[70] For example, see the interview by Mike Chinoy, entitled "Chen on Taiwan: It's the Democratic Republic of China," CNN.com, May 23, 2002.

[71] Taiwan's investment on the mainland, by some estimates, increased 30 percent in 2001. See "WSJ Sees Feasibility…," *Taiwan Central News Agency*. For early reports that investment was slowing in early 2001 see "'China fever' Cooling: MOEA," *Liberty Times*; "Taiwan Approves Major Investment Plans in China," *The China Post*, May 21, 2002, in FBIS 05/21/02 (CPP20020521000201).

[72] See "China and North East Asia," *Asia Monitor*, vol. 9, no. 2 (February 2002), p. 9; see also Francis Li, "Taiwan More Optimistic About Economic Recovery," *Taipei Journal*, March 8, 2002, in FBIS 03/08/02 (CPP20020308000217).

[73] Lillian Lin, "Taiwan's Jobless Rate Drops Slightly to 4.98% in April," *Taiwan Central News Agency*, May 22, 2002; "Approved Foreign Investment in Taiwan Up Sharply," *Taiwan Economic News*, February 22, 2002.

[74] See Joyce Huang, "Taiwan: DPP Blames Opposition for Bear Economy," *Taipei Times*, November 11, 2001, in FBIS 11/11/01 (CPP2001111130000207); and "Former Taiwan President Blames KMT for Bad Economy," *Taipei News*, November 11, 2001, in FBIS 11/11/01 (CPP200111113000217).

75 "Chen 'Emboldened' by Strong American Support, Lien Chan Says," *Taipei Times*, May 14, 2002, <www.taiwansecurity.org>.

76 To the contrary, there are reports that Chen's foreign efforts have been quite popular, see "Chen's Diplomacy Wins Kudos," *Taipei Times*, May 20, 2002.

77 "Cross-Strait Volume Up 12.9 Percent in Jan.-Feb.," *Taiwan Central News Agency*, April 29, 2002, in FBIS 04/29/02 (CPP20020429000300).

78 Interviews with CCP experts, Beijing, January 2002.

79 See "WTO has Mixed Impact on Taiwan-China Relations" *Taipei Journal*, May 3, 2002, FBIS 05/03/02 (CPP20020503000117).

80 See Sadanand Dhume and Susan V. Lawrence, "Buying Fast Into Southeast Asia," *Far Eastern Economic Review*, March 28, 2002; and David Kruger and Ichiyo Fuyuno, "Innovation: Flight to China-Japan's Industry Fights Back," *Far Eastern Economic Review,* April 25, 2002.

81 James Kynge, "China's Burden," *Financial Times*, January 3, 2002.

82 Nicholas R. Lardy, "When Will China's Financial System Meet China's Needs?" Center for Research on Economic Development and Policy Reform, Working Paper No. 55, Stanford University, 2000; and Edward S. Steinfeld, *Forging Reform in China: The Fate of State-Owned Industry*, Cambridge: Cambridge University Press, 1998. For the need for depoliticization of banking at the center, see Bruce Gilley and David Murphy, "Why China Needs a Real Central Bank," *Far Eastern Economic Review*, May 24, 2001; Kynge, "China's Burden," *Financial Times*; Peter Wonacott, "Strategy Revealed in Collapse of Chinese Investment Trust," *Wall Street Journal*, February 15, 2002.

83 While the state no longer takes in nearly as much of its tax revenue from SOEs as it did earlier in the reform period, it is now directly and heavily taxing the banks on the profits from the small percentage of high performing loans that they make. In essence, the state is still taxing the individual depositor and hiding fiscal deficits via the SOEs. David Lague, "Non-performing Loans: A Finger in the Dyke," *Far Eastern Economic Review*; and John Langlois, "Taxing China's Banks into Oblivion," *The Wall Street Journal*, October 12, 2000.

84 The estimates of NPLs were made by the governor of the central bank, Dai Xianglong, in January 2001. Since the banking system has expanded considerably in the past few years and since AMCs have purchased a substantial amount of debt from SOEs, the implication of Dai's statement is that NPLs have actually gone up, not stabilized, in those years. See Kynge, "China's Burden," *Financial Times*. For an excellent summary of these problems, see Nicholas Lardy, "China's Worsening Debts," *Financial Times*, January 22, 2001. I am grateful to Edward Steinfeld for helpful comments on this point.

85 See Susan V. Lawrence and David Murphy, "Graft Storm Hits Bank's Listing," *Far Eastern Economic Review*, February 28, 2002; and David Lague, "The Great Kaiping Bank Robbery," *Far Eastern Economic Review*, May 30, 2002.

86 As a result, although SOEs now account for far less than half of the economy, they still control 70 percent of fixed assets and 80 percent of working capital. "Enter the Dragon," *The Economist*, March 10, 2001. Edward Steinfeld claims that until a few years ago, the close relationship between state banks and SOEs was largely a result of direct government pressure on banks to provide loans for political reasons. After that pressure stopped, the persistence of this prac-

tice is more puzzling. Steinfeld blames a series of factors, especially a false belief among bankers and SOE managers alike that exposure to market forces domestically and internationally will somehow magically render efficient the irrationally organized and poorly managed SOEs. The market's Darwinian selection mechanism has not been allowed to take hold, partly because banks are gambling that the institutions that already owe them money might just turn profitable and be able to repay that money. Also, local government officials, including bank officials, fear the social implications of SOE bankruptcy. These beliefs about the market and the refusal to allow bankruptcies affect the debt-equity swap market as well. The Chinese asset management companies (AMCs) that do buy up the debt of the companies are forced to pay inflated prices. Since AMCs are government institutions relying on 10-year government bonds that will be difficult to repay, Beijing is just kicking the can down the road. Unsurprisingly few foreign investors have leapt at the chance to purchase China's decrepit and massively indebted SOEs. See Edward Steinfeld, "Free Lunch or Last Supper: China's Debt Equity Swaps in Context," *The China Business Review*, July–August 2000, pp. 22–27; and Steinfeld, "Market Visions: The Interplay of Ideas and Institutions in Chinese Industrial Restructuring," unpublished manuscript, November 2000; Joe Studwell, "Blindness Over Beijing's Economic Woes," *Wall Street Journal*, February 22, 2002; Xiaobo Hu "The State, Enterprises, and Society in Post-Deng China: Impact of the new Round of SOE Reform," *Asian Survey* vol. 40, no. 4 (July/August 2000), pp. 641–57; and Langlois, "Taxing China's Banks into Oblivion," *Wall Street Journal*.

[87] David Lague, "Non-performing Loans: A Finger in the Dyke," *Far Eastern Economic Review*.

[88] "Enter the Dragon" *The Economist*. In 2001, China's stock of FDI was at $350 billion, third only to the United States and the United Kingdom. China is also now the second biggest target for new FDI.

[89] Meng Yan, "Record High for China's FDI," *China Daily*, January 15, 2002; and Wonacott, "Economic Growth," *Asian Wall Street Journal*.

[90] For the 2000 downturn in export growth, see "China: Finance Chief Sounds Alarm on Exports," *South China Morning Post*, July 13, 2001; and *Asia Monitor*, vol. 9, no. 2. For foreign exchange reserve figures, see Kynge, "China's Burden," *Financial Times*.

[91] Craig S. Smith, "Capital Leaps Forward in China," *The New York Times, Week in Review*, June 3, 2001. Moreover, private Chinese citizens are now able to invest in "B shares" previously reserved for foreign and institutional investors. The increased liquidity that this policy shift created helps explain some of the increased FDI. Wonacott, "Economic Growth," *Asian Wall Street Journal*.

[92] By one calculation, from 1991 to 1997 (the beginning of the Asian financial crisis) the share of GDP produced by the private economy increased from 2.6 percent to 24.5 percent. Neil Gregory, Stoyan Tenev, and Dileep Wagle, "China's Emerging Private Enterprises: Prospects for the New Century," *International Finance Corporation*, World Bank, 2000, p. 11, Table 2.1.

[93] This is true largely because of Chinese citizens' high savings rates (near 40 percent), the state banks' near monopoly status in accepting savings accounts, the limited and unstable nature of Chinese stock markets, and the inconvertibil-

ity of the currency, so that it is difficult for ordinary Chinese citizens to move savings abroad. These factors distinguish the Chinese economy from those that were shattered in the 1997 Asian financial crisis, where individual citizens had incentives to run on banks as soon as they seemed insolvent. In addition, individual home mortgages and consumer credit have become popular in Chinese urban centers and, perhaps for the first time, have provided state banks with a large market for steady, profitable, and relatively secure loans. "China's Banks: China's Misunderstood Banking Sector," *Barclays Asian Monthly*, May 1999, pp. 5–17; and Ben Dolven, "Consumer Credit: Credit Where Credit is Due," *Far Eastern Economic Review*, February, 22, 2002. According to Kathy Wilhelm, "Bank loans to consumers soared 137% [in 2000] to 337 billion [renminbi]; most of the loans were mortgages." See "Window of Opportunity," *Far Eastern Economic Review*, May 3, 2001. On the importance to banks, see Wonacott, "Economic Growth," *Asian Wall Street Journal*. More competition in the Chinese financial system flowing from WTO accession might challenge the state bank monopoly. If a precipitous banking crisis were to occur, the government would have little choice but to use its foreign exchange reserves to bail out branches of its largest banks or, perhaps less wisely, simply to print new money.

[94] See David Murphy, "Riding the Tiger of Trade," *Far Eastern Economic Review*, November 22, 2001; "China's Unemployment Pressure to Increase in Next Five Years," *Hong Kong Tongxun She*, February 18, 2002, in FBIS 02/18/02 (CPP200218000078); and "Li Peng Urges Active Handling of Opportunities, Challenges After Joining WTO," *Xinhua*, March 2, 2002, in FBIS 03/02/02 (CPP 20020306000230). For two different views on agriculture, see Bruce Gilley, "Agriculture: Farmers Need Freedom to Grow," and Gilley, "How to Build A Rebellion," *Far Eastern Economic Review*, November 29, 2001.

[95] Kynge, "China's Burden," *Financial Times*, and Kynge, "Few Sectors Will Remain Untouched," *Financial Times*, November 13, 2000. Under the original bilateral U.S.-PRC agreement agricultural tariffs were to be reduced from 21 percent to 17 percent with quotas phased out and subsidies reduced. It appears that the Bush administration has allowed a small increase in the low-level subsidies allowed Chinese agriculture in the latest round of negotiations. See Craig R. Smith, "Obstacles to China's WTO Entry Erased in Talks with U.S.," *The New York Times*, June 10, 2002.

[96] See Erik Eckholm, "China's Inner Circle Reveals Big Unrest," *The New York Times,* June 3, 2001; a second extremely frank report can be found on the website of the State Statistical Bureau. It is entitled "Qingnian nongmin shi dangjin Zhongguo zui da de zhengzhi" (The greatest politics of China today are peasant youth), <www.stats.gov.cn/gqgl/gqglwz/200105080006.htm>. The article outlines how religion and radical politics appeal to disgruntled Chinese rural youth under 30 years of age and how many small political movements have formed around the leadership of radical youth leaders and could prove dangerous if they successfully appeal to more moderate elements of society. In the late 1990s, a bold publisher ran a series of books on China's social and economic problems. Perhaps the most critical and popular of these was He Qinglian, *Xiandaihua de xianjing* (The modernization trap), Beijing: Contemporary China Publishers, January 1998.

[97] David Hsieh, "China Jobless Figure Enters Danger Zone," *Straits Times*, June 15, 2002.

[98] David Murphy, "Labor Unrest: Nothing to Celebrate," *Far Eastern Economic Review*, April 4, 2002; and Erik Eckholm, "Order Yields to Lawlessness As Maoism Recedes in China," *The New York Times*, May 29, 2002.

[99] Joe Studwell, "Blindness over Beijing's Economic Woes," *Wall Street Journal*, February 22, 2002.

[100] Susan Lawrence, "Going West: Hu Are You?" *Far Eastern Economic Review*, October 25, 2001.

[101] See Susan Lawrence, "Wen Jiabao is no Zhu," *Far Eastern Economic Review*, March 14, 2002; and Charles Hutzler, "China's New Generation of Leaders Keep a Low Profile as They Push for Reforms," *Wall Street Journal*, January 3, 2002.

[102] Speech by Vice President Hu Jintao, Washington, DC, May 1, 2002.

[103] For example, the director of the new Institute of International Strategic Studies at the Central Party School is Wang Jisi, a scholar widely known and respected in the United States for his moderation, foresight, and in-depth knowledge of the United States and its allies. For an analysis, see Ray Cheung, "Peers United in Praise of Likely Top Policy Adviser," *South China Morning Post*, May 30, 2002, in FBIS 05/30/02 (CPPP2002053000013).

[104] Edward D. Mansfield and Jack L. Snyder, "Democratization and the Danger of War," *International Security*, vol. 20, no. 1 (Summer 1995), pp. 5–38. This theme is explored in more detail in Richard K. Betts and Thomas J. Christensen, "China: Getting the Questions Right?" *The National Interest* (Winter 2000/2001), pp. 17–30.

[105] James Kynge, "China's Binding Ties," *Financial Times*, May 10, 2001; Tkacik, "Taiwan Dependence: Trade and Investment Dimensions of Cross-Strait Politics"; and Robert S. Ross, "The Stability of Deterrence in the Taiwan Strait," *National Interest* (Fall 2001), pp. 67–76.

[106] Author interviews in Beijing and Shanghai, 2000 and 2001. One of the interesting things about these discussions is that people who vigorously disagree with this proposition still recognize that many of their colleagues hold it. As with many strategic issues in China, there is a debate about the limits of U.S. resolve on Taiwan.

[107] See, for example, Kynge, "China's Binding Ties," *Financial Times*.

[108] Interviews, Beijing, January 2001 and January 2002.

[109] For example, Yan Xuetong, formerly of a Chinese intelligence agency and currently a professor at Tsinghua University, argues confidently about U.S.-China relations, "No matter what happens [in relations], it won't hurt economic cooperation. Both sides understand that." Michael M. Phillips and Charles Hutzler, "U.S. Official Urges Beijing to Avoid Provocations during Trade Review," *Wall Street Journal*, June 8, 2001.

[110] "Hu Jintao yu Meiguo fuzongtong Qieni juxing huitan" ("Hu Jintao and U.S. Vice President Cheney hold talks), *Jiefangjun Bao*. Apparently Wolfowitz misspoke when he went so far as to state that the United States "is opposed to" Taiwan independence. For the quotation, see Greg Trodore, "US calls for closer military ties," *South China Morning Post*, May 31, 2002.

JAPAN

*Eric Heginbotham and
Richard J. Samuels*

I s Japan becoming a "normal" nation—one willing to apply military force in a wider range of circumstances than homeland defense? If so, will it become a more capable political and military partner to the United States? Recent events have led some analysts to answer these questions in the affirmative.[1] Japanese measures to support the U.S. military in Afghanistan after September 2001 and post-Cold War debate about Article Nine of the Constitution have been hailed as evidence of a significant shift in Japanese foreign policy toward both "normality" and closer collaboration with the United States. American strategists who had exhorted Japan to "show the flag" during America's war on terrorism welcomed the response.

Examination of both long- and short-term developments suggests that change has been misrepresented and overstated. That noted, major change in Japanese security policy has not been constrained exclusively, or perhaps even primarily, by constitutional or normative inhibitions on the use of force.[2] Rather, Japan's current foreign policy direction reflects a long-

Eric Heginbotham is Senior Fellow at the Council on Foreign Relations. Richard Samuels is Ford International Professor of Political Science and Director of the Center for International Studies at the Massachusetts Institute of Technology. The authors are grateful for the comments they received from Richard Ellings, Aaron Friedberg, George Gilboy, Benjamin Self, Michael Swaine, and Christopher Twomey on earlier drafts of this essay. Thanks are also due to Jocelyn Roberts and Michael Hatada who made heroic efforts to find trade and investment data.

held elite concern for the importance of economic security and the low utility of military action, with pacifism and constitutional constraints frequently invoked to support preferred policies. Hence, even should pacifism continue to decline in Japan—and we acknowledge that it remains an important element in Japanese political discourse, even if sometimes used instrumentally—there may be significantly less change in Tokyo's foreign policy than is anticipated in the United States. Many conservative political leaders are reluctant to use force, not because they are morally opposed to its employment or because they fear public disapproval at the polls, but because they question its efficacy in a world where, they believe, economic power is more important.

Change at Last or Change at Least?

During the U.S. operation in Afghanistan, Japanese naval vessels were deployed far from Japan's littoral waters, but the support was limited to a small-scale logistical effort far from the scene of combat. While this support was more extensive than any previously offered the United States, it was diluted by teams of high-level Japanese politicians and diplomats dispatched to reassure the Muslim world that Tokyo was in fact not engaged in the conflict. Decision-makers in the governing Liberal Democratic Party (LDP) declined to implement the bolder package of military measures suggested by Prime Minister Koizumi Junichiro shortly after the September 11 attacks. The LDP leadership debated and carefully calculated Japanese national interest and, while it agreed that some assistance to Japan's U.S. ally was necessary, it also felt that maintaining strong ties with regional states (especially oil-producing states) required that military support be limited to symbolic measures far from the scene of actual fighting.[3]

To be sure, Japan's military shield is larger, more legitimate, and more convincing than at any time since 1945. With the end of the Cold War and the further rise of the United States as the preeminent actor on the world stage—and after considerable domestic debate—military power is now openly a part of the Japanese security discourse. Japan steadily increased its defense budget during the 1980s and 1990s to the point where Japanese defense spending is second only to the United States, and is comparable to that of Britain, Germany, and France. In East Asia, Japan has the most powerful navy and air force after the United States, and it is well ahead of China in its defense and military procurement budgets.[4] China's naval surface tonnage today is only 77 percent as large as Japan's and is far less sophisticated.[5] Japan's air force is equally impressive. It backs up a substantial force of 160 F-15s and 28 F-2 fighters (an F-16 derivative, 130 of which will be produced) with sophisticated airborne early warning aircraft (including 10 E-2C and 4 Boeing E-767 AWACS), capabilities not enjoyed by the Chinese.[6] Its pilots have between 50 percent and 100 percent more training hours than Chinese pilots, and its training system is more technologically sophisticated.[7] This combines to give the Japanese air-to-air and strike capabilities unmatched by the Chinese air force.

But Japan has sharpened its mercantile sword as well. Today Tokyo conducts its economic diplomacy more independently in the pursuit of Japan's interests than ever. Investment in Iran, trade with Libya, technological assistance to Cuba, and economic cooperation with Burma challenge U.S. preferences and, in the cases of Iran and Libya, Japanese policy openly rejects the legitimacy of U.S. sanctions. If "normal" nations are defined by their active and independent pursuit of the national interest, Japan has long since arrived. Thus, there is evidence of change—automatically following the U.S. lead on high profile international issues is no longer Japanese policy. Note, for example, Koizumi's open rejection of President George W. Bush's call for the replacement of Yasser Arafat as president of the Palestinian National Authority in June 2002.[8] But there is also evidence of continuity—concern for international commerce remains as salient a feature of Japan's security policy calculus as concern for international political stability. Japanese national interests are still defined as often in economic terms as in terms of the military balance of power. In this sense, then, "comprehensive security" remains Japan's security policy touchstone.

Under comprehensive security Japanese leaders employ a dual hedge designed to protect the state against two types of threats simultaneously: military and economic. Both are considered equally important strategically for Japan's long-term independence and prosperity. In each of these areas (military and economic security) Japan's strategies, and even its partners, may be different. Okamoto Yukio, a former senior diplomat and leading policy advisor, recently put this bluntly: "America can be Japan's ally in security affairs, but I do not think it can be an ally in economic affairs."[9]

Japanese diplomats recognize that there will always be tensions between the military and economic components of its strategy, and they direct efforts at finding paths that enable pursuit of both simultaneously. Tokyo's hedge against military threats continues to revolve around maintaining the U.S.-Japan military alliance, complemented with efforts to foster cooperative security regimes in the region. Its hedge against economic threats focuses on developing strategic economic and political relationships with a variety of states, including those with complementary economies (i.e., those, unlike North America and Western Europe, that do not compete in the same high value-added manufacturing sectors), which provide raw materials or markets and serve as bases for Japanese outward investment

and production. These states include several that the United States identifies as present or potential military security threats.

In the short- to mid-term, Japan is likely to continue incrementally
strengthening both the military and economic components of its security
strategy, but it is unlikely to undertake any fundamental change in the way
in which it balances them. Barring a major external shock (such as a direct
attack on the Japanese homeland or a global economic collapse), Japan's
foreign policy status quo is most likely to change if politicians assume
greater control over the bureaucracy, if the balance of power within the
bureaucracy shifts away from the economic ministries, or if the conservative LDP regime collapses as a result of continued economic under-perfor-
mance. The collapse of the LDP could give rise to either a new center-right
or a center-left government, either of which might wish to diversify Japan's
security options, moving away from what some in each camp see as excessive reliance on the United States. In either case, political reform is likely
to take decades to unfold. Hence this essay focuses on how new challenges
to Japan's established approach to international relations will likely produce evolutionary change in its foreign policy.

This chapter is divided into six parts, beginning with a description of
"comprehensive security" as it is currently constituted. Using this as a
baseline, Japan's response to September 11 is examined and explained.
Third, important ongoing developments in Asia that impinge on Tokyo's
security policy and how those have or have not been affected by the events
of September 11 are assessed. Fourth is a discussion of Japan's likely stand
on scenarios involving those states that President Bush described as members of an "axis of evil"—Iraq, Iran, and North Korea. The fifth speculates
about how domestic political change will affect Japan's foreign policy. The
conclusion revisits the baseline to assess how both short and long term events
are likely to affect Japan's more general approach to foreign policy.

Baseline: Comprehensive Security and the Dual Hedge

Japan's comprehensive security doctrine—an omnibus threat assessment—
is not new; it is well documented and widely understood in Japan and
abroad.[10] It starts from the idea that economic security is at least as important as military security, and posits that diplomacy ought to accommodate
military, economic, and associated resource interests simultaneously. It
emphasizes that security comes in many forms, and that policy instruments
from the economic, technological, and even cultural realms, as well as
military ones, can secure the nation. Makino Noboru, the former head of
the Mitsubishi Research Institute, wrote that "although national supremacy
was once a product of military power, it is now decided primarily by eco-

nomic power. Economic power is, for its part, decided primarily by the ability to generate technology."[11] Then deputy foreign minister, and current ambassador to the United States, Kato Ryozo, wrote in a December 2000 article that "Japan realized after the long drawn out war [World War II] that it is more beneficial for the nation to seek to build up its power by putting emphasis on the economy and technology development than by trying to win more land power."[12] And the January 2000 *Report of the Prime Minister's Commission on Japan's Goals in the 21st Century* predicted that "in the twenty-first century the use of military might to secure national development and settle disputes will increasingly lose legitimacy."[13]

Thus, while military security is widely accepted as one pillar of the larger comprehensive approach, it is assigned a low utility for all but home-land defense. That, combined with the high costs associated with its use and (especially) with the continued willingness of the United States to in-dulge Japanese "cheap riding," has focused Japanese discussion of mili-tary security on the maintenance of the alliance with the United States. While the range of elite opinion on this issue has widened in recent years, Prime Minister Koizumi responded to questions on military security during a June 2001 press conference by insisting:

> I do not feel that I have to make extra efforts in particular on security. That is because Japan's basic stance is to ensure its secu-rity with the Japan-U.S. security alliance serving as a basis. That is the way it has been, and it will remain so in the future.[14]

Still, change has occurred in Japan's defense posture. Some of this has come in response to episodic U.S. prodding, but even when its U.S. ally has seemed most determined to convince Japan to bear a greater military burden, Japanese leaders have carefully avoided specific commitments and often have proceeded quietly to reverse course after American pressure has subsided. In response to strong U.S. pressure for greater burden-sharing in efforts against the Soviet Union, for example, Japanese defense spending in 1987 broke the one percent of GNP barrier for the first time in 21 years—only to fall below that threshold once again three years later, after that particular issue had declined in salience in American eyes. Similarly, de-spite officially expanding the Japanese defense perimeter to 1,000 nautical miles in 1981 and agreeing on new defense guidelines in 1997, the Japa-nese government refused to stipulate what type of crises might trigger what particular military response. During the war in Afghanistan, the Japanese "showed the flag," but the enabling legislation explicitly limited the dis-patch of Japanese forces to this one event, rather than using the opportu-nity to reaffirm the broader alliance or to reinterpret the Constitution, as some politicians had preferred. Former prime minister Nakasone Yasuhiro lamented the lost chance: "[The terrorist attacks] posed a rare opportunity to change the interpretation. However, it has become a case of forfeiting that opportunity."[15]

Japanese leaders have arguably made more lasting adjustments to their security policy vis-à-vis the United Nations than vis-à-vis the United States. During the 1990–91 Gulf War, Prime Minister Kaifu Toshiki and LDP Secretary General Ozawa Ichiro engineered the first legislation allowing dispatch of Japanese forces, under the auspices of the United Nations and in a non-combat capacity.[16] In September 1992, Japanese soldiers participated in UN peacekeeping operations in Angola and Cambodia, the first time since 1945 that Japanese troops were deployed abroad. With those precedents set, Japanese forces were subsequently deployed to Mozambique, Rwanda, Honduras, the Golan Heights, and Bosnia. Since September 11, the government has further relaxed limitations on the use of force in a move to satisfy international demands for a Japanese contribution to global peace and security. These measures have enhanced Japan's diplomatic stature even as they have given Japan a nascent alternative to U.S. demands for closer bilateral military cooperation.

Clearly, military security has not been ignored, but it is routinely subordinated in a strategic debate focusing on how to increase aggregate state power—specifically, advancing Japan's economic position. The pages of Japanese foreign policy journals are filled with articles on national strategy by senior staff members from Keidanren (the Japanese Federation of Economic Organizations), the economic ministries, and even individual Japanese corporations. These business elites address the U.S.-Japan security alliance, constitutional revision, and the strategic balance in Asia, and their views are taken seriously. Less is heard from retired military officers and academic specialists on security studies. Indeed, perhaps the largest misunderstandings in the U.S. strategic community about Japan's foreign policy derive from its proclivity to take Japan Defense Agency (JDA) views as representative of Japan's own strategic community, or to assume its views carry significant weight in the policy debate. Many senior positions in the JDA are assigned to officials dispatched from the other ministries, and, while the agency is respected for its technical capability, it is not responsible for Japan's strategic planning. Former LDP faction chief Kato Koichi spoke to this clearly when he explained why Japan should protect its economic relations with the Muslim world and not dispatch Aegis-equipped vessels to assist U.S. operations in Afghanistan. "It is natural for the Defense Agency to desire the use of the Aegis," he said, "but lawmakers and the Foreign Ministry should think more strategically."[17]

September 11 and the Afghan War

On September 19, Prime Minister Koizumi announced a seven-point plan of action that appeared to signal Japan's Self-Defense Force (SDF) would play a prominent role in America's war against the Taliban and the Al Qaeda network.[18] The first measure—citing UN Security Council Resolution 1368—was an unambiguous pledge to dispatch the SDF to assist the United States in its military response to terrorism. Other measures included the strengthening of SDF protection of U.S. bases in Japan, intelligence gathering on behalf of the anti-terrorist coalition, emergency aid to Pakistan and India, humanitarian assistance to Afghan refugees in bordering states, and special efforts to calm the roiling seas of the international economy.

The Koizumi cabinet and the media focused most attention on the dispatch of SDF forces overseas. This was to include three components. First, naval ships were to provide medical, transport, and logistical support for U.S. forces undertaking strikes against Afghanistan. Secondly, the Maritime Self-Defense Force (MSDF) would quickly dispatch ships and aircraft to the Indian Ocean to collect intelligence. Specifically, Japanese officials discussed the dispatch of Japan's most capable warships, 7,800-ton Aegis destroyers and P-3 aircraft, to operate from Diego Garcia and secure the U.S. rear area while the United States conducted offensive operations. Third, other SDF elements would be dispatched to offer humanitarian aid to refugees.

After a decade of obfuscatory debate about whether or not Taiwan was located "in the areas surrounding Japan," many believed that with this announcement, Prime Minister Koizumi had taken a long-awaited giant step in the transformation of Japanese foreign policy. And, indeed, domestic political circumstances in late September 2001 appeared propitious for the success of Koizumi's plan. Apart from the Socialist and the Communist parties, which between them controlled only eight percent of the Diet, there was little identifiable pacifist opposition to the deployment of military forces. Throughout September, Hatoyama Yukio, the leader of the main opposition Democratic Party of Japan, expressed strong support for cooperation with the United States, although he was later unable to deliver the full endorsement of his party. The head of the Liberal Party, Ozawa Ichiro, did not oppose deployment in principle, but argued that it would require more explicit backing from the United Nations. Editorials in the *Yomiuri Shimbun* and the *Sankei Shimbun* wholeheartedly supported Japanese participation, and the *Asahi Shimbun* offered conditional approval. Only the *Mainichi Shimbun*, concerned about Japan's standing in the Muslim world, opposed a military response. Most important, Prime Minister Koizumi's cabinet enjoyed overwhelmingly high approval ratings, and some form of military support for the United States was backed by a majority of the Japanese public.[19] Given this support, the LDP government would have had little difficulty implementing most of the plan had it been committed to the task.

In the event, however, the LDP did not wish to execute Koizumi's plan. Early dispatch of SDF vessels was vetoed during a September 27 meeting of the LDP General Council (which includes only former secretaries general of the party). One of the participants, Nonaka Hiromu, said, "I am worried the current policy of making Japan visible and mobilizing the SDF is moving our country in the wrong direction."[20] The day after the General Council meeting Yamazaki Taku, the sitting LDP secretary general, met with Prime Minister Koizumi and advised caution.

LDP opposition to a high-profile military role was not limited to one or two individuals; it included a number of faction chiefs and former prime ministers, in addition to the former and present party secretaries general mentioned above. Many of these conservative party luminaries were self-identified nationalists who opposed high-profile military action explicitly on the grounds of the damage such measures would do to Japan's economic interests in the region. Even the more moderate former faction head, Kato Koichi, who headed the hastily assembled Lower House Counter-terrorism Committee, reported that the government decided against the dispatch of Aegis destroyers against the wishes of the Defense Agency:

> It [was] wiser for Japan to consider how it could contribute [to the peace and reconstruction of Afghanistan] after the Taliban than to dispatch Aegis vessels—an action that would lead Arab nations to believe that Japan has provided heavy military assistance.[21]

Former Prime Minister Hashimoto Ryutaro expressed similar concerns about the reaction of the Muslim world. In early October, he was sent to Egypt and the United Arab Emirates as a special government envoy, where he also met with Yasser Arafat of the Palestinian Authority. In a subsequent interview, Hashimoto explained his mission:

> In the current situation, the important Japanese roles are to provide support for refugees, transportation, and medical care.... However, we do not engage in combat. That is the message the Japanese government has sought to convey in the countries I visited.... I was really shocked to realize that the message had not gotten through, and an image was being formed that Japan was waging war along with the United States and Britain.[22]

He was, he assured the reporter, able to convey Japan's true position. Even the openly hawkish former Prime Minister Nakasone Yasuhiro opposed Koizumi's initial plan on similar grounds, proclaiming that "any globally-minded politician worth his salt should be exploring measures that would please the Arab world and bring honor to Japan at the same time."[23] And Nakasone should know. As Minister of International Trade and Industry in 1973, he negotiated an explicit quid pro quo with Saudi Arabia, agreeing to Japanese recognition for Palestinian autonomy in exchange for Japan's exclusion from the Arab oil embargo.[24]

The Iranian Connection

Japan's political-economic relationship with Iran was of singular importance in its response to September 11. More than a full year earlier, anticipating that the United States would lift Iranian sanctions when they expired in July 2001, the Japanese began to establish what the business magazine *Toyo Keizai* called a "foothold before U.S. companies begin to participate in force."[25] Although Congress renewed the sanctions, Japan announced a package of business deals with Iran that could amount to $6–$12 billion in new investment. The political groundwork for the package was established well before September 11. In September 2000, Iran's government spokesman, Ayatollah Mohajerani, visited officials in Tokyo, clearing the way for a visit by President Mohammad Khatami two months later. Subsequent business consultations culminated in a visit to Tehran by Japan's Trade Minister, Hiranuma Takeo, who brought with him a delegation of 80 businessmen representing 34 Japanese companies.[26] Proposed deals included: 1) the development of the massive new Azadegan oil field (with Royal Dutch Shell holding a minority stake); 2) repair of the loading facilities at Kharg Island, from which 90 percent of Iran's oil is exported; 3) introduction of natural gas-powered buses in Tehran; 4) new telecom businesses related to oil and gas pipelines; 5) modernization of refineries in Tehran, Tabriz, and Isfahan; 6) measures to save energy at the Ahwaz steelworks; and 7) remodeling the plants of Tehran Cement Company. Despite a later start than its European competitors, the size and breadth of these deals, their coordination in Tokyo, and the high-profile political backing they have received promise Japan strategic advantages in the Gulf far in excess of any it once enjoyed via the now defunct Khafji concession in Saudi Arabia.[27] Although this major package of deals had been negotiated before the attacks on the United States, they had not yet been signed; the details were to be completed by late October 2001, and ultimately were signed as scheduled.

With these strategic transactions in the balance, much of Japan's early post September 11 regional diplomacy revolved around discussions with Iranian officials about measures to alleviate problems associated with the expected influx of Afghan refugees. This concern was reciprocated by Iran, which assured Japan of a steady flow of oil throughout America's military campaign.[28] With the United States seeking to shore up support for its military activities in Afghanistan among that country's neighbors, Japan found itself poised to seize an epochal opportunity to assist in and benefit from any potential rapprochement between Iran and the United States.

Ultimately, it was these concerns that won the day, and Japan undertook the minimum military commitment it could while still being able to announce to the U.S. side that it had done more than wave its checkbook at the alliance.[29] No Aegis-equipped ships were dispatched to the Indian Ocean. No P-3s were sent to Diego Garcia. No medical teams for either refugees or U.S. soldiers were sent. No SDF personnel were deployed for refugee relief work in Pakistan. Rather, several C-130s, loaded with blankets and relief supplies landed, disgorged their goods at Islamabad airport, and quickly took to the air. Logistical support was provided to U.S. forces, but it did not include weapons or ammunition, and it arrived after the Taliban had been routed. Japanese support consisted of two SDF tankers shuttling fuel to the U.S. fleet. Destroyer escorts were provided for the tankers, but served little if any military function.[30]

It was a remarkably deft move. Japan's military response enabled Defense Agency Director General Nakatani Gen to go to Washington and take credit for a contribution to the U.S. war effort while at the same enabling Hashimoto to argue that Japan was not waging war alongside the United States. Secretary of Defense Donald Rumsfeld stressed the differential capabilities of U.S. allies and professed pleasure with all that Japan was doing within the limits of its Constitution. In a joint press conference with Nakatani, Rumsfeld said, "we appreciate what they're doing a great deal, and it is helping, and it is important."[31] A few days earlier, at a ceremony marking the sixtieth anniversary of the Japanese attack on Pearl Harbor, President Bush proclaimed that "today we take special pride that one of our former enemies is now among America's finest friends: We're grateful to our ally, Japan, and to its good people. Today our two navies are working side by side in the fight against terror."[32]

Since Washington did not actually need, or even seek, a specific Japanese contribution to its military campaign, and since the war reinforced the most valuable element of the alliance, American forward deployment in Asia, the U.S. government was understandably pleased with the Japanese response. Still, by distancing itself from U.S. actions, Japan had engineered significant collateral benefits for itself. One month after President Bush's gushing appreciation for Japan's military role in the Arabian Sea, LDP Secretary General Yamazaki returned from a mission to the Middle East and reported that the "meetings were very effective," adding, "I think they carefully listened to our opinions because we were calling for peace from a different point of view than that of the United States and Europe."[33]

Japan's Response vs. Other American Allies

The Japanese response to September 11 must be compared to those of other states. The British played the most active role, flying strike missions with the United States and inserting special forces on the ground. Australia, a nation with the population no larger than Tokyo, conducted air strikes after deploying a squadron of F-18s to Diego Garcia. Even Jordan, with its own delicate domestic political balance and significant security concerns (and without any formal alliance with the United States), provided security for U.S. special forces and established a field hospital in Mazar-e-Sharif, the scene of one of the largest battles in the war. Importantly, other countries with constitutions that repudiate war acted more boldly than Japan. The German government responded immediately to the terrorist attacks of September 11 with full support for the United States, and Chancellor Gerhard Schroeder staked the future of his government on legislation that would permit Germany to join the allied response. German warships led an international squadron patrolling waters off Somalia to interdict supplies bound for Al Qaeda groups there. A unit armed with Fuchs nuclear, biological, and chemical warfare vehicles was dispatched to Kuwait to prepare for possible use in the region. German special operations forces took part in offensive combat operations (including *Operation Anaconda*) inside Afghanistan, and at least 700 soldiers participated in the international peace-keeping force designed to maintain order after the fall of the Taliban. The Italian government offered an armored regiment, attack helicopters, fighter jets, and made four warships available to the United States. Italy conducted advanced reconnaissance in mid-December and offered the use of its nuclear, chemical, and biological warfare specialists, and its troops began arriving in Afghanistan before January 2002.[34]

International comparisons and the absolute level of military support aside, what precedents might Japanese deployments have set and what are the implications for the future of Tokyo's security policy? This was, after all, Japan's first military deployment in support of the United States and the first since World War II.[35] Perhaps its own past military activities might offer a better standard of comparison than Italian or German actions. The Japanese or, more likely, the U.S. government could use these support operations to demonstrate precedent and undermine arguments about the constitutional or legal limits on Japanese forces. But there are several reasons not to expect these actions to lead Japan toward a more active military role—at least as a U.S. alliance partner. First, the legislation approving the dispatch stipulates that the SDF cannot use force or operate in an area where combat is likely. Second, the law enabling the dispatch of MSDF tankers was limited to two years' duration and to the Afghan operation in particular. Third, Japanese lawmakers made the dispatch conditional on UN approval of the operation. Taken together, and in the context of meticulous Japanese efforts to stipulate their implications, these restrictions would appear to limit the possibilities for precedence. In fact, the legislation and the operation it enabled may have done more to tie the Japanese military to multilateralism than it does to strengthen the U.S.-Japan alliance.[36]

Japan's Preferred Role as "Mediator" Ascendant

By proposing that Japan could coordinate the international effort to pre-pare for the post-Taliban rebuilding of Afghanistan, Tokyo found it could simultaneously fulfill its obligation to the United States and consolidate its position in the region—without incurring the political-economic risks associated with military action. Prime Minister Koizumi raised the idea of a Tokyo peace conference with President Bush when they met during the annual APEC meeting on October 20. Japanese officials explained that Japan had been working with all parties to the Afghan conflict since 1996 and that Tokyo therefore had access to virtually all of the relevant parties, *better* access to some, in fact, than did the United States.[37] Japan's relationship with Iran thereupon shifted from being a point of contention with the United States to a potential benefit. Its relationships elsewhere in the region likewise served Japan well. Despite having officially cut off new official development assistance (ODA) projects in Pakistan after that country's nuclear tests in 1998, for example, Japan remained its largest donor.[38] And Japan's standing among some Arab states was enhanced by the fact that it had been providing substantial financial assistance to Palestine since 1993.[39]

Although such a meeting would ostensibly focus on political affairs inside Afghanistan and the future shape of its government, the larger hope, in the words of one newspaper editorial, was that Japan would "serve as an intermediary between Western nations and the Muslim world."[40] Although a successful meeting would cost Japan—in the form of side payments and other incentives—the costs would be more than recovered by the opportunities for Japan's economic diplomacy that hosting the conference would confer.[41] Thus, while Japanese military planning moved forward at a deliberate pace, the focus of Japan's response after October 20 shifted to securing a leading role in post-Taliban Afghan reconstruction. As it did so, the incentives to soften Japan's apparent military involvement increased.

Ultimately, Japan's effort to maximize its gains while minimizing its exposure was only partly successful. Although the United States welcomed

Japanese leadership on this issue, agreed that Japan should co-chair an organizational meeting in November 2001, and signed off on Koizumi's proposed Tokyo conference in January 2002, France, Germany, and Britain all objected vehemently to such a high-profile Japanese role. They argued that, having placed troops in harm's way, they had risked more than the Japanese and were entitled to take a leading political role after the war.[42] The United States yielded. The European Union (EU) and Saudi Arabia were added as co-chairs for a Washington conference that was downgraded from ministerial to vice-ministerial status. The meeting to decide on an interim Afghan government was held in Bonn in December 2001, and by the time the Tokyo conference was convened, its purpose had been reduced to that of soliciting and organizing donor contributions for the physical rebuilding of the country—an important, but not terribly glamorous, job.[43]

The Europeans may have outmaneuvered Japan in the Afghan endgame, but Japan was able to achieve most of its objectives. Japan consolidated its budding relations with Iran, further enhanced relations with Pakistan, positioned itself to recover its position in Saudi Arabia, and established itself as an interested party in the Middle East and Central Asia, capable of playing an independent role and willing to play partner to those who may have differences with the United States. Its failure to gain a preeminent role in Afghanistan itself may lead it to refine its tactics further, but its overall success will only confirm its general strategic direction.

Continuing Asian Developments

Although they lack the drama of recent events in the Middle East and Central Asia, there are at least two developments in East Asia that will affect Japanese security policy in the short to medium term. The first is the growing support among East Asian states for efforts to achieve greater regional economic integration, including both multilateral and bilateral free trade agreements (FTAs). The second is the continued rise of Chinese power.

Regional Economic Integration

Region-wide support for integrating the East Asian economies grew stronger over the last decade, especially in the wake of the 1997–98 Asian financial crisis.[44] After investor confidence plummeted, the regional economies were unable to control massive capital outflows. They stood by helplessly as foreign reserves declined, stock markets collapsed, and currencies depreciated. Central banks intervened to defend currency values and raise interest rates, and they tightened capital and exchange controls, but individual governments could do little on their own; they recognized that the absence of region-wide coordination cost them dearly.

There has long been a powerful constituency within Japan for an Asian trading bloc. Many in the Ministry of Economy, Trade, and Industry (METI, formerly the Ministry of International Trade and Industry—MITI), the Ministry of Foreign Affairs (MOFA), and the Japanese business community supported the idea of an East Asian Economic Caucus (EAEC) when Malaysian Prime Minister Mahathir Mohammad first proposed the idea in 1990. During the early 1990s, strong U.S. opposition dissuaded Tokyo from signing on to the idea, but domestic support never waned. METI and MOFA officials often promote Asian regionalism in the media and are often joined by business leaders. A June 2001 study by Keidanren placed East Asian economic integration first on its list of foreign policy priorities. In particular, it called for the conclusion of FTAs with South Korea and Singapore and for using those relationships to create a network of FTAs, with Japan at the hub, that would ultimately engage all the states in the region.[45] And at the bureaucratic level, METI's 2002 white paper reflects a shift in the internal balance of power within that ministry, with proponents of economic regionalism gaining relative to advocates of strengthening the World Trade Organization (WTO) and other free trade-oriented international organizations.[46] Even absent a grand strategic regional architecture, Japan's ODA and its outward direct investment—often coordinated by METI and backed by MOFA—have helped advance the cause of economic integration by creating integrated networks of Japanese producers and their associated suppliers across the region.[47]

While their competitive impulses have by no means been eliminated, and while their failures have often been conspicuous, Asian states have accelerated their efforts to further economic integration. In 1997, the members of the Association of Southeast Asian Nations (ASEAN) asked China, Japan, and South Korea to participate in an ad hoc "ASEAN+3" summit. The scope of the group's first meetings was limited to discussions of how the region might cope with the financial crisis, but ASEAN+3 soon assigned itself a more ambitious agenda, one that includes discussion of how to compete with and balance against the North American Free Trade Agreement (NAFTA) and the EU.[48]

Although it is premature to suggest that Asia has developed a stable and effective response to European or North American economic regionalism, ASEAN+3 has provided East Asian integration with a new modality and with an energy it had hitherto lacked.[49] In 1999 the group expanded the scope of its discussions to include social, political, and security issues. In 2000, ASEAN+3 had its first meeting of finance ministers and reached an agreement to stabilize currency exchange rates during a financial crisis. At the same time, a study group was established to consider an ASEAN+3

FTA. The following year Prime Minister Mahathir began lobbying for the establishment of an ASEAN+3 secretariat, finding support from South Korea, China, Japan, and Singapore.[50] At the same time, South Korea's Kim Dae Jung has backed a proposal to change the ASEAN+3 group's name to the East Asian Community, a shift that would permit the group's summit meetings to be held in Northeast Asia.

There is no question that the diplomacy driven by these efforts has already had a significant impact on the interactions among states in the region. In particular, it has affected the competition between Japan and China for regional leadership. A Japanese-led Asian FTA has long faced two obstacles. The first has been concern about opposition from the United States, Japan's largest trading partner. These concerns have been overcome, as U.S. policy has become more unilateral on other fronts, as the United States has reduced its opposition to Asian regional integration, and as Japan's neighbors have taken the initiative to proceed without Tokyo. The second obstacle—the political imperative to protect Japanese agriculture—has proven more difficult. The LDP survives as the governing party thanks in large measure to electoral support from farmers and financial support from their powerful lobby. As a result, the LDP government has stubbornly re-fused to make concessions on agriculture in its trade negotiations. When Tokyo concluded its FTA with Singapore in January 2002, Japanese offi-cials were quick to point out that Singapore has no significant agricultural production. As if just to make sure that the LDP's constituents would not miss this point, Tokyo insisted that the bilateral FTA exclude goldfish and orchids, two of the very few agricultural products that Singapore *does* ex-port. Japan thereupon wasted no time in moving forward with negotiations on a bilateral FTA with Australia (also excluding agriculture), and with South Korea, which is as eager as Japan to exclude agricultural products from such agreements.

Meanwhile, China has openly challenged Japan's hub-and-spoke ap-proach to regional integration. In November 2000 Beijing proposed its own China-ASEAN FTA, which was accepted by ASEAN a year later to the open consternation of Tokyo.[51] While all states have endorsed the ideal of a comprehensive regional agreement, China's move challenged Japanese economic leadership in the region. Japan, stymied by domestic political dynamics, stumbled along as China set the pace, shape, and direction of regional trade institution building.[52]

For example, in January 2002 Prime Minister Koizumi departed on a hastily organized tour of Southeast Asian states, during which he proposed a Japan-ASEAN Comprehensive Economic Partnership (CEP). This CEP would cover not just trade, but would also enable closer cooperation on investment, education, employment, and technology development. Ultimately, he hoped, the partnership would encompass not just all the ASEAN+3 states, but also Australia and New Zealand. But the Japanese initiative was hastily assembled and inconsistently explained. While Koizumi's proposed ASEAN+5 included Australia and New Zealand during his January swing through Southeast Asia, those two states were replaced with Hong Kong and Taiwan in his speech to the Boao Forum in April.[53] Koizumi's efforts were met with limited enthusiasm. He was left grasping for attention at a *Chinese*-sponsored Boao Forum (billed as the "Asian Davos") in May 2002, where he announced that "the region must increase cooperation to compete economically against the North American Free Trade Agreement and the European Union."[54] While Japan will surely be a central participant in any ultimate regional trade regime, it remains unclear if Tokyo (host to the lowest level of inward FDI in the industrial world) is capable of making the concessions necessary to bring these plans to fruition under its leadership.

Sino-Japanese competition and Japanese investment and trade policies notwithstanding, the drive to integrate the Asian economies and to institutionalize multilateral economic and political relations has already had a generally positive impact on regional international relations. As negotiations on the ASEAN-China FTA have proceeded, multilateral discussions between those parties on a code of conduct for the South China Sea have taken on added urgency, with a first round of talks held in March 2000 and with all sides agreeing to exercise restraint until a formal agreement can be reached. The former Commander in Chief of the U.S. Pacific Command, Admiral Dennis Blair, hailed a recent "decline in tension in the South China Sea between China and rival claimants" during a February 2002 visit to Hanoi.[55] Peace in the South China Sea and the recognition of the right of passage of third-party shipping is obviously of great interest to each of the states in the region. Multilateral agreements have been reached to combat piracy, enabling the Japanese Coast Guard (the Maritime Safety Agency) to sail far from Japanese littoral waters to play a regional security role with the support of China and its Southeast Asian neighbors for the first time.

While Japan is not about to abandon its military alliance with the United States, new opportunities presented by regional economic integration, together with its own proclivity for a comprehensive approach to security, are encouraging it to explore other arrangements with its neighbors designed to enhance confidence and complement its U.S. alliance. In February 2002, Nakatani Gen suggested that Japan should work toward the development of an "Asian NATO" that would include, among others, China and Russia.[56] While Nakatani's proposal called for something more akin to an Asian version of the Organization on Security and Cooperation in Europe (OSCE) than to NATO, it represents an important and relatively new element in Japanese security thinking. It suggests that even mainstream elites are willing to think outside the box of the bilateral alliance without calling for its abrogation or insisting that either UN-guaranteed collective security or autonomous defense are its only possible alternatives. The opposition and the business community have joined this chorus. A policy analyst in the Democratic Party argues for "the establishment of an Asian multilateral security framework," and the Japanese Association of Corporate Executives (Keizai Doyukai) has called for greater attention to organizations that can promote confidence building among the region's states.[57] Japanese elite opinion confirms these preferences: In a recent survey, only 11 percent of Japanese elites thought that the U.S. alliance should be strengthened, while more than half said it should be weakened and 12 percent said it should be abrogated. Meanwhile, nearly three-quarters of these elites thought that "building and strengthening a regional framework to promote peace and dialogue in Asia" was a "very important" security option.[58]

Sino-Japanese Relations

Tokyo's dual hedge comes into clearest relief in its China policy. Japan continues to assiduously maintain its U.S. alliance and marshal autonomous defense capabilities to hedge against future military threats from this quarter, while it simultaneously cultivates cooperative political and economic relations with China in order to buttress its economic position vis-à-vis the United States and Europe.

After reducing its military budget during the 1980s, China has increased its defense spending rapidly in recent years, narrowing the gap between China's spending and that of Japan. Although the ratio of official Chinese to official Japanese spending only returned to its 1980 level in 2002, China's success in developing its industrial and technological base has allowed it to reduce the gap (in relative terms) between the quality of its forces and those of Japan. Moreover, by focusing more of its defense efforts on air and naval capabilities, China has made gains in these areas. Japan's lead in naval tonnage, for example, was cut from about 35 percent in 1989 to around 29 percent by 2001.[59] In the short term, however, China's military strength is but a shadow of what Japan once faced from the former Soviet Union, whose naval tonnage was some 250 percent that of Japan's in 1989 and whose technology was more comparable.

After declining somewhat immediately after the Cold War, Japanese public support for the U.S. alliance has increased in recent years, and outright elite opposition remains low. Japan has also repositioned its own military forces from the north, where they once stood opposite Soviet troops, to the south, where they now face China. In December 2001, the Japanese Coast Guard—a force that is almost as large as the entire Chinese surface combat fleet and in several respects better equipped—pursued and sank what is believed to be a North Korean spy ship near Chinese territorial waters.[60] This was Japan's first use of military force since World War II. Still, Japan has avoided strong unilateral measures in the pursuit of military security where danger is not imminent, and China is cooperating with Japanese efforts to raise the vessel.

Although China's growing military budgets have contributed to Japanese sentiments in favor of reducing its economic aid to China, any sense of immediate threat from China is balanced by the prospect of economic gains from the relationship. The prevailing elite view is that China is at worst a hypothetical future threat. Most see reason for hope that China can be successfully integrated into the international system, especially if it is not isolated or contained. Moreover, in contrast to the late 1970s and early 1980s, a 2000 public opinion survey indicates that more Japanese favor reducing Japan's military budget (14 percent) than increasing it (11 percent). Some 62 percent favors maintaining the current spending level—more than at any time since the surveys began.[61]

Despite some concerns about the future shape and direction of Chinese power, the level of military threat has not been sufficient to deter Japan from pursuing closer regional bilateral cooperation. In addition to giving China a stake in international stability and encouraging its development in peaceful directions, closer regional cooperation with Beijing offers Japan strategic advantages in its economic position. There is more here than the (not inconsiderable) value of the bilateral relationship itself. Competition for regional leadership notwithstanding, Tokyo realizes that good relations with China also contribute to achieving the greater prize—effective regional economic cooperation to balance U.S. and European economic power.

Japan and China have already achieved a great deal. Japan conducts nearly twice as much trade with China, as a percentage of its total trade, as does the United States. This trade, moreover, again relative to total trade grew faster than that of the U.S.-China trade between 1990 and 2000.

China is Japan's second largest trade partner and the largest recipient of its aid in Asia. China is also the largest recipient of Japanese outward FDI, having served as a preferred production base for Japanese firms since the rise of the yen and U.S. protectionism encouraged them to move offshore during the mid-1980s.[62] U.S. investment in China, once far behind Japan's, has only recently surpassed Japanese levels in absolute terms despite the much larger size of the U.S. economy.

Table 4.1. Japanese and U.S. Trade with China

		1990	1995	2000
Japan	Exports to China (as % of total Japanese exports)	6.7	11.2	12.1
	Imports from China (as % of total Japanese imports)	6.1	11.5	15.1
	Total trade with China (as % of Japanese total trade)	6.4	11.4	13.4
United States	Exports to China (as % of total U.S. exports)	3.0	4.5	4.0
	Imports from China (as % of total U.S. imports)	5.2	7.8	9.6
	Total trade with China (as % of U.S. total trade)	4.2	6.4	7.5

Source: International Monetary Fund, *Direction of Trade Statistics,* 1997, 2000, and 2001 editions. Data for China includes trade with Hong Kong and Macao.

Table 4.2. Japanese versus U.S. Investment in China

	1990	1995	2000
Ratio of Japanese to U.S. FDI in China	12 : 1	15 : 1	0.8 : 1

Source: Organization for Economic Cooperation database, <www.sourceoecd.org>. Exchange rate conversion based upon IMF standard.

METI's analysts highlight the direct benefits of increased Japanese economic interaction with China. China was responsible for 40 percent of East Asia's growth during the 1990s, and its economic reforms will, in METI's view, "encourage dynamic changes in the industrial and trade map for East Asia as a whole, boosting the region's competitiveness still further as one of the world's key manufacturing centers."[63] METI sees the Chinese economy as continuing to be complementary to that of Japan. It observes that most Chinese high-end development has been among parts suppliers, increasing China's value as both a production base and trade partner. The most important competition taking place in China, it concludes, is not between Chinese firms and Japanese ones, but rather between the companies of advanced industrial states.[64]

Despite this, Japanese and Chinese manufacturers do compete in some sectors. Japanese fears of the economic consequences of industrial out-migration, what they refer to as "hollowing," are not unfounded. China's continued economic growth poses challenges to Japan's sunset industries, a point stressed by Japan's China hawks. Prime Minister Koizumi, however, has sided with METI and Keidanren, which represents Japan's larger, technology-based firms. During the Boao Forum he put a decidedly positive spin on Sino-Japanese economic competition by acknowledging the need for the structural adjustment of the Japanese economy through the phasing out of older industries: "I see the advancement of Japan-China economic relations not as a hollowing out of Japanese industry but as an opportunity to nurture new industries in Japan."[65]

In dismissing the concerns of the China hawks so directly, Prime Minister Koizumi has reaffirmed Japanese policy promoting amicable Sino-Japanese relations as essential for regional integration and Japanese economic security. He is joined by business leaders who worry that Japan will lose all if it confronts Chinese power. In the February 2001 issue of *Gaiko Foramu*, Fujino Fumiaki of the Itochu Trading Company wrote that the development of ASEAN+3 integration depends on the backing of both China and Japan. "In the midst of all this," he continues, "I believe it will be necessary for Japan and China to become stronger partners. If Japan does not exercise joint leadership in Asia with China, we [Japan] will be left behind."[66] A 2001 report by Keidanren makes a similar point, arguing that Japan and China "should avoid binding themselves to the narrow confines of a bilateral relationship. The two countries should map out a broad-based strategy of cooperation and build a bilateral relationship in a multilateral setting encompassing Asia and the world as a whole."[67]

Although Japanese apprehension of China has received much attention in the western media, Sino-Japanese relations have been institutionalized during the past decade. Whether the byproduct of regional integration or of strategic choice, the Japanese prime minister now meets either the Chinese prime minister or the chairman of the Communist Party several times a year. Many of their regular meeting venues are of recent origin: the APEC summit meeting (since 1993); the ASEAN+3 summit (since 1997); a Sino-Japanese bilateral summit (since 1998); within the trilateral summit among China, Japan, and South Korea (since 2000); and the Boao Forum (since 2002). Negotiations preceding and following each of these various meetings at the highest political levels, as well as others scheduled for the economic and foreign ministers, enable both countries' government officials to meet and troubleshoot at the working level.

Of course, common economic interests and the institutionalization of relations have not and will not prevent problems and crises from challenging Sino-Japanese relations. In recent years there have been several highly visible incidents that threatened to disrupt bilateral relations. Incursions by Chinese navy-affiliated research ships into Japan's exclusive economic zone (EEZ) during 1999 and 2000; Prime Minister Koizumi's visits to the Yasukuni Shrine in August 2001 and April 2002; Japanese tariffs on Chinese agricultural products and China's retaliation against Japanese electronics imports in 2001; Japan's pursuit and sinking of a North Korean spy ship in China's EEZ in December 2001; and China's intrusion into Japan's consulate in Shenyang in May 2002 to seize a family of five North Korean refugees, all raised nationalist temperatures in both countries.

But a combination of sustained political will and the use of the increasingly dense set of institutionalized connections between the two governments allowed for the resolution of each of these problems—in every case significantly faster and more satisfactorily than predicted by many observers. When, for example, Chinese maritime incursions into the Japanese EEZ began to adversely affect Japanese public opinion toward China, Mori Yoshiro raised the issue with Zhu Rongji during the October 2000 bilateral summit in Tokyo, and Zhu quickly promised to resolve the problem. Beijing agreed to provide prior notification to Tokyo in case the former wished to conduct further oceanographic surveys in Japanese economic zones. At the height of the "mushroom war," Koizumi and Jiang met for 30 minutes on the sidelines of the Shanghai APEC meeting and agreed to resolve the difference. In the case of the sinking of the North Korean "mystery ship," Li Peng arrived in Tokyo in April 2002 for a bilateral summit and delivered the message that China would allow Japan to salvage the vessel.

This string of particularly contentious incidents signals that there remain many threats to full Sino-Japanese rapprochement at the level of public opinion. Certainly, Prime Minister Koizumi's two visits to the Yasukuni Shrine inflamed passions in China (and in Korea as well). Likewise, the unauthorized entrance of Chinese military police into Japan's Shenyang consulate compound in May 2002 had a similar effect on Japanese public opinion (as did the earlier naval incursions). Although nationalists in both Japan and China sought to exploit and enlarge the friction, none has succeeded to date. Japanese popular perceptions of China are reasonably positive.[68] And at the official level, determined political leadership on both sides has ameliorated the worst effects of openly provocative actions.

Clearly, the emphasis Japanese leaders have placed on comprehensive security has tilted them toward maintaining a positive working relationship with China. That relationship has already become more institutionalized than most analysts have expected. While this progress certainly can come undone, any Japanese leader seeking to steer a newly confrontational course on China policy will face formidable roadblocks erected by the bureaucracy and business interests. Japanese leaders are likely to be more preoccupied fending off U.S. pressure to strike a hardline posture vis-à-vis the PRC than fending off their own China hawks. In June 2002, reporters from the *International Herald Tribune* asked Prime Minister Koizumi if Japan would increase its defense commitment in Asia in light of U.S. distractions elsewhere. In reply, he said, "I do not subscribe to the view that China is a threat. The fact that the Chinese economy is becoming more powerful does not necessarily mean that it will pose any military danger." He noted that during the 1980s, some in the West had held similar fears about Japan. Rather than building up Japan's military forces, Koizumi suggested that the challenge was "how Japan will be able to cooperate in terms of regional stability, with the premise that Japan will not use force."[69]

Japan and the "Axis of Evil"

China is not the only—or even the most likely—litmus test of the health of the U.S.-Japan alliance. Japanese security policy is more likely to be tested in the short term if the United States decides to take offensive action against any of the three states identified by President Bush as belonging to the "axis of evil": Iran, Iraq, and North Korea. Since U.S. security concerns with those states are related more closely to the proliferation of weapons of mass destruction (WMD) than to the war on terrorism, existing legislation cannot provide Japan a framework for action. How closely will Japan cooperate with the United States in the event of military action to preempt WMD proliferation by the Bush administration? Will it permit the unfettered use of U.S. bases for an operation it cannot support politically?

Reaction in Tokyo to President Bush's January 2002 State of the Union speech in which he first identified the "axis of evil" was mixed. While there may have been less open indignation with U.S. moralizing in Tokyo than in European capitals, many Japanese officials expressed concern with Bush's position. They were not confident about how much and under what conditions Japan could assist the United States militarily. JDA Director Nakatani Gen questioned the tie between Iran, Iraq, and North Korea and the September 11 attacks, and suggested that the "axis of evil" designation might have been intended for a domestic audience.[70]

As a variety of Japanese officials and newspapers quickly observed, President Bush denounced the "axis of evil" without specifying the conditions under which the United States might act. While this naturally makes it hard for Japanese planners to respond, on some points there is little doubt that Japan's position is likely to be less forthcoming than the United States might demand or expect. Tokyo officials have, without exception, welcomed the prospect of mediating between the United States and various other parties—the European states, other Arab states, Iran, North Korea, and China.[71] However, there has been considerably less enthusiasm about the prospects of playing any significant role in military undertakings. Although Prime Minister Koizumi expressed support for President Bush in the abstract, JDA Director Nakatani Gen, LDP Secretary General Yamazaki Taku, and Deputy Cabinet Secretary Abe Shinzo each expressed concerns about the legal basis of possible Japanese military support for U.S. action against any of these states.

A Military Campaign in Iraq

Japanese officials and commentators have focused on Iraq as the most probable target of U.S. military action. Japan's level of participation in any possible strike against Iraq will depend on four factors: 1) whether the United States can tie Iraq to the events of September 11; 2) whether and how the United Nations authorizes action; 3) the degree of support and participation of America's European allies; and 4) the reaction of Arab states to U.S. action. In no event, however, is Japan likely to be among America's most visible supporters. At best it will mix political support with very indirect military support, but it will almost certainly not do more than it did to assist U.S. operations in Afghanistan.

Several Japanese observers have argued that non-participation in any possible U.S. military action would jeopardize the alliance, but others counter that Japanese support for the war against terrorism had fortified the alliance. With the United States satisfied that Japan will not allow demonstrations to disrupt the use of Japanese bases, the larger question is whether or not the LDP can reprise its legislative initiatives in support of new U.S. action. As noted above, current legislation enabling support for U.S. operations in Afghanistan only covers events associated directly with the September 11 attack on the United States, Al Qaeda, and the Taliban. In a February 2002 statement, Nakatani Gen observed that a good explanation for the connection between Iraq and Al Qaeda would have to be established before Japan could participate in, or even provide rear area support for, an invasion of Iraq. While the Diet could consider new legal measures, Nakatani Gen's general caution on both of these questions was highlighted by his conclusion that "the United States is fully aware of Japan's constitutional constraints and is unlikely to press it hard to take such a step."[72]

The history of Japanese involvement in the Middle East indicates that political and economic concerns, especially Japan's oil diplomacy, will be at least as important as any legal constraints on action. Japan has few if any direct interests in Iraq itself, but since the oil crises of 1973 and 1979, Tokyo's concern for its image in the Arab world has been a primary driver in virtually all of its regional relations—even those with nations or groups that themselves produce no oil or do not control oil exporting routes. Regional support for U.S. efforts against Iraq would be necessary for Tokyo to undertake anything more than issuing vague and conditional statements of approval. Still, even support from prominent Arab leaders may be insufficient to calm the nerves of Japanese officials if popular opinion in important Arab states remained volatile. Hence, anything less than an attack by Iraq on one of its neighbors, and the subsequent consolidation of regional opinion behind a multinational operation, would be unlikely to elicit Japanese direct military support for U.S. operations beyond perhaps the same type of largely symbolic assistance it provided during the Afghan campaign.

The position of other U.S. allies, especially the Europeans, will also influence Japanese decision-making. Being singled out as the most high-profile non-participant in the 1990–91 Gulf War coalition affected Japanese foreign policy thinking for more than a decade. A reprise of broad European support for a military campaign would put immense pressure on Japan to provide token non-combat military assistance for U.S. operations. The more likely absence of broad European support, however, would remove much of the pressure for a Japanese military role on the ground.

While each of these factors will affect Japan's final decision, Japanese military support for U.S. operations against Iraq seems highly unlikely. One face-saving option under consideration is for Japan to continue or even expand its role in Afghan-related operations in the Arabian Sea during a U.S. campaign against Iraq. This would allow Tokyo to contribute to what the United States regards as a single war without having to pass new legislation or having to shoulder the international political risks associated with specific support for an operation against Iraq. Moreover, by freeing up U.S. resources for what will at that time be more demanding operations in Iraq, Japan will also be contributing something plausibly valuable to the war effort in that theater.[73]

Mediating between Iran and the United States

Although Japan is even more unlikely to take an active military role in any U.S. military action against Iran, no such action appears imminent. Rather, the United States appears intent on applying diplomatic pressure in an effort to dissuade Iran from developing nuclear weapons and to desist from backing anti-Israeli militia groups. As part of that effort, Washington has asked Tokyo to raise these issues directly with Tehran in their bilateral discussions.[74] Tokyo has been willing to do this and will almost certainly continue to do so, as long as its role as mediator does not interfere with the development of bilateral relations with Iran. Indeed, this role works to eliminate potential friction that might have arisen as a result of Tokyo's 2001 break with the sanctions unilaterally imposed on Iran by the United States.

Foreign Minister Kawaguchi Yoriko dutifully raised U.S. concerns during her May 2002 visit to Tehran. Although it is difficult to gauge what effect Kawaguchi's delivery of the U.S. message on nuclear weapons and support for terrorism might have had, Iranian President Mohammad Khatami used the opportunity to blast the United States, contrasting its belligerence with Iran's "good relations with Japan," based on "mutual respect and the relaxation of tensions."[75] Much if not all of Kawaguchi's time in Tehran was devoted to other issues—joint Japanese-Iranian efforts to solve the refugee problem along Iran's border with Afghanistan, the expansion of cultural ties between the two countries, statements of Japanese support for Iranian political reform, and the further consolidation of bilateral economic ties. Although Japan did not emphasize its economic interests publicly during the trip, Iranian news sources quoted a Japanese spokesman in Tehran as saying that "Japan is keen to upgrade bilateral relations with Iran especially in the economic field."[76] This is particularly important for oil. In 2001, when Japan's crude oil imports declined by nearly six percent overall and Middle East imports declined by five percent, crude oil imports from Iran increased by more than two percent. In fact, Iran, which now accounts for nearly one-tenth of Japan's total crude oil imports, was the only source from which Japan increased its oil imports last year.[77] Moreover, while Japanese oil imports from Saudi Arabia and the United Arab Emirates, Tokyo's two largest Gulf sources, declined between 1995 and 2000, imports from both Iran and Iraq increased.[78]

It follows that Japan is very unlikely to support coercive U.S. policy towards Iran. Having already demonstrated a willingness to stand up to the United States on Iran, Tokyo would be far more likely to attempt to dissuade the U.S. government from applying elevated economic sanctions or military action. In July 2001 Japanese Trade Minister Hiranuma Takeo stated that in signing investment deals in Iran, Tokyo would not bow to U.S. pressure in boycotting energy projects, even if confronted by American officials.[79] He also assured Iran that Tokyo would back its bid for WTO membership, despite expected American opposition.[80] And in February 2002, after President Bush's "axis of evil" speech, a MOFA spokesman reiterated that "the government of Japan and the Islamic Republic of Iran have maintained friendly relations with each other, and I do not see any change in our policy toward Iran."[81] Without clear provocation from the Iranian side, Japanese support for an aggressive U.S. policy is highly unlikely.

Confronting North Korea

Several general circumstances make Japanese support for U.S. military action against North Korea more likely than in the cases of Iraq or Iran. First, Korea falls clearly within Japan's "surrounding area," within which events impinge directly on Japanese security. Second, war on the Korean

Peninsula has long been a likely scenario, and it is widely assumed that maintaining the alliance will depend on Japanese support for U.S. operations during that contingency. These warnings are broadly accepted. Third, unlike Iraq and Iran, where Japanese economic interests are directly in play, Tokyo has virtually no commercial stake in North Korea. Although important economic relations with South Korea and China might be adversely affected by war on the peninsula, there are fewer actors to consider than in either of the Middle Eastern scenarios. Finally, U.S. public opinion on the question of Japan's appropriate role would be likely to translate into particularly strong American political pressure brought to bear in the event of conflict. Thus, a plausible case can be made that Japan will provide rear area support for U.S. forces in the event of war in Korea, contingent on a few relatively easily met criteria.

This is not to suggest, however, that Japan will necessarily agree with or support U.S. decisions that might be seen as leading to war. In mid-1994, Tokyo opposed a preemptive U.S. attack on North Korean nuclear facilities at Yongbyon.[82] More recently, Nakatani Gen noted that North Korea had nothing to do with the Al Qaeda network and was critical of its inclusion in the "axis of evil."[83] We should therefore expect that Japan's decision on the degree of backing to give the United States will largely depend on the degree of support forthcoming from Seoul and Beijing. Japan is unlikely to back moves opposed by these two actors, although once a war begins, it may feel little choice but to provide material backing (including the deployment of military assets in non-combat roles) for U.S. operations.

Domestic Politics and the Long-Term Prospects for Foreign Policy Change

In the long run, the best prospects for a shift in Japanese foreign policy are associated with a broader change in Japan's governing system: either a shift in the balance of power between politicians and bureaucrats or a shift in relative power within the bureaucracy itself. The former (strengthening the hand of politicians vis-à-vis the bureaucrats) could endow Japan with a significantly more decisive style of foreign policy, even if the content of that foreign policy might become more difficult to predict. The latter possibility (rebalancing power within the bureaucracy) is more likely to produce constitutional crises, policy gridlock, and a general loss of confidence among Japanese in their own democratic system—if it is not accompanied by reforms that ensure greater political oversight.

Currently, comprehensive security is not only accepted as a guideline for political action, it is also hard-wired into the nation's political and administrative structures. Although the Diet is formally the "highest organ of state power," Japan's politicians and jurists defer to their bureaucrats on matters of constitutional interpretation and rely upon them to a remarkable degree for the execution and formulation of foreign policy. Complicating their task of gaining control over the bureaucracies they nominally oversee, is the fact that politicians appoint relatively few officials. At the same time, the economic ministries tend to have a disproportionate voice within the bureaucracy. Both of these phenomena—the power of the bureaucracy and the power of economic ministries within the bureaucracy—are illustrated in the case of the Cabinet Legislation Bureau, where career bureaucrats, seconded from other ministries and without representation from the JDA, control the interpretation Article Nine of the Constitution. It is these individuals, none of whom were elected by voters or appointed by political leaders, who have determined that collective defense violates the Constitution of Japan.[84]

Political reform undoubtedly would produce changes in the style and content of Japanese foreign policy, and there are several leaders who would likely take Japan in new directions. Ishihara Shintaro, currently the governor of Tokyo, is well known for anti-U.S. and anti-Chinese positions and for supporting closer ties to Southeast Asian states. Ozawa Ichiro opposed the post-September 11 anti-terrorism legislation because it was too closely linked to U.S. unilateral responses, and not linked closely enough to UN multilateralism.[85] While it is difficult to predict whether a more decisive leadership would result in a stronger U.S. alliance, in a tilt towards Asia, or in a greater commitment to multilateralism, it is clear that political reform would have important consequences for Japanese foreign policy. That said, it is unlikely that this change will come soon, if at all. Evolutionary change is underway, but the "iron triangle," the pejorative term used to describe the collusion of business, the bureaucracy, and politicians, continues to serve as a powerful brake. The electorate has responded to calls for structural reform, propelling politicians such as Prime Minister Koizumi to the fore. Koizumi's fortunes, however, have waned with his inability to overcome entrenched interests and deliver reform.

Change might also come to Japanese foreign policy if there is a shift in the balance of power within the bureaucracy, specifically if the JDA can increase its influence vis-à-vis the economic ministries. But, since the agency has yet to earn the trust of the Japanese people, this will not suffice to establish the legitimacy it would need to be an effective advocate for policy change. In recent months, the JDA has escorted U.S. warships out of port without political approval, secretly lobbied the United States to pressure Japan to provide additional military assistance to the war on terrorism, and collected personal data on citizens who had filed requests for data under the new freedom of information law.[86] The JDA seeks ministerial status, but in the eyes of many Japanese it has yet to assume the responsibilities of democratic governance. Without confidence in the oversight capacity of political authorities, the strengthening of the JDA is more likely to result in internecine bureaucratic and political warfare than it is to strengthen Japan's international role. Knowing this, Japanese politicians are, for the most part, reluctant to strengthen Japan's military. Absent either of the changes discussed above, preference for tinkering at the margins of comprehensive security will remain dominant.

Conclusion: Baseline Revisited

As we have seen, there was both more and less to Japan's response to September 11 than meets the eye. Japan made sure that the United States had unfettered access to its bases there and broke with precedent in offering military assistance. In addition, Japan used its good offices to mediate between the United States and Iran, a key state in the region. Ultimately, however, Japan demurred from the high-profile military action that Prime Minister Koizumi had outlined soon after the attacks. But it was not the normative and institutional constraints often associated with Japan's postwar pacifism that deterred Japan from executing Koizumi's program. Instead, key internal debates centered on how to balance the perceived need to "show the flag" in support of its U.S. security guarantor with the desire to avoid jeopardizing relationships with Middle Eastern oil exporters and their allies. In the end, Japan limited its military contributions to largely symbolic measures. Moreover, the legal authority for Japan's response was explicitly designed to preclude its use as a precedent in future conflicts.

Japanese behavior during the war on terrorism demonstrates continued adherence to a well-established doctrine of "comprehensive security" and to an evolving tactic of "double hedging." On the one hand, Japan relies on its alliance with the United States as a hedge against military threats. On the other hand, it relies on different partners, including some that the United States identifies as present or potential adversaries, as a hedge against economic uncertainties and dangers. Using the U.S. alliance as a military shield and other economic relationships as a mercantile sword requires Japan to rely on diplomacy for the sometimes tricky task of harmonizing the military and economic aspects of its strategy. Specifically, it has to reassure the United States that it is becoming a military partner, while reassuring the others that it is not. In the context of the war in Afghanistan, this required the dispatch of the MSDF far from Japanese littoral waters but not close enough to the battlefield to prevent Japan's many special envoys from denying that their military participated in the war on terrorism when representing Japan to the Muslim world.

Japan is by no means the only U.S. ally seeking collateral benefit from its participation in the war on terrorism. Moreover, it is amply clear that Japan has provided the United States what the U.S. Defense Department arguably most wants—a military platform in East Asia. Given this, it is not surprising that the United States warmly welcomed Japan's contribution to the anti-terrorism campaign. However, by highlighting differences between the positions of the United States and Japan in the Middle East and by positioning itself in opposition to U.S. policy on Iran and Palestine, Japanese diplomacy has complicated U.S. regional strategy. Ironically, at the same time that Japanese and American officials have celebrated the newly strengthened alliance, Japan's dual hedge has become ever more pronounced, revealing just how much U.S. and Japanese policy preferences have diverged.

Divergence in U.S. and Japanese preferences seem even more pronounced in East Asia. Japan's Asian neighbors, including China, now rival the United States as Tokyo's most important economic partners. Policymakers recognize the complementary nature of their economies and view them as indispensable supply and production bases. The accelerating trend toward regional integration, while challenging Japanese leaders to confront domestic protectionist sentiments in sunset industries and in agriculture, has also opened new horizons for the further rationalization of Japanese trade and production networks. The economic potential and strategic importance of regional integration requires Tokyo to maintain positive relations with Beijing. Hence, even as Japan maintains its alliance with the United States as a military hedge against future uncertainties, it is taking measures to ensure that Sino-Japanese relations remain on an even keel.

Continued economic difficulties in Japan seem to be reinforcing comprehensive security more than weakening it. On the one hand, uneasiness with the relative decline in Japan's position vis-à-vis its neighbors, especially China, reinforces the conviction that the U.S.-Japan alliance continues to fulfill an important function as a hedge against uncertain military futures. On the other hand, Japan's economic problems, and those of its neighbors, have given Tokyo's leaders a sense of shared interest in creating regional economic relationships that could cushion the Japanese economy against some of the demands being placed upon it. Those interests, in turn, have led Japan to foster stronger ties with regional states, including China. In the short to mdeium term, we can expect some national leaders who might be more outspoken than their predecessors on foreign policy, but it is unlikely that any of them will have the luxury of focusing on foreign policy, and to the extent that they do, they will be unlikely to effect any essential transformation in Japan's approach to security.

Japan's double hedge will continue to frame any Japanese decisions about support for the United States in a battle with the "axis of evil." Straightforward Japanese support for U.S. action is unlikely except, as outlined above, in the most propitious of circumstances—including UN-sanctioned military operations, as well as broad support from European and other states in the region. It is more likely that the alliance will be strained should the United States seek significant additional military support from Japan and force the Japanese government to choose between what it will view as an immoderate military ally and its commercial partners.

Endnotes

1   See, for example, The Atlantic Council, "New Frontiers for U.S.-Japan Security Relations," *Policy Paper*, February 2002; William Breer, "Japan's Contribution to the Campaign Against Terror," *Japan Watch*, Center for Strategic and International Studies, October 18, 2001; John Miller, "Japan Crosses the Rubicon?" *Asian-Pacific Security Studies,* vol. 1, no. 1 (January 2002); and Debra R. Little, "Peacekeeping: Japanese Style," paper prepared for presentation to the Midwest Political Science Association, Chicago, April 25–28, 2002. Ozawa Ichiro, *Nihon Kaizo Keikaku*, Tokyo: Kodansha, 1993 (English translation published as *Blueprint for a New Japan: The Rethinking of a Nation*, Louisa Rubenfien, trans., New York: Kodansha, 1994) was the first call for a "normal" Japan.

2   Thomas U. Berger, "From Sword to Chrysanthemum: Japan's Culture of Anti-Militarism," *International Security*, vol. 17, no. 4 (1993), pp. 119–50; Glenn D. Hook, *Militarization and Demilitarization in Contemporary Japan*, London: Routledge, 1996; and Peter J. Katzenstein, *Cultural Norms and National Security: Police and Military in Postwar Japan*, Ithaca: Cornell University Press, 1996. Each of these works examines the normative and institutional constraints on Japanese security policy. Sabine Fruhstuck, and Ben-Ari Eyal, "'Now We Show it All!' Normalization and the Management of Violence in Japan's Armed Forces," *The Journal of Japanese Studies*, vol. 28, no. 1 (Winter 2002), pp. 1–40, explores the sociology of anti-militarism in contemporary Japan.

3   For a detailed account of Japan's response to September 11, see Christopher Hughes, "Japan's Security Policy and the War on Terrorism: Steady Incrementalism or Radical Leap?" unpublished paper, Centre for the Study of Globalisation and Regionalisation, University of Warwick, 2002.

4   These comparisons are calculated using exchange rate values and estimates of defense-related expenditures not included in official budgets. Some analysts use purchasing power parity (PPP) multipliers to assess the actual value of monies spent on defense. If this is done, China's spending exceeds Japan's. While nominal exchange rate calculations do not provide perfect comparisons, figures derived using PPP multipliers can be misleading because they fail to account for incorporated technologies and misrepresent the cost of imported equipment.

[5] Tonnage calculated using International Institute of Strategic Studies (IISS), *The Military Balance, 2000–2001*, London: IISS, 2000 and Jane's, *Jane's Fighting Ships Yearbook 2001–2002*, New York: Jane's Information Group, 2001. Surface combat ships over 1,000 tons are counted. The Chinese navy has only a handful of truly modern warships, while virtually all of Japan's warships incorporate cutting edge engines, electrical generation, radar and communications, and missile systems. Its newest warships, including both the Murasame-class and Kongo-class, incorporate the vertical launch system (VLS), vastly increasing their defensive and offensive firepower, and the latter is equipped with the Aegis radar system. A report by the Center for Naval Analyses (CNA) concludes that the Chinese navy will not be a regional navy until 2020. See Christopher D. Yung, *People's War at Sea: Chinese Naval Power in the Twenty-first Century*, Alexandria, Va.: Center for Naval Analysis, March 1996.

[6] Long-term problems with the Chinese air force are documented in Kenneth W. Allen, Glenn Krumel, and Jonathan D. Pollack, *China's Air Force Enters the 21st Century*, Santa Monica, Calif.: RAND, 1995.

[7] Flight hours are reported in IISS, *Military Balance*.

[8] *Yomiuri Shimbun*, June 28, 2002.

[9] "Paradaimu wa kawatta no ka? 'jiyu' kara 'anzen' no jidai ni" (Paradigm shift? From the age of "free" to the age of "secure"), *Gaiko Foramu*, January 2002, p. 36.

[10] Eichi Katahara explores "comprehensive security" in Eichi Katahara, "Japan's Concept of Comprehensive Security in the Post-Cold War World," in Christopher P. Twomey and Susan L. Shirk, eds., *Power and Prosperity: Economics and Security Linkages in Asia-Pacific*, New Brunswick: Transaction Publishers, 1996. For the origins of comprehensive security in nineteenth century ideas about the relationship of military and techno-economic power, see Richard J. Samuels, *"Rich Nation, Strong Army": National Security and the Technological Transformation of Japan*, Ithaca: Cornell University Press, 1994. Eric Heginbotham and Richard J. Samuels, "Mercantile Realism and Japanese Foreign Policy," *International Security*, vol. 22, no. 4 (Spring 1998), pp. 170–202, derive a model of "mercantile realism" from the concept. For more on comprehensive security as a baseline, see Kenneth B. Pyle and Eric Heginbotham, "Japan," in Richard J. Ellings and Aaron L. Friedberg, eds., *Strategic Asia 2001–02: Power and Purpose*, Seattle, Wash.: The National Bureau of Asian Research. For a dissenting view, see Bill Emmott, "The Economic Sources of Japan's Foreign Policy," *Survival*, vol. 34, no. 2 (Summer 1992), pp. 50–70.

[11] Makino Noboru, *Chuo Koron*, July 1990, p. 111.

[12] Kato Ryozo, "Nichibei domei no kudoka osoreru" (Fear of the hollowing of the U.S.-Japan alliance), *Chuo Koron*, December 2000, pp. 81–82.

[13] "The Frontier Within: Individual Empowerment and Better Governance in the New Millenium," report of the Prime Minister's Commissions on Japan's Goals in the 21st Century, January 2000.

[14] "NHK Carries Koizumi's Q&A Session After Summit Talks with Bush," June 30, 2001. On April 27, 2001, Prime Minister Koizumi insisted at a press conference that the U.S. alliance is the "most important element in Japan's national interest. His statement is cited in National Institute for Defense Studies, ed.,

East Asian Strategic Review, 2002, Tokyo: National Institute for Defense Studies, 2002.

[15] *Kyodo Voice*, December 1, 2001.

[16] Mike Mochizuki, "Japan and the Persian Gulf Crisis: The Lessons Learned," paper prepared for the Center for National Security Studies, Los Alamos National Laboratory, February 1992.

[17] *Yomiuri Shimbun*, December 7, 2001.

[18] The plan can be found at Foreign Press Center, "Japanaese Government's response to Terrorist Attacks in the United States," September 28, 2001, <www.fpcj.jp/e/shiryo/jb/0141.html>.

[19] According to a September 25, 2001, public opinion survey by *Nihon Keizai Shimbun*, Koizumi enjoyed a 79 percent popularity rating. Support for military cooperation with the U.S. depended on both the wording of the question and the sponsoring agent of the survey. According to a September 26 survey by *Yomiuri Shimbun*, 87 percent favored cooperation, including 56 percent in favor of intelligence gathering and sharing. A September 24 survey by *Asahi Shimbun* found that 48 percent of Japanese approved of retaliatory strikes and that 48 percent approved of the SDF transporting supplies, including weapons and ammunition. On this latter question, 41 percent were opposed.

[20] *Kyodo News Service*, September 28, 2001.

[21] *Yomiuri Shimbun*, December 7, 2001.

[22] Hashimoto also took the opportunity to point out that "no one" in the U.S. State Department can speak Pushtun and that "if one cannot communicate, one cannot provide medical care…. For Afghanistan, Japan is the safest and most trustworthy country." *Mainichi Shimbun*, October 26, 2001.

[23] *Kyodo Voice*, December 1, 2001.

[24] Nakasone reminisces about this in *Asahi Shimbun*, October 31, 2001. Sam Jameson reminds us that, when Iranian militants seized the U.S. embassy in Tehran in 1979, Prime Minister Ohira Masayoshi responded "without a hint of blame or condemnation of Iran." *Japan Times*, November 29, 2001.

[25] *Toyo Keizai*, November 7, 2000.

[26] *Deutsche Presse-Agentur*, September 20, 2000, and July 18, 2001.

[27] *Nihon Keizai Shimbun*, October 19, 2001. When it is in full operation, the daily oil output of the Azadegan field is expected to be twice that of the Khafji field. For background on Japanese energy diplomacy see Robert A. Manning, *The Asian Energy Factor: Myths and Dilemmas of Energy, Security, and the Pacific Future*, New York: Palgrave, 2000.

[28] *Jiji Press*, October 23, 2001.

[29] National Institute for Defense Studies, *East Asian Strategic Review, 2002*, refers to the "casting off of checkbook diplomacy," p. 37.

[30] Apart from the possibility of small terrorist suicide boats, which the tankers themselves would be as capable of handling as destroyers would, there was no credible naval threat. U.S. tankers generally are not escorted (except when they are actually traveling with the fleet) and escorts would only add to the total burden of refueling without contributing materially to the mission.

[31] Department of Defense transcript, December 10, 2001, <www.defenselink.mil/news/dec2001/t12102001_t1210jda.html>.

[32] Cited in National Institute for Defense Studies, 2002, p. 39.

[33] *Daily Yomiuri*, January 16, 2002.

[34] *Chicago Tribune*, December 21, 2001.

[35] During the Korean War, Japan dispatched large numbers of technical workers, many of them former soldiers and sailors, to Korea to assist U.S. forces.

[36] This is also the conclusion of Hughes, "Japan's Security Policy and the War on Terrorism."

[37] A series of Taliban and anti-Taliban faction leaders (including the exiled Afghan king and representatives of the Northern Alliance) had been brought to Tokyo for talks, and Japan felt confident that it could use the relationships it had cultivated with these factions to broker a post-war settlement. Taliban leaders came to meet Japanese MOFA officials in Tokyo in February 1996, July 1998, and March 2000. Anti-Taliban faction leaders visited in June 1997, March 1998, and March 2000. MOFA press conferences discussing these visits can be found at <www.mofa.go.jp/region/middle_e/afghanistan/index.html>.

[38] Japan continued to supply funds for technical cooperation, grass-roots grant assistance, emergency humanitarian aid, and continuing projects. Budgets in many of those categories (e.g., grass-roots assistance) increased substantially. "Continuing projects" were defined very liberally, so that, for example, a new $35 million budget for "phase two" of a tunnel project was approved in the summer of 2001. Most importantly, Japan rescheduled Pakistan's $822 million in debts. Data from speech by Numata Sadaaki, the Japanese Ambassador to Pakistan, May 27, 2000, <www.japanemb.org.pk/ambassador/ambspeech_ english_spunion_27may00.htm>. Data on tunnel project from July 2001 report by Japan Bank for International Cooperation, <www.jbic.go.jp/autocontents/ english/news/2001/000023>.

[39] *Mainichi Shimbun*, October 26, 2001.

[40] *Mainichi Shimbun*, September 25, 2001.

[41] Besides, Japanese ODA had long provided a net benefit to Japanese firms. See David Arase, *Buying Power: The Political Economy of Japan's Foreign Aid*, Boulder, Colo.: Lynne Rienner, 1995; and Robert M. Orr, Jr., *The Emergence of Japan's Foreign Aid Power*, New York: Columbia University Press, 1990.

[42] Interestingly, some in the Japanese press accused the Europeans of opportunism, using their participation in the war to pursue mercantile gains. See for example Taniguchi Nagayo, "Tai-tero renkei ni miru EU shokoku no kokueki arasoi" (The EU nations' struggle for national gains in the anti-terror coalition), *Chuo Koron*, January 2002, pp. 152–60.

[43] On these events, see *The Daily Yomiuri,* November 27, 2001.

[44] See Stephan Haggard, *The Political Economy of the Asian Financial Crisis*, Washington, DC: Institute for International Economics, 2000, and William W. Keller and Richard J. Samuels, eds., *Innovation and Crisis: Asian Innovation after the Millennium*, New York: Cambridge University Press, 2002.

[45] Keidanren, "Towards the Implementation of Strategic Trade Policies: A Grand Design of Japan's Policy as a Nation Built on Trade," June 2001. A May 2001 report by the Keizai Doyukai arrived at similar conclusions. "Building regional partnerships in East Asia" was the first of seven recommendations. See Keizai Doyukai, "Heiwa to hanei no nijuisseiki o mezashite" (Aiming toward a peace-

ful and prosperous twenty-first century), April 25, 2001.

[46] *Yomiuri Shimbun*, June 26, 2002.

[47] See Walter Hatch and Kozo Yamamura, *Asia in Japan's Embrace: Building a Regional Production Alliance*, Cambridge: Cambridge University Press, 1996.

[48] In a January 2002 meeting, Mahathir told Prime Minister Koizumi that "Europe is one bloc, while the United States has NAFTA, but Southeast Asia does not have an organization representing us. Therefore, we need to strengthen ASEAN Plus Three as a necessary balance." See Ito Shingo, "Japan, Malaysia Seek Common Asian Voice," *Agence France-Presse*, January 10, 2002.

[49] In Japan and other member states, the development of ASEAN+3 has received considerable attention, a fact to which any quick survey of the Japanese Foreign Ministry's web page, <www.mof.go.jp>, will attest. For a Japanese perspective on the development of this organization, see National Institute for Defense Studies, *East Asian Strategic Survey, 2001*, Tokyo: National Institute for Defense Studies, 2001.

[50] See David Chelliah Kovilpillai, "China, Japan, South Korea, ASEAN Keen on EAEG, East Asian Summit," *Malaysia General News*, November 6, 2001. Until now, most ASEAN+3 initiatives have been managed by the ASEAN Secretariat in Jakarta, with the cooperation of ad hoc teams dispatched by various ministries and associations from Japan, China, and South Korea.

[51] Although the ASEAN states have historically been reticent to open their markets quickly to outsiders, the Chinese offered attractive terms. The arrangement provides for China to unilaterally open its doors to free trade by 2006, while ASEAN must reciprocate by 2010. David Wall, "Koizumi's Trade Pitch Misses its Target," *Japan Times*, April 21, 2002. The February 2002 issue of *Chuo Koron* featured a collection of essays on the challenge posed by the China-ASEAN FTA and the danger to Japan of being marginalized as Asian regional economic integration proceeds. The consensus view was that the ability of Japan to remain a regional leader would depend upon its ability to enact domestic reforms. See the essays by Kuroda Atsuo, Otsuji Yoshihiro and Shiraishi Takashi, and Mahathir Mohammad in particular, pp. 58–99.

[52] Cindy Sui, "Southeast Asia Plans Mega Free Trade Zone with China, Japan, South Korea," *Agence France-Presse*, November 5, 2001. During the November 2001 ASEAN+3 summit, members of the Chinese delegation were quoted as predicting that Japan and South Korea would need time to resolve agricultural issues before they moved ahead with an FTA, but they also expressed their willingness to move ahead with a region-wide FTA. It is also worthy of note that during those same summit, China, Japan, and South Korea moved to establish annual trilateral meetings of their economic and foreign ministers.

[53] David Wall, "Koizumi's Trade Pitch Misses its Target," *Japan Times*, April 21, 2002.

[54] "Asian Free Trade Zone May Accelerate 'Liberalization'," *New Straits Times*, April 16, 2002.

[55] "Vietnam, China Reach Agreement in Border Talks," *Agence-France Presse*, February 28, 2002.

[56] "'Ajia-ban NATO ga hitsuyo' nakatani boeicho chokan ga koen de" (Defense agency chief Nakatani: "there is a need for an Asian NATO"), *Asahi Shimbun*.

[57] Sugawa Kiyoshi, "Time to Pop the Cork: Three Scenarios to Refine Japanese Use of Force," *CNAPS Working Paper*, Brookings Institution (June 2000); and Keizai Doyukai, ed., "Heiwa to hanei no nijuichi seiki o mezashite."

[58] National Institute for Research Advancement, *Japan's Proactive Peace and Security Strategies*, Tokyo: National Institute for Research Advancement, 2001.

[59] For Japanese views on China's future, which acknowledge the possibility of its continued growth but highlight the danger of political instability (or collapse), see Nakanishi Teramusa, "Bei-chu no hazama de nihon torubeki kokusai senryaku to wa" (The international strategy Japan should pursue as it is squeezed between the United States and China), *Ronso*, March 1, 2001; and Samejima Keiji, ed., *2020 Nen no Chugoku* (China in 2020), Tokyo: Nihon Keizai Shimbunsha, 2000. For a variant on this theme which suggests that political problems will slow China's growth, see Kuroda Atsuo, "'Chugoku kyoiron' mo 'chugoku hokairon' mo ayamari da" (Both the "China threat theory" and the "China collapse theory" are incorrect), *Chuo Koron*, February 2002, pp. 58–67.

[60] The Japanese Coast Guard includes 48 armed ships over 1,000 tons for a total of 100,000 tons. The Chinese navy's surface warfare fleet totals 124,000 tons, and the Chinese Customs Service, its closest equivalent to Japan's Coast Guard, deploys no ships in this category. While the Japanese Coast Guard is armed with guns rather than missiles, its ships are equipped with good communications and navigation gear, deploy as many helicopters aboard ship as does the Chinese navy, and could be used in conjunction with the MSDF to expand the coverage of the fleet.

[61] *Heisei 13 Nenban Boeicho Handobukku* (2001 Self-Defense Agency Handbook), Tokyo: Asagumo Shimbunsha, 2001, p. 749. The ratio of those favoring increased spending to those favoring reductions has increased since the mid-1990s, but it remains significantly lower than it was during the 1970s and 1980s.

[62] Figures are from Ministry of Finance, <www.mof.go.jp>.

[63] Ministry of Economy, Trade and Industry, White Paper on International Trade 2001, "Key Points," p. 13.

[64] Ministry of Economy, Trade, and Industry, "East Asia as the Hub of a Mega-Competition Era," *White Paper on International Trade 2001*, p. 32. For the views of Japan's most distinguished China hawk, see the papers by Ambassador Okazaki Hisahiko, <www.glocomnet.or.jp/okazaki-inst/okazaki-eng.html>.

[65] Clay Chandler, "China's Rivals Slow to Grasp Export Might: Beijing Building Trade Powerhouse," *Washington Post*, May 25, 2002. Chandler predicts that Southeast Asian states will face stiff competition from China in their primary export sectors and may be damaged by China's economic rise. Japanese firms, however, do not export in similar sectors. In a separate interview, Koizumi reflected the views of Japanese business elites when he suggested Japan should respond to Chinese growth by restructuring its economy, not confronting Beijing politically. See David Ignatius and Thomas Crampton, "A Confident Koizumi Keeps His Sails Set," *International Herald Tribune*, June 20, 2002.

[66] Fujimura, Takayoshi, Ohashi Hideo, Fujino Fumiaki, and Yokota Jun, "WTO kamei ato no chugoku o yosoku suru" (Forecasting China after WTO accession), *Gaiko Foramu*, February 2001.

[67] Keidanren, "Japan-China Relations in the 21st Century: Recommendations for

Building a Relationship of Trust and Expanding Economic Exchanges Between Japan and China," February 20, 2001.

[68] According to a 2000 government survey, 50 percent of all Japanese have positive feelings toward China, while 46 percent have negative feelings. These figures show that China is significantly more well-liked in Japan than, for example, Russia (with 16 percent favorable and 79 percent unfavorable), and it was about as popular as South Korea (48 percent favorable and 47 percent unfavorable). *Naikaku Daijin Kanbo Seifu Kohoshitsu Hen, Heisei 12 Yoron Chosa Nenkan* (2000 public opinion yearbook), Tokyo: Zaimusho Insatsu Kyoku, p. 83.

[69] David Ignatius and Thomas Crampton, "A Confident Koizumi Keeps His Sails Set," *International Herald Tribune*, June 20, 2002.

[70] *Jiji Press*, February 17, 2002.

[71] On Japan as a mediator between the United States and these states, see, for example, *Sankei Shimbun*, February 19, 2002.

[72] *Jiji Press*, February 17, 2002.

[73] Dispatch of a Japanese Aegis destroyer to the Arabian Sea prior to the commencement of U.S. operations reportedly was requested by U.S. officials for this purpose. There is some question about the possibility that this request originated with Japanese military officials. See *Asahi Shimbun*, April 22, 2002, and May 6, 2002.

[74] See *Tokyo Kyodo*, February 19, 2002. President Bush raised the issue personally with Koizumi, acknowledging that he understood "Iran is important to Japan," but nevertheless suggesting that Japan could use its relations with Iran to persuade it to change its behavior. *Sankei Shimbun,* February 19, 2002.

[75] "'We will not give way to America's threat,' Iranian president says to Foreign Minister Kawaguchi," *Mainichi Shimbun*, May 6, 2002.

[76] *Iran Republic News Agency*, May 4, 2002. The official Japanese Foreign Ministry website carried no news of Minister Kawaguchi's economic discussions.

[77] *Deutsche Presse-Agentur*, April 30, 2002.

[78] U.S. Department of Energy, 2002.

[79] *Deutsche Presse-Agentur*, July 8, 2001.

[80] *Deutsche Presse-Agentur*, July 9, 2001.

[81] MOFA press conference, February 12, 2002, <www.mofa.go.jp/announce/press>.

[82] Don Oberdorfer, *The Two Koreas*, Indianapolis: Basic Books, 1997, pp. 318–20 and Leon Sigal, *Disarming Strangers: Nuclear Diplomacy with North Korea*, Princeton: Princeton University Press, 1999, p. 118.

[83] *Jiji Press*, February 15, 2002.

[84] For more on the extraordinary power of the Cabinet Legislation Bureau, see Nakamura Akira, *Sengo Seiji Ni Yureta Kenpo Kyujo* (Article Nine that shook world politics), Tokyo: Chuo Keizaisha, 2001 and Nishikawa Shinichi, *Shirarezaru Kancho: Naikaku Hosei Kyoku* (The agency that must be known: the Cabinet Legislation Bureau), Tokyo: Gogatsu Shobo, 2000.

[85] For analysis of Ishihara and Ozawa see Richard J. Samuels, *Machiavelli's Children: Leaders and their Legacies in Italy and Japan*, Ithaca: Cornell University Press, forthcoming.

[86] See Sasaki Yoshitaka, "Strict Civilian Control Needed over SDF," <www.asahi.com/english/asianet/hatsu/eng_hatsu011213e.html>.

KOREA

Nicholas N. Eberstadt

Despite the deep mutual hostility between the two Korean states, and the official programmatic commitment each maintains to the eradication of the other's political system, a truce has held in the Korean Peninsula for almost half a century (thanks largely to the U.S.-ROK military alliance, codified in the 1953 Mutual Defense Treaty and instantiated in the 37,000 soldiers Washington still billets in the South, that has provided an indispensable element of deterrence in the peninsula's military equation). To be sure, maintaining peace in Korea has been a high-maintenance, high-tension operation, and on more than one occasion over the past five decades it has seemed as if the mission might fail.[1] Yet as was noted in last year's *Strategic Asia* report, the security situation in the Korean Peninsula has seemed relatively calm of late—by any recent historical measure, quite uncharacteristically so—and that calm has held, extending the peninsula's period of unusually clement diplomatic weather by another full year.

Korea's Current Season of Calm

In part, today's relative calm can be explained by the character and tenor of relations among the great Pacific powers in the Korean peninsula and beyond it. Although these remain far from the diplomatic Elysium envi-

---

Nicholas Eberstadt holds the Henry Wendt Chair in Political Economy at the American Enterprise Institute in Washington, DC. He would like to thank Lisa Howie, Heather Dresser, and Wonchol Noh for their research assistance.

sioned in Kant's *Perpetual Peace*,[2] it is nevertheless fair to argue that at the dawn of the twenty-first century the overall level of cooperation between Beijing, Moscow, Tokyo, and Washington was higher than at any point in the previous hundred years.

But surely no less important to the peninsula's relative calm has been the ostensible progress toward an inter-Korean reconciliation spelled out under Republic of Korea (ROK) President Kim Dae Jung's "sunshine policy" of engagement with the Democratic People's Republic of Korea (DPRK) and epitomized by the unprecedented Pyongyang summit of June 2000, and the subsequent award to President Kim of the 2000 Nobel Peace Prize. While there have been precious few new milestones of inter-Korean comity since the Pyongyang summit—the past two years instead have witnessed a succession of North Korean rebuffs of South Korean entreaties for dialogue—the present state of inter-Korean relations still qualifies (by past performance) as unusually constructive and cooperative. Some put the case in even stronger terms: in June 2002, for example, the ROK ambassador to Washington proclaimed "the tension level on the Korean peninsula is now at an all time low."[3]

Be this as it may, beneath Korea's surface calm forces were gathering that could potentially change the security balance in the peninsula in a radical and destabilizing manner. Three factors in particular were marked in last year's chapter for continued attention: 1) the DPRK's abysmal economic performance, insofar as continuing decline will eventually invite systemic failure unless reversed; 2) Pyongyang's multifaceted programs for developing weapons of mass destruction (WMD), since enhanced North Korean WMD capabilities could dangerously undermine deterrence in the Korean peninsula; and 3) unattended problems in the U.S.-ROK military alliance, since these problems, though relatively minor today, could eventually undercut public support for the arrangement if not addressed and corrected. Over the past year none of those issues has been substantively redressed. To the contrary, each of these "wild cards" for Korean security has stayed in play—and developments over the past year appear to have raised, rather than reduced, the risk that any of these might be shown.

Although quantitative data on North Korean economic performance are remarkably scarce, the balance of available evidence suggests that the economy is still deteriorating and declining (a descent mitigated, but not corrected, by humanitarian assistance from abroad and other forms of foreign aid). Revitalization of the North Korean economy cannot be achieved in the absence of a decisive shift toward a more pragmatic and open economic policy. By all appearances, Pyongyang remains opposed to such a turn, and the country's physical and human capital continues to decay.

With respect to North Korea's WMD programs, the 1994 "Agreed Framework" is supposed to have "frozen" the DPRK's nuclear program, and Pyongyang's "Dear Leader" Kim Jong Il has publicly promised a conditional moratorium on ballistic missile launches until at least 2003. Neither of these assurances, however, is altogether reassuring. North Korea's launch moratorium precludes neither the export of missiles nor the development of new systems—and in March 2002 CIA Director George Tenet testified that North Korea was indeed using missile sales to Muslim states to finance its own missile development program.[4] That program evidently proceeds apace, for while Pyongyang has not test-fired an *entire* ballistic rocket since 1998, in 2001 a top State Department official confirmed reports that North Korea had been detected test-firing a rocket engine for its long-range Taepo Dong missile series.[5] As for North Korea's nuclear program, a U.S. National Intelligence Estimate (NIE) released in December 2001 declared "the intelligence community judged in the mid-1990s that North Korea had produced one, possibly two, nuclear weapons."[6] As commentators noted, however, this was actually a new revelation, and not simply old news. In the mid-1990s, the U.S. intelligence community had specifically concluded that the DPRK probably possessed enough plutonium to potentially construct a bomb, whereas now it was indicating that the North Koreans had actually succeeded in engineering the weapons themselves.[7] The implication was that new information on covert North Korean nuclear activities was in hand—an implication furthered in April 2002, when, for the first time, the State Department declined to certify to Congress that North Korea had "halted definitively" its nuclear program, as the existing "Agreed Framework" requires.[8]

But perhaps the most noteworthy developments over the past year concerned the U.S.-ROK security alliance or, more specifically, the building frictions in that relationship. Significantly, since the September 11 terrorist attacks on the United States, those frictions have not only continued to accumulate, but seem to have done so with gathering speed. The increasing complications in the U.S.-ROK relationship stand in stark contrast to post September 11 trends in Washington's relations with all of Korea's neighbors, as U.S. security interactions with Russia, Japan, and even China have notably improved.

It should be emphasized that although the contradictions within the U.S.-ROK alliance are mounting, the troubles to date appear to be entirely manageable and ultimately remediable—assuming that they are given the attention, consideration, and effort necessary to resolve them. To do so, moreover, is surely in the interests of the United States, considering the importance of the U.S.-ROK military alliance to America's position in East

Asia (to say nothing of its salutary effects on the East Asian economic environment). For the relationship to enjoy a healthy middle age, however, it is incumbent upon the alliance's exponents to demonstrate that it has a compelling and continuing rationale. That case, unfortunately, is not being presented by Washington today. Instead, America's level of policy interest in Korea—surprisingly, not only South Korea, but also in North Korea— seems distinctly less intense today than years immediately past.

It is not that U.S. policymakers have been entirely silent about Korean affairs. Well before September 11, the incoming Bush administration loudly advertised its suspicions about the sincerity and trustworthiness of the North Korean regime—implicitly calling into question the viability of Seoul's "sunshine policy" (not to mention the agreements with North Korea that Washington had already entered into under the Clinton administration). After September 11, Washington's attitude toward Pyongyang hardened appreciably, as famously illustrated by the president's depiction of the DPRK as a member of an international "axis of evil"[9] in the January 2002 State of the Union address. A significantly new approach toward Korea policy was indicated, indeed all but promised, by the administration's words. But instead, no Korea policy whatever has been expounded publicly (or, so far as can be told, formulated internally). In consequence, over a year and a half into the president's term, U.S. policy toward the Korean Peninsula proceeds as if on autopilot, continuing largely on its own earlier inertia, without much evident attention from top Washington policymakers.

There are, of course, explanations for Washington's new attitude of detachment. With an international war against terrorism underway, the administration must perforce prioritize—and any distant land not currently convulsed by crisis, or imminently threatened by it, is accorded a lower priority in U.S. foreign policy today than immediately before September 11. Washington's seeming insouciance about spelling out and implementing the new Korea policy may also reflect an implicit judgment that the matter can wait—or that the objectives envisioned will be easier to accomplish, for whatever reasons, in the foreseeable future.

Yet it is not self-evident that time is on Washington's side in Korea— or that the trends now working to alter the extant security balance in the peninsula can be expected to correct themselves apart from U.S. planning and guidance. On the contrary, in light of forces already in motion in North Korea, South Korea, and the United States, the "summer calm" in the peninsula looks increasingly unsustainable. Forecasts for the following season are at this juncture highly variable—but many of the contingent outcomes would promise the United States a Korean security environment more complex, contentious, and immediately challenging than the one it faces today.

Northeast Asian Security Relations
After September 11: The Doughnut and the Hole

The attacks that leveled the World Trade Center and left the Pentagon in flames on September 11, 2001, had immediate and worldwide reverberations. The direct strategic consequences of the attack and Washington's response was to reinforce still further America's already extraordinary, post-Cold War preeminence in world affairs.[10] Particular reverberations, of course, varied from one regional theater to the next. One of the most interesting, and perhaps surprising, patterns was observed in Northeast Asia: that is to say, the Korean peninsula and the surrounding countries.

On the one hand, for the three other great Pacific powers—China, Japan, and Russia—the tenor of relations with Washington, and the degree of cooperation with U.S. international security policies and objectives directly (and in some instances remarkably) improved in the aftermath of September 11. On the other hand, in Korea itself, U.S. relations with both governments of the divided peninsula showed signs of greater strain.

One might argue, of course, that a new chill in U.S.-DPRK relations was entirely predictable, given the easily conjoined facts that President Bush immediately pledged to "rally the world" in a war against terrorism[11] and that the State Department had reaffirmed its designation of the DPRK as a state sponsor of terrorism just a few months earlier.[12] But the increasing awkwardness in Washington's relations with Seoul was striking, and also arguably unique, at least among countries bound to the United States through a standing security treaty. To the extent that the events of September 11 had recast the strategic landscape in Northeast Asia, from an American perspective something like a doughnut was taking form. That is, a ring of increasingly solid (or at least serviceable) bilateral relationships was developing between Washington and the countries surrounding the Korean peninsula, while the post-September 11 responses to the United States from within the peninsula itself left something of a hole at the region's center.

Russia, Japan, and China

In Northeast Asia, the country that effected the most dramatic post-September 11 change in its relations with the United States was without question the Russian Federation. By the time the smoke from the September 11 assaults had cleared, Russian international policy had executed a virtual *volte face*: "mulitpolarity" was out and partnership with the United States was in. As William Wohlforth documents in this volume, Putin immediately and unhesitatingly pledged his country's assistance to the U.S. response against Al Qaeda.[13] Moscow provided high-value intelligence, overflight rights, and former Soviet bases in Central Asia for the U.S.-led campaign in Afghanistan. The redirection of Russian foreign and security policy, however, extended much further than the war on terror alone. In the months following September 11, Moscow purposely set about eliminating old irritants in the U.S.-Russian relationship and acquiesced in important aspects of U.S. strategic policy that it had heretofore battled against (such as U.S. withdrawal from the Anti-Ballistic Missile treaty, NATO expansion, etc.).

Moscow's historic post-September 11 tilt toward the United States did not settle all previously disputatious issues in the U.S.-Russian relationship. Major disagreements remained over Russian policy toward Iraq and Iran (especially Moscow's ongoing assistance for Iran's nuclear program). In the Korean peninsula, Russia is still cool to the idea of a long-term stationing of U.S. forces (i.e., after hypothetical unification)[14] and as recently as May 2002 reportedly was discussing possible avenues of "military technical cooperation" with the DPRK.[15]

Even so, Moscow's international realignment directly increased the strategic freedom of U.S. action in the world—and in the Korean theater as well. This latter point was highlighted in March 2002, when the Defense Department's *Nuclear Posture Review*—a document describing U.S. contingency planning for nuclear strikes against Russia, Iran, North Korea, and four other countries—was leaked. The revelation provoked a furious reaction from Tehran and Pyongyang, but Moscow appeared unperturbed. Indeed, Russian Defense Minister Sergey Ivanov publicly emphasized that he had discussed the issue with U.S. officials, and that they provided satisfactory explanations.[16] Coming as it did from the head of the Red Army, Ivanov's signal was especially disturbing for the "rogue states" from which Moscow was disassociating its interests.

There was nothing like this dramatic shift in the case of Japan. For a half a century, changes in Tokyo's approach to international security has come in cautious increments, and that tradition was not changed by the terror attacks on America. Nevertheless, as the United States declared its open war on international terrorism, Japan moved toward a more conspicuously supportive role in that particular struggle—and toward a somewhat more active defense posture more generally.

Japan's first substantive response to the September 11 attacks was to pass "counter-terrorism" legislation in October 2001, permitting the Maritime Self-Defense Forces to deploy the Japanese fleet to the Indian Ocean in support of the U.S.-led campaign in Afghanistan. Then, in December 2001, Japan's military marked another postwar first. After challenging a suspicious ship that had entered Japanese waters, a Japanese coast guard craft gave chase, pursuing the boat into the waters of China's exclusive economic zone (EEZ). When the unidentified vessel shot at the Japanese craft, the coast guard returned fire, sinking it, and evidently killing its entire crew. It was widely rumored that the vessel in question was North Korean.[17] And in February 2002, sources in the Japanese government revealed that Tokyo and Washington were planning working-level talks on the proposed U.S. national missile defense (NMD) system. By meeting with Americans to discuss the possibilities and implications of a U.S. system, Tokyo sent an unusual signal of official support to President Bush, who in May 2001 had called for a concerted effort to develop NMD to protect the U.S. homeland from overseas ballistic attack and redoubled his urgings after the September 11 assault.[18] At much the same time—shortly after President Bush caused considerable consternation in much of East Asia by labeling Pyongyang part of an international "axis of evil"—Prime Minister Koizumi publicly backed the president's assessment, remarking that "this is a manifestation of the strong will to continue to fight terrorism. North Korea has to come to appreciate that the determination is real."[19]

Japanese security strategy in the aftermath of September 11 may still best be described as a "hedge," as Eric Heginbotham and Richard Samuels argue in this volume.[20] But circumstances in Japan have clearly changed—and in a direction congruent with U.S. international security objectives in Northeast Asia. In 1994, during the height of that year's North Korean nuclear crisis, American officials were not at all sure that Japan would have permitted Washington to use U.S. bases to supply forces in Korea in the event of a conflict.[21] In the post September 11 environment, the risks of a breach in U.S.-Japanese defense cooperation in the event of a crisis in the Korean peninsula looked smaller than they had been in the recent past—and perhaps smaller than ever before in the postwar period.[22]

U.S. relations were distinctly more contentious with China than with the other two Pacific powers at the dawn of the twenty–first century. But as it happened, Sino-American cooperation increased, and diplomatic interactions deepened over the past year. In April 2002, Secretary of State Colin Powell testified to the Senate that U.S.-China relations had "improved markedly" over the previous 12 months.[23] The events of September 11 were instrumental in this shift.

As Thomas Christensen details in his chapter in this volume, China lent its immediate (if measured) support to the initial U.S. campaign against terror. And as the campaign unfolded, the tempo of top-level diplomatic contact between Washington and Beijing also accelerated. Personal relations can matter in global politics, and both Washington and Beijing were deliberately augmenting this scarce commodity. From Beijing's standpoint, the decision to side with Washington in the international war on terror and to pursue improved ties with America after September 11 was hardly an act of disinterested altruism.[24] The improvement in Washington's relations with Beijing, furthermore, may prove to be only temporary; in his chapter, Christensen warns that the current U.S.-China "honeymoon" is built on fragile foundations, and elsewhere Aaron Friedberg has argued there are deep and fundamental reasons to expect today's relatively cordial phase of Sino-American relations to return to a more familiar rivalry.[25] Be that as it may, for the time being China's adjusted approach toward the United States has increased, not reduced, Washington's international freedom of maneuver. In the Korean peninsula, the adjustment has had both immediate consequences and important longer-term implications.

In immediate terms, a closer degree of Sino-American cooperation makes it that much more difficult for Pyongyang to "play" China against the United States in its own international strategy. Even before September 11, China seemed to be laying down limits for Pyongyang in this regard. President Jiang's September 3–5, 2001, visit to the DPRK, for example, conspicuously ended without the traditional Sino-North Korean joint communiqué. Unofficially, Chinese sources claim that the joint statement foundered on a number of sticking points, one of which was Beijing's unwillingness to join Pyongyang in a call for a U.S. troop pullout from the Korean peninsula. Pyongyang's opportunities for leveraging China against the United States are more qualified today than at the time of Jiang's trip.

Over the long run, however, China's most important strategic signal for the United States in Korea may paradoxically have been recorded in Central Asia—and not in something China did, but in what it failed to do: China did not object when the United States stationed U.S. forces at military bases in several Central Asian countries, and then used those bases and forces to stage its swift and devastating campaign against Al Qaeda and the Taliban in Afghanistan.

Kyrgyzstan and Tajikistan were two of the countries from which the U.S. operations were conducted—and both share long borders with China. For many years western strategists, recalling the events that led to China's fateful entry into Korea in October 1950, have speculated whether China would ever tolerate a stationing of U.S. forces along its borders. (The question takes on a special salience in thinking about the future of a unified Korean peninsula under a democratic government that might wish to maintain security ties with the United States.) The answer to the most openended version of these speculations is now known. Yes, there are indeed conditions under which Beijing will accept the entry of U.S. troops and the establishment of U.S. bases in bordering lands. Moreover, the Kyrgyzstan-Tajikistan example seems to suggest, with respect to Korea's future security, that Beijing would be inclined to regard the still hypothetical issue of an American military presence in a united Korea with an eye toward its own perceived benefits and costs—a posture more promising from a U.S. vantage point than some have heretofore assumed.

North Korea

The DPRK's post-September 11 response to Washington was not totally antagonistic. It is apparently true, as one report put it, that the North Korean government quickly sent a "private communication" to the State Department (via the Swedish embassy in Pyongyang), "expressing sadness for the catastrophe" and "making it clear that Pyongyang had nothing to do with the attacks."[26] In addition, on September 12, 2001, a spokesman for the DPRK Foreign Ministry stated tersely that the attacks were a "very tragic and regretful incident", that "the DPRK is opposed to all forms of terrorism," and that "this stance will remain unchanged."[27] Apart from these two official expressions, however, Pyongyang's reaction to the terror attacks and America's unfolding anti-terror campaign has been one of unremitting hostility toward Washington. Characterized though they may have been by programmatic opposition before September 11, Washington and Pyongyang's positions have subsequently moved even farther apart.

Even as Pyongyang was carefully distancing itself from September 11 for foreign audiences, it was indicating to its own populace that these were the natural and even deserved consequence of American policy. As Kongdan Oh has noted, on domestic DPRK radio, the September 11 attacks "were described not as terrorism but as 'unprecedented surprise attacks' [*supkyok sagon*]." DPRK internal broadcasts further suggested "that the 'root of this incident lay in Bush's unilateral foreign policy of putting only U.S. interests above all else.'"[28] (North Korea's domestic listeners would probably have found it confusing, if not baffling, to hear their government describe those attacks on the United States as "terrorism." According to DPRK doctrine before and since September 11, "terrorism" is defined as the threatening actions of "imperialist" states, and the United States, as the paramount western state, qualifies as the global "kingpin of terrorism.")[29]

Despite (or more precisely because of) the DPRK's "principled opposition to terrorism," Pyongyang came out unequivocally against U.S. military operations in Afghanistan, warning the day after the campaign commenced that "the U.S. should not be a source of vicious cycle of terrorism and retaliation that may plunge the world into the holocaust of war."[30] Thereafter, Pyongyang steadily criticized U.S. military involvement in Afghanistan, highlighting reports of casualties and seizing joyfully on any perceived sign of setbacks for U.S. forces.[31]

North Korea vented its ire about many other post-September 11 changes in U.S. foreign and security policy as well, particularly those viewed as limiting the DPRK's own freedom of motion. Pyongyang's pronouncements skewered Japan for its closer military cooperation with Washington.[32] Without criticizing Russia by name, Pyongyang's media also bitterly commented that "unexpected changes are taking place in international relations. An ally in the last century appears as an enemy...."[33] But Pyongyang was most alert to, and critical of, the United State's multifaceted plans for long-term security mobilization in the wake of the terror attacks. It blasted the emergency supplement to the FY 2002 U.S. defense spending and decried the sharp (15 percent) proposed increase in the president's FY 2003 defense budget as "an expression of the dominationist nature of the U.S." as a grave threat to world peace and stability.[34] It sounded a harsh drumbeat against America's evolving plan for a NMD system, reacting with particular opprobrium to the announcement that Washington would be establishing a Missile Defense Agency within the Department of Defense.[35] It was, of course, vitriolic about the "axis of evil" statement (and, even by its own high standards, waxed unusually *ad hominem* in its excoriation of President Bush).[36]

But Pyongyang's most pointed and continuing verbal assault on U.S. policy concerned what it asserted to be Washington's growing interest in using military force directly against North Korea. The United States, Pyongyang alleged in December 2001, was targeting North Korea for war after Afghanistan.[37] By June 2002, after revelation of the aforementioned *Nuclear Posture Review* and President Bush's West Point speech (which mentioned the possibility of pre-emptive U.S. strikes against terrorism),[38] Pyongyang declared that it was expecting a surprise attack from the United States, possibly nuclear in nature.[39] North Korea, its media declared, was "ready enough" for war,[40] and, if war came, it intoned, "the choice of strike, which the United States likes to babble about impertinently, does not belong to the United States alone."[41] Although one might think there was little room for perfecting the invective North Korea had deployed against America over the previous 50 years, Pyongyang proved the contrary in April 2002 by labeling the U.S. "imperialists" the "century-long sworn enemy of the Korean people" in a special article in the party's daily paper.[42]

North Korea's public counter to the new post-September 11 environment was two-pronged. On the one hand, Pyongyang argued that recent events had only reaffirmed the prescience of its "military-first politics," and the regime reinforced its official commitment to augmenting the country's defense capabilities.[43] On the other, North Korea intensified its longstanding call for the United States to withdraw troops from the Korean Peninsula— a potentially significant gambit about which more is discussed later.

What we may note for now is that North Korea's opposition to America's more assertive post-September 11 policy took place almost exclusively in the realm of rhetoric. North Korea's posture toward the United States may have been increasingly confrontational, but it was a stance almost entirely disconnected from visible actions—actions that might provoke tangible responses from America's foreign policy apparatus or the mighty military machine behind it. The tone of its declarations notwithstanding, Pyongyang was laying low.

As will be argued, Pyongyang's relative restraint in external behavior seems to betoken in part a conscious innovation in its unification strategy—a new approach in its old quest to decouple South Korea from the United States. But after September 11, a new measure of caution in Pyongyang's external policy was also a perfectly rational reaction to what was clearly, from the DPRK's standpoint, an increasingly unfavorable international situation. North Korea was unquestionably more vulnerable and exposed after September 11 than before. The terrorist attacks had precipitated an international realignment much to the immediate global advantage of Pyongyang's "sworn enemy"—and the swift and almost seamless course of its Afghanistan campaign showed that enemy's military power to be even greater than previously understood.

South Korea

"President Kim's administration did not become one of the strongest supporters of the anti-terrorism campaign."[44] Kongdan Oh's assessment of the ROK's response to the events of September 11 wells with understatement. Perhaps no other U.S. military ally was so conspicuously unwilling to participate in the post-September 11, America-led reveille against terrorism. A brief recap of events makes the point.

In the hours after the world learned about the catastrophes in New York and Washington, literally dozens of heads of state phoned President Bush to express their sorrow, convey their sympathy, and affirm their solidarity with the United States. President Kim Dae Jung was apparently not one of these. Instead, according to his staff, he decided instead simply to "sen[d] a letter of condolence to U.S. President George W. Bush over the plane attacks in the United States."[45] It was evidently not until a week after the attacks, and in a phone conversation specifically requested by President Bush, that the two leaders talked directly.[46]

This is not to say that the Blue House was not busy in the wake of the announcement of the attacks. Barely hours after those grim reports, Kim's administration revealed its own initiative to cope with the unfolding global crisis: a proposed joint declaration with Pyongyang condemning international terrorism.[47] Among the many questions begged by this curious diversionary device was the substantive issue of what the DPRK's assent would actually have signified; the library of international diplomacy, after all, contains a small shelf of documents that North Korea has signed but failed to honor. These and other questions proved moot, however, for the effort in diplomatic craftsmanship was put to rest when Pyongyang refused even to consider it.[48]

A day after the attacks on the United States, NATO, for the first time in its history, invoked its charter's mutual defense clause (Article 5) to declare that its signatories would respond to the assault on the treaty's American member.[49] The ROK is also bound to the United States by a military treaty with a mutual defense clause (the Mutual Defense Treaty of 1953). The provisions of the latter treaty, however, can be read to mean that mutual defense is only required of the members in the case of "external armed attack" taking place "*in the Pacific area,*"[50] and the ROK did not volunteer to read the language of the treaty otherwise. NATO members' reading of their post-September 11 charter obligations was less legalistic. Technically, objections could have been raised that the attacks on the U.S. were not from a country, and that the response would likely be out of area—but neither reservation was lodged.

The hesitancy of ROK authorities to side squarely with the United States immediately after the terror attacks was mirrored in the South Korean public's response. In a poll one week after news of the attacks against New York and Washington, less than 40 percent of surveyed South Koreans opined that the United States should react with immediate military force. The distinct majority preferred Washington to address the problem in "a humane way." If the United States did pursue military retaliation, only a razor-thin 46–42 percent plurality favored joining the campaign.[51]

By such soundings, South Korea's level of public support for joint action with the United States was indistinguishable from that of, say, Peru, a neutral South American nation. Among the European members of NATO, by way of contrast, in almost every case an overwhelming majority of the public agreed that their country should participate in military action against international terrorism. In some NATO countries, those levels of public support were 20 or 30 percentage points above South Korea's. In Italy and the Netherlands, for example, the affirmative response was 66 percent; in France, 73 percent; in Britain, 79 percent; and in Denmark, 80 percent.[52]

As the anti-terror campaign unfolded, a number of America's military allies offered to put their own forces in harm's way in and around Afghanistan. Some, like Germany, had never made any such commitment in the past. The ROK, on the other hand, focused strictly upon limiting the amount of support that might be expected of it. South Korea's news agency, Yonhap, revealed its government's negotiating position:

> The government is said to be mulling rendering medical, transportation and engineering support worth 500 [million] U.S. dollars, which amounts to the support given to the country during the Gulf War, *in case Washington makes an official request*.[53] [emphasis added]

In an earlier U.S. military campaign in Asia—the war in Vietnam—the ROK had committed two divisions of troops; at their peak, over 50,000 South Korean soldiers were in Vietnam, and, over the course of that war approximately 300,000 served in Southeast Asia. As the years passed, South Korea increasingly regarded its involvement in Vietnam as embarrassing or shameful. In the critical, modern reading, it was the act of a military dictator (ROK President Park Chung Hee), renting out troops to the great power (the United States) to which he was beholden.[54] No offers of military participation were forthcoming this time. On the other hand, the South Korean government's irritation over those burdens that it was assuming in the American-led war on terror could not be successfully hidden.

Shortly after the start of the Afghanistan campaign, for example, a major South Korean weekly carried a story, reportedly sourced by ROK military and intelligence officials, claiming that the United States was angling to "pressure" and "rip off" South Korea through unequal burden sharing in that war. According to one anonymous ROK intelligence officer, "Recently, we have often seen American CIA agents coming in and going out. They have spread malignant, and unconfirmable, information to make the Korean intelligence nervous and strained." The article went on to explain that this "'pressure-putting operation' is intended to coax as much money as possible from South Korea in the name of a share of war expenses."[55] Though the journal publishing this article was private—and thus should not be presumed to express an official government viewpoint—it is noteworthy that, just weeks after that article appeared, the publisher-president of the magazine was appointed chief of the ROK Government Information Agency (and thereby official Blue House spokesman).[56]

After the fighting in Afghanistan had concluded, an indignant South Korean Ministry of National Defense source told the ROK press that the United States had repeatedly requested South Korea to send troops—including possible combat troops—to the front. According to the report:

> The official hastened to add that [South] Korea has "not even considered" the possibility of participating in combat operations in

Afghanistan. "Likewise," he said, "we turned down [the U.S.] request for Korean airborne troops in Afghanistan last year...."

The [most recent U.S.] verbal request was made despite Korean rejection of about 10 earlier similar requests.... The official complained that the frequent requests amounted to pressure by the United States to get [South] Korean troops into the ongoing action in Afghanistan.[57]

Blue House officials responded to the story by saying they had never received a formal request from Washington for combat troops in Afghanistan and "that it was unlikely that such a request would be delivered as ground operations in Afghanistan are nearing completion."[58]

In addition to the issue of possible burden-sharing, there was one other aspect of the U.S. anti-terror campaign against Al Qaeda that seemed to raise extraordinary sensitivities in official circles in Seoul: any indications that North Korean aid had been extended to the forces in the Al Qaeda/ Taliban coalition. Less than three weeks after the terror attacks in New York and Washington, for example, news items surfaced that a former Taliban security officer was claiming he had seen a North Korean in Afghanistan training local forces in the use of chemical weapons.[59] Although the item was highly newsworthy—and presumably of particular interest to the Korean public—the South Korean government stonewalled the report, studiously avoiding any official comment. Later, when a South Korean paper reported that the United States had seized North Korean-manufactured weapons in Afghanistan and had tracked phone calls between Pyongyang and Kabul, the government reacted with unconcealed anxiety. A South Korean intelligence official extenuated that "these communications could have been exchanged between the Pyongyang authorities and [sources] unrelated to the Taliban"; another government official declaimed that weapons sales for North Korea were merely "a means of bringing in foreign currency" and that such DPRK sales were commonplace in regions of turmoil or instability.[60]

It should be emphasized that none of the western allies in the Afghanistan operation have yet suggested that Pyongyang played a role in supporting Al Qaeda or the Taliban, and press reports of possible North Korean involvement are to date unconfirmed. What was noteworthy here, however, were not the possible matters of fact under discussion, but the ROK government's reactions to them. For while the ultimate success of the U.S.-led international campaign against terror would arguably rest on developing the best possible intelligence about the workings of the international terror network—and sharing that information with the western electorates whose support would be required for the prosecution of the effort—Seoul's first impulse concerning possible North Korean linkages with international terror was to evade, deny, or excuse.

In sum, as the international war against terror began to unfold, South Korea and the United States appeared to be working at cross-purposes in some fundamental respects, and, as the campaign progressed, these signs of divergence became gradually more evident. A simple but important contradiction underlay these divergences: the U.S. international defense posture looked to be increasingly mismatched with the peninsular objectives of the ROK government—whose territory and populace the United States was committed by treaty to defending. The North Korean question was at the heart of this difference between friends.

When the Bush administration looked at Pyongyang, it saw a "rogue state" (a term formally renounced under the Clinton administration, but officially resurrected shortly after Bush came to office). The Kim Dae Jung government, on the other hand, hoped that Pyongyang would be its partner in peninsular peacemaking. In ways that Washington does not seem to appreciate fully, the North Korean government has been working, with some limited success, to cultivate those South Korean hopes—with an eye toward weakening the U.S.-ROK military alliance. The current complexities of this extended relationship can be best understood by examining strategies and constraints for the three state actors in question—North Korea, South Korea, and the United States.

Pyongyang's Waiting Game

The North Korean state today is under extraordinary and ever mounting pressure—and there seems to be little the regime can do to remedy the situation. To begin, the DPRK's economic situation is absolutely dire, and its economic prospects remain grim. Although the ROK's Bank of Korea (BOK) suggests that North Korea experienced its third straight year of GDP growth in 2001—and that output was back up to the level before the official food crisis was announced in 1995[61]—the BOK's methodology for such calculations is opaque and the results are irreproducible. Other indications of DPRK economic performance convey a less optimistic impression.

According to official South Korean reconstructions based on reports by its trade partners, for example, North Korea's commercial exports remain extraordinarily weak. In 2001, by these South Korean estimates, the DPRK's total exports of civilian merchandise amounted to less than $1 billion[62]—that is to say, under $50 per capita. Urbanized, literate, industrial North Korea's per capita capacity for generating foreign exchange is thus on par with the most miserable and turmoil-beset regions of sub-Saharan Africa.[63]

Domestic and external economic achievements, furthermore, are such that the DPRK has been unable to put an end to the ongoing national food emergency it first officially acknowledged in 1995. In June 2002, a spokesman for the UN World Food Program warned that North Korea's hunger disaster was poised to erupt anew, barring additional humanitarian assistance.[64] In other words, immediate famine would only be forestalled through the continued kindness of strangers. By 2002, tens of thousands—some said hundreds of thousands—of North Korean citizens were border-crossers foraging for sustenance in China, and many hundreds of these unfortunates were applying for, and receiving, sanctuary in South Korea.[65]

While a consequential proportion of its population had been reduced to living literally hand to mouth, Pyongyang was also apparently neglecting the basic investments that would be needed to rebuild the country's industrial infrastructure. Calculations by two South Korean economists made the point clear. Their study concluded that North Korea was caught in a "poverty trap"—that depreciation of outworn facilities exceeded investment in new plants, so that the country's productive capacity was gradually eroding. By their estimates, North Korea's capital stock could be expected to decline by roughly 1.7 percent a year, absent policy changes.[66] Though that figure may have been excessively precise, the downward trajectory that their study predicted looked all too plausible.

As last year's study argued, an economic turnaround in the DPRK will require a much more pragmatic economic policy, and new economic direction in North Korea, for its part, will require major departures from past positions on three interconnected issues—the regime's attitude toward: 1) economic opening; 2) its WMD program; and 3) the right of the Republic of Korea to co-exist on the peninsula as a legitimate state. Over the past year, precious little movement on any of those fronts has been evidenced.

With regard to "economic opening," North Korean policy pronouncements over the past year have inveighed against the global world economy and have urged (if possible) even greater vigilance against "ideological and cultural infiltration"—Pyongyang's formulation for contact with the outside world.[67] Though in some quarters hopes of an impending North Korean economic opening were lifted by Kim Jong Il's January 2001 seemingly symbolic visit to Shanghai, expectations seem to be much lower today—not least so in China. At a June 2002 conference in Beijing with over a dozen Chinese specialists on Korean affairs, for example, not one of those experts volunteered the assessment that Kim Jong Il's China visits had actually commenced a process of redirecting the North Korean economy.[68]

(As this volume was going to print, news reports began to circulate suggesting that North Korea was implementing a major round of wage increases, exchange rate devaluations, and rationing system overhauls. The precise details of these changes remained unconfirmed—and Pyongyang had made no official announcements about them.)

On the WMD front, it is perhaps significant that North Korea continues to extol its self-styled "military-first politics" (as noted above).[69] Beyond dispute, however, was that almost eight years into the "Agreed Framework," North Korea continues to prevent inspectors from the UN International Atomic Energy Agency (IAEA) from conducting the unimpeded visits that would permit an independent determination about the suspect nuclear program that occasioned the Agreed Framework in the first place.[70]

As for North Korea's stance on the legitimacy of the South Korean government, suffice it to say that the "South Korean National Defense Front" (SKNDF)—a fictitious South Korean organization issuing purportedly homegrown cries for an end to the South Korean "police state" and expulsion of its American masters—resounded in North Korea's press and airwaves as usual.[71] Pyongyang was more circumspect about the Kim Dae Jung government when it was using its own voice than when it was engaging in acts of political ventriloquism. Even so, official DPRK commentators averred that the United States' aim on the peninsula is to "fixate…the colonial military occupation of South Korea"[72] and stated that "South Korea has become a great open-air prison, in which people are unable to exercise political rights but are held hostage to fascist force of arms."[73] Governments that regard other governments as independent, sovereign, and legitimate do not ordinarily describe them in such terms.

With an ossified, decaying industrial base and little evident willingness to embrace the sorts of economic or diplomatic measures that might help revitalize it, Pyongyang's would appear to have extremely circumscribed room for strategic maneuver. Yet recently, North Korea seems to have devised a campaign for influencing the international environment from within its self-imposed straitjacket.

Sundering the U.S.-ROK military alliance has always been an objective of paramount importance to North Korean leadership, as last year's study explained. Unchanging DPRK doctrine has held for decades that U.S. military power in Korea is the primary obstacle preventing Pyongyang from unifying the peninsula on its own terms.[74] This seemingly "unchanging" state has actually been deploying new stratagems in this old quest. What is evident today in Pyongyang's external behavior is a forbearance notable in its own right, and all the more striking in contrast with the DPRK's historic *modus operandi.*

That forbearance, to be sure, stands out mainly against the past pattern of North Korea's international activities. By any other measure, North Korea's military posture would still qualify as extraordinarily provocative and its state rhetoric as almost uniquely vicious. What must be noted, however, is that North Korea is today engaged in a prolonged—and wholly unprecedented—effort to present an attractive face to the outside world. This effort, moreover, significantly predated the post-September 11 U.S. war on international terrorism. It therefore cannot be dismissed purely as quiescence born of a healthy respect for a reassertive adversary.

Consider that for three full years, between the Yellow Sea naval clashes of June 1999 and June 2002,[75] North Korea provoked no major border incidents with South Korea. In 1999 Pyongyang also issued a declaration that promised (albeit equivocally and conditionally) to suspend all launches of North Korean ballistic missiles. No new missiles have yet been launched, and Kim Jong Il has publicly extended this test-flight moratorium until 2003. Under the terms of the U.S.-DPRK Agreed Framework, North Korean nuclear development is ostensibly suspended—and, at least as yet, the U.S. intelligence community has offered no evidence of any covert North Korean program. Although not yet exactly civil, North Korea's public diplomacy is no longer regularly freighted with the most violent utterances of past years (threats to turn Seoul into a "sea of fire" and the like). No less portentous than any of this, Pyongyang hosted the celebrated and highly successful visit by South Korean President Kim Dae Jung in June 2000 and promised that Kim Jong Il would make a reciprocal visit to the South "at the appropriate time"—occurrences and promises all but unimaginable in earlier years.

It is in these particulars that proponents of "sunshine policy" base their claims for success. But it is not only combatants in the South Korean political arena who find the case for a "new North Korea" to be compelling. In the wake of the Pyongyang summit, many governments long skeptical of Pyongyang's purposes finally extended diplomatic recognition to the DPRK; at this writing, for example, 13 of the European Union's 15 states and the EU itself have normalized ties with North Korea.[76]

If Pyongyang has deliberately restrained its impulse for traditional brinkmanship diplomacy over the past several years, it has, however, continued and even intensified its campaign to oust the U.S. military from South Korea. According to South Korean accounts, Kim Jong Il reportedly indicated during the Pyongyang summit that he might acquiesce to a future U.S. troop presence in Korea under certain conditions—hints greeted as spectacular news by some in the South. Irrespective of what the Chairman may or may not have said once in private, North Korea's public stance on the

U.S.-ROK military alliance is absolutely unambiguous: it must be scrapped—and U.S. soldiers must leave Korea immediately.

Since the Pyongyang summit (as was noted last year), Chairman Kim has opined publicly on the U.S. troop issue on three occasions. In late June 2000, in an interview with a Korean-American reporter, he confided, "President Kim Dae Jung's image ha[s] not been so good among our people. For instance, he has advocated continued U.S. military presence in our country even after unification has been realized...."[77] In June 2001, in an *Itar-Tass* interview, Kim Jong Il declared "the whole world knows that the United States has forcibly occupied half of our country's land and is constantly threatening us."[78] And in August 2001, in the aforementioned joint declaration with President Putin during Kim Jong Il's Moscow visit, the DPRK side avowed that "the pullout of U.S. forces from South Korea is a pressing issue which brooks no delay."[79]

Moreover, from the DPRK's standpoint, the June 2000 Pyongyang summit was an instrument for increasing the pressure to oust U.S. forces from the South. The first point of the post-summit "North-South Declaration" signed by Kim Dae Jung and Kim Jong Il reads as follows:

> The North and the South agreed to solve the question of the country's reunification independently by the concerted efforts of the Korean nation responsible for it.[80]

For the DPRK, such usage of the word "independent" is well-known and long-established code language. In the North Korean lexicon, an "independent South Korea" is defined as a South Korea that is no longer stationing U.S. forces or bound to the United States by a military alliance. It is therefore highly significant that North Korea managed to insert this point into the joint statement. (Perhaps distracted by the euphoric symbolism of the visit, President Kim Dae Jung unwittingly fell into the trap.)

In the months since the attacks on New York and Washington, Pyongyang has redoubled its cries for the South to "honor the June 15 declaration"—meaning that U.S. forces in the peninsula be shown the door. "The U.S. troops in South Korea," inveighed North Korea's *KCNA*, "are the source of all misfortune and suffering of the Korean people, and their withdrawal from the South...is the task the United States should undertake before all others."[81] The troop presence, intoned *Minju Choson*, is a "cancer-like... obstructi[on]...."[82] The United States, the *Nodong Sinmun* explained:

> is the key force that opposes our country's peaceful unification....
> We have to firmly adhere to the principle of national independence
> in accordance with what was announced in the Joint Declaration

and cooperate with our compatriots instead of "cooperating" with foreign forces.[83]

With the U.S. military now unleashing operations in a war against terrorism that was indefinite in duration but potentially global in scope, the DPRK began to fix on a new and more intellectually sophisticated rendition of an old argument, maintaining that North and South were being commonly endangered by the designs of the peninsula's alien troops.

"Frankly speaking", the North Korean media implored in March 2002, "the United State's keeping its forces in South Korea is not to protect someone and guarantee safety."[84] Embracing the late-Cold War notion of "enemy imaging," Pyongyang agued that "the rumors of a threat of our southward aggression the United States is clamoring about are a reversed version of [the rumors about] a northward aggression.... U.S. forces are tasked with a mission to light the fuse of a new Korean war."[85] Couching its contentions in soft-left, anti-globalization language, the regime in Pyongyang warned that:

> Today the U.S. imperialists are scheming to make the Korean people kick off a game of killing each other by igniting the flames of war on this land. It is a cunning intention of the U.S. imperialists to make the Korean people fight against each other, making a profit out of the two contestants.[86]

There was a newly solicitous tone in Pyongyang's entreaties toward the South. In April 2002, Pyongyang pleaded that:

> The people in the North and the South...are the same people who lived on the same land by inheriting the same blood generation after generation.... Today's grave situation created on the Korean peninsula is not a result of internal discord within our nation but a product of the U.S. imperialists' interference....[87]

Consequently, Pyongyang proposed, the task before the South Korean citizenry was twofold. One the one hand, the ultimate objective of Koreans in North and South must be to oust U.S. forces from the peninsula. The burden for accomplishing this mission would fall upon South Koreans, but Northerners would lend moral support in their effort:

> It is natural that a broad segment of the South Korean people is energetically waging a struggle to oppose the United States' criminal hostile policy toward the DPRK and to withdraw U.S. imperialist forces of aggression occupying South Korea. This struggle is getting active support from all fellow countrymen.[88]

On the other hand, South Koreans had to understand that North Korea's defense buildup was a necessary countermeasure to malign U.S. maneuvers and was being undertaken in the interest of all Korean compatriots. "Our enhancement of self defensive military capability," Pyongyang explained in April 2002, "is not targeted at South Korea but at thoroughly preparing for the U.S. imperialists' aggression."[89]

A North Korean paper for overseas Koreans advised in June 2002:

> It is essential to support the strengthening of the North's military power unsparingly. ... [War has been prevented in Korea] not because the United States is concerned about the catastrophe the South Koreans would suffer because [of] the North's superb military power that has thwarted a war the United States might have wished to wage on this land ten times; and that has safeguarded peace on the Korean peninsula.[90]

In the past, North Korea's international diplomacy has not been successful in persuading the unconvinced (to put it mildly). But if an objective of North Korea's tactical recalibration since 1999 has been to foster conditions conducive to a U.S. pullout from South Korea, one would have to conclude that the program has been—within the DPRK's clear limits of maneuver—rather more effective than past schemes.

Given Pyongyang's comparatively "pacifistic" external policy during the years under consideration, North Korean arguments for a U.S. troop withdrawal seemed inherently that much more acceptable. Very few South Koreans, to be sure, would concur today with all points in Pyongyang's brief for a U.S. troop pullout. But Pyongyang's anti-American contentions almost certainly resonated with a wider spectrum of the South Korean public in the immediate post-September 11 period than they ever had before. Perhaps even more consequentially, while Pyongyang's case hardly persuaded policymakers in Seoul to shift their course, the DPRK's anti-American accusations were received more sympathetically in current government circles than had any previous North Korean offerings been received by ROK administrations since the foundation of South Korea.

What distinguishes current North Korean policy toward the U.S.-ROK alliance from all previous renditions is the large and conscious measure of patience and restraint it seems to require of Pyongyang. Curiously, North Korea's new approach to dissolving the U.S.-ROK alliance looks like a waiting game—an implicit calculation that self-control will reap strategic dividends. Strange as it may sound, given all of the DPRK system's chronic afflictions, North Korean leadership seems to be betting that time is on its side—at least, as far as the U.S.-ROK military alliance is concerned.

Seoul's Sunshine Policy:
Torn Between Washington and Pyongyang

In June 2002 President Kim Dae Jung declared that "the possibility of military confrontation is lessening" in the Korean peninsula, and that "the situation" was indeed "heading toward stability and peace."[91] Coming when Kim's assertions did—on the eve of the second anniversary of the Pyongyang summit—they unavoidably brought to mind a few inconvenient facts. Among these were the reminders that Kim Jong Il had still not made good on his promised reciprocal visit to the South and that official North-South dialogue had essentially been in abeyance over the previous 20 months. (Ironically, just days after President Kim's words North Korean gunboats sank a South Korean naval vessel in the Yellow Sea.) The remarks underscored once again the President Kim's implacable confidence that his approach to North Korea policy would surely result in reconciliation with the DPRK regime—and eventually, in a lasting peace on the peninsula.

President Kim's North Korea policy is by no means universally acclaimed in South Korea: the ROK public remains deeply ambivalent about the approach its government should take toward Pyongyang. Nevertheless, the policy continues to resonate within broad circles of the electorate and the ROK government—largely, of course, because of what are said by proponents to be its tangible achievements to date and its promising prospects for the future. Some of the reasons for the policy's attraction in South Korea, however, have nothing to do with either its achievements or its prospects.

Domestic Wellsprings of "Sunshine"

One powerful extrinsic factor buoying the South Korean public's support for a conciliatory policy toward the DPRK is historic in nature—the ROK's transition from military rule to constitutional democracy. That process, which has taken place just in the past decade and a half, has given the South Korean populace the opportunity to join together with other affluent western democracies in aspirations and outlook. The South Korean public, like so many other OECD electorates, is eager to enter into a peaceful and prosperous millennium (so famously termed "the end of history" by Francis Fukuyama,[92] echoing Hegel and Kojève, wherein international conflict does not distract attention from the public's own preferred purposes). Indeed, with the memory of military rule still so vivid, South Korea's electorate may be especially allergic to unnecessary martial commitments. Irrespective of popular estimates of Pyongyang's current intentions, there is a widespread and entirely natural longing in the South to be rid of the "North Korean threat" and to move away from the burdens that such a threat entails.[93]

A second powerful factor militating for the current "sunshine" search for diplomatic breakthroughs with the DPRK is sheer political exigency. Within the confines of domestic South Korean politics, the Kim Dae Jung administration has little room for maneuver, and the president's leeway for movement continues to narrow. Consequently, from the Kim government's standpoint, the imperative of securing a conciliatory response from the North has taken on an ever-growing importance, for this is one area in which the president can pursue his own policy agenda relatively free from constraints of his domestic political opposition.

Despite his international acclaim, Kim Dae Jung is caught in a political vise at home. Kim's ruling coalition is no longer in charge of the country's legislative branch, having essentially lost control of the National Assembly to the ROK's main opposition party in September 2001. In practical terms, the loss of the National Assembly now prevents the president from following through on the unfinished items of his domestic agenda—a list including, but not limited to, health care reform, education reform, corporate reform, and financial reform.

The National Assembly would not have switched hands if Kim's government had not already lost much of its initial luster. The South Korean electorate is today deeply dissatisfied with the country's political and economic situation. In late 2000, three out of four South Koreans surveyed said the nation was "not on the right track."[94] Last year, according to an amazing finding of the *Korea Democracy Barometer*, "a plurality of South Korean citizens [rated] the Kim Dae Jung government more negatively *than the past military government headed by former General Chun Doo Hwan*" (emphasis added).[95] And in early 2002, an in-depth survey of ROK "next generation leaders" (persons in their 30s and 40s) found that fully 92 percent described themselves as "dissatisfied" or "very dissatisfied" with "the way things are going in [South] Korea these days."[96]

Particularly disappointing to many in South Korea was the Kim Dae Jung administration's limited success in addressing the country's corporate and financial weaknesses—conditions that lay behind the country's 1997 crisis of international liquidity and precipitated the IMF-led "rescue package" that greeted Kim when he assumed the presidency in February 1998. Although the ROK enjoyed a vigorous economic rebound under Kim's presidency—with GDP growth averaging over 7 percent a year for the three years from 1999 to 2001[97]—relatively little progress was made in resolving the underlying structural problems of "Korea, Inc.," to whit, an economy dominated by *chaebol* (business conglomerates) whose growth was predicated on unbankable loans and a banking sector willing to dispense them. While South Korea's defenders could point to a number of specific measures the country had implemented to redress these problems, by 2002 foreign observers were giving South Korea's economic reform effort very poor marks. In June 2002, for example, Moody's Investors Service ranked the South Korean banking industry's financial strength as 70 out of 79 countries assayed, and gave Korean banks an overall rating of D-minus (meaning they were not "investment-eligible" grade).[98] In June 2002 the Economic Freedom Network released its latest survey of "Economic Freedom of the World."[99] South Korea came in at 38—tied with such economies as Jamaica and the Philippines, and rated behind Argentina and Costa Rica.[100] South Korea's low grades reflected in some important measure the country's all too hesitant movement toward rule of law and transparency in economic life, for the ROK was regarded as a corrupt society by foreigners and South Korean citizens alike. Transparency International's 2001 "Corruption Perceptions Index," for example, rated South Korea 42 out of 91 countries surveyed—below virtually every OECD country save Mexico, and below such Middle Eastern societies as Jordan and Tunisia too.[101] If anything, South Korean citizens rendered an even more critical verdict. A 2002 poll of South Korean high school students, for example, reported that fully 90 percent of the respondents regarded the ROK as a "corrupt" society.[102]

Any further progress in economic reform—or on any other part of Kim Dae Jung's domestic agenda—looks altogether unlikely in this fifth and final year of his presidency. As the chilly *Korea Democracy Barometer* readings attest, South Korean evaluations of Kim's first four years of domestic achievements are by no means generally positive. (As one South Korean political expert put it, despite President Kim's vocal promise to reform the country's politics, "the reduction of the number of parliamentary seats to 273 from the previous 299 is the only political reform the president has implemented."[103]) Mired as he now is in his own family's legal and financial scandals,[104] and increasingly criticized as a corruption-plagued, do-nothing president,[105] Kim Dae Jung's popularity has plummeted. Currently President Kim's approval ratings hover at only 20–30 percent—down from almost 90 percent at his inauguration.[106]

But while President Kim may be down, he is not yet out. Previous South Korean presidents have suffered even greater ratings drops (President Kim Young Sam was down to single-digit approval ratings when he left office). And seething public dissatisfaction hardly spares Kim's political rivals. To judge by the surveys, many of Kim's opponents are held in even lower public regard. Most importantly, Lee Hoi Chang—de facto leader of the parliamentary opposition and now presidential nominee for the principal opposition party (the Grand National Party or GNP)—regularly garners approval ratings lower than Kim Dae Jung's own.[107]

Similarly, while President Kim may be low on political options today, he is not entirely bereft of them. Given the semi-paralytic state of his presidency, Kim's best chance for burnishing his legacy and bolstering support for his party's presidential nominee this election year, a not entirely unrelated matter, now lies not in prospective achievements within the domestic realm, but rather in the prospects of eliciting a powerful symbolic gesture from without—more specifically, from Pyongyang. Considering the precarious balances and the deep, seemingly structural divisions that characterize politics in the ROK, moreover, it would not be unreasonable to imagine that such a gesture might end up making the difference between victory and defeat for the candidate who proposed to continue Kim Dae Jung's "sunshine" policy in a tight presidential race this coming December.

Despite continuing difficulty in bilateral relations, evidenced by the June 2002 gunboat incident, the possibility of an election-influencing "peace breakthrough" is not dead in the water. South Korean polls show that while 70 percent of the public believes Pyongyang deliberately engineered the shoot-out, nearly 60 percent nevertheless want the sunshine policy to continue.[108] As recently as April 2002, President Kim sent former General Lim Dong Won, effectively co-architect of his "sunshine policy," to Pyongyang on a mission to jumpstart the "Korean peace process"; if public sentiment holds and North Korean posture permits, more impromptu missions could well follow the latest naval clash. It is worth recalling, furthermore, that President Kim has previously choreographed such "breakthroughs" to coincide with the South Korean electoral calendar: his historic visit to Pyongyang, for example, was announced just three days before the country's April 2000 National Assembly elections.

Growing Seoul-Washington Strains

In other bilateral relations, popular sentiments and political constraints in the ROK make for an increasingly complex relationship between the South Korea and the United States—or more properly, between the Kim Dae Jung administration and the Bush government. On the one hand, South Korean security policy still relies crucially on a defense guarantee from the United States against outside aggression—and implicitly presumes that guarantee will continue into the indefinite future. On the other hand, President Kim's political reputation—and the future of his cherished sunshine policy—are now both critically dependent upon a goodwill overture from North Korea (against whom Washington is pledged to defend Seoul). Should such an overture not be forthcoming, furthermore, the Kim administration would have strong incentives not to blame Pyongyang for the failure (since a revealed lack of sincerity on the DPRK's part would fatally discredit the "sunshine" theory), but rather to fault the Bush presidency. Sure enough, in 2001 and 2002 Kim's administration (and party) repeatedly indicated that responsibility for the impasse in inter-Korean reconciliation efforts lay not at Pyongyang's door, but rather at Washington's.

The proposition that Washington is interfering in the Korean people's quest for peninsular peace is a vintage tenet of North Korean ideology— but today that accusation seems to be corroborated by the government of South Korea. Quite predictably, these peculiar circumstances led to an inflammation of anti-American suspicions in portions of the South Korean body politic not customarily susceptible to the affliction.

Relations between the Kim government and the Bush administration did not get off to a swimming start. Just weeks after Bush's inauguration, and apparently without prior consultation with Washington, Kim issued a joint communiqué with Russian President Putin, in which he praised the 1972 ABM Treaty as a "cornerstone of strategic stability."[109] Since the new U.S. President was intent upon pursuing a national missile defense system and the ABM treaty expressly prohibited NMD, Kim's surprise decision in effect placed Seoul with Russia and against the United States on a key point of global U.S. security policy. (In the face of the ensuing controversy, President Kim retracted this position on U.S. NMD and repeatedly expressed his "regret over the unnecessary misunderstanding.")[110] Almost immediately thereafter, Kim visited Bush in Washington to press him to embrace Seoul's approach to reducing tensions with North Korea. In a series of Washington meetings described in the South Korean press as a "disaster" for President Kim,[111] Bush countered that Washington would not rush into negotiations with Pyongyang and would take its time reviewing North Korea policy overall; Bush also pointedly emphasized his misgivings about North Korea's trustworthiness as a negotiating partner, remarking publicly that "we're not certain as to whether they're keeping all terms of all agreements"[112] and "I do have some skepticism about the leader of North Korea."[113] But as has been shown above, difficulties in the Seoul-Washington relationship increased appreciably after the events of September 11, and most of these differences directly or indirectly concerned North Korea policy.

Some government and party figures were willing to criticize openly the purportedly adverse U.S. influence on inter-Korean relations, especially after September 11. In December 2001, for example, a spokesman for the president's Millennium Democratic Party (MDP) insisted that "there are clear signals North Korea is trying to be more cooperative," but suggested that Washington was sabotaging the sunshine policy: "It's very disappointing...The United States delivers ultimatums and threats, and of course North Korea feels it has to react."[114] In the National Assembly, one representative of Kim Dae Jung's party responded to President Bush's "axis of evil" speech by declaring Bush himself to be "evil incarnate."[115] Perhaps most significantly, in April 2002 presidential confidant and envoy, Lim Dong Won, indicated to the National Assembly on his return from a mission to Pyongyang that the Bush administration was responsible for Kim Jong Il's failure to visit the South. According to a press report on the proceeding:

> [Lim said that] Chairman Kim [Jong Il] originally thought of visiting Seoul in March of [2002], but the visit failed to take place due to unfavorable conditions, including DPRK relations with the U.S. Bush administration.[116]

More commonly, however, these post-September 11 objections to U.S. North Korea policy were couched indirectly, and on an unattributed basis. To cite a few examples:

- a "diplomatic source" complained in December 2001 that dialogue between the United States and North Korea was unlikely to resume soon because this was "not a priority issue for the Bush administration";[117]
- anonymous government officials in January 2002 confided that they had urged the Bush administration to tone down its anti-Pyongyang rhetoric ("in order to allow Pyongyang to save face and come to the negotiating table");[118]
- a "Seoul official" responded to the State Department's annual *Country Reports on Human Rights Practices* with the comment, "We are concerned that the North's antipathy to the United States may deepen on the occasion of the human rights report";[119]
- in April 2002 an ROK Foreign Ministry official sourly noted that, because Washington decided not to remove the DPRK from its list of terror-sponsoring states, "there will be no specific change in the status quo as the United States seems to think the North has failed to take steps pertinent to anti-terror efforts";[120] and
- in June 2002, in a none-too-subtle signal that it believed the Bush administration did not understand how to manage its relations with the DPRK, a "senior [Blue House] official" let it be known that Seoul had urged the United States to assign the deputy secretary of state rather than the ambassador for the Korean peace process to upcoming U.S.-North Korea talks: in his words, "I hope that Washington will send a senior official to Pyongyang for a quick fix of their relationship…However, it seems to be easier said than done."[121]

Sentimental Fallout

The continuing official intimation that the United States was poisoning Seoul's efforts to improve its relations with the Pyongyang—inadvertently or otherwise—naturally struck a nerve with many South Korean citizens. According to opinion surveys, the South Korean public has divided feelings about the sunshine policy. Depending upon the most recent event in North-South relations, the particular aspect of the policy under consideration, and the specific wording of the pollsters, reactions could be elicited on a spectrum ranging from the resoundingly negative to the enthusiastically favorable. (Unsurprisingly, South Koreans indicated overwhelming opposition to "one-sided give-aways," but overwhelmingly supported "avoiding another conflict in the Korean peninsula.") On the central issue of the efficacy of the sunshine policy, the South Korean public was almost evenly split. According to a June 2002 survey, 50 percent of citizens concurred that "North Korea has changed as a result of sunshine policy," while 48 percent disagreed.[122]

For the half of the South Korean public that believed President Kim's North Korea policy was achieving genuine results, purported American interference in the peninsular reconciliation process would mean the United States was directly harming ROK national interests. Even among South Korean skeptics of "sunshine," the notion that the United States was subverting their government's inter-Korean policy could provoke strong nationalistic reactions.[123] Negative public assessments of U.S. policy toward Korea, and of the United States itself, consequently became more common.

Poll results illustrate the new climate of opinion. In April 2002, a survey of college freshmen in the Taegu and Kyongsang area found that 75 percent of respondents judged the "axis of evil" remark to "hinde[r] North-South relations, which had been improving through the implementation of the 15 June joint declaration."[124] The fact that this survey was seized upon by the North Korean media may suggest it was unrepresentative, but other polls reported correspondingly critical assessments of U.S. Korea policy.

In February 2002, for example, a poll by the weekly *Sisa* found that "most South Koreans believe the United States' tough stance against North Korea is the prime obstacle to inter-Korean reconciliation, and felt that America throws its weight around the world unnecessarily."[125] According to another opinion poll, South Korean adults disapproved of Bush's formulation by a lopsided 56–36 majority, with 47 percent of respondents attributing those remarks to Bush's "domestic problems in the U.S.," and only 13 percent agreeing that the words actually reflected "the military threat posed by the North." The same survey found that South Koreans blamed the United States over North Korea for "the rising tension on the Korean peninsula" by a 38–31 plurality. Moreover, whereas a mere 11 percent of those polled thought the "U.S.'s hawkish stance toward the North" would promote inter-Korean relations, fully 50 percent believed it would "aggravate" them.[126] By spring 2002, many South Koreans would evidently agree with a prominent Seoul columnist's contention that the "U.S., not the North, is a barrier" to better North-South relations.[127]

One can make too much of such passing soundings, of course. In both elite and popular circles in South Korea, the United States enjoys a deep wellspring of trust and respect, and continues to be very positively regarded on the whole. Anti-Americanism, conversely, seldom succeeds in striking a responsive chord in public discourse. During the June 2002 World Cup jointly hosted by Japan and South Korea, for example, radical students from the Hanchongnyon attempted to mobilize viewers and fans into mass protests against the United States. Their effort was a conspicuous failure—and indeed seemed to generate embarrassment and irritation over their antics.[128]

A New Presidential Contest

Less epiphenomenal than transient opinion surveys, however, are political choices. In April 2002, President Kim Dae Jung's MDP party nominated former National Assembly member Roh Moo Hyun as its candidate for president in the coming December elections. A dark-horse candidate until late this past spring, Roh has spent relatively little time on the national stage (two terms in the National Assembly, and a brief stint as a cabinet minister in the Kim Dae Jung government). Consequently, his electoral agenda is not as well known as those of more perennial aspirants to the ROK's highest office. It seems apparent, however, that Roh has a significantly different attitude toward the United States from any previous serious candidate for the South Korean presidency.

A former labor lawyer and human rights activist, Roh publicly agitated for the ouster of U.S. forces from South Korea as late as 1990.[129] Roh insists he subsequently had a change of heart and avers he now strongly supports the alliance. Nevertheless, his precise views about that alliance are unclear and are further clouded by an element of apparent self-contradiction. (In a radio interview in April 2002, for example, he reportedly claimed that he "never gave a thought to withdrawal of U.S. forces from the Korean Peninsula."[130]) What is indisputable, however, is that Roh is virtually alone among contemporary South Korea political figures in having *never* visited the United States. At his age (he is now 56), such an achievement can be understood to require something like a continuing act of will—and can easily be seen as a political signal in and of itself.

Roh's own reaction to questions about this lacuna on his résumé tends to reinforce such impressions. In April 2002, he stated that in the past:

> Leaders without legitimacy had to visit the U.S. and bow to get Washington's endorsement. I will visit America if I have business there, or leisure time, but I will not go simply to have pictures taken for political purposes.[131]

Indications of Roh's disposition toward the United States may have been further revealed when the South Korean press reported that his foreign policy advisor in April 2002 issued this warning to U.S. officials: "Though Roh may not be entirely palpable to the U.S. Republican Party's taste, don't think about trying to interfere in Korea's presidential election and keep your hands off the ruling party's nomination race."[132]

At this writing (almost five months before the presidential vote), guesses about the outcome of the race still remain hazardous. South Korean domestic politics are extraordinarily volatile—partly because the role of political parties is arguably more fragile and less institutionalized in ROK than in any other OECD country.[133] South Korean domestic politics are a highly factional affair, with crosscutting cleavages separating voters by region, class, education, and age. It is worth noting that no candidate has ever won an absolute majority of votes in an open Korean presidential election. Throughout the spring of 2002, public opinion polls showed Roh far ahead of any likely challenger. In June, however, the MDP suffered serious losses in South Korea's regional (gubernatorial) elections; these were followed by setbacks in the country's August parliamentary by-elections, and Roh slipped behind GNP presidential nominee Lee Hoi Chang.

Any number of factors could sink Roh's presidential hopes: an unexpected crisis with North Korea (main rival Lee is an outspoken proponent of a tougher posture toward the DPRK and a staunch supporter of the ROK-U.S. alliance[134]); a successful effort by his opponents to define him as "radical" (most South Korean voters today characterize themselves as moderate, or slightly conservative[135]); or an infelicitous but memorable turn of phrase during the heat of the campaign (Roh has a something of a record for retracting off-the-cuff remarks). But a number of factors also favor Roh's candidacy. First, specialized surveys suggest he is the strong and indeed unmistakable favorite of the South Korean press corps.[136] Other things being equal, he can therefore expect comparatively favorable campaign coverage. Second, North Korea has, during the Kim Dae Jung administration, seemingly attempted to influence specific electoral or legislative votes in South Korea;[137] since Pyongyang incessantly reviles "traitor Lee Hoi Chang" in its pronouncements,[138] it is possible that North Korean policy may try to stimulate the "Roh wind" through its own actions. Third, while at this writing the ROK presidential race is a match-up between two candidates, the past three races have fielded three major candidates, and today's most likely prospects for a third major candidate (e.g., 1997 presidential aspirant Rhee In Je; former President Park Chung Hee's daughter, Park Geun Hye; or *chaebol* scion and World Cup games chairman, Chung Mong Joon) would all likely drain more votes from Lee than from Roh.

Today, the plain fact is that Roh is potentially electable. He might well win the coming ROK presidential election. And if he does not, he is not likely to be the last major ROK presidential candidate to cast a colder eye on the United States than Washington has heretofore been accustomed. Polling data show that Roh's strongest base of support lies in South Koreans in their twenties and thirties, and in the ROK's more educated strata.[139] As today's younger, more educated generations move into positions of greater influence and responsibility in South Korea, it would seem entirely reasonable to anticipate a more active and questioning approach to the country's alliance with the United States.

ROK Defense Policy and the "North Korean Threat"

However the 2002 ROK presidential election may unfold, South Korean developments already point to nascent contradictions in the logic of the U.S.-South Korean military alliance. For now, South Koreans and their government seemed increasingly inclined to regard North Korea as something other than an urgent and immediate military threat. Yet the U.S.-ROK military alliance is explicitly premised on just such a security risk. South Korea's own military strategy seems implicitly to presume a continuing, if not indefinite, U.S. defense commitment to the ROK. How such a commitment could retain public support in both the ROK and the United States in the absence of a clear and present danger from North Korea, however, is a question that has gone unaddressed.

By the summer of 2002, important segments of the government, the legislature, and the electorate in South Korea were sending signals that they believed North Korea was no longer the security problem it had been in the past—and by some soundings, that South Korea's true security problems in the region lay elsewhere:

- In February 2002, a survey of 67 ROK lawmakers revealed that the great majority—almost two thirds—designated *Japan* as the greatest threat to Northeast Asian regional security.[140]
- By late 2001, a growing minority of South Koreans professed the belief that North Korea was not a terrorist state; according to one

poll, 38 percent sided with the DPRK's somewhat extreme assertion that North Korea was not involved in any kind of terrorism and did not support terrorists.[141]

• Most portentously, South Korean defense doctrine was under serious reconsideration. The South Korean Ministry of National Defense had deferred publication of its 2001 annual white paper because the Kim Dae Jung government could not resolve the contentious issue of whether Pyongyang should be designated as the ROK military's "main enemy." In 2002, this issue again assumed center stage. Once again, ROK defense circles resisted the idea of dropping the "main enemy" designation for DPRK forces. When it became clear that the 2002 white paper could not reclassify North Korea without a stir, the Kim Dae Jung government cancelled the white paper altogether.[142]

These general attitudes and inclinations have already begun to transform South Korea's patterns and trends of defense expenditures. Like all other free peoples, the South Koreans had determined that they would vote themselves a "peace dividend" after the end of the Cold War. While absolute levels of real military spending rose somewhat between 1989 and 2001, the ROK's level of "military burden" fell sharply, from 4.1 percent of national output in 1989 to 2.7 percent (see Figure 5.1).[143] Most of the decline in South Korea's military burden, it should be noted, preceded Kim Dae Jung's accession to office. Just before September 11, the ROK's defense commitments were lower than those of the United States (where defense expenditures equaled about 3 percent of output in 2000) and only slightly higher than those of European NATO states in the new "Europe whole and free" (whose military burden in 2000 was 2.2 percent of output).[144]

Furthermore, not all of South Korea's military expenditures at the start of the new century were devoted to meeting a possible North Korean military challenge. Quite the contrary, ROK defense allocations were being increasingly invested in systems only tangentially related to potential DPRK aggression, but integral to the development of a regional "force projection" capability. Until it joined the Missile Technology Control Regime (MTCR) in 2001 (under Washington's strong urging), for example, South Korea was quietly working on developing a medium-range missile capacity of its own.[145] South Korea has also directed its military procurements toward submarines (19 are already in the fleet,[146] and nine more were contracted in 2001[147]), Aegis-class destroyers,[148] amphibious transport vessels,[149] and naval-launched attack helicopters,[150] and air-refueling aircraft.[151]

These defense expenditure and allocation decisions suggest something like a long-term strategy. Evidently, decision makers in Seoul (and not simply

Figure 5.1. South Korea's Military Burden

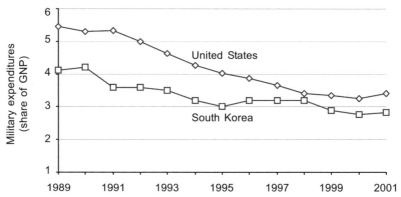

Source: Department of State, Bureau of Verification and Compliance; 2000–01 data from Department of Commerce (Bureau of Economic Analysis), ROK Ministry of National Defense (Policy Planning Bureau), and ROK National Statistical Office.

those under the current Kim Dae Jung government) have been gradually downgrading their assessment of the urgency of the "North Korean threat" and have begun to prepare their forces for a "post-DPRK security environment" in which operational capacities beyond the confines of the Korean peninsula will matter. The logic of this implicit strategy, however, flies in the face of the current U.S.-ROK military alliance. For now, the rationale for U.S. military presence in the Korean peninsula is to deter the "North Korean threat."[152] If that threat is no longer consequential, the current justification for the alliance no longer obtains. While the ROK is now investing in a military that can reach out from the Korean peninsula into the ambit of the Northeast Asian neighborhood, its capabilities are minimal in relation to its neighbors and are likely to remain minimal for some time to come.

Estimates by Charles Wolf Jr. and his colleagues at RAND make the point (see Table 5.1). They attempted to calculate and project trends in military capital stock, the infrastructure necessary to produce armaments and material and thus to sustain war-fighting capacity for a number of Asian states up to the year 2015. In the year 2000, by their reckoning, South Korea's military capital stock was dwarfed by both Japan's and China's: Japan's was at least two-and-a-half times larger, and China's might be four times as large. Yet by 2015, even positing continuing growth and military investments by South Korea and slow growth in Japan, South Korea's military capital stock would still look like a "shrimp among whales." At best, by these figures, the ROK would have two-thirds the military capital stock of Japan, and at worst less than one-fifth that of China.[153]

Presuming any turbulence in the neighborhood, an independent defense posture would simply be too risky. South Korea's defense spending plans

Table 5.1. Estimated and Projected Military Capital Stock

	Military Capital Stock ($bn constant)		
	2000	2005	2010
Based on nominal exchange rates (XR)			
Korea	30.8	35.3	43.5
China–Stable growth	69.0–78.0	84.0–106.0	106.0–138.0
China–Disrupted growth	69.0	82.0	97.0
Japan	154.3	149.7	156.4
Based on purchasing power parity (PPP)			
Korea	61.4	70.4	86.8
China–Stable growth	241.0–276.0	295.0–339.0	372.0–485.0
China–Disrupted growth	238.0	282.0	333.0
Japan	111.5	107.4	112.2

Source: Charles Wolf, Jr., *Asian Economic Trends and Their Security Implications*, Santa Monica, Calif., RAND, 2000. Note: Data shown in 1998 constant dollars.

would make sense if (and perhaps only if) the North Korean threat receded, while the American security commitment to the ROK endured. This indeed seems to be what the current government in Seoul is hoping for. President Kim Dae Jung has repeatedly advocated a continuing U.S. troop presence in Korea on into the future, declaring that U.S. forces are "of help in promoting the [South Korean] national interest no less than an increased [ROK] defense budget."[154] Unfortunately, an explication of a post-DPRK role of U.S. forces in Korea has not yet been offered to the South Korean or the American public. For the moment, Seoul is thus in the curious—and ultimately untenable—position of endorsing the long-term cantonment of foreign forces from the very government that it holds to be inflaming inter-Korean tensions and hampering North-South reconciliation.

Washington: Korea Policy on Hold

On March 6, 2001, as President Kim Dae Jung was arriving in Washington for his talks with President Bush, Secretary of State Colin Powell told reporters that "U.S. policy on North Korea is in complete agreement with what the South Korean government is pursuing,"[155] adding that the Bush administration planned "to pick up [with the DPRK] where President Clinton and his administration left off…. Some promising elements were left on the table, and we'll be examining those elements."[156]

The following day, in the midst of the Bush-Kim meeting, Powell stepped out of the Oval Office to inform the press that North Korea was "a threat…we have to not be naïve about the threat." If "there are suggestions that there are imminent negotiations [between Washington and Pyongyang]," he continued, "that is not the case."[157] Powell went on to emphasize that

President Bush "understands the nature of the regime in Pyongyang and will not be fooled" by it.[158]

The next day, in Senate testimony, Powell branded the DPRK as a "despotic" regime, indicated that the United States might want to revisit the KEDO nuclear reactor deal with North Korea, suggested that reduction of North Korea's enormous conventional army should probably be on the Washington-Pyongyang agenda,[159] and added that North Korea is a "failed society that has to somehow begin opening if it is not to collapse. Once it's opened, it may well collapse anyway."[160]

With this succession of jarringly inconsistent public statements, Powell demonstrated that the new Bush administration did not have a single, coherent voice on North Korea policy. The episode, of course, could be explained. Coming as it did barely six weeks after the president's inauguration, many key foreign policy positions for the incoming administration were still unfilled, and the Bush team had already announced that the United States' North Korea policy was to undergo a thorough "review." Yet today—almost a year and a half later, and over a year after the official completion of that "review," Washington has still not divulged the details or objectives of its North Korea policy.

Washington's attitude toward Pyongyang is unmistakably tougher than that of its predecessor—and the posture has toughened further in the wake of September 11. Washington's attitudes and actions on North Korea, however, often seem disconnected and have sometimes been in direct conflict. Before September 11 and after it, the Bush administration's policy toward North Korea—and thus toward the Korean peninsula as a whole—was in a state of drift, rife with unresolved contradictions but lacking the top level attention that could resolve them. Powell's March 6 protestations notwithstanding, what was clear in the highest levels of the new Bush administration was that Washington did *not* want to continue with North Korea where the Clinton team had left off. U.S. policy had fallen into a system of material rewards for the North Korean regime.

One of these diplomatic dysfunctions has been described as "money for talks."[161] If the DPRK agreed simply to show up at meetings, the United States would announce a new shipments of "humanitarian assistance." More money was available for tangible actions. In 1999, after U.S. intelligence had identified a suspicious underground facility in North Korea that might violate its non-proliferation commitments, the Clinton administration provided at least 500,000 tons of food aid in return for North Korean permission to inspect the site.[162] In the final months of Clinton's term, according to the administration's point-person on North Korea policy, Washington was offering to compensate Pyongyang if it ceased missile exports. (Those negotiations did not fix on a figure, but "several hundred million dollars a year" was viewed within the Clinton administration as a reasonable figure.[163]) As one of Bush's advisors pointedly remarked the week of Kim Dae Jung's Washington visit, "I'm kind of tired of the old pattern where they shoot off a missile and we send them a bucket of wheat."[164]

While relative consensus prevailed on what North Korea policies the Bush administration wished to avoid, there was less uniformity about just what the administration wanted to pursue—or exactly how it should do so. In May 2001, Powell declared that the United States would "re-engage" North Korea "at the time and place of our choosing."[165] Early the next year Powell said instead that the United States would talk with the DPRK "any place, any time, without any preconditions."[166] President Bush announced the formal completion of the North Korea policy review in early June 2001[167]—but the new U.S. approach, alternatively described as "discriminate dialogue"[168] or a "comprehensive approach"[169] was never entirely spelled out.[170] One year later, the Bush administration still did not seem to have worked through its North Korea strategy. In April 2002, Pyongyang indicated it was finally interested in resuming talks with Washington, but in May 2002 a Bush administration official confided to reporters that "there is no consensus in the administration on the way forward" with North Korea.[171] In June 2002, according to a report in the *Washington Post*:

> "Fundamental questions have still not been answered," about how to respond to [North Korea's recent dialogue] overture, said one official involved in the discussions. "The problem is, people are operating from different assumptions. Some people think North Korea is sincere. Some don't. The way forward is not clear."[172]

A few days later, Deputy Secretary of State Richard Armitage reiterated the message of U.S. indecision: "Once we have made up our mind," he assured the Japanese press, "we will of course go to our South Korean and Japanese friends...."[173] (In late July 2002, Secretary of State Colin Powell met briefly and informally with North Korea's foreign minister at the ARF meeting. What this meeting portends for U.S.-DPRK relations remains to be seen.

What, exactly, accounts for this dilatory approach to Korea policy by the Bush administration—a repose on its face curious not only because of the Korean Peninsula's prominence in overall U.S. security strategy, but also because of the administration's purported "assertiveness" and predisposition to "unilateral" action? Three possible explanations may be adduced.

The first is, of course, September 11. With the United States suddenly under attack, and facing the outset of what promised to be a prolonged and wide-ranging war against terrorism, the U.S. government's immediate pre-occupations were with protecting the nation and its assets from additional assaults, readying a military response against the culpable terrorist groups, and building the international diplomatic coalition to facilitate these counterblows. All other foreign policy considerations took second stage. An in-depth re-examination of a Korea policy for the post-September 11 era was an effort that would demand considerable attention from the highest levels of the administration—but their attention was trained elsewhere.

A second possible hypothesis is that the Bush administration may have calculated that the "correlation of forces" (as Leninist strategists once put it) was with it in the Korean Peninsula—and therefore there was no urgent need for executive action. With the rapid and decisive destruction of Al Qaeda forces in Afghanistan and the overthrow of the Taliban regime, America's global military credibility increased palpably; after the mobilization Washington was evidently preparing to deploy against Iraq, its credibility might be expected to weigh that much greater. In South Korea, moreover, the presidential election was on the horizon, and a candidate rather more in sympathy than Kim Dae Jung with the Bush administration's international security attitudes stood a good chance of winning the vote. By this hypothesis, Washington's delay in formulating a North Korea policy reflected in part the implicit judgment that pursuing the administration's preferred course, whatever that might be, would be easier at a later juncture, both because coordination with Seoul would be less onerous and because Pyongyang would take U.S. policy points that much more seriously.

There was a third explanatory factor—this one distinctly less hypothetical than the second. The fact of the matter was that the Bush administration at its highest levels was deeply divided over the appropriate approach to the North Korean problem. Although the new team in Washington was often typecast simply as "conservative" by its domestic and international critics, that smug epithet neglected important distinctions in the philosophies and dispositions of the administration's key decision makers.[174] On the North Korean question, the Bush administration's foreign policy team seemed be split between two camps: those favoring what one scholar termed "hawk engagement"[175] and those favoring regime change.

Proponents of "hawk engagement" held that North Korea's international conduct could be improved, and its menace to the rest of the world reduced, through more intensive diplomatic interaction with the regime—but through an interaction premised upon strict reciprocity, including tangible penalties for adverse DPRK behavior. Advocates of regime change, by contrast, maintained that the DPRK was one of those governments whose commitment to destabilizing activities and dangerous objectives was so fundamental that the regime's conduct could not be reliably ameliorated through ordinary diplomatic modalities; the safer path, to this way of thinking, was to encourage the wholesale replacement of the existing governmental structure. In the aftermath of September 11, it should be noted, regime change came to assume a new prominence in U.S. international security strategy. With Deputy Defense Secretary Paul Wolfowitz's September 13 notification to the world that the United States would be "ending states that sponsor terrorism,"[176] active and even pre-emptive intervention to unseat dangerous governments became a new and central focus of U.S. government security policy and was applied in Afghanistan within a matter of weeks.

In theory, hawk engagement and regime change need not be mutually exclusive strategies. In the face of hostile and unsatisfactory responses to attempts to "engage" a troublesome state, hawk engagement could pave the way for, reinforce, and justify subsequent regime change efforts.[177] In practice, however, the advocates of hawk engagement and regime change seemed to find few common points of departure for a new, robust, North Korea policy. And since neither group managed to attain decisive influence over the formulation of policy, while each maintained a measure of veto power over the other, the result was little North Korea policy at all.

In consequence, America's North Korea policy in the immediate post September 11 period was characterized by a curious admixture of aggressive language and passive response. Despite the administration's insinuation that Pyongyang was not living up to the terms of all its agreements with Washington, and the secretary of state's indication that the U.S. might want to rewrite some of those agreements if it continued in them, the State Department reaffirmed in August 2001 that all existing agreements signed by the DPRK and the United States were valid.[178] Despite the Bush administration's recurrent thematic emphasis of the clear and present dangers posed by missile development in rogue states—North Korea most specifically included—the deputy secretary of state demurred, saying that, "there is nothing in and of itself wrong with that," when it was confirmed, in July 2001, that the DPRK been caught test-firing rocket engines.[179] Even after the president had labeled North Korea part of the "axis of evil" and avowed that "I will not stand by as peril grows closer and closer,"[180] top officials at the State Department volunteered to reporters that the United States did not want to topple the government of Kim Jong Il.[181]

To judge by actions alone, that last claim would have seemed incontestably true—for in the first 18 months of the Bush administration, Washington's only practical interaction with the North Korean state was in subsidizing it. Under the new administration, Washington adhered strictly to the existing interpretation of the "Agreed Framework," and continued to provide Pyongyang will free heavy fuel oil at a tempo of half a million tons a year. The Bush administration also continued the practice of shipping food aid to the DPRK, while expressing "concern[s] about restrictions placed on food aid monitoring,"[182] and it committed over a quarter of a million tons between Bush's inauguration and late June 2002. By performance specifications, Washington's new North Korea policy had much in common with the old one, and no one in the highest levels of the administration seemed prepared to correct that awkward continuity.

But the inescapable corollary of indecision and disarray in North Korea policy was lack of clarity in Washington's security policy toward South Korea—the treaty ally. Accordingly, at the very moment when questions in South Korea were mounting about the purposes and objectives of the U.S. forces stationed in the ROK, Washington was singularly unprepared to answer them.

Pressures for Change

As the year 2002 progresses, it appears as if the Korean peninsula's season of relative calm may be nearing its end. The peninsula's recent period of comparative tranquility was made possible by a most unusual conjuncture of policies on the part of the governments in Seoul, Washington, and Pyongyang. As has been shown, that conjunction is inherently unstable, and therefore should not be expected to endure indefinitely. But as it happens, three events loom on the horizon, any one of which could bring the "peaceful" balance known in Korea in recent years to an immediate end by significantly altering the policies of one or more of the governments involved in this triangular relationship.

In 2003, Pyongyang's self-imposed moratorium on the test-launch of long-range missiles is due to expire. If Pyongyang chooses to use that milestone as the occasion for missile firings, the DPRK's period of relative restraint in its external behavior will have come to an end; Washington and Seoul's postures toward Pyongyang would also correspondingly toughen.

The year 2003 is also the "target date" specified in the Agreed Framework for the completion of the first of two light-water reactors (LWRs) that the KEDO consortium is building for the DPRK in return for a verifiable freeze on its nuclear program, eventual satisfactory IAEA inspections, and ultimate dismantling of existing North Korean nuclear facilities.[183] As of mid-summer 2002, however, the cement for this plant had not yet been poured. Even if construction proceeded smoothly and without interruption, it would be many years before the generators at Kumho could be activated. According to the Agreed Framework document, moreover, the reactors in question will not be built until the DPRK has clarified questions about the government's pre-Framework nuclear activities—and nearly eight years into the Framework, Pyongyang has resisted the IAEA inspections that would supply the needed information. Pyongyang's incentives for averting inspections are apparent. If it were determined that the DPRK had indeed processed the amounts of fissile material that the U.S. intelligence community suspects, international non-proliferation claxons would be sounded—to North Korea's ultimate and obvious disadvantage. If, on the other hand, it were determined that North Korea had never generated enough plutonium to qualify as a nuclear power, U.S. and international security policy could treat the country with considerably less consideration than it has been accorded over the past decade. In all, the particulars of the impasse in the KEDO LWR program provide ingredients for an end to the prevailing quiescence in Pyongyang-Seoul relations.

Both the missile and the LWR problems, however, are conceivably open to deferral, turning as they do on the pleasure of decision-makers in Washington and Pyongyang. The third looming issue in triangular relations cannot be similarly postponed—this is the December 19, 2002, presidential election in the ROK. Upon any reasonable handicapping of that race today, one of two men will emerge as president-elect: Lee Hoi Chang of the GNP or Roh Moo Hyun of the MDP. If Lee is victorious, South Korea's sunshine policy will be finished—and the unstable balance in relations between the three governments will be overturned. North Korea's loathing for Lee is undisguised; North-South relations will most likely move back to the bared-fang *modus operandi* that preceded Kim Dae Jung's accession.

If, on the other hand, Roh should win, U.S.-ROK relations could move into entirely uncharted waters. If President Roh Moo Hyun is as intent upon cultivating good ties with Pyongyang as candidate Roh seemed to be, and if he views the United States as the impediment to inter-Korean reconciliation that his campaign sometimes indicates it to be, the U.S.-South Korean alliance could not help but suffer. In this eventuality, the summer calm of the past several years would come undone—but in a much different manner from the other potential crises driven by impending events in the peninsula, albeit possibly every bit as far-reaching in security implications.

Last year's study argued that it was incumbent upon U.S. and South Korean policymakers to elucidate to their electorates the rationale for their nations' long-term military alliance—the common security objectives of the partnership and the threats it was forged, at great and continuing expense, to overcome. Absent a clear exposition of the alliance's current purpose by South Korean and U.S. leadership, the U.S.-ROK military could not presume continued and unquestioning public support. Over the past year, no such brief has been offered, either in Washington or in Seoul. It is hardly self-evident that the alliance has grown healthier over the interim—or that this inadversion has left Washington and Seoul better equipped to confront the security challenges that could face them in the not-too-distant future.

Endnotes

1   For accounts of perceived "war threats" over the past generation, see William H. Gleysteen, *Massive Entanglement, Marginal Influence: Carter and Korea in Crisis,* Washington, DC: Brookings Institution,1999, and Donald Oberdorfer, *The Two Koreas: A Contemporary History,* New York: Basic Books, 2001.

2   Immanuel Kant, *Perpetual Peace,* New York: Columbia University Press, 1939.

3   James Morrison, "Peace Policy Defended," *Washington Times,* June 18, 2002. The ambassador in question was Yang Sung Chul.

4   "Worldwide Threat Converging Dangers in a Post 9/11 World," testimony of Director of Central Intelligence George Tenet before the Senate Armed Services Committee, March 19, 2002 (as prepared for delivery), <www.cia.gov/cia/public_affairs/speeches/senate_select_hearing_03192002.html >.

5   "'Nothing wrong' with North Korean rocket motor tests: top US official," *Agence France-Presse,* July 6, 2001.

6   National Intelligence Council, *Foreign Missile Developments and the Ballistic Missile Threat through 2015,* December 2001, p. 9, <www.cia.gov/nic/pubs/other_products/unclassifiedballisticmissilefinal.htm>.

7   See Notra Trulock, "Going nuclear in North Korea," *Washington Times,* June 25, 2002.

8   "Bush refuses to certify N. Korea abiding by nuclear deal," *Japan Economic Newswire,* April 2, 2002; "Bush releases 95 million dollars for North Korean nonproliferation", *Agence France-Presse,* April 3, 2002.

9   The other members being Iraq, Iran, "and their terrorist allies." For the text of the speech see "President Delivers State of the Union Address", January 29, 2002, <www.whitehouse.gov/ news/releases/2002/01/20020129-11.html>.

10 To add further ballast to the argument that this "American moment," far from being inherently unstable and transitory, may instead prove to be enduring and "systemically stable." See William C. Wohlforth, "The Stability of a Unipolar World," *International Security,* vol. 24, no. 1 (Summer 1999), pp. 5–41.

11 David Espo, "Bush says nation will fight back, recover from 'acts of war'," *Associated Press,* September 12, 2001.

12 See Department of State, Office of Coordinator for Counterterrorism, "Overview of State Sponsored Terrorism," *Patterns of Global Terrorism 2000,* April 30, 2001, <www.state.gov/s/ct/pgtrpt/2000/2441.htm>.

13 See William Wohlforth's chapter in this volume. See also Leon Aron, "Russia's Choice," *AEI Russian Outlook,* Winter 2002. For a more skeptical reading of Russia's policy in the wake of September 11, see Vladimir Votapek, "Russia and the United States," in Janusz Bugaski, ed., *Toward an Understanding of Russia: New European Perspectives,* New York: Council on Foreign Relations, 2002, pp. 183–209, especially pp. 191–94.

14 See, for example, "US forces should leave South Korea eventually: Russia,"

Agence France-Presse, May 19, 2002.

[15] Dmitry Zaks, "Russia defends North Korea ahead of Bush visit," *Agence France-Presse*, May 20, 2002. On the Korean Peninsula, pre-September 11 Putin government policies were redolent with anti-American mischief. In July 2000, after a trip to Pyongyang, Putin cast himself as a qualified defender of North Korea's missile program, backing the claim that the DPRK's rocket program was intended for "peaceful space research," and promoting an opaque scheme that would have had third countries launch Pyongyang's satellites in return for a moratorium on rocket launches from North Korea. In August 2001, on the occasion of Kim Jong Il's visit to Moscow, Putin signed a DPRK-Russia joint declaration which sympathized with North Korea's call for a U.S. troop pullout from South Korea. Earlier in the year, Putin had also raised the issue of U.S. troop withdrawal with President Kim Dae Jung during his visit to Seoul.

[16] Angela Charlton, "Russia satisfied with U.S. explanations on nuclear strike plan; Iran, N.Korea hit back," *Associated Press*, March 15, 2002.

[17] See, for example, Mari Yamaguchi, "Boat sinks after gunbattle with Japanese coast guard; no sign of survivors," *Associated Press*, December 22, 2001; and "Growing Concern Over Japan's Military Projection," *Korea Times*, December 26, 2001.

[18] *Sankei Shimbun*, February 16, 2002; translated as "US, Japan 'Top Leaders' Likely To Agree To Start Joint Missile Defense Research Talks," FBIS-EAS-2002-0216, February 16, 2002; "Japan, U.S. to hold working-level security talks in April," *Kyodo News Service*, March 17, 2002.

[19] *Sankei Shimbun*, February 17, 2002; translated as "Japan to Support Bush's 'Axis of Evil' Statement at Bilateral Summit," FBIS-EAS-2002-0216, February 17, 2002.

[20] See Eric Heginbotham's and Richard Samuels's chapter in this volume.

[21] Kenneth Pyle, "Japan's Immobilism," *NBR Analysis*, vol. 9, no. 4 (September 1998), p. 23. The very real uncertainties of that period are reflected in Pyle's observation that "if conflict had ensued and American forces had not had access to Japanese bases, Defense Secretary Perry later said, 'it would have been the end of the alliance'."

[22] It should be noted that Japan's present utility in U.S. strategy in East Asia turns not only upon the government's willingness to assist in the forward-deployment of U.S. forces, but also in the Japanese economy's ability to serve as an engine of prosperity for the region and the world. While trends in the former have been guardedly favorable of late, the same can hardly be said about the latter.

[23] "Powell Upbeat on U.S.-PRC Relationship," *China Post*, April 26, 2002.

[24] China has its own worries about Muslim minorities, and is well aware of the security threats that Muslim separatist, radical, or terrorist movements could entail. Moreover, international terrorism could make for serious dislocations in the world economy, on which Beijing may be more dependent than is widely understood. Thomas Rawski's analysis of recent Chinese economic data argues that its growth rate since 1998 is lower than officially claimed. If true, the repercussions for Beijing of a shock to the world economy would be more severe.

[25] Aaron L. Friedberg, "11 September and the Future of Sino-American Relations," *Survival*, vol. 44, no. 1 (Spring 2002), pp. 33–50.

26 *Yonhap News Agency* (Seoul), September 24, 2001; reprinted as "South Korea reports North sent private anti-terrorism message to USA," in *BBC Monitoring Asia Pacific—Political,* September 24, 2001.

27 "DPRK stance towards terrorist attacks on U.S.," *Korea Central News Agency* (hereafter KCNA), September 12, 2001, <www.kcna.co.jp/item/2001/200109/news09/12.htm#2>.

28 Kongdan Oh, "9/11 Terrorism: What It Means for the US and Korea," *International Journal of Korean Unification Studies*, vol. 10, no. 2 (2001), pp. 59–78, especially p. 76.

29 "U.S. imperialists warned not to act rashly," *KCNA*, December 9, 2001, <www.kcna.co.jp/item/2001/200112/news12/09.htm#6>.

30 "DPRK Denounces U.S.'s Retaliatory Attacks on Afghanistan," *KCNA*, October 9, 2001, <www.kcna.co.jp/item/2001/200110/news10/09.htm#10>.

31 For example, *Nodong Sinmun*, May 18, 2002; translated as "DPRK Article Views US Position in 'Long-Term War' in Afghanistan", FBIS-NES-2002-0603, June 10, 2002.

32 For example, "Japan's moves to tighten military alliance with U.S. denounced," *KCNA*, September 25, 2001, <www.kcna.co.jp/item/2001/200109/news09/25.htm#2>.

33 "Strengthening of army called for," *KNCA*, October 28, 2001, <www.kcna.co.jp/item/2001/200110/news10/28.htm#5>.

34 "DPRK Condemns U.S. for Sharply Increasing Military Budget," *Xinhua* (Beijing), February 8, 2002.

35 "North Korea Denounces US Plans for Creating Missile Defence Agency." *BBC Monitoring International Reports*, January 10, 2002.

36 See, for example, "U.S. Is 'Empire of Devil' in 'War Hysteria': Pyongyang Returns Answers to Bush's 'Axis of Evil' Rhetoric," *People's Korea*, February 13, 2002,<www.korea-np.co.jp/pk/175th_issue/ 2002021204.htm>; *Chollima*, May 2002, translated as "DPRK Popular Magazine Chollima Analyzes 'Axis of Evil' Speech," FBIS-NES-2002-0614, June 19, 2002.

37 Pyongyng Broadcasting Station, December 9, 2001, translated as "DPRK Daily Denounces US for Targeting DPRK as 'Next' After Afghanistan," FBIS-EAS-2001-1209, December 12, 2001.

38 For the text, see "President Delivers Graduation Speech at West Point," June 1, 2002, <www.whitehouse.gov/news/releases/2002/06/20020601-3.html>.

39 See *Pyongyang Central Broadcasting Station*, June 17, 2002, translated as "Pyongyang radio slams US anti-terror campaign as cover to conquer world," *BBC Monitoring Asia Pacific —Political,* June 17, 2002; KCNA, June 24, 2002, reprinted as "North Korean paper denounces US strategy based on pre-emptive strikes", *BBC Monitoring Asia Pacific—Political*, June 24, 2002.

40 "N. Korea says it is 'ready enough' for war," *Kyodo News Service*, January 13, 2002.

41 "North Korean Radio Says US President's 'Violent Remarks' Cannot be Overlooked," *BBC Monitoring International Reports*, February 2, 2002.

42 *Nodong Sinmun*, April 2, 2002; translated as "DPRK Special Article Denounces US 'Imperialists' as 'Sworn Enemy'," FBIS-EAS-2002-0405, April 19, 2002.

43 See "Strengthening of army called for," *KNCA*, October 28, 2001, <www.kcna.co.

jp/item/2001/200110/news10/28.htm#5 >; *Nodong Sinmun*, May 16, 2002, translated as "DPRK Political Essay 'Love The Future' Urges Upholding Military First Politics," FBIS-EAS-2002-0518, June 10, 2002; *Minju Choson*, May 19, 2002, translated as "DPRK Stresses Military-First Politics as 'Lifeline' of Socialism," FBIS-EAS-2002-0531, June 7, 2002.

[44] Oh, "9/11 Terrorism: What It Means for the US and Korea," *Journal of Korean Unification Studies*, p. 75.

[45] "South Korea on alert for attacks on US forces," *Agence France-Presse*, September 12, 2001.

[46] "U.S., S. Korean Presidents Vow To Eradicate Terrorism", *Xinhua*, September 19, 2001.

[47] *Digital Chosun Ilbo*, September 15, 2001, reprinted as "ROK Daily Criticizes Idea of N-S Joint Terrorism Statement," FBIS-EAS-2001-0914, September 15, 2001.

[48] *Yonhap*, September 16, 2001, reprinted as "ROK, DPRK Begin Talks; DPRK 'Lukewarm" About Anti-Terrorism Declaration," FBIS-EAS-2001-0916, September 16, 2001.

[49] Suzanne Daley, "For The First Time, NATO Invokes Joint Defense Pact With United States," *The New York Times*, September 13, 2001.

[50] The text of the U.S.-ROK Mutual Defense Treaty is available at <www.yale.edu/ lawweb/avalon/ diplomacy/korea/kor001.htm>. The text of the NATO charter is available at <www.nato.int/docu/basictxt/treaty.htm>.

[51] "Koreans Divided Over US Response to Terrorist Attacks," *Digital Chosun Ilbo*, September 19, 2001.

[52] For a detailed exposition of international public opinion data from the week following the attacks, see Karlyn Bowman, "The World Reacts," *The American Enterprise*, December 2001, p. 60.

[53] *Yonhap*, September 15, 2001, reprinted as "South Korean, US foreign ministers to discuss terrorist attacks, North policy," *BBC Monitoring Asia Pacific—Political,* September 15, 2001. Additionally, the ROK Foreign Minister, in his capacity as chairman of the 56th UN General Assembly, committed himself to expediting a vote on a resolution condemning the terror attacks.

[54] Nicholas Evan Sarantakes, "In the Service of the Pharaoh? The United States and the Deployment of Korean Troops in Vietnam, 1965–1968," *Pacific Historical Review*, vol. 68, no. 3 (August 1999), pp. 425–49. For data on the financial aspects see Woo Jung-en, *Race to the Swift: State and Finance in Korean Industrialization*, New York: Columbia University Press, 1991, pp. 92–97.

[55] *Sisa*, October 25, 2001, partially translated in People's Korea, October 31, 2001, <www.korea-np.co.jp/pk/169th_issue/2001103103.htm>.

[56] *Yonhap*, January 16, 2002, reprinted as "South Korea: New Director of Information Agency Named," *BBC Monitoring International Reports*, January 16, 2002.

[57] Lee Chul Hee, "Defense official cites 'pressure' on troops," *Joongang Ilbo*, May 28, 2002.

[58] Kim Min Bai, "Cheong Wa Dae Denies Combat Troop Request," *Digital Chosun*, May 28, 2002.

[59] Kathy Gannon, "War On Terrorism," *AsianWeek*, September 29, 2001; and

Yonhap, September 29, 2002, reprinted as "North Korean Allegedly Trained Bin Ladin's Followers: ROK News Agency," FBIS-EAS-2001-0929, October 1, 2001.

[60] *Kyonghyang Sinmun*, translated as "ROKG Said To React 'Sensitively' to Reports on DPRK Weapons Seizure in Afghanistan," FBIS-EAS-2001-1220, December 21, 2001.

[61] ROK Bank of Korea, "Gross Domestic Product of North Korea in 2001," May 15, 2002, <www.bok.or.kr/bokis_attach/040524north-gdp(2001).doc>.

[62] See "Inter-Korean Trade Down," *Xinhua*, January 23, 2002, The ROK Unification Ministry places 2001 DPRK exports to South Korea at $176 million, and *Yonhap*, June 26, 2002, reprinted as "North Korean trade increase for third consecutive year—South agency," *BBC Monitoring Asia Pacific—Political*, June 26, 2002. The Korea Trade-Investment Promotion Agency (KOTRA) estimates North Korea's 2001 exports to the rest of the world to have been $650 million. Those two cited sums total $826 million. Assuming North Korea's population was about 23 million, that would make North Korea's calculated per capita export level about $36 in 2001. It is true that North Korea's imports are estimated to have increased since 1998. Those increases, however, have been financed largely by overseas assistance and remain dependent upon such aid flows.

[63] Per capita dollar-denominated exports of goods and services for sub-Saharan countries for 1999 derived from World Bank, *World Development Indicators 2001*, CD-ROM.

[64] "North Korea facing new food crisis, WFP warns," *Deutsche Presse-Agentur*, June 20, 2002.

[65] See John Pomfret, "More N. Koreans Seek Asylum in Beijing," *Washington Post*, June 12, 2002; and Robert Marquand, "Escape from hunger, fear in N. Korea," *Christian Science Monitor*, July 25, 2002.

[66] Yoon, Deok Ryong and Park, Soon Chan, "Capital Needed for North Korea's Economic Recovery and Optimal Investment Policy," *Policy Analysis 01-08*, Korea Institute of International Economic Policy, 2002 (in Korean), cited in Yoon Deok Ryong, "Economic Development in North Korea: A Possible Time Line for North Korean Transformation," in Korea Economic Institute, *Korea's Economy 2002*, Washington, DC: KEIA, 2002, pp. 69–75.

[67] See *Kyongje Yongu*, November 20, 2001, translated as "DPRK Decries Imperialists' Scheme to Control World Through Globalization," FBIS-EAS-2002-0103, January 14, 2002; *Nodong Sinmun*, March 24, 2002, translated as "DPRK Stresses Fight Against Imperialism as Revolutionary Stance," FBIS-EAS-2002-0329, April 5, 2002; and *Minju Choson*, May 7, 2002, translated as "DPRK Calls For Vigilance Against Infiltration of 'Imperialist' Ideas, Culture," FBIS-EAS-2002-0531.

[68] For a summary of proceedings, see "Conference Report: Promoting Cooperation in the Korean Peninsula and Northeast Asia," Institute of Asia-Pacific Studies, Chinese Academy of Social Sciences, Beijing, June 6–8 2002 , <www.keia.org/conference%20full%20reportrev.doc>.

[69] Pyongyang recognizes the tradeoff between guns and butter and officially acknowledges its own choice: "Although our people are leading somewhat difficult daily lives and cannot live in abundance like others, they regard possessing

a powerful military as something as [*sic*] the greatest pride." *Pyongyang Central Broadcasting Station*, April 2, 2002, translated as "Despite 'Somewhat Difficult Daily Lives' North Koreans To Strengthen Military," *BBC Monitoring International Reports*, April 6, 2002.

[70] Reportedly, North Korea's current position is that the IAEA inspections can wait until the year 2005. "IAEA to warn Pyongyang on inspections," *Joongang Ilbo*, June 11, 2002; "Nuclear watchdog to make new bid to see North Korean sites," *Agence France-Presse*, June 18, 2002.

[71] FBIS offers 120 separate North Korean media appearances of SKNDF between September 11, 2001, and this writing (July 1, 2002)—and that is not meant to be an exhaustive list.

[72] *Pyongyang Broadcasting Station*, March 5, 2002, reprinted as "Koreas: North Warns US Forces in South Threat to World Peace," *BBC Monitoring International Reports*, March 10, 2002.

[73] "DPRK Special Article Denounces US 'Imperialists' as 'Sworn Enemy'," FBIS.

[74] Selig Harrison, an American who has been allowed extensive conversations with North Korea's party and military leadership over the course of 30 years of visits to the DPRK, argues that Pyongyang no longer is interested in absorbing and communizing the South. See Selig S. Harrison, *Korean Endgame: A Strategy for Reunification and U.S. Disengagement*, Princeton: Princeton University Press, 2002. His accounts make important and interesting reading, but whether they are convincing turns on one's judgments about the nature of the evidence he adduces. (The problem of North Korea's "strategic deception" was addressed in last year's report.) For now, perhaps the most authoritative insight into the thinking of North Korean leadership on the unification issue comes from the words and actions of Kim Jong Il. In August 2000, he told a visiting media delegation from the ROK that the passage in the party charter calling for the subversion of the South Korean system "can be changed at any time." *Yonhap*, August 13, 2000, reprinted as ""North Korean leader says party charter 'can be changed at any time'," *BBC Monitoring Asia Pacific—Political*, August 13, 2000. Today, two years later, the charter remains unchanged.

[75] Doug Struck, "Koreans Accusatory After Boat is Sunk," *Washington Post*, June 30, 2002.

[76] Since the April 2000 announcement that President Kim would travel to Pyongyang for a June 2000 summit, eleven countries of the Organization for Economic Cooperation and Development have normalized or reestablished their diplomatic ties with the DPRK: Australia (May 2000), the United Kingdom (December 2000), Netherlands (January 2001), Belgium (January 2001), Turkey (January 2001), Canada (February 2001), Spain (February 2001), Germany (March 2001), Greece (March 2001), Luxembourg (March 2001), and New Zealand (March 2001). The European Union announced the normalization of relations with North Korea in May 2001. For a sympathetic assessment of EU policy toward the DPRK, see James Miles, "Waiting North Korea Out," *Survival*, vol. 44, no. 2 (Summer 2002), pp. 37–50.

[77] "Interview with General Secretary Kim Jong Il", June 30, 2001, <http://www.korea-np.co.jp/pk/144th_issue/ 2000072502.htm>.

[78] "General Secretary Kim Jong Il Answers Questions Raised by Itar-Tass," Au-

gust 1, 20001, <www.www.korea-np.co.jp/pk/166th_issue/2001080101.htm>.

[79] "DPRK-Russia Moscow Declaration," *KCNA*, August 5, 2001, <www.kcna.co.jp/contents/20010805.htm#1>.

[80] "North-South Joint Declaration," available on *People's Korea* website, <www.korea-np.co.jp/pk/142th_ issue/2000061501.htm>.

[81] Cited in *Yonhap*, January 10, 2002, reprinted as "ROK's Yonhap: N.K. Demands USFK's Pullout from SK as a Precondition for Dialogue", FBIS-EAS-2002-0110, January 11, 2002.

[82] "North Korea demands 'cancer-like' US troops withdraw from the South," *Agence France-Presse*, April 18, 2002.

[83] *Nodong Sinmun*, May 3, 2002, translated as "DPRK Stresses Importance of 'Fundamental Principles' of Fatherland," FBIS-EAS-0515, May 20, 2002.

[84] "Koreas: North Warns US Forces in South Threat to World Peace."

[85] *Nodong Sinmun*, "DPRK Says Withdrawal of USFK 'Fundamental' for Peace on Korean Peninsula," May 3, 2002, translated as "DPRK Stresses Importance of 'Fundamental Principles' of Fatherland," FBIS-EAS-0515, May 20, 2002.

[86] *Nodong Sinmun*, April 6, 2002, translated as "DPRK Article Urges South Korea To Fight US 'Imperialists' Together," FBIS-EAS-2002-0412, April 19, 2002.

[87] *Nodong Sinmun*, "DPRK Articles Urges South Korea To Fight US 'Imperialists' Together."

[88] *Nodong Sinmun*, March 1, 2002, translated as "DPRK Party Organ Urges Stronger 'Anti-US Struggle' in ROK," FBIS-EAS-2002-0301, March 4, 2002.

[89] *Pyongyang Central Broadcasting Station*, April 2, 2002, translated as "North Korean Paper Urges South to Drive Out US Forces," *BBC Monitoring International Reports*, April 4, 2002.

[90] *Tongil Sinbo*, June 8, 2002, carried in *Choson Ilbo*, June 24, 2002, reprinted as "DPRK Reportedly Urges ROK To 'Unsparingly' Support Strengthening of DPRK Military," FBIS-EAS-2002-0624, June 25, 2002.

[91] Ser Myo Ja, "Kim notes a tendency to peace on peninsula," *Joongang Ilbo*, June 5, 2002.

[92] Francis Fukuyama, *The End of History and the Last Man*, New York: Free Press, 1992.

[93] There is an analogy here between ROK attitudes and those of the Western European democracies—somewhat in contradistinction to those of the American public. For an examination of the European-U.S. distinction, see Robert Kagan, "Power and Weakness" *Policy Review*, no. 113 (June/July 2002).

[94] *Yonhap* News Service, October 9, 2000, reprinted as "ROK's Yonhap: Three Out Of Four Discontent With Current Society," FBIS-EAS-2000-1009, October 10, 2000.

[95] Cited in Samuel S. Kim, "The Korean Peninsula and Northeast Asia Security: US Policy Options," in Michael Kraig and James Henderson, eds., *US Strategies for Regional Security*, Muscatine, Iowa: Stanley Foundation, 2001, p. 60.

[96] William Watts, "Next Generation Leaders In The Republic of Korea: Opinion Survey Report and Analysis", unpublished paper from Potomac Associates, Washington, DC, April 2002.

[97] *Korea Insight* (Korea Economic Institute of America), vol. 4, no. 7 (July 2002), p. 4.

[98] Hwang Soon-hyun, "Moody's Gives D grade to Korean banks," *Digital Chosun Ilbo*, June 24, 2002.

[99] "ROK 38th in Global Freedom Ranking," *Korea Times*, June 26, 2002.

[100] For more details see James Gwartney and Robert Lawson, *Economic Freedom of the World: 2002 Annual Report*, Vancouver, BC: Fraser Institute, 2002, <www.freetheworld.com>.

[101] Transparency International, *2001 Corruption Perceptions Index*, <www.global corruptionreport.org/download/data_and_research.pdf>.

[102] Damien McElroy and Roger du Mars, "Corruption stains the land of the white envelope," *Sunday Telegraph* (London), June 23, 2002, p. 5.

[103] "President Kim Draws Praise, Blame on Occasion of Fourth Anniversary," *Korea Herald*, February 25, 2002.

[104] Seo Yoona, "President Apologizes for Sons' Misdeeds," *Digital Chosun Ilbo*, June 21, 2002.

[105] "President facing political crisis," *Korea Herald*, April 24, 2002.

[106] "President Kim Draws Praise, Blame on Occasion of Fourth Anniversary," *Korea Herald*, February 25, 2002.

[107] In a survey in autumn 2001, for example, only 38 percent of respondents said the president was "doing a good job"—but the corresponding tally for Lee was 33 percent. *Kyonghyang Sinmun,* October 7, 2001, translated as "ROK Opinion Poll Shows Falling Approval Rating for President," FBIS-EAS-2001-1008, October 9, 2001.

[108] *Digital Chosun Ilbo*, July 7, 2002, reprinted as "Poll: 'Most' South Koreans Consider Sea Clash as DPRK's 'Premeditated Provocation'," FBIS-EAS-2002-0707, July 8, 2002.

[109] Patrick E. Tyler, "South Korea Takes Russia's Side in Dispute over American Plan for Missile Defense," *The New York Times*, February 28, 2001.

[110] "Kim Addresses U.S. concerns over missile defense stance," *Korea Herald*, March 9, 2001.

[111] For example, "Sunshine At Stake," *Korea Herald*, March 15, 2001.

[112] David E. Sanger, "Bush Tells Seoul Talks With North Won't Resume Now," *The New York Times*, March 7, 2001.

[113] David E. Sanger, "It's North Korea. Go Figure," *The New York Times*, March 11, 2001.

[114] Doug Struck, "U.S. Warnings Worry Seoul," *Washington Post*, December 19, 2001

[115] Kim Hyung Jin, "Parliamentary session paralyzed after MDP lawmaker lambasted opposition leader Lee," *Korea Herald*, February 19, 2002. The lawmaker in question was subsequently moved to retract his words.

[116] *Chosun Ilbo*, April 9, 2002, translated as "DPRK Leader Reportedly Planed To Visit ROK in Mar 2001," FBIS-EAS-2002-0409, April 11, 2002.

[117] *Yonhap*, December 4, 2001, reprinted as "Diplomatic 'Source' Says DPRK-US Dialogue Not 'Priority' for US," FBIS-NES-2001-1205, December 6, 2001.

[118] *Korea Times*, January 17, 2002, reprinted as "ROKG Official: ROK To Ask US To 'Tone Down' Anti-DPRK 'Rhetoric' at Summit," FBIS-EAS-2002-117, January 18, 2002.

[119] Kim Ji Ho, "U.S. human rights report casts further clouds over relations with

North Korea," *Korea Herald*, March 6, 2002.

[120] Shim Jae Yun, "Seoul Urges Washington to Take NK Off Terror List," *Korea Times*, April 21, 2002.

[121] Oh Young Jin, "ROK Wants US to Talk Directly to Kim Jong-il," *Korea Times*, June 26, 2002.

[122] *Yonhap*, June 16, 2002, translated as "ROK Opinion Poll Shows Majority Support for 'Sunshine Policy'," FBIS-EAS-2002-0616, June 18, 2002.

[123] Such emotions are never far from the surface in Korean politics. In part, this is due to Korea's legacy as a playground for great power politics in the late nineteenth and early twentieth centuries. It also speaks to an earlier history: Korea's subservience to China in the old East Asian order of tributary relations. To this day, Pyongyang uses the term, *sadaejuii*, awkwardly translated as "flunkeyism" , for that tributary system as a term of opprobrium for the Koreans it accuses of working for the interests of foreign countries. Unlike most epithets from the North, this one evidently still stings in the South.

[124] *Pyongyang Central Broadcasting Station*, April 11, 2002, translated as "DPRK Cites ROK Student Poll on Anti-US Sentiment, Desire for Reunification," FBIS-EAS-2002-0411, April 15, 2002.

[125] *Joongang Ilbo*, February 27, 2002, reprinted as "ROK People 'Wondering If US Is True Ally', Skating Call Biggest Reason for Worsening Opinion," FBIS-CHI-2002-0227, February 28, 2002.

[126] "Six in 10 Koreans say Bush's 'Axis of Evil' Remark Inappropriate," *Korea Times*, February 10, 2002.

[127] Kim Young Hie, "U.S., not the North, is a barrier," *Joongang Ilbo*, May 10, 2002.

[128] See Jo Hui Cheon, "Government to Crackdown on Anti US Protests," *Digital Chosun Ilbo*, June 7, 2002; Son Min Ho, "Protests fall on deaf ears," *Joongang Ilbo*, June 10, 2002; Joo Sung-Goo, "A Disgraceful Celebration," *Korea Herald*, June 12, 2002.

[129] *Korea Herald*, April 3, 2002, reprinted as "ROK MDP's No Mu-hyun Refutes Accusations on USFK Issue, Expresses Support for USFK," FBIS-EAS-2002-0402, April 3, 2002.

[130] "Candidate speaks his mind on R.O.K.-U.S. relations," *Joongang Ilbo*, April 24, 2002.

[131] *Chosun Ilbo*, April 29, 2002, reprinted as "ROK MDP Presidential Candidate No 'More Progressive' Than President Kim," FBIS-EAS-2002-0429, April 30, 2002.

[132] "Roh's Aide Urged US Not to Meddle in Election ," *Korea Times*, May 2, 2002; "Roh Sacks Aide over Controversial Remarks On U.S." *Korea Herald*, May 2, 2002.

[133] In South Korea, indeed, political parties often seem to enjoy the half life of certain rare elements in the periodic table. The constant state of flux is illustrated by the fact that President Kim's current ruling party is not the same one under which he was elected to the presidency.

[134] For Lee's view on North Korea policy and the US-ROK military alliance, see Lee Hoi Chang, "Korea at the Crossroads: The Challenges Ahead," lecture delivered conjointly to the Heritage Foundation and the American Enterprise

Institute, January 23, 2002; <www.heritage.org/shorts/20020124korea.html>.

[135] Hong Yeong Lim, "Koreans See Themselves As Moderates," *Digital Chosun Ilbo*, May 1, 2002.

[136] "Korean Journalists Favor Noh as Next President, Survey Shows," *Korea Herald*, January 7, 2002. In this survey, 62 percent of the journalists questioned reported that they favored Roh.

[137] In 2000, for example, North and South Korea announced that President Kim would be visiting Pyongyang on April 11—three days before the ROK's National Assembly elections. Similarly, on September 2, 2001, ROK Unification Minister Lim Dong Won was scheduled to face a parliamentary no-confidence vote over the alleged failure of his sunshine policy, the day before Pyongyang suddenly offered to resume inter-Korean talks. It may be noted that Pyongyang's actions did not influence events in the direction the DPRK might have hoped: Kim's party lost seats in the elections, and Lim failed the no-confidence vote.

[138] In Pyongyang's estimate, Lee is "human scum fawning on his U.S. master," "a nation-selling traitor," and is under a "political death sentence." See, *inter alia*, *KCNA*, "Reckless remarks of 'GNP' president condemned," January 21, 2002; *Nodong Sinmun*, April 6, 2002, translated as "DPRK Decries Grand National Party for Basic Policy Line Towards North," FBIS-EAS-2002-0412, April 16, 2002; *Nodong Sinmun*, June 7, 2002, translated as "DPRK Says 'No Future' for Traitor to Nation Ti Hoe-ch'ang," FBIS-EAS-2002-0617, June 24, 2002; and *Pyongyang Central Broadcasting Station*, June 18, 2002, translated as "North Korea blames South politician for blocking joint declaration," *BBC Monitoring Asia Pacific—Political*, June 18, 2002.

[139] See *Chosun Ilbo*, May 2, 2002, translated as "Age Gap in Approval Ratings for Presidential Candidates Viewed," FBIS-EAS-2002-0521, May 23, 2002.

[140] Kim Hyung Jin, "S. Korean Lawmakers See Japan As No. 1 Threat To Regional Security," *Korea Herald*, February 25, 2002.

[141] *Digital Chosun Ilbo*, December 2, 2001, reprinted as "ROK Poll Shows Local Terrorism Concerns, Mistrust of DPRK Anti-Terror Stand," FBIS-EAS-2001-1202, December 3, 2001.

[142] *Dong-a Ilbo*, April 26, 2002, translated as "Background of ROK's Possible Drop of Term 'Main Enemy', Repercussions Viewed," FBIS-EAS-2002-0426, April 29, 2002; *Digital Chosun Ilbo*, April 28, 2002, reprinted as "ROKG Urged To Consider Military Concerns To Decide on 'Main Enemy'," FBIS-EAS-2002-0428, April 29, 2002; Lee Chul Hee, "No paper, so no need to identify an 'enemy'," *Joongang Ilbo*, May 25, 2002; "Sunshine Policy Ousts White Paper," *Korea Times*, May 25, 2002.

[143] *Yonhap*, August 10, 2001, reprinted as "South Korea's defence budget drops to 2.7 percent of GDP in 2001," *BBC Monitoring Asia Pacific—Political*, August 10, 2001.

[144] International Institute for Strategic Studies (IISS), *The Military Balance 2001–2002*, London: IISS, 2001, Table 34.

[145] Don Kirk, "South Korea Launches Missile In Its First Test Since Last Year," *The New York Times*, November 23, 2001; and James Risen, "South Korea Seen Trying To Extend Range of Missiles," *The New York Times*, November 14, 1999.

[146] IISS, *The Military Balance 2001–2002*, p. 198.

[147] "Shipbuilding sector booming with new orders," *Korea Herald*, December 7, 2001.

[148] "Seoul to Begin Building 7,000-Ton Aegis-Class Destroyer Next Year," *Korea Times*, October 23, 2000.

[149] "Seoul to Select Contractor for Destroyer Project in May," *Korea Times*, December 27, 2001.

[150] Prasun K. Sengupta, "Force projection with naval helicopters," *Asian Defense Journal*, January 2002, pp. 38–42.

[151] "Seoul to Begin Building 7,000-Ton Aegis-Class Destroyer Next Year," *Korea Times*, October 23, 2000.

[152] Although some U.S. analysts believe that South Korean forces are capable of deterring a conventional military attack from the DPRK on their own. See, for example, Bruce Bechtol, Jr., "Who Is Stronger? A Comparative Analysis on the Readiness and Capabilities of the North and South Korean Militaries," *International Journal of Korean Unification Studies*, vol. 10, no. 2 (2001), pp. 1–26. See also Michael O'Hanlon, "Stopping a North Korean Invasion: Why Defending South Korea is Easier than the Pentagon Thinks," *International Security*, vol. 22, no. 4 (Spring 1998), pp. 135–70.

[153] Charles Wolf, Jr., *Asian Economic Trends and their Security Implications*, Santa Monica, Calif.: RAND, 2000, <www.rand.org/publications/mr/mr1143>.

[154] *Yonhap*, January 8, 2002, reprinted as "President Kim defends presence of US forces in South Korea," January 8, 2002.

[155] "South Korean President Kim Dae Jung to meet with Bush," *Deutsche Presse-Agentur*, March 6, 2001.

[156] *Yonhap*, March 7, 2001, translated as "US Sec of State Powell's Remarks on DPRK Policy Viewed," FBIS-EAS-2001-0307, March 12, 2001.

[157] David E. Sanger, "Bush Tells Seoul Talks With North Won't Resume Now," *The New York Times*, March 7, 2001.

[158] "Bush and Kim have 'frank' talks on North Korea," *Deutsche Presse-Agentur*, March 7, 2001.

[159] Ben Barber, "Powell wants a reduction in size of N. Korea's million-man army," *Washington Times*, March 9, 2001.

[160] "U.S. in no hurry to develop NKorean policy—Powell." *AFX-Asia,* March 8, 2001.

[161] The term is Marcus Noland's. Such a pattern was denied by the Clinton administration; Noland documented it, however, in his *Avoiding the Apocalypse: The Future of the Two Koreas*, Washington, DC: Institute for International Economics, 2001, p. 186.

[162] Here again, the Clinton administration declared there was no *quid pro quo*— but Pyongyang insisted Washington had agreed to pay "an inspection fee." See Nicholas Eberstadt, *The End of North Korea*, Washington, DC: AEI Press, 1999.

[163] Michael R. Gordon, "How Politics Sank Accord on Missile with North Korea," *The New York Times*, March 6, 2001.

[164] Sanger, "It's North Korea. Go Figure," *The New York Times*.

[165] *Yonhap*, May 15, 2001, reprinted as "ROK's Yonhap: U.S. to Resume Talks with N.K. after Policy Review: Powell," FBIS-EAS-2001-0515, May 16, 2001.

[166] U.S. Department of State, International Information Programs, "Powell Says Iraq Must Allow Arms Inspections," February 17, 2002, <http://usinfo.state.gov/regional/nea/iraq/text/0217pwl.htm>.

[167] Jane Perlez, "U.S. Will Restart Wide Negotiations With North Korea," *The New York Times*, June 7, 2001.

[168] *Joongang Ilbo*, May 17, 2001, reprinted as "ROK Paper Views US Policy on 'Discriminative Dialogue' with DPRK," FBIS-EAS-2001-0517, May 21, 2001.

[169] *Yonhap*, June 8, 2001, reprinted as "ROK's Yonhap: Summary of ROK Foreign Minister's Interview With Reporters After Holding Meeting With Powell", FBIS-EAS-2001-0608, June 11, 2001.

[170] As Larry Niksch observed, Bush's June 6, 2001, statement on the conclusion of the North Korea policy review "sets out priorities and objectives but omits the crucial issue of strategy." Larry Niksch, "How To Assess Bush's North Korea Policy," *Chosun Ilbo*, November 3, 2001. The need to elucidate the policy and strategy was vitiated by Pyongyang's refusal to enter the proposed talks.

[171] Nicholas Kralev, "Officials mixed on renewing dialogue: weigh 'sincerity' of Pyongyang," *The Washington Times*, May 24, 2001.

[172] Peter Slevin, "What To Say To North Korea?" *Washington Post*, June 3, 2002.

[173] Oh Young Hwan, "U.S. seen settling its policy on North," *Joongang Ilbo*, June 6, 2002.

[174] For a study that appreciated some of these differences, and their potential ramifications for East Asia policy, see Andrew Scobell, "Crouching Korea, Hidden China: Bush Administration Policy Toward Pyongyang and Beijing," *Asian Survey*, vol. 42, no. 2 (March/April 2002), pp. 343–68.

[175] The term was coined by Professor Victor Cha of Georgetown University. See his "Korea's Place in the Axis," *Foreign Affairs*, vol. 81, no. 3 (May/June 2002), pp. 79–92, and his earlier "The Rationale for 'Enhanced' Engagement of North Korea," *Asian Survey*, vol. 39, no. 6 (November/December 1999), pp. 845–66.

[176] Elisabeth Bumiller and Jane Perlez, "Bush and Top Aides Proclaim Policy of 'Ending' States that Back Terror," *The New York Times*, September 14, 2001.

[177] Hawk engagement and regime change advocates might also be able to settle on mutually agreeable strategic objectives, such as "regime transformation."

[178] *Joongang Ilbo*, August 10, 2001, translated as "Anonymous US Official Says DPRK-US Communique Still Valid in Bush Administration," FBIS-EAS-2001-0810, August 13, 2001.

[179] *Yonhap*, July 10, 2001, translated as "ROK Yonhap Article Notes US 'Soft' Attitude to DPRK," FBIS-EAS-2001-0710, July 13, 2001.

[180] Michael R. Gordon, "Broadening Of 'Doctrine'," *The New York Times*, January 30, 2002.

[181] Zeno Park, "South Korean Presidential Envoy to Leave for Pyongyang Next Week," *Agence France-Presse*, March 28, 2002.

[182] "US gives 100,000 tons of food aid to North Korea," *Agence France-Presse*, June 7, 2002.

[183] The Agreed Framework is available on the KEDO website, <http://kedo.org/pdfs/agreedframework.pdf>.

RUSSIA

William C. Wohlforth

After the September 11, 2001, terrorist attacks against New York and Washington, Russian President Vladimir Putin gathered 21 leading Russian politicians to his Kremlin office to solicit their views about Russia's options. One advocated support for the Taliban, two supported siding with the United States, and the rest argued that Russia ought to remain strictly neutral. Having heard them out in silence, Putin thanked them for their advice and declared his intention to offer unconditional support to the U.S.-led coalition against terrorism. Once the president had made his views clear, the assembled guests who had expressed opposition to the pro-American course fell quickly and insincerely into line.[1]

This story captures a pervasive view of Russia's new geopolitical stance in world affairs: the shift occurred after September 11, it represents a fundamental break with Russia's previous strategy, and its fate hinges for the time being on one man's vision and political skills. If this view is right, significant changes in Russia's behavior in Asia might follow. At a general level, the age-old uncertainty about Russia's true geopolitical identity might finally be resolved in favor of Europe. More practically, Moscow might be more inclined to alter its relationships with China, India,

William Wohlforth is Associate Professor of Government at Dartmouth College. He is grateful to Richard Ellings, Aaron Friedberg, James Wertsch, Michael Wills, and Enders Wimbush for their helpful comments on earlier drafts, and to Jocelyn Roberts and Loren Runyon for research assistance.

Japan, Korea, and Iran in ways that meet with favor in western capitals. The turn to the West might also produce a different and more pliable Russian partner in the South Caucasus and Central Asia—one that is less competitive and more focused on the economic bottom line.

This view is popular and accords superficially with the evidence, but it misses much of the real story. This chapter shows that what is driving the new approach is not an imagined choice between East and West—which has been and will continue to be driven largely by hard geographical and economic realities—but rather Russians' more forthright recognition of their country's post-imperial power and interests. Indeed, the key to understanding Russian strategy over the past decade and for the next decade and longer is that imperial retrenchment takes a long time. The loss of formal sovereignty over former imperial territories is just the beginning. Disengagement from areas long under imperial rule and management of the resulting security and economic challenges are anguishing, often chaotic, and always lengthy processes. Adjustment to a new and humbler international role is never swift or smooth. For an empire that was not defeated and dismembered in war, the proper measure of time for imperial retrenchment is a generation.[2] What is new and important about Putin is what he represents: the first post-collapse generation in leadership and its promise of a more effective post-imperial grand strategy.

This chapter proceeds in four sections. The first analyzes the key background cause of Moscow's strategic reappraisal, the interaction between Russia's ongoing decline and its hierarchy of strategic objectives. The second assesses the strategic interactions that brought this underlying cause to the fore, the failure of the "multipolar" strategy Russia was pursuing before September 11. These two sections provide the critical context for the third, which tracks Moscow's strategic shift, showing that the case for an adjustment had been building since 2000, and, indeed, that the Putin team had begun to engineer it well before September 11. The final section sets forth the trajectory Russia's Asian strategy is most likely to follow over the next decade.

The Realities Behind Russia's Asia Policy

Much of the existing literature on Russian foreign policy has been marked by wild gyrations in response to events. The Russian elite's anguished reactions to NATO's campaign against Serbia over Kosovo, for example, convinced many analysts both in Moscow and abroad that Russia had irrevocably chosen an anti-western—especially anti-American—geopolitical stance.[3] This was close to the conventional wisdom until Putin's post-September 11 support for the U.S. campaign against terror, when the op-

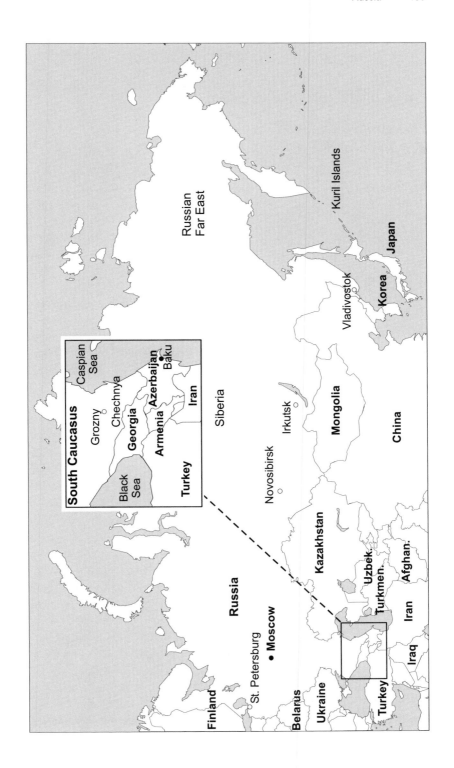

posite view suddenly came to the fore. It is impossible to read this literature without concluding that much research on Russian strategy has suffered from too much focus on Russian elite commentary as opposed to
close analysis of underlying constraints.

Decline

Russia has experienced the greatest peacetime decline of any major power
in history. The Soviet Union entered a period of relative economic decline
beginning in 1975. Decline accelerated in the 1980s, and in the 1990s it
reached near catastrophic proportions. This quarter century of nearly un-
interrupted decline, with all the anguished acceptance of brutal trade-offs
it has imposed, has been the single most important driver of Russian international behavior.[4] Moreover, relative decline will continue to frame Russian strategy in Asia and overall for many years to come, even if the Russian economy continues to grow in absolute terms.

In 2001 Russia's GDP amounted to 9,041 billion rubles, which works
out to $309 billion at the official rate of exchange or $1,235 billion according to the World Bank's purchasing power parity estimate.[5] Even the more
generous estimates place Russia's GDP at about the size of Brazil's, or one-
ninth that of the United States' and one-quarter of China's. Even if Russia
averages steady six percent annual average economic growth, the gap
between the size of its economy and those of the countries of the Organization for Economic Cooperation and Development countries will continue
to widen in the short-term (unless the rich countries enter a Japan-scale
recession). The gap with China will probably widen even faster. Thus, even
if Russia can sustain the economic recovery begun in 1999, which most
economists doubt, it will still decline relative to most other players in Asia
(with the possible exception of Japan) and globally.

Russia's decline transcends economic indices to encompass a demographic meltdown (the population is shrinking by 750,000 per year), a public health crisis, the catastrophic degradation of the environment, an educational system in crisis, and the systematic breakdown of social and physical infrastructure throughout the country.[6] Any one of these would be a
headline-grabbing crisis in a stable, rich country. In combination, these
multiple crises will present impoverished Russia and its comparatively weak
state with gargantuan challenges for decades to come. Even if Russia sus-
tains respectable rates of economic growth, its population will continue to
decline and age and it will face the daunting economic costs of today's
deep and well-documented social, institutional, and infrastructural crises.

Russia's relative military power will continue to decline as well. Between 1992 and 1998, Russia experienced what was probably the steepest

peacetime decline in military spending by any major power in history.[7] Even after the defense budget increases began in 1999, outlays in 2000 remained less than 40 percent of those in 1992. Weapons procurement declined even more dramatically after 1991, and by 2000 only 20 percent of Russia's operational weapons stocks were modern, compared to 60–80 percent in NATO countries.[8] Maintenance and training are dismal; personnel problems are dire and getting worse.[9] Most important, to date nothing serious has been done to advance real military or defense industrial reform.[10] Thus far, the policy appears to have been one of malign neglect—let the military self-destruct until a more propitious moment arrives to begin to construct a modern armed force from the rubble. Initial indications are that Putin is continuing the previous policy, but even if real military reform is in the works, it is a tremendous task that will demand further reductions in forces long before real capabilities increase.

Ultimately, Russia faces a tough trade-off between reform, which entails increased budgetary outlays for fewer professional soldiers, and weapons modernization, which entails increased budgetary outlays for developing new-generation arms. Even if Russia opts for the latter, which is favored by the top brass and is the fastest way to make Russia look stronger on paper (though, given poor training, probably not in practice), the current estimate is that the money will not be available until 2008–10 at the earliest.[11] Moreover, even if economic growth is robust and substantially increased defense spending is forthcoming, the new money is unlikely to go to increased purchases of existing weaponry, most of which is already outdated compared to NATO systems, but rather into researching and developing new systems.[12] Hence, even under optimistic assumptions is it very unlikely that absolute Russian military capability can increase before 2010. Meanwhile, however, the military capabilities of all Russia's potential great power rivals in Asia—China, Japan, and the United States—are increasing rapidly. Hence, Russia faces the prospect of continued relative decline in conventional military power both globally and in Asia.

In short, even in classical realist terms that ignore economic interests, Russia faces every incentive to avoid alienating any other great power—east, west, or south. Historically, there is only one clear case of any major power choosing to initiate a rivalry with another great power from a position of economic weakness comparable to what Russia now faces relative to Japan and China, to say nothing of the United States: Japan's famously ill-fated decision to take on the United States, which occurred when it accounted for only one-fifth of U.S. GDP.[13] By favorable purchasing power parity estimates, Russia today produces roughly one-fourth China's or Japan's GDP, and one-ninth of America's.

Table 6.1. Russia's Military Decline in Asia

	1993	2001
The Pacific Fleet		
Submarines	66	10
Nuclear ballistic missile	20	5
Nuclear non-ballistic missile	9	2
Other nuclear fueled	17	3
Other non-nuclear fueled	20	0
Principal surface combatant vessels	49	10
Cruisers	14	1
Destroyers	7	7
Frigates	28	2
Other surface ships	340	99
Naval aviation	319	81
Combat aircraft	220	55
Armed helicopters	99	26
Ground Forces in Siberian, Transbaykal and Far Eastern Military Districts[a]		
Divisions[b]	52	19
Tank	7	2
Motorized infantry	35	12
Machine gun/artillery	7	4
Artillery	3	1

Source: International Institute for Strategic Studies, *The Military Balance, 1993–1994* and *2000–2001*, London: Oxford University Press, 1994, 2001. Notes: a) In 1999, the Transbaykal and Siberian Military Districts were combined into one Siberian Military District; b) The number of sub-divisional units increased between 1993 and 2001, but not enough to compensate for the general decline in the number of divisions.

Geography dictates that Russia be an Asian country, but not necessarily an Asian power. As Table 6.1 shows, even in quantitative terms, Russia's military decline in Asia has been precipitous. Historically, Russia has only managed to act in Asia as a great power when China was weak and when Russian governments have been willing and able to devote the fantastic resources that a real strategic presence in the East demands.[14] Long, expensive, and slow transportation lines, the North-South flow of rivers, soil quality, problematic coastal geography, and, most important, the inhospitable climate make it very expensive to deploy and maintain a significant strategic presence in Russia's far eastern and south-eastern provinces. The two historical periods in which Russia seriously endeavored to overcome these obstacles—the late-Tsarist and Soviet eras—were short-lived. In both periods, Russia's status as an Asian great power rested mainly on military capabilities; these capabilities themselves rested on an extremely tenuous material base; and the effort strained Russia to the breaking point, contributing in both cases to imperial overstretch and collapse. The conditions that facilitated those bids for Asian great power status do not apply today and certainly will not apply for the next 10 to 15 years.

The Hierarchy of Strategic Objectives

Like all states, Russia's interests encompass security, prestige, and welfare. The fundamental question for Russians remains how to balance among those objectives. For the last decade, that question has been answered for Moscow by the exigencies of precipitous decline.

Russian governments and elites overwhelmingly do not believe that traditional security threats from other great powers are the major concern now or for the policy relevant future, if for no other reason than their confidence in existential nuclear deterrence. Russia's two post-Soviet presidents (as well as the last Soviet one); all its defense ministers, foreign ministers, chiefs of staff, and national security advisors; and all of its official doctrines on national security, military policy, and foreign policy have stated unequivocally that the territorial conquest of Russia by the United States or any other major power is not a concern on the policy relevant horizon.[15] Threats from regional powers—Turkey featured in this role in the mid-1990s—have also been discounted in recent years. The trend over the last decade has generally favored increased emphasis on other threats, such as secessionism, demographic decline, health and environmental decay, drug smuggling, and terrorism.

Nevertheless, long-term threats from other great powers do concern Russian officials. America's unrivalled primacy in the scales of interstate power is worrisome to Moscow. While it may not portend the loss of sovereignty via old-style territorial conquest, it does threaten Russia's autonomy and prestige. Taken individually, U.S. policies on missile defense, NATO expansion, Iran/Iraq, the Caspian Basin, and Central Asia do not threaten Russia's core security, but together they are troubling indicators of what Washington can do—and what it might do in the future if the trend toward unipolarity continues.[16] Moreover, increased power gives the United States increased leverage on many issues, which constrains Russia's room to maneuver.

The other great power that figures seriously in Russian threat assessments is China. Indeed, some Russian strategists recognize that over the long term China presents a more serious land-power challenge than the United States.[17] Notwithstanding its military successes in Iraq, Kosovo, and Afghanistan, there is little evidence that the United States will have the capability or intention to take and hold large swaths of territory in Asia. The only state that can conceivably generate that kind of power is China.

Given continued economic growth and modernization, China will have the option to become Asia's most formidable land power.[18] Yet at the same time, China is a prime client for Russian arms and it appears to Moscow as the best partner in countering the near-term problem of U.S. unipolarity.

After security, the second priority is prestige or international status. The Russian political elite's well-known affection for international prestige is alive and well. It has its roots mainly in history (St. Petersburg and Moscow played the roles of great powers for over three centuries), size (Russia has been the largest polity on earth for most of the last 400 years), and location (situated in central Eurasia, even an economically weak Russia is in some sense a "global power" that can affect the strategic desiderata of numerous crucial regions). Russians are united on the need to prevent the further erosion of Russia's prestige and to create the conditions for the country's reemergence as a full-fledged great power. Concern over international prestige is also a powerful tool in Russian domestic politics. Sensitivity to this issue is stronger in Russia than it is elsewhere if for no other reason than the trauma inflicted by the country's precipitous decline over the past quarter-century. Moreover, national prestige is the ubiquitous and sometimes potent ideology of the military establishment, which has suffered a decade of humiliation, defeat, and downsizing. Any Russian government—even the most pragmatic—can ill afford to ignore the collective self-esteem of the elite it wishes to govern.

The third strategic priority is modernization: namely, the rejuvenation of Russia's economy and the creation of the institutions necessary for its continued growth. Rhetorically, modernization was already a high priority when Leonid Brezhnev and his sclerotic successors held sway in the late 1970s and early 1980s. By the time Mikhail Gorbachev was selected party leader, the pent-up demand to take real action had become critical. The failure of Gorbachev's modernization effort led to Russia's subsequent drive to modernize via liberalization. The meager results attained thus far have only strengthened the modernization imperative. While some domestic factions may question whether liberalization is the best route, none questions the basic modernization imperative. Given 25 years of national decline, no Russian government can ignore the overpowering need to reverse the trend and create the conditions for sustained growth.

Debates about Russian foreign policy, both inside the country and abroad, center on the nature and strength of trade-offs among these priorities and their proper ordering overall and on specific issues. While there is no simple answer to this question that is true for all policies in all regions, a general trend is evident: economic decline has driven redefinitions of Russia's security and prestige interests. Overall, the more Russians recognize the extent of their country's decline, the more importance they place on the modernization imperative and the more inclined they are incrementally to scale back their expectations for international status and to pare down their security agenda. Indeed, the shift from the baseline multipolar strategy to Putin's pragmatic accommodation with the United States is just the latest instance of this dynamic.

The Baseline: Russia's "Multipolar" Policy

The key to understanding Russian foreign policy is that perceptions of power have consistently lagged behind real decline. The first wrenching intellectual adjustment to decline occurred in the late 1980s, as the Soviet leadership realized that it could not sustain its alliance system and so could not end the Cold War on equitable terms. Still, from roughly 1989 until 1993 Moscow acted as if it had the power to sustain bipolarity. That is, even after the formal loss of the outer and inner empires, Russians still acted as though their country remained a superpower—inferior to the United States, to be sure, but well above all the rest. Moscow's first swing to the West under Boris Yeltsin in 1991–93 thus took place under the optimistic assumption of Moscow's continued superpower standing.[19] The second agonizing reappraisal came in 1992–94, as Russians realized that the distribution of power had undergone a massive shift, leaving the United States as the sole remaining superpower.

As this realization set in, Russian leaders and elite commentators began to speak incessantly of the dangers of a unipolar world and the need to take action to create or preserve multipolarity. By the mid-1990s, there appeared to be an elite and official consensus on this approach.[20] At the global level Moscow presented itself as the key organizer of a "multipolar" coalition to rein in U.S. power. As prime minister, Yevgeny Primakov's tenure at the helm of Russian foreign policy inaugurated a parade of ostensibly anti-U.S. diplomatic combinations: the "European troika" of France, Germany, and Russia; the "special relationship" between Germany and Russia; the "strategic triangle" of Russia, China, and India; and, most important, the "strategic partnership" between China and Russia. At the same time, Moscow sought to sustain a special relationship with Iran, buttressed by exports of nuclear technology and arms. Closer to home in the "near abroad," Russian officials insisted that, although the formal sovereignty of the other former Soviet republics should be respected, Russia's interests demanded a sphere of influence in the former Soviet territory.

This strategic approach is the baseline against which to assess Putin's post-September 11 tilt toward the West. A great many analysts in both Russia and the West—and even some officials—took the geopolitical language used to describe this strategy at face value. They believed that Moscow genuinely was on course to become the linchpin in a new Eurasian anti-hegemonic coalition that would reorder world politics and end America's unipolar moment.[21] Viewed in that light, the strategic choice to bandwagon with Washington appears to be a watershed reversal of historic proportions. In fact, this view is not so much wrong as exaggerated. Russia's multipolar strategy was far subtler (and somewhat less coherent) than the language with which policymakers and pundits tended to describe it.

The Baseline Strategy in East and South Asia

The language Primakov, Foreign Minister Igor Ivanov, and other Russian officials used to describe their policy was misleading on two counts. First and most important is the plain fact that Russia never counterbalanced U.S. power—neither globally nor in Asia. Balancing power involves taking specific actions alone or in concert with others that promise to provide some counterweight to America's overweening capabilities—actions, moreover, that would not have been taken if the United States had not been so powerful. The most reliable way to balance power is to build up one's own capabilities. Needless to say, Russia's multipolar strategy did not entail any such "internal balancing." Russia has not increased its own military capabilities to check the United States' unrelenting accretion of power. As noted, military spending declined precipitously in absolute terms through most of the 1990s, and no Russian leader expended the political capital needed to begin the military reforms that would be necessary to squeeze more capabilities out of a smaller economy.

Neither did Russia engage in "external balancing"—that is aggregating its power in alliance with other states in a meaningful way. Russia's treaty relationships with China and India simply are not such power-aggregating alliances. All three powers continued to cooperate closely with the United States on a very large range of security and economic matters—behavior bearing scant resemblance to any normal understanding of balancing. Analysts sometimes stress that these treaties contain language that hints that they might eventually become real alliances.[22] But such warnings miss the point. All states technically have the option to conclude alliances whenever they want. Alliances assume strategic significance less by the specific language of the treaty documents than by the effect of the signatories' actions on their actual power to defend against or attack another state. The relationship with India amounts to a Soviet holdover based on the Friendship Treaty of 1971 whose language implied weak security obligations even in the Cold War, and a largely symbolic Declaration on Strategic Partnership signed by Putin and Indian Prime Minister Atal Behari

Vajpayee in 2000. The Russia-China Treaty on Good-Neighborliness, Friendship, and Cooperation signed in July 2001 capped over a decade of improving bilateral ties but it similarly lacks anything resembling a mutual defense clause.[23] While the treaty obligates the signatories in a general sense to maintain the global equilibrium and to consult each other in the event of security threats, neither it nor any public Russo-Chinese agreement entails any observable or costly commitment to counter U.S. power.

At the core of Russia's relationships with India and China are major arms sales and extensive military coproduction arrangements. Russia's interest in these exports is not driven by the need to counterbalance U.S. power. Rather, they are desperately needed to slow the inexorable decline of Russia's military industrial complex. Given the collapse of domestic orders (in 2001, only 10 percent of Russian defense firms received state orders), Russia's defense sector possesses massive excess capacity.[24] Exports are a crucial lifeline for a military industry producing less than one-third of its 1992 output, and rapidly losing technological competitiveness. The defense sector provides income and welfare services to hundreds of thousands of workers and their families; provides the economic lifeblood of dozens of cities, many located in Russia's Asian provinces; and enriches numerous managers and public officials. The evidence concerning Russia's Asian arms relationships overwhelmingly indicates that they have little to do with U.S. power. The United States could cut its defense outlays by two-thirds tomorrow, and Moscow would remain just as eager to sell weaponry to Beijing and New Delhi. Indeed, the United States is eager to sell arms to India, so the issue is clearly not India's capability to balance the United States but rather competition for market share. Moreover, while arms sales to its Asian clients do alter local power balances, not even the most alarmist interpretation of them suggests that they will provide a genuine counterbalance to U.S. power overall.[25]

Second, Moscow's multipolar rhetoric was misleading because the bulk of Russia's security relationships in East and South Asia have little to do with America's global hegemony and regional presence. If the United States were only half as powerful as it is today, Russia would still seek rapprochement with China and would still face a powerful incentive to work with rather than against Beijing in the effort to manage the security problems created by its own imperial retrenchment. The Soviet Union's effort to contain China in the 1970s and 1980s strapped its capabilities and contributed significantly to its imperial overstretch. Today, a much weaker and still weakening Russia has to preserve amicable security ties and has a strong interest in developing economic relations with a much stronger and growing China.

Aside from arms transfers, the partnership with China has three elements: regional, economic, and multipolar. The last item received the most attention; the first two are where most of the concrete actions have taken place. During the 1990s, the two sides demarcated most of their 4,000-kilometer border (several islands in the Ussuri River remain contested).[26] They sought to cooperate on cross-border trade and immigration issues. They endeavored to boost bilateral trade, although politicians in both capitals have only a limited ability to affect the underlying demand in each country for the other's goods. And they instituted confidence-building measures and negotiated limits on troop deployments in the region.

The Multipolar Strategy and
Russian Primacy in the South Caucasus and Central Asia

The baseline strategy in the South Caucasus and Central Asia was more complicated because the security problems created by Russian imperial retrenchment were far more serious, the economic stakes larger, and the anguish over the loss of empire far greater. The overall pattern of policy was more consistent with genuine geopolitical imperative of retaining regional hegemony in order to limit the penetration of outside powers. The imperative to secure regional hegemony from a relatively weak economic base appeared to lend Moscow's behavior in the former Soviet zone, which Russians dub the "near abroad," a strong geopolitical and competitive cast. The policy was very frequently justified as the local analogue to the global multipolar strategy, especially when Russian officials needed to justify the high economic costs the policy sometimes imposed. That is, Russia's central role as the organizer of a great Eurasian balance against U.S. hegemony demanded that American security and economic influence in the former Soviet space be kept to a minimum, even if it implied heavy subsidies for regional actors or other economic losses.

Strategies of geopolitical and geoeconomic denial led to a series of Kiplingesque tactical aims, all of which were reactive: prevent the Central Asian states from establishing a corridor to the Indian Ocean (the Tedjen-Serakhs railway); foil the possible transportation axis connecting Turkmenistan and Uzbekistan via Afghanistan and Pakistan; oppose the "Europe-Caucasus-Central Asia" (TRACECA) transportation corridor (the restoration of the "Great Silk Road"); and, most notably, oppose the Baku-Ceyhan oil pipeline project. Russian policy in the South Caucasus and Central Asia could be seen as being guided by classical geopolitical objectives: to prevent the emergence of a "new rimland" along the southern reaches of the post-Soviet space and in southeastern Europe, which would have the effect of transforming Russia into a peripheral northeastern Eurasian state, located off the main trade routes, unable to bring to fruition its full geopolitical potential. A large body of specialists' literature documents Moscow's costly use of its remaining natural resource and economic assets to purchase regional predominance.[27]

But even in Central Asia and the South Caucasus, the baseline multipolar strategy tended to obscure the main dynamics behind Russian activity in the region, which were increasingly motivated by commercial and local concerns. There are economic rents to be gained by control over transshipment of petroleum resources in the Caspian Basin, and Russia has an interest in maximizing those rents that is independent of any need to counterbalance U.S. primacy. Washington, meanwhile, has been the driving force behind pipeline projects that bypass Russia and has no difficulty justifying the potentially high economic costs of its preferred routes by referring to security gains. These facts lent a competitive cast to the international politics of the region that was unrelated to the security problems created by U.S. primacy.

In addition, imperial retrenchment left behind real security problems in the South Caucasus that tended to draw in Russia. Retaining an interest in its erstwhile provinces, Russia increasingly lacked the means to exercise sway as a benign hegemon. The policy levers available to Moscow were limited: a traumatized, ineffective, and occasionally insubordinate military establishment; a sometimes unreliable intelligence establishment; and economic influence resulting from its control over transport infrastructure and the asymmetrical dependence of local states. Local regimes themselves often exacerbated the post-colonial security dilemmas that prompted Russian intervention. Nationalist mobilization in Armenia and Azerbaijan fed the Nagorno-Karabakh conflict, as Georgian nationalism sparked separatism in Abkhazia, Ajaria, and North Ossetia. Given such predictable postimperial conflicts and the absence of any outside power willing and able to devote the resources necessary to provide benign security regimes, for better or (usually) for worse, the region ended up with the old imperial metropole as the security provider of last resort.

A similar logic applies to Central Asia. Although Russian officials remained deeply suspicious of American intentions in the area, trends in Russia's security role the region were not directly linked to counterbalancing the United States. Russian imperial retrenchment left behind serious security challenges in Central Asia. Particularly explosive is the triangular relationship among the Uzbeks, Tajiks, and Kyrgyz, who form sizeable minorities in each other's countries and share the fertile and overpopulated Fergana Valley. Ethnic tensions in the region are exacerbated by interstate rivalries. Uzbekistan, with roughly half the region's 50 million population, periodically seeks to assert its preponderance, provoking resistance from the smaller states.[28] After 1998, Tajikistan and Uzbekistan aided each other's rebel movements.[29] Kyrgyzstan, which owns most of the water resources of the region, has threatened to cut off supplies to its neighbors if they do not take into account Bishkek's interests. Uzbekistan, in turn, has made similar threats regarding its gas supplies. Last but not least, poverty and poor governance have greatly stimulated the production and trafficking of drugs from Afghanistan via Central Asia to Russia and Europe.

Increasingly, Moscow defined its interests in this complex mosaic in terms of defense from Muslim extremism supported from outside the former Soviet space. Russian officials and analysts conjured up the image of post-Soviet Central Asia as a buffer zone between Russia, where some 13 percent of the population is Muslim, and the forces of militant Islamism to the south. In this view, Russia's support for the Northern Alliance and its own border guards in Tajikistan were necessary to prevent Taliban-supported radicals from destabilizing Tajikistan, and then possibly Uzbekistan, and perhaps even Kazakhstan with its 8,000 kilometer-long and virtually indefensible border with Russia.

Thus even Russia's official framing of the security challenge to the region was ultimately disconnected from the global distribution of power and U.S. unipolarity. The multipolar strategy still played a role in part because Russia increasingly coordinated its regional policies with China. As in East Asia, the region has been marked by relative Russian withdrawal and Chinese advance—though the extent of this power shift has often been exaggerated—and anti-unipolar rhetoric served to obscure this uncomfortable reality.[30] Both powers defined the security challenge to the region in similar terms, finding it convenient to locate the source of the problem in Afghanistan rather than the systematic intolerance of the local post-colonial authoritarian regimes and their mutual rivalries. As in the Caucasus, the long list of post-colonial problems created strong local demands for outside involvement, which in practice meant Russian involvement given the lack of plausible outside security managers. Moscow had an incentive to coordinate its polices with China, especially given that Beijing's initiatives were aimed at tackling problems Russian officials placed at the top of their own national security threat list: terrorism, organized crime, Muslim "extremism," and separatism.

None of this is to deny that the multipolar policy was real. In fact, it consumed a great deal of the foreign ministry's energy, and the rhetoric surrounding it was loud and consistent. Russian officials and the foreign policy elite in Moscow put a great deal of intellectual energy into articulating the strategy and developing its theoretical underpinnings.[31] It provided the main intellectual framework for Russia's pre-September policies in East, South, and Central Asia. But although Russians articulated the strategy in terms of balance of power theory, in reality the strategy had no effect on, and little to do with, the global distribution of capabilities.

Rather than aggregating power to rein in the United States, the policy's real goal was much more modest: to try in concert with other players to get the United States to alter specific policies. In other words, it was not power balancing, but policy bargaining—more typical of coalition politics among allies or even in domestic politics than the military balancing of the Cold War or the nineteenth century. Russia sought to present itself as the linchpin member of global coalitions aimed at countering specific U.S. policies, such as NATO expansion, Iraq, the Balkans, and missile defense. Each of Russia's putatively geopolitical "axes" was in response to a particular U.S. policy initiative. Thus, on an official visit to New Dehli in December 1998, Primakov called for a strategic alliance of Russia, China, and India. The immediate impetus was an effort to deliver some rebuff to the recent U.S. bombing of Iraq. India's Prime Minister Vajpayee was cautious about the idea, but he began to warm to it slightly during NATO's air war against Yugoslavia. The Kosovo operation marked the high water mark for the Asian strategic triangle. One issue on which the three capitals could agree was their intense disapproval of armed NATO intervention against a sovereign state in support of separatists without U.N. Security Council authorization. Yet even at the peak of their indignation, no concrete action was forthcoming because the three powers differed in the intensity of their opposition to different U.S. policies, India-China bilateral relations remained problematic, and New Delhi pursued a policy of improving ties with Washington. As a result, none of the three members demonstrated willingness to pay any significant military, economic, or political price to punish NATO for its perceived transgression in the Balkans.

Similarly, the multipolar rhetoric surrounding the essentially pragmatic Russia-China partnership correlates with the two countries' disapproval of specific U.S policies. For example, the Friendship Treaty contains a laundry list of U.S. policies the two sides opposed. Article 11 stipulates support for the principles and norms of international law, which means that the two sides oppose any repetition of the Kosovo scenario anywhere in the world and any revision of international treaties (e.g., the Anti-Ballistic Missile [ABM] Treaty). Articles 11 and 12 reinforce both parties' commitment to the treaty, while Article 12 enjoins both to maintain the "global strategic balance and stability." In short, the sole "multipolar" aspect of this treaty was an attempt to signal Washington that it could pay some unspecified price if it unilaterally abandoned the ABM Treaty.

Touting the multipolar dimension had other potential benefits as well. Underlying resentment of U.S. power does offer a useful rallying point for stimulating cooperation on other issues. In the period prior to September 11, Russian and Chinese leaders highlighted their desire for a world of reduced U.S. influence not because this is a goal toward which they actually took real steps, but rather because it was one general principle on which they could agree. Even if the main objectives are local, coordination among regional powers can have the attractive potential side benefit of enhancing bargaining power vis-à-vis Washington. Thus it can pay to talk up the counterbalancing potential of any prominent coordination effort among major powers that excludes the United States if only as a signal in an ongoing bargaining game. The rhetoric surrounding the June 2001 summit of the Shanghai Cooperation Organization (SCO) was a classic example of this dynamic in play.

The Turn: September 11 in Context

Ultimately, however, Russia's multipolar strategy imposed major costs. It diverted attention from the real nature of Russian behavior in world politics, which amounted to chaotic and often reactive imperial retrenchment, combined with the search for entry into a world economic system dominated by the United States—the very power against which the whole multipolar strategy was ostensibly directed. Recognition that the baseline strategy forced Russia consistently to operate beyond its ability in world politics even as it potentially soured relations with the necessary U.S. partner is the critical shift that explained Putin's specific response to the September attacks.

Russia's Strategic Reappraisal

In January 2000 the independent Council on Foreign and Defense Policy published a report entitled "A Strategy for Russia" that presented a comprehensive critique of the multipolar approach. What commanded attention was less the Council's direct influence on the government (although its membership does boast a number of well-connected political, academic, and, especially, business figures) than the fact that the same group had played a prominent role in publicizing the multipolar policy in the first place.[32] The most important criticism was that the old policy simply did not work. It did not maximize Moscow's bargaining leverage either with Washington or the other main players in the policy counterbalancing game. As Vladimir Lukin, vice president of the State Duma and a stalwart advocate of multipolar diplomacy, going back to his scholarly writings in the Brezhnev era, asked: "What dividends did we get? None that I can see."[33] On each issue with the United States from 1993 to 2000, Moscow stated opposition in unambiguous terms and then ended up backing down humiliatingly. By so publicly and clearly backing down from such loudly stated positions, Moscow squandered its limited prestige and advertised its weakness.

The thrust of the report's argument was that the multipolar approach was beyond Russia's limited capabilities. Russia clearly lacks the power to affect the polarity of the international system, and underlying trends toward multipolarity will occur independent of Russian diplomacy. If local hegemony in the former Soviet space and global multipolarity were each daunting objectives, their combination was formidable indeed. Confidence in Russia's ability to play such a major role in world politics owed much to the rise in geopolitical theory in the country in the 1990s, after the demise of Gorbachev's idealistic new thinking and the liberal enthusiasm of the early Yeltsin years. Such an agenda only can be made to look plausible by ignoring Russia's weaknesses and assuming that location and size remain decisive in world politics.[34] If one thinks of power as economic might rather than territorial extent, however, there would be little reason to think that Russia's $1 trillion economy should be a linchpin player between the U.S. and the European Union's roughly $10 trillion each, on the one hand, and the $4.5 trillion economies of Japan and China, on the other.

The old approach also scattered Russia's limited foreign-policy energies around the globe, preventing a necessary concentration on priority issues. It constrained Russia's flexibility, trapping it into taking a lead position in most global anti-U.S. policy coalitions. Other powers, such as the EU and China—often with greater interests at stake and far greater capabilities—were letting Russia do the dirty work of seeking to constrain the United States, all the while making lucrative deals with Washington on the side. Why should Russia, often the weakest player, always lead the charge? Moreover, if relations between any of the other multipolar partners and Washington were to deteriorate seriously, between Beijing and Washington over Taiwan, for example, Russia might have been drawn into a confrontation in which it had no stake and which it could not afford.

Disenchantment with the multipolar policy, even in its modest policy-balancing form, shows how declining relative power has slowly shifted Russians' assessments of their essential interests by forcing them to accept trade-offs among different security objectives. The key judgment here is that Russia would prefer to balance the United States if it could do so at a bearable cost. The concentration of power in U.S. hands is worrisome in a general sense to many Russians. Some believe it impinges on their optimal security policies in several key areas, and all believe it challenges their prestige. Nevertheless, the pursuit of prestige is hard to justify when it is not connected to direct security threats and imposes heavy costs. The security problems created by the concentration of power in the United States are simply not the most salient for Moscow, and so Russia was ultimately unwilling to pay the costs of policy balancing. Balancing the United States on these issues takes resources away from more pressing needs. Indeed, declining relative power has caused Russians progressively to pare down their security agenda. As a result, the list of issues where U.S. unipolarity appears to threaten Russian interests has grown shorter even as the list of pressing near-term and local threats has lengthened.

Concerning the near abroad, a growing number of Russian analysts identified the fundamental incoherence of the previous policy: the economic, local, anti-Islamist, and anti-unipolar elements all contradicted each other, resulting in an over-committed posture that strapped Russia's meager resources.[35] The Council recommended a new and more modest strategy of selective engagement (*izbiratelnaya vovlechennost*) and retrenchment (literally "concentration"—*sosredotochivanie*). The Putin administration saw no benefit in adopting those catchphrases to describe its approach to foreign policy. The report, however, reflected the growing disenchantment with the old approach in elite and governing circles, and accurately anticipated the general policy direction in which the Putin team was already headed.

Pre-September Shifts

Vladimir Putin's ability to manage Russia's sprawling state apparatus was limited, especially at first. But the easiest thing to change is language, and Putin immediately shifted the official discourse about Russia's power and interests. More clearly than his two immediate predecessors, he stressed the imperative of economic growth. He set the tone when he was still prime minister and acting president, posting an article on the government's website in December 1999 in which he stressed that "it will take us fifteen years and an eight percent annual growth of our GDP to reach the per capita GDP level of present-day Portugal...."[36] In his maiden state of the union address, he insisted that "the growing rift between the leading states and Russia is pushing us toward becoming a third-world country."[37] Putin is justly known in Russia for his prudence and circumspection. From the outset, he mastered ambiguity as a leadership strategy—a necessity, given the domestic constraint under which he initially operated. Hence the interminable Russian debate over "who is Vladimir Putin?". But a general strategy of ambiguity calls attention to those few things about which a leader speaks clearly. Putin's blunt talk about the imperative of Russia's modernization got through. His stark comparison of great Russia to the EU's poorest member stuck: it may be the most quoted comment Putin has ever made.

None of his predecessors ever spoke so bluntly about the limits to Russian power and the challenges lying ahead.

It is important to stress that the new leadership was only making more explicit a set of policy imperatives that had been gaining converts in Russian official and elite circles for nearly two decades. By the late 1980s, the Soviet leadership and much of the elite had internalized the connection between economic performance, security, and great power status. Even then, the realization was gaining ground that the opportunity costs of remaining isolated from the world economy were growing rapidly. Moreover, it was clear to many segments of Moscow's policy establishment that declining economic competitiveness was partly the result of isolation from the global economy and that it had profound effects on the country's longer-term national security.[38] The experience of the 1990s only hammered that connection home.

The new team also sought to distinguish itself by highlighting the greater realism with which it was going about the modernization task in comparison with its predecessors. Putin was not shy about spelling out the larger foreign policy implications of the modernization imperative. It meant gaining access to western financial and trading organizations. In the near term, this implies qualifying for WTO membership and removing special EU and U.S. trade restrictions on Russia. Over the longer term, it means establishing a reliable institutional framework for relations with Russia's most important trading partner and source of investment capital, the EU. But Putin was at pains to stress the hard-bitten realistic nature of his approach this task, as opposed to the dreamy liberalism of the early Yeltsin years. That first effort to enter the West was based on an overestimation of Russia's bargaining power. Now, a reduced but scrappier Russia was ready to take on the West with its eyes open. As Putin put it, "no one is going to war with us in the modern world... but no one is really waiting for us either, no one will help us specially. We have to fight for our place in the economic sun."[39]

In addition, over the course of 2000–01, the new national security team shifted Russia's official priorities away from concern over unipolarity and toward more local issues such as terrorism and organized crime. In the first six months of his presidency, Putin signed several heavily promoted policy documents: Russia's official concept of national security, its foreign policy concept, and its defense doctrine.[40] All three contain strong anti-unipolar language, but Putin and his associates influenced the final drafts to emphasize the requisites of modernization and newer threats from terror and organized crime. The document they had the strongest hand in drafting— the security concept released by the national security council—is the most forthright in insisting that economic decline, institutional decay, organized crime and corruption, terrorism and separatism are the main threats to Russia's national security.

Reorienting the actual strategic behavior of a sprawling, poorly governed state like Russia is a much more daunting task than altering rhetoric and official doctrines. Nevertheless, significant changes were already underway before September 2001. Commentators focused on Putin's frenetic travel and summit schedule during his first year in office, which included high-profile meetings with nearly every major antagonist of the United States in international relations. At summits with Jiang Zemin, Vajpayee, and other Asian leaders, Putin maintained Russia's official multipolar line. Less often noted, however, was the substantive economic focus of much of his diplomacy.

In East Asia, Russia backed off the multipolar emphasis in relations with China and made immediate efforts to take a more realistic and bottom-line oriented approach to the strategic partnership. In the months leading up to September 2001, all the usual preconditions for an intense bout of multipolar diplomacy were in place. Resentment of U.S. hegemony had been stoked by the prominent unilateralist tendencies and rhetoric of the early Bush administration, the galvanizing push of U.S. plans concerning missile defense, the new administration's cooler and more distant stance toward both Russia and China, and the EP-3 spy plane incident. Yet even in this hothouse atmosphere for nurturing a serious anti-U.S. policy alignment, the parties were reluctant to commit publicly to real policy coordination. While they were together in Shanghai to initial the SCO's founding documents, Presidents Putin and Jiang Zemin did express their opposition to U.S. efforts to develop a missile defense system. Yet when the two leaders met again a month later at the signing of their friendship treaty—amid a chorus of punditry about a new Moscow-Beijing "axis"—Putin responded to a question about joint Sino-Russian opposition to U.S. plans for a national missile defense (NMD) system by stressing that "Russia plans no joint actions with other states in this sphere, including China."[41] In other words, not only were Russia and China not combining to counter U.S. power, Russia was not even inclined to coordinate with Beijing to undermine U.S. policy.

In the spring and summer of 2001, Putin oversaw a sustained effort to improve relations with the United States, as well as a weaker but measurable attempt to add impetus to ties with Japan. There was evidence of a warming trend between Washington and Moscow even before the two presidents met in Slovenia in June 2001. Putin began slowly to shift Russia's policies on NATO expansion and ABM—two of the three remaining objectives of the multipolar strategy (the other being Iran/Iraq). He talked about joining NATO, or at least selling arms to new NATO members, and bruited the idea of Russian participation in U.S. ABM projects. These were initial and reversible overtures, but they all led away from the baseline strategy.

In March 2000, Putin restated an earlier offer to return two of the disputed Kuril Islands to Japan and created momentum toward a breakthrough in negotiations over normalization. Although the islands negotiations soon bogged down in familiar ruts, modest progress was evident in other areas.[42] Military contacts between the two countries increased after a visit by Russia's defense minister in December 2001 that led to regular exchanges of delegations between security institutions and expanded confidence-building measures.

Perhaps the most spectacular pre-September initiative in Asia was Putin's re-engagement in Korean affairs. In July 2000 and August the following year, he and North Korea's Kim Jong Il exchanged visits after a decade-long freeze in the two countries' relationship. Russian officials argued that rebalancing Moscow's relations between North and South Korea would aid their expressed interest in re-engaging the strategic dialogue on the peninsula after years of having been shunted aside by Beijing and Washington. In addition, the Russians hoped to prod the North Koreans to abandon their missile program in order to defuse one U.S. argument for missile defense. But much of the substance of the meetings concerned economic relations with both Koreas: connecting the trans-Siberian railway to the North Korean rail network and the inter-Korean railway; refurbishing power plants and other facilities constructed with Soviet aid in the 1950s and 1960s (with Moscow refusing barter transactions and attempting to induce South Korean banks and firms to finance the projects); and, of course, possible arms sales to both Koreas "within the limits of reasonable sufficiency."[43]

In South and Southeast Asia change was less notable but still detectable. Emblematic of the new approach was Russia's decision to abandon its naval base in Vietnam's Cam Ranh Bay before its lease was to run out in 2004—making a point of stressing that economic ties should henceforth be at the forefront of relations between the two countries.

In Central Asia, Putin attempted to lend coherence to Russian policy by stressing the anti-terrorist dimension of security policy (as well as his trademark focus on the economic bottom line). In a January 2001 speech to the foreign ministry, Putin underlined the threat from international terrorism and the need for international cooperation to combat it.[44] Accordingly, Moscow renewed its efforts to increase and institutionalize Russian security cooperation in the region, with improved ties to local militaries.

One of the most important developments in Russian military policy was an effort to restructure and redeploy Russian forces to deal with new threats from Central Asia. At the May 2001 summit of the Commonwealth of Independent States (CIS) in Yerevan, the sides agreed on the creation of a "Collective Rapid Deployment Force" for regional contingencies. The force consists of units from Kazakhstan, Kyrgyzstan, and Tajikistan (with unspecified Russian elements) under the leadership of a Russian officer with command and control facilities in Bishkek. But most of these measures were declaratory and organizational. The ability of forces actually to deploy jointly and deal with real contingencies depends on transportation equipment, facilities, and training, and for all of these things Russia's Defense Ministry lacked the necessary funds.

To be sure, the states of the South Caucasus and Central Asia remained so vulnerable that even a weakened Russia exerted intense pressure on them, and Moscow loomed large in local security calculations. But the fundamental reality underlying policy was that even in these neighboring regions Russia's capabilities faced severe limits. The war in Chechnya remained a major drain on Russia's military resources. Officials acknowledge over 4,000 combat deaths and 12,000 wounded since 1999, and independent experts put the number much higher.[45] The budgetary costs of the Chechen conflict may approach $1 billion annually.[46] Despite announced troop reductions, the Russian Ministry of Defense keeps over 40,000 troops in the republic, as well as a major support structure in the North Caucasus Military District, which has become the ministry's largest at over 75,000 troops. The war has not only poisoned morale and stalled reform, but it is even depleting Soviet Cold War munitions stocks dating back to the 1960s, which are not being replenished.[47]

In 2001, Russia had 25,000 troops deployed abroad, three-quarters of whom were garrisoned in the Asian near abroad (9,000 in Armenia and Georgia and 8,000 in Tajikistan).[48] Though the numbers are impressive, Russia's real military capabilities are quite limited in the region. The 201st division in Tajikistan, once charged with a "peacekeeping" mission, has been upgraded to a permanent military base. However, it stands very isolated, alongside the 14,500 Russian-led but overwhelmingly Tajik-manned border guards. In mid-2000, the Russian General Staff decided to place a 50,000-strong rapid deployment corps near the Russo-Kazakhstan border to be used to intervene in an emergency anywhere in Central Asia. But as of 2002, it remained a paper force whose transformation to operational status would require time and money. The capability for rapid Russian force projection is virtually nonexistent. Russia's airlift capacity is too limited to move large forces rapidly; rail remains the only realistic option.

Given these limitations, Moscow faced incentives to cooperate with China in the region, and to manage that cooperation through the "Shanghai Five" (Russia, China, Kazakhstan, Kyrgyzstan, and Tajikistan), which gained a sixth member when Uzbekistan joined at the June 2001 summit that institutionalized the grouping as the SCO. Despite the multipolar rhetoric that accompanied the summit, developments on the ground were already trumping the anti-American card as an impetus for regional cooperation. Moscow's official preoccupation with international terrorism and the change in Washington's attitude toward the Taliban as a result of the 1998 embassy bombings in Africa set the stage for increased U.S.-Russian cooperation in Central Asia. Russia participated in joint training of Central Asian states under the auspices of NATO's Partnership for Peace program. Following the joint statement on Afghanistan of the 2000 Moscow summit, a U.S.-Russian working group on counter-terrorism was established and began to hold regular meetings.

Post-September Shifts

The pre-September trajectory was moving steadily from the baseline multipolar strategy toward a more pragmatic policy of selective accommodation that is more sensitive to Russia's limited capabilities, the overpowering necessity for modernization, and the economic costs and benefits of foreign policy. In the year leading up to the terrorist attacks, Vladimir Putin and his economic and foreign policy advisors had stressed in terms clearer than those used by any of their predecessors that Russia's only salvation was sustained economic growth, and that the main route toward that object lay to the west—that is, in gaining full membership in the global economy whose institutions and practices are dominated by the United States and the EU. Moreover, the attacks on the United States came after several years of building Russian dissatisfaction with multipolar diplomacy, and after Moscow had refashioned its security policy in Central Asia explicitly as a response to the terrorist threat from Afghanistan—linked, of course, with its own brutal campaign against separatism in Chechnya. And, finally, Russian officials were increasingly aware that they lacked the military capability to address to their own and their allies' satisfaction the security challenge in Central Asia even in the oversimplified terms in which they portrayed it.

If these prior conditions make Putin's decision to join the U.S. anti-terror coalition a foregone conclusion, they did not dictate the decisive nature of the response. Putin was the first foreign leader to call President Bush after the World Trade Center and the Pentagon were attacked. Over the next two weeks he met with advisors and political leaders to weigh options. He then laid out what Russia was prepared to do: 1) exchange intelligence on international terrorists; 2) open Russian air-space for humanitarian flights; 3) encourage the Central Asian states to offer military bases for the counter-terrorist campaign; 4) cooperate in search-and-rescue operations; and 5) expand assistance to the Northern Alliance in its campaign against the Taliban. By all accounts Russia delivered. U.S. officials described Russian-supplied intelligence on the Taliban and Al Qaeda as high volume and high quality. Russian supplies did get to the Northern Alliance in short order. Russian forces did materially assist alliance forces in tunnel clearing operations and elsewhere in Afghanistan. President Bush later lauded Russia's contribution to the Afghan campaign as the most important from any ally in the war against terrorism except Britain.

Beyond the immediate decision to cooperate with the United States in the campaign against the Taliban and Al Qaeda, three significant changes occurred. First, Putin used the event to accelerate the strategic shift toward selective accommodation and retrenchment that was already underway. The trend toward de-emphasizing multipolarity now encompassed both rhetoric and behavior. The centerpiece of the effort was a retreat on issues where Putin knew Russia would eventually have to compromise: NATO and the ABM Treaty. Once Russia further softened its stance on these issues, the path was open to major improvements in relations with the United States, signified by Russia's signing a strategic arms reductions treaty during George Bush's May visit to Moscow and St. Petersburg, and formally joining the new NATO-Russia Council later that month. Adding weight to these modest policy moves was a dramatic increase in the clarity with which Putin and other top officials described the rapprochement with the West.[49]

The shift altered the tone of the strategic partnership with China. In effect, Russia chose to defect from the multipolar policy coalition against U.S. abrogation of the ABM Treaty and NATO expansion. Putin's relaxed reaction to the announcement of formal U.S. withdrawal from the treaty in December 2001 put the nail in the coffin of that coalition, while his acceptance of a revamped Russian role in the NATO-Russia Council pulled the rug out from years of campaigning against that organization's role in international security. The immediate implication was clear. Russia's role in the anti-terror campaign meant that it did not need China—or the threat of closer security ties to China—to enhance its importance to Washington. More fundamentally, it reflected the long-germinating assessment that Russia's forward-leaning stance on multipolarity only set it up to be suckered by China (and the Europeans) as they shrank from paying the up-front political costs of confronting Washington.

The U.S. and Russian response to September 11 also undermined the modest momentum that had been building behind the SCO. The main impetus behind the strengthening of the organization (including Uzbekistan's decision to join it in 2001) had been the terrorist threat emanating from Afghanistan. Now, the SCO's Central Asian members were hosting the U.S. military, which went on to accomplish the membership's cherished goal of destroying the Taliban. To restore a certain degree of normalcy in the post-Taliban era, SCO foreign ministers met in Beijing in early January to assess the new situation in the region. Russia's immediate response was, as in much of its diplomacy in recent years, to make a virtue of necessity. Russian Defense Minister Sergey Ivanov explicitly linked the SCO to the global anti-terror coalition. With the formation of the NATO-Russia Council whose mandate explicitly highlights counter-terrorism, he stressed, Moscow has indeed become a crucial link in a Eurasian counter-terrorist coalition encompassing two regional security organizations covering the North Atlantic and Central Asia.[50] The SCO officials agreed to set up a regional counter-terrorism agency and an emergency response mechanism. But the organization's structure, mode of operation, rules for accession, participation of observers, and membership criteria all remain ill-defined. And, most important, it has yet to redefine its goals in response to the U.S. role in regional security.

Russia in Asia after the Turn

When Putin met German Chancellor Gerhard Schroeder in March 2002, the conversation was notable for its focus on economic issues, and especially on Russian energy exports to the EU. After the meeting, Putin made a point of stressing that the EU must treat Russia as an equal—mentioning both the benefits Europe obtains from stable Russian supplies and the costs that would accompany any restriction in those deliveries.[51] At the same time, Putin was bandwagoning with the United States on nearly all issues—upsetting European diplomats' own assumption that Russia could be counted on to lead most anti-U.S. policy coalitions. On Putin's next visit in May, Europeans detected increased pressure on a variety of issues, ranging from energy contracts to the visa status of Russians transiting to and from Kaliningrad after EU accession by Poland and Lithuania. In response, EU diplomats were able to give on one issue, the granting of "free market" status to the Russian economy (Washington soon followed suit).

In a nutshell, this episode captures Russia's strategy over the medium term. The strategy is focused on modernizing Russia so that it has a chance to recover as a real great power in the middle decades of this century. In the medium term, that means exploiting Russia's existing resources to finance the creation of the institutions and relationships it needs to succeed over the long term. And the chief resource Russia has at its disposal now is petroleum. Russia is becoming a petro-power in order to create the preconditions for its reemergence as a full-fledged great power. In the meantime, it will use the influence it gains as a major oil and gas power—with the limits created by the need to maintain a reputation as a reliable supplier—mainly to leverage its way into better economic arrangements that further its modernization objective.

Russia's Non-Choice:
The Realities Behind New Strategic Pragmatism

The new strategy explicitly recognizes what the old multipolar approach obscured: there can be no serious discussion of a choice of emphasis between east and west. For if traditional military concerns rule out a great power role in Asia for Russia, economic incentives will pull Russia consistently westward. The geographical center of Russia's economy is in the West. Eighty percent of Russians live in the European portion of their country. The city of Moscow has as many inhabitants as the entire Far East. Analysts in Russia and abroad have expressed grave concerns about the under-population of Siberia and the Far East, as the decline in subsidies from Moscow prompted a major outmigration.[52] The real problem, however, is that the northeastern and, in all likelihood, the southeastern sections of Russia are currently overpopulated as a result of uneconomic "strategic investment" by Soviet authorities.[53] If Russia continues to reform its economy on market principles, much of the current industrial activity in the Far East will relocate or become unviable and the federal government will face ongoing pressure to minimize subsidies. The major economic activity that will remain profitable will be resource extraction—a much smaller employer than manufacturing. And the payrolls of oil, gas, and mineral concerns will decline as new investment and technology increases the productivity of those activities.

European Russia, by contrast, has good access to the world market, with excellent ports and good road, rail, and pipeline links. In light of these realities, the direction of Russia's trade not surprisingly is weighted heavily to the West (see Figure 6.1). Germany and the United States are Russia's top trading partners. Belarus and Ukraine are quantitatively far more important in Russia's trade than either China or Japan. Oil and natural gas are Russia's main exports, and Europe is the main customer for both. Military hardware remains an important export for Russia, with yearly sales averaging $3.2 billion from 1995 to 2001. Exports of nuclear material and technology are also important; they earned Russia an average of $2.2 bil-

Figure 6.1. The Geography of Russia's Trade, 1996–2000

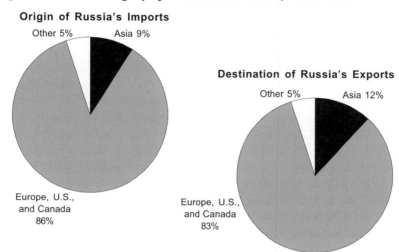

Source: Calculated from International Monetary Fund, *Direction of Trade Statistics*, Washington, DC: IMF, 2001. Note: Asia defined as the countries and territories included in NBR's Strategic Asia Program; Europe as the EU plus countries of Central and Eastern Europe.

lion annually in 1995–97. Both of these export categories loom large in Russia's Asian trade portfolio, but together they account for less than five percent of Russia's exports.

Russia's growing need for investment capital will continue to draw Russia westward. Russia will not sustain high growth rates without massive investment. Russians debate whether foreign direct investment (FDI) is necessary for a country with substantial unrealized domestic investment potential.[54] The debate is largely moot, for Russia's investment needs outstrip any realistic estimate of domestic and foreign supply. The average age of Russian industrial plants and equipment is 17 years (three times higher than the OECD average).[55] By all accounts, Russia's basic infrastructure—transportation systems, pipelines, power lines, water supply, sewer systems, and the like—is in urgent need of renewal. Over the next 20–25 years, former Economics Minister Yevgeny Yasin estimates that Russia will need more than $2 trillion in infrastructure investment, some of which will have to come from abroad.[56] The electricity monopoly alone may need $50–70 billion simply to prevent increased power shortages. Sectors with great promise, such as oil and gas, need massive investment to realize their potential. In many cases, only FDI will do because technology, strategic partnerships, marketing arrangements, and access to foreign research and development (R&D) are as important as raw financial resources. Given Russia's priority stake on developing technology and capital-intensive

industries, as well as the dramatically enhanced role of FDI, strategic partnerships, joint ventures, outsourcing, and other transborder production
activities in precisely those sectors, the economic opportunity costs to
Russia of exclusion from the world economy are growing rapidly.[57] And
the source of FDI is the West (see Figure 6.2).

Russia, in short, cannot be truly Eurasian, but rather is fated to remain, for some time to come, a European country with territory in Asia. It

Figure 6.2. The Geography of FDI in Russia, 1999–2000

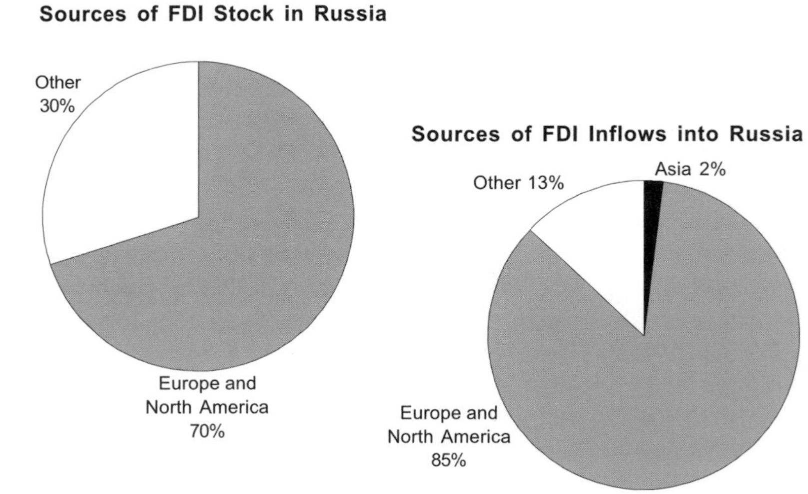

Sources of FDI Stock in Russia

Sources of FDI Inflows into Russia

Source: Calculated from United Nations Conference on Trade and Development, *World In-
vestment Report 2001: Promoting Linkages*, New York: UNCTAD 2001; and UNCTAD, *World
Investment Report 2000: Cross-Border Mergers and Acquisitions and Development*, New York:
United Nations, 2000. Note: Asia defined as the countries and territories included in NBR's
Strategic Asia Program; Europe as the EU plus Switzerland.

faces overpowering incentives to conduct itself in world affairs in a manner that will maximize its chances of securing profitable trade and investment relationships with Europe and the United States. That said, Moscow's
hold on its sparsely-populated and resource-rich Asian territories will remain militarily vulnerable. It will long remain interested in promoting exports of military hardware and petroleum products to major Asian clients.
Russia's increasingly profitable and politically influential gas and oil industries will create particularly strong incentives to seek marginal gains in
growing Asian markets. And Japan remains an as yet untapped potential
source of FDI. While Russia will retain its strongest ties to the West it
cannot afford to alienate the East.

Russia's Interests and Levers of Influence in Asia

Over the next 10–15 years, Russia will have no interest in any confrontation among great powers globally or in Asia. Moscow can be counted on to use the limited means at its disposal to forestall such an outcome. In particular, Russian officials will continue to work feverishly to preserve the pragmatic core of the strategic partnership with China. Russia's main levers of influence in Asia will be arms sales and resource exports. The major dynamic will be the reduced salience of the former in favor of the latter.

Moscow's record arms sales of recent years are mainly of upgraded products from the Soviet military industrial complex.[58] They are possible only because Russian military concerns inherited the best facilities of the Soviet defense industry, on which Moscow had lavished human and material resources throughout the Cold War.[59] But domestic orders dried up after 1991, and the sector consequently is burdened with massive overcapacity. It is largely unrestructured, populated by far too many uncompetitive firms with too many employees on their payrolls, and suffers from a chronic shortage of funds for R&D and investment. Between 1992 and 1998, the share of the government's military R&D expenditure declined from 12.8 percent to 0.5 percent of total spending. Russia's science and technology base—already weak in some militarily important areas such as microelectronics—began to collapse. A 1998 report of the Russian Federation's audit office concluded that on current trends, the Russian defense industry would "lose the capability to develop advanced technologies and world-level industrial models by 2005."[60]

Most major arms exporters produce 80–90 percent for the domestic market. Russia's military industrial complex, by contrast, sells far more weaponry to foreign clients than to its own armed forces. In 1999 and 2000, Russia sold three times more weapons abroad than at home.[61] Revenues from these sales keep some important military plants (many located in the Russian Far East) running and allow marginal increases in R&D spending that permit some upgrading of select weapons systems but only very limited development and construction of new systems.[62] The result is intense pressure for codevelopment and production agreements with willing partners. Two countries with great incentives and much to offer in this regard are India and China, although Russia's arms exporters are working feverishly with Brazil and other countries in search of similar deals. Russia's arms exports were up dramatically in 2001, and exporters are in for another banner year in 2002—owing mostly to deals with Beijing and New Dehli.[63]

But foreign sales and partnerships simply cannot substitute for massively increased domestic demand and financing, which is not going to be forthcoming on the scale needed for the sector to retain its current competitiveness. Hence, the spectacular export deals of today obscure the real story, which is that the Russian defense industry is declining. While it will remain an important player, it will become increasingly uncompetitive with its rivals in world arms markets over the next decade and a half—especially in the market for the more advanced systems. That leaves three scenarios for China and India. They can continue to rely on the Russian connection, which, given declining Russian competitiveness, will mean locking themselves into serious technological inferiority. They can develop the capacity to produce a higher proportion of their top military systems indigenously (something they have thus far proved unable to do). Or they can diversify their supply of high-end weapons systems (something India might do). Under any of these three scenarios, the geopolitical significance of Russian arms sales in Asia will decline.

While Russia will face a powerful incentive to maintain its arms relationships, over the next 10–15 years its interests will increasingly become preoccupied with the development of natural resource export markets in Asia. At present Russia is primarily a European oil and gas market operator, owing to the combination of transport costs and limited pipeline infrastructure. But the country wants to go beyond that within the next 10 years. The Putin team has already made a concerted effort to refashion Russia's external image in Asia from a corrupt basket case wallowing in great power fantasies to an emerging energy superpower whose natural resources could become the linchpin of major projects and networks of pipelines throughout Asia. After Putin's March 2001 visit to Seoul, Russia and South Korea announced close cooperation to promote the Irkutsk (Kovykta) gas project, involving an $11 billion pipeline to bring gas down from Siberian fields through China and North Korea, and then to the industrial heartland of South Korea. They also consulted on South Korea's participation in projects to develop oil and gas fields on Sakhalin and other Russian regions.[64] Other pipeline projects currently in discussion or planning phases include an oil pipeline from Sakhalin to Japan, South Korea, and Taiwan (or a shorter line to a Russian trans-shipment terminal); a Russia-China oil pipeline from Siberian fields running either through Mongolia or North Korea into China; natural gas pipelines to China and South Korea; and a trans-China gas pipeline.[65]

The key to Russia's prospects as an oil power is its latent ability to increase production. Optimism about Russia as the coming oil power is lodged less in the size of its reserves (ranked eighth in the world) than the level of its current exports (second in the world) and its potential (and apparent eagerness) to increase those exports substantially. To realize that potential, Russia will need large amounts of investment. The deals that Russia has already signed with partners in Asia and elsewhere, and, indeed, major elements of Putin's new foreign policy strategy, hinge on the ability to raise exports.[66] The deterioration of its oil infrastructure and the technological capacity of its oil firms are the chief obstacles to increasing exports. And a key to overcoming those obstacles is investment—some of which will have to be foreign–and joint ventures with western firms. For example, just developing Russia's share of Caspian oil may take more than $225 billion over the next 10 years.[67] Siberian projects will demand major investments in order to tap new supplies and reduce recovery and shipping costs.[68] Thus, Russia's medium-term strategy brings it full circle: To be a major petro-power in the East, it needs investment capital and technology obtainable mainly in the West.

Will Russia Stay the Course?

Russian decline forecloses most major alternatives to a general policy of accommodation with the major powers. The choice of strategy within the range of possibility will be strongly influenced by the relative costs and benefits of the mix of policy levers available to Moscow. The analysis here suggests that Russia's traditional geopolitical tools, military power and the military industrial complex, will continue to decline relative to its geoeconomic tools, primarily, over the medium term, its oil and gas industries. It follows that whoever occupies the presidential office will face strong incentives to maintain and even deepen the current pragmatic course.

An important corollary of the analysis developed in this chapter is that, while it reflects deeper causes than Putin's personal preferences and his immediate response to September 11, Russia's strategic turn is a less dramatic departure than the conventional wisdom holds. The previous multipolar approach was never a real anti-U.S. balancing policy. It was part bargaining tactic, part sop to domestic prestige anxiety, and, perhaps, part self-delusion. The biggest change has been to move official rhetoric closer to the reality of what Russia is doing, and is capable of doing, in world politics. The real policy changes have been subtler, amounting to acquiescence to U.S. policies that Russia was powerless to stop, some of which arguably enhanced its security. The rest of Russia's activities in world politics have largely continued as before.

It follows that there is considerable room for deepening the strategy. As of summer 2002, there were numerous indications that Russia was on course to do just that. Press reports documented building pressure in the Russian government to rein in the Ministry of Atomic Energy's export policy to Iran by insisting on stricter inspection regime for the Bushehr reactor project than Tehran has been willing to accept.[69] Russia cooperated with the United States in pushing through "smart sanctions" on Iraq; and, while Russia remained officially opposed to an invasion, some officials hinted to western interlocutors that, as long as Russian oil companies' leases in Iraq were honored by a post-Saddam regime, Moscow would do little to stand in the way. If Russia continues to reduce its opposition to U.S. Persian Gulf policy, one of the main remaining irritants in Russian-U.S. relations would be removed. In Asia, that would leave arms sales to China and India as a potential problem. That issue is not likely to be removed soon, but its significance will probably wane over the long haul and, in any case, all sides have proven able to manage it thus far.

As noted at the outset of this chapter, however, the new foreign policy course is genuinely unpopular with important sectors of the Russian elite, and most observers believe that it is far more likely to be reversed than deepened. It is extremely difficult to assess the precise nature and strength of the domestic constraint on Russia's foreign policy.[70] Moscow pundits were initially skeptical, but most swiftly fell in line. Intense media criticism in the winter of 2001–02 may have been part of a ploy to enhance Moscow's bargaining leverage with the West. After all, much of the popular media is controlled or influenced by the Kremlin, and such criticism had waned considerably by the summer in any case. Still, it is impossible to rule out the chance that Putin or his successor will be confronted with domestic political incentives for a more anti-American stance that outweigh the economic and international incentives stressed so far in this chapter.

Nevertheless, the evidence suggests that this scenario will be less likely in the coming decade than it was in the 1990s because the nature of the domestic constraint is changing rapidly. While many analysts remain fixated on Russia's military and traditional foreign policy elites, business elites matter as well. To be sure, few of Russia's business sectors have developed sophisticated lobbying operations, but indirectly their preferences will weigh on any Russian president interested in sustaining economic growth. And, on balance, their preferences are increasingly oriented toward integration and the West. Three changes are particularly noteworthy. First, not only is Russia's trade weighted toward the West (see Figure 6.1 above), but trade is assuming more importance in Russia's economy overall. In 1994, for example, exports were equivalent to about 24 percent of the Russian economy; by 2000, this figure had grown to 42 percent.[71] Second, by fits and starts, important Russian companies are restructuring along western lines, resulting in a net decline in preferences for protection from foreign firms. An example is the dramatic changes in the oil sector over the last two years.[72]

Third, the biggest exporters, which play a major role in the Russian economy and in supplying the government's revenues, are increasingly oriented toward the West. In 2000, 50 percent of Russian exports were in oil and gas. Europe and the United States are where Russia's oil and gas giants sell most of their products, borrow most of their money, locate most of their own outward FDI, secure most of their foreign partnerships, and get most of their inward FDI. Increasingly important parts of the power and metals industries, as well as telecommunications, civilian air transport, banking, and finance, also have growing market and investment incentives to favor a generally integrative course.[73] Even the interests of traditionally anti-western sectors are changing at the margins. The nuclear industrial complex, whose relationship with Iran has long vexed western policymakers, is actually split, with some sectors that have benefited immensely from cooperation with the United States. The military industrial complex is a major commercial competitor with U.S. defense contractors and is strongly oriented toward the Asian strategic triangle if only to preserve market share. Nevertheless, even that sector contained many firms with partnerships and other relationships with western firms.[74]

The new policy turn, in short, accords with the general material interests of most of the powerful actors in the Russian economy. Foreign policy pragmatism is an easy sell to hard-nosed businessmen as well as the largely isolationist public. This is no guarantee for its stability, but it suggests that the staying power of the new orientation is greater than a quick reading of Moscow's public foreign policy discourse would suggest.

The most probable cause of an alteration in the strategic course over the near to medium term is tactics. One effect of Putin's turn toward the United States is to remind the Europeans and Chinese that Russia should not be taken for granted. In time, Russia will give the United States such a reminder. Given the economic interests at play, the most likely tactical shift will be toward Europe, however, rather than China. The EU is Russia's most important trading partner, and many Russians would prefer to build relations with it at the expense of the United States. Given America's role in international economic institutions, as well as its continued close relationship with Europe, however, the old game of playing on inter-alliance contradictions has been put aside for the time being. When conditions are ripe, Russia may again decide to team up with Europe and against the United States on some important policy issue. Each time Moscow engineers such subtle tactical shifts, the punditocracy will talk about fundamental and epoch-making transformations. If the analysis here is right, however, for a decade at least, they will be wrong.

Conclusion

Russia's new foreign policy course is a response to the country's continued decline as well as to the lack of plausible strategy for recovering great power status other than modernization via integration into the world economy. While its significance should not be oversold, Russia's adoption of a more coherent grand strategy based on a clear-eyed appraisal of its real potential is a noteworthy development. A still weakened but much more purposeful Russia is on the horizon.

The bottom line is that increased Russian realism augurs for strategic stability in Asia. The fact that Russia's geopolitical weight, such as it is, has shifted slightly away from China is the least significant implication, and, in any case, the most militarily significant aspect of that relationship—arms transfers—is set to continue. Far more important are the positive dividends of Moscow's more sober appraisal of its power and interests. While students of international relations sometimes equate realism and power politics with conflict, a realistic appraisal of power relations is generally preferable to wishful thinking. A realistic and weakened Russia can have no interest in reigniting great power rivalry in the region and indeed can be expected to do whatever is in its limited capabilities to forestall such an outcome. At the same time, a Russia with its aspirations and potential in sync is more likely to concentrate on the mundane tasks of governance and development and is less likely to destabilize the region through its own further decline and dissolution. Russia thus looks less primed to present Asia with either a dangerous great power threat or a tempting power vacuum than it did in the mid- to late 1990s. A Russia that is more realistic about its power is also more apt to seek entry to Asia's economic and security arrangements on terms that are acceptable to the other major players and thereby more prone to be welcomed by them.

Endnotes

[1] This story is based on a report of the meeting by the Russian liberal politician and leader of the Yabloko Duma faction Grigory Yavlinsky, who was in attendance. See Yavlinsky, "Domestic and Foreign Policy Challenges in Russia," at the Carnegie Endowment for International Peace Briefing, Washington, DC, January 21, 2002. <www.ceip.org/files/events/yavlinskytranscript013102.asp>.

[2] On the timescale for imperial retrenchment, see Dominic Lieven, *Empire: The Russian Empire and its Rivals*, London: John Murray, 2000.

[3] See, for example, Andrei P. Tsygankov, "The Final Triumph of the Pax Americana? Western Intervention in Yugoslavia and Russia's Debate on the Post-Cold War Order," *Communist and Post-Communist Studies*, vol. 34, no. 1 (2001), 133–56.

4   Data on this decline are presented in Stephen G. Brooks and William C. Wohlforth, "Power, Globalization and the End of the Cold War: Reevaluating a Landmark Case for Ideas," *International Security*, vol. 25, no. 3 (Winter 2000/2001), pp. 5–53.

5   Central Intelligence Agency, *The World Factbook, 2001*, <www.odci.gov/cia/publications/factbook/index.html> and World Bank, *World Development Indicators 2001*, Washington, DC: World Bank, 2001.

6   See Murray Feshbach, "The Demographic, Health and Environmental Situation in Russia," draft report presented at the Liechtenstein Institute on Self-Determination Conference "The Future of the Russia State," Triesenberg Liechtenstein, March 14–17, 2002; and Feshbach, "Russia's Demographic and Health Meltdown," testimony to U.S. Congress, Joint Economic Committee, *Russia's Uncertain Economic Future*, Washington, DC: Government Printing Office, 2002.

7   Christopher Hill, "Russian Defense Spending," in Joint Economic Committee, *Russia's Uncertain Economic Future*, p. 168. According to Hill's calculations, defense spending represented about $50 billion in 2000—or five percent of GDP. This falls between Russia's official statistics (2.7 percent of GDP) and the four percent stated by the Stockholm International Peace Research Institute (SIPRI) database on military expenditures, <http://first.sipri.org>, on the one hand, and the International Institute for Strategic Studies' estimate of eight percent (IISS, *The Military Balance: 2001–2002*, London: Oxford University Press, 2002), on the other.

8   "Only 20% of Russian Arms are Modern," RFE/RL *Daily Report*, May 21, 2001.

9   "Every Third Potential Conscript Said Not Fit for Military Service," *ITAR-TASS*, May 23, 2002.

10 See Dale R. Herspring, "Recreating the Russian Military: The Difficult Task Ahead," draft report presented at the Liechtenstein Institute on Self-Determination Conference "The Future of the Russia State," Triesenberg Liechtenstein, March 14–17, 2002.

11 Ibid., pp. 6–7.

12 Hill, "Russian Defense Spending," p. 180.

13 Calculated from GDP estimates in Angus Maddison, *Monitoring the World Economy, 1820–1991*, Paris: Organization for Economic Cooperation and Development, 1995.

14 For an excellent, concise analysis, see Robert S. Ross, "The Geography of the Peace: East Asia in the Twenty-First Century," *International Security*, vol. 23, no. 4 (Spring 1999), pp. 81–118.

15 See "Osnovnye polizheniia voennoi doktriny Rossiskoi Federatsii," *Izvestiia*, November 19, 1993, p. 1; the debates on doctrine in "Military Doctrine of the Russian Federation (Russia)," *Voennyi vestnik* (English edition), nos. 13–14, 1992, pp. 2–34; "Russian Military Doctrine Today in Light of the New Realities," *Zarubezhnaya voennoie obozrenie* 1994:2 as translated and reprinted in JPRS-UFM-94-005; and, for the recent version, "Voennaia Doktrina Rossiskoy Federatsii," <www.scrf.gov.ru.>.

16 See William Zimmerman, *The Russian People and Foreign Policy: Russian Elite*

and Mass Perspectives, Princeton: Princeton University Press, 2002, which shows that Russian elite threat perceptions are better explained by their assessments of specific U.S. policies than by overall U.S. power.

[17] Officials are supposed to watch their words on this issue, but they sometimes slip, as when Defense Minister Igor Radionov listed China among Russia's "main potential enemies." Quoted in Alexander Lukin, "Russia's Image of China and Russian-Chinese Relations," *Brookings Institution Working Paper*, June 2001, p. 15. For the debate, see Aleksandr G. Yakovlev, "'Tretiya ugroza:' Kitaai—Vrag No. 1 dlya Rossii?" *Problemy Dal'nego Vostoka*, no. 1 (January 2002), pp. 48–61, and sources cited therein.

[18] Ross, "The Geography of the Peace: East Asia in the Twenty-First Century."

[19] A good sampling of the distribution of assessments in the period is provided by the Foreign Ministry Conference on "A Transformed Russia in a New World," reported in *International Affairs* (Moscow), April–May 1992.

[20] See the result of a poll of foreign policy elites reported by Gudrun Dometeit, "Vision of Greatness," *Focus* (Munich), June 3, 1996, pp. 235–38, reprinted and translated in Foreign Broadcast Information Service—Daily Report: Central Eurasia (hereafter FBIS-SOV) 96-109; D. Furman, "O venshne-politicheskikh prioritetakh Rossii," *Svobodniai mysl'* 1996: 13–18. A comprehensive review is provided by Hannes Adomeit, "Russia as 'Great Power' in World Affairs: Image and Reality," *International Affairs* (London), vol 71, no.1: 35–68.

[21] A notable example was the press commentary that accompanied the signing of the China-Russia Friendship Treaty in July 2001. Thus, for example, William Safire warned that "a future recombination of China and Russia… would challenge America's status the world's sole superpower" in "Putin's China Card," *The New York Times*, June 18, 2001, and Martin Sieff seriously pursued an analogy between the Sino-Russian Friendship Treaty and the Hitler-Stalin Pact: "Russia-China Pact Echoes 1939," *UPI*, July 10, 2001 in Johnson's Russia List, no. 5349, (July 17, 2001).

[22] See, for example, Nikolai Sokov, "What is at Stake for the United States in the Sino-Russian Friendship Treaty?" *PONARS Policy Memo*, no. 200 (September 2001).

[23] For a detailed analysis of the treaty, see Elizabeth Wishnick, "Russia and China: Brothers Again?" *Asian Survey*, vol. 41, no. 5 (September–October 2001), pp. 797–821.

[24] Kevin P. O'Prey, "Arms Exports and Russia's Defense Industries: Issues for the U.E. Congress," in Joint Economic Committee, *Russia's Uncertain Economic Future*.

[25] The major effect is on the power assessments in whose shadow bargaining over the Taiwan issue takes place. See Thomas Christensen, "China," in Richard J. Ellings and Aaron L. Friedberg, eds., *Strategic Asia 2001–02: Power and Purpose*, Seattle, Wash.: The National Bureau of Asian Research, 2001.

[26] Local tensions over the contested islands are detailed in Oleg Zhunusov, "Spornye ostrova otob'yut u Kitaya s pomoshch'yu pontonov," *Izvestiya*, July 19, 2002, p. 2.

[27] This voluminous body of literature is dissected in Douglas W. Blum, "Do-

mestic Politics and Russia's Caspian Policy," *Post-Soviet Affairs*, vol. 14, no. 2 (April–June 1998), pp. 137–64; and Blum, "Globalization and the Caspian Region," in *Succession and Long-Term Stability in the Caspian Region*, Cambridge, Mass.: BCSIA, 2000. Another excellent recent discussion is Pavel Baev, "Russia Refocuses its Politics in the Southern Caucasus," Caspian Studies Program of the John F. Kennedy School of Government, Working Paper No. 1 (July 2001).

[28] For more on interstate rivalries in Central Asia, see Martha Brill Olcott's chapter in this volume.

[29] Kenneth Weisbrode, *Central Eurasia: Prize or Quicksand? Contending Views of Instability in Karabakh, Ferghana and Afghanistan*, Adelphi Paper No. 338, 2001.

[30] For the background, see Martha Brill Olcott, *Central Asia's New States: Independence, Foreign Policy, and Regional Security*, Washington, DC: United States Institute of Peace, 1996. For more recent analysis of the Russian and Chinese roles that confirm these initial trends, see Christensen "China," and Rajan Menon, "Russia," in Ellings and Friedberg, eds., *Strategic Asia 2001–02*.

[31] Indeed, the logic has been exhaustively set forth in books by Primakov and Ivanov. Yevgeny Primakov, *Gody v bolshoi politike*, Moscow: Kollektsiia Sovershenno sekretno, 1999; Igor S. Ivanov, *Novaia rossiiskaia diplomatiia: desiat let vneshnei politiki strany*, Moscow: Olma-Press, 2001.

[32] "Strategiia dlia Rossii IV," <www.svop.ru>.

[33] Gregory Feifer, "Forum Argues over Russia's Place," *Moscow Times*, in Johnson's Russia List, no. 6282, May 1, 2002.

[34] Even moderate foreign policy thinkers, to say nothing of the geopolitical theorists popular with Ministry of Defense and General Staff officers, fell prey to this bias. As Sergei Rogov, director of the Russian Academy of Sciences Institute of the United States and Canada, put it: "due to the size of its territory and population, as well as its military and scientific potential, and as a great Eurasian power, [Russia] can become a leading participant in a multipolar world, playing an active role in resolving problems in which it has an interest." Rogov, "Kontory Rossiiskoy geopolitikoi," *Nezavisimaya gazeta—stsenarii,* no. 3 (March 1998), p. 5.

[35] Iuriy Shishkov, "Russia i SNG: neudavshchiysya brak po raschetu," *Pro et Contra*, vol. 6, no. 1–2 (Winter–Spring 2001), pp. 91–106.

[36] "Rossia na poroge tysiacheletiia," December 31, 1999, <www.gov.ru>.

[37] BBC Monitoring, July 8, 2000, in Johnson's Russia List, no. 4391, July 9, 2000.

[38] See Brooks and Wohlforth, "Power, Globalization and the End of the Cold War."

[39] Text of Putin's state of the nation address to the Russian parliament, as translated by BBC monitoring, reprinted in Johnson's Russia List, no. 6195 (April 19, 2002).

[40] The most recent drafts of all three documents are available at the Security Council's website: <www.scrf.gov.ru/documents/documents.htm>.

[41] <http://pravda.ru>, July 19, 2001.

[42] Alexei Zagorsky, "Three Years on the Path to Nowhere: The Hashimoto Ini-

tiative in Russian-Japanese Relations," *Pacific Affairs*, vol. 74, no. 1 (Spring 2001), pp. 75–93.

[43] Interfax/ITAR-TASS (Moscow), January 9, 2001; and Roald Saveliev, "The New Russian Leadership's Foreign Policy and Russian-Korean Relations," *Far Eastern Affairs*, no. 2 (2001), pp. 10–15.

[44] Full text of Putin's speech in the Russian Foreign Ministry on January 26, 2001, reported by <http://strana.ru> in Johnson's Russia List, no. 5054, January 27, 2001.

[45] "Russian Military Publishes Chechnya Death Tolls," *Reuters*, July 22, 2002, reprinted in Johnson's Russia List, no. 6365, July 23, 2002.

[46] IISS, *Military Balance 2001–02*, estimate for 2000, p. 108.

[47] Pavel Felgenhauer, "Paying for the War in Chechnya," *Moscow Times*, April 26, 2001, in Johnson's Russia List, April 29, 2001.

[48] IISS, *Military Balance*, pp. 117–18. Estimate excludes the approximately 14,500 border troops in Tajikistan who are Tajik conscripts serving under Russian officers.

[49] For a good example, see the interview with Igor Ivanov reported in, "Svetlana Babaeva, 'Igor' Ivanov: Glavnoa-stoby vneshnyaya politika ne privodila k raskolu vnutri strany," *Izvestiya*, July 10, 2002, p. 1.

[50] Dmitry Safonov, "Sergey Ivanov Views Shanghai Cooperation Organization's Antiterror Mission," *Izvestiia*, May 15, 2002, FBIS-CHI-2002-516.

[51] Interfax, *Oil & Gas Report*, April 19–25, 2002 in FBIS-SOV-2002-0418.

[52] See, for example, Vilia Gelbras, "Rossia i Kitai: Voprosy sobiraniia geoekonomicheskikh prostranstv," *Polis-politicheskiie issledovanie*, no. 6 (1995), pp. 32–54.

[53] Vladimir Kontorovich, "Economic Crisis in the Russian Far East: Overdevelopment of Colonial Exploitation?" *Post-Soviet Geography and Economics*, vol. 42, no. 6 (2001), pp. 391–415; and Allen C. Lynch, "The Roots of Russia's Economic Dilemmas: Liberal Economics and Illiberal Geography," *Europe-Asia Studies*, vol. 54, no. 1 (January 2002), pp. 31–49.

[54] See sources reported in Ksenia Yudaeva, Konstantin Kozlov, Naltalya Melentieva, and Natalya Ponomareva, "Does Foreign Ownership Matter? The Russian Experience," Working Paper No. 2001/027, Moscow: New Economic School, 2001.

[55] Keith Bush, *The Russian Economy in March 2002*, Washington, DC: Center for Strategic and International Studies, 2002, p. 23.

[56] Cited in World Bank, "Russian Economic Report," no. 2 (January, 2002), <www.worldbank.org.ru>.

[57] Richard Ericson, "The Russian Economy" draft report presented at the Liechtenstein Institute on Self-Determination Conference "The Future of the Russia State," Triesenberg Liechtenstein, March 14–17.

[58] For example, the Su-30 MKK fighter-bombers sold to China are upgraded versions of the Su-27, a late 1970s design; and the Project-636 Kilo class submarines Beijing purchased in June 2002 are improved versions of the standard Kilo that entered service in the Soviet Navy the early 1980s.

[59] Gregg Austin and Alexey D. Muraviev, *The Armed Forces of Russia in Asia*, London: Tauris, 2000, chapter 10.

60 Ibid., p. 235.

61 IISS, *Military Balance, 2001–2002*, p. 111.

62 Stockholm International Peace Research Institute, *SIPRI Yearbook 2001: Armaments, Disarmament, and International Security*, London: Oxford University Press, pp. 230–31.

63 Alexey Komarov, "Russia Chalks up Record Defense Sales," *Aviation Week and Space Technology*, January 7, 2002.

64 Interfax, *Oil & Gas Report*, March 2–8, 2001.

65 EIA Report, "Russia: Oil and Natural Gas Pipelines," March 2002 <www.eia.doe.gov>; and Mikhail Klasson, "Gazprom Breaks into Asia," *Moscow News*, July 17, 2002.

66 Edward Morse and James Richard, "The Battle for Energy Dominance," *Foreign Affairs*, March/April 2002.

67 Bush, "Russian Economy," p. 23, reporting an EBRD estimate.

68 U.S. Department of Energy, Energy Information Agency, Country Report, "Russia," April 2002.

69 See, for example, "Russia Ending Involvement in Iranian Reactor," Stratfor, June 28, 2002, in Johnson's Russia List, no. 6330, June 30, 2002.

70 The best public opinion research suggests that the Russian populace is much more isolationist than militant or anti-American, implying support for Putin's bottom-line orientation to foreign policy. The same research documents much more geopolitical and skeptical attitudes among the elite, ratifying the impression conveyed by the Russian press. See Zimmerman, *The Russian People and Foreign Policy*.

71 William H. Cooper, "Russia's Economic Performance: Entering the 21st Century," in Joint Economic Committee, *Russia's Economic Future*, p. 13.

72 U.S. Department of Energy, Energy Information Agency, "Restructuring the Energy Sector."

73 For a comprehensive report, see Sergei Medvedev, ed., *Business Elites and Russia's European Policy*, UPI (The Finnish Institute of International Affairs) Working Paper No. 26 (2000).

74 David Bernstein, *Commercialization of Russian Technology in Cooperation with American Companies*, Stanford, Calif.: Stanford University Press, 1999; and David Holloway, ed., *The Anatomy of Russian Defense Conversion*, Stanford, Calif.: Stanford University Press, 2001.

CENTRAL ASIA

Martha Brill Olcott

T he September 11 terrorist attacks on the United States and subsequent U.S. military action in Afghanistan brought Central Asia into the news, reminding the international community of the strategic importance of the region and the consequences of ignoring the region's problems. Ousting the Taliban eliminated a major security risk for the Central Asian states, and the renewed western interest in the region created an opportunity for these states to "get it right" by redressing the mistakes of the first decade of independence.

For all of President George W. Bush's initial reluctance for the United States to engage in "nation-building,"[1] this is precisely what his administration is now doing, in Central Asia as well as in Afghanistan. The United States is taking an active role in facilitating economic and political institution building as well as cooperation in security relations.

U.S. troops are now stationed in the region, at the Khanabad base in Karshi, Uzbekistan, and at Kyrgyzstan's Manas airfield (now renamed Peter Ganci in honor of a New York City fire fighter who was killed in the

Martha Olcott is Senior Associate at the Carnegie Endowment for International Peace. She wishes to thank Marat Umerov and Karlis Kirsis, who were junior fellows in the Carnegie Russia-Eurasia Program in 2001–02, for their work on the tables, footnotes, and fact checking. She also benefited from the advice of Aaron Friedberg, Richard Ellings, Francine Frankel, Erica Johnson, and Enders Wimbush, who read earlier drafts of this chapter.

attack on the World Trade Center). U.S. forces have also made use of facilities in Tajikistan and have been given limited landing rights in Kazakhstan as well. In addition, Turkmenistan has been a major transit point for humanitarian assistance bound for Afghanistan.

The ouster of the Taliban was a very positive development from the point of view of the Central Asian states, as the leaders of most of these countries saw the ideological nature of the former Afghan regime as threatening to their secular visions of nationhood. The region's leaders were also bothered by the high level of toleration that the Taliban clerics showed for drug traders and international terrorist groups such as the Al Qaeda network. The degree of perceived threat varied over time and from state to state, but, from late 1999, all of the region's leaders except Turkmenistan's Saparmurad Niyazov strongly supported the goal of regime change in Afghanistan. A deepening sense of fear set in throughout the region after a series of terrorist bombings in Tashkent in February 1999,[2] and later that summer when an armed incursion by the Afghan-based Islamic Movement of Uzbekistan (IMU) captured villages in Kyrgyzstan and took several foreigners hostage.[3]

This chapter outlines the five Central Asian states' development in their first decade of independence, examining how each regime approached issues of political and economic reform, and assessing the rise of radical Islamist groups across the region. It then looks at the geopolitics of Central Asia before September 11, 2001, both in terms of inter-state relations and the roles and influences of major external powers such as Russia, China, Turkey, Iran, and the United States. The subsequent section examines the extent to which the Central Asia strategic environment has changed post-September 11, marked especially by the major increase in U.S. influence in the region. A concluding section looks ahead and suggests how this changed strategic landscape might affect political and economic development within the states, and explores some of the risks and opportunities of greater U.S. engagement in the region.

Central Asia's Second Chance

The regime change in Afghanistan provides the states of Central Asia with much desired breathing room. Homegrown opposition groups will now have to go further afield for their training and work harder to raise the money to sustain their operations. The reconstruction of Afghanistan, should it go fairly smoothly, will also benefit the Central Asian states by allowing for the development of new transit corridors across Afghanistan, creating relatively rapid access to the ports of Pakistan, and opening the possibility of supplying India with Central Asian oil and gas.

The increased U.S. presence in the region and the potential benefits of rebuilding Afghanistan, however, will not provide answers to the major problems that the Central Asian states face if there is no will to reform within the states themselves. The Central Asian states all face serious crises in the years to come. Although the states vary in the degree of severity of their difficulties, in every instance serious reform is required. All of these nations must still undergo the transfer of power to a new generation, and at best they have introduced only a few institutions to attempt this in a democratic fashion. The Central Asian states all have strong presidential systems, and are headed by men who either served as heads of Soviet republic communist parties or as senior Soviet officials.[4]

While some of the states of the region have made considerable progress in their transition to market economies, others have not begun. Corruption is endemic throughout Central Asia and there is little protection of private property. The Central Asian states all have rapidly growing populations. They are all still reforming education and health-care systems, but some are not doing as well as others, leaving fertile breeding grounds for activism by radical Muslim groups that are indigenous to the region.

The Central Asian states remain interdependent in unusual ways, a legacy of having been part of a single state. There are shared hydroelectric and other energy systems, imprecise national boundaries, and highways built with little regard to those boundaries. While these features are not necessarily bad, the Central Asian states lack effective bilateral or multilateral institutions to manage the potential conflicts that their intimate geography and shared Soviet history might create. One reason for this lack of institutions is that each of these states is still striving to create an international identity separate from that of each of its neighbors. In trying to do so, however, each has been hampered by the somewhat erratic engagement of regional as well as global powers. Although the United States was quick to recognize all five newly independent states, initially Washington was content to take a backseat to Russia in the region. This situation began to change when U.S. and Western European firms became more interested in developing the sizeable Caspian oil and gas reserves. These projects were still largely in the exploration phase in September 2001, and western strategic engagement with these states was limited.

Sharing borders with three of the five Central Asian states, China has long had an interest in the region. China, like Russia, has not hurried to maximize its strategic advantage. By contrast, Turkey and Iran saw in the creation of independent states in Central Asia potential to shift the geostrategic balance to their respective advantages, but they lacked the resources to become a deciding influence in any of these countries.

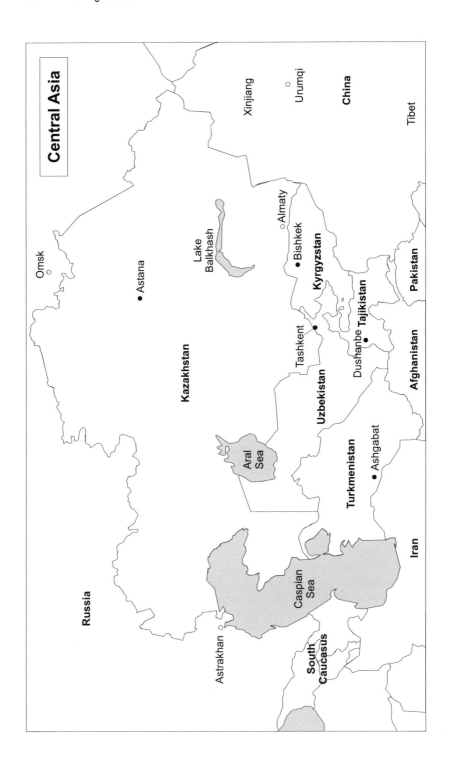

Perhaps more than anything else that happened in the last decade, the opening of U.S. military bases in the region, formally marks of the end of the Russian and Soviet empires. Interestingly, Russia has tolerated, supported, and even appreciated the insertion of U.S. power into Central Asia, largely because the increased U.S. presence came in pursuit of a goal that Russia long wanted but was incapable of achieving—the defeat of the Taliban. Russia's influence in the region was already diminishing through a combination of Moscow's greater sense of its own limited capacities and the simultaneous growth in confidence by the leaders of some of the Central Asian states, most particularly Presidents Karimov of Uzbekistan and Nazarbayev of Kazakhstan, both of whom were the architects of increasingly complex and multi-vectored foreign policies.

Now these multi-vectored policies are yielding fruit. The United States seems unlikely to leave Central Asia any time soon and is developing long-term strategic relationships with several of the region's states. It has signed a long-term security partnership with Uzbekistan, which seems to ensure continued U.S. investment in programs designed to reform that country's military. Moreover, the United States may gradually extend similar offers to other Central Asian states. There has also been a commitment to increase U.S. spending for upgrading border security throughout the region and for improved narcotics interdiction. Slowly but surely the United States, as a lone superpower, is bringing this region at least partly under its security umbrella in ways that are certain to have an impact on the region's former and aspiring hegemons.

It is less clear, however, that the expanded U.S. role in Central Asia (and the conversely diminished Russian role) will in and of itself reduce or change the nature of the security risks that emanate from this region, although it does admittedly make U.S. intervention or preemptive action easier if Washington believes its interests are directly threatened.

Creating Nations in Central Asia: The First Decade

While the leaders of each of the five Central Asian nations embraced independence in December 1991 as a form of statehood restored, in reality none of these five countries had a history of modern independence. The five Central Asian states, as currently defined, were Soviet-era creations, and the current national boundaries do not reflect natural geographic divides, nor do they closely reflect historic patterns of land usage.

In the 1920s Stalin carved five Soviet republics out of the Russian colonial acquisitions of Turkestan (southern Kazakhstan, eastern Turkmenistan, Kyrgyzstan, Uzbekistan, and Tajikistan), the Transcaspian military district (the rest of Turkmenistan), and the so-called Kyrgyz Steppe

Table 7.1. Economic Conditions in Central Asia (2000)

	Population (m)	Per capita GDP ($)	GDP growth (%)	Inflation (%)	Unemployment (%)
Kazakhstan	14.9	1,225.0	9.6	13.2	6.0
Kyrgyzstan	4.7	275.2	5.1	18.7	5.6
Tajikistan	6.2	159.9	8.3	32.9	2.5
Turkmenistan	5.4	552.5	17.6	8.3	...
Uzbekistan	25.0	252.3	4.0	24.2	0.6

Source: European Bank for Reconstruction and Development, *Transition Report 2001*, London: EBRD, 2001.

(the rest of Kazakhstan). The Russians had gained control of northern Kazakhstan by treaties signed with the local Kazakh nobility in the first half of the eighteenth century. They had then extended their territory southward through conquest in the middle of the nineteenth century, subduing Kazakh (known then as Kirghiz) and Kyrgyz (known as Karakyrgyz—black Kyrgyz) tribes and defeating the Khan of Kokand (1864), the Khan of Khiva (1873), and the Emir of Bukhara (1868). The administrative boundaries of the Soviet republics were modified many times, and were designed to leave large irredentist populations scattered throughout the region.

A decade ago it made good sense to think of the region as a coherent whole with a single set of problems that might have been addressed through a coordinated and integrated response. Today most observers of the region recognize that this view is overly simplistic. Kazakhstan, Kyrgyzstan, Tajikistan, Turkmenistan, and Uzbekistan have all evolved in different ways over the past decade, and each has taken on a distinct identity.[5]

Kazakhstan

Prior to September 11, there was a growing sense of U.S. disappointment with all the Central Asian states. The one partial exception was Kazakhstan, which seemed to stand out—at least economically. In fact, Kazakhstan had always stood somewhat apart from its other Central Asian neighbors. In Soviet times, these five republics were referred to as "Middle Asia and Kazakhstan." Kazakhstan had the largest Russian population of all the Central Asian republics, and ethnic Russians outnumbered ethnic Kazakhs for most of the post-World War II period. Ethnic Russians began leaving Kazakhstan in the late 1980s, when legislation requiring that they learn the Kazakh language was introduced. The pace of exit increased dramatically after independence, and over 1.5 million Russians left the country in its first decade of existence. The mines, refineries, and factories of northern Kazakhstan were critical to the Soviet Union's industrial output, but these industries nearly ground to a halt when the inter-republic linkages of the Soviet Union were broken in the early 1990s. Northern Kazakhstan was also fully dependent upon oil and electricity supplied by Russia, and the country accumulated hundreds of millions of dollars of inter-state debt trying to keep its factories running and municipal utilities functioning.

Nevertheless, compared with its Central Asian neighbors, Kazakhstan made the most headway in its economic transition. This is partly due to its vast natural resources and human potential and partly because it has engaged in macro-economic reforms, introducing a freely convertible currency, the most modern banking sector in the region, and a functional stock exchange (although it still lacks stocks to be traded). The tax structure has been reformed, and the pension system reorganized, making it more market-driven. Attention also has been paid to reforming the health care and educational systems. The government of Kazakhstan, though, has wasted a lot of money that could have gone to the reform effort, including billions of dollars that were spent on moving the nation's capital from Almaty to Astana (formerly Akmolinsk).

Most of Kazakhstan's hopes for the future rest with the development of its oil fields, which, if current optimistic estimates of these assets are confirmed, could make Kazakhstan the fifth largest oil producer in the world. Kazakhstan has received $13 billion in foreign direct investment since independence, most of it in the oil and gas sector.[6] According to the U.S. Energy Information Administration, Kazakhstan's oil reserves are estimated to be in the range of 5.4–17.6 billion barrels. Most of the expected oil production growth will come from three fields: Tengiz, Karachaganak, and Kashagan. The Tengiz field, with an estimated 6–9 billion barrels of recoverable oil reserves, is being developed by the TengizChevroil joint venture. Chevron was initially invited to develop this field by Soviet president Mikhail Gorbachev, but later negotiated a new contract with the Kazakh government. The Karachaganak field, which is being developed by a consortium led by Britain's BG Group and Italy's Agip, has estimated recoverable reserves of two billion barrels of oil and gas condensate, as well as 17 trillion cubic feet of natural gas making it the country's largest deposit. The offshore Kashagan field could contain up to 40 billion barrels of oil, at least 10 billion of which are thought to be recoverable. Agip KCO operates Kashagan, which could be the largest oil discovery in the past 40 years.

Kazakhstan has proven natural gas reserves of between 65 and 70 trillion cubic feet, ranking it in the top 20 countries in the world. In 1997, an international consortium of Agip, ChevronTexaco, and Lukoil (Russia) signed a $7–$8 billion final production-sharing agreement to develop the field for 40 years, with a planned investment of $4 billion by 2006. Thus far, development of the field has concentrated on gas condensate. Kazakhstan's other significant producing areas include the Tengiz, Zhanazhol, and Uritau fields, with the undeveloped offshore areas also believed to hold large amounts of natural gas. Nevertheless, because of the lack of developed pipeline infrastructure to link the natural gas fields in the western part of the country to consumers in the south, Kazakhstan must import natural gas to meet domestic demand.

Much could still happen to derail or delay the plans for development of resources in this landlocked state. For now, the only "sure-thing" is the development of the Tengiz oil field, which currently produces 37,000 tons of oil daily. The development of TengizChevroil was initially delayed for several years by difficulties in negotiating transit terms. The rights to develop the Tengiz field were contingent on Chevron accepting that oil would be exported by a pipeline running across Russia, which was to be built by the Russian- and Omani-dominated Caspian Pipeline Consortium. The Russian company Transneft was designated the pipeline operator. In 1997 Mobil was brought in as an additional investor in the project, and the pipeline was finally opened in 2001.[7] ChevronTexaco owns 50 percent of the TengizChevroil project and 20 percent of the Karachaganak Integrated Organization (KIO), which is developing the giant Karachaganak field (originally a Texaco project) in northwestern Kazakhstan. This project, though, is still at the exploratory stages.

The real challenge for Kazakhstan will be to manage its oil revenues in a way that benefits the country's population. To this end, Kazakhstan created a National Oil Fund in 2001 and is regularly depositing funds in it. The success of this project requires greater economic transparency in the country's oil industry, however. While investor confidence in Kazakhstan is regularly reported as increasing, at the same time, there is a feeling of vulnerability fueled by the rumors of corruption around the president and his family.

Many fear that President Nazarbayev will set up a political dynasty, and his daughter Dariga and son-in-law Timur Kulibayev (who is the dominant figure in Kazakhstan's national oil and gas company) are both rumored to be potential successors. The leader of Kazakhstan since 1989, Nazarbayev did not faced serious competition in his 1991 or 1999 presidential bids. His major competitor in the latter election, former prime minister Akezhan Kazhegeldin, was barred from running because he acquired a "criminal record" when his political party (the Republic Party) held an unsanctioned meeting.

Two Kazakh parliaments were disbanded before their term was completed, the first in 1993 when Boris Yeltsin eliminated the communist-era

Russian parliament, and the second in 1995 on a legal technicality.[8] The latter occurrence was justified as necessary to permit Kazakhstan to proceed with its macroeconomic reforms, which were introduced through presidential decree. Over the past 10 years the Kazakh parliament has gone from a raucous unicameral body that debated legislation with vigor, and sometimes forced its will on a reluctant president, to a bicameral body, with an upper house that is effectively hand-picked by the president and a lower house that is also generally reluctant to cross him.

Political opposition is dangerous in Kazakhstan, as elsewhere in the region. Independent newspapers are subject to harassment, and reporters have been beaten up and editorial offices burned. Kazakhstan's chief opposition figure, former prime minister Kazhegeldin, lives in exile under constant risk of extradition, having been tried in absentia on charges of having absconded with state funds. Nazarbayev's attempts to intimidate Kazhegeldin backfired in a rather embarrassing, and potentially quite serious way. When the Kazakh government asked the Swiss to investigate the former prime minister's Swiss holdings, the investigation turned up evidence of bank accounts belonging to the Kazakh president as well. This incident in turn helped trigger a U.S. Department of Justice investigation into the behavior of certain U.S. oil companies and their intermediaries, as well as that of the Kazakh government.[9] Eventually, the Kazakh government admitted to the existence of a $1 billion "secret foreign currency fund" that had been deposited in Swiss banks in 1996. Kazakh authorities maintain that much of this money went to pay off pension arrears, to support the national budget, and that the remaining $212.6 million has been deposited into the country's new National Oil Fund.[10]

Although the U.S. government was disturbed by the political trends in Kazakhstan and its officials were quietly pressuring the Kazakh government to democratize their political institutions, the emphasis of U.S. policy was on improving the investment conditions in Kazakhstan. Most importantly, the United States tried to convince the Kazakh government to send its oil from the off-shore Kashagan field along the U.S.-supported Baku-Tbilisi-Ceyhan pipeline route, bypassing Russia and Iran.

Kyrgyzstan

If U.S. officials held out the hope that reform might still eventually bear fruit in Kazakhstan, there was little reason for enthusiasm about developments in Kyrgyzstan. Kyrgyzstan had initially seemed the most promising of all the Central Asian states from the point of view of U.S. policymakers. President Askar Akayev was viewed as a scientist and not a traditional communist party official. Although Akayev has a doctorate and worked as a physicist, most of his career was spent in the science sections of the party bureaucracy. Akayev was head of the republic's Academy of Sciences in October 1990, when he was chosen to be president of the Kyrgyz SSR.

Akayev initially styled himself the "Thomas Jefferson of Central Asia," and Kyrgyzstan was the first state in the region to engage in macroeconomic reform, introducing its own currency as part of an International Monetary Fund macro-stabilization program in May 1993. Kyrgyzstan was also the first of the post-Soviet states (excluding the Baltic nations) to enter the World Trade Organization (WTO), which it did in 2000. President Akayev was the only Central Asian leader to back Boris Yeltsin at the time of the August 1991 coup attempt, and, until the mid-1990s, the country seemed likely to make a rapid transition to a democratic political system.

Since the early days of independence, however, the range of acceptable political activity in the country has been steadily diminishing. President Akayev has been elected president three times: in 1991, 1995, and 2000 (the last was facilitated by a 1998 Constitutional Court decision that the original two-term rule of the Kyrgyz constitution did not apply to the president because the country adopted a new constitution in 1993). Although President Akayev promises that he will step down when his term expires in 2005, his critics claim that the former scientist will again seek constitutional modifications to allow him yet another term in office.

Initially, according to the country's constitution of 1993, Kyrgyzstan had a parliamentary-presidential government, but a referendum of October 1994 created a two-house legislative system, consisting of the People's Representative Assembly and the Legislative Assembly. The intent of this move was to make the legislature malleable and to transform the country into a strong presidential system. Even after these changes, similar to those Kazakhstan, Kyrgyz leaders have been unwilling to support free and fair elections for their much weakened legislatures, and the subsequent parliamentary elections have been filled with irregularities.

Over the past several years the amount of political space available to critics of the Akayev regime has been declining steadily. Many of the country's independent media outlets have been fined and closed, in some cases precisely because they made allegations about presidential corruption. Some prominent critics of the president have also been sent to jail, including the country's most popular politician, Feliks Kulov, the leader of the opposition Ar-Namys (Dignity) party, who is serving a lengthy prison term on what appear to be politically motivated charges.

The 2000 Kyrgyz presidential election was criticized by the Organization for Security and Cooperation in Europe (OSCE) for failing to meet international standards. The campaign was flawed well before the balloting, as several candidates were eliminated because they failed to pass a closed-door exam in Kyrgyz, including some whose native language was Kyrgyz.[11]

Many feel that President Akayev has turned away from his commitment to democratic transition because of the country's difficult economic transition. Although Kyrgyzstan has experienced positive economic growth rates in recent years, much of this has come from the development of its giant gold mine, Kumtor, a joint venture with Canada's Cameco. For example, while Kyrgyzstan's industrial output reportedly grew 6 percent in the first half of 2001, if companies developing the Kumtor gold field are factored out industrial output actually fell 5.4 percent during this period.[12]

One major problem is that, despite some lingering ties from the Soviet period, Central Asia has failed to develop any sort of regional market, which has left the tiny economy of Kyrgyzstan cut off from Russia by trade barriers in Kazakhstan and cut off from the markets of Uzbekistan by the policies of economic isolation that Tashkent has pursued. As a result, over the course of the first decade of independence, Kyrgyzstan went from a country that the international development community felt had great promise to one that the donor community is now using as a laboratory for trying strategies for poverty alleviation.[13]

Tajikistan

Political life in Tajikistan spiraled out of control immediately after the failed August 1991 Communist coup in Moscow, and from 1992 to 1997 the country was engulfed in a devastating civil war, which was fought between the Moscow-backed Tajik leadership and the Muslim-led United Tajik Opposition (UTO) for control of the central government.[14]

After the August coup, which had been supported by Kakhar Makhkamov, Tajikistan's communist party secretary and president, an active pro-democracy movement in the country's capital city of Dushanbe and an ambitious and frustrated former Communist Party leader, Rahmon Nabiev, mobilized large groups of people, including devout villagers, who were brought to Dushanbe with the help of Tajikistan's increasingly powerful religious leaders. In the face of this public pressure, Makhkamov resigned in 1991 and was replaced by Nabiev, who quickly fell out of favor with both the pro-democratic and pro-Islamic groups. Large demonstrations in the spring of 1992 turned into factional fighting, along regional as well as ideological lines. Nabiev was forced to resign in May 1992, and a coalition government was formed, headed by Akbarsho Iskandarov, who served as chairman of the parliament. After six months of fighting, the Iskandarov government was overthrown in November 1992, with the support of Russian troops based in the country.[15] Tajikistan's current president, Emomali Rahmonov, seized power at the time, and was then elected president in November 1994.

A provisional cease-fire was brokered in October 1994, although a lasting peace agreement was not reached for several more years and violence continued. The five-year civil war ended in June 1997, when international mediation led to a largely successful process of national reconciliation and the warring sides signed peace accords in Moscow. The accords formalized power-sharing by bringing together communists, representatives of some Tajik Islamist groups, and democrats in a coalition government.[16]

Politics in Tajikistan had long been centered around regional ties, with the communists garnering support in Khujad and Kulob provinces, Islamist groups drawing much of their support from Kurgan Tiube, and democrats largely finding support in Dushanbe. While President Rahmonov, head of a former Soviet collective, is still seen largely as a factional leader, favoring the interests of his native Kulob region, the critical feature of power-sharing formalized by the national reconciliation agreement was that it brought other regional groups into the government and provided representation for some of the Islamist groups that had been part of the UTO.

Tajikistan's civil war also had many hidden costs for neighboring states. Even today, the Rahmonov government's control over Tajikistan's territory is far from complete, and this has created new and more serious risks for those living in neighboring states. The presence of Islamists in Tajikistan's government has worried the leaders of neighboring Uzbekistan, Kyrgyzstan, and Kazakhstan, who view this as a dangerous precedent for the region as a whole. The drugs smuggled from Tajikistan have undermined its economy and led to the corruption of law enforcement in southern Kyrgyzstan, a situation that made that country's southern border more porous to militant groups like the Islamic Movement of Uzbekistan. The IMU has been able to seek sanctuary in or passage through Tajikistan, and its activities have become more violent since early 1999.[17]

While Tajikistan's government of reconciliation may have angered some of its neighbors, U.S. and international financial engagement in Tajikistan increased in 1998–99 after the formation of the coalition government. The international donor community began an aggressive program of macroeconomic reform, and, like Kyrgyzstan, Tajikistan is working with the international financial community to develop poverty alleviation strategies.[18] Moreover, although everyone recognized that the Tajikistan still has a long way to go, most outside observers thought that things were moving in the right direction at the time of the country's tenth anniversary.

At the same time, assistance from the International Monetary Fund (IMF) has been periodically suspended because of what is believed to be the deliberate manipulation of official statistics, and the debt burden of that nation has been increasing steadily since the appointment of the reconciliation government. While some of this budgetary manipulation is certainly sheer negligence, many in the Tajik government also have had a strong vested interest in concealing the economic impact of Tajikistan's narcotics trade, which some estimate as equal to over 50 percent of GDP. This trade was undoubtedly facilitated by the atmosphere of lawlessness that pervaded the country in the aftermath of the civil war.

Turkmenistan

Tajikistan is not the only country in the region in which there is reason to have little confidence in official statistics. There have also been complaints about data from Uzbekistan, but Turkmenistan is the most problematic for those interested in using statistics as a guide to economic performance. Unlike the Tajiks, officials in Turkmenistan have no interest in cooperating with international financial institutions.

Given their energy resources, the Turkmen should not be poor, and they certainly did not expect that the first decade would bring them relative economic hardship rather than prosperity. The Turkmen government was initially so bullish on the country's prospects that it promised free utilities and long, paid vacations for the population. Despite official reports of economic growth, credible sources indicate a steady impoverishment of the urban and rural populations that belies the statistics that are being published.

Turkmenistan has substantial oil reserves and is second to Russia among the post-Soviet states in the size of its gas reserves.[19] Gas, though, is a much more problematic commodity to develop than oil, as it is completely dependent upon the availability of a readily accessible market. Turkmenistan's geographic isolation has been a serious handicap in this regard, as it must ship its gas through either Iran or Russia, both of which also have gas to export.[20]

Turkmenistan very much wanted to limit its dependency upon the Russian pipeline system, and its policy toward Afghanistan, providing the Taliban *de facto* recognition (although never *de jure*), was partly motivated by this economic goal. In fact, the Turkmen government briefly allowed its officials formally to champion the Taliban cause, and Turkmenistan's Foreign Minister Boris Sheikhmuradov went to Washington in 1996 to press the Clinton administration to recognize the Taliban government. One of the reasons the Turkmen so vigorously pursued recognition for the Taliban regime was their desire to see Unocal build a pipeline to transport Turkmen gas from giant Dauletabad field in southeastern Turkmenistan across Afghanistan for sale in Pakistan and hopefully in India as well. Due to the harsh behavior of the Taliban and instability in Afghanistan, however, Unocal abandoned this project in November 1998.

Turkmenistan's foreign policy has sometimes been difficult to understand and seems to genuinely reflect the rather perverse personality of the country's first and only president, Saparmurad Niyazov. Niyazov, who has dubbed himself Turkmenbashi (head Turkmen), has created a cult of personality that outstrips even that of Stalin in its extremes and is highlighted by a rotating gold-plated statue of the president that dominates the skyline of the capital city of Ashgabat. Billions of dollars were spent in rebuilding the main streets of the city, and some of this money is reported to have come from the drug trade.[21]

Niyazov was declared president for life by the country's parliament in December 1999. His face is everywhere, appearing on everything from yogurt containers to the national currency. Instead of a logo his picture is beamed in the corner of all the national television broadcasts. He has sharply cut back the required level of education in the country and mandated the study of his life, his family, and a moral code (Rukhnama) that he has claimed to have personally authored. For a time he even floated a rumor that he was immortal, like a prophet, until some of Turkmenistan's Muslim neighbors objected to this as blasphemous.

Niyazov also believed himself capable of reshaping how the international system functioned, or at least how it influenced newly independent states such as his own. As a result Turkmenistan has pursued a Niyazov-inspired doctrine of "positive neutrality" and opted for non-engagement in most of the regional and super-regional initiatives that have been put forward. Presumably it was because of his interest in non-engagement that Niyazov refused to commit his country's gas to a U.S.-backed Trans-Caspian Pipeline that would run under the sea and join up with the proposed Baku-Ceyhan pipeline system, which is to be built from Azerbaijan, across Georgia, and on to Turkey's Mediterranean coast. Supporting the U.S. project, though, would improve access to gas markets that the Turkmen president seems so desperate to obtain.

Uzbekistan

Uzbekistan's President Islam Karimov is often compared to Turkmenistan's leader, although the comparison is not terribly useful. Karimov is certainly a strong and autocratic figure, and a leader who frightened all his neighbors with the prospect of future Uzbek hegemonic behavior.[22] At the same time, however, Karimov has a much more coherent, and even predictable, vision of national interest, given his background as a Samarkandi-born,

Soviet-era economic planner and communist party official. As someone from Samarkand (the historic seat of the fourteenth-century Central Asian empire) and as a person rumored to be of both Tajik and Uzbek ethnic stock, Karimov believes that Uzbekistan has a historic mission to lead in Central Asia, regardless of the attitude of its neighbors or the international community. This belief drove him to carve out a model of political and economic development supposedly in keeping with the national culture rather than accepting strong international direction.

The Uzbek government initially worked with the IMF, reaching an economic stabilization agreement in 1995 that was designed to support the new national currency (the Uzbek som), only to abandon the agreement a year later in favor of an economic protectionist strategy. Karimov, often against the recommendations of his economic advisors, believed that the country could preserve its system of price supports and subsidies if Uzbekistan's two primary export-earning commodities—cotton and gold—remained under state control. At the same time that Karimov was retaining strong central control on the export industries, he was also delegating more economic and social responsibility to traditional local institutions, such as the *mahalle,* which are neighborhood-level government councils.

Karimov's economic strategy was a logical complement to his political program of squelching opposition among the population. In the last years of Soviet rule, Uzbekistan was becoming more politically diverse, with two pro-democracy political parties, Erk (Liberty) and Birlik (Unity), and a growing Islamic revival that was sparked in part by the appointment of a dynamic young *mufti,* Muhammad Yusuf (also known as Mamayusupov) to head the country's religious establishment. The communist party elite was also becoming far less monolithic in its worldview. Many of the country's reformist figures were more comfortable with Vice President Shukrullo Mirsaidov than with the rigid and authoritarian President Karimov, but Karimov dismissed Mirsaidov in early 1992 and forced the leaders of Birlik and Erk into exile.[23] Since then, the only legal political parties have been those created by the government. The country's Islamic revival was much more difficult to contain.[24] Mamayusupov was removed from office in November 1992, but radical Muslim groups, centered in Andizhan and Namangan, continued to gain support from the thousands of young underemployed men who lived in the densely populated Fergana Valley.[25]

The civil war in Tajikistan fueled the Uzbek government's fear of the violent nature and seeming uncontrollability of the population and was often used as an explanation for why the Central Asian countries should proceed slowly with democratization. The civil war also, particularly in Uzbekistan, served to reinforce economic conservatism, as the government was frightened of what would happen if human security was somehow compromised and social welfare commitments were not maintained. This led to the enforcement of price supports long after neighboring Kazakhstan and Kyrgyzstan had abandoned them, and, fearful of traders from neighboring states profiting from Uzbekistan's lower prices, fostered an atmosphere of economic isolation.

Added to this was the situation in Afghanistan. Even before the Taliban took power in Afghanistan and allowed Al Qaeda to establish itself in the country, the disorder in Afghanistan complicated the process of state-building throughout Uzbekistan. During Tajikistan's civil war, opposition groups were able to take refuge in Afghanistan, and Islamist groups in particular (from both Uzbekistan and Tajikistan) found it a welcome refuge even in the Afghan territories dominated by the Northern Alliance. From the point of view of the Uzbeks, the instability in Afghanistan knew no borders with Tajikistan, and the presence of Russian border guards on the Tajik border was only a minimal confidence-building measure.

The Uzbek government had been targeting leaders of Islamist groups since the mid-1990s, but after explosions in Tashkent left 15 dead in February 1999, it began to target radical Muslims much more directly. Blame for these explosions was laid on the IMU, and the Uzbek government began to rigorously enforce border restrictions in an effort to keep out potential terrorists.[26] Following the Tashkent bombings, the Karimov regime intensified its campaign against individuals and groups considered to be religious extremists. Over 7,000 people were arrested, including people with known associations with seditious groups, but also people who were, or appeared to be, devout, such as bearded men, or women in modest dress.[27]

IMU activities became more violent in early 1999. This was especially true during the final years of the Taliban regime in Afghanistan because the IMU was free to increase its numbers and practice terrorist techniques in the Al Qaeda-supported training camps in Afghanistan. The IMU has mainly conducted small-scale armed attacks in Central Asia, including car bombings and hostage-taking, and it made incursions into Kyrgyzstan, Uzbekistan, and Tajikistan. While the group's early attacks focused on Uzbek targets, its operations moved closer to the Uzbek-Kyrgyz border as the IMU infiltrated the mountainous areas of southern Uzbekistan in the spring and summer of 2000. The IMU has also conducted attacks more openly, its members withdrawing to villages and disguising themselves as locals rather than retreating to the mountains following an attack.

The largest of Uzbekistan's radical Islamist groups, the Hizb-ut-Tahrir, had experienced a dramatic increase in its membership in the mid-and late 1990s.[28] The leadership of the Hizb-ut-Tahrir calls for believers to unite and return Islam to the purity of its founding through the creation of a new caliphate. The Hizb-ut-Tahrir was gradually outlawed not only in Uzbekistan but in all the other Central Asian states except Turkmenistan, where it seems to lack a significant presence. Following massive arrests, adherents of the movement went underground in Uzbekistan, but their numbers continued to increase in the border regions of Kazakhstan and Kyrgyzstan.

The Tashkent bombings further hardened the Uzbek government's determination to both delineate and defend its national boundaries, including such steps as placing land mines along some of the border areas shared with Tajikistan and Kyrgyzstan. While the various states of the region are steadily moving toward delineating their borders in ways that are mutually acceptable (Uzbekistan having begun the process quite unilaterally in 1999), the management of Uzbekistan's borders with Turkmenistan, Kyrgyzstan, and Tajikistan were a particular problem. The Kazakhs and Kyrgyz also began to better protect their borders (although they did not mine them), and national demarcation commissions for determining the Kazakh-Kyrgyz and Kazakh-Uzbek borders were organized. The latter commission was organized after armed clashes in 2000.

Visa requirements introduced by some of the Central Asian states have also created new divisions and hardships. Turkmenistan was the first to introduce visa requirements for visiting the country in 1999, a requirement that applied to all foreign visitors including citizens of the Commonwealth of Independent States, but the decision by Uzbekistan to introduce a visa regime for citizens of neighboring countries (excluding residents of some border communities) later that same year introduced more serious hardships. These restrictions further impeded interstate commerce and trade within the region and provided visible proof that the Soviet-era linkages were irreversibly being destroyed, with very little replacing them.

The Geopolitics of Central Asia Before September 11

Independence was not anticipated by any of the Central Asian states, nor did the international community envision it for them. As a result, the relationships that they developed with their more powerful neighbors all had a relatively tentative quality during the decade following the collapse of the Soviet Union. Russia remained a visible, and often irritating presence in the region, but an increasingly ineffective one. China sought to protect its national interests in this area but was mostly interested in positioning itself to fill the strategic void it saw as eventually developing. The United States was drawn to the region by the oil and gas reserves of the Caspian Sea and tried to keep Russia and Iran from controlling them. Turkey and Iran both saw the independence of these states as part of their respective senses of historic destiny, but neither had the resources to compete directly with the Russia, China, or the United States.

Four of the leaders of the Central Asian states were very interested in carving out a unique international presence for their nations, and by so doing claiming a future role for themselves and solidifying their hold on power. Askar Akayev vowed to make Kyrgyzstan the Switzerland of Central Asia, while Nursultan Nazarbayev claimed that Kazakhstan was a bridge between Europe and Asia. Saparmurad Niyazov tried to create a new international status for Turkmenistan. Uzbekistan's Islam Karimov strove to make his country the most powerful military nation in Central Asia, and one that was not dependent on Russia for meeting its security needs.

Interregional Relations

As the Central Asian leaders tried to place these international postures into coherent foreign policies, they were forced to deal regularly with one another to manage their common affairs. The leaders of Kazakhstan, Kyrgyzstan, and Uzbekistan first joined together in 1993 to form a regional organization. Initially called the Central Asian Union, its membership and purpose has been redefined several times. It was expanded in 1998 to include Tajikistan and is now called the Central Asian Economic Community. Turkmenistan steadfastly refused to participate in any of these formal agreements, citing its doctrine of "positive neutrality." The organization is still much more of a photo opportunity for the region's leaders than a functioning interstate institution. Although there is a small permanent bureaucracy and an inter-state bank has been established to fund development projects, the organization's impact has been relatively limited.

Although these states claimed that they were interested in closer cooperation, their actions gave the opposite impression. Highways were recut to make each state less intertwined with its neighbors. Uzbekistan (in part through international assistance) has rerouted many of its principal highways to allow travelers to avoid entering Kazakhstan, Kyrgyzstan, and Tajikistan on their journeys between two points within the country. The process has been costly but made it easier for the Uzbeks to introduce full passport control and customs regimes on all of its borders.

Uzbekistan's actions prompted the Kyrgyz Republic to seek assistance funds to redirect some of its highways in the southern part of the country to facilitate travel within Osh and Jalalabad provinces. Kyrgyzstan was the only Central Asian state to join the WTO in this period, and was consequently the only one to subscribe to WTO standards for uniform tariffs and an open (and predictable) trade regime. Transit trade across Kazakhstan remained difficult for the Kyrgyz, and their goods were subjected to high tariffs at the national border, and separate "fees" to be shipped across each of the Kazakhstan's provinces.

Kazakhstan, too, began refashioning its highway and rail systems with international assistance. In the Kazakh case, though, it will take several billion dollars to fully disentangle the country's transit system with that of Russia and will require laying hundreds, and possibly even thousands, of kilometers of new road and rail-bed.

Recutting Central Asia's road system addresses some of the problems of intrastate commerce, but does nothing for interstate transport. All of these countries are land-locked—and goods from Uzbekistan must cross two countries to reach port—which means that customs barriers and difficult border crossings are real detriments to timely transport of goods from this region to market. Geography also reduced the commercial viability of alternative transit routes, endorsed by both the European Bank for Reconstruction and Development (EBRD) and the Asian Development Bank (ADB). The Europeans in particular were interested in helping the Central Asian states develop alternate transport routes that by-passed Russia, and sponsored the multi-billion dollar TRACECA project, but the rebuilding of roads and railroad lines will take decades.[29]

Another source of tension between the Central Asian states has been the fact that all were still bound together by the hydroelectric grids and gas pipelines laid in Soviet times and by the fact that water in the Aral Sea basin (which includes southern Kazakhstan and the other four Central Asian states, as well as part of Afghanistan) is delivered by the Amu Darya and Syr Darya Rivers that originate in Tajikistan and Kyrgyzstan, respectively. In Soviet times most of the water was allowed to flow to the downstream users, and this water is critical to the survival of the cotton industry in both Uzbekistan and Turkmenistan. Since the collapse of the Soviet Union, an interstate water coordination council, based in Uzbekistan, has managed water usage, and the criteria for distribution of water has remained largely unchanged. This has been a source of constant consternation to both Kyrgyzstan and Tajikistan, which have had to meet the costs of maintaining large reservoirs built in the Soviet-era. Both states would prefer to use this water for generating additional electricity in order to make them less dependent upon gas supplies from Uzbekistan. Uzbekistan has cut off the gas to all its foreign customers when Tashkent felt that unpaid bills had grown too large. Kazakhstan, which relies on gas from Uzbekistan but also supplies electricity for parts of Uzbekistan, has retaliated on occasion by cutting back on the electricity that it supplies to Uzbekistan.

The Central Asian states have refused international efforts to help them reorganize their interstate water system, claiming that they have managed the division of water for thousands of years unassisted. Beginning in 1998, Kazakhstan, Uzbekistan, and Kyrgyzstan did make some headway on managing the waters of the Syr Darya, and in 2001 the Kazakhs began contributing to the upkeep of the Kyrgyz reservoir system. However, water allocations and electricity and gas prices are still negotiated on an annual basis.

Russia's Continuing Influence in the Region

In the first years of independence, Russia had used its position as energy supplier to maintain an economic hold on a number of post-Soviet states, including Kazakhstan, which was dependent upon Russia for much of the electricity used in its northern reaches, and for most of the oil and gas used there as well. Eventually Kazakhstan gave equity stakes in its hydroelectric station, RAO-UES, the partly state-held Russian United Energy System, in return for debt forgiveness.

Energy debts were only one means of Russia's attempts to control Central Asia. In the early 1990s, Moscow believed that the Russian national interest should prevail over efforts by other Soviet successor states to define and advance national interests of their own.[30] Initially, Russia sought institutional solutions to advance this goal, including the CIS and the Tashkent Collective Security Agreement. These arrangements failed to develop into multilateral organizations with clout, largely because the leaders of the newly independent states did not want to delegate authority to them. Uzbekistan's Islam Karimov and Turkmenistan's Saparmurad Niyazov were particularly unwilling to empower organizations in which Russia sought to represent the interests of its former republics. The leaders of the other three Central Asian states were more interested in retaining close ties to Russia;[31] all participated actively in collective security arrangements and joined an economic union that included Belarus and Ukraine.[32]

Slowly, Russia began to reduce and redefine its engagement in Central Asia. While Russian nationalists, intellectuals, and policy advisors still share the opinion that Russia's destiny is inextricably tied to these former colonies, those charged with making and implementing Russian policy have came to realize that they are not in a position to realistically implement this goal. Moreover, at many critical junctures the Russians opted for non-engagement. Russia's decision not to support the ruble zone was a prime example of this policy withdrawal. Had the Russians been willing to keep subsidizing the price-support structure of the Central Asian economies in late 1993, all but Kyrgyzstan would have stayed in the ruble zone and Russia would have continued to dictate the terms of their economic development. However, economic reformers were more interested in controlling inflation than in the attainment of more ephemeral neo-imperialist goals.

Russia's level of military engagement and cooperation with these states has also steadily diminished. Even before September 11, the Tashkent Collective Security Agreement, signed on May 14, 1992, was virtually dead following the withdrawl of the Uzbeks in April 1999. And it is hard to say with certainty how much support Russia would have given any of the leaders in Central Asia before September 11. Little help was offered to Bishkek after incursions by the IMU in the summer of 1999 and the summer of 2000. By the late 1990s, the government in Moscow had realized that it had limited resources and had to make difficult choices about where and how to assert Russian influence in neighboring countries. Russian leaders hoped that the Shanghai Five, which was founded by China, Russia, and three of the Central Asian states in April 1996, would provide a new means for Moscow to maintain its security interests in the Central Asian region.[33] China, as a major driving force in the organization, had similar hopes.

China's Ascending Role in the Region

The Shanghai Five was initially conceived as a confidence-building measure for China, Russia, Tajikistan, Kyrgyzstan, and Kazakhstan as they delineated and demilitarized the Sino-Soviet border that they had inherited upon the collapse of the Soviet Union. The delineation of these borders has been a tumultuous political process in Kyrgyzstan and Kazakhstan because both countries view China as an age-old rival that historically was more feared than Russia. In both Kazakhstan and Kyrgyzstan, the delineation of boundaries has led to land transfers that favor the Chinese, and opposition politicians in Kyrgyzstan are so incensed by the treaty agreed with China that they have demanded President Akayev be impeached.[34]

The concession of territory by Kyrgyzstan and Kazakhstan was recognition of China's potential for regional hegemony. All of the region's leaders have been eager to establish close ties with the Chinese and to ingratiate themselves with the leaders in Beijing. Kazakhstan and Kyrgyzstan have had foreign ministers who speak Chinese and have appointed ambassadors fluent in Chinese. For all the nervousness about China, there is also a strong fascination with what many see as China's economic miracle and admiration for China's combination of a seemingly tightly controlled political regime with high rates of economic growth. China is an increasing economic force in the region (see Table 7.2), and trade with China has been an important source of capital accumulation for small entrepreneurs, who then reinvest their profits in more permanent enterprises.

China has also managed to gain control of a share of Caspian energy reserves, partly to meet its own energy needs and partly to increase its geopolitical influence in the region. In 1997 the Chinese National Petro-

Table 7.2. Central Asia's Trade with China (2000)

	Exports ($m)	Imports ($m)	Trade balance ($m)	Exports (% share of total)	Imports (% share of total)
Kazakhstan	671	155	516	7.3	4.2
Kyrgyzstan	44	37	7	8.8	6.7
Tajikistan	3	12	-9	0.4	1.8
Turkmenistan	8	16	-8	0.3	0.9
Uzbekistan	11	44	-33	0.5	2.1

Source: IMF, *Direction of Trade Statistics*, Washington, DC: IMF, 2001. Note: China total includes trade with Hong Kong and Macao.

leum Company won a tender and a 60 percent stake in the Zhanazhol and Kenkiyak oil fields in Aktobe, Kazakhstan.[35] Originally, the Chinese committed to the construction of a $9.6 billion pipeline, but the current version of the project calls for the staged construction of a 2,900 kilometer pipeline, beginning with a section running from Kenkiyak (in Aktobe) to Atyrau, in late 2002. The total cost is now envisioned at under $3.5 billion, of which less than $200 million has been authorized.[36]

The thrust of China's policy in Central Asia throughout the first decade of these states' independence has been to position Beijing to protect and develop its security interests in the region. The granting of independence created new security threats to the Chinese, as it increased the demands for independence or greater autonomy by the Uighurs and other Turkic Muslim minorities who live in northwestern China. Nationalists in the Central Asian states sometimes provided support for these groups, and large diaspora Uighur communities in Kazakhstan and Kyrgyzstan were politically active in the early 1990s. Under strong pressure from China, both the Kazakh and Kyrgyz authorities sharply curtailed the activities of the Uighur nationalists, whom the Chinese maintain are terrorists.[37]

Turkey and Iran

In contrast to the Chinese, the Turkey and the Iran saw little downside to the independence of the Central Asian states, and the leaders of both countries were eager to use arguments of historical and cultural affinity to advance their economic and geopolitical interests in the region. The Turks fared much better than the Iranians in becoming an important economic partner for these states, in large part because of U.S. pressure to keep Tehran diplomatically isolated (see Tables 7.3 and 7.4). Turkey also had the stronger economy, and Turkish entrepreneurs were eager to invest in projects in Central Asia. Turkish businessmen were not as put off by the corruption in the region as many of their European counterparts, and they were

Table 7.3. Central Asia's Trade with Iran (2000)

	Exports ($m)	Imports ($m)	Trade balance ($m)	Exports (% share of total)	Imports (% share of total)
Kazakhstan	204	13	191	2.2	0.4
Kyrgyzstan	7	9	-2	1.4	1.6
Tajikistan	13	8	5	1.7	1.2
Turkmenistan	242	91	151	9.7	5.1
Uzbekistan	...	...	...	...	...

Source: IMF, *Direction of Trade Statistics*, Washington, DC: IMF, 2001.

Table 7.4. Central Asia's Trade with Turkey (2000)

	Exports ($m)	Imports ($m)	Trade balance ($m)	Exports (% share of total)	Imports (% share of total)
Kazakhstan	64	143	-79	0.7	3.9
Kyrgyzstan	7	27	-20	1.4	4.9
Tajikistan	58	4	54	7.4	0.6
Turkmenistan	186	253	-67	7.4	14.1
Uzbekistan	78	91	-13	3.7	4.3

Source: IMF, *Direction of Trade Statistics*, Washington, DC: IMF, 2001.

able to gain a foothold in the region's construction, food processing, and textile industries. Turkey's president Turgut Ozal (1989–93) was an especially strong supporter of the idea of Turkey's partnership with the newly independent Turkic states (Azerbaijan, Turkmenistan, Kazakhstan, Kyrgyzstan, and Uzbekistan) and gathered the leaders of these countries for a series of summit meetings, hoping that this would lead to a more formal multilateral organization.

The Turks see themselves as natural leaders in the region and have tried to be a driving force behind the cultural and linguistic revival of these nations. Turkey annually offers scholarships to thousands of students from the region, it has provided support for the introduction of the Latin alphabet to replace the Cyrillic one,[38] and it has made its television programs available at preferential rates. These were all policies that met with the approval of Washington, as they were seen as helping to diminish the role of Russia and thus strengthening the independence of the regional states. Some U.S. technical assistance money for the region was funneled through Turkey, but the cornerstone of the U.S. policy of strengthening Turkey's role was the promotion of the Baku-Tbilisi-Ceyhan pipeline to ship Azerbaijani oil and gas to market through Georgia and Turkey rather than through Russia. As already noted, the United States also strongly supported the construction of a Trans-Caspian Pipeline to move Turkmen gas and Kazakh oil into this new pipeline system.

While all of the Central Asian states are eager for close ties with Turkey (including Tajikistan), they have not been as willing to cozy up to the Turks as Ankara or Washington might want. Nor have any of the Central Asian states been willing to cut ties with Iran. Kazakhstan and Turkmenistan have not fully endorsed Washington's oil and gas pipeline strategy. Turkmenistan ships gas through Iran and would like to obtain international financing to ship even more via that route. President Nazarbayev regularly reaffirms Kazakhstan's interest in eventually shipping part of its offshore oil to market through a new pipeline to link these fields with Iran. The Iranians also enjoy a close relationship with the government of Tajikistan, and Tehran has been a source of cultural and educational materials for the revamped Tajik education system.[39] The Iranians also played a decisive role in helping negotiate the national reconciliation agreement in Tajikistan.

As a Caspian littoral state, Iran has been involved in much of the debate about how the resources of the sea should be divided. Because the Iranians have the least valuable sector of the Caspian, they oppose the division of the sea into national sectors. Nevertheless, Kazakhstan, Azerbaijan, and Turkmenistan are steadily moving toward the development of their declared national sectors. Moreover, Russia has reached agreement on demarcation with Kazakhstan and is likely to reach agreement with both Azerbaijan and Turkmenistan in the near future.[40] These agreements represent a policy reversal for the Russians, and, given Moscow's willingness to see Caspian oil development move forward, the realists who dominate Tehran's oil and gas sector began to understand that Iran's best chance of prospering from Caspian oil and gas would be from its transit.

In general, the Iranians have high hopes of benefiting from improved transport and communication routes throughout Central Asia, and the Iranian government has always placed more emphasis on improving commercial relations with these states than on ideological goals. The Iranian leaders have by and large managed to convince the Central Asian leaders that Iran's Islamic revolution poses no direct threat to them.[41] Iran's cultural influence in the region is especially limited because none of the Central Asian states are Shi'a Muslim and only the Tajiks have linguistic ties with the Persian spoken in Iran.

United States

While the Central Asian leaders have all maintained regular contacts with the Iranians, they have been careful to not jeopardize their relationship with the United States. All five leaders have always been interested in strengthening ties to the United States, and most have been willing to go to great lengths to arrange official visits to Washington simply because the "face-time" with a U.S. president was seen to solidify their political position at home. Moreover, cooperation with the United States and NATO had long seemed the best prospect for these states to modernize their militaries, but before September 11 the United States (and the NATO countries more generally) had little interest in funding Central Asia's rapid entry into a global security system. All the same, the U.S. military presence in the region was growing, especially after the terrorist bombings in Tashkent in February 1999 and the incursions by the IMU into Kyrgyzstan in the summers of 1999 and 2000.

The U.S. strategic interest in Kazakhstan dated from independence, in large part because Kazakhstan inherited a part of the Soviet nuclear arsenal.[42] Between January 1992 and September 2000, the U.S. government spent more than $190 million on programs to reduce weapons of mass destruction (WMD) and address other nonproliferation concerns in Kazakhstan, which were mostly funded by the Cooperative Threat Reduction Program. Part of this money was used to fund a seven-year agreement (signed in December 1993) to destroy Kazakhstan's nuclear silos. All the nuclear warheads that Kazakhstan inherited were returned to Russia by the end of 1995, and 147 missile silos were gradually destroyed as well.[43]

In addition, Uzbekistan, Kazakhstan, and Kyrgyzstan were all active members of NATO's Partnership for Peace, and annually participated in regional cooperation exercises with U.S. forces. It had initially been the U.S. intent to form a single regional peacemaking force to be dispatched in the event of ethnic conflict, but U.S.-led training exercises held in the region in 1997 and 1998 were marked by a great deal of competition between the various Central Asian militaries.[44]

In subsequent years, U.S. assistance to the Central Asian states has been bilateral in focus, and it was increasing even prior to the Afghanistan conflict (see Table 7.5 overleaf). U.S.-Uzbek security cooperation increased after the February 1999 terrorist bombings in Tashkent, and in May 1999 two cooperative agreements were signed between the U.S. Department of Defense and the Uzbek Defense Ministry. At that time the United States made it clear that it had no interest in gaining basing rights from the Uzbeks.[45] A small group of special forces was sent to Tajikistan in August 2001 as part of an anti-Taliban operation, and special forces were engaged in training in Uzbekistan.[46] However, the scale of U.S. engagement came nowhere close to meeting the training and supply needs of these states, leaving Central Asia with a growing security void.

Table 7.5. Cumulative U.S. Aid to Central Asia, 1992–2000

	Total U.S. assistance ($m)					
	Kazakh.	Kyrgyz.	Tajik.	Turkmen.	Uzbek.	NIS[a]
USAID[b]	273.0	141.5	47.2	33.9	83.9	419.1
WMD/Nonproliferation[c]	190.5	4.2	neg.	1.2	8.0	155.1
Other security[d]	10.5	6.8	...	3.7	10.3	91.6
Training/Education reform[e]	42.3	23.2	13.5	10.1	29.0	36.0
Democracy[f]	2.4	1.4	0.1	0.4	2.1	18.9
Trade/Investment[g]	6.9	0.2	neg.	neg.	1.1	343.3
Business development[h]	4.4	1.5	1.7	0.2	0.9	11.7
Energy/Environment[i]	3.4	...	...	...	...	0.4
Social/Humanitarian[j]	277.1	384.1	253.6	146.5	151.7	...
Other[k]	10.4	11.0	0.3	10.4	13.4	7.6
Total Assistance	820.9	573.9	316.4	206.4	300.4	1083.7

Source: Office of the Coordinator of U.S. Assistance to the NIS, *U.S. Government Assistance to and Cooperative Activities with the New Independent States of the Former Soviet Union*, FY 2000 Annual Report, January 2001. Notes: a) For programs active in more than one country of the Newly Independent States; b) U.S. Agency for International Development: includes programs on economic restructuring, democratic transition, trade, investment, energy, environment, and other sectors; c) WMD/nonproliferation-related security programs; d) Other security programs; e) Training exchange and education reform programs; f) Democracy programs; g) Trade and investment programs; h) Business and economic development programs; i) Energy and environmental programs; j) Social sector and humanitarian programs; k) Cross-sectoral and other programs (including Peace Corps).

Geopolitics in Central Asia After September 11

Security Cooperation with the United States

Following September 11, there is a real chance that Central Asia's security void will be filled, largely by the introduction of U.S. troops and increased military cooperation between regional states and the principal U.S. allies in the war on terrorism. It is still too soon to know how much direct military assistance will be forthcoming, however. It is unclear whether U.S. troops will remain in the region, and it is also difficult to predict what orders U.S. troops would receive if their host regime were on the verge of being toppled by internal forces. Nonetheless, the growing U.S. military presence in Central Asia does change the geopolitical balance in the region.

The Central Asian states have all signed on to support the U.S.-led war on terrorism, although each is making a distinct contribution. The Uzbek and the Kyrgyz governments are playing the most active roles by granting the United States the rights to maintain military bases on their territories. Uzbekistan's Karze-Khanabad base is serving as a forward area for U.S. activities and humanitarian assistance going to northern Afghanistan, and the United States is said to be investing nearly half a billion dollars in Afghanistan's refurbishment.[47] The United States opened the Peter Ganci Air Base in Kyrgyzstan, just on the edge of the country's main commercial airport in Bishkek, on a one-year renewable agreement.[48] The infrastructure being built in Kyrgyzstan, however, suggests a continuing U.S. presence, as the base includes a gymnasium complex, which is rumored by insiders to be a telltale sign of a longer-term commitment. The base also houses 1,800 troops (half from the United States) and F/A-18 fighter planes and French Mirage jets, which are flying missions in Afghanistan. There are conflicting accounts on how much the base benefits ordinary Kyrgyz citizens. The airport is rumored to be owned or managed by a privately held group, which is said to be receiving the landing fees. Most of the supplies used on the base come from outside of Kyrgyzstan, and U.S. soldiers do not mix much with the local society.[49]

U.S. military cooperation with the other Central Asian states is more limited. A small detachment of about 60 U.S. troops is based in Tajikistan, where the focus is on refueling planes going into or out of Kandahar. The Tajiks had wanted a larger U.S. engagement, both to help reduce their dependence on the Russian military and to help modernize their armed forces and refurbish their decaying military facilities. The Kazakhs were more cautious about expanding military cooperation with the United States, although between October 2001 and May 2002 Kazakhstan's airspace was crossed in over 600 forays made by the coalition. In addition, during Secretary of Defense Donald Rumsfeld's May 2002 trip to the region, Kazakhstan's leaders announced that three airfields in southern Kazakhstan could be used by the United States in the case of emergencies.[50] The Turkmen have been the most aloof, insisting on preserving the country's neutrality in all military conflicts, and were reported as having refused the German air force the use of Turkmen bases in connection with a counterterrorist operation.[51] However, about a third of all humanitarian assistance being shipped to Afghanistan has gone through Turkmenistan.

Russia's Diminished Role and China's Ascendancy

On the surface, this increased U.S. presence in Central Asia has not come at the expense of Russia, in part because both the United States and Russia have been careful to define participation in the war on terrorism as activity that is beyond their normal treaty obligations. The improved U.S.-Russian relationship has helped Russia maintain the façade of being a great power in the region, and President Putin has tried hard to convey an image of Russian participation in this part of the world. Russia continues to be an important international partner of all of these states, and an impor-

Table 7.6. Central Asia's Trade with Russia (2000)

	Exports ($m)	Imports ($m)	Trade balance ($m)	Exports (% share of total)	Imports (% share of total)
Kazakhstan	1,784	2,460	-676	19.5	66.7
Kyrgyzstan	65	133	-68	12.9	24.0
Tajikistan	259	105	154	33.0	15.6
Turkmenistan	1,029	255	774	41.1	14.3
Uzbekistan	602	302	300	28.3	14.3

Source: IMF, *Direction of Trade Statistics*, Washington, DC: IMF, 2001.

tant trade partner as well—accounting for a far greater share of trade turnover for each of these states than any other country (see Table 7.6). With the greatly enhanced U.S. presence in the region, however, it has become increasingly difficult for Russia to use the multilateral institutions that it created to structure its relationships with the Central Asian states.[52]

As an example, with all the Central Asian leaders in attendance at the March 2002 summit, the CIS leaders vowed to reinvigorate the organization and transform it into something like the European Union, but no specific policy recommendations were made to build toward this goal.[53] Moreover, at the May 13, 2002 summit of the Eurasian Economic Community (EEC), which includes Kazakhstan, Kyrgyzstan, Tajikistan, Russia, and Belarus, there was talk of an expanded membership, but Putin's bid to chair the organization failed, guaranteeing that this organization would be of secondary importance to Russia for the foreseeable future.[54] One day later, at the tenth anniversary summit of the Collective Security Organization (the renamed Collective Security Treaty), which includes Kazakhstan, Kyrgyzstan, Tajikistan, Russia, Belarus, and Armenia, the assembled presidents could not agree on creating a joint military force under the command of the Russian General Staff and instead settled for an agreement on the trading of weapons and military hardware at a preferential price.

The Russian military, however, is unwilling to be fully eclipsed in Central Asia. Russian border guards still have principal responsibility for patrolling the 1,500 kilometer border between Tajikistan and Afghanistan, and they continue to have troops from the 201st Motorized Brigade based in Tajikistan. In late April 2002, President Putin announced that Russia would beef up its naval forces in the Caspian Sea and would hold large-scale military exercises there. The Russians also have a newly organized 1,500-man CIS collective rapid deployment force based in Bishkek, and Russian military leaders have regularly suggested that, as the U.S.-led coalition takes responsibility for ensuring security in Afghanistan, the Russian-led CIS forces would guarantee security within Central Asia.[55]

The U.S. military presence has not changed the shared Russian and Chinese commitment to greater security cooperation in Central Asia or for the planned roles of the Shanghai Cooperation Organization. In recent months there has been talk of the SCO working in concert with the CIS collective security force to help stem challenges from Uighur "terrorist" groups, which purportedly have ties with the Uighur communities in Kazakhstan and Kyrgyzstan.[56] There has also been a small SCO anti-terrorist center organized in Bishkek.

The organization continues to have a public presence that is almost undiminished from what it was before September 11. SCO members have supported the creation of a formal secretariat, to be housed in Beijing, but the emergence of this organization as something more than a consultative body has been slowed substantially by the introduction of a U.S. military presence in the region. For a while in early 2002, it was even rumored that President Karimov would withdraw his country from membership in the SCO because of the increased interaction with the United States. Although the Uzbeks decided to remain in the SCO, Karimov's participation is said to have gone from enthusiastic to tepid.[57]

While the future role of the SCO is still difficult to predict, the introduction of U.S. forces in the region is unlikely to be more than a temporary setback for the Chinese. Beijing is determined that China will play a leading role in the geopolitics of Central Asia, and its size and economic potential seem to ensure that it will. For the Chinese, the U.S. military presence may be little more than a temporary annoyance.

Iran and Turkey

Iran is a state that has not fared well in the Central Asian region in recent months. Initially, the Iranians hoped that the war on terrorism would offer an opportunity for improved cooperation with the United States. Instead Iran was labeled part of the "axis of evil," in President George W. Bush's January 2002 State of the Union address. But the Iranians are determined not to be fully eclipsed, and in April 2002 President Mohammad Khatami took a trip through the region, meeting with all five Central Asian presidents and reaffirming Iran's interest in improving bilateral relations. During the Khatami visit the Kazakhs expressed continued interest in exporting oil through Iran,[58] the Kyrgyz and Iranians signed an agreement on renewed cooperation, and even Karimov, long the most wary of Central Asia's leaders, signed a number of agreements designed to facilitate improved cooperation in transportation and the fight against terrorism.

The U.S. presence in Central Asia has been of only indirect benefit to Turkey. As the only NATO country with cultural affinities to the Central

Asia, Turkey could be called upon to play a greater role in the military reform of these countries. The increased direct U.S. military engagement in Central Asia, however, makes Turkey less necessary as a U.S. surrogate, a role that it was frequently called upon to play in the last decade.

Impact on Interregional Relations

The relationships between the Central Asian states and Afghanistan have obviously been affected by the actions that the United States took in the wake of the September 11 attacks. Diplomatic relations have been restored, but movement across Afghanistan's borders is still closely monitored and restricted to prevent the flow of refugees from Afghanistan into Tajikistan, Uzbekistan, and Turkmenistan. Improved trade relations between the Central Asian states and Afghanistan are still largely a prospect for the future, and the big development projects that could be of considerable benefit to all the states of the region are in the earliest planning stages and will be difficult to finance. As an example, the project of greatest potential interest to many of these states—the construction of oil and gas pipelines across Afghanistan—is not likely to obtain international funding for several years. Morevoer, sponsors have not been found for the big hydroelectric projects in Tajikistan and Turkmenistan that would produce more electricity for Afghanistan. International investors remain very cautious about the prospects that the new Afghan government, led by Hamid Kharzai, will be able to fully restore order and successfully manage the economic and political transition necessary for Afghanistan to become a stable transit zone.

As long as disorder prevails, Afghanistan will remain a source of sanctuary for radical Islamist and other opposition groups from Central Asia, and, given the ethnic makeup of the border regions in Afghanistan, particularly for those from Uzbekistan or Tajikistan. The defeat of the Al Qaeda network means that these groups will enjoy a much more meager kind of hospitality than when Osama bin Laden was helping to bankroll them, but the mountain regions of Afghanistan offer natural cover. Although the Taliban-run *madrassas* have been closed down, radicals from Central Asia are still able to transit across Afghanistan to receive training elsewhere. Moreover, most Central Asians who embraced radical Islamism did so because of religious training they received in their own or a neighboring Central Asian country, and this situation is unlikely to change even with official efforts to eliminate unsanctioned mosques and *madrassas*.

Finally, the opium and heroin produced from Afghanistan's poppy crops remain a ready source of income for radical groups throughout Central Asia. While the U.S. government has repeatedly stated a goal of eliminating Afghanistan's drug trade, efforts to curtail the cultivation of poppies only scratch the surface of the problem. Funds allocated by the United States and the Europeans were only sufficient to buy up a small part of the 2002 crop.[59] Afghanistan also remains an arms bazaar and serves as a source of small arms for Central Asia, which already had a lot of small arms and larger weapons available after the breakup of Soviet forces.

Conclusion: Whither Central Asia?

As the discussion here has shown, in the first ten years of independence, none of the Central Asia leaders were particularly inclined toward reform, yet regional development requires considerable restructuring of local political systems, health and education infrastructure, regional trade ties, and economic policies. Will the increased international attention to the region since September 11 give the Central Asian states a new opportunity to get things right? Will the U.S. military presence increase regional stability, encourage the Central Asian leaders to liberalize the political and economic systems in their countries, and strengthen multilateral economic and security mechanisms in the region?

While the developments in the war against terrorism do not in and of themselves change the face of political life in the region, they do show that alliance with the United States has done little to compel Central Asia's leaders to introduce democratic reforms. It has also done little to make these states more secure from the internal threats that they were already facing. Overall, the outlook for reform is not positive. The one partial exception is Uzbekistan, where President Karimov believes that the tragedies of September 11 created a one-time opportunity to build a close strategic relationship with the United States.

In pursuit of this new opportunity, President Karimov visited Washington in March 2002 and signed five separate agreements on cooperation with the United States. The most important of these is the broad-based "United States-Uzbekistan Declaration on the Strategic Partnership and Cooperation Framework," which commits the Uzbek government to support democratic reforms in return for the U.S. promise to "regard with grave concern any external threat to the security and territorial integrity of the republic of Uzbekistan."[60] The United States and Uzbekistan also agreed to cooperate on nuclear nonproliferation.[61] While the Karimov government has made a number of promises to reform, virtually nothing has happened since September 11 to increase the popularity of Karimov's authoritarian regime and the Uzbek government is sure to face enormous challenges and opposition to its economic and political reform programs.

In fact, opposition in many of the Central Asian countries has crystallized and become seemingly more effective since September 11. In

Turkmenistan, Niyazov fears disloyalty on the part of his government and regularly rotates state officials in and out of office. In recent months the full savagery of the president's power has been unleashed upon political revivals within the Turkmen elite.[62] Nevertheless, Turkmenistan's opposition movements do seem to be gaining power. Upon resigning from his post as Turkmenistan's ambassador to China, former foreign minister Boris Sheikhmuradov formed an opposition party, the People's Democratic Movement of Turkmenistan, which seems to have much greater support within Turkmenistan than earlier opposition efforts, and several prominent Turkmen diplomats also have joined the movement.[63]

Opposition forces in Kyrgyzstan have also begun to press more seriously for President Akayev's resignation. A cycle of mounting national protests was triggered in March 2002, when police fired on groups of peaceful demonstrators in the city of Dzellabad, leaving seven dead. They were protesting the arrest of Kyrgyz legislator Azimbek Beknazarov, chairman of the parliamentary committee on judicial and legal affairs, who had repeatedly called for Akayev's impeachment because of the treaty on borders that he had signed with China.[64] Demonstrations grew so severe that in May 2002 the prime minister and his entire cabinet resigned and a temporary standoff was achieved. While President Akayev has made some political concessions as a result of increased U.S. pressure, Kyrgyzstan's independent media remains a target of the regime, and in May 2002 former vice president Feliks Kulov, who has become an important symbol for democratic opposition groups, was sentenced to three more years in prison and barred from ever holding political office.[65]

Pro-democracy activists in Kazakhstan have been increasing pressure on the Nazarbayev regime as well. Despite the fact that President Nazarbayev has continued to provide strong rhetorical support for the need to democratize Kazakhstan, actions taken by the him and his senior officials provide little evidence that the country's leaders intend to commit to democratic reform. In response, a group of key reformers left the government in November 2001 and formed a political movement called Democratic Choice.[66]

To date, none of the countries of the region has held a free or fair election for president or parliament, and the region's legislative bodies serve as little more than a rubber-stamp. Nevertheless, four of the five states in the region are weak and at risk, and even the leader of the region's most prosperous state, Nazarbayev of Kazakhstan, could face ouster by an angry and increasingly disempowered political elite. Other regional leaders are even more likely targets of a coup, especially Turkmenistan's Niyazov. With increasing pressure from opposition groups, questions of succession are imminent and the international response will be crucial.

As the United States defines its future policy toward Central Asia, what options will enable it to take advantage of this opportunity to form new strategic relationships within the region? If Uzbekistan is any indication, agreements with the regional leaders for cooperation and funding show promise. The 2003 aid allocations being considered for the Central Asian states, however, are small relative to the needs of these states, and they do not give the United States any real influence on the domestic policy choices being made by the various Central Asian regimes. U.S. values, especially those related to political and economic rights of citizenship, remain a hard sell in the region.

Central Asia's leaders do not currently feel beholden to the United States. If anything, the region's leaders now feel that the United States needs them more than they need it. None is convinced that the U.S. presence in the region will be long term, or even whether this would be desirable. The Central Asian leaders may have accurately assessed U.S. intentions in the region: First and foremost, U.S. troops were sent to Central Asia to facilitate the protection of U.S. citizens and not to bolster the stability of this region. The current campaign against terrorism, for all its reach, does not protect the Central Asian leaders against Islamist critics of their regimes. Islamists in Kyrgyzstan and Tajikistan will continue to train ethnic Uzbek youths, and the region's radical movements are likely to become more difficult for their weak governments to control. The importance of narcobusiness in Tajikistan cripples other forms of security efforts nationwide, while the Kyrgyz government seems to be fraying under growing popular protest in the south, where Islamist groups are strongest.

All this means that the United States could face some ugly choices in Central Asia in the years, or even months to come, as to whether U.S. forces will openly assist the non-democratic leaders of these newly allied states to stay in power. Whatever choices Washington makes, the outcome is likely to reinforce the U.S. desire to make its presence in the region as temporary as possible. Whatever happens, both Russia and China remain eager to fill any new security voids that may develop in Central Asia.

Endnotes

[1] Remarks by President George W. Bush, September 25, 2001, Federal News Service, September 26, 2001.

[2] Uzbekistan's President Islam Karimov was the apparent target of six car bomb explosions in Tashkent on February 16, 1999, which killed 15 people (including two attackers) and wounded 150 others. The Uzbek government blamed the attacks on the Islamic Movement of Uzbekistan (IMU). Intercon, *Daily Report on Russia*, February 23, 1999.

³ In the summer of 1999, several hundred militants invaded Kyrgyzstan twice and took hostages. Those hostages included Kyrgyz officials and four Japanese geologists. The latter were released only after payment of a large ransom.

⁴ Nursultan Nazarbayev was elected first secretary of the Kazakh Communist party in 1989 and served as Chairman of the Kazakh Supreme Soviet from 1989 to 1990 and as president of the Kazakh Soviet Socialist Republic (SSR) from 1990–91. In 1991 he became independent Kazakhstan's president. Nazarbayev had his term extended to 2000 by a referendum held in April 1995. His last re-election was held in January 1999, a year before it was scheduled. Constitutional changes in 1998 extended the presidential term to seven years, removed restrictions against Nazarbayev seeking a new term, and awarded the first Kazakh president extensive political privileges in retirement.

Askar Akayev was first elected president of the Kyrgyz SSR in October 1990. In October 1991, he ran uncontested for the presidency of independent Kyrgyzstan, and was reelected in December 1995 and in October 2000.

Emomali Rahmonov served as the head of state and Supreme Assembly chairman in Tajikistan from November 1992, until November 1994, when he was elected president. He was last reelected on November 6, 1999.

Saparmurad Niyazov, then first secretary of the Communist Party of Turkmenistan, was elected president of the Turkmen SSR in October 1990. Niyazov was elected president of independent Turkmenistan in June 1992. In January 1994, Niyazov's rule was prolonged until 2002 and in December 1999, his rule was extended indefinitely.

Islam Karimov, then first secretary of the Central Committee of the Uzbek SSR, was elected president of Uzbekistan in December 1991. President Karimov's original term was extended for an additional five years by a national referendum held in March 1995. He was last reelected in January 2000.

⁵ These identities reflect the history and cultures of the peoples involved. There has always been competition between the oasis agricultural settlements located between the Syr Darya and Amu Darya rivers (present-day Uzbekistan) and the pastoral nomads who lived in the mountains and steppe lands just beyond (Kazakhstan and Kyrgyzstan). The nomadic group was comprised of mixed Mongol and Turkic stock; the Turks having migrated from east of the Tien Shan Mountains to the Anatolian Plain. The original population of the oasis settlements was indigenous Persian, who gradually intermarried with the Turkic peoples who came to live among them and with the Mongol aristocracy of Genghis Khan's family who ruled them. The oasis settlements also competed with the Turkmen tribesmen just to their west, who, as their name implies, were largely Turkic in origin.

⁶ See U.S. Department of Energy, Energy Information Administration, *Kazakhstan Country Analysis Brief*, <www.eia.doe.gov/emeu/cabs/kazak.html>.

⁷ The Caspian Pipeline Consortium is comprised of the following owners: Russia (24 percent), Kazakhstan (19 percent), Chevron (15 percent), Lukarco (12.5 percent), Mobil (7.5 percent), Rosneft-Shell (7.5 percent), Oman (7 percent), British Gas (2 percent), Adjip (2 percent), Oryx (1.75 percent), Kazakoil/Amoco (1.75 percent).

⁸ In early March 1995, the constitutional court of Kazakhstan ruled in favor of

Tatyana Kvyatkovskaya, a journalist from the Abylaykhan electoral district of Almaty. Kvyatkovskaya charged that the electoral districts for the 1994 election had been disproportionately drawn. The constitutional court ruled that the entire 1994 parliamentary elections had been unconstitutional.

9   *Agence France-Presse*, September 24, 2001.

10 *RFE/RL Newsline,* April 18, 2002, <www.rferl.org/newsline/2002/04/180402.asp>.

11 Chinara Jakypova, "The Challenge of Governance in the Central Asian Countries (an Example of Kyrgyzstan)," paper prepared for the International Peace Academy conference on Security in Central Asia, Vienna, July 2002.

12 U.S. Department of Commerce, Business Information for the Newly Independent States (BISNIS), "Commercial Overview of the Kyrgyz Republic, chapter 2, <www.bisnis.doc.gov/bisnis/country/ 0110overviewch2_kg.htm>.

13 By June 2001 the annual cost of debt relief was 130 percent of GDP. On June 29, 2001, Kyrgyzstan's Finance Minister Temirbek Akmataliev told a meeting of the State Commission on Foreign Aid and Investments that the country's foreign debt had reached $2 billion, which was one-third higher than annual GDP. *RFE/RL Newsline*, July 2, 2001, <www.rferl.org/newsline/2001/07/020701.asp>.

14 During the Tajik civil war, the UTO was bolstered by the members of the Islamic Movement of Uzbekistan (IMU), which is mostly comprised of militant Muslim extremists from Uzbekistan but includes other Central Asian nationalities and ethnic groups as well. The importance of assistance from Afghanistan to Tajikistan's Islamist movement is a much debated issue—with Ahmed Rashid most strongly arguing its significance.

15 Muriel Atkin, "Tajikistan: Reform, Reaction, and Civil War," in Ian Bremmer and Ray Taras, eds., *New States, New Politics: Building the Post-Soviet Nations*, Cambridge: Cambridge University Press, 1997, pp. 602–627.

16 According to the agreement, implementation of which was delayed, the government promised to lift the ban on all parties of the UTO in order that parliamentary elections could take place in 2000.

17 For additional details on the IMU, see this chapter's section on Uzbekistan.

18 In 1999, 83 percent of Tajikistan's population lived below the national poverty line, according to *Poverty Reduction, Growth and Debt Sustainability in Low-Income CIS Countries*, Washington, DC: World Bank and International Monetary Fund, February 4, 2002, p. 9.

19 Turkmenistan has 546 million barrels in proven oil reserves, with possible reserves (mainly in the western part of the country and in undeveloped offshore areas in the Caspian Sea) of up to 1.7 billion barrels as well as some of the world's largest deposits of natural gas, with proven natural gas reserves of approximately 101 trillion cubic feet.

20 Save for relatively limited amounts of gas across Iran, the government in Ashgabat has been almost entirely dependent upon Russia's Gazprom to purchase its gas. The Russians and Turkmen have had great difficulty reaching agreement over the price and form of payment for this gas, and at various times in the mid-1990s the Turkmen simply withheld their gas from market rather than take the heavily bartered deals that Russia was proposing.

21 According to a report by *Deutsche Welle*, Turkmenistan's regime has engaged in systematic narcotics trafficking and has forged ties with poppy producers in Afghanistan. Rustem Safronov, "Turkmenistan's Niyazov Implicated In Drug Smuggling," Eurasia Insight, March 29, 2002 <www.eurasianet.org>; See also: *Turkmenistan's Political Crisis—Inside The Niyazov Regime: A Discussion With Boris Sheikmuradov*, Washington, DC: Carnegie Endowment for International Peace, April 29, 2002 <www.ceip.org/files/events/sheikmuradov042902 transcript.asp>.

22 As a symbolic gesture of Uzbekistan's hegemonic intentions, Karimov declared Timur (Tamerlane, 1370–1405), who built a fourteenth-century empire in Central Asia, a national hero and commemorated him in downtown Tashkent with a statue and a large museum.

23 Mohamed Saleh, leader of the Erk party, took refuge in Turkey in late 1993. Abdurakhim Pulatov, from Birlik, left for the United States in November 1994. See Olivier Roy, *The New Central Asia*, New York: New York University Press, 1997, pp. 132–33.

24 There were several charismatic Muslims preaching in these years—men who had received their first training in underground schools in the 1970s and also in the looser conditions of the late Soviet-era were able to travel to and study in other Muslim countries.

25 Abuhjabber Abduvahitov, "Islamic Revival in Uzbekistan," in Dale Eickelman, *Muslim Politics*, Bloomington: Indiana University Press, 1993.

26 Founded in 1996, the IMU seeks to overthrow the existing Uzbek regime and establish an Islamic state, a goal most of its members subscribed to well before the organization was formalized by Juma Namangani (Juma Khodjiev) and Tahir Yuldashev.

27 U.S. Department of State, Bureau of Democracy, Human Rights, and Labor, *Uzbekistan, Country Report on Human Rights Practices—2001, March 4, 2002* <www.state.gov/g/drl/rls/hrrpt/2001/eur/8366.htm>. *See also Human Rights Watch World Report 2001*: Uzbekistan <www.hrw.org/wr2k1/europe/uzbek istan.html>.

28 See: Ahmed Rashid, *Jihad: The Rise of Militant Islam in Central Asia*, New Haven, CT: Yale University Press, 2002; and International Crisis Group, "The IMU and the Hizb-ut Tahrir: Implications of the Afghanistan Campaign," *Central Asia Briefing*, January, 30, 2002 <www.intl-crisisgroup.org/projects/ asia/centralasia/reports/A400538_30012002.pdf

29 The TRACECA Program was launched at a conference in Brussels in May 1993, bringing together the five Central Asian republics and the three South Caucasian republics. TRACECA is a program of EU-funded technical assistance to develop a transport corridor on a west-east axis from Europe, across the Black Sea, through the Caucasus and the Caspian Sea to Central Asia. To date the TRACECA program has financed 25 projects (valued at 35 million euro) and 11 investment projects for the rehabilitation of infrastructure (47 million euro).

30 Russian Foreign Minister Andrey Kozyrev stated on September 30, 1993, that Russia had a special right to intervene in the former Soviet republics to protect human rights, "particularly those of ethnic minorities." *Keesing's Record*

of World Events, vol. 39, no. 10 (October 1993), p. 39693.

31 In 1994 Nazarbayev floated the idea of a Euro-Asian Union that would replace the CIS by binding the states even more closely together while simultaneously putting them on a more equal footing. See Martha Brill Olcott, *Kazakhstan: Unfulfilled Promise*, Carnegie Endowment for International Peace, 2002, pp. 38–39.

32 For more on the Customs Union, see Martha Olcott, Anders Aslund, and Sherman W. Garnett, eds., *Getting It Wrong: Regional Cooperation and the Commonwealth of Independent States*, Washington, DC: Carnegie Endowment for International Peace, 1999, pp. 170–72.

33 For more on the Russia's involvement in the Shanghai Five, or the Shanghai Cooperation Organization as it was renamed in June 2001, see William Wohlforth's chapter in this volume.

34 The Kyrgyz parliament eventually ratified the border agreement in May 2002, giving the Chinese much of the disputed Uzeng-Kuush drainage area.

35 Access Industries took control of the Kazakh government shares in 2001, in part because of the difficulty that the Kazakh government was having in working with the Chinese in managing the project.

36 Interfax, *Central Asia and Caucasus Business Report*, vol. 5, no.16, April 15–21, 2002.

37 See Rashid, *Jihad*, pp. 70–71.

38 The change of alphabet is for the national languages; Russian continues to be written in Cyrillic. The Kyrgyz, Kazakhs, Uzbeks, and Turkmen have all made the switch. The Tajiks have reintroduced the Arabic alphabet, with the support of the Iranians.

39 Iranian textbooks are more easily adapted to immediate use than the Turkish ones, as written Tajik and Persian are virtually interchangeable, whereas only Turkmen is in the same Turkic language grouping as Istanbul Turkish.

40 Kazakhstan and Azerbaijan signed a bilateral deal on the median-line principal, which divides the two countries' respective sectors of the Caspian Sea. Russia and Kazakhstan had largely negotiated an agreement before September 11, but it was finalized in May 2002, when Russia and Kazakhstan signed a protocol on the equal division of three oil fields in the northern Caspian (Kurmangazy, Tsentralnoe, and Khvalynskoe). Under that protocol, each country has 50 percent stake in developing the deposits, and the median line dividing their respective sectors of the Caspian was also determined. This augmented the 1998 agreement, under which Kurmangazy was in Kazakhstan's sector of the Caspian and the other two fields were in the Russian sector. *Financial Times*, April 27, 2002; Kazakhstan Daily Digest, May 14, 2002 <www.eurasianet.org>. Russia and Azerbaijan were expected to sign a similar agreement in June 2002, but disagreement over "technical issues" prevented the finalization of the deal. Statements from both sides indicate the agreement will be signed soon. Sergei Blagov, "Second Bilateral Caspian Deals Prove Elusive," *Asia Times Online*, June 11, 2002 <http://atimes.com/c-asia/dfl1ag01.html>.

41 Uzbekistan's Islam Karimov does not seem to fully believe this claim, and he has kept his country's relationship with Iran more formal than friendly.

[42] The Central Asian states fall under the operational control of the U.S. Central Command (CENTCOM), whose commander in chief, General Tommy Franks, visited the region in September 2000 and again in May 2001. U.S. interest in the region was also marked during the command of his predecessor General Anthony Zinni (August 1997–August 2000).

[43] This program was renewed in May 2002, as Kazakhstan still has six remaining silos located at a test range in the south of the country. See *RFE/RL Newsline*, May 17, 2002, <www.rferl.org/newsline/2002/05/170502.asp>.

[44] Originally, these exercises were known as CENTRASBAT activities.

[45] Ambassador Stephen Sestanovich, the State Department special envoy for the Newly Independent States, made this statement at the conclusion of the May 1999 meeting of the U.S.-Uzbekistan joint commission. See Bruce Pannier and Zamira Echanova, "U.S. signs security agreements with Uzbekistan," *RFE/RL Newsline*, May 26, 1999, reprinted in *Asia Times Online*, May 28, 1999 <www.atimes.com/c-asia/ae28ag01.html>.

[46] *BBC Monitor* August 19, 2001 and August 20, 2001.

[47] Mikhail Khodarenok, "Starshego brata sdali za milliard dollarov." *Nezavisimaya Gazeta*, January 30, 2002.

[48] Associated Press, "Pentagon Studies Central Asia Forces," April 30, 2002 <www.nytimes.com/aponline/national/AP-U.S.-Central-Asia.html>.

[49] Edmund L. Andrews, "Bustling U.S. Air Base Materializes in the Mud," *The New York Times*, April 27, 2002.

[50] Embassy of the Republic of Kazakhstan, *Kazakhstan News Bulletin*, vol. 2, no. 16 (May 8, 2002).

[51] Roman Streshnev, "Sojuzniki Sobirajutsja Gostit' Dolgo," *Krasnaya Zvezda*, January 24, 2002, p. 3.

[52] See Olcott, Aslund, Garnett, *Getting It Wrong*, Washington, D.C.: Carnegie Endowment for International Peace, 1999.

[53] It is unusual for all five of the Central Asian leaders to attend a multilateral meeting, and Turkmenistan's Niyazov made an especially rare appearance. The CIS summit was held at a skiing resort of Chimbulak in Kazakhstan on March 1, 2002. "CNG stanet Evrosoyuzom," *Kommersant*, March 4, 2002.

[54] Officially Putin recommended reelecting Kazakhstan's Nazarbayev to be the chairman of the EEC.

[55] Vladimir Socor, "Kyrgyzstan's Hosting of U.S. Forces Irritates Moscow," *Monitor*, April 26, 2002, vol. 8, no. 82, p. 2.

[56] See press conference with Valery Nikolayenko, Secretary General of the CIS Collective Security Council, May 7, 2002, *Federal News Service*, May 8, 2002.

[57] Uzbekistan withdrew from GUUAM in 2002, a multilateral organization linking it with Georgia, Ukraine, Azerbaijan, and Moldova.

[58] Paul Starobin, "The Next Oil Frontier," *Business Week*, May 27, 2002.

[59] According to reports, gangs form Tajikistan, Kyrgyzstan, Kazakhstan, Uzbekistan, and Azerbaijan are flocking to the Russian Far East to sell heroin. The flow of drugs from Central Asia to Vladivostok, Nakhodka, and Khabarovsk dates back to 1998, when Iran closed its border with Afghanistan and western law enforcement agencies started cracking down harder on heroin trafficking to Europe and the United States. Rampant organized crime in the Russian

Far East makes it harder for businesses to operate and is a powerful lure to Central Asian and Caucasian newcomers. Velisarios Kattoulas, "Russian Far East: Crime Central," *Far Eastern Economic Review*, May 30, 2002.

[60] Uzbekistan also reaffirmed its "commitment to further intensify the democratic transformation of its society politically and economically." In addition, the United States also agreed to provide assistance to the Uzbek government for the implementation of democratic reforms in priority areas such as strengthening civil society, establishing a multi-party political system and independent media, strengthening non-governmental structures, and improving the judicial system. For the complete text of the "United States-Uzbekistan Declaration on the Strategic Partnership and Cooperation Framework," see Department of State website, <www.state/gov/r/pa/prs/ps/2002/8736pf.htm>.

[61] Under this agreement, the United States will facilitate the repatriation of enriched uranium fuel from a research reactor in Uzbekistan to Russia and will help the Uzbek government convert the reactor to low-enriched uranium fuel. U.S. Department of Energy, *DOE News*, March 12, 2002.

[62] For example, former Security Chief Muhammad Nazarov was dismissed in March 2002, charged with "premeditated murder, procuration of women, abuse of power, bribe-taking, illegal arrests, the manufacture and sale of counterfeit documents, seals, stamps and blank forms, embezzlement, and the abuse of power," and given the maximum sentence of 25 years in prison. *Interfax News Bulletin*, May 7, 2002.

[63] These include a group of pro-democracy activists known as Azadliq ("freedom"), which was organized during the Gorbachev reforms, and the United Turkmen Opposition, formed by Turkmenistan's first foreign minister, Avdy Kuliev, and former oil and natural gas minister, Nazar Suyunov.

[64] Beknazarov was charged with abuse of office while he was a local official in Toktogul. Sadji, "An Early Defeat for President Akaev," *Prism*, vol. 8, no. 4 (April 2002), part 4.

[65] Kulov was charged with abusing his position as head of national security in 1997–98.

[66] Two of the group's organizers were quickly arrested: Mukhtar Ablyazov, for alleged malfeasance when serving as head of Kazakhstan's power industry, and Gaklimzhan Shakiyanov, for purported abuses committed while Akim of Pavlodar Oblast. Some of the independent newspapers that tried to report these events experienced mysterious fires.

SOUTH ASIA

Stephen P. Cohen

O n September 11, 2001, the world learned that the United States was terribly vulnerable to a concerted terrorist attack. Two South Asian states, Afghanistan and Pakistan, were close to the heart of the problem. Both showed that terrorist organizations can be found where aggressive ideologies intersect with maldeveloped societies: Afghanistan was a state that had been commandeered by terrorists; Pakistan had the potential to move in the same direction. The terrorists who attacked the United States were trained in and directed by Al Qaeda leaders based in Afghanistan; in turn, Pakistan was supportive of the Afghan regime and cultivated its own home-grown Muslim radicals, many of whom supported Al Qaeda.

This discovery has transformed the world's understanding of South Asia. Until the September attacks, most attention had been devoted to India, the region's rising power. New Delhi was seen by the Clinton and Bush administrations as a possible Asian strategic partner, and Indians, Americans, and others spoke of New Delhi extending its economic, military, and cultural influence throughout the Indian Ocean area and working closely with the United States in keeping regional peace. But September 11 set in motion complex diplomacy that sorely tested the new Indian-U.S. relation-

Stephen Cohen is Senior Fellow in the Foreign Policy Studies Program at the Brookings Institution. He wishes to acknowledge the research assistance of Eric Longenecker and Sunil Dasgupta of the Brookings Institution and Meena Mallipeddi of Stanford University, and the helpful suggestions of Polly Nayak, visiting fellow at Brookings. Thanks are also due to Francine Frankel, Aaron Friedberg, Jack Gill, and Enders Wimbush for comments on an earlier draft.

ship and revived U.S. ties to Islamabad. It also produced a major India-Pakistan crisis that just might lead to a fundamental transformation of regional politics. This transformation in turn could liberate India from its "Pakistan problem," enabling it to play a more significant role as a major Asian power rather than a mere regional one.

This chapter addresses the major post-September 11 concerns of U.S. policymaking toward South Asia. First, the chapter summarizes the mixed regional picture that existed on the eve of September 11, when Pakistan seemed to be in decline, India was seen as a rising power, and the tensions between them appeared to be manageable.

Next, it examines the regional consequences of September 11. The most visible was the U.S. military operation in Taliban-controlled Afghanistan, which opened the door for the restoration of a free Afghan state. Another consequence of September 11 was the revival of close U.S.-Pakistan relations, which raises the prospect of a long-term U.S. commitment to helping Pakistan contain its own Muslim radicals and cease its support for such groups in Afghanistan and the Indian-governed portions of the state of Jammu and Kashmir. Defying past experience, the U.S.-Indian strategic relationship was also strengthened, and the United States has good relations with both South Asian powers for the first time in 50 years, raising the question as to whether Washington will use this position to help both states move toward some kind of agreement on Kashmir and other issues.

The chapter then addresses the six-month crisis of 2001–02. This standoff was the latest in a series of increasingly frequent and intense India-Pakistan confrontations. Like its predecessors it had the potential to escalate rapidly to a nuclear war, with profound strategic implications for Asia and the United States.

The chapter concludes with an examination of U.S. choices in this region of Strategic Asia. Is South Asia a new area of engagement for American diplomacy? If so, will this engagement focus largely on a rising India or will it encompass the still-powerful, but troubled, Pakistan? Washington must weigh the relative importance of a number of interests and devise a policy that balances the new concern with global terrorism with earlier concerns about preventing a nuclear war in South Asia and strategic cooperation with an emerging India.

Before September 11: A Strategic Snapshot

On the eve of September 11, India was widely seen to be "rising" by many American observers, Pakistan was clearly floundering, and the Taliban seemed to have established itself as the dominant force in Afghanistan, albeit one that had made important enemies around the world.[1] The nuclear

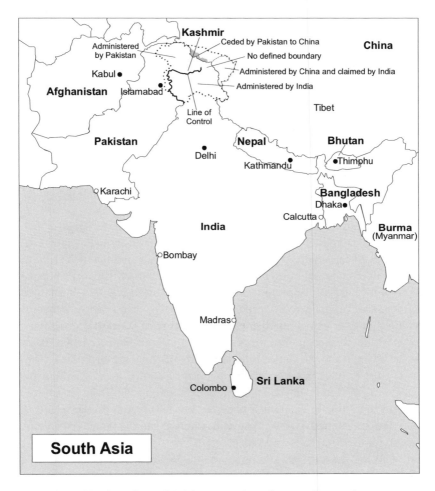

Kashmir
Administered by Pakistan
Ceded by Pakistan to China
No defined boundary
Administered by China and claimed by India
Administered by India
China
Kabul ●
Islamabad
Afghanistan
Tibet
Line of Control
Pakistan
Nepal
Bhutan
Delhi ●
Kathmandu
● Thimphu
Karachi ○
Bangladesh
Dhaka ●
Calcutta ○
India
Burma (Myanmar)
Bombay ○
Madras ○
Colombo ●
Sri Lanka

South Asia

programs of both India and Pakistan continued apace. Internal unrest continued in Nepal and Sri Lanka, but this had few strategic implications since New Delhi permitted friendly outside powers (Canada, Britain, Israel, and the United States) to work with regional governments to contain extremist and separatist movements. As for China—an important non-regional player in South Asia—its military and political support for Pakistan continued. China's growing trade ties with New Delhi did not translate into progress in resolving the long-standing India-China border dispute.

There was widespread consensus that India had ridden out the storm of anger triggered by its nuclear tests of May 1998, and that accommodation by the major powers, especially the United States, was at hand. One Indian commentator noted that by early 2001 "India was basking in new diplomatic glory. It had resisted the coercive measures of the international community, reordered relations with the major powers to its advantage, and managed an armed conflict with its nuclear neighbor with some responsibility and political success."[2] India sought, and soon received, tacit U.S. acceptance of its new nuclear status, as Washington searched for ways to modify the elaborate sanctions regime. India's economy continued to grow at a healthy rate, although there were several soft areas, especially manufacturing. India's domestic politics appeared chaotic, faction ridden, and violent in many states, but this is to be expected of a country undergoing several simultaneous economic, class, caste, and ideological revolutions. Democracy may not have been the best framework to foster rapid economic growth, but it certainly was the only one that could hold together this gigantic and complex state-civilization.

In contrast, Pakistan was widely perceived to be on the verge of failure. When the military seized power in October 1999, some Pakistanis acknowledged that their state had "failed," but also noted that it had failed four or five times earlier, most dramatically when half of Pakistan's population—East Pakistan—became the state of Bangladesh in 1971. The natural comparison with India reinforced this judgment. Pakistan's official economy was flatlined or worse; its core institutions were in shambles; it was supporting the Taliban regime in Afghanistan, which alienated two major states—China and the United States; and in mid-1999 it precipitated a limited war with India in the Kargil region of the disputed state of Jammu and Kashmir. This war resulted in a humiliating withdrawal of Pakistan's forces and set in motion the coup that removed Prime Minister Nawaz Sharif; it also saw the United States siding with India against Pakistan openly and firmly for the first time in 50 years.

Pakistan was also becoming an ideologically divided state, and even the return of the military to power in October 1999 could not stem the increase in domestic terrorism. This trend was epitomized by the systematic assassination of Shi'a physicians, which contributed to an exodus of some of Pakistan's most talented professionals. Senior police officers acknowledged that terrorists could strike in Pakistan at any time and any place that they wanted. Paradoxically, these issues were more freely debated in the Pakistani press than they had been for years, and Pakistan's non-governmental organizations were thriving, perhaps because so many state institutions had collapsed.

In sum, South Asia presented a mixed picture in late fall 2001. Relations between India and Pakistan were badly strained, with India refusing to resume its strategic and political dialogue until Pakistan ceased its support for insurgents and terrorists in Kashmir. Unwilling to restrain even its own domestic extremists, Islamabad continued its support of the Taliban

in Afghanistan and allowed a variety of Kashmir-oriented groups to operate from its territory and those parts of Kashmir that it controlled.

Nevertheless there were promising developments. India-Pakistan cross-
border trade had greatly increased,[3] and in early 1999 a promising summit
between Pakistani Prime Minister Nawaz Sharif and Indian Prime Minister
Atal Behari Vajpayee was held in the Pakistani city of Lahore. This meeting set out a full menu of arms control and confidence building measures,
none of which were consummated. The goodwill in India engendered by
this summit vanished after Pakistan initiated a military probe across the
Line of Control (LOC) at Kargil later that year. Indians were infuriated when
it was revealed that General Pervez Musharraf (as army chief) was planning the Kargil incursion even as the Lahore summit was in progress.

A second summit was held on July 14–16, 2001, in the Indian city of
Agra between Vajpayee and General/President Musharraf—who had displaced Sharif. Agra was a spectacular failure, with each side accusing the
other of bad faith. It was also South Asia's first televised summit and had
a negative impact on public opinion in both countries. Pakistanis concluded
that President Musharraf acquitted himself well on enemy territory, while
the Indian impression was that he was an arrogant huckster who upstaged
Vajpayee. In truth, neither side had prepared well for the meeting and there
were political and bureaucratic elements on both sides who were pleased
that it failed.

As for outside powers, China was playing its diplomatic cards very
carefully, while the United States actively sought an expanded relationship with India. Beijing did nothing to damage its good relationship with
Pakistan, but it was alarmed by Islamabad's support for Afghanistan's radical Taliban regime. The Taliban allowed Afghanistan to be used for the
training of radical Chinese Muslims, especially minority Uighurs.[4] The
Chinese pursued a policy that would enable them to pressure Afghanistan
to cease this support, and on the very day of the World Trade Center/
Pentagon attacks Beijing signed an aid agreement with the Taliban.

The Bush administration built upon the Clinton administration's "discovery of India" and set out to create a comprehensive and positive relationship with New Delhi. It valued India's expanding political and economic
power and its democratic political order. Strategically, New Delhi was also
viewed as a potential counterweight to a rising China. Like its predecessor, the Bush administration recognized the potential political importance
of Indian-Americans, and sought to harmonize its foreign policy goals in
South Asia with the desires of this affluent community. The Bush administration accelerated the process of normalization by shifting U.S. non-proliferation policy away from preventing India (and Pakistan) from acquiring

nuclear weapons to one of encouraging them to be more responsible nuclear powers. South Asia was not considered an area of imminent crisis—but the events of September 11 were soon to alter the circumstances.

Consequences for South Asia

Shortly after the September 11 attacks, Washington uncovered a link between the hijackers and South Asia. The terrorists all had ties to Al Qaeda, and the headquarters of this foundation-like organization, with its separate fundraising and operational wings and a grant-making arm, was situated in Afghanistan, with cells in dozens of countries around the world. Afghanistan's Taliban regime allowed Al Qaeda to operate freely, but the Taliban were in turn dependent upon Al Qaeda. Complicating matters further, the Taliban were backed by countries nominally friendly to the United States, notably Saudi Arabia, the United Arab Emirates, and Pakistan.

Washington was confronted with a cascading series of tasks in South Asia, each generating more and more demands on U.S. military and diplomatic resources. Any attempt to strike back at Al Qaeda would mean a confrontation with the Taliban, and any action in Afghanistan would require Pakistan's assistance. In turn, this would entangle the United States in the complex India-Pakistan dispute.

Nearly a year after the terrorist attacks, some of the original U.S. objectives in South Asia have been achieved, notably the destruction of the Taliban, the eviction of Al Qaeda from its Afghan stronghold, and the beginning of a new era for the Afghan people. However, September 11 also brought to the surface some of the fundamental contradictions in Pakistani policy, exacerbated a major India-Pakistan crisis, and caused a number of other powers to reassess their South Asia policies.

Afghanistan: Total War in a Small Place

The Taliban regime not only tolerated Al Qaeda, it was militarily and financially dependent upon it. There may be cases of state-sponsored terrorism, but Afghanistan was an example of a terrorist-sponsored state, since Al Qaeda provided the Taliban with armed units, financial assistance, and a link to the outside world. After the Taliban rejected the U.S. demand to turn over Afghanistan's "guests," the Bush administration launched *Operation Enduring Freedom* (OEF), against Al Qaeda and the Taliban.

OEF had two aims. The first was total war against Al Qaeda, obliterating it as an organization and killing, capturing, and punishing the top leadership and as many of its cadres as could be located. The Bush administration invoked the language of total war against what was viewed as an implacable and unscrupulous enemy. The war against Al Qaeda escalated to a war against "international terrorism." This was originally defined as terrorism directed against the United States, but ultimately included any group that America identified as "terrorist." There is still no precise definition of terrorism, but it has been long understood to include unprovoked attacks on unarmed and innocent civilians. This has led India, Israel, and Russia to press the United States to support their own counter-terrorist operations—however defined. One consequence has been that the United States modified its "war on terrorism" to include groups other than Al Qaeda that had also been active in Kashmir.

This phase of the war went better than most military experts predicted. Although there are no reliable casualty figures (or even good estimates of Al Qaeda's numbers), the organization is now reduced to small-scale operations in Afghanistan.[5] OEF was extended to Pakistan's Federal Administered Tribal Area (FATA) in April 2002.[6] These operations generated considerable information about Al Qaeda's global networks, yet only a few of the top leaders have been captured or killed and the organization may still be able to mount large-scale terrorist attacks. Several terrorist attacks in Pakistan, including the bombing of a church in Islamabad, a suicide car bomb that killed over a dozen French technicians in Karachi, the murder of U.S. journalist Daniel Pearl, and an attack on the American Consulate in Karachi show signs of Al Qaeda involvement, although no organization has claimed responsibility for them.

One factor that may abbreviate the U.S. commitment to Afghanistan is the prospect of significant military action against Saddam Hussein's regime in Iraq, and informed observers have urged Washington to first complete the task in Afghanistan.[7] Without a strong foreign presence, either in the form of U.S. units or the International Security Assistance Force (ISAF), or a cohesive Afghan army, there is a risk that Afghanistan's neighbors may once again seek allies and friends among the warlords. This outcome is made more likely by active Iranian and Indian efforts in Afghanistan, the latter exploiting its strong ties to the dominant Tajik element in the Afghan army.[8] Pakistan regards such influence as threatening to its own interests in Afghanistan, fearing that India will provoke the Pushtuns to revive claims for a greater "Pakhtunistan," which would include parts of Pakistan. The major concern that all parties will face, perhaps by mid-2003, is the question of what America will do if Afghanistan should fall once again into civil war while the United States is preoccupied elsewhere.

Pakistan: A New Alliance with the United States

September 11 has produced closer ties between the United States and Pakistan. It has also revealed and intensified the fissures within Pakistani

society, placing those ties at risk. Recognizing that Islamabad's cooperation would be vital to any operation in Afghanistan, the Bush administration turned to Pakistan within a day of the attacks, wielding sticks but also
offering carrots. Washington made seven demands of Islamabad, and
Pakistan's President Pervez Musharraf agreed at once to the U.S. ultima-
tum. These demands included: 1) stopping Al Qaeda operatives at the
Pakistan border and ending all logistic support for Osama bin Laden; 2)
providing blanket overflight and landing rights to the United States; 3)
access to Pakistani naval and air bases and along the border; 4) immediate
intelligence and immigration information; 5) condemnation of the September 11 attacks and the curb of "all domestic expressions of support for
terrorism against [the United States], its friends or allies"; 6) termination of
fuel shipments to the Taliban and the flow of Pakistani volunteers going
to join the Taliban in Afghanistan; and 7) breaking diplomatic relations with
Afghanistan and providing assistance to the United States in bringing
down the Taliban and Al Qaeda if the evidence strongly implicated Al
Qaeda and the Taliban continued to harbor it and bin Laden.[9]

President Musharraf had no choice but to accede to U.S. demands.
Almost bankrupt, Pakistan was vulnerable to economic pressure; it was
also diplomatically isolated because of its support for the Taliban and its
toleration of radical Muslim movements on its own territory.

The newly expanded India-United States relationship subsequently had
little direct impact on U.S. operations in Afghanistan, but it provided Washington with political leverage, as it made credible the implied threat that if
Pakistan did not cooperate with the United States the latter might side with
India on Kashmir and other issues.

Besides hosting over 2,000 members of the international press corps
and 3,000 Americans on temporary duty, Pakistan provided significant assistance to the war effort. Musharraf retired or transferred some of the senior
officers associated with Pakistan's support for the Taliban; several air bases
were made available to the United States, and part of the Karachi airport
became a logistical staging ground. Pakistan allowed its airspace to be used
by U.S. and allied aircraft for OEF operations in Afghanistan, and some
U.S. forces joined with Pakistani troops to carry out operations within
Pakistan itself. Finally, Islamabad has shared intelligence with the United
States and shows signs of intensifying its drive against domestic radicals.

In return for Pakistan's cooperation, Washington lifted nuclear sanctions, suspended the "democracy" sanctions that had been in place since
the 1999 coup, and put together a package of nearly $1 billion in debt re-
lief.[10] Pakistan also received at least one payment of $100 million for the
use of its air bases, but Washington refused to sell it any new weapons.

The United States and Pakistan are now uneasy partners in a marriage of strategic convenience. Pakistan expressed the hope that Washington would become more active on the Kashmir dispute, but the United States was in no mood to endanger its new relationship with New Delhi. Pakistan also asked for military equipment and sought economic help in the form of increased textile quotas (textiles are Pakistan's most important export), but the Bush administration was unable to persuade Congress, and the feeling persists among Pakistanis that Washington wants to keep their country on a short tether, just as the feeling persists in Washington that Pakistan remains unhealthily fixated on Kashmir. However, the subsequent India-Pakistan crisis did lead Washington to pledge that it would pursue the Kashmir problem in exchange for President Musharraf's pledge to cease Pakistan's support for cross-border "militants."

Pakistan's Islamic Dimension

A quarter of the world's Muslims live in South Asia. India, Bangladesh, and Pakistan each have about 130 million Muslims, and Pakistan was the only modern state founded explicitly as a homeland for Muslims. However, South Asian Islam is notable for its diversity and variety. The attacks of September 11 and the subsequent fighting in Afghanistan were seen by the region's Muslims through very different lenses.

Operation Enduring Freedom was accepted in Bangladesh and by Muslims in India even if it was not admired. Aside from a few fringe groups that supported the Taliban, most of the nearly 300 million Muslims in these countries saw the U.S. response as justified, if harsh. There were no Indians or Bangladeshis on the aircraft that slammed into the Pentagon and World Trade Center buildings. The most important "civilizational faultline" in South Asia does not fall between the predominately Muslim states (Pakistan and Bangladesh) and predominately non-Muslim ones (India, Sri Lanka, Nepal), but within the overwhelmingly Islamic Pakistan.

While most Pakistanis practice a moderate form of Islam, the civilizational faultline that really counts runs through the middle of Pakistan. A violent, aggressive Islam has taken root in South Punjab, parts of the Northwest Frontier Province (NWFP), and in some urban areas, including the metropolis, Karachi. In these regions organized gangs, usually based on one or another Sunni or Shi'a sect, terrorize the population and wage war with each other and against the Pakistani government. They are often affiliated with a sympathetic *madrassa,* which acts as a recruiting ground for pro-Taliban fighters. Ideologically-linked *madrassas* form a circuit that extends through different parts of Pakistan and terror and death squads travel through the countryside almost at will. When OEF began, these *madrassas* turned out volunteers to fight the Americans, and thousands of young Pakistanis were captured or killed in Afghanistan.

Al Qaeda and the Taliban have a strong presence in Pakistan, especially in the Northwest Frontier Province and parts of Punjab. While there were no Pakistanis among the September 11 hijackers, several of them were trained in Pakistan or had passed through Pakistan on their way to the frontlines of Afghanistan or Kashmir. One senior Al Qaeda leader was captured in a joint operation in the Punjab city of Faisalabad. This means that Pakistan is a "sea" in which Muslim radicals swim, but it does not necessarily mean that Pakistan is becoming a radical Islamic state.

Pakistan's Muslim parties and movements are very diverse. Some seek to foment a global Islamic revolution, others would be content to introduce more Islamic elements into Pakistan itself. The former would use Pakistan as a base camp for global revolution. They are bitterly angry at the military and other members of the Pakistani establishment and they constitute the greatest risk to foreigners living in Pakistan, as well as to the Pakistani leadership. The brother of Pakistan's interior minister was assassinated by one such group in December 2001. They are also strongly anti-American, not only because of Washington's support for Israel and the present Saudi regime, but because of U.S. support for moderate Pakistani governments over the years. Finally, most of these groups are fervent Sunnis and anti-Shi'a. Although small in numbers, these radical groups have been willing to employ deadly force within Pakistan against liberals, "secularists," Shi'a, and now foreigners. Although they represent a threat to public order and are capable of assassination and murder, they do not have wide political support.

The Muslim groups and parties located toward the center of Pakistan's political spectrum do have more support, but even then it does not compare with the "normal" political parties, the Pakistan People's Party (PPP) and the Pakistan Muslim League (PML). The most centrist Islamic party, the Jamiat-i-Ulema-Islami, is also the largest and best-organized, although it also has done poorly at the polls. Its ideology has spread widely in the army, the bureaucracy, and in some of the universities, especially in Punjab. The Jamiat has forced the two major parties to become more "Islamic" than they might have been otherwise.

The Jamiat propagates the view that Pakistan should be a modern but Islamic state, and, by participating in electoral politics, it acknowledges the legitimacy of western-derived institutions such as parliament. The Jamiat was a proponent of nuclearization, but it has also been a critic of the military, especially after the army withdrew its covert support for the party. It regards Musharraf as particularly threatening because of his "secular" tendencies. While bitterly critical of India, the Jamiat's leadership craves acceptance in the international community and thus presents a moderate face to the world. The Jamiat also sees itself as an advocate of modernity, envisaging Pakistan as a marriage of Islam and technology.

Ethnic, linguistic, and economic issues, not religious ones, have dominated Pakistani politics. The power of the religious parties derived from the patronage of the state; from Zia's time onward the religious parties were used to balance the secular (and more influential) PML and PPP. The religious parties have never polled more than 2 to 3 percent in a national election, and some now question whether the parties' street power can threaten any military regime or democratically elected government or whether they will ever have the votes to win a free election.[11] The World Trade Center attacks did not strengthen radical Islam in Pakistan—or anywhere else in South Asia—but they did illuminate the deep fissures that exist between moderate and radical Muslims in these societies.

Pulling Up the Roots of Terrorism and Reforming Pakistan

Pakistan's size (it will soon become the world's fifth most populous state), ties to many Arab and other Islamic states, nuclear capabilities, and critical location make its survival important to many powers. Yet its weakened administrative structures, especially an ineffective system of revenue collection and a corrupt and timid judiciary, will continue to cripple it. Moreover, the fundamental fear of India and its obsession with Kashmir will continue to constrain Pakistan's ability to reform.

Pakistan has many possible futures, some of them unpleasant and dangerous. It could split up into its constituent ethnic/linguistic units or civil war might break out. A more likely scenario would be the emergence of an autocracy, perhaps inspired by Islamic precepts. In each of these cases, Pakistan is likely to produce more, not fewer, Muslim extremists, and its nuclear weapons program is likely to accelerate, not slow down. A failing Pakistan could spew out terrorists and fissile material, or even whole nuclear weapons, and would be a matter of grave concern to its powerful neighbors, especially Iran, China, and India.

When he came to power in 1999, General Musharraf indicated that he sought to turn Pakistan into a moderate, liberal, Muslim state along the lines envisioned by Mohammed Ali Jinnah, Pakistan's most important founding father. This plan and Pakistan's opposition to terrorism were forcefully restated in a dramatic speech delivered in Urdu over Pakistani television on January 12, 2002.[12] Musharraf proclaimed that no internal extremism would be tolerated and no safe-havens for terrorists operating across Pakistan's borders would be provided. He stated that Pakistan itself had been a victim of terrorism (referring both to sectarian violence, but perhaps also alluding to Indian actions), and rejected his predecessor's support for Muslim militants. A joke made the rounds in Pakistan after the speech that if the pious Zia *died* in 1988 he was finally *buried* in 2002.

Islamabad's support for the Taliban and the Kashmiri jihad had important domestic political consequences for Pakistan. Most of the Islamists had a tie to Pakistan's security establishment. In fact, Pakistan's employment of militants and religious extremists dates back to operations in East Pakistan, when the army used militant Muslim groups to intimidate dissident Bengalis. The victims included intellectuals and educators, many of whom were murdered. The alliance between the army and violent militants was strengthened by Zia and his successors who gave the Inter-Services Intelligence Directorate (ISI) an overt role in domestic politics. Various militant Pakistani outfits were used to intimidate Pakistani political parties. The Afghan and Kashmir operations strengthened domestic Islamists, who were publicly defiant of Islamabad even after the military coup in 1999—perhaps because many of them felt they still had official support.[13]

There was a deeper problem with Pakistan as well. It had once been a moderate Islamic state, and under Ayub Khan in the 1950s and 1960s even military rule was applied with a light touch. It was on the verge of reaching the middle tier of the global economy in the 1960s and East Asian experts were encouraged to study Pakistan's model developmental programs. But by the late 1990s Pakistan's very identity was deeply contested. One of the first states to be created on the basis of a shared religious identity, a "homeland" for Indian Muslims, Pakistan had strayed far from the vision of Mohammed Ali Jinnah.[14] Jinnah had envisioned a secular, democratic state, tolerant of its own religious minorities (Hindu or Christian) and of different Islamic sects (Pakistan has a 12 percent minority Shi'a community, plus other sects such as the Ahmediyyas). However, it has been very difficult to translate this vision into contemporary political realities; while lip-service was paid to Jinnah, in practice Pakistan was becoming an increasingly backward-looking and bigoted state.[15]

After Musharraf's January 12 speech, there was a series of highly publicized murders of foreigners, continuing sectarian violence, and additional evidence that Al Qaeda and the Taliban had made Pakistan their new home base. Despite his public pledges, Musharraf is either unwilling or unable to crack down on Pakistan's home-grown Muslim radicals. The difference between "unable" and "unwilling" is the substance of a major debate that is raging in India, the United States, and Pakistan itself.

Some would argue that this shows how little control the government has over radicals and that Musharraf needs to be supported, even strengthened, as he attempts to rid Pakistan of these elements. Those who hold this position, including many senior U.S. officials with extensive contact with Musharraf and the Pakistani government, note that Musharraf and the army have reversed their Afghanistan policy and that with additional inducements—and perhaps additional pressures—the United States can convince them to do what is in Pakistan's own interest.

On the other hand, there are experts, especially in India, but also in the United States, who would frame the problem differently. They assert that Musharraf is *both* unable and unwilling to abandon the Islamic radicals, because they have penetrated into his own army and intelligence services as well as the deeper crevices of Pakistani society.[16] They point to the mushroom growth of the *madrassas*, the open display of arms, and the defiance of the government and conclude that Pakistan's problems are too deeply rooted for even a well-intentioned reformist general to tackle—and many doubt whether Musharraf is well-intentioned.

Pakistanis have themselves embarked upon a major debate about their state's support for Islamist militants, including those operating in Kashmir. This debate has expanded to include the future of Pakistan's entire foreign policy and the very identity of the Pakistani state. The supporters of Muslim militancy argue that Pakistan must abandon its dependency upon the United States and support the Islamists against India, ultimately forcing India to come to the bargaining table or even triggering a wider revolution in India itself.[17] This view, which parallels that of Hamas and Hezbollah and other radical groups attacking Israel, is not widely supported, but it is held by those in influential positions in Pakistan's security establishment and it dominates the more Islamist and militant political parties.

Yet the mainstream of Pakistan's establishment, which also supported this policy for at least a decade or more, now has second thoughts and more accommodating strategies are being widely discussed. For the first time since 1990, Pakistani intellectuals are speaking out on the Kashmir problem, many of them suggesting publicly what has been known privately for well over a decade—that Pakistan cannot sustain this kind of operation in the face of Indian resistance, international opposition, and resentment among the Kashmiri Muslims themselves, who regard their "liberators" as no less ruthless than the Indian security forces.[18]

Musharraf has come out publicly in favor of the more moderate position, but he continues to walk a narrow line between the militants and the moderates. He lacks charisma, popular support, and an efficient civilian administrative structure. His power base is in the army—he appointed all of the powerful corps commanders to their present positions. However, a series of large-scale public protests could make him dispensable as far as his colleagues are concerned, and there is always the possibility that a cabal of officers might depose him, and the risk of assassination remains high.[19] Musharraf's "victory" in a stage-managed referendum that asked the Pakistani people to support him in the presidency for another five years badly eroded his legitimacy. His most important asset is that at the moment there is no other military or political figure who can plausibly challenge him, nor does it seem likely that he will be abandoned by his powerful foreign supporters, including the United States, Saudi Arabia, and China.

The full restoration of democratic government and efficient rebuilding of the Pakistani state is a long and difficult journey. Although most members of the Pakistani elite are formally committed to the restoration of democracy, they are also uncomfortable with the idea of mass democratic politics. Politics is still the avocation of the rich and influential, seen more as a civic obligation than a career. In terms of democratization, Pakistan is ahead of many Arab states, but behind the thoroughly politicized and democratized India, Sri Lanka, and even Bangladesh. Pakistan is not likely to see a truly democratic state emerge until some kind of accord is brokered between the military and the politicians. It is a state that has an army that cannot govern but yet not allow civilians to rule. Pakistan's army is strong enough to prevent state failure, but it is not imaginative enough to impose the changes that might transform the state.[20] Pakistan's future remains uncertain, but there is no doubt that it has a core of able, trained officials and an elite that could transform the country. Transformation will require international support, the abandonment of quixotic foreign policy goals, and India's tolerance.

In sum, there is no certainty that Pakistan will become a normal state, but a high degree of certainty that if it fails to do so, it will have strained relations with most of its neighbors and even with states further afield, especially if it becomes a base for Islamist terrorism on a wider scale.

Angry India

The events of September 2001 led to closer ties between India and the United States. They seemed to validate India's views regarding the threat of Islamic terrorism and increased India's sense of righteousness. They also enhanced India's willingness to threaten Pakistan with the use of force.

India had long argued that Pakistan was a particularly dangerous state, supporting terrorism in India and Afghanistan, and New Delhi was frustrated by Washington's seeming apathy toward the issue. The attacks of September 11 seemed to vindicate India's position that terrorism rather than nuclear proliferation or Kashmir was the major strategic issue in South Asia. This argument was generally accepted, but it was also recognized that India's policies in Kashmir were partially responsible for the rise of separatist feelings. After the attacks, New Delhi immediately found a more attentive audience in Washington and other western states as far as terrorism-related matters were concerned. India was, however, taken aback by the simultaneous revival of close U.S.-Pakistan ties following September 11.

To India's chagrin, Pakistan was transformed overnight from a "failing state" to a "frontline" state, and became the recipient of western (especially American) attention, aid, and praise. The United States tried to balance its interests: while there were loans to Islamabad to rescue it from economic catastrophe and some sanctions were lifted, Washington tried to accommodate India by pressing Islamabad to cease its support for Muslim radicals and for cross-LOC operations in Kashmir. The Bush administration also assured Indian leaders that the forces based in Pakistan and military and economic assistance provided to Pakistan were designed to assist the war against terrorism, and were not directed against New Delhi.

Despite the events of September 11, Washington also wanted to preserve President Bush's "one big idea" concerning South Asia. This idea was that India was the regional power that counted, and that there was an opportunity for long-term strategic, economic, and political cooperation between two states that were once characterized as "estranged democracies."[21] Thus, Indian-American military cooperation increased dramatically, much of it designed to improve India's counter-terrorist capabilities.

The two countries also revived earlier plans for defense cooperation. Indian forces are expected to train alongside their U.S. counterparts in Alaska, the first significant new arms sales to India in over a decade were announced in April 2002, and U.S. and Indian special forces have engaged in joint training in Agra. This was an especially symbolic choice because Agra is the location of the Taj Mahal and the site of the failed India-Pakistan summit.[22]

As for Kashmir, the most visible issue dividing India and Pakistan, the Bush administration at first demonstrated that its pre-September 11 pro-India policy was intact by steadfastly refusing to discuss "mediation" between India and Pakistan over Kashmir. Indeed, two days after President Bush met President Pervez Musharraf, the United States also ruled out "facilitation"—a lesser form of engagement.[23] This policy was to change only two months later.

The Operational Code of the Indian Strategic Elite

The events of September 2001 strengthened the core beliefs of the Indian strategic elite. These include assumptions about India's special quality as a state, its place in the world, and the policies of other important states.[24]

Indians of all political stripes, including many leading Muslims, believe that India is a distinct civilizational entity. Like China, India embodies a distinct and great civilization in a single state. The Indian strategic community accepts the notion of "civilizational" competition, and Samuel Huntington's arguments are well-known and appreciated in New Delhi. According to this worldview, India is viewed as having been culturally and politically influential throughout the world. The means by which India spread its influence were morally sound, since its civilization and culture were spread by example, not the sword. Other great civilizations, including Europe, Islam, and China, owe much to India for its unique contributions to their cultural, philosophical, and moral growth. This suggests, to India's leaders, that there is a historic obligation or duty to restore Indian influence in Asia and the world and that states opposing India's restoration to the front ranks are either ignorant, malign, or jealous of India's greatness.

September 11 strengthened this belief in India's civilizational distinctiveness in two ways. First Indian civilization is explicitly compared with Islam and the conclusion is that India is both enduring and moderate. The Indian elite believes that "Indian-ness" will persist and prevail. There are Indians who assert a more militant Hindu-based civilizational identity, and those (such as the Nehruvians), who praise India's secular qualities (made possible, many would argue, by the tolerance built into polytheistic Hinduism), but both groups agree that the pluralist, complex Indian civilizational core is well-suited to the modern world, certainly more so than militant Islam, and perhaps more so than the materialist West. The events of September 11 and their aftermath strengthened the belief in India's civilizational distinctiveness. The September attacks seemed to show that India was not the only civilization under attack by radical Islam and that the West and India must form a defensive coalition.

As for method, the Indian strategic elite believes that while force should not be the *first* policy option, it is the *ultimate* option. India did lose its historically preeminent position because it was reluctant to defend itself against the invasions of Muslim and European adventurers. The impact of September 11 was to strengthen the argument that India has achieved moral superiority by its restraint, so that when it does eventually use force against its enemies—especially Pakistan—it will be even more in the "right." Like water building up behind a dam, the longer India waits to retaliate against its enemies, the greater the flood will be, but it will be a morally just flood. Thus, the inhibitions against using force now seem to be lower than ever before. The examples of the United States, which acted swiftly in Afghanistan in response to the attacks, and of Israel, which responded to Palestinian terrorist attacks, are cited as proper models for a vigorous and proud

India to emulate. When the 2002 crisis between India and Pakistan ended, Prime Minister Vajpayee exulted that India had won a "victory," but without a battle.

India's Relations with Pakistan, China, and the United States

The attacks of September 11 and the subsequent terrorist acts in India have temporarily tilted the balance between India's doves and hawks in terms of how they view India's relations with Pakistan, China, and the United States. Indian moderates, who advocated accommodation with Pakistan and China, are now hard to find. Few Indians publicly argue for an understanding, dialogue, the benefits of trade, or cultural exchanges with Pakistan. The attacks in Kashmir and New Delhi brought into public discourse a view that was once only uttered privately: Pakistan is an accident of history, and must be forced to its knees or destroyed. This is not yet the dominant view, but its growth over the past few years is striking, stimulated in part by intense television coverage of the Kargil war, the failed Agra summit, and the 2002 crisis.

India's highly vocal and politically ascendant hawks fall into three categories: those who would lure Pakistan into a military confrontation, leading to a final triumph over the Pakistan army (the aborted 1987 *Brasstacks* model[25]); those who believe that Pakistan merely needs a push in the form of increased support for separatist forces in the Sind, NWFP, and Baluchistan, which would lead to a civil war and the breakup of Pakistan (the 1971 model); and those who believe that India's greater economic potential will enable it to naturally dominate Pakistan and persuade its outside supporters that Pakistan is a failed state (the Soviet model). If India were to achieve a seven percent or even a five percent annual growth rate—instead of the three percent it had managed over the past decades—then New Delhi could play a significant role in Asia *and* cope with the residual threat from Pakistan; its advanced technologies would put it in a different league, its relative domestic order would make it more stable than Pakistan, and in any case Islamabad was (before September 11) quickly losing whatever friends it had. It was thought that India's economic growth would leave Pakistan behind, forcing it to recognize India's dominance. This view proved overly optimistic as it underestimated the difficulty of turning economic potential into political pre-eminence and actual growth and it ignored the assets available to even a struggling Pakistan.

While India did double its GDP from the time major economic reforms were initiated (in 1992), growing an average of six percent every year, growth is now slipping, and India will do well to achieve five percent growth in 2002. This weak performance is not the result of some cyclical movement;

analysts fear that India faces the prospect of "permanently sluggish economic growth" unless radical measures are taken to restructure the economy.[26] India also lacks a strategic economic asset—it is not a source of energy resources, it produces no vital raw materials, and it lacks a manufacturing capacity of consequence. The one bright spot, its niche role in the software industry, is just that—a niche, not a dominant presence.[27]

These three positions have in common two ideas: that Pakistan is a fundamental threat to India and that Islamabad is inherently vulnerable. They differ only in their estimate of the risk and cost of a direct Indian military initiative, but the events of September 11 and December 13, (the date of the militants' attack on the Indian parliament) gave the military option new life, in part because the long-range strategy of economic domination seems to be less realistic.

China raises the most disagreement among Indian strategists. Some still argue that accommodation with China is possible, but the realists who dominate the current BJP-led coalition argue that India and China will inevitably clash since China is inherently expansionist, is still a colonial power in Tibet and Xinjiang, and fears the example of Indian democracy and the expansion of Indian-U.S. strategic ties, especially in the Indian Ocean region. The September 11 attacks did nothing to change these views dramatically, but Indians have noted that it was China that urged Pakistan to join the war on terrorism and restrain its own Muslim extremists. There is clearly a convergence of interests between India and China in this regard, as there is between India and the United States.

The United States is seen by the core "realist" group of Indian strategists as a once-misguided state that now recognizes (albeit not fully) India's rightful role in South Asia, and its potential as a partner out-of-region. However, Indian leaders see Washington as an immature power that still does not know its own interests and cannot be relied upon in matters of vital importance to New Delhi. A strategy of appearing to accommodate Washington's *idée fixe* of the week is acceptable, as long as it does not compromise long-standing Indian principles and enduring interests.

India's Domestic Factor

Events following the attacks of September 11, including developments within India, demonstrated that while India seeks recognition as a rising state, its political elite remains preoccupied with domestic politics. The dominant ruling party, the BJP, governs by the consent of a shaky and heterogeneous coalition, and coalition partners regularly extract concessions from the BJP which weakens it own core support of hardline Hindus. Indian politics remains violent and chaotic, and the violence is not confined to the poorest and most backward states. It was Gujarat, one of India's richest states, that in February–April 2002 saw the mass murder of almost 2,000 Muslims and the transformation of over 100,000 into domestic refugees.[28] The BJP is also divided internally between modernizers and those who would favor a closed, autarkic economy, and the party has found it difficult to undertake systematic economic reform at a pace that would significantly change India's role as the dominant power in a problematic region. Even the new U.S.-Indian relationship is held hostage to this weak economic performance, and while the United States has officially ignored the mass killings in Gujarat, additional slaughters are likely to bring wider international condemnation, making it even more difficult for New Delhi to allow outside powers to play a diplomatically helpful role in Kashmir.

While September 11 increased Indian distrust—even hatred—of Pakistan, made China seem less of a threat and more of an ordinary competitor, and led to expanded U.S.-Indian cooperation on a range of issues, these attitudinal shifts may be temporary. Only a few years ago India and Pakistan were practicing highly-praised summitry, there was deep distrust of China, and the United States was seen as implacably hostile to a rising India. Given the very low levels of trust and understanding between the major players in South Asia, the wheel of opinion could turn again quickly, and as is noted below, change might come via domestic developments within India or Pakistan.

The Compound Crisis of 2002

History may yet judge that the most important event to occur in South Asia in 2001–02 was not the overthrow of the unsavory Taliban regime by U.S. and allied forces, but the extended crisis between India and Pakistan. This prolonged stand-off threatened to escalate into a major, and possibly nuclear war, but its denouement opens a new opportunity for India to establish a normal relationship with Pakistan. If this opportunity is lost, then crisis will become the normal state of affairs in South Asia.

Regional Crises

The crisis of 2001–02 was the latest in a series that began in 1987. The first was triggered by the Indian military exercise code-named *Brasstacks*. This exercise involved provocative Indian military deployments in the Rajasthan-Sind area. Pakistan responded in kind, the Indians paused, and the crisis evaporated. It was only later that the international community learned how close the two countries had come to war. This was the last conflict in which the two countries might have waged a purely conventional war; some time between that 1987 and 1990 both acquired simple nuclear weapons.

The second crisis occurred three years later, lasting from January to May of 1990. This crisis was the product of domestic political instability in both countries, the eruption of separatist violence in Kashmir, and serious misjudgments in Islamabad and new Delhi.[29] The 1990 crisis was intensified by the belief that India and Pakistan each had a few nuclear weapons. Subsequent press reports alleged (incorrectly) that Pakistani nuclear weapons were moved in the middle of the crisis, making the 1990 crisis a more threatening event in public perception than it really was.

Although alarms were sounded in 1992 and 1993, both turned out to be false. In May 1998 both India and Pakistan tested a variety of nuclear weapons, declaring themselves to be full-fledged nuclear weapons states. They have also engaged in competitive and well-publicized missile-testing programs. Only 16 months after the tests (and after the apparently successful Lahore summit) India and Pakistan fought a limited war in the Kargil region of Kashmir. This exercise in limited war was instigated by the Pakistani army when it infiltrated guerillas and regular army forces across the contested LOC, threatening India's position in the Siachin Glacier region as well as the town of Leh to the southeast.[30] Unfamiliar with the response of both a mass democracy and the international community, the four Pakistani generals (including Musharraf) who planned the operation believed that India could be forced to the negotiating table and that dialogue over Kashmir would ensue. Instead, they precipitated South Asia's first televised war and generated massive suspicion, even hatred, in India, emotions that were intensified by the failed Agra summit of July 2001.

Several hundred troops were killed at Kargil, and for the first time in 30 years India launched air strikes. These targeted Pakistani forces and irregulars who had infiltrated into Indian-administered Kashmir. India also pulverized Pakistani positions with artillery and the ground, air, and naval forces of both countries were mobilized.

Relations between India and Pakistan had scraped bottom. Both sides were extremely suspicious of the other's motives, and there was no popular support for détente. Kashmir was the main focal point of the rivalry, but the two states could not even agree on how to talk about it. India insisted that Pakistani support for "terrorism" be stopped before a dialogue began; Pakistan claimed that India's refusal to talk about Kashmir increased the risk of nuclear war in South Asia. The crisis of 2002 was to transform this debate, perhaps decisively.

Kashmir Redux

Kashmir remains one of the world's most complex disputes. Indians and Pakistanis are divided as to whether their fundamental differences are territorial (e.g., Kashmir), involve authority over people (e.g., Kashmiris, but also India's Muslims), or ideological. The complexity of this dispute gives it some of the qualities of a civil war, with domestic, economic, international, ideological, and military factors all intertwined. There are those on both sides who argue that they will never have a normal relationship until one side or the other gives in completely—whether on the territorial issue, the "people" issue, or the ideological issue—or all three.

India's strategy, as the status quo power, is eventually to settle for a compromise solution, approximately the present LOC with some adjustments. This would leave the prize of Kashmir, the Vale, in Indian hands. New Delhi would continue to maintain a large security presence in the state, while attempting to micro-manage Kashmiri politics—or at least those Kashmiris living under its control. New Delhi sees time as on its side, and assumes that sooner or later Pakistan will lose interest as the Kashmiris become more closely tied to India. This strategy has not shown results in the last 40 years, but many Indian officials argue that 40 or 50 years is nothing—what counts is that India not show signs of weakness on Kashmir, lest other provinces and regions of the country seek a separate status also, leading to the eventual breakup of India.

Pakistan's approach to Kashmir combines four motives: a desire for revenge, a desire for justice, a desire to keep the larger and more powerful India off balance, and a desire to divert public attention from domestic economic and political problems. The revenge factor flows from India's management of the vivisection of the old Pakistan in 1971. Even Pakistanis who acknowledge that West Pakistan had alienated East Pakistanis still regard the Indian intervention as evidence that India does not accept the legitimacy of Pakistan—or would like to reduce Pakistan to a vassal state, turning their country into "West Bangladesh."

A sense of grievance and injustice also pervades Pakistani attitudes. Most Pakistanis think that India has flouted all standards of decency in its relations with Pakistan, and Kashmir is seen as the most outrageous example of India's disregard for international principles. The Pakistani army sees Kashmir as a way of keeping India off balance, and has been merciless in its attempt to disrupt Indian rule there by any means, even at the cost of thousands of Kashmiri lives. It is likely to continue this strategy if only to ensure that Indian forces are bogged down in Kashmir, and unable to confront Pakistan proper across the international border.

Finally, successive Pakistani governments have used the Kashmir issue to generate national unity and patriotism. This is a "cause" that seemingly unites all Pakistanis, according to the government, and the government-sponsored academic and think-tank community, and the Pakistani "establishment" in general. However, public opinion polls support the impression that Pakistani attitudes on Kashmir fluctuate greatly. Pakistanis in Sind, Karachi, and Baluchistan care much less about Kashmir than those living in Punjab and Islamabad, and, in hard economic times, the salience of the issue slips even further.

Kashmir is the most important single conflict in the subcontinent, not just because its territory and population are contested, but because larger issues of national identity and regional power balances are embedded in it. "Solving" the Kashmir dispute means addressing these larger concerns, and they cannot be addressed without new thinking.

Terrorism in Kashmir: Deed and Response

In October 2001 a group of armed militants attacked the Kashmir state assembly in Srinagar, killing 38 people. The chief minister of the state, Farooq Abdullah, called on India to strike at militant training camps across the LOC and in Pakistan. Subsequently, an attack on the Indian parliament building on December 13 killed 14 people. Parliament was in session, and several senior parliamentarians and government officials narrowly escaped injury. Indians were infuriated and the Indian government, blaming Pakistan for the attack, announced a total military mobilization. It suspended ground and air links to Pakistan, reduced the size of its diplomatic establishment there, and threatened the one bilateral agreement that works, the 1960 Indus River Treaty.[31]

The December 13 attack heightened the already intense Indian debate over the proper response to terrorist attacks. At one extreme, reflecting the views of some hawks in Vajpayee's cabinet and elements of the military, the Pakistani provocations were described as acts of war and seen as justifying a military response.[32] Indian moderates urged patience and dialogue, but as each attack took place, their voices were silenced, and Indian opinion eventually was overwhelming in favor of some military response against the camps. Many also urged that India attack Pakistan itself, removing what was described as the ultimate cause of terrorism.

After four months of continuing low-level terrorist attacks and some incidents along the LOC, another atrocity took place on May 14, when 33 soldiers and their families were killed in a suicide/terrorist attack on the Kaluchak army camp in Jammu. This heightened the sense of crisis, as New Delhi put even greater pressure on Washington to force Pakistan to turn over 20 named individuals accused of terrorism and to stop militants from crossing the LOC. New Delhi may have had a third goal: forcing a change in the Pakistani leadership. By mid-May there was widespread speculation that limited military action could break out at any moment.

A High-Risk Response

What was India's strategy, given the inflamed state of public opinion and the reality of terrorism in the heart of New Delhi? Early in the crisis, India's strategy of choice was characterized as "coercive diplomacy" by Brajesh Mishra, the national security advisor. Pakistan called it "brinkmanship" and tried to depict India as an irresponsible provocateur. A more neutral term would be compellence—the threat of escalation to compel an adversary to carry out an action. Compellence's twin, deterrence, is the threat to use force to dissuade an adversary from moving. When deterrence works *nothing* happens, when compellence works *something* happens.

India's compellence strategy was aimed more at the United States than Pakistan. New Delhi guessed correctly that Pakistan would ignore its demands but it hoped that the United States would take the threats more seriously. From Washington's perspective there were a number of reasons to do so. There was a possibility that the U.S. war on terrorism would be disrupted by an India-Pakistan war, and that conflict in South Asia might even go nuclear, creating a crisis with world-wide implications. Washington was also faced with a demand from a new "natural" ally, a state it viewed as a rising power and a potential balancer of China. Finally, India was taken seriously because it was threatening to do exactly what the United States had accomplished in Afghanistan and what Israel was doing (with U.S. support) in the Middle East.

The Indian government thus successfully reframed the South Asian debate over peace and war. Echoing the U.S. and Israeli responses to terrorism, Indian officials argued that the issue facing the international community in South Asia was no longer "Kashmir" but terrorism. India refused to discuss Kashmir until terrorism ended, the same position held by Israel (and backed by the United States). This strategy neutralized Pakistan's long-standing argument that peace would come to South Asia once India began to negotiate on Kashmir. India ran the risk of being labeled the aggressor because of its threat of war, but it correctly judged that it had found a way to bring international pressure to bear upon Pakistan.

This was not the first time that India tried compellence. During the Kargil conflict in 1999 it abandoned its earlier assertion that nuclear weapons would deter all war in South Asia, and moved to the position held by Pakistan—that nuclear weapons deter nuclear and large-scale war, but provide the opportunity for "limited" conventional war with due regard for the risks of escalation to a nuclear conflict. Pakistan has for many years supported what it termed "militants" to compel India to come to the negotiating table and discuss Kashmir; ironically, India arrived at the same strategy, and successfully turned it against Pakistan.

While Indian forces were fully mobilized as early as December 18, they were kept in the field for a full six months after the roll-out of the compellence strategy. Even after the crisis appeared to be resolved in mid-June, Indian officials, while claiming a "victory without war," again threatened war should Pakistan not comply with India's demands.

Compellence does carry some risks, and it has to be carefully applied to be effective. There is always a danger that the response of the other side may be miscalculated or that it will simply not comply with a demand. In this case India was not pressuring Pakistan directly, but was applying pressure on the United States and other countries, which would, in turn, apply pressure on Islamabad. Pakistan was correctly seen as vulnerable to such indirect pressure, in part because its economy was so weak, and in part because it had been compromised by its support of the Taliban and its tolerance of radicals on its own territory. India had placed Musharraf in a corner: if he argued that he did not want to stop the militants, then he would be admitting guilt; if he argued that he could not stop them, he would be admitting incompetence, inviting his own removal.

There was also the risk that Pakistan would not have taken seriously India's threat, and that India would have to do something to retain its credibility. In this case, New Delhi kept its military on high alert from mid-December 2001, despite considerable hardship. In fact, the government emphasized the army's anger and kept up a steady stream of public threats. It also stressed the nature of the attacks: two of them (the attacks on the Kashmiri legislature and on the Indian parliament) were on the democratic institutions so highly valued in the West, and which Pakistan lacked, and one of them, the attack at Kaluchak, had targeted women and children.

Finally, to be effective in persuading third parties, the demands made by a state engaged in compellence should echo the policies of major powers. India ensured that its demands on Pakistan resembled those of the United States vis-à-vis states alleged to be supporting terrorism and those of Israel on the Palestinian leadership. Indian diplomacy thus put Washington in a position where it was being asked to support Indian policies that mirrored its own and where failure to support such policies could trigger a major war and undercut Pakistan's support for the war on terrorism.

Military Calculations: Conventional Forces and the Nuclear Balance

No comprehensive military strategy will work without adequate military force. A rational leadership will initiate the use of force only if it believes that doing so will help achieve its political objectives, that it can manage the response of the other side, and that it is willing to move up the ladder of escalating force.

Throughout the 2002 crisis there were repeated assertions by each side that the military balance was in its favor. From an outside perspective, the "objective" military balance, determined by simply counting numbers, appears to favor India, though not overwhelmingly so. The force ratios are such that neither side can undertake a major conventional attack with a high degree of confidence in its success, and both sides remain vulnerable to low-level pin-pricks, all of which have the potential for escalation. Both sides also recognize that a nuclear exchange of any consequence would be devastating to their respective societies, and that "victory" in such a war would be Pyrrhic.

During the 2002 crisis it was frequently asserted that the conventional military balance overwhelmingly favored the much bigger India.[33] India did defeat the Pakistan army in East Bengal in 1971, it successfully pushed back most of the Pakistani encroachment in the recent Kargil conflict, and Indian officials and publicists boasted that they would put Pakistan in its place once and for all if it did not cease its meddling in India.

This was not the view from Pakistan's army headquarters in Rawalpindi. Senior officers there were confident they could deter any large-scale Indian attack and respond effectively to small-scale incursions. As the crisis began to mount they argued that while Indian forces could mass at any place along the international border or the LOC, Pakistan had adequate reserves to meet and stop them. Pakistan also had the option of moving across the LOC in Kashmir or the international frontier at several points. It planned to do this in 1987 when it threatened a counter-attack against the then turbulent Punjab. Rightly or not, some Pakistani generals believed that India's Sikh population was not loyal to New Delhi, and some ideologues argued that India's vast Muslim population (numbering 130 million) was a potential fifth column, especially after the Gujarat riots. This confidence in its own ability to defend Pakistan goes hand in hand with the army's deep distrust of New Delhi, and its assumption that India had a wider goal, the destruction of the state of Pakistan.

Actual ratios of Indian superiority were not overwhelming and the figures do not account for the qualities of leadership, morale, intelligence capabilities, logistics, doctrines, and the role of outside powers in pushing the military outcome in one direction or another.

The actual ratio of critical weapons between India and Pakistan has not changed for many years, and still hovers around 2:1 for aircraft, and 1.5:1 for tanks and armored personnel carriers. India has a substantial naval advantage (5:1), but the Pakistan navy would be fighting a defensive battle, and any Indian attacks on ships bound for Pakistani ports would immediately involve other countries, since Pakistan's own merchant navy

Figure 8.1. Military Balance Ratio: India vs. Pakistan

a) Land Forces

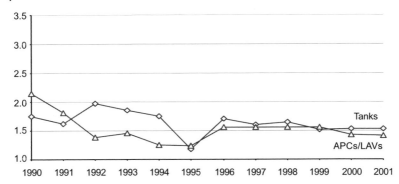

b) Naval Forces

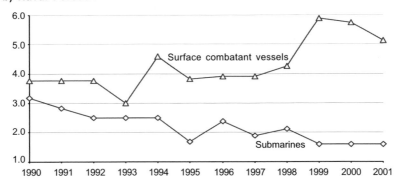

c) Air Forces

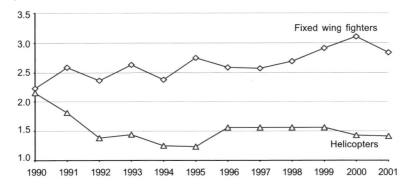

Source: International Institute of Strategic Studies, *The Military Balance*, New York: Oxford University Press, various editions.

is quite small. India, in turn, would have to be wary of Pakistan's small but fairly modern submarine fleet.

Moreover, India's larger army is tied down in internal security duties in a number of places, especially Kashmir. There are substantial shortages of officers at lower ranks, and the quality of equipment of both military establishments is not significantly different. Neither country comes up to western standards, although the warfighting skills of both far surpasses that of most non-western military establishments.

In early 2002 the outcome of a short conventional war between India and Pakistan was hard to predict. It might have been another inconclusive conflict. The way in which a conventional war might escalate to the nuclear level has been discussed at length but is un-knowable. India probably did not have conventional dominance, but its strategy of compellence succeeded because of the risk that Pakistan would eventually have been forced to move up the escalation ladder to the use of nuclear weapons.

India and Pakistan went overtly nuclear in 1998, and since then they have slowly assembled nuclear doctrines, picking up bits and pieces from strategic and tactical nuclear doctrines of the United States and other major powers. The crisis of 2002 accelerated this process, but their doctrines, like their weapons and missiles, are still new, and raise questions about the stability of the relationship between these fledgling nuclear powers. Table 8.1 summarizes recent estimates of current Indian and Pakistani nuclear capabilities, as well as their delivery systems, which for Pakistan are largely missiles and for India are largely aircraft.

Until recently there were no substantiated reports that nuclear weapons had been deployed to operational field commands. Most academic analysts assumed that India and Pakistan had not "mated" their nuclear warheads with delivery systems (aircraft or missiles), and that warheads were stored in an unassembled form.[34] These assumptions may be incorrect and, according to a study of the 1999 Kargil crisis by a senior American official, the United States was then convinced that Pakistan had deployed its nuclear weapons.[35] There are still no reliable public estimates of the "strategic warning time" of each state—the time it would take them to assemble, mate, and deploy nuclear weapons. This could be a matter of days, hours, or even minutes. In a crisis, uncertainty over the preparedness of the other side (or ignorance of one's own capabilities) could lead to consideration of a pre-emptive strike, and the revelation that Pakistan had deployed its nuclear force in 1999 may itself influence regional strategic planning. The region's nuclear status appears to be in flux, and almost all independent observers now agree with the assessment of the Central Intelligence Agency that the possibility of a nuclear conflict between In-

Table 8.1. South Asian Weapons of Mass Destruction

India	Pakistan
NBC Weapons	**NBC Weapons**
Nuclear Weapons High amounts of plutonium and small quantities of enriched uranium, enough for 45–95 warheads (only 30–35 likely have been made). India claimed its 1998 tests yielded 43 kilotons; independent observers argue the yield was 12 kilotons.	Nuclear Weapons High amounts of weapons-grade uranium and small quantities of plutonium (all believed to be used for weapons), enough for 30–52 nuclear warheads. Pakistan claimed its 1998 test yields were up to 35 kilotons.
Biological Weapons Not known to have been produced. Maintains a research program for biological weapons defense, and has a biological and genetic modification research program.	Biological Weapons Not known to have been produced. Has the resources and technological capacity for a limited biological weapons research program.
Chemical Weapons Chemical weapons manufactured, but destroyed before India signed the Chemical Weapons Treaty. A large chemical industry could be a source for dual-use chemicals potentially usable as weapons.	Chemical Weapons Not known to have been produced. Research had progressed far enough to produce chemical weapons, and Pakistan has imported numerous dual-use chemicals.
Primary Delivery Systems	**Primary Delivery Systems**
NBC-Capable Aircraft Fighters and ground attack aircraft: 84 Jaguar S(I) (4,775 kg), 135 MiG-27M (3,000 kg). Bombers: 5 TU-142 F Bear (20,000 kg, ASW), 4 TU-22M3 Backfire (24,000 kg, leased). Potential nuclear delivery aircraft (if modified): 40 Mirage 2000H, 63 MiG-29, 16 Su-30K.	NBC-Capable Aircraft Fighters and ground attack aircraft: 42 A5 Fantan (2,000 kg), 16 Mirage III (4,000 kg), 52 Mirage 5 (4,500 kg). Potential nuclear delivery aircraft (if modified): 32 F-16 A/B (5,450kg) (believed more likely than above).
Ballistic Missiles Short range: 12–75 Prithvi-1 (1,000 kg) on 3–5 launchers (not nuclear-capable).	Ballistic Missiles Short range: 80 Hatf-1 (not nuclear capable), 30 M-11 (NBC-capable), and unknown number of Shaheen-1 (may be nuclear-capable).

Medium Range: Tested Agni and Agni-2 (both 1,000 kg, and both may be NBC capable).	Medium Range: 12 Ghauri (500–750 kg) (NBC capable). Tested Shaheen-2 (1,000 kg) and Ghauri-2 (750–1,000 kg) (both NBC capable).
Potential Delivery Systems	**Potential Delivery Systems**
Cruise Missiles Various air-, submarine-, and ship-launched anti-ship cruise missiles. One indigenous ground-launched, land attack cruise missile.	Cruise Missiles Various ground-, air-, and ship-launched anti-ship cruise missiles.
Towed and Self-Propelled Artillery 4,400 various howitzers (75mm–155 mm).	Towed and Self-Propelled Artillery 1,700 various howitzers (85mm–203 mm).
Multiple Rocket Launchers 100, including BM-21 (122mm) and Pinacha (214mm). None are nuclear-capable.	Multiple Rocket Launchers 45 Azar (122mm). None are nuclear-capable.
WMD Defense	**WMD Defense**
Air Defense 2,500 various air defense gun vehicles (23mm–40mm), 1,800 various personal, vehicle-mounted, and towed surface-to-air missiles.	Air Defense 2,000 various air defense gun vehicles (14.5mm–57mm), 1,400 various personal, vehicle-mounted, and towed surface-to-air missiles.
Missile Defense Working to build a limited system based on several dozen Russian S-300MV air defense systems.	Missile Defense No interceptors or radar systems sufficient for even limited detection or defense capabilities.

International Institute for Strategic Studies (IISS), *The Military Balance 2001–2002* for missile, aircraft, and artillery inventories; Office of the Secretary of Defense, *Proliferation: Threat and Response,* (January 2001) for nuclear, chemical, and biological weapons inventories; Center for Defense and International Security Studies, *Cruise Missile Tables,* for cruise missile inventories; Federation of American Scientists, *Military Analysis Network* and *WMD Resources,* for information on capabilities of delivery systems and history of nuclear testing; the Stockholm International Peace Research Institute's *FIRST Database* and the Bulletin of Atomic Scientists' website were consulted for nuclear arsenals and delivery systems.

dia and Pakistan was higher in the spring of 2002, and the chance of war was higher than at any point since 1971.[36]

Pakistan has a straightforward view of nuclear weapons, derived from the Pakistan army's contacts with NATO nuclear training teams in the 1950s. Nuclear weapons are *weapons,* to be used according to the threat facing the state. Tactically, they could be used on the battlefield to make up for

Pakistan's deficiency in conventional forces. Strategically, they could be used against Indian cities should Pakistan be on the verge of total defeat (or of losing a major part of its territory, as it did in 1971 when East Pakistan fell to Indian forces). As its nuclear doctrines are still evolving, Pakistan has not made clear where the line would be drawn between a tactical and a strategic use of nuclear weapons, and ambiguity is an inherent component of any deterrent strategy. As the 2002 crisis progressed, Pakistan discovered that the world no longer regarded a first-use doctrine, even at the tactical or battlefield level, to be politically acceptable, and India skillfully exploited Pakistan's statements that Islamabad would use nuclear weapons if the threat was great enough.

More provocatively, the Pakistani army had very early developed the idea that once the region went nuclear, then Pakistan could be more open in its support of Kashmiri separatists and other Islamists operating against India.[37] Pakistan would use its nuclear umbrella as a way of pursuing a low-intensity war against India, and it was assumed that India would not risk responding at the conventional, let alone the nuclear level.

The Indian view has always been more complex, and derived from civilian thinking about nuclear weapons. The Indian strategic elite was once highly critical of the use of nuclear weapons. Even used as a deterrent, they were scorned as immoral weapons of the strong used against the weak, allowing a cheap victory by advanced, western, technological powers over less-developed Asian ones.[38] Indians prefer to think of their power as entirely defensive and thus entirely *moral*. There thus arose a discrepancy after India tested and declared itself to be a nuclear weapon state. On the one hand, India had a purely defensive military strategy, developed in the context of conventional weapons, which emphasized territorial denial and defense. On the other hand, India was beginning to manufacture nuclear weapons—the deterrent par excellence.

India developed a novel theory of nuclear weapons that framed its new nuclear status in acceptable moral as well as strategic terms. The result was a theory of nuclear weapons that was dissociated from war.[39] Developed by K. Subrahmanyam, General K. Sundarji and others, this theory had three components. The first was that India's nuclear weapons were not instruments of war, but were designed entirely to *prevent* nuclear war, and would only be used if India were attacked by nuclear weapons. India's response would be swift and certain: the aggressor would be punished. India's nuclear weapons would remain "moral" in that they would only be used against an aggressor. The second part of this doctrine combines morality with grand strategy. India's nuclear weapons would allow it to pressure other nuclear weapons states to reduce or eliminate their nuclear forces, thus paving the way for global disarmament, and, incidentally, increasing India's relative power, since in a nuclear-armed world India would be among the few nuclear "haves." Finally, a "principled" no-first-use doctrine was announced. All of this culminated in the idea of a "non-military" nuclear weapon, strongly criticized both by nuclear "realists" such as Bharat Karnad and by nuclear abolitionists such as Kanti P. Bajpai.

Kargil was powerful evidence to Indians that their "draft" nuclear doctrine—the government has not actually declared it to be government policy—was inadequate. India's nuclear weapons did not deter Pakistan from this operation; if anything, becoming a nuclear weapons state made the Indian security establishment over-confident. The recent Indian pronouncement of a "limited war" doctrine was the logical response. Indians believed in extended deterrence, but after Kargil they came to the conclusion that they had an ineffective low-level response and a high-level response that was not credible. Defense by punishment did not work because India could not attack high-value Pakistani targets for fear of retaliation on its own cities. Now, India is moving to a limited war doctrine, trying to retain a façade of "victory" in a situation where compromise and blurred results are inherent. This new doctrine is disliked by politicians as it gives the military more of a role in decision-making. Indian politicians are also uncomfortable with the limited war doctrine because it pushes India closer to the actual use of nuclear weapons, moving India in the direction of Pakistan's first-use doctrine.

India claims that it is prepared to "win" a war that by definition is kept limited in intensity or scope. However, it takes two sides to limit a war and there is always a temptation for either side to escalate to prevent defeat. Kargil was typical: India claimed victory although it suffered significant casualties; Pakistan claimed victory because of India's losses. It may be that both sides tacitly understood that this was the way in which the war would end. To some extent, the 2002 crisis also ended this way, with each side claiming to have "won" a victory that was made possible by its powerful military capabilities.

The 2002 crisis led to further evolution in the nuclear doctrines of both India and Pakistan. The public side of the process began with a widely circulated statement by the chief of Pakistani nuclear planning to a group of Italian scientists—who carried the message immediately to India. The gist of Pakistan's evolved position is that it had a number of "red lines," i.e. actions by India that would trigger the use of nuclear weapons. These included an economic or sea blockade, a military threat in the plains, meddling in Pakistani politics, a cut-off of water from the Indus River, and other activities. In return, the Indian chief of the army staff, General S.

Padmanaban, held a press conference in which he declared that India's "no first use" doctrine might be more flexible than previously thought. Not only would India respond to a direct nuclear attack on India and Indian forces by a nuclear counter-attack at a time and place (and magnitude) of India's choice, but New Delhi might use nuclear weapons if they were first used *anywhere* by Pakistan, including Indian military forces on Pakistani soil. In response, President Musharraf gave an interview to the German magazine *Der Spiegel* in which he reiterated Pakistan's position: if the pressure from India became too great, "as a last resort the [use of the] atom bomb is also possible." A government spokesman, probably Rashid Qureshi (Musharraf's close confidant and press spokesman) elaborated: "Only if Pakistan were threatened to disappear from the map, the pressure of our people to take this option would be too great. Then it will be valid. In an emergency also, the atom bomb."[40]

In comparison with India, Pakistan's case was much simpler. Pakistan's nuclear doctrine was developed entirely by the armed forces (and almost entirely by the army). It was strongly influenced by early NATO doctrine— NATO and U.S. teams used to lecture at Pakistan's Staff College on this subject. Nuclear weapons are seen as the great equalizer, and Pakistan allows for their first use in the face of a large Indian conventional attack, let alone an Indian nuclear strike.

Since 1990, Pakistan has used the risk of escalation to nuclear war to shield a policy that combines an element of punishing India with an attempt to compel it to offer concessions on the Kashmir issue. The tests of 1998 emboldened Islamabad in this strategy: if pain will force the Indians to change their policies on Kashmir, more pain will speed up the process. For Pakistan there was no need to change its military doctrine after 1998, it was simply more effective when nuclear weapons came out into the open. There has been a recent softening of the *presentation* of Pakistani policy by Musharraf, but not a fundamental change in the strategy of pursuing a limited undeclared war against India, leaving open the possibility of a limited nuclear war.

Domestic Factors

A final component of the 2002 crisis was domestic political uncertainty in both India and Pakistan just at the moment the crisis reached a peak in March and April. Two developments were particularly important; one was the decline in General Musharraf's popularity and the other was an outbreak of communal violence in Gujarat.

General Pervez Musharraf came to power in 1999 without much popular support, but he was not personally disliked. He held a referendum on

April 30, 2002 in an attempt to solidify his position as Pakistan's national leader, but this was widely seen in Pakistan as a crudely manipulated victory. For India, Musharraf's dismal performance raised the possibility of his departure from power, either by a coalition of political opponents, the army, or one of Pakistan's outside supporters, notably the United States. Balancing their desire to remove Musharraf was the Indian concern—shared by many Americans—that his successor might not be a more pliable civilian or even a moderate-liberal general, but one of the hawks that had come to a position of influence after the 1999 coup. India oscillated, therefore, in its personal attacks on Musharraf. Privately, Indian leaders expressed their dislike for him, but for the most part they publicly suggested that he would be acceptable if he yielded to Indian demands on cross-border movements.

The other important domestic event took place in India. When New Delhi made its demands of Islamabad in December and placed its forces on alert, most Pakistanis regarded the Indian buildup as motivated by elections scheduled for February 14–21, 2002. The elections passed, but Indian pressure showed no sign of softening—and Pakistanis assumed that New Delhi was merely waiting for an appropriate moment to cut its losses and abandon its provocative armed diplomacy.

Instead, relations between the two countries took a nasty turn, giving a new twist to what Pakistanis still regarded as a synthetic crisis. On February 27 a train carrying radical Hindu extremist volunteers returning from a pilgrimage in Ayodhya was attacked by a Muslim mob and at least 60 passengers, including women and children, were burned alive in a railway carriage in Gujarat. Hindus retaliated, killing at least 2,000 Muslims in the state, ironically once Mahatma Gandhi's home.[41] Thousands more were relocated to camps, fearful of returning to their homes and businesses. The BJP chief minister in Gujarat refused to resign over the violence and explained that the Hindu retaliation was "understandable." The killings continued for the next three months.

For most Pakistanis, Gujarat was further evidence that India was now governed by intolerant Hindus, and the "idea" of Pakistan as a homeland for India's Muslims was strengthened. On the Indian side, government officials accused Pakistan's intelligence agencies of masterminding the original attack on the train.

India's first televised, communal bloodbath interacted with the larger India-Pakistan standoff. Many nationalists, and especially those on the Hindu right, saw an opportunity to teach India's Muslims a "lesson" by attacking Pakistan, arguing that a short, sharp war would cut Pakistan down to size, and that the only language the Pakistani generals understood was force. Until the passions faded, Pakistanis were even less likely to support any concessions on Kashmir, and Pakistani militants argued that support for the Kashmiris was doubly justified after Gujarat. Despite a few very hawkish speeches, even Vajpayee was under attack from the Hindu right for being "soft" on Pakistan.

Resolving the Crisis

As in 1999, U.S. intervention proved to be decisive in defusing the 2002 India-Pakistan crisis. For years, the Indian government had formally resisted the idea of a more active U.S. role in the India-Pakistan conflict, while the Pakistani government eagerly sought the intervention of outside powers. These positions were modified when India accepted a U.S. role in pressuring Pakistan in Kargil. New Delhi's rigid insistence on bilateralism in its dealing with Pakistan was again bent to give U.S. diplomacy an opportunity to "deliver" Musharraf in 2002. The BJP-dominated government was supported in this view by virtue of its alliance partners as well as some opposition leaders who openly favored a more active U.S. role.[42]

Washington's first high level engagement took place in January, with telephone calls from President Bush to the leaders of both countries, followed by a visit from Secretary of State Colin Powell. However, the crisis persisted through the successive months as India continued to insist that its conditions be met before it would draw down its forces along the border and the LOC. Other countries played complementary roles, but it was renewed U.S. intervention that finally ended the crisis in mid-June.[43]

Washington knew that the cross-border infiltrations were continuing, but it did not have information about the numbers or the identity of the infiltrators. Further, the Bush administration was preoccupied with events elsewhere, notably the breakdown of Israeli-Palestinian relations and the continuing war against Al Qaeda and the Taliban in Afghanistan, which had spread to Pakistan. There was little inclination to put pressure on Islamabad when the latter's support was vital to the U.S. war on terrorism.

Yet India persisted, continuing the military build-up and issuing increasingly threatening statements. By May it was widely believed that a war was inevitable, and much of the public discussion was simply over whether and when the conflict might escalate to a nuclear exchange. Indian officials fanned the war fever by releasing information about India's nuclear command and control arrangements, and there was suddenly a burst of publicity about nuclear protection and the availability of fallout shelters. India's leading news magazine carried a vivid account of the consequences of a nuclear war for Indian cities.

However, when Pakistani officials stated that they would have no recourse but to use nuclear weapons if India were to invade in large numbers, New Delhi quickly accused Pakistan of playing a dangerous game of nuclear brinkmanship, and reiterated India's position of "no-first-use." This may have been unpersuasive to experts, but it had the desired effect of alarming a number of governments, and these, led by the United States, began to put more pressure on Musharraf to halt cross-border infiltration.

On May 13–15, U.S. Assistant Secretary of State for South Asia Christina Rocca visited New Delhi and Islamabad, but she failed to make headway in conversations with regional leaders, in part because her visit coincided with the Kaluchak attack.[44] In the meantime, the United States issued a warning to its citizens that they leave India (earlier travel warnings were already in effect for Pakistan), and it airlifted non-essential government personnel and dependent family members back to the United States.

This warning was justified in terms of the objective risk to Americans should major war break out between India and Pakistan, but it certainly had other consequences. The travel advisory was a signal that India might not be such a good place to invest after all. Investment in India was already in decline. In the three weeks after the May attack on the army camp, investors pulled at least $48 million out of the Bombay Stock Exchange. The Indian software industry was hurt by the postponement of visits from foreign clients, and Indian businessmen were shocked, informing both their U.S. counterparts and the Indian government that the travel ban would have grave consequences for India's already staggering economy.

The U.S. decision also demonstrated to the Indian government that, while the United States sympathized with Delhi's concern about terrorism, there would be a tangible price to pay if India were to persist in keeping the region in crisis. Washington seemed to be saying publicly that the new U.S.-Indian relationship could not be counted on to provide absolute support under all circumstances, especially in a conflict with a state that was still an important partner in the U.S. war against terrorism.[45]

When Deputy Secretary Armitage returned to South Asia in June, he ratcheted up the pressure on both India and Pakistan. In Islamabad he extracted a commitment from General Musharraf to "permanently" stop cross-border infiltration, and in turn he committed the United States to a more proactive role in resolving the Kashmir dispute. Armitage conveyed Musharraf's commitment to New Delhi and the Indians had, at the time of writing, expressed their satisfaction with Pakistan's actions on the ground. New Delhi decided to allow Pakistani flights to use Indian airspace, the Indian navy began to move away from the Pakistani coast, and some army and air force units were removed from alert status. However, India has continued to threaten military action if Pakistan does not adhere to commitments made to U.S. officials.

The seriousness of Pakistan's pledges fell into question right after they were made, as Musharraf gave an interview to *Newsweek* that linked his commitment to a "permanent" halt to infiltration to Indian actions in Kashmir.[46] A hasty clarification was obtained, and the two countries each celebrated a victory of sorts: Pakistan boasting that its diplomacy had finally convinced the United States to pressure India on the Kashmir conflict, and India boasting that it had, through the United States, extracted a statement from Pakistan that it would cease support for cross-border terrorism.

Consequences

How did the crisis of 2002 affect the strategic balance in South Asia and the futures of India and Pakistan? While the picture of the dénouement is still incomplete, it is possible that the outcome represented a gain for both India and Pakistan, although it was a victory that came at a steep price.

In Pakistan's case the crisis could represent a turning point in the country's internal debate about its own future—and it could indicate that Pakistan will devote more of its energies to domestic reform and less to developments in neighboring states. If the United States stays engaged in the region and if India begins to accommodate legitimate Kashmiri concerns, then Musharraf can plausibly argue that the concessions he made on cross-border infiltration will work to Pakistan's advantage. However, some political parties already accuse him of selling out the Kashmiris, and his own political future will depend greatly upon U.S. and Indian willingness to address the Kashmir issue as well as to provide support for Pakistan's fragile economy and weak institutions.

India took a bold step and gambled that its high-stakes coercive diplomacy would pay off. The BJP-led coalition took such a step in 1998 when it tested nuclear weapons; this move resulted in less objective security for India, but an enhanced reputation for boldness and a willingness to accept short-term economic losses (sanctions in 1998 and reduced investment in 2002) to achieve a strategic objective. The 2002 crisis will burnish India's reputation for the risky gambit, but, as in 1998, New Delhi will have to follow through to avoid looking foolish or mendacious. If there is no progress on Kashmir, another crisis is inevitable and U.S. support might not be so forthcoming. If India does follow through on Kashmir, then the 2002 crisis will be seen as the springboard to a statesmanlike handling of India's "Pakistan problem."

The India-Pakistan rivalry hurts both states, and the prognosis is that unless there is sustained and effective intervention by outside powers, including the United States, crises like 2002 will recur with unpredictable consequences. If this is the region's future, then India and Pakistan will have dealt themselves out of a larger Asian strategic community; indeed, they will increasingly be seen as a threat to the peace and stability of the rest of Asia. The interest of outsiders in preventing a war will be balanced by their wariness in getting involved in what is seen as an intractable conflict and India and Pakistan will be even less attractive as potential allies or strategic partners.

U.S. Policy: Old Problems, New Opportunities

From the perspective of official Washington, South Asia was for many years a strategic backwater where no vital U.S. interests were at risk. By 1989 nonproliferation had replaced the Cold War as the issue that framed U.S. regional policy. A broader approach was considered by the Clinton administration in 1996, but it was shouldered aside by the 1998 Indian nuclear tests. By 1999, however, Washington had decided that a long-term relationship with India was feasible, a policy enthusiastically endorsed by the new Bush administration. However, neither administration thought that Kashmir deserved a special initiative, and neither responded strongly to India's complaints about Pakistani-sponsored terrorism. Afghanistan was regarded as a side-show, a failed state with a terrorist problem.

September 11 shifted U.S. priorities, and for most of 2002 U.S. policy has tried to harmonize a complex set of strategic, economic, and political interests with the new post-September 11 focus on fighting terrorism. This reorganization has been a difficult process but three major trends have emerged. They include a new interest in the task of state-building in Afghanistan and Pakistan, moving the India-Pakistan relationship from one of recurring crises to one framed by a peace process, and protecting the pre-September 11 relationship with India.

State-Building in Afghanistan and Pakistan

In this era of globalization, any place on earth can quickly become relevant to the United States. Friends and trading partners can be found anywhere, but so can terrorists who can also communicate by cell phone, email, and fax and travel to their targets via the airlines of their intended victims.

Previously dismissed as marginal, Afghanistan and Pakistan took center-stage in 2001 and 2002, and their domestic politics suddenly became the stuff of headlines. The Bush administration is reassessing its opposition to nation-building in South Asia, although some of its officials remain more wary than others.[47] Nevertheless, the increasing interdependence of the world will force the administration to address the "nation-building" problem, as one of the emerging threats to the United States is not from over-militarized and nuclear-armed states, but from maldeveloped ones.

Afghanistan and Pakistan are states with acute domestic problems. Their problems are different—Afghanistan lacks the most basic state institutions, especially an army,[48] whereas Pakistan's state institutions are in gross imbalance and the army is excessively powerful.[49] There will have to be different remedies for each state, but there can be no doubt that if their domestic political orders are ignored, then, as an American ambassador to Pakistan remarked, the cost will be measured in American lives.

The first phase of Washington's war on terrorism required Pakistan's logistical and political support to prosecute the war against the perpetrators of September 11. The next phase, rooting out terrorism's causes, must necessarily focus on Pakistan. The problem facing Pakistan is not one of total state failure, but shaping the kind of nation-state that Pakistan will become. Some of its alternative futures are frightening, others are more benign. Assuming the end goal is a liberal, modern state, functioning in the global system at peace with its neighbors, there is a very long road ahead, and no guarantee that Pakistanis are willing or able to traverse it.

Support for the reinstitutionalization of Pakistan is a worthy goal but Pakistan's progress must be carefully monitored over the next few years and all aid programs should have benchmarks and mechanisms that will immediately flag problems. The bulk of assistance and training programs should go to rebuilding Pakistan's enfeebled civilian institutions. Such support for Pakistan's "civil society" will be useless, however, unless attention is paid to the Pakistani army, likely to remain the most important political force in the country for years. Over a decade systematically excluding Pakistanis from U.S. training and educational facilities did not narrowed rather than broadened the outlook of the army. While the courts, the educational system, and political parties all need help to bring it up to modern standards, the army must also come to understand how it can play a positive role in Pakistan's development. Officers of all grades need to be exposed to the West and to developing states that have a balanced civil-military relationship. National security issues will remain the army's primary concern, but some officers understand that the army cannot be a parasite on the state and that domestic disorder and chaos may be the greatest security challenge facing Pakistan today. If the Bush administration or Congress calculates that there is any prospect of a "normal" Pakistan, then they must expand greatly their support for the development and re-professionalization of Pakistan's crumbling civil and military institutions.

From Crisis to Process

For at least 15 years, several major initiatives tried to bridge the gap between India and Pakistan. Most of these were private, funded by foundations and governments. There was a widespread belief that increased trade between India and Pakistan would promote peace (by giving important elites in each country a stake in good relations with the other); that cultural exchanges and personal diplomacy would help (by showing each side that the other also wanted peace); or that various "confidence building measures" and arms control arrangements would make it easier for the governments to engage in reasoned dialogue over critical issues. One war and several crises later, it is evident that private diplomacy and good intentions are not enough. Unless there is a more weighty effort, India and Pakistan are likely to continue moving from crisis to crisis.

The attacks of September 11 have created a unique opportunity for U.S. statecraft to shift from intermittent attempts at crisis prevention to a more lasting effort to build a process that features political reconciliation. The Kashmir problem is not likely to be solved soon, but, like the Middle East, it is important that all sides see that politics rather than the gun (or terrorism) is the way to achieve success.

If its engagement in the India-Pakistan dispute is to deepen, Washington will have to address the Kashmir issue, even if a resolution to this conflict is not at hand. It was unwise for National Security Advisor Condoleezza Rice to insist that the United States would not only decline the role of mediator but that it would not "facilitate" an India-Pakistan dialogue.[50] This studied disinterest was abandoned as the 2002 crisis reached its peak in June. In a post-crisis visit to South Asia, Colin Powell noted that progress on Kashmir was "on the international agenda," and that the United States would "lend a helping hand to all sides."[51] Powell and other officials stressed the importance of forthcoming elections in both India and Pakistan as a first step in a "broader process" that begins to address Kashmiri grievances and leads India and Pakistan back to dialogue. While these remarks were welcomed in Islamabad, which is desperate for any international attention on the Kashmir issue, New Delhi remains hostile to any formal third party role and particularly skeptical of the motives of the United States and Britain.[52] So far, India shows little inclination to ease the task of U.S. diplomacy by making any new gestures in Kashmir, or allowing international observers to view the forthcoming election.

While some informed Indian observers indicate that the resolution of the 2002 crisis gives Prime Minister Vajpayee a third opportunity to engage Pakistan in a substantive dialogue,[53] there is no indication that the Indian foreign policy bureaucracy, the hard-line BJP leadership, or the BJP's coalition partners are in any rush to renew talks with Musharraf. All prefer to let Washington put pressure on Islamabad and wait until domestic changes in Pakistan throw up a new and perhaps more pliable leadership.

Thus, the new U.S. attempt to promote an India-Pakistan dialogue on Kashmir and other issues may not bring quick results. There are three things that the United States could do to ensure that this opportunity for creative diplomacy is not lost.

First, the Bush administration could adopt a policy taken in 1999 by the Clinton administration: that the LOC was inviolable. Reiterating this position, which New Delhi warmly applauded, would begin the process of the United States defining for itself what it thinks a suitable final arrangement for Kashmir might look like.

Second, Washington needs to consult more widely with close allies and key countries in developing a coordinated policy on India-Pakistan normalization. While the British government is closely linked to current U.S. diplomatic initiatives, nothing has been done to associate such states as France, Japan, and other major allies with a concerted attempt to promote dialogue. Beyond this, it is also important (as experience in the Middle East shows), to share ideas with such powers as China and Russia, both of which have considerable influence in South Asia.

Third, distrust of the United States still runs very deep in New Delhi. Pakistan may be vulnerable to outside pressure because of its economic and political weakness, but India can afford to do nothing, which ensures that nothing will be done. If the Bush administration believes that the risk of nuclear war is as great as its spokesmen have stated, then clearly more needs to be done to persuade New Delhi that a U.S.-led initiative to kickstart a peace process in South Asia will ultimately work to India's advantage. Washington needs to demonstrate that it does not "equate" India and Pakistan, except in the sense that both are important, and now nuclear-armed states. U.S. interests in each are quite different, although there is a powerful international interest in ensuring that the two states do not go to war or launch nuclear weapons against each other. This argument will be effective among Indians who believe that it is in New Delhi's interest to have a moderate, stable Pakistan as a neighbor, it will not be persuasive among those Indians who deny Pakistan's right to exist or who still view Washington as a strategic threat to a rising India.

While it is important that Washington pursue the idea of a regional "dialogue," it should be aware that making U.S. engagement in South Asia contingent upon India-Pakistan cooperation is a formula for failure. If a peace process or a strategic dialogue cannot be initiated and nurtured, then the framework of U.S. policy should take the form of parallel bilateralism, working with each country in such a way that specific American interests are advanced. These interests include non-use of nuclear weapons, the containment of terrorism, avoidance of another India-Pakistan war, and some degree of military or strategic cooperation with India or Pakistan. At the same time, Washington should be prepared to deal with another, and perhaps more serious crisis between India and Pakistan in the next few years.

Expanding Relations with India

U.S. policy on the eve of September 11 had the long-term objective of developing a closer relationship with India. Its high technology, professional military, shrewd, realistic political leadership, and rapid economic growth suggested that India could be an important partner. Additionally, its democratic government and the large Indian-American community provided an incentive for close ties with New Delhi. This new policy downplayed Pakistan, a state that was seen as unhelpful at best and a failure at worst, and saw India as a possible balancer of a rising China.

For their part, Indian strategists no longer question the United States' global military and economic dominance and appear to have abandoned the idea of joining with other states in some kind of grand coalition to counter Washington. India is still struggling with its own internal economic, social and political revolutions, and the bloodbath of Gujarat was a reminder of the fragility of Indian democracy (and its strength—since the communal riots did not spread beyond the state). In short, from the Indian perspective Washington is an attractive strategic partner, and Indian officials see a close relationship with the United States as enabling India to "carve out a space for itself in a unipolar world."[54] India seeks to work closely with America in areas of common interest, and resist U.S. pressure to change fundamental Indian policies on key issues (such as Kashmir, or the nuclear deterrent). This means that the prospects for U.S.-Indian cooperation in strategic Asia will be limited, but will still be of a magnitude unimaginable five or ten years ago.

The last two years saw a dramatic increase in joint U.S.-Indian activities, although they do not add up to an alliance. The two countries are still in the learning phase as they discover that cooperation (including intelligence-sharing) is possible on counter-terrorism, developments in the Indian Ocean, environmental problems, energy research (so far, other than nuclear power), space, countering piracy in the Indian Ocean region, and consultation on various regional security issues. This is a spectacular achievement given the previous inability of the two countries to talk to each other in a civil fashion. Various administrative mechanisms designed to further these contacts were put in place by the Clinton administration, and the Bush administration has expanded them. Still, it should be remembered that the practical implementation of a policy of cooperation is hampered by resistance in the bureaucracies of both states, with the United

States dragging its feet on the release of dual-use and high-technology items and Indians still suspicious of U.S. motives and the penetration into India of American cultural, economic and political influence.

Other areas of cooperation could include nuclear weapons and proliferation. Having destroyed the United States' unrealistic anti-proliferation policy by its 1998 tests, India now tries to project itself as a responsible nuclear weapons state. Additional proliferation would only devalue its nuclear currency, and New Delhi does not want to see a world of 20 nuclear weapons states. India might agree to limits on its own program in exchange for assistance in the civilian power sector and symbolic membership in the club of major nuclear powers if it can be assured that this does not represent the American camel's nose in the Indian nuclear tent. One way the United States might address Indian anxiety would be to remove New Delhi from the "sensitive technology" control list. This would be a signal to the Indian strategic and scientific elite that Washington does not fear a democratic nuclear India—even if it disagrees from time to time with the policies New Delhi pursues.

Beyond its immediate neighborhood, India can be expected to play a more important role in what once were the outer reaches of the British Raj's sphere of influence. This is of special importance to the United States, and Indian power and U.S. interests match up well in the Middle East, Central Asia, and Southeast Asia. Here is where a balanced middle power such as India might make a difference, and it would be wise to consult with India about these regions. However, it is unlikely that New Delhi would antagonize states that provide it with vital oil and gas, and a future Congress government, probably allied with one or more "left" parties, might be more cautious about supporting a U.S. military action against Iraq.

As for India's strategic rivalry with China, it would be unwise for Washington to assume that India will be part of a military coalition that will contain a rising China. India's relevant power here is the power of an idea, democracy, which may be a greater strategic weapon in an era when nuclear war inhibits the use of force.

The most serious mistake that Washington can make is to under- or over-estimate India's identity as a piece on Asia's strategic chessboard. India is not a pawn, but it is not quite yet in China's league, and it is a great distance from becoming a major economic power. India wishes to play an independent role in Asia; and one of its role models is France, a formal American ally that has not hesitated to criticize Washington while often pursuing an independent line simply to emphasize its independence. Both U.S. and Indian officials have used the term "natural alliance" to describe the new relationship between these two countries, but the vagueness of the concept is self-evident. India can shoulder part of the burden of the war on terrorism and join the larger project of stabilizing parts of the world that are ungovernable. It can also be a responsible nuclear weapons state, and find a way to accommodate its impossibly persistent rival Pakistan. Such an India will have moved very far toward acquiring the status of a great power that its leaders (and its well-wishers) hope for it.

Endnotes

1. For two studies that took note of India's strategic emergence, see Ashley J. Tellis, "South Asia," in Richard J. Ellings and Aaron L. Friedberg, *Strategic Asia: Power and Purpose, 2001–02*, Seattle, Wash.: The National Bureau of Asian Research, 2001, and Stephen Philip Cohen, *India: Emerging Power*, Washington, DC: Brookings Institution Press, 2001.

2. C. Raja Mohan, "The Enigma of India's Arrival," *The Hindu*, September 2, 2001.

3. Exact figures are unavailable because much trade goes through third countries, but figures from India's Commerce Ministry and various trade organizations indicate a 20 percent surge in Indian exports to Pakistan and a substantial increase (eight percent) of Indian imports from Pakistan between 2000 and 2001. George Iype, "Indo-Pak trade Surges Despite Border Tension," *India Abroad*, March 29, 2002.

4. Before the war began in Afghanistan India displayed the corpses of dead Uighur fighters that it encountered in Kashmir, and Chinese officials have been reported as claiming that over 300 Uighur Muslims from Xinjiang were captured in Afghanistan fighting with Taliban and Al Qaeda forces. Eric Eckholm, "China: Muslims in Afghanistan," *The New York Times*, May 28, 2002.

5. By early May 10, 2002, British and U.S. commanders had announced that large-scale combat had virtually ended in Afghanistan. *Financial Times*, May 9, 2002.

6. Dexter Filkins, "Border Operations," *The New York Times*, April 28, 2002. There have been doubts, however, about Pakistan's enthusiasm for the war and whether General Musharraf will take a softer line toward Muslim extremists than either India or the United States would like. See Edward Luce and Farhan Bokhari, "An Undemocratic Friend," *Financial Times*, April 20, 2002.

7. Anatol Lieven, "Finish the War in Afghanistan First," *Financial Times*, March 25, 2002; Elie Krakowski, "How to Win the Peace in Afghanistan," *The Weekly Standard*, July 1, 2002.

8. India has agreed to train the Afghan military, a move that is certain to accelerate Pakistani concern. *Indian Express*, May 5, 2002.

9. *Washington Post*, January 29, 2002.

10. These concessions will require a fresh congressional waiver in September 2002, a month before the scheduled elections that will presumably restore civilian government to Pakistan.

11. This is the view of a recent study by the International Crisis Group, "Pakistan: The Dangers of Conventional Wisdom," <www.intl-crisis-group.org/projects/showreport.cfm?reportid=578.>.

[12] For an authorized translation see President Pervez Musharraf's *Address to the Nation*, January 12, 2002, <www.pak.gov.pk/public/president_address.htm.>.

[13] For a comprehensive discussion of the move of militancy to Pakistan, and the links to ISI, see Bob Drogin, Josh Meyer, and Eric Lichtblau, "Al Qaeda Gathering Strength in Pakistan," *Los Angeles Times*, June 26, 2002.

[14] For surveys on the idea of Pakistan see Akbar S. Ahmed, *Jinnah, Pakistan and Islamic Identity: The Search for Saladin*, Karachi: Oxford University Press, 1997.

[15] See Stephen Philip Cohen, "The Nation and the State of Pakistan," *Washington Quarterly*, vol. 25, no. 3. (Summer 2002), pp. 109–22.

[16] The government has banned several of the groups that it originally covertly sponsored, including Lashkar-e-Toiba and Jaish-e-Mohammad, but past experience indicates that these groups may reform under another name, or that their members may simply join other radical outfits, with or without the approval of the Pakistan army.

[17] For an informed but hardline anti-Indian position on Kashmir see many of the publications of Pakistan's FRIENDS Foundation, such as General Aslam Beg, "Kashmir: The Latent Dimensions," June 2002, <www.friends.org.pk.kashmir%20/tge%katebt%dimensions.htm>.

[18] For an informative discussion of Pakistan's ruling political elite, see Mushahid Sayed Hussain, "Whither Pakistan's Establishment," *The Nation* (Lahore), June 18, 2002.

[19] One such attempt, led by a mid-level officer of the paramilitary Rangers, apparently went awry.

[20] Cohen, "The Nation and the State of Pakistan," *Washington Quarterly*.

[21] For an overview see Dennis Kux, "India's Fine Balance," *Foreign Affairs*, May/June 2002. For a survey of Indian-U.S. relations, see Dennis Kux, *Estranged Democracies*, Washington, DC: National Defense University Press, 1996.

[22] Shyam Bhatia and Desikan Thrunarayanapuram, "Military to Train with U.S. Forces in Alaska," *Washington Times*, April 19, 2002. This training, the first Indian operations in North America, would be of special relevance to the Indian army, which faces both Pakistan and China across formidable mountain ranges.

[23] T. V. Parasuram, "No U.S. mediation or facilitation on Kashmir," *Press Trust of India*, February 15, 2002. National Security Advisor Condoleezza Rice also sided with India's view that the attack on the Indian parliament was carried out by "terrorists," contradicting Musharraf's public statements.

[24] For an overview, see Stephen Philip Cohen, *India: Emerging Power*, and for a recent statement of the Indian "realist" perspective see Bharat Karnad, *Nuclear Weapons and Indian Security*, New Delhi: Macmillan India, 2002.

[25] *Brasstacks* was a series of provocative military exercises that nearly started an Indo-Pakistani war in 1987. For an overview of the conflict, see Kanti Bajpai, P. R. Chari, Pervez Cheema, and Sumit Ganguly, *Brasstacks and Beyond: Crisis Perception and Management in South Asia*, New Delhi: Manohar, 1995.

[26] See Edward Luce, "India seeks new life in 'second generation' plan," *Financial Times*, February 25, 2002. Various economists argue that India faces high capital costs that leave Indian firms uncompetitive even within the country, making them fearful of a more open investment regime. Indian firms are also badly supported by the country's creaky infrastructure: only a few can afford their

own power generation, telecommunication systems, and port facilities. Additionally, India's labor laws have made it difficult for companies to restructure redundant or inefficient facilities. U.S. officials have bluntly and publicly shared their alarm about stagnation in the Indian economy and the consequences for U.S.-India trade relations. See the addresses on "U.S.-India Economic Relations" by Ambassador Robert D. Blackwill, New Delhi, January 28, 2002; and "Unleashing India's Vast Growth Potential," remarks by Deputy U.S. Treasury Secretary, February 7, 2002. The view is shared by India's most adventurous business association, the Confederation of Indian Industries. See its series, "State of the Economy," and "India Economic Policy Update," <www.ciionline.org>.

[27] Growth in the coming decade depends primarily in the government's ability to deregulate further sectors of the economy, but especially agriculture, which still employs the majority of India's labor force and holds the key to rural prosperity. The other critical policy measure has to occur in the privatization program, which has been extremely slow and unrewarding in helping bring down the fiscal deficits. The growth sectors such as software, telecommunications, entertainment, back-office services for foreign firms, but also education and healthcare-related fields, will provide the excitement for globalization and more economic reforms. Joydeep Mukherjee, "View from the Silk Road: Comparing Reform in China and India," *Standard and Poor's CreditWeek*, February 2, 2002.

[28] European reports indicate that at least 2,000 Muslims were killed, others put the figure at less than 1,000. For one account see Celia W. Dugger, "Religious Riots Loom over Indian Politics," *The New York Times*, July 27, 2002.

[29] See P.R. Chari, Pervaiz Iqbal Cheema, and Stephen Philip Cohen, *The Compound Crisis of 1990*, Routledge, forthcoming.

[30] Leh is the central Indian army garrison for the defense of the contested India-China border. The LOC is the name used after 1971 for the earlier cease-fire line; it is not a formally recognized boundary, but represents the positions held by the two armies after their various conflicts; it regularly undergoes minor adjustment as one side or the other presses forward and seizes posts—or loses them in subsequent counter-attacks.

[31] This treaty has never been challenged by either side. Any manipulation of the flow of water would be devastating for Pakistan, and government officials in Islamabad have declared that such a cut-off would be regarded as an act of war.

[32] Brahma Chellaney, "An Act of War," *Hindustan Times*, December 18, 2001.

[33] For example see Farhan Bokhari, "Tests Underline Pakistan's Conventional Arms Weakness," *Financial Times*, May 27, 2002.

[34] For an American assessment, based on unclassified sources, see Andrew Winner and Yoshi Toshihara, "Nuclear Stability in South Asia," Institute of Foreign Policy Analysis, <www.ifpa.org/textonly/new/nuk-stab.htm>.

[35] See Bruce Riedel, *American Diplomacy and the 1999 Kargil Summit at Blair House*, Philadelphia: Center for the Advanced Study of India, 2002.

[36] Testimony of CIA Director George Tenet before the Senate Armed Services Committee, March 18, 2002. See *Washington Times*, March 19, 2002.

[37] For an early discussion of Pakistan army views see Stephen P. Cohen, *The Pakistan Army*, Berkeley: University of California Press, 1985.

[38] Indira Gandhi once called the idea of deterrence "immoral."

[39] For an overview of Indian strategic nuclear thinking see Ashley W. Tellis, "India's Nuclear Doctrine," *NBR Analysis*, vol. 12, no. 2 (May 2001).

[40] Abbas Rashid, "Raising the Specter of Last Resort," *Daily Times* (Pakistan), April 15, 2002.

[41] The larger figure is the estimate of official western observers. Edna Fernandes, "Diplomats Say Killings in Gujarat State are Genocide," *Financial Times*, April 25–26, 2002.

[42] Jairam Ramesh, "Kautilya: Viewpoint," *India Today*, December 24, 2001.

[43] At one time or another Japan, Denmark, Canada, Iran, and several other states, notably China and Russia, offered their services as intermediaries in the crisis. Russia even invited Musharraf and Vajpayee to Moscow for further talks after a summit meeting in Almaty. The Indians declined the invitation, waiting for U.S. emissaries to bring the crisis to an end.

[44] For an U.S. version of what transpired during Armitage's visit, and the subsequent visit by Secretary of Defense Donald Rumsfeld, see Glenn Kessler, "A Defining Moment in Islamabad—U.S. Brokered 'Yes' Pulled India, Pakistan from Brink of War," *Washington Post*, June 22, 2002.

[45] The United States, unlike Britain and the European Union, had said nothing about the Gujarat killings, and may yet benefit financially in terms of Indian purchases of civilian and military aircraft. Jyoti Alhotra, "Friendly nations to get our shopping list," *Indian Express*, June 25, 2002.

[46] Lally Weymouth, "Voices from a Hot Zone," *Newsweek*, July 1, 2002. See also Armitage's discussion of Indian and Pakistani positions in the transcript of an interview with the *Financial Times*, June 23, 2002.

[47] For an explication of the Pentagon's views, as expressed by Deputy Secretary Paul Wolfowitz, see Fred Hiatt, "Underachieving Afghanistan," *Washington Post*, May 20, 2002. For a statement of senatorial concern about Kabul's security problem see James Dao, "Top Lawmakers Urge Bush to Expand Afghan Force Beyond Kabul," *The New York Times*, June 29, 2002.

[48] For several informed perspectives on Afghanistan's prospects as the center of a new regional order in Central Asia and as a viable state, see the contributions of S. Frederick Starr and Marvin G. Weinbaum, respectively, in The Asia Society, Asian Update Series, *Afghanistan's Reform Agenda: Four Perspectives*, New York: The Asia Society Issues Program, March 2002.

[49] Cohen, "Nation and State of Pakistan," *Washington Quarterly*.

[50] After the 2002 crisis was resolved Prime Minister Vajpayee used the term approvingly in describing a suitable U.S. role in Kashmir. See Lally Weymouth, "Voices from a Hot Zone," *Newsweek*.

[51] Press Briefing by Sectary of State Colin L. Powell, July 28, New Delhi, Department of State.

[52] For a blunt statement of India's increasing resistance to U.S. engagement on Kashmir—except to pressure Pakistan—see the address of the newly-appointed Foreign Secretary, Kanwal Sibal, to the Confederation of Indian Industries, July 10, 2002, <http//cgi.rediff.com/cgi-programs/print/printpage.cgi>.

[53] See C. Raja Mohan, "Vajpayee: Third time Lucky?," *The Hindu*, June 20, 2002.

[54] Kanwal Sibal address.

SOUTHEAST ASIA

Sheldon W. Simon

S outheast Asia's political and economic variety covers the gamut from powerful and effective governments (Singapore) to the early stages of state-building, national identity, and cohesiveness (East Timor, Laos, and Cambodia) and points in between where political pluralism is still fragile (the Philippines, Thailand, and Indonesia). Although 10 of Southeast Asia's 11 members form the Association of Southeast Asian Nations (ASEAN), this organization has been of limited utility in recent regional crises such as the 1997–98 Asian financial crisis, the 1999 secession of East Timor from Indonesia, and the current U.S. war on terrorism in the wake of the September 11 attacks on the United States.

This chapter assesses Southeast Asia in the wake of September 11 and the reactions of the region's core states to U.S. efforts to create effective regional anti-terrorist cooperation. The focus is on those Southeast Asian states where terrorist cells operate and where there is at least some evidence that these cells aid one another across national boundaries—Indonesia, Malaysia, the Philippines, and Thailand. Radicals in Southeast Asia constitute a relatively small minority of the Muslim community throughout

Sheldon Simon is Professor of Political Science at Arizona State University and Director of Southeast Asian Studies at The National Bureau of Asian Research. He wishes to particularly thank Richard Ellings and Michael Wills for their insightful comments on earlier drafts of this paper, and Loren Runyon who prepared the tables and figures. Special thanks go to Aaron Friedberg for his guidance in sharpening the implications of this study.

the region, though Islamist cells have been discovered in Indonesia, Malaysia, Singapore, and the Philippines. While there is some evidence of transnational cooperation among the radicals, for the most part their activities are confined to the countries in which they are located. None seriously threatens any government's viability. However, without continued economic growth and a more equitable distribution of national wealth, particularly in Indonesia and the southern Philippines, as well as reduced corruption and coercion, particularly by political elites in Malaysia, Indonesia, and the Philippines, the conditions which nurture militants will persist.

These conditions, of course, vary among the core states in Southeast Asia. Malaysia's Prime Minister Mahathir Mohamad has used the war on terrorism to strengthen his party's position by painting the Muslim opposition as supportive of terror. Indonesian officials have eschewed confrontation with radicals, fearing an electoral backlash in the world's largest Muslim democracy. The Philippines, recently with direct U.S. military and financial assistance, has cracked down on the most extreme terrorists in the south, the Abu Sayyaf, while negotiating power-sharing arrangements with two much larger Muslim political movements. In Thailand, persistent low-level violence in the south does not appear to be linked to the region's Islamists.

U.S. anti-terrorist actions are focused on the southern Philippines, where U.S. Special Forces are advising the Philippine military, although not actually participating in the hunt for terrorists. In the rest of the region, Washington offers assistance to upgrade law enforcement capability, intelligence sharing, and ways to interdict and freeze terrorist finances. While the Bush administration hopes to reestablish military ties with Indonesia as a key component of Washington's anti-terrorist, Southeast Asian coalition, U.S. congressional strictures preclude this until those Indonesian military officers responsible for atrocities in East Timor are brought to justice. Exchange of intelligence with the United States on terrorist activities has been formally established with Malaysia, Singapore, and Thailand following FBI Director Robert Mueller's visit to Southeast Asia in March 2002.

Southeast Asian states on their own have begun to work together. Statements condemning terrorism and urging intelligence sharing and collaboration among law enforcement authorities have been issued by ASEAN and the ASEAN Regional Forum (ARF). However, the most effective anti-terrorist cooperation has been bilateral, particularly between Singapore and Malaysia. The latest development, though, is a counter-terrorism agreement among Malaysia, the Philippines, Indonesia, and Thailand to monitor their porous borders, across which illegal migration is ubiquitous. The efficacy of all these new joint efforts is problematic, however, given the limited surveillance and interdiction capabilities of Southeast Asian states.

In sum, Southeast Asian states recognize the importance of collaborating to fight transnational terrorism, but their capabilities to do so are limited, and the political challenge of Islamists varies greatly from state to state. U.S. offers of assistance are generally welcome, though no Southeast Asian government wishes to be seen as pandering to U.S. demands, especially since many Southeast Asian Muslims insist that the U.S. war on terrorism is really an attack on Islam. Emphasizing the distinction between Islamist terrorists and the vast majority of peaceful Muslims is essential for both the United States and its Southeast Asian partners.

Southeast Asia and the War on Terrorism

The U.S. war on terrorism came home to Southeast Asia in December 2001–January 2002. In these two months, authorities in Singapore and Malaysia arrested dozens of Islamists who had organized clandestine cells in each country's capital. Targeting U.S. and other western embassies as well as U.S. forces in Singapore, the cells included Indonesians, Malaysians, and Singaporeans and were also linked to individuals in the Philippines. The transnational and covert nature of these groups stunned regional security officials, for, until their discovery, it had been generally believed that although Islamism existed in Southeast Asia, it neither dominated the region's faithful nor had become radicalized.

In the aftermath of the September 11 terror attacks on the United States, all Southeast Asian governments supported the UN Security Council resolutions condemning the attacks. Moreover, at their November 2001 summit in Brunei, all ASEAN leaders agreed to adopt a declaration on joint action to counter terrorism. Yet, at the same meeting, ASEAN representatives stressed that "at the international level, the UN should play a major role in this regard."[1] ASEAN was not about to offer a *carte blanche* endorsement for unilateral American actions against terror, especially since U.S. officials were speculating that Al Qaeda elements might shift their operations to the Philippines and Indonesia as they fled Afghanistan.[2]

Indeed, while localized violence could be found in Indonesia and the Philippines before September 11, these flare-ups were not part of the work of a global network. Rather, they were movements for autonomy or independence (Aceh and Papua in Indonesia, and Mindanao in the Philippines) or communal conflicts over who would control particular regions (the Malukus and Sulawesi in Indonesia). While regional intelligence organizations were aware of some Malaysians involved in Indonesia's Laskar Jihad paramilitary, in general, these groups were small and homegrown.[3] Nevertheless, Malaysia's Defense Minister Najib Tun Razak acknowledged that Malaysian militants might well have contacts with Al Qaeda "at the international level," while dismissing the possibility that Al Qaeda cells were present in Malaysia.[4]

More disturbing is that the "sleeper cells" disrupted in Malaysia and Singapore had been in place for up to eight years. They communicated with supporters in Indonesia and the Philippines, and several members were trained by Al Qaeda in Afghanistan. Malaysia may have been the center for this coterie of cells because Kuala Lumpur does not require visas for citizens from Muslim countries.[5] In effect, these groups exploited the porous borders among the Southeast Asian states. Joining smugglers, gun-runners, and human and narcotics traffickers—persistent security threats of previous years—are now Islamist terrorists. Clearly, Southeast Asia's strategic environment had become more precarious after the events of September 11. How prepared was the region to cope?

In contrast to China, its neighbor to the north, Southeast Asia was weaker politically, economically, and militarily. While the 10 Southeast Asian states (East Timor, the putative eleventh, was a UN protectorate from its 1999 referendum until it obtained formal independence in May 2002) meet regularly for political, economic, and security discussions in ASEAN as well as ARF—an organization encompassing all Asian-Pacific states, exclusively devoted to regional security, and led by ASEAN—these groups manage to avoid dealing with the core security concerns of their members.[6] Since formal decisions in both ASEAN and the ARF require consensus, controversial concerns such as the future of the South China Sea islands or drug smuggling across national borders seldom appear on their agendas. Instead, the ARF works best when developing cooperative strategies for peripheral security concerns that yield benefits for all at reasonable national costs. These include measures to deal with piracy, ocean pollution, regional haze, and transnational crime. In these deliberations, no blame is allocated. Rather, proposed multilateral solutions presume that all governments want to resolve the problems they face in common. In fact, however, lying beneath this placid surface remain mutual suspicions among most ASEAN members: Indonesia, Malaysia, and Singapore have long-term concerns about each other; Thai-Burmese relations are strained over drug trafficking and hundreds of thousands of Burmese refugees in Thailand; friction in Philippine-Malaysian relations exists over lawless elements from Mindanao illegally resident in eastern Malaysia; and Thai-Malaysian relations sometimes flare over an irredentist movement in southern Thailand with cross-border affinity to Malaysia. While these tensions have been contained and even transcended through ASEAN membership, they nevertheless have inhibited security cooperation on core issues such as efforts by religious extremists to destabilize regional governments.

On the economic dimension, the major security concern revolves around the ability of two of Southeast Asia's worst performing economies to provide hope to their populations and pull them out of poverty. Destitution in both Indonesia and the Philippines makes jobless young people vulnerable to religious extremism. For these countries, and Southeast Asia more generally, renewed foreign investment is a key to economic recovery. However, Japan's economic woes and competition from China, where labor costs are a fraction of those in Thailand and Malaysia, have inhibited Southeast Asia's rebound. The biggest investment banks are not optimistic about Southeast Asia's short-term prospects.[7]

ASEAN is losing in head-to-head competition for investment funds with China.[8] In 2001, ASEAN economies received just 17 percent of the foreign direct investment (FDI) that flowed to developing countries in Asia, down from over 60 percent in the early 1990s. China, which had received just 18 percent of the FDI a decade ago, now obtains 61 percent. Moreover, ASEAN seems to be retreating from its free trade commitments, agreeing in September 2000 to allow Malaysia not to meet its obligation to lower tariffs on car imports from other Southeast Asian countries. This retreat can only further discourage foreign investors who were anticipating a larger regional market as the ASEAN Free Trade Area (AFTA) emerges as a reality later this decade.[9]

Furthermore, Southeast Asian economies have not generated increased domestic demand because they have delayed structural reforms. Instead, they continue to depend on exports to pull them out of the doldrums. Thailand's exports of goods and services were 66 percent of GDP in 2001, compared to 39 percent in 1996. Electronic equipment accounts for over half of the total exports from Malaysia, Singapore, and the Philippines, but this sector has suffered as a result of this glut. Even Singapore went into recession in 2001, although it has shown signs of recovering by mid-2002. Nevertheless, there are some encouraging signs: several Southeast Asian states have rebuilt current account surpluses, cut short-term debt, and replenished foreign exchange reserves. In short, their overall financial conditions are significantly stronger than they were on the eve of the 1997–98 financial crisis, if not their medium-term prospects.[10]

Militarily, Southeast Asian states had put their armed forces modernization programs on hold after the 1997–98 financial crisis.[11] By September 11, ASEAN states had just begun to reorder the navy and air force equipment they had planned to acquire in the mid-1990s. These plans were designed to enhance their ability to monitor and control sea and air spaces around their territories. Porous borders are ubiquitous throughout the region, as manifested by fishery poaching, piracy, and illegal population

Table 9.1. Economic Conditions in Southeast Asia

	GDP growth (%)		Inflation (%)		Growth in exports (%)	
	1996	2001	1996	2001	1996	2001
Indonesia	8.0	3.3	-39.6	11.5	5.8	-9.8
Malaysia	10.0	0.4	3.5	1.4	6.9	-8.8
Philippines	5.8	3.4	9.1	6.1	17.7	-16.2
Singapore	7.7	-2.0	1.3	1.0	6.4	-11.9
Thailand	5.9	1.8	5.9	1.7	-1.9	-7.0

Source: Asian Development Bank, *Asian Development Outlook 2002.*

Table 9.2. Investment Trends in Southeast Asia

	Foreign direct investment (% of GDP)		Gross domestic investment (% of GDP)		Debt/service ratio (% exports)	
	1996	2001[a]	1996	2001	1996	2001
Indonesia	3.0	8.0	30.7	17.0	37.9	44.8[b]
Malaysia	0.0	...	41.5	24.8	11.0	6.0
Philippines	2.0	1.0	23.1	16.6	12.7	16.4
Singapore	10.0	8.0	37.1	24.3	...	...
Thailand	1.0	3.0	41.6	22.0	13.9	17.4

Source: Asian Development Bank, *Asian Development Outlook 2002.* Notes: a) Data for 1999 or 2000 (most recent year available); b) Data for 2000.

movements—which now include terrorists. Moreover, Southeast Asian armed forces engage only in minimal collaboration across their boundaries. Although a few bilateral exercises occur, for the most part these have not been extended to the multilateral level. Nor is there interoperability among the services. Naval and air force modernization, therefore, unless undertaken with some sensitivity to common security challenges, will remain within the confines of exclusively national needs.

Radical Islam: The Region's New Security Challenge

On the eve of September 11, the security environment in Southeast Asia seemed remarkably tranquil. None of the region's states contemplated war. Despite underlying suspicions, such as ethnic concerns, international security problems tended to be bilateral, focused on border difficulties, and were either low level or, if serious, as with the South China Sea islands, postponeable for several years. New security concerns came onto the regional agenda in the 1990s involving transnational problems for which traditional military capabilities provided only a partial solution. These new issues included piracy, drug and human trafficking, illegal migration, transnational crime and money laundering, and regional environmental threats.[12] While dissident movements in Malaysia, Indonesia, the Philippines, and Thailand were often communal and frequently engaged in violence, their actions were localized. Little attention was paid to their transnational potential.

In the wake of September 11, however, U.S. officials feared that Al Qaeda operatives might seek refuge and activate operations in Southeast Asiadue to its porous borders, weak internal security, large populations of urban and rural poor, and armed extremist groups, both Muslim and non-Muslim. Al Qaeda's ideology discounts national borders and attempts to rally a transnational Muslim nation to overthrow moderate Muslim governments and eliminate the western support that helps sustain them.[13]

Globalization has augmented terrorist capabilities. The rapid proliferation and decreasing cost of communications technology, such as satellite phones and e-mail, enable these groups to maintain a hierarchy even though they are divided into many small geographically dispersed cells. The Internet permits terrorist organizations to transfer funds around the world. With state-of-the-art encryption technology, terrorists can clandestinely purchase explosives and an array of weapons online.

During the 10-year Afghan war against the Soviet Union, a large number of Muslims from Indonesia and Malaysia joined the *mujahidin* in their battle against the Soviets. While in Afghanistan, they were exposed to radical Islam and trained in guerrilla warfare. Upon their return, these individuals formed the cores of such organizations as Jemaah Islamiya and Kumpulan Mujahidin Malaysia (KMM) in Singapore and Malaysia and their counterparts in Indonesia. As Kumar Ramakrishna of Singapore's Institute of Defense and Strategic Studies puts it:

> The basic problem is that as long as sizable pockets of disgruntled, anti-American young Muslims remain in countries from Nigeria to the Philippines, there will always be a radical Islamic movement posing an existential threat to Western and especially U.S. interests.... Basically, Muslims the world over must be persuaded that Islam *can* coexist with modernity, and it is possible and desirable to be both a good Muslim and still be thoroughly engaged with a modern capitalist world system.[14]

Until then, however, Southeast Asia, among other regions, must contend with radical groups such as the Singaporean-Malaysian cells that were disrupted at the beginning of this year. Interrogations of those arrested revealed a well-organized network stretching across Southeast Asia com-

Table 9.3. Islamist Militant Groups in Southeast Asia

Name: Abu Sayyaf	**Based:** Basilan, Philippines

Area of Operation: Philippines - Sulu, Zamboanga, and Manila; East Malaysia
Strength: Estimated 200 core members, with a significant number of sympathizers on Basilan
Goals: To establish an Islamic state
Activities: Bombings; assassinations; kidnapping; piracy; extortion
Terrorist Links: Some members fought in Afghanistan and may be linked to Al Qaeda

Name: Islamic Defenders Front (IDF)	**Based:** Jakarta, Indonesia

Area of Operation: Indonesia - Java and Sumatra
Strength: Unknown; no more than 1,000 members and sympathizers have attended rallies
Goals: To oppose the U.S. presence in Southeast Asia and establish an Islamic state
Activities: Bombings, protection rackets, violent demonstrations
Terrorist Links: Some members may have received funds from Al Qaeda

Name: Jemaah Islamiya	**Based:** Malaysia

Area of Operation: Indonesia, Malaysia, Philippines, and Singapore
Strength: Unknown, 200 in Malaysia alone
Goals: To establish a single Islamic state uniting the Muslim populations of maritime Southeast Asia
Activities: Planned attacks on U.S. and other western targets
Terrorist Links: Al Qaeda has trained some operatives and may provide some funding

Name: Kumpulan Mujahidin Malaysia (KMM)	**Based:** Malaysia

Area of Operation: Indonesia, Malaysia, Philippines, and Singapore
Strength: Less than 100 poorly armed members
Goals: To establish a single Islamic state uniting the Muslim populations in maritime Southeast Asia
Activities: Bombings, assassinations; planned attacks on western targets
Terrorist Links: Possible ties to terrorists in the Philippines and Indonesia; some members fought with the Afghan *mujahidin* and some have trained with Al Qaeda; has received some equipment from the MILF

Name: Laskar Jihad	**Based:** Java, Indonesia

Area of Operation: Indonesia - Java, Malukus, and Sulawesi
Strength: At least 2,000–3,000 core members, with thousands of sympathizers
Goals: To establish an Islamic state in Indonesia
Activities: Terrorism and guerrilla-style warfare against Christian communities
Terrorist Links: Some members may have received funds from Al Qaeda; some members are also soldiers in the Indonesian armed forces

---

Name: Moro Islamic Liberation Front (MILF)   **Based:** Philippines
Area of Operation: Philippines - Mindanao
Strength: 10,000 to 15,000 well-trained fighters
Goals: To establish an Islamic state
Activities: Currently engaged in peace talks with the Philippine government
Terrorist Links: Ties with Muslim militants in Indonesia; some operatives have trained with Al Qaeda

Name: Moro National Liberation Front (MNLF)   **Based:** Philippines
Area of Operation: Philippines - Mindanao
Strength: Almost 6,000 well-trained fighters; now integrated into the Philippine armed forces
Goals: Originally to establish an Islamic state; now seeking greater local autonomy for Mindanao
Activities: Reached peace agreement with the Philippine government in 1996
Terrorist Links: Abu Sayyaf and the MILF split off from MNLF after the 1996 peace agreement was struck

---

Sources: U.S. State Department, *2001–2002 Patterns of Global Terrorism*; Federation of American Scientists, *Intelligence Resource Program*; International Institute for Strategic Studies, *The Military Balance 2001–2002*; Devi Asmarani, "Jakarta groups took millions from Al-Qaeda," *Straits Times*, April 30, 2002; Chris Wilson, "Indonesia and Transnational Terrorism," Australian Dept. of the Parliamentary Library, Foreign Affairs, Defense and Trade Group, October 11, 2001.

parable in many ways to those organized by Osama bin Laden's lieutenants in Europe. One western diplomat, after reviewing evidence about the Singaporean and Malaysian cells, stated: "[This was] not a rogue group. There was a management hierarchy and a functional breakdown. It was like a KGB cell."[15]

The transnational linkages of the Singapore-based Jemaah Islamiya included an Indonesian hard-line Muslim teacher Abu Bakar Ba'asyir as leader, and a regional council based in Malaysia. Below the council were individual cells active in Malaysia, Singapore, and the Philippines.[16] None of these groups is large, however; the biggest is the KMM with fewer than 90 poorly armed members. Their grandiose designs for establishing Islamic states in Southeast Asia are pipedreams. Nevertheless, the Singapore group possessed fake passports and was beginning to collect explosives for truck bombs from the MILF in the Philippines. These were to be used against U.S. institutions and American citizens in the city-state.[17]

While some of the terrorists arrested in Singapore and Malaysia had been to Afghanistan and Pakistan where they imbibed radical ideas, most were home grown; and several had been educated at Abu Bakar Ba'asyir's radical *madrassa* (religious school) in central Java. The school became a training ground for radicals in Java, most notably Laskar Jihad.[18] However, as Donald Emmerson, a noted Stanford University Indonesia specialist, pointed out in congressional testimony in January 2002, armed Muslim groups in Southeast Asia do not possess and are not interested in acquiring "global reach." As for Laskar Jihad, the Aceh Freedom Movement (GAM), and Abu Sayyaf in the Philippines, none is looking to expand operations beyond their self-proclaimed boundaries.[19]

Nevertheless, some Southeast Asian radical Islamists had global linkages. A former Malaysian army captain and Al Qaeda operative met with two of the September 11 hijackers in September and October 2000 in Malaysia and transferred at least $35,000 to them. While U.S. intelligence officials believe Malaysia has been a central location for regional Islamist terrorism, Prime Minister Mahathir rejects the suggestion that his country could be a staging point and has refused to extradite the former army captain to the United States.[20]

However, on its own Malaysia has cracked down on potential extremists, including a decision in late January 2002 to deport half of the 900,000 registered Indonesian workers in the country on the grounds that they constituted a security risk. Kuala Lumpur has also tightened border controls. But each Southeast Asian state has developed its own counter-terrorist policy, with collaboration only developing slowly (see below). Thus, in July 2000,when Indonesian authorities discovered Al Qaeda members in Jakarta planning to bomb the U.S. embassy, the suspects were deported instead of arrested. Indonesia's reticence toward Islamist radicals within its territory has caused regional resentment and has forced other Southeast Asian countries to deal with the spillover from Indonesia on their own.[21]

There is additional evidence of linkages among Southeast Asian Islamic radicals. Investigators in Singapore point to the MILF in the Philippines as providing guerrilla and explosives training in its Mindanao camps for some of the terrorists detained in Singapore. The Jemaah Islamiya in Singapore and Malaysia has a broad regional goal of overthrowing Southeast Asian secular governments and creating an Islamic state linking Malaysia, Indonesia, and the southern Philippines. Radical groups in Malaysia and Singapore also raised money for Muslim militants in Indonesia and the Philippines.[22] Moreover, the Philippines has become the key location for terrorists to acquire explosives for use throughout Southeast Asia.[23]

In hopes of obtaining a statement representative of moderate Islam condemning the extremists, Prime Minister Mahathir addressed the April 2002 meeting of the Organization of the Islamic Conference (OIC). He urged that all attacks on civilians, "including human bomb attacks by Palestinians," be classified as acts of terror. The OIC rebuffed the proposal, refusing to label any Palestinian acts terrorist. While the OIC condemned terrorism in the abstract, each member defines the concept operationally according to its national needs. Mahathir's hope for a united conference condemnation was not realized.[24]

In sum, even among Southeast Asian policy intellectuals there is little consensus on whether radical Islam pervades the region or on the seriousness of its threat to incumbent governments. At the June 2002 Asia-Pacific Roundtable—the annual Track II meeting of regional security professionals in Kuala Lumpur—the relationship between radical Islam and terror generated considerable debate but no agreement. Most argued that Southeast Asian Islamist radicals were, for the time being, small in number and minimally linked to the vast majority of their co-religionists.

The security specialists at the roundtable were less concerned with the threat to their countries by Islamist radicals than with the perception that the Bush administration's anti-terror policy would make their countries targets for U.S. retaliation. Among even the moderate Muslims at the meeting, the U.S. war on terror became conflated with a general attack on Islam, despite American denials that this was so. The chief causes of this suspicion of U.S. policy are what many perceive as a "one size fits all" view of Islamist radicals from Washington, that is, the American belief that all Islamist radicals are somehow linked to Al Qaeda and are targeting the United States as well as U.S. interests and citizens abroad. The other problem is what is perceived as a U.S. bias toward Israel in the Israel-Palestine conflict. If the United States could convince Tel Aviv to endorse the Saudi Arabian peace initiatives, Southeast Asian security specialists believe much Muslim anger would dissipate.[25] In any case, the view from Southeast Asia is that U.S. actions since September 11 have been exacerbating radical activities in the region rather than assisting in their containment.

The Core ASEAN States, U.S. Actions, and
The Security Challenge of Islamist Radicalism

Southeast Asia has presented the United States with a variety of responses to September 11. Enthusiastic endorsement for President Bush's war on terrorism characterized the Philippines, with quieter backing from Singapore. Thailand's support was more tentative, and Indonesia and Malaysia tempered their sympathy with warnings that the United States not target Islam generally. Southeast Asia's prominence in U.S. concerns about terrorism is derived from alleged links between Al Qaeda operatives and the Abu Sayyaf and MILF in the Philippines, past contacts with Islamists in Indonesia and Malaysia, ties to the Jemaah Islamiya in Singapore, and apprehension that Southeast Asia's porous borders and Muslim populations provide a hospitable location for Al Qaeda to regroup after the war in Afghanistan.

The governments of the ASEAN core (Singapore, Malaysia, Indonesia, the Philippines, and Thailand) unanimously condemn terrorism. However, their collaboration with the United States varies both substantively and in degree of enthusiasm. In discussions with moderate Muslim governments, the United States points out that the vast majority of the victims of Islamist-based terror are Muslims themselves. Southeast Asia's own moderate Muslim leaders insist that the faithful denounce terrorists who corrupt the message of Islam and paint an image of Muslims as vicious, violent, and cruel contrary to the peaceful, tolerant, and egalitarian character that is the heart of the religion.[26]

Singapore

The most surprising terrorist development in Southeast Asia was the discovery of an Islamist group in Singapore that was plotting to bomb western embassies and U.S. military personnel on the island. Of the 15 arrested, all but one were Singaporean. Given the city-state's tight internal security, it is remarkable that such a large group had gone undetected for so long, though local officials claimed they had been monitoring it for some time. Interrogation revealed that cell members had contacted Al Qaeda about funding, but that Osama bin Laden's organization did not follow up. The suspects also insisted that Singapore itself was not a target, only western interests located there. Singapore maintains close security ties with the United States, including a permanent U.S. naval logistics office. U.S. ships and aircraft regularly use the island's ports and military airfield. Singapore is sharing intelligence with the United States and its ASEAN neighbors on terrorism. Because Singapore is predominantly Chinese and non-Muslim, it has maintained a low-profile in regional anti-terrorist cooperation.

Indonesia

Deputy U.S. Defense Secretary Paul Wolfowitz, a former ambassador to Indonesia, characterizes the country as one that "practices religious tolerance and democracy, treats women properly, and believes Islam is a religion of peace."[27] And, indeed, the bedrock of Islam in Indonesia—the world's most populous Muslim country—consists of a pair of moderate broadly based organizations, Muhammadiya and Nahdlatul Ulama, which claim memberships that total one-fourth of the population. They advocate the maintenance of a clear boundary between politics and religion. Nevertheless, Indonesia is an ideal hiding place for terrorists with its weak central government, chronic corruption, lagging law enforcement (some of whose members have been co-opted by militants), lax banking regulations, and porous borders stretched over an archipelago of 17,000 islands.

Radical Muslim groups operate in Indonesia. The Islamic Defenders Front (IDF) had threatened to attack U.S. installations and foreigners even before September 11, and the militant Laskar Jihad has battled Christian Indonesians in Sulawesi and the Malukus. Although these groups may have received some funding from Al Qaeda, they deny they are tools of Osama bin Laden's organization. Indeed, while they "talk the talk" of jihad, their activities are more akin to local terrorizing. The IDF ran protection rackets in Jakarta, while Laskar Jihad has directed its militancy entirely against Christians in eastern Indonesia.[28] Neither has pretensions of carrying their hostilities beyond Indonesia.

Ironically, radical Islamism is a product of Indonesia's post-Suharto democratization. During the strong man's reign (1966–98), any manifestation of Muslim militancy was harshly suppressed; but with Suharto's exit, Islamist political activities—along with many others of various political stripes—have flourished. Elements in both the national police and the military (Tentara Nasional Indonesia—TNI) have backed these groups; and even those who oppose their actions are fearful of a Muslim political backlash that a crackdown might precipitate.[29] Moreover, the activities of radical Islamist groups with their high political profile could increasingly set the terms of the 2004 parliamentary elections. Vice President Hamzah Haz, closely linked to the Islamists, may be trying to establish a Muslim political bloc for a presidential campaign in 2004. He has been shielding hardliners from international pressure to combat terrorism in the belief that a motivated bloc of up to 15 percent of the electorate could help win over a larger number of moderates.[30]

Members of Al Qaeda have slipped into and out of Indonesia over the past several years with millions of dollars to fund radical Muslim organizations, help recruit new members, and provide military training. Plans were made by some Yemeni radicals to blow up the U.S. embassy in 2000 and 2001, but when their plot was uncovered the men fled before they could be arrested.[31] Indeed, in general, Indonesian authorities refuse to detain Islamist radicals for fear of large-scale protests that could be used by Muslim opposition parties against President Megawati Sukarnoputri. Even when Singapore and Malaysia asked Indonesia to detain Abu Bakar Ba'asyir, the Indonesian cleric linked to Jemaah Islamiya, Jakarta demurred, saying it had no evidence Ba'asyir had committed any crime.[32]

The former head of Indonesia's armed forces, Admiral Widodo, acknowledged that an international terror network has penetrated the country and that neighboring states are concerned that Indonesia not become a safe haven. This admission may have been an effort to conciliate an angry charge from Singaporean senior minister Lee Kwan Yew that Indonesia was "one

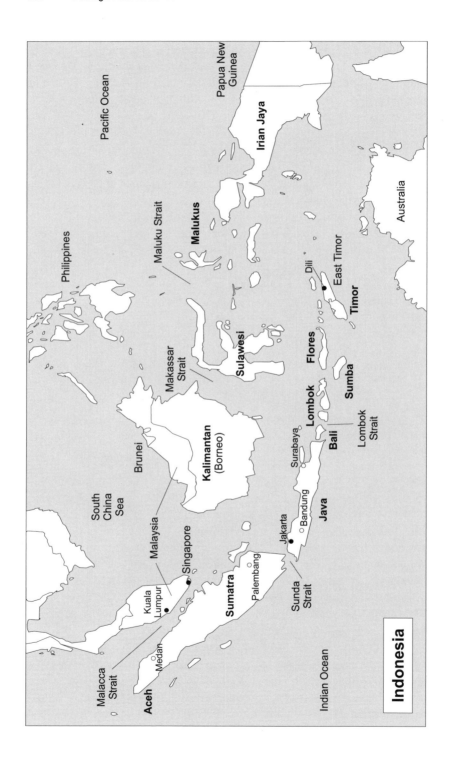

of the dens of terrorism." Indonesian citizens have been arrested in Singapore, Malaysia, and the Philippines. In March 2002, three were detained while boarding a plane in Manila and charged with transporting C-4 explosive materials.[33]

While some Indonesian officials admit there is a terrorist problem, they have often had to back down. For example, in December 2001, the director of Indonesia's intelligence agency, in an effort to persuade the government to become more active in the war on terrorism, announced that Al Qaeda had set up terrorist training camps in the country. In response, several Islamist organizations denounced him, and the government retreated, probably fearing a nationwide backlash.[34] Exacerbating these problems has been the spring 2002 Israeli military incursion into the Palestinian West Bank, widely covered in the Indonesian media, providing a further opportunity for Islamist radicals in Indonesia to expand their membership and public profile. Moderate Islamic leader Hasyim Muzadi warned that "the Israeli action would be used to provoke certain religious followers to perpetrate violence here."[35]

Nevertheless, there have been some encouraging signs. The Indonesian parliament passed a money laundering law in March 2002, authorizing the government to investigate unusual financial transactions. The Indonesian chief of police agreed that new laws on terrorism were essential to give the authorities the right to detain suspects.[36] Additionally, the leaders of moderate Muslim organizations, representing the great majority of the country's population, have agreed to raise their voices "to safeguard the presence of civil society in Indonesia." These leaders agree that the U.S.-initiated war on terrorism should not be construed as a war on Islam, contrary to the charges of the radicals.[37] In April 2002, Nahdlatul Ulama and Muhammadiya leaders, alongside Indonesian Christian organizations, launched a national "moral movement" to restore peace across the archipelago. Whether these voices of tolerance, moderation, and the rule of law can ultimately curtail regional, communal, and ethnic violence remains to be seen. Thus far, however, the Indonesian government has shied away from any overt confrontation with the radicals, some of whom maintain connections at the highest levels in Jakarta.

Despite these calls from Muslim leaders, many Muslims are wary of the U.S. war on terrorism, and Washington has faced a much cooler reception in Indonesia than in the Philippines. Although the U.S. military had close relations with Indonesia's armed forces during the Cold War, relations soured in the 1990s over human rights abuses, particularly in the events leading up to and immediately after East Timor's 1999 secession vote. The U.S. Congress subsequently cut off all assistance to the TNI until the government brought those responsible for atrocities to justice. Nevertheless, the Bush administration wants to restore military ties as a step toward suppressing terrorist cells it believes operate in Java and Sulawesi. U.S. combat troops are out of the question; however, Paul Wolfowitz has spoken of helping Indonesia form an internal peacekeeping force.[38]

With close military cooperation unlikely for the foreseeable future, the United States has turned to Indonesia's law enforcement sector for counterterrorist cooperation. Working with the Indonesian police and customs agencies, Washington initially provided $10 million to deal with terrorism. It has also offered to train Indonesians on intelligence techniques and provide expert assistance for the banking community to counter money laundering. These activities have remained low profile because Jakarta publicly proclaims that it needs no U.S. assistance to deal with terrorism. Yet American and Indonesian defense officials are meeting, and in the Pentagon's 2002 Supplemental Defense Appropriations bill earmarked $21 million for Indonesian counter-terrorism training.[39] The TNI's access to these funds will continue to be restricted as long as the Indonesian army protects officers involved in egregious human right violations. It is improbable that high-ranking officers will be prosecuted, however. To do so would split the armed forces at a time when they are essential in containing communal and separatist conflicts. Nevertheless, there is no doubt that Indonesia's armed forces would welcome the restoration of normal relations with the U.S. military—70 percent of its equipment comes from the United States, and because of the Leahy Amendment in the U.S. Congress, less than half of that hardware remains operational.[40]

Although Indonesia's cooperation with the United States has been low profile, and even though Jakarta will not detain individuals identified by its neighbors or the United States as terrorists, there are reports of cooperation between U.S. and Indonesian intelligence agencies. This cooperation has had almost the same effect as arrests. For example, in January 2002, the CIA notified its Indonesian counterpart of an Egyptian cleric in Indonesia who was linked to Richard Reid, the shoe bomber on the December 2001 flight from Paris to Miami. Egyptian authorities requested his extradition, and Indonesian intelligence detained him and deported him to Cairo. He had no lawyer nor court hearing and was spirited out of the country to Egypt on a U.S.-registered Gulfstream jet. Interrogation techniques in Egypt do not take into account international conventions prohibiting torture. U.S. intelligence has used this approach to apprehend alleged Al Qaeda operatives in cooperation with local authorities in Africa, Central Asia, and the Balkans, from which they are sent to Egypt or Guantanamo Bay.[41]

Malaysia

In contrast to Indonesia's President Megawati Sukarnoputri, who fears the ability of her political opposition to use Islamist radicalism against her fragile government, Malaysia's long-serving Prime Minister Mahathir Mohamad has no such qualms. Seizing the aftermath of September 11 as an opportunity, he has tarred the major opposition Pan-Malaysian Islamic Party (PAS) with a terrorism brush, placing it on the defensive. Also unlike Indonesia and its new found civil liberties, Malaysia has held approximately 100 suspected terrorists under its Internal Security Act, interrogated them, and shared some of the results of these interrogations with the United States since September 11.[42]

Because PAS condemned the U.S. war on terrorism as a war against Islam and renewed its insistence that Malaysia adopt *shari'at* (Islamic) law for all its citizens, the opposition coalition, which had included non-Muslim Chinese and moderate Muslims, disintegrated by late 2001. Mahathir claimed that PAS supported the Taliban. By contrast, the prime minister averred that the ruling coalition, Barisan Nasional, has demonstrated that moderate Islam and modernization are compatible.[43] Despite Malaysia's relatively weak economy, pervasive corruption, economic dominance by its Chinese minority, and radical religious factions, Mahathir has managed to project an image of commitment to modernization and religious pluralism, while cracking down on extremists, augmenting border controls, and deporting foreigners—mainly Indonesians—who pose security risks.

In condemning radical Islamism, Mahathir has ridiculed its *ulama* (religious scholars) as uneducated "deviants" who are mistaken in their interpretation of Islam: "These are political *ulama* who are willing to misinterpret Islam for political reasons."[44] The United States has applauded the strong stand Mahathir has taken against terrorism. Assistant Secretary of State for East Asia and the Pacific James Kelly stated in Kuala Lumpur in April that "the U.S. has been gratified by the contribution made by your prime minister, the Malaysian government, and the Malaysian people to the international effort to eradicate terrorism."[45] Kelly's statement seems to reverse the FBI's claim just a few months earlier that Malaysia was a den for terrorists who met there to plan actions elsewhere. In effect, the Malaysian prime minister has used the war on terrorism to marginalize his political opposition at home and improve security ties with the United States, while avoiding an open endorsement of U.S. anti-terrorist policies.

Thailand

Thailand's initial response to the September 11 attacks on the United States disappointed Washington. At first, the Bangkok government seemed to adopt a position of neutrality both because of residual anger at the United States for not doing more to help Thailand during the 1997–98 financial crisis and because of American opposition to Supachai Panitchapakdi's candidacy to head the World Trade Organization. Moreover, Prime Minister Thaksin Shinawatra was also concerned about what the Muslim minority in southern Thailand—at times roiled by what it perceived as lack of attention from the central government—might do.

Nevertheless, Thailand joined the coalition against terror, authorizing U.S. use of U-Thapao air base for the war in Afghanistan. Thailand's National Security Council was tasked with formulating measures against terrorism, with particular attention to the use of Thai territory for illegal arms transfers and money laundering. However, a limited budget, primitive technologies, and rivalries among the country's security agencies that inhibit cooperation over a national area of 514,000 square kilometers, render Thai efforts problematic.[46]

The vast majority of the population in the three southern Thai provinces of Pattani, Yala, and Narathiwat are Muslim with both ethnic and historical links to northern Malaysia, and transportation links from there to the rest of Buddhist Thailand are limited. Unrest flared in the southern provinces in March 2002 when seven policemen were killed at the same time as bombs went off at several public places. Responsibility for these events is unclear, however. Local authorities cite conflicts between the police and army units in the area and personal vendettas. Other observers believe the attacks bear the trademark of Muslim separatists.[47] The attacks show planning and coordination, and there is evidence for both explanations. On the one hand, police operations have cracked down on narcotics activities run by local criminal gangs but have been unwilling to share the credit with local army units. On the other hand, an army spokesman attributes at least some of the attacks to a local Muslim separatist group, some of whose members were trained by Al Qaeda in Afghanistan. In fact, both interpretations could be correct since government corruption, organized crime, and separatist militancy are frequently linked in the Thai south.[48]

The symbiotic relationship between terrorism and criminal activities has been underlined by the former commander-in-chief of the U.S. Pacific Command, Admiral Dennis Blair. In testimony before a U.S. Senate committee, Blair cited the earnings of Wa drug cartels from Burma as linked to terrorist movements.[49] Burma has become the world's top heroin producer as well as the manufacturer of illegal methamphetamines, most of which end up in Thailand. Thai security forces estimate that more than 700 million "meth" tablets were smuggled into Thailand, mostly by the Wa, in 2001.[50] Listed as Thailand's number one national security problem, Admiral Blair's explicit connection of drugs to terrorism may well yield additional U.S. funding for Thai interdiction operations. Nevertheless, despite Blair's specification of the Wa as a major narcotics supplier, the United States has not designated it a terrorist organization.

The United States is involved in Thai drug interdiction operations through technical assistance provided by U.S. Special Forces who are working with Thai Interagency Task Forces (elite units, army, and border police) in Chiang Mai province along the Burma border. Particularly worrisome is evidence in 2002 that the Shan State Army (SSA), previously cooperative with the Thais in anti-drug activities, may now be collaborating with the drug-producing United Wa State Army. In a March clash, a number of the drug suspects killed were SSA soldiers.[51]

In sum, Thailand is assisting U.S. counter-terrorist efforts by offering use of an air base (U-Thapao) and strengthening its efforts to control illegal arms transfers and money laundering. Moreover, in 2002, the annual *Cobra Gold* military exercise (see below) incorporated a counter-terrorist scenario for the first time. While Thailand must cope with a protracted, sometimes violent Muslim autonomy movement in the south, the authorities in Bangkok do not see Islamist terror as a serious national challenge. They are more concerned with ongoing border skirmishes with Burmese forces and drug cartels, none of which is related to Islamist terrorism.

Philippines

Faced with a ruthless, if small, radical insurgent Islamist group in the southern Philippines—the Abu Sayyaf—and a persistent communist insurgency in Luzon, President Gloria Macapagal-Arroyo saw some immediate benefits in associating the Philippines with the U.S. war on terrorism. In desperate need of U.S. aid for a sputtering economy and military assistance to armed forces whose hardware had deteriorated to an almost unusable state, the Philippine offer of political support to Washington was accompanied by a substantial shopping list.

Soon after the September 11 attack, President Arroyo enunciated an anti-terror policy that matched those of America's NATO allies. This included close cooperation with the United States; making Philippine air space and facilities available, including Clark air base and Subic port, to transiting U.S. forces; the enactment on September 30 of anti-money laundering legislation; and even combat troops for Afghanistan if requested by the United Nations.

The Philippines is particularly keen on obtaining U.S. arms and technical assistance to enhance its ability to suppress a radical Muslim insurgent movement, the Abu Sayyaf, which operates from the southern Philip-

pines but has also conducted a kidnapping raid in Malaysia's Sabah. Abu Sayyaf's kidnappings have reportedly netted the group some $20 million in ransoms, some of which goes to buy support from the local population in Mindanao and some to purchase arms and other supplies. While a number of Philippine analysts believe that the Abu Sayyaf has simply become a criminal gang, the September 11 attacks led to greater scrutiny of the organization, including its earlier links to Al Qaeda.

U.S. officials have stated that the Abu Sayyaf's links to Osama bin Laden are sufficient reason to expand military assistance to the Philippines, though there is no evidence of a recent relationship, probably because kidnapping proceeds have provided the Abu Sayyaf with enough money.

President Arroyo's visit to Washington in November 2001 as Southeast Asia's most vocal supporter of the U.S. war on terrorism was rewarded with sizeable military and economic assistance: $100 million in military aid was immediately provided over a five-year program with another $150 million under negotiation. The package included a C-130 transport plane, helicopters, a patrol boat, armored personnel carriers, 30,000 M-16 rifles, and counter-terrorist training. Economic assistance amounted to $49 million in 2001 with another $61 million committed to development projects for 2002. The combination of U.S. government, financial institution, and private sector investment pledges over several years constitutes a package estimated at $4.6 billion.[52]

In late January 2002, the United States began to deploy 600 U.S. soldiers, including Special Forces, to the southern Philippines where Muslim resentment against the Christian central government is as old as the Philippines itself. Upon the invitation of President Arroyo, the U.S. contingent participated in *Balikatan 02*, a joint training exercise that previously had always taken place in Luzon or the Visayas, well out of harm's way. This time, however, the exercise was carried out at least partly on the island of Basilan, where Abu Sayyaf held two Americans and a Filipina hostage until Philippine forces destroyed the small group holding the hostages in a June 2002 encounter that left the Filipina nurse and the male American hostage dead and the female Amreican hostage wounded. From a professional military perspective, *Balikatan 02* offered counter-terrorist training, particularly in the use of up-to-date equipment, including night-vision capability and state-of-the-art communications. Small numbers of Americans were assigned to Philippine forces as advisors but not as combatants.

President Arroyo's invitation has led to considerable controversy within the Philippine Congress and vocal opposition from the country's political left, though it has elicited support from the Catholic Bishops Conference which, in the early 1990s, had strongly opposed a U.S. military presence in the Philippines. The Philippine president has calculated that the political fallout is more than compensated by U.S. military and economic aid, which will improve the capacity of the armed forces to combat insurgencies and pump resources into the economy.

From the American perspective, the deployment of U.S. forces to the Philippines, albeit under the guise of a training exercise, constitutes the next location for the U.S. war on terrorism after Afghanistan. Deputy Secretary of Defense Wolfowitz stated that the destruction of the Abu Sayyaf "would be a small blow against the Al Qaeda network," though he emphasized that military action would be carried out exclusively by Philippine troops.[53] The exercise lasted until the end of July 2002, and at the time of writing negotiations about possible subsequent exercises were underway. The U.S. commander is Brigadier General Donald Wurster, the head of

Special Operations Command in the Pacific, an indicator of how important Washington sees this deployment. The Bush administration may have selected Abu Sayyaf because it appeared to be a relatively easy win early in the war. With Philippine approval, the United States was also able to strengthen its military presence in Southeast Asia.

In fact, Abu Sayyaf's current connection to Al Qaeda is problematic. While the group was formed in the early 1990s and in its early days proclaimed religious fervor, it has become a criminal gang engaged in murder and kidnapping for ransom, striking not only in the Philippines but also in Malaysia. The group's focus is the southern Philippines; it possesses neither the intention nor the capability to strike the United States. Although it may have had some early contacts with Al Qaeda operatives in the mid-1990s, there is no evidence that these have continued, especially since Abu Sayyaf now funds itself through kidnappings. Rather than an Al Qaeda clone, Abu Sayyaf is more in the tradition of southern Philippine pirates. In late April 2002, reports surfaced of the payment of a $300,000 ransom to the group for the release of the American hostages—to no avail. The payment was arranged by elements of the Philippine police who chose not to inform the army because of previous military moves to appropriate portions of ransoms for themselves. Such lack of cooperation among Philippine security agencies also hampered previous hostage rescue efforts.[54]

The main issues in the U.S.-Philippine joint exercise, which in many respects is a search and rescue operation, are who commands the U.S. participants and what are their rules of engagement? The understanding appears to be that the Americans serve only as advisors, do not engage in combat, but can defend themselves if attacked. How all this plays out in the fog of battle, however, is an open question. As for who commands, U.S. law and practice require that U.S. officers command American forces. However, the Philippine constitution prohibits the operation of foreign combat forces on Philippine soil—a major reason for the U.S. deployment being called a training exercise. Discussions between the two countries' defense and foreign policy leaders apparently led to an understanding that Philippine officers had "authority" over the forces they lead, including U.S. advisors, but U.S. officers retained "command" (perhaps a distinction without a difference). Through mid-2002, U.S. advisors have only been assigned to the Philippine forces at the battalion level, meaning that they do not go out on patrols in search of the Abu Sayyaf. By mid-year, however, both U.S. and Philippine officials were discussing the assignment of U.S. advisors to the company level, enhancing patrol effectiveness.[55]

There are other risks for the U.S. forces in Zamboanga and Basilan. One is that Abu Sayyaf not be confused with the MILF, a much larger dissident organization with armed forces that is engaged in negotiations with Manila. Moreover, some former rebels who had fought with the MILF and Moro National Liberation Front (MNLF), the latter now governing part of Mindanao, have defected again to the rebel side. If Philippine forces with American advisors clash with these groups, the whole basis of the U.S. presence is undermined.[56] Another possibility is that the Abu Sayyaf may try to seize a propaganda advantage from the U.S. presence by recasting the conflict as a fight by foreign Christians against righteous Muslim warriors. An additional disturbing feature is the Philippine army's reputation in Muslim-controlled areas. It has employed some of the same terrorist tactics as its adversary. Since the Abu Sayyaf has no uniforms and can melt back into the civilian population, the parallel with the Vietnam War should be disturbing to U.S. armed forces.[57]

The MILF has adopted a cautious attitude toward U.S. participation in the hunt for the Abu Sayyaf. While insisting they have no quarrel with the Americans, the MILF warns that if its camps are attacked, it will respond. Some eight MILF battalions are reported to be encamped on Basilan. They are better organized, equipped, and led than the generally rag-tag Abu Sayyaf.[58] Curiously, some MILF leaders have asked the United States to intervene on their behalf in negotiations with Manila, arguing that, as the former colonial power, which in 1946 ceded the Muslim islands of Mindanao to a Christian Philippines, Washington has a "moral responsibility" to assist their struggle for independence. No friend of the Abu Sayyaf, the MILF has also reportedly offered to assist the Philippine army in crushing the terrorists. Far from an altruistic offer, the MILF fears an extension of anti-Abu Sayyaf fighting to Mindanao, which is the Front's main base.[59]

On the other hand, since the mid-1990s, a variety of foreign Islamist militants including Indonesians, Malaysians, and Thais have passed through MILF camps in Mindanao, both giving and receiving training. Moreover, there are close ties between Islamists and MILF cadres in Indonesia's Sulawesi. One captured Indonesian told Philippine authorities that he had provided explosive training learned from Al Qaeda in Afghanistan to MILF camps in Mindanao from 1996 to 2000. The Philippines is also holding several other Indonesians who entered the country illegally and have been identified as members of the militant Jemaah Islamiya.[60]

Complicating the Philippine confrontation with Islamic separatists has been the revival of the Philippine communist party's military arm, the Maoist New Peoples Army (NPA). Estimated at approximately 12,000 guerrillas, a number of clashes have occurred over the past few years. In addition, the NPA is reactivating operations in Mindanao, particularly worrisome if it coordinates activities with the MILF.[61]

President Arroyo hopes to see the U.S. presence in the southern Philippines extended in time and scope to include civic action such as the construction of roads and water systems. However, some Philippine nationalists have raised concerns that any extension of U.S. military activities after the Abu Sayyaf are routed would be construed as the beginning of a permanent American military presence in the country.[62] Although both the Philippine and U.S. governments deny such intentions, skepticism is widespread in the Philippines.

Nevertheless, in late April 2002, emboldened by public opinion polls showing that three-fourths of Filipinos surveyed supported U.S. actions in Mindanao, President Arroyo announced the deployment of additional U.S. civic action forces to Basilan to improve medical care and living conditions for some of the country's most neglected rural areas. While some Filipino nationalists opposed any U.S. expansion, others who had been initially skeptical about U.S. intentions, such as Senator Aquilino Pimentel from Mindanao, now welcomed the enhanced presence of U.S. engineers who "would have a salutary effect on the whole *Balikatan* exercise."[63]

Multilateral Security Cooperation

Both Secretary of State Colin Powell and Assistant Secretary of Defense Paul Wolfowitz have pointed to U.S. cooperation with the Philippine armed forces as a model for dealing with local terrorist organizations. According to Admiral Blair, "the focus of our activities is to make sure that Asia is not the last bastion of Al Qaeda, to make it as inhospitable as possible."[64] The idea is to buttress local counter-terrorist efforts and capabilities and not to take a direct combat role as in Afghanistan. Hopefully, U.S. support for friendly governments would help them "root out the terrorist infrastructure and terrorist organizations that are there." For that, equipment, intelligence, training, and good tactical doctrine are required; U.S. assistance is designed to augment these capabilities.[65]

Following their success for surveillance in Afghanistan, Washington has sent unmanned aerial vehicles (UAVs) over Basilan. Flying from bases in Okinawa and elsewhere in Asia, their deployment implies that the United States has obtained permission from other Asian states to use their territories in post-September 11 action. U.S. and Philippine officials are also discussing a new treaty that would provide "access rights" for U.S. forces, whereby they could pre-position supplies and benefit from permanent overflight privileges. In addition to increased military and economic aid, a more institutionalized U.S. military presence could help the Philippines balance China's growing naval deployments in the South China Sea among the Spratly Islands.[66]

Admiral Blair has emphasized the importance of Asian multilateral cooperation in the war on terrorism, noting linkages among terrorist and international criminal activities ubiquitous in the region, particularly drug smugglers and money launderers. The terrorists and criminal gangs share "centers of gravity,…people, money, transportation networks, and sanctuaries." According to Blair, military-to-military cooperation must be strengthened to cope with these challenges.[67]

On a different dimension, the United States continues to promote security multilateralism in its various annual military exercises in Southeast Asia. In *Team Challenge 2002*, PACOM has linked the Philippine *Balikatan* exercise with *Cobra Gold* in Thailand. The latter is the most elaborate U.S. joint and combined forces event in the region. Occurring over two weeks in May, the 2002 exercise expanded on the peace operations scenario introduced the previous year. Now a trilateral event involving Singapore, an additional 14 nations have sent observers including China and Vietnam for the first time, as well as Russia, France, and India. From America's point of view, *Cobra Gold* serves several ends: some degree of interoperability among the participants, a display of U.S. military technology and professionalism, and a demonstration that armed forces can collaborate for nonhostile purposes such as peacekeeping and disaster relief. *Cobra Gold 2002* deployed 14,000 U.S. personnel, the largest number in the history of the exercise, and 7,000 Thais alongside a small number of Singapore's forces. Moreover, this year's exercise introduced an anti-terrorism component, simulating raids on terrorist camps with naval and air cover. Critics wondered, however, whether large-scale military assaults on jungle bases are applicable to what are more likely to be small groups of terrorists operating in urban areas. Additionally, it is improbable that Southeast Asian governments would permit a massive invasion of their territories to round up terrorists. Rather, these critics suggest, an emphasis on collaborative intelligence gathering and subsequent police action would be more useful.[68]

Finally, the United States has had a warship regularly patrolling the Strait of Malacca to protect oil tankers and merchant ships against possible terrorist attacks. Admiral Blair asked Indonesia, Malaysia, and Singapore to mount their own joint patrols of the Strait. In April, U.S. and Indian media announced that the Indian navy has joined the United States in patrolling the strategic strait.[69]

Prospects for Regional Cooperation in the War Against Terrorism

While the United States focuses on following Al Qaeda's trail wherever it may lead, Southeast Asian governments have also discovered that regional cooperation is essential for countering transnational terror cells. Their enthusiasm for this enterprise varies, however. Three distinct approaches to anti-terrorism cooperation coexist. The most effective is direct government-to-government contacts, followed by ASEAN declarations, and finally proclamations from ARF—the first time this security dialogue body has dealt with an imminent security threat, if only rhetorically.

Interstate cooperation (and its problems) center on the Singapore-Malaysia-Indonesia nexus. With the discovery of Jemaah Islamiya in Singapore, associated with Al Qaeda and with cells in Malaysia and Indonesia, the need for regional cooperation was clear. Malaysia and Singapore have collaborated via intelligence exchanges and the incarceration of terrorist suspects, a sharp shift from past practice. Both countries have urged Indonesia to detain specific individuals such as Abu Bakar Ba'asyir, the Indonesian cleric whose Islamist school educated a number of the Jemaah Islamiya and KMM terrorists currently in jail in Singapore and Kuala Lumpur. Indonesia, however, has refused, citing its new democratic procedures but also reflecting President Megawati Sukarnoputri's fear of an Islamic backlash were she to comply. While Indonesian authorities claim to be cooperating with their neighbors, in fact little seems to have been done.[70] By contrast, Kuala Lumpur sent the former MNLF leader Nur Misuari back to Manila in January 2002 after he fled the Philippines for Malaysia following a short-lived though bloody insurrection. Similarly, on a tip from Singaporean intelligence, the Philippines arrested five suspected Indonesian members of Jemaah Islamiya and made them available for questioning by Singaporean and Indonesian officials.[71]

While the Indonesian parliament has enacted a law on terrorism, it has not been enforced because of the president's concern over public reaction. Nor has Indonesia cooperated with other countries in halting money laundering, ending up on the blacklist of the international Financial Action Task Force.[72] In an effort to appease its neighbors, Indonesia has talked with Malaysia and the Philippines about trilateral maritime patrols to combat smuggling, illegal arms shipments, and narcotics. However, with the partial exception of Malaysia, none of these countries has the ships to interdict these activities.[73]

Insofar as terrorist organizations threaten Southeast Asia as a region, ASEAN should be concerned. Charged with assisting its members' quest for security and stability, one of ASEAN's underlying principles is that no state should subvert an ASEAN partner. Since terrorist cells with transborder activities operate in the Philippines, Malaysia, Indonesia, and Singapore, ASEAN has begun to address these concerns. Nevertheless, because terrorist groups operate both domestically and internationally, ASEAN cooperation runs up against the association's *noninterference principle*. This requires each nation to agree before ASEAN can investigate, make recommendations, or take action with respect to the internal affairs of a member even though these internal problems precipitate external effects.

ASEAN foreign and interior ministers have been meeting to discuss how the region's members can cope with transnational terrorism, but little has been accomplished. The members agreed to share intelligence and to ensure there would be no safe haven for terrorists. An understanding was reached among the Philippines, Malaysia, Indonesia, and Thailand that any warrant issued for cross-border criminal activity would be honored by each country.[74] However, this can lead to complications. In March 2002, three Indonesians were arrested in the Philippines as alleged members of the Jemaah Islamiya. The arrests were made after a tip from Indonesian intelligence. Regardless of the truth of the allegations, in fact the three are associated with the political party of the Indonesian People's Consultative Assembly Chairman Amien Rais, a potential presidential candidate. His supporters have accused Indonesian intelligence of trying to undermine Rais. Subsequently, after personal intervention by President Megawati with President Arroyo, two of the suspects were repatriated to Indonesia, leaving the third to stand trial. The larger point is that cases of this kind involving nationals of one country subverting another demonstrates how the international anti-terrorism campaign tears at the fabric of regional unity and collides with ASEAN's non-interference principle.[75] To put it another way, how obstructive is the non-interference principle to regional cooperation against terrorism? Given the plethora of meetings in 2002 among ASEAN states leading to pledges to harmonize laws covering extradition, criminal investigations, and prosecutions, future efforts should reveal whether the non-interference principle has been transcended.[76] The fact that terrorists cross borders for training, supplies, and operations may be sufficient to generate serious Southeast Asian efforts to address the politics of religious radicalism—though perhaps not yet in Indonesia.

Malaysia, Indonesia, and the Philippines initialed an anti-terrorism cooperation treaty in May 2002 to which Thailand has since adhered. The treaty provides for the creation of a joint committee to determine how maritime and land border cooperation among the signatories can be implemented. However, whether this new arrangement adds to the undertakings already in place remains to be seen.[77]

On a broader scale, the ARF, too, has convened a series of workshops to strengthen security cooperation on combating terrorism. Their subjects include financial measures, border control and immigration, and security for air travel and major international events. The terrorist financing workshop is attempting to craft international standards on how to identify and terminate terrorist financing and money laundering. ARF members are urged to freeze terrorist assets within their jurisdictions and close terrorist access to the international financial system. Each member is also asked to establish a financial intelligence unit that will share information on these issues. Of course, these recommendations can only be implemented through voluntary national compliance.[78]

At its July 2002 meeting in Brunei, the ARF responded positively to U.S. counter-terrorist requests with a Statement on Measures against Terrorist Financing that lays out specific steps the members agree to take to fight terrorism. The statement claims that members will block terrorists' access to each country's financial system, freeze terrorist assets, exchange financial information, provide technical assistance to each other, and report on the progress of these efforts. While this statement is unprecedented as an action commitment by ARF members and mandates counter-terrorism cooperation by members' law enforcement agencies, it is still not a binding agreement (comparable to a treaty). Nor does it include a common definition of terrorism so that Indonesia, for example, which refuses to detain the head of Jemaah Islamiya, may have a different vision of terrorism than Malaysia and Singapore, which have asked Indonesia to act against the group. Nevertheless, both ASEAN and the ARF have made strong formal statements against terrorism and have pledged to cooperate in an area that is bound to involve their members' domestic affairs. If these new pledges are implemented, both regional organizations could make significant progress toward enhancing regional security and validating their relevance in a new international context.[79]

One of the most promising signs that Asian states are getting serious about counter-terrorist collaboration was a three-day Singapore gathering in early June 2002 of defense ministers from Southeast Asia, the United States, China, Japan, India, and Russia along with legislators, academic experts, and European defense officials. Convened by London's International Institute for Strategic Studies, the conclave was the first ever gathering of Asian defense ministers and was equally stunning in that it also included an official from Taiwan's National Security Council.[80]

One focus of attention was Indonesia's reticence to collaborate with its neighbors in rooting out terrorism and its training grounds. Deputy Defense Secretary Wolfowitz, representing the United States at the conference, affirmed the Pentagon's desire to resume military relations with Indonesia, a goal equally pursued by Jakarta. Indonesia's Defense Minister Matori Abdul Djalil told Wolfowitz and a U.S. congressional delegation that the TNI had made several important reforms, including putting the military under civilian control and establishing tribunals for human rights violations. Even without restored military ties, the Pentagon has asked Congress to fund a plan for training and equipping domestic peacekeepers in Indonesia to help quell sectarian violence and for assisting the Indonesians in establishing their own counter-terrorism unit.[81]

Whether the defense ministers' meeting will become an annual event has yet to be decided. There did seem to be a consensus among the ministers that if transnational terrorism is to be stopped, ongoing collaboration among security institutions is essential. A Philippine proposal for the creation of a multinational counter-terrorism center to facilitate the exchange of information among law enforcement, defense, and security agencies generated particular interest.[82] These meetings could portend a new level of Southeast Asian security collaboration commensurate with the challenges the region faces. Once again, the proof will lie in implementation.

Major External Actors and Southeast Asian Security

China

China continues to engage Southeast Asia as part of a long-term strategy of political reassurance and mutual economic benefit. These linkages include a new Sino-ASEAN Free Trade Area agreement to be implemented over a 10-year period as well as growing investment. The latter is concentrated in natural resources, for which China's industrial appetite is insatiable. While the overall amount of Chinese FDI in ASEAN is modest—$108 million approved in 2000—the trend line for the past several years is upward.

China is particularly attracted to Indonesia's abundant natural resources—oil, gas, timber, palm oil, and coal. In January 2002, China's state-owned oil company, CNOOC, purchased a Spanish oil company's Indonesian assets for $585 million, making China the biggest offshore oil producer in Indonesia. Moreover, Indonesia and China are negotiating for the latter's acquisition of a 22 trillion cubic foot natural gas field in West Papua which, if consummated and developed, would provide a steady supply for Guangdong province in southern China.[83]

From Southeast Asia's viewpoint, traditional suspicions of Beijing's intentions are being ameliorated as China increasingly is seen as an important economic partner, alongside the United States, Japan, and the European Union—able to help the region recover from its economic recession. China's investment strategy also demonstrates that Beijing's WTO membership need not be at the expense of Southeast Asian business interests. Nevertheless, China's total approved Southeast Asian investment in ASEAN countries in 2000 was only 20 percent of its total outward investment, revealing that Chinese companies are mainly interested in *global* business opportunities.[84] Still, Beijing is trying to assuage ASEAN's concerns that China is now attracting 60 percent of the foreign investment going to Asia compared to only 30 percent for ASEAN, a reversal from the early 1990s.[85]

Beijing is also promoting regional infrastructure expansion designed to increase road, rail, and shipping links between China and Southeast Asia. It is building an east-west highway from Shanghai through Yunnan province to Burma, and another through Laos that will connect with northern Thailand. The latter, if connected to Thailand's system, will become part of the pan-Asian highway going all the way to Singapore. Expanded commercial shipping on the upper Mekong River and a new Chinese-built port south of Rangoon increase trade opportunities for China's southwestern provinces in Southeast Asia. While Southeast Asia welcomes enhanced economic interactions, there is concern in Thailand particularly that illegal Chinese immigration will follow commercial trails just as it has in Burma, where northern cities are heavily populated by Chinese merchants who have crossed the border.

China's reaction to America's war on terrorism in Southeast Asia has been mixed. There is concern that terrorist cells in the region provide "a pretext" for the United States to create new bases "around the world." At the same time, Chinese authorities acknowledge that Washington has legitimate interests in Asia that entail a military presence.[86] However, Beijing fears the possibility that the U.S. Navy might once again obtain access to Vietnam's Cam Ranh Bay naval base since the Russians have opted to leave. Chinese media have implied that the presence of U.S. forces in Vietnam would be viewed as a hostile act. Hanoi has assured China that it has no plans to sign a military access agreement with any country.

India

India continues to expand its "Look East" policy in Southeast Asia. Prime Minister Atal Behari Vajpayee visited Singapore and Cambodia in early 2002, offering aid to the latter and economic cooperation to the former. The "Look East" policy is also part of India's quest for energy security as it seeks oil and gas supplies from Burma, Vietnam, and Indonesia. Seeing the Strait of Malacca remain in friendly hands, then, constitutes the strategic rationale for Indian naval escorts there. Nevertheless, India's political and economic profile in Southeast Asia pales compared to China's. The latter is a member of the active ASEAN+3 group, which is exclusively East Asian; India is merely an ASEAN dialogue partner, a more limited relationship. Trade between ASEAN and India was $8.5 billion in 2001 compared to China's $41.6 billion. Delhi has its own Southeast Asian highway project to link India with Burma and Thailand; however, it remains only a plan at this point.

Both China and India are also engaging Southeast Asia on security issues. China is working with Burma, Thailand, Laos, and Vietnam to counter drug trafficking, while India is cooperating with the Malacca Strait states in anti-piracy patrols. These activities are compatible with U.S. interests as well, since they all serve to combat transnational crime and reduce resources that could be used to fund terrorism.[87]

Japan

Japan's strategic relationship with Southeast Asia goes back decades. Tokyo's official development assistance (ODA) and investments, inaugurated in the 1950s and 1960s, became one of the bases for the region's post-World War II recovery and development. Diplomatic activism over the past decade followed these investment, trade, aid, and loan initiatives.

Strategically, Japan's most important contribution to Southeast Asia has been indirect—the provision of bases for America's East Asian military presence. In recent years, Japan's prolonged economic malaise has led to a significant reduction in ODA to Southeast Asia. Moreover, its inability to resolve structural economic difficulties has tarnished its state-led development model. By contrast, should China be able to sustain its economic growth over the next 20 years—a big assumption—its influence in Southeast Asia may well surpass Japan's.

Japan is attempting to compete with China's Sino-ASEAN Free Trade Area proposal by exploring prospects for a similar arrangement. However, so far, only Singapore has signed on. The sticking point for the rest of the region is Japan's highly protected agricultural sector that undermines Tokyo's appeal as a free trade partner.

Japan has played a more active political role in Southeast Asia since the 1990s. Among a number of initiatives are aid in the reconstruction of Cambodia and East Timor, as well as participation in peacekeeping in both countries. Tokyo has also attempted to convince the Burmese junta to negotiate with Nobel Prize laureate and opposition leader Aung San Suu Kyi to form a government of reconciliation. Moreover, Prime Minister Koizumi Junichiro has promoted cooperation with ASEAN on a variety of transnational issues including terrorism, piracy, energy security, infectious diseases, the environment, narcotics, and human trafficking.[88]

More broadly, under its recent Defense Guidelines with the United States, Japan has sent Maritime Self-Defense Force destroyers and supply ships through Southeast Asia to provision U.S. and British naval vessels in the Indian Ocean as part of the war against the Taliban and Al Qaeda in

Afghanistan. This was the first time Japan has assisted forces in combat zones since World War II. Moreover, Japan is operating almost half of its C-130s by flying U.S. equipment and personnel to Singapore and Guam. Thus, Japan plays an important if ancillary role in the war on terrorism through Southeast Asian waters and air space.[89]

In sum, major power roles in Southeast Asia are in flux, and each has varying agendas. China's emphasis is the promotion of economic partnerships designed to de-emphasize its competitive acquisition of foreign investment and rivalry in global trade. Territorial disputes in the South China Sea are on the back burner, particularly because of Beijing's concern over Taiwan's political recalcitrance and military buildup. India demonstrates a growing interest in Southeast Asia as an economic and security partner. Delhi's long range goal is to provide an alternative to future domination by China. Yet since India has neither the economic nor political presence in the region to be a major player, it is linking its security role to the United States, still the dominant external actor in East Asia, with joint naval counter-terrorist patrols through the Strait of Malacca. Japan's agreement to the post-September 11 expansion of defense relations with the United States places its naval and air forces in transit through Southeast Asia to assist U.S. deployments in the Indian Ocean. Tokyo's protracted financial stagnation, however, has reduced its economic importance in the region. Finally, Washington has raised its security profile in Southeast Asia since September 11, with the deployment of military advisors to the Philippines, the addition of a counter-terrorist scenario to *Cobra Gold*, and behind-the-scenes support for regional counter-terrorist collaboration among Malaysia, Indonesia, Thailand, and the Philippines. These new U.S. policies are a subject of debate within the region among governments and security specialists.

Conclusion

Has the struggle against transnational terrorism become the new framework for security collaboration within Southeast Asia as well as between the ASEAN states and great powers? What effect does this putative collaboration have on the ASEAN states' jealously guarded noninterference norm? So far, anti-terrorist cooperation is essentially bilateral, as are other security issues. Nevertheless, even bilateral cooperation can effect significant political changes. Australia and Indonesia, previously antagonistic because of Canberra's military role in defending East Timor's post-referendum independence, have reestablished security ties. As part of this renewed relationship, Australia has provided Indonesia with five fast coastal patrol craft. The focus of this new security relationship is the Timor Gap where human smuggling into Australia and piracy are ubiquitous.[90]

While Indonesia finds itself increasingly isolated in Southeast Asia as its neighbors deplore Jakarta's lack of cooperation in counter-terrorist efforts, the United States is attempting to buttress Indonesia's capabilities to deal with home-grown insurgents. Pentagon officials visited the Indonesian capital in late April 2002 to meet with TNI leaders for wide-ranging security talks. A recent U.S. State Department document provided the rationale for these new approaches to Indonesia:

> Southeast Asia is second only to South Asia as a priority in counter-terrorism, and Indonesia is of primary concern in that region as an area where domestic, regional, and al Qaeda-related terrorists may transit or operate....[91]

Although military-to-military ties continue to be precluded because of congressional human rights sanctions, a policy dialogue among defense civilians of the two countries has been reestablished. In effect, these talks constitute efforts by the United States to appeal to the professionalism of the Indonesian armed forces, to urge the TNI to withdraw its support and protection from Islamist militant groups, and to counter ethnic separatism and communal violence in a more even-handed way. This amounts to U.S. political involvement in Indonesia's domestic troubles. To help Indonesia cope, the U.S. State Department has proposed an initial $8 million to train and equip a domestic peacekeeping force so that the central government can respond more rapidly to destabilizing events. The State Department believes such a force would facilitate the rapid restoration of order, weaken extremist groups, and serve counter-terrorism goals. An additional $8 million will be offered for civilian counter-terrorism units whose members would be vetted by the FBI and U.S. intelligence agencies to ensure that no one with a history of human rights violations was included. However, Indonesia had not responded to these offers by mid-2002.[92]

India's involvement in the U.S. war on terrorism has further linked South to Southeast Asia. Joint patrols in the Strait of Malacca with U.S. and Indian naval vessels to protect merchant ships has been welcomed by Malaysia and the international Piracy Reporting Center in Kuala Lumpur. India's naval base in the Andaman Islands near Indonesia's territorial waters is the primary port for Delhi's ships.[93]

Thus, the war on terrorism has led to some new collaboration within Southeast Asia and among the ASEAN states, the United States, Japan, and India. Nevertheless, Al Qaeda remains elusive. No Southeast Asian government acknowledges it has discovered an Al Qaeda cell on its territory, though Al Qaeda has sought individual recruits for training. Ironically, the organization with the strongest links in the past to Al Qaeda, the MILF in the southern Philippines, is not on the U.S. terrorist list. Moreover, the Philippine government is negotiating with the MILF to see if it can be peacefully incorporated into the political structure of Mindanao. Toward that end, an agreement was reached in Malaysia that provides the MILF with a role in Mindanao's governance.

Washington's sometimes contradictory actions as a global power have also interfered with the war on terrorism in Southeast Asia. A move in Congress to extend trade preferences to Andean countries in order to wean their economies away from narcotics may lead to the unintended consequence of thousands of Muslim workers losing their jobs in the southern Philippines. Ecuador and Colombia might displace the Philippines for the tuna market in the United States. The hardship this would create in Mindanao could well neutralize joint U.S.-Philippine efforts to ameliorate the conditions that breed insurgencies. In effect, U.S. efforts to fight the drug trade in Latin America may harm the war on terrorism in Southeast Asia.[94]

While American assistance for Southeast Asia to prosecute the war on terrorism has been generally welcome, over the long run Southeast Asian states must change the political-social-economic milieu in which terrorism breeds. Specifically, these changes should include socio-economic development in the southern Philippines, economic recovery in Indonesia, the restoration of law and order in the Malukus and Sulawesi, and, still in Indonesia, a political solution to the conflicts in Aceh and Papua (Irian Jaya). Internal security resources in Southeast Asia are low. Until these capabilities are enhanced and the socio-economic deficits erased, terrorism will continue to flourish regardless of outside efforts to eradicate it. Hunting down terrorists deals with the symptoms but not the underlying disease.

Finally, the United States must be cautious in its rush to embrace moderate Muslim leaders in Southeast Asia. Militants are attempting to paint their moderate co-religionists as U.S. puppets. For Washington to embrace them too openly could be a political "kiss of death." Moreover, the United States should not push Southeast Asian states to accept a larger military presence. As Brad Glosserman of the CSIS/Pacific Forum in Honolulu warns: "A heavy-handed U.S. effort to [play] a military role in combating terrorism in Indonesia or Malaysia would be an affront to those countries and destabilizing..." given popular suspicions of U.S. intentions.[95] The exception to this stricture is the Philippines, an American ally, where the government welcomes a U.S. military counter-terrorist role. However, even for the Philippines, Southeast Asian specialists caution that the United States not extend the fight beyond the universally despised Abu Sayyaf to, for example, the MILF, with which regional governments have helped broker peace arrangements with Manila.

An effective counter-terrorism policy for Southeast Asia must add a substantial public diplomacy component to counter the widespread belief that the United States is unilateralist and indifferent to the Muslim world. Support for moderate nongovernmental organizations is one approach. Another is to ensure that ranking U.S. government officials aver America's continued interest in Southeast Asia's progress and that Washington's focus is not exclusively military and counter-terrorist. The United States must be sensitive to the region's development, trade, and investment needs. It should demonstrate that U.S. engagement is a long-term, multifaceted commitment and that Southeast Asia means more than simply one more element in a global anti-terrorism strategy.

Endnotes

[1] Cited by Mohammed Jawhar Hassan, "Terrorism: Southeast Asia's Response," *PacNet Newsletter*, no. 1, Honolulu: Pacific Forum/CSIS, January 4, 2002.

[2] Deputy Defense Secretary Paul Wolfowitz's remarks cited in James Dao and Eric Schmitt, "U.S. Sees Battles in Lawless Areas after Afghanistan," *The New York Times*, January 8, 2002.

[3] Hassan, "Terrorism: Southeast Asia's Response," p. 2.

[4] Two of the men identified as September 11 hijackers are believed to have visited Malaysia in 2000. See Seth Mydans, "15 Held in Singapore Said to Have Al Qaeda Ties," *The New York Times*, January 8, 2002.

[5] Raymond Bonner and Seth Mydans, "Sleeper Cells in Singapore Show Al Qaeda's Long Reach," *The New York Times*, January 26, 2002.

[6] For an assessment of Southeast Asia's security situation prior to the events of September 11, see Sheldon W. Simon, "Southeast Asia," in Richard J. Ellings and Aaron L. Friedberg, eds., *Strategic Asia 2001–02: Power and Purpose*, Seattle, Wash.: The National Bureau of Asian Research, pp. 269–97.

[7] Credit Suisse, First Boston, Goldman Sachs, and Merrill Lynch have all pared back their Southeast Asian operations. See Wayne Arnold, "In Southeast Asia, a Wary Optimism," *The New York Times*, April 4, 2002.

[8] Leif Rosenberger, *Asia-Pacific Economic Update 2002*, Honolulu: U.S. Pacific Command, 2002, p. 27.

[9] Ibid., p. 28.

[10] Ibid., pp. 29–30.

[11] For a discussion of the effects of the financial crisis on Southeast Asian armed forces, see Sheldon W. Simon, "Asian Armed Forces: Internal and External Tasks and Capabilities," in Simon, ed., *The Many Faces of Asian Security*, Lanham, Md.: Rowman and Littlefield, 2001, pp. 49–70.

[12] For an extended discussion of this new security agenda, see Simon, ed., *The Many Faces of Asian Security*.

[13] A good analysis of Al Qaeda's potential in Southeast Asia is found in Kumar Ramakrishna, "Addressing Transnational Security Threats in the Asia-Pacific Region," paper presented to the 2002 Pacific Symposium, National Defense

University, Washington, DC, February 20–21, 2002.

[14] Ibid., pp. 6 and 8.

[15] Quoted in Bonner and Mydans, "Sleeper Cells in Singapore Show Al Qaeda's Long Reach," *The New York Times.*

[16] Ibid.

[17] Seth Mydans, "Suspects in Singapore are Linked to Al Qaeda and Plans for anti-U.S. Attacks," *The New York Times*, January 12, 2002.

[18] Jane Perlez and James Brooke, "Indonesian in Terror Inquiry Lauds bin Laden," *The New York Times*, January 25, 2002.

[19] Emmerson's congressional testimony is summarized in Don Pathan, "Terrorist War Ships to South Asia," *The Nation* (Bangkok), January 24, 2002, in FBIS, January 25, 2002 (FBIS-EAS-2002-0124).

[20] Philip Shenon and David Johnston, "Suspect Calls Malaysia a Staging Area for Terror Attacks," *The New York Times*, January 31, 2002.

[21] "Anti-Terrorism War Causing Southeast Asian Discord," Stratfor.com, January 29, 2002.

[22] William Depasupil, "MILF Talks Peace, but Pursues Terrorist Aims," *Manila Times*, February 1, 2002, in FBIS, February 4, 2002 (FBIS-EAS-2002-0201); see also "New Terrorist Group with Links to September 11 Uncovered," *Washington Post*, February 3, 2002; and Raymond Bonner, "How Qaeda Linked Up with Malaysian Groups," *The New York Times*, February 7, 2002.

[23] Doug Struck, "Philippines is Seeking Four Tons of Explosives," *International Herald Tribune* (Singapore), March 19, 2002; and *GMA-7 Television* (Manila), March 15, 2002, in FBIS, March 18, 2002 (FBIS-EAS-2002-0315).

[24] "What Do You Mean 'Terrorist'?" *The New York Times,* April 7, 2002; " 'Islamic Unity' at Odds with Geopolitical Realities," Stratfor.com, April 4, 2002; "Malaysian Minister Describes OIC Meeting on Terrorism as Unsuccessful," *Bernama* (Kuala Lumpur), April 3, 2002, in FBIS, April 4, 2002.

[25] An extensive discussion of Southeast Asian security specialists views of radical Islam and the U.S. war on terrorism at the June 2002 Asia Pacific Roundtable may be freund in Brad Glosserman, "Southeast Asia's Words of Warning," *PacNet Newsletter 2002*, no. 24, Honolulu: Pacific Forum/CSIS, June 14, 2002, pp. 1–2.

[26] Hassan, "Terrorism: Southeast Asia's Response," p.3.

[27] Cited by Kumar Ramakrishna, "Addressing Transnational Security Threats in the Asia-Pacific Region," p.12.

[28] Nyier Abdou, "The Asian Connection," *Al Ahram Weekly* (Cairo), January 24–30, 2002; and Sheldon W. Simon, "Mixed Reactions in Southeast Asia to the U.S. War on Terrorism," *Comparative Connections—An E-Journal on East Asian Bilateral Relations*, vol. 3, no. 4 (January–March 2002), pp. 1–2.

[29] Tom Raquer, "Growth of Laskar Jihad in Indonesia," Honolulu: U.S. Pacific Command, March 24, 2002.

[30] *The Jakarta Post*, June 1, 2002, in FBIS, June 4, 2002.

[31] Raymond Bonner and Jane Perlez, "Qaeda Moving into Indonesia, Officials Fear," *The New York Times*," January 23, 2002.

[32] Perlez and Brooke, "Indonesian in Terror Inquiry Lauds Bin Laden," *The New York Times.*

33 Kompas (Jakarta), February 12, 2002 and March 18, 2002 in FBIS, February 17 and March 20, 2002 respectively. See also *Media Indonesia*, March 20, 2002 in FBIS, March 22, 2002.

34 Bonner and Perlez, "Qaeda Moving Into Indonesia, Officials Fear," *The New York Times*.

35 Quoted in "Upsurge in Israeli-Palestinian Conflict Impacts Southeast Asia," Stratfor.com, April 8, 2002.

36 *Kompas*, April 2, 2002, in FBIS, April 3, 2002; and *Jakarta Post*, April 5, 2002, in FBIS, April 6, 2002.

37 *Jakarta Post*, March 25 and 27, 2002 in FBIS, March 26 and 28, 2002 respectively.

38 Jane Perlez, "The Helping Hand Gets Limp Shakes," *The New York Times*, April 7, 2002.

39 *Media Indonesia* (Jakarta), January 29, 2002, in FBIS, January 30, 2002. See also *Wall Street Journal*, January 18, 2002; and Sadanand Dhume and Murray Hiebert, "Indonesia: A Slow March," *Far Eastern Economic Review*, January 17, 2002.

40 Jane Perlez, "Indonesia Resumes U.S. Military Talks, Pleasing the Pentagon," *The New York Times*, April 25, 2002. See also Jason Sherman, "U.S. Seeks Aid for Indonesians to Fight Terrorism," *Defense News*, April 28, 2002.

41 Rajiv Chandrasakaran and Peter Finn, "Secret Transfers: The CIA is Orchestrating the Transport of Terrorist Suspects to Outside the United States," *Washington Post, Weekly Edition*, March 18–24, 2002.

42 Raymond Bonner, "Indonesian Cleric Suspected of Being a Terrorist Leader," *The New York Times*, February 3, 2002; *Malaysiakini* (Petaling Jaya), February 2, 2002, and May 12, 2002, in FBIS, February 5 and May 13, 2002.

43 Raymond Bonner, "Malaysia's Canny Autocrat Grows Stronger Since September 11," *The New York Times*, February 9, 2002.

44 *Malaysiakini* (Petaling Jaya), April 2, 2002 in FBIS, April 3, 2002 (FBIS-EAS-2002-0402).

45 "Malaysia's Mahathir Criticizes PAS for Backing 'Deviant' Islamic Scholars," *Malaysiakini*, April 16, 2002, in FBIS, April 17, 2002 (FBIS-EAS-2002-0416).

46 See the discussion in "Thailand: The Next Stage," conference report from the School of Advanced International Studies, Southeast Asia Program, Johns Hopkins University, November 30, 2001, pp. 28–29. See also the *Bangkok Post*, January 22, 2002 in FBIS, January 23, 2002.

47 Varying accounts may be found in the *Bangkok Post*, March 22 and 23 in FBIS, March 25, 2002; *The Nation* (Bangkok), March 19, 2002 in FBIS, March 20, 2002; and *Krungthep Thurakit* (Bangkok), March 21, 2002 in FBIS, March 22, 2002.

48 *Krumthep Thurakit* (Bangkok), March 27, 2002 in FBIS, March 29, 2002; and "More Violence on Horizon in Thailand," Stratfor.com, March 27, 2002.

49 Cited in the *Bangkok Post*, March 18, 2002 in FBIS, March 19, 2002.

50 *Agence France-Presse* (Hong Kong), March 20, 2002 in FBIS, March 21, 2002. See also General (ret.) Teerawit Putamanonda, "Thailand's Defense Concept and Transnational Threats," paper presented at the 2002 Pacific Symposium, National Defense University, Washington, DC, February 20–21, 2002, p. 4.

[51] *The Nation* (Bangkok) editorial on drugs, March 12, 2002; and the *Bangkok Post*, March 26, 2002, in FBIS, March 21 and 27, 2002, respectively.

[52] Overview of Philippine foreign policy by the Honorable Teofisto T. Guigona, Jr., during a new year briefing to the diplomatic corps, January 16, 2002, <www.dfa.gov.ph/archive/speech/guinguna/nyearbriefing.htm>.

[53] Seth Mydans, "Muslim Separatists Terrorize Filipinos with Kidnappings for Money and Marriages," *The New York Times*, January 13, 2002.

[54] Eric Schmitt, "U.S. and Philippines Setting Up Joint Operations to Fight Terror"; James Brooke, "Unease Grows in Philippines on U.S. Forces"; Raymond Bonner, "Given $300,000, Abductors Refuse to Free 2 Americans," *The New York Times*, January 16 and 19, and April 27, 2002 respectively.

[55] Eric Schmitt, "American troops will begin tighter operations with Filipinos," *The New York Times*, June 20, 2002.

[56] "Philippines Rebel Presence in Military Endanger U.S. Troops," Stratfor.com, January 16, 2002; *Philippine Daily Inquirer*, February 12, 2002, in FBIS, February 13, 2002; and *The Manila Times*, January 17, 2002 in FBIS, January 18, 2002.

[57] Jane Perlez, "Philippine Army Eagerly Awaits New U.S. Gear," and Nicholas Kristof, "Sleeping with the Terrorists," *The New York Times*, February 12, 2002.

[58] *The Manila Times*, January 17, 2002, in FBIS, January 18, 2002; and *The Nation*, February 22, 2002, in FBIS, February 25, 2002.

[59] "Muslim Militants Just Love America," *Far Eastern Economic Review*, March 21, 2002; "Philippines: Hunt for Abu Sayyaf worries MILF rebels," Stratfor.com, June 12, 2002.

[60] Anthony Davis, "Manila's Grasp on Peace Slips," *Jane's Defense Weekly*, April 3, 2002; and the *Philippine Daily Inquirer*, April 11, 2002, in FBIS, April 12, 2002.

[61] *Philippine Daily Inquirer*, April 16, 2002, in FBIS, April 17, 2002.

[62] *Philippine Daily Inquirer*, April 16, 19, and 23, 2002, in FBIS, April 17, 20, and 24, 2002.

[63] Quoted in the *Philippine Daily Inquirer*, April 20, 2002 in FBIS, April 22, 2002.

[64] Eric Schmitt, "U.S. and Philippines Setting up Joint Operations to Fight Terror;" *The Manila Times*, January 24, 2002, in FBIS, January 25, 2002; and Eric Schmitt, "Hurdle Leapt, U.S. Will Help Philippines Battle Rebels," *The New York Times*, January 30, 2002.

[65] Schmitt, "Hurdle Leapt, U.S. Will Help Philippines Battle Rebels," *The New York Times*.

[66] Thomas Ricks and Alan Sifress, "Spy Planes Seek Out Philippine Guerrillas," *The Washington Post*, February 21, 2002; and Raymond Bonner, "U.S. and Philippine Governments Revive Old Relationship," *The New York Times*, March 4, 2002.

[67] Admiral Blair's address to the 2002 Pacific Symposium at the National Defense University in Washington, DC, cited in *Washington Post*, February 22, 2002.

[68] Robert Karniol, "China to Observe 'Cobra Gold'," *Jane's Defense Weekly*, January 30, 2002; Xinhua (Beijing), April 12, 2002, in FBIS, April 15, 2002;

Bangkok Post editorial, June 2, 2002, in FBIS, June 3, 2002.

[69] Murray Hiebert and Susan Lawrence, "Hands Across the Ocean," *Far Eastern Economic Review*, March 14, 2002; *The Hindustan Times* (New Delhi) and *The Washington Times*, April 19, 2002.

[70] *Kompas* (Jakarta), January 9, 2002 in FBIS, January 10, 2002.

[71] *The Manila Times*, January 29, 2002 in FBIS, January 30, 2002; *The Jakarta Post*, February 5, 2002 in FBIS, February 6, 2002.

[72] "Indonesia Reform Process Grinding to a Halt," Stratfor.com, March 22, 2002; *Bernama* (Kuala Lumpur), April 9, 2002 in FBIS, April 11, 2002.

[73] *Bangkok Post* editorial, February 25, 2002 and *The Nation* (Bangkok), February 21, 2002, FBIS, February 26 and February 22, 2002 respectively.

[74] "Anti-Terrorism Campaign Chips Away at Asian Regional Unity," Stratfor.com, April 11, 2002; *Wall Street Journal*, April 22, 2002.

[75] *Bangkok Post*, May 6, 2002 and *Bernama* (Kuala Lumpur), May 7, 2002, in FBIS, May 9, 2002.

[76] "ASEAN," *Far Eastern Economic Review*, May 30, 2002; and the *Bangkok Post*, June 2, 2002, in FBIS, June 3, 2002.

[77] *Draft Report of the ARF Workshop on Terrorist Financing*, Honolulu, March 24, 2002; *The Nation* (Bangkok), April 18, 2002 in FBIS, April 19, 2002.

[78] Sadanand Dhume and Susan Lawrence, "Buying Fast into Southeast Asia," *Far Eastern Economic Review*, March 28, 2002.

[79] For an optimistic assessment of the July 2002 ARF Statement against Terrorist Financing, see Brad Glosserman, "The ARF Breaks New Ground," *PacNet Newsletter*, no. 32, Honolulu: Pacific Forum/CSIS, August 9, 2002.

[80] Normally, the ARF brings together member foreign ministers, while U.S. PACOM provides an annual venue for Asia Pacific chiefs of staff to meet.

[81] Barry Wain, "British Think Tank Persuades Asia to Attend Security Forum," *Wall Street Journal*, May 30, 2002; and Eric Schmitt, "Pentagon Official Warns Asians to Guard Against Terror," *The New York Times*, June 1, 2002.

[82] Jason Sherman, "Asia Tackles Terror," *Defense News*, June 10–16, 2002.

[83] Dhume and Lawrence, "Buying Fast into Southeast Asia," *Far Eastern Economic Review*.

[84] Jane Perlez, "U.S. Envoy Campaigns for Trade Pacts on Asian Trip," *The New York Times*, April 7, 2002.

[85] Cited by Lyall Bracken in "Gains for Beijing in an Otherwise Gloomy Quarter," *Comparative Connections*, vol. 3, no. 4 (January–March 2002), p. 1.

[86] Ibid., p. 2

[87] Ibid., pp. 4–6; and "Southeast Asia to Benefit from India-China Rivalry," Stratfor.com, April 15, 2002. See also "India May Join Malacca Straits Patrol," *Far Eastern Economic Review*, March 21, 2002.

[88] An excellent discussion of Japan's security interests in and cooperation with Southeast Asia is found in Lam Pang-Er, "Trading Places? The Leading oose and Ascending Dragon," *Comparative Connections*, vol. 4, no. 1 (April–June 2002).

[89] Jason Sherman, "U.S. Seeks Japanese Aid in Terror Fight," *Defense News*, April 21, 2002.

[90] One-third of the world's pirate attacks occur around the Timor Gap, presenta-

tion by Australian General Simon Willis at the Pacific Symposium 2002, National Defense University, Washington, DC, February 21, 2002; and "Isolated Indonesia Eyes Australia for Support," Stratfor.com, February 11, 2002.

[91] Quoted in Jason Sherman, "U.S. Seeks Aid for Indonesia to Fight Terrorism," *Defense News*, April 28, 2002.

[92] "U.S. Aid for Indonesian Force," *Far Eastern Economic Review*, May 7, 2002.

[93] *The Straits Times* (Singapore), April 23 and 24, 2002.

[94] Keith Bradsher, "Quandary in Trade," *The New York Times*, May 21, 2002.

[95] Brad Glosserman, "Southeast Asia's Words of Warning," p. 2.

STRATEGIC ASIA

SPECIAL STUDY

ISLAM AND ASIAN SECURITY

Robert W. Hefner

The violence of September 11, 2001, and the Afghanistan campaign that followed raised troubling new questions about security in the Muslim world. Nowhere have these questions taken on greater urgency than in the diverse Muslim communities of Central, South, and Southeast Asia. Although most westerners identify Islam with the Arab Middle East, some 60 percent of the world's 1.2 billion Muslims resides in Asia. The Muslim population inhabits a swath of territory stretching from the mountains and deserts of Central Asia to the rice paddies and cities of tropical Southeast Asia. Lacking an Arab or Persian cultural core, Asian Muslims display far greater ethnic and civilizational variation than their Middle Eastern counterparts. Although small numbers of believers can be found in almost all Asian countries, Muslims are an especially important presence in the 11 countries where they comprise an outright majority (the five Central Asian states, Afghanistan, Pakistan, Bangladesh, Malaysia, Brunei, and Indonesia) and in the five others where they constitute a politically prominent

Robert Hefner is Professor of Anthropology and Senior Research Associate at the Institute on Religion and World Affairs, Boston University. The author wishes to thank Donald Emmerson, Aaron Friedberg, and Michael Wills for their valuable criticisms of an earlier draft of this paper.

religious minority (India, northwest China, Singapore, southern Thailand, and the Philippines).

It is not simply the demographic girth of Asian Islam that has captured policymakers' attention. During the long jihad against Soviet occupation (1979–89) and the fierce Taliban campaign against rival Muslims (1994–2001), an estimated 50,000 volunteers from 60 Muslim countries traveled to Afghanistan to join with the *mujahidin* (jihad fighters). Tens of thousands more made their way to conservative Islamist *madrassas* (religious schools) along Pakistan's border with Afghanistan where the Taliban leadership had studied earlier. In these fiercely independent institutions, students were instructed in an ideologized and entirely untraditional variant of their faith. They learned, among other things, that the Muslim community is locked in a fight to the finish with belligerent unbelievers led by the United States and Israel in alliance with Russia, India, and other secular powers. A peculiar response to globalization, this *jihadi* Islam blends the modern preoccupation with state power and global inequalities with an austere social conservatism, not least of all as regards the status of women and non-Muslims. In the late 1990s, after Osama bin Laden established his training camps in Afghanistan, 6,000 foreign nationals went a step further, undergoing initiation into the now infamous Al Qaeda.[1]

Although no precise estimate is possible, many of the foreigners who fought alongside the Taliban or joined Al Qaeda were from Asia. Most of the Asian recruits came from Pakistan and the Central Asian states, especially Uzbekistan. However, hundreds more came from more distant places such as Indonesia and the southern Philippines. Some of these remained behind in Afghanistan after completing their training, eventually joining the Taliban resistance to the American campaign. Others, however, returned to their homelands determined to do battle, not so much with Israel and the United States, but with secular and moderate Muslims in their own countries. In the 1990s, this radical Islamism was making itself known in places like Indian Kashmir, the southern Philippines, and China's Xinjiang region—areas where poverty and ethno-religious inequalities inclined some Muslims toward a radicalized interpretation of their faith. In the five former Soviet republics of Central Asia, 70 years of communist repression of Islam gave way in the 1990s to a great Islamic resurgence. In a handful of years, tens of thousands of mosques and *madrassas* were built for the region's almost 50 million Muslims.[2] Most of the newly pious were apolitical or politically moderate. At the margins of the mainstream community, however, militants worked to take advantage of popular disaffection with regime corruption, economic depression, and *apparatchik* repression to incite revolutionary change. Even in countries like Singapore, Malaysia, and Indonesia, where Muslim politics had long been moderate, the 1990s saw efforts by *jihadi* militants to expand their radical networks. No Islamist Internationale directed the radicals' efforts. Few of their organizations received direct support from Al Qaeda. Nonetheless, with their global finances, keen sense of mission, mastery of new communications, and hostility to moderate Islam, the radicals constituted a militant reserve willing and able to take advantage of any weakening of the political center. The Asian financial crisis of 1997–98 and the September 11 attacks in the United States provided two such opportunities.

The events of September 11 raised troubling questions about the breadth and depth of the new *jihadi* radicalism. The questions were given special urgency after the collapse of the Taliban regime in late 2001. This flushed remnants of the Taliban and Al Qaeda into Pakistan and the Central Asian states. It also gave rise to concerns that, under pressure from the American-led alliance, Al Qaeda might attempt to reposition some of its forces away from the front lines of conflict to territories like Kyrgyzstan, Kashmir, northwest Pakistan, the southern Philippines, and Indonesia.[3] In all of these locales, rugged terrain and weak state administration enhanced the prospects for safe haven. The discovery of Al Qaeda cells in Malaysia, Singapore, and the Philippines at the end of 2001 raised fears that the network was indeed spreading.

The seriousness of these developments makes it imperative to go beyond reports in the mass media and attempt a balanced assessment of Muslim politics and its implications for security in Asia. This assessment is difficult because the Asian Muslim community is more culturally and politically diverse than its counterpart in the Arab Middle East. The purpose of this chapter is to provide just such a comparative assessment of Asian Muslim politics. The discussion begins with an overview of the social and political history of Islam in the region—important because it offers insight into the great variety of cultures that influence Muslim politics today. It then turns to the impact of the Islamic resurgence that swept Muslim Asia in the 1980s and 1990s, and whose primary trait was not a particular political orientation, least of all anti-western, but growing piety among Muslims previously indifferent to the ritual demands of their faith.

Having sketched this background, the next section of the chapter assesses the way in which developments since September 11 have impacted state and society in Muslim Asia. As the global campaign against terrorism has advanced, its impact has been anything but uniform. Because other chapters in this book provide country-specific assessments of post-September 11 events, the discussion here focuses on transnational linkages within and between Central, South, and Southeast Asia. The final section examines future trends for Muslim politics in Asia and the relative impact of Islamist radicalism on regional security, and offers several observations for consideration with regard to U.S. policy toward Muslim Asia.

It is clear that *jihadi* Islamists have been able to take advantage of globalizing trends in the media, markets, and politics; in so doing, their movements have introduced a destabilizing element into politics and society in Muslim Asia. Although the threat posed by these movements is real, analysts need to distinguish between the radicals resolutely opposed to the global order and the far larger community of ordinary Muslims indifferent or opposed to radical appeals. Over the long term, the most effective policies toward Muslim Asia will be those that contain extremism while working with, rather than against, the Muslim majority's aspirations for social and economic improvement.

Legacy

Commentators from Muslim Asia often make a point of saying that their region has traditionally been more tolerant and moderate than the Muslim Middle East. This alleged difference often is explained with reference to the fact that unlike the early Islamic expansion in the Middle East and North Africa, Islam arrived in Asia not on the heels of conquering Arab armies but through the peaceful activities of traders, mystics, and high-minded rulers.[4] Arabs did play a role in the early diffusion of Islam in Asia. Arab traders had established themselves in trading ports in southern China and caravan centers in Central Asia by the end of the seventh century. Arab armies made incursions as well, reaching Central Asia in 650 and the western border of the expanding Chinese empire in 751. An Arabic-speaking kingdom was established in northern India in 711.[5] Even after Arab rulers had long since disappeared from Asia, Islamic schools in Egypt and Arabia continued to host Muslim students from the continent. During the great migrations of the late nineteenth and early twentieth centuries, hundreds of religious scholars (*ulama*) from southern Arabia established themselves in the booming cities of colonial Asia, going on to play a role in the religious reformation that swept the region at that time.[6]

Notwithstanding these influences, it is true that Islam in Asia acquired a civilizational ballast different from that of the Arab Middle East. The Arab kingdoms established in Central Asia gave way in a little more than a century to Muslim polities led by indigenous rulers. From that period on, rulers in Central and South Asia looked to Persian and Turkic rather than Arab prototypes for their models of civilizational excellence. In Southeast Asia, the Muslim kingdoms were from the beginning led by native potentates.[7] Most conversion to Islam occurred well after the first centuries of the Arab expansion, was the fruit not of Arab labors but of Asian Muslims, and generally took place in an undramatic and incremental fashion.

Even where formal conversion occurred, it typically did not entail an immediate rupture with local traditions, a fact that helps to explain the complex tapestry of Muslim traditions across Asia today. On the steppes of north-central Asia, the conversion of Kazakh nomads to Islam was still going on as late as the seventeenth century; to this day, many Kazakhs identify as much with their ethnic traditions as they do with Islam. In the Indian subcontinent, many Muslims participated in mystical activities with Hindus at the shrines of saints deemed holy to both religions, practices that declined only with the Islamic reform of the late nineteenth century.[8] In insular Southeast Asia, conversion to Islam began in the thirteenth century but continued until the eighteenth. The public culture of Islam in Southeast Asia was also distinctive. Prior to the Islamic resurgence of the 1970s, few women wore veils, the cloistering of women (*purdah*) was rare, and the application of harsh Islamic criminal laws, such as the stoning of adulterers or severing of thieves' hands, was almost unknown.[9]

These historical details aside, the early history of Islam in Asia illustrates a point directly relevant for policy analysis today—that the spread of Islam in the continent was not accompanied by the Arabization or imperial unification seen in the Middle East. Islam in Asia did not bring a uniform political culture or, least of all, ideological agreement. In what are today Pakistan and Afghanistan, sectarian rivalries between majority Sunnis and minority Shi'a created a bitter legacy that endures to this day. (Shi'ism is virtually absent from Southeast Asia, but is found as a minority tradition in South and Central Asia.)[10] On the Southeast Asian islands of Sumatra and Java, Muslims united to do battle against Hindu-Buddhist rulers at the beginning of the sixteenth century. After the Muslim triumph, however, the alliance gave way to bloody dynastic wars between coastal and interior kingdoms, each committed to a different profession of Islam. This variety in Indonesian Islam exists to this day. In Central Asia, questions of Islamic piety have been regularly drawn into ethnic conflicts, such as those pitting Kazakhs and Kyrgyz, casual in their profession of Islam, against puritanical Uzbeks. In these and other examples, conversion to Islam did not serve as a melting pot for Asia's varied social groups, but added yet another ingredient to the ethno-religious stew.

European colonialism took this ethnocultural fragmentation and relocated it within the borders of what were to become modern Asia's nation-states. The Spanish took all but the southern (Muslim) islands of the Philippines in the sixteenth and seventeenth centuries, leaving the task of conquering the Muslim south to the United States after the Spanish-American war. The Dutch stole into portions of Indonesia in the seventeenth and eighteenth centuries, completing their conquest of the archipelago only at the beginning of the twentieth. The British encroached on Muslim-ruled India from the mid-eighteenth century. Having welcomed Muslim sojourners for almost a thousand years, the Chinese moved west into eastern Turkestan in the eighteenth century. The Russians annexed Siberia in 1650, then pushed south in 1715 to invade the Kazakh steppe, and brought most of present-day Uzbekistan, Turkmenistan, Kyrgyzstan, and Tajikistan under their dominion at the end of the nineteenth century.

These historical facts speak directly to contemporary political realities. The absence of a great Arab expansion and the ethnic fragmentation of Asia's Muslim states ensured that Muslim Asia brought a legacy of fractious division and intra-Muslim rivalry to the twentieth century. European colonialism maintained and, in some cases, worsened these divisions. Unlike the Muslim Middle East, Muslim Asia witnessed no serious attempt to foster a pan-Asian Islamic nationalism. The changes experienced in the modern era were instead broadly consistent with the pluricentrism long characteristic of Asian Islam.

Religious Reform and Resurgence

If modern developments did not foster political unity among Asian Muslims, they nonetheless did usher in basic changes in the profession of Islam. In the late nineteenth and early twentieth centuries, European colonial rule brought telegraphs, railways, and, in insular Asia, steamships. These new technologies increased Asian Muslims' communications with the Middle East, as well as their participation in the annual pilgrimage (*haj*) and in schools in Egypt and Arabia. The Europeans also brought printing presses that allowed for the mass production of Islamic books and newspapers. European influence stimulated the growth of new forms of civic and political association, some of which paved the way for the independence movements that swept South and Southeast Asia after the Second World War.

The development of modern communications, education, and urbanization in twentieth century Asia challenged existing patterns of authority in the Muslim community. In cities with large numbers of educated Muslims such as Delhi, Lahore, Singapore, and Batavia (present-day Jakarta), the first decades of the twentieth century saw the appearance of a new class of modernizing reformers, intent on removing Islam from the hands of rulers, Sufi mystics, and classically-trained religious scholars traditionally responsible for the management of the religion. The reformers were determined to use the machinery of modern education and bureaucratic organization to purify Islam of local cultural accretions. In so doing, they hoped, Muslims would respond more effectively to the challenge of the West. The modernist message met with little enthusiasm in remote parts of Asia and in backward countries like Afghanistan; in Asia's bustling cities, however, it had great appeal.[11]

During and immediately after the great nationalist struggles of the mid-twentieth century, however, politics in Muslim Asia continued to be dominated by nationalist and socialist appeals rather than Islamist ideologies. Aside from a few formulaic references to the Prophet, the main political groupings in Muslim Asia relied little on Islamic precedents in devising their plans for government. The world's largest majority-Muslim country today, Indonesia in the late 1950s boasted the largest communist party in the non-communist world. Even in Pakistan, a country founded as a homeland for South Asia's Muslims, voters consistently rejected Islamist appeals to turn the nation into an Islamic state.

Religious developments during the late 1970s and 1980s, however, challenged the nationalists' hegemony and established the parameters for an ideological contest that is still raging in Muslim Asia today. The primary characteristic of the resurgence was not so much political as it was an increase in mosque construction, religious education, pilgrimage to Mecca, and Islamic publishing—in short, public piety. The precise causes of the increase in religious piety varied from country to country, as did its political disposition.[12] However, the fact that the resurgence brought Islamic ideas and organizations into public prominence meant that, if and when political rivalries intensified, some among the contestants would be tempted to use Muslim symbols for their mobilizational appeals. In the Soviet Union's Central Asian republics during the 1980s, non-Russians responded to Russian dominance by asserting their identity as Muslims.[13] Even in Pakistan and Indonesia, where the ideals of nationhood were officially multiethnic, national politics had long been dominated by leaders from large ethnic groups. Against this perceived slight, many members of smaller ethnic groups affirmed their common identity as Muslims.[14]

There was also a transnational influence on the resurgence. After the rise in petroleum prices during 1973, Saudi Arabia and several other Middle Eastern states increased their assistance to Muslim organizations in Asia. Most of the Middle Eastern donors directed their largesse toward groups willing to promote a theologically conservative interpretation of Islam. In the aftermath of the Soviet occupation of Afghanistan in 1979, this assistance took a military tack. Saudi Arabia and the Gulf states joined the United States to provide $10 billion in military assistance to Afghan *mujahidin* fighters. Pakistan's powerful Inter-Services Intelligence (ISI) directorate managed most of this assistance and directed the lion's share to conservative Islamists. Committed to their own puritanical interpretation of Islam, the Saudis went along with this conservative bias. On a lesser scale, Libya also became active in the provision of international assistance from the late 1970s.[15]

Although Iran had offered a dramatic demonstration of Islam's revolutionary potential a few years earlier, ultimately it was the *mujahidin* struggle in Afghanistan that had the most decisive impact on the rise of radical Islamism in Asia. Afghanistan became a training ground for tens of thousands of militant Muslims from Asia and the rest of the Muslim world. Some of the military assistance intended for *mujahidin* made its way into the hands of militants in Uzbekistan, Xinjiang, and Southeast Asia. The Afghan model of Muslim politics was deeply conservative, even anti-modern, especially as regards the status of women and non-Muslims. It was premised on an alliance between two types of radicals previously not prone to collaboration: transnational Islamists like Osama bin Laden, with wildly utopian visions of international revolution, and local Muslims frustrated by regional and ethnic inequalities. The small network of radical internationalists had found what it hoped would be its mass base.

Radicalization

To discuss the resurgence in purely political terms, however, obscures the fact that the great majority of people drawn into the revival were not motivated by political concerns. In the Soviet republics of Central Asia, for example, apolitical Sufi orders were more popular in the 1980s than was political Islam.[16] The majority of newly pious in India, Malaysia, and Indonesia were moderate in orientation. Muslims in Malaysia and Indonesia in particular were prominent in the ranks of local democracy movements.[17]

Although the resurgence was for most Muslims a matter of personal religiosity, it nonetheless benefited the radical fringe. The resurgence contributed to the further fragmentation of Muslim religious authority and to the growing debate among Muslims over the political uses of Islam. While mainstream Muslims are not united in their political views, radical Islamists share certain common convictions. They emphasize three points: that the essence of Islam is *shari'at* (literally "the way," such as divine law or commandment); that only *shari'at* can solve the world's problems; and that only one understanding of *shari'at* is allowed. The science and culture of classical Muslim civilization, the grappling of modernist Muslims with the challenges of our age, and traditional scholars' awareness that God's will allows diverse interpretations—these and other achievements of earlier Muslim civilizations are cast aside for a totalizing and millenarian understanding of the law.

In idealizing *shari'at* in this manner, the radicals differ both from traditional Muslims and moderate reformers. For most ordinary Muslims, *shari'at* is not the sum total of Islam's message, any more than the Ten Commandments are is all that there is to their faith for traditional Christians. Sufi mystics and pietistic Muslims may insist that devotionalism and spiritual peace, not public punishment or (least of all) state power, are what is central to Islam. Even many Muslim traditionalists, who agree that *shari'at* must be upheld, will insist that its interpretation is varied and its implementation best left to individuals and communities, not government bureaucrats. Moderate Muslims in Iran, India, Indonesia, and Malaysia take this reservation one step further. They point out that to surrender responsibility for religion to the state is to invite religion's subordination to petty rulers and party bosses.[18]

By itself, however, the conservative interpretation of the *shari'at* need not be radicalizing. Saudi Arabia has long applied Islamic law, and, although starkly conservative, is not known for revolutionary adventurism. The romance of *shari'at* becomes more seriously destabilizing where warfare, corruption, and social disintegration undermine established authorities and create a public thirst for radical change. In circumstances like these, the delicate balance of interests that underlies the everyday practice of Islam may be destroyed, and the totalizing appeals of radical Islamists may for the first time receive a broad hearing. In calling for a statist and totalitarian profession of Islam, of course, radical Islamism bears more than a passing resemblance to another modern millenarian offspring, Marxism-Leninism. The similarity is not merely ideological. Radical Islamists use a system of organization that relies on underground networks and militant cells similar to that pioneered by Lenin. Where, as in the Central Asian states in the 1990s, authoritarian rulers repress even moderate Islam, those activists best able to weather the storm tend to be radicals equipped with this combination of absolutist ideology and ruthless organization.

Afghanistan in the 1980s and 1990s was a prime example of just such a destruction of the moderate tradition of Islam and the rise of radical Islamism. The Soviet invasion in 1979 came on the heels of several years of internal conflict. The occupation (1979–89) and subsequent civil war destroyed the country's traditions of Muslim pluralism and diversity. As Larry Goodson notes, "the Afghan War totally destroyed the progress toward nation building of more than two centuries. It also destroyed much of the country."[19] Out of a population of 23 million, two million were killed; an equal number were seriously injured. Two million Afghans were internally displaced, and six million fled the country entirely. Half of the country's 24,000 villages were destroyed. Many of its cities were reduced to rubble.[20]

Beyond its physical horrors, the war also destroyed the pluralist fabric of Afghan life. Prior to the Soviet occupation, Afghanistan had a reputation as a deeply Islamic society. However, a people's commitment even to conservative Islam is not the same as political extremism. "Traditionally Islam in Afghanistan has been immensely tolerant—to other Muslim sects, other religions, and modern lifestyles.... Until 1992, Hindus, Sikhs, and Jews played a significant role in the country's economy."[21] The country's low rates of literacy and general backwardness had served to insulate rural Muslims from the calls for puritanical reform emanating from Pakistan and Saudi Arabia. In this regard Afghanistan resembled its neighbors in Soviet Central Asia more than it did Iran or Pakistan.[22]

Twenty years of warfare, however, allowed what had once been a radical fringe to move to the center. The war against the Soviets wreaked havoc with the economy. Opium production and drug trafficking moved into the gap, creating an alliance of Islamist revolutionaries and drug traffickers. In addition, "the war destroyed the pre-war elites and the social system that supported them, leading to the development of new political elites... founded on a newly prominent role for youths and Islamist ideologues."[23] The Taliban leaders were not recruited from mainstream society or the ranks of traditional religious authorities but from among youths living in refugee camps located in Pakistan's North-West Frontier Province, Baluchistan Province, and Tribal Areas. Most of the *madrassas* in which these youths were trained were operated by Pakistanis associated with the Jamiat-i-Ulema-i-Islami (JUI), an ultra-conservative and anti-western group.[24]

Although *madrassas* have long played a role in Islamic education, the *jihadi madrassas* had appeared only in the 1980s. This was a decade of crisis in Pakistan's educational system, with many poor youths unable to afford public education. Neighboring Afghanistan was at the same time in the throes of Soviet occupation. With the help of donors in Saudi Arabia and Pakistan, and with the full knowledge of Pakistani and western intelligence services, the *madrassas* took advantage of the crisis to direct their appeals toward Afghan refugees and Pakistan's poor. Long before the Taliban's rise in 1994, the conservative *madrassas* had become a training ground for militants from South and Central Asia. The future leaders of the *jihadi* groups fighting in Indian Kashmir, such as the Harkat-e-Jihadi Islami, were also alumni of these schools.[25]

If the Afghan case sheds light on the conditions that allow a radical fringe to transform itself into the vanguard of Islamist revolution, it also reveals the limits of the example. No other Muslim society in contemporary Asia has experienced the devastation of Afghanistan. None has seen its religious, intellectual, and political elites so thoroughly decimated. These facts remind us of how unusual Afghanistan's experience was, and of the improbability of a revolutionary Islamist movement on the scale of that country's arising in other parts of Muslim Asia.[26]

However, if a radical movement on the scale of Afghanistan's seems a remote possibility, extremist-inspired conflict and political instability do not, particularly where established regimes experience a crisis of legitimacy. Over the last decade Islamist extremists have succeeded at implanting themselves in most countries in Muslim Asia. Effective policy requires a clear understanding of the scale of their organization, which varies greatly from country to country, as well as the varied impact of September 11.

Central Asia

After the collapse of the Taliban in late 2001, no area of Muslim Asia seemed more likely to experience radical destabilization than the former Soviet republics of Central Asia: Turkmenistan, Uzbekistan, Kazakhstan, Kyrgyzstan, and Tajikistan. In addition to their proximity to Afghanistan and their troubled administrations, all five states have citizens who had traveled to Taliban training camps in Afghanistan. Earlier, hundreds of Central Asian students had also trained in Pakistani *madrassas* linked to the JUI and other hardline groups. Worse still, several radical Islamist groups, such as the Islamic Movement of Uzbekistan (IMU—discussed below and in Martha Olcott's chapter in this volume), had direct ties with Al Qaeda.

Prior to 2001, all of the Central Asian states had experienced some Islamist unrest. The five are predominantly Muslim, although Kazakhstan and Kyrgyzstan have large Russian minorities as well.[27] All had experienced an Islamic religious revival after Soviet authorities relaxed restrictions on Muslim activities in the late 1980s. The resurgence took on political overtones in the 1990s in response to the region's deepening political crisis.

The problems these countries faced at first had little to do with religion. They were in severe economic decline in the 1990s, a slide which had begun the previous decade as a result of the economic downturn in the Soviet Union. The decline was compounded by the Soviet withdrawal of subsidies to the republics in 1990, prior to the collapse of the Soviet Union in December 1991. The change left the states' economies unable to accommodate the large numbers of young people entering the work force each year.[28] Even when a country is endowed with oil and gas resources, as in Turkmenistan, Uzbekistan, and Kazakhstan, political instability and corruption made foreign firms reluctant to invest. The economic instability in turn increased the role played by heroin trafficking in several states. Traffickers made deals with Islamist paramilitaries on the model of their arrangements with *mujahidin* fighters in Afghanistan.

Table 10.1. Muslim Central Asia—Economy (2000–01)

	GDP ($bn)	GDP growth (%)	Inflation rate (%)	Unemployment (%)	Poverty (%)
Kazakhstan	22.5	9.6	13.2	3.7	35[a]
Kyrgyzstan	4.4	5.0	18.7	7.5	51[b]
Tajikistan	2.4	8.3	24.0	2.7	80
Turkmenistan	7.2	17.6	13.3	...	neg.
Uzbekistan	12.0	4.0	44.3	0.4	...

Sources: World Bank, *World Development Indicators 2002*, for GDP, GDP growth, and inflation; World Bank, *Country Notes*, for inflation; Asian Development Bank, *Key Indicators of Developing Asian and Pacific Countries* for unemployment and poverty. Notes: a) Data from 1996 survey; b) Data from 1997 survey (World Bank).

Table 10.2. Muslim Central Asia—Population (2000–01)

	Population (mil.)	Pop. growth (2000)	Muslim share of pop. (%)	Muslim pop. (mil.)	Refugee pop. (000s)
Kazakhstan	14.9	-0.4	47	7.0	119.5
Kyrgyzstan	4.9	1.0	75	3.7	9.8
Tajikistan	6.2	0.2	85	5.3	18.1
Turkmenistan	5.2	2.0	89	4.6	14.5
Uzbekistan	24.8	1.4	88	21.8	40.9

Sources: World Bank, *World Development Indicators 2002*, for population and population growth; Department of State, *Country Background Notes*, for Muslim share of population; Muslim population is calculated; UNHCR, *2001 Population Statistics* for refugee population.

In the end, however, the states weathered the economic downturn of the 1990s and seemed to be on their way to recovery in 2001. Even with the conflict in neighboring Afghanistan, their economies managed to achieve rates of growth in 2001 that ranged from five percent to seven percent in Uzbekistan and Tajikistan to more than 10 percent in Turkmenistan and Kazakhstan.[29] Today the economic circumstances do not appear nearly as dire as analysts had feared in the mid-1990s. The more vexing question as regards the five states and the future of political Islam concerns their ongoing political transitions. Government in Central Asia is still dominated by ex-communist *apparatchiks* who, rather than inviting moderate Muslims to join the political process, have blocked their access. Repression has weakened the moderate Muslim opposition while strengthening the extremists. The precise balance of power among Muslim groupings, however, varies greatly by country.[30]

Kazakhstan

With its booming economy, large Russian minority, and many secular Muslims, Kazakhstan remains the least vulnerable to radical destabilization. The Kazakhs were latecomers to Islam, and their urban middle class is the most westernized in Central Asia. Where the Islamic resurgence has taken hold, it has typically taken on pietistic or mystical tones, emphasizing personal devotion rather than public politics. When radicals like those in the IMU (which, despite its name, is active across Central Asia) have attempted to launch initiatives in Kazakhstan, they have met with limited success, typically only among the two to three percent of the population that is ethnically Uzbek.

A more serious influence on radical Muslim politics in Kazakhstan has been the repressive hand of the state itself. The government is led by President Nursultan Nazarbayev, the former first secretary of the Kazakhstan Communist Party, and now the leader of its successor, the Unity Party. Nazarbayev has recently signaled his intention to create a family dynasty, passing the presidency to his daughter and the internal security apparatus to her husband. Repression of Muslim organizations has pushed small numbers of young activists underground, into the ranks of the IMU and the Hizb-ut-Tahrir. The latter is a pan-Central Asian organization dedicated to the overthrow of existing regimes and the imposition of *shari'at* law.[31] Although the IMU has launched guerrilla attacks in the south of Kazakhstan, its appeal so far has been limited. This could change, however, if moderate Muslims continue to be excluded from the political process and from the benefits of economic growth.

Uzbekistan

If Kazakhstan seems as yet resistant to radical destabilization, neighboring Uzbekistan appears more vulnerable.[32] With almost half of Central Asia's population and two of its most important religious centers (Bukhara and Samarkand), Uzbekistan has long been the cultural and political heartland of Muslim Central Asia. Ethnic Uzbeks were among the region's first converts to Islam, and they were also responsible for some of its greatest cultural achievements.

Uzbekistan has been slow to implement structural reforms in the economy. Nonetheless, the country's agricultural sector recovered in 2000, led by cotton exports. The country's vast energy and mineral reserves and sizable industrial sector ensure that the economy remains reasonably diversified. Although like its neighbors it has a high rate of population growth, Uzbekistan may yet be able to provide economic opportunities for young people entering the workforce. Here again, however, the most serious influence on Muslim politics is not the country's economy, but rather an authoritarian regime and the powerful Islamist underground movement that has arisen to oppose it—the IMU.

Like most of the Central Asian leaders, the president of Uzbekistan, Islam Karimov, is a former first secretary of the Communist Party who in recent years has refashioned himself as an ethnonationalist. Karimov has been the most assertive of Central Asia's leaders in the post-Soviet period. He has defied Moscow's wishes, threatened his Central Asian neighbors, and refused to court even a moderate opposition. In 1992 Karimov suppressed a democratic coalition, which, with its mixture of liberals and moderate Muslims, was among Central Asia's most enlightened. Shortly thereafter, Karimov directed his aim at Muslim organizations, accusing even moderate Muslims of having ties to the Afghan *mujahidin*. After an assassination attempt against Karimov in February 1999, the regime arrested thousands of Muslims and pro-democracy reformers on the suspicion that they had conspired against the president.

Uzbekistan has nonetheless become an important supporter in the war on terrorism. Karimov was among the first Central Asian leaders to allow joint exercises with NATO troops, which began in 1998. He had also allowed his intelligence services to cooperate secretly with U.S. intelligence officers several years earlier as part of an effort to track Osama bin Laden.[33] In the fall of 2001, Karimov permitted the United States to station 1,000 troops on bases several hundred kilometers from the Afghan border. Since September 11, his regime has been the largest beneficiary of western military aid in Central Asia.

The Islamic Movement of Uzbekistan

The IMU, with 2,000 to 3,000 fighters, was established at a meeting in Kabul in 1998, although its leadership and organization had taken shape 10 years earlier, when the Soviet Union was at war in Afghanistan and Central Asia was beginning its slide into political-economic crisis. That leadership came not from the ranks of religious scholars but from among young, alienated graduates of the Soviet social and educational system. For most of its existence, the IMU's leader was Tohir Abdouhalilovitch Yuldeshev, known later by his battle name Juma Namangani. An ardent backer of the Taliban, Namangani (who was killed in Afghanistan in November 2001) was a man of action, who combined military prowess with a superficial understanding of Islam. In 1987 he served as a conscript with Soviet forces in Afghanistan. There he is said to have developed such respect for his Afghan opponents that he underwent a reversion to his birth religion.[34] Back in Uzbekistan, Namangani made contacts with Muslim activists, slowly developing the network of militants that was to become the core of the IMU.

Some among Namangani's aides had studied in Saudi Arabia in the late 1980s. There they secured the financial backing of Saudi-based Uzbeks, descendants of fighters who had fled the Soviet Union after the last great Muslim revolt against Soviet rule in the 1920s (the so-called Basmachi rebellion). Having won financial backing, the young activists returned to Uzbekistan in the early 1990s. Working from the mosques and schools springing up across the country at that time, Namangani and his friends quickly attracted a hard-core following of several hundred men. Buoyed by their rapid growth and alert to the opportunities presented by the collapse of the Soviet Union, Namangani went public in early 1992, demanding that Karimov implement Islamic law. From their urban strongholds, Namangani's associates formed vigilante patrols that forced women to adopt conservative dress and required men to attend the Friday prayers.

At first Karimov seemed uncertain as to how to respond to the militants, but in March 1992 he cracked down, and the IMU leadership fled to Pakistan, Saudi Arabia, and Afghanistan. Like the Taliban, with whom they would eventually collaborate, several of the future IMU leaders used their travels to make contact with JUI officials in Pakistan. The JUI raised funds for the Uzbek militants and agreed to sponsor dozens of Uzbek students at *madrassas* along the Pakistan-Afghanistan border. During the first Chechen war against Russia (1994–96), Namangani traveled to Chechnya to meet with rebel commanders; he also made fund-raising excursions to Turkey. His base of operations during these years was a conservative *madrassa* in Peshawar, Pakistan. From there he made trips into Uzbekistan and Tajikistan, organizing the underground cells that, after 1998, came to comprise the armed wing of the IMU.[35] During these same years, the IMU leadership became involved in drug trafficking. Before their military setbacks in the fall of 2001, IMU leaders were thought to control the largest share of the region's booming heroin trade.

Although the majority of its recruits are ethnic Uzbeks, the IMU has followers in other Central Asian states. Indeed, despite its close identification with Uzbekistan, the organization is dedicated to the creation of Islamic states across the region. On numerous occasions this commitment has been translated into action. During 1992–93, militants linked to Namangani crossed from Uzbekistan into Tajikistan to assist Muslim fighters involved in the Tajik civil war. That conflict ended in 1997, but the IMU took advantage of Tajikistan's weak government to operate bases inside the country, from which it launched raids into Uzbekistan during 1999 and 2000. As Namangani and his associates escalated their campaign against Karimov, they established contacts with Osama bin Laden. He agreed to provide the group with communications equipment and automatic weapons. The Taliban also allowed the IMU to establish military bases on the northern Afghani border adjacent to Uzbekistan. The continuing IMU threat in Kyrgyzstan and Uzbekistan prompted the United States, Russia, China, and several other nations to increase their military assistance to the two countries, and in September 2000, the Clinton administration placed the IMU on its list of international terrorist organizations.

When the U.S.-backed alliance began operations in Afghanistan in the fall of 2001, the IMU stepped up its assistance to the Taliban, fighting alongside until the regime collapsed. The severity of the U.S. bombing in northeastern Afghanistan and the collapse of the Taliban regime have dealt a serious blow to the IMU. The IMU may have lost several hundred fighters in Afghanistan, although the smaller of its two military wings is thought to have stayed on the sidelines of the conflict. U.S. bombing is also thought to have destroyed the largest of the IMU bases along the Afghanistan-Uzbekistan border. However, a large body of the IMU probably remains intact, and its surviving leader, Tohir Yuldash, has political skills that Namangani lacked. Moreover, although compromised by battle losses and arrests, the IMU appears still to have an extensive underground network in Uzbekistan. Rather than the major guerrilla incursions attempted by Namangani in 1999 and 2000, the organization in years to come may shift to a campaign of targeted violence against the Karimov regime.

The greatest hope for the IMU is that Karimov's repressive regime will give rise to a new generation of *jihadi* fighters. Karimov's policies toward Muslims have changed little since September 11. Many practicing Muslims in Uzbekistan "do not want to belong to any of the Islamist political groups but remain deeply resentful of the government's policy on religion…. The conditions that helped create and sustain the IMU remain unchanged."[36] Although the improved security situation has encouraged moderates in the government to press for reforms, hardline figures around Karimov continue to resist these calls. The arrest and torture of thousands of Islamists in secretive groups like the Hizb-ut-Tahrir keep the likelihood of future unrest high.

Hizb-ut-Tahrir

The Hizb-ut-Tahrir's leadership has gone underground since September 11. Nonetheless, western intelligence reports indicate that the organization has continued to recruit new members and has transformed itself into the largest Islamist movement in Uzbekistan, and perhaps all of Central Asia. Officially the organization's leaders forswear violence, but their organization is dedicated to the overthrow of the existing regimes in Central Asia and their replacement with a unified Islamic state (caliphate). This ambition has brought them squarely into conflict with the governments in the region, especially in Uzbekistan, where thousands of Hizb-ut-Tahrir followers have been arrested and tortured. Since September 11, some of the rank and file in Hizb-ut-Tahrir have been so outraged by the repression that they have indicated a willingness to take up arms against the government. "The failure of the Karimov government to distinguish between moderate Islamist forces in Uzbekistan and more radical elements only tends to radicalize larger and larger segments of the religious community."[37]

Kyrgyzstan and Tajikistan

The future of the other three Central Asian states, especially Tajikistan and Kyrgyzstan, will depend heavily on the outcome of the political struggle unfolding in Uzbekistan. None has a hardline movement comparable in size to that in Uzbekistan. Having at first experimented with political pluralism and a moderate policy toward Islam, Kyrgyzstan was pressured by Uzbekistan to curtail its democratic reforms and crack down on Muslim organizations in the mid-1990s. Neighboring Tajikistan has experienced an equally somber evolution. One quarter of Tajikistan's six million people are ethnic Uzbeks, and tensions between the two ethnic groups threaten stability. Radical Islamists, including the IMU, occasionally mount operations in the country. However, the growing strength of Tajik nationalism, the moderation of most Tajik Muslims, and public anxieties about the threat from Uzbekistan have encouraged Tajik Muslims to downplay religious differences in favor of broad-based cooperation.[38]

In the short term, the continuing presence of U.S. forces in Central Asia, as well as assistance from the United States, Russia, and Western Europe, will limit the possibility of a full-blown IMU revival. At the same time, however, the chances of serious political unrest, particularly in Uzbekistan, remain high. The Hizb-ut-Tahrir is now the region's most powerful Islamist organization. Although its leaders officially renounce violence and have distanced themselves from Al Qaeda, state repression may yet push them toward violent action. Over the long term, political stabilization and Muslim moderation will depend on efforts to reorient Central Asia's economies and, most important, initiate reforms that allow all its people to participate in the political process in a meaningful and peaceful manner.

China—Xinjiang

Muslims have lived in China for 1,300 years. They played a key role in the medieval caravan trade through western China and Central Asia, as well as in southern China's maritime trade with India and Southeast Asia. Estimates of the number of Muslims in China today range from 17.5 million (the official 1990 figure) to 36 million. The actual number probably lies toward the lower end of this range. The Muslim population is spread across China, with almost all counties reporting some Muslim residents.[39]

Specialists of Islam in China distinguish the 8.6 million Hui, who, despite significant variation in their own customs, have adopted many elements of Han Chinese culture, from the mostly Turkic-speaking Muslims who preserve more distinct ethnic identities. With a population of more than seven million, the largest of these latter groups is the Uighur. Unlike the widely dispersed Hui, Uighurs are concentrated in northwestern China in Xinjiang Autonomous Region. In recent years unrest of a broadly Islamist cast has been seen among this ethno-religious minority. Little is known about the organization and leadership of the Uighur groups involved in the most militant actions other than that some hope to establish an independent homeland called East Turkestan. Mainstream Uighur leaders reject calls for an independent state, but have appealed to Chinese authorities for greater political autonomy.

After September 11, Beijing attempted to take advantage of the U.S. campaign against terrorism by escalating their crackdown on Uighur activists. In December 2001, a foreign ministry spokesperson claimed to have proof that Uighur separatists were part of the "bin Laden clique."[40] According to another report, China claimed that 10,000 Uighurs had traveled to Pakistan and Afghanistan for religious and military training.[41] This figure is certainly too high, although some Uighur students have studied in JUI *madrassas* in Pakistan and some fought alongside the IMU and Taliban in northern Afghanistan. While praising Chinese officials for cooperating with the counter-terrorism campaign, U.S. authorities have resisted efforts to link Uighur separatists to Al Qaeda. At a meeting in Beijing on December 6, 2001, General Frank Taylor, U.S. ambassador-at-large for counter-terrorism, said that the "legitimate economic and social issues" in northwest China needed "political solutions, not counter-terrorism."[42]

The restlessness in Xinjiang has less to do with Islam than it does the region's recent political and demographic transformation. The Qing dynasty conquered much of the region in the 1750s.[43] The Uighurs chafed under Chinese rule, but they were able to keep most of their social and religious institutions intact well into the twentieth century. When the Chinese state weakened in the 1930s, Uighur nationalists declared their independence, first in 1933 and then again in 1944, although Chinese authorities were able to suppress both initiatives.

When the People's Republic of China was founded, the population of Xinjiang was still 90 to 95 percent Muslim. Determined to enhance control of his border territories, however, Mao Zedong in the 1950s encouraged the mass migration of Han Chinese to the region. This remains the government's policy today, and the 2000 census put the share of Chinese in Xinjiang at 40 percent of the total population, as opposed to 47 percent who are Uighur. Although fertility rates among the Uighurs are considerably higher than among Chinese, the Chinese population continues to grow at twice the Uighur rate due to immigration.[44]

During China's Great Leap Forward (1958–61) and the Cultural Revolution (1966–76), the government placed strict limits on ethnic and religious associations in Xinjiang. Mosques and Quranic schools were closed, religious publications were banned, and residents were barred from traveling to Muslim countries. Restrictions were eased in the 1980s, in keeping with a general softening of state policies on minorities. These were the same years of Islamic resurgence in neighboring Central Asia, and the revitalization had a strong effect in Xinjiang. Uighur youths traveled to Central Asia for religious education; a smaller number went to Pakistan and Afghanistan for military training; and a Uighur separatist party was established in October 1993.

Chinese authorities responded by reimposing travel restrictions and launching a general crackdown on separatists in late 1996. In February 1997, the government suppressed a Uighur protest near the border with Kazakhstan at a cost of 300 lives. Shortly thereafter, Uighur separatists escalated their attacks on government officials. In 1997 the government blamed Xinjiang rebels for a bombing in Beijing. Indian officials have also reported capturing Uighurs among Pakistani-backed guerrilla units fighting in Indian Kashmir.[45]

Chinese authorities have responded to these events by encouraging even more Han migration and penalizing Uighurs too zealous in their profession of Islam. In the months since September 11, the repression has increased. China also bolstered its forces on the border with Pakistan and Afghanistan, tightened visa controls on visitors from Islamic countries, and provided military assistance to Central Asian governments fighting Muslim militants.

Despite the Chinese crackdown, unrest in Xinjiang continues. The majority of Uighurs appear realistic about their long-term prospects and aspire to greater autonomy within China rather than independence. Although China seems reluctant to make concessions, unrest in the region seems resolvable under a political framework sensitive to these concerns. Nevertheless, Xinjiang's wealth of mineral and oil resources and location, bordering Central Asia to its west and Russian Siberia to the north, means that the region is of great strategic importance to China. For these reasons, it is unlikely that Chinese authorities will grant heightened political autonomy to Xinjiang's Uighurs in the near future.

Pakistan and India

Since September 11, the political situation in South Asia has become the most dangerous in all of Muslim Asia. This is so not because of the sentiments of the Muslim community as such, but because Muslim affairs in this region implicate two states that each have nuclear weapons, a large army, and a history of antipathy for the other. India's Muslim population comprises 12 percent of the country's total, estimated at one billion. Muslims are found in most portions of the country, with the largest numbers concentrated in the northern and western states as well as in booming commercial cities. Prior to the traumatic partition of Pakistan and India in 1947, Muslims comprised a full quarter of the population of British India. Muslims who chose to remain in India are varied in ideological orientation. As a minority in a majority Hindu society, most accept the legitimacy of the nationalist state and support multiconfessional parties. The notable exception to this pattern is the Muslim population in Jammu-Kashmir.

The rise of the Hindu nationalist movement during the 1980s and 1990s has greatly complicated the situation of India's Muslims. Hindu nationalists have made a point of emphasizing that India is not a multireligious state but a Hindu nation. Violent communal conflicts like those that followed the destruction of the Ayodhya mosque in December 1992 and the riots in Gujarat in March 2002 have tarnished India's tradition of civic tolerance.[46] It is only in the disputed state of Kashmir, however, that tensions like these have taken on dangerously destabilizing proportions. Some 70 percent of Kashmir's population is Muslim, although there is a large Hindu minority in the south of the state and a smaller Buddhist minority in the east. At the time of partition in 1947–48, the state was ruled by a Hindu maharaja who opted to join India rather than Pakistan. For Pakistani Muslims, the incorporation of Kashmir into India flew in the face of their country's founding principle, that Pakistan should be a homeland for the subcontinent's Muslims. Over the next 25 years, Pakistan and India went to war three times over the territory: in 1947, 1965, and 1971. In the 1947 conflict, Pakistani forces were able to win a large portion of the northwest of the state but were unable to take its economic and demographic heartland, the Srinagar Valley.[47]

These three wars in Kashmir involved conventional armies. The conflict took a more ominous turn in 1989, however, with the outbreak of a guerrilla insurgency. Today, some two dozen Muslim secessionist groups operate in the state. Their organization is irregular, with most groups operating independently of one another. Estimates put the strength of the guerrilla force in the thousands.[48] Officially the Indian government has a force of 125,000 in the state, but Pakistani officials estimate the total as more

Table 10.3. Muslim South Asia—Economy (2000–01)

	GDP ($bn)	GDP growth (%)	Inflation (%)	Unemployment (%)	Poverty (%)
Afghanistan	6.9	...	...	...	...
Bangladesh	48.9	5.9	2.4	2.5	35.6[a]
India	466.7	3.9	4.0	...	26.0[b]
Pakistan	71.3	4.4	4.4	5.9	34.0[b]

Sources: World Bank, *World Development Indicators 2002*, for GDP, GDP growth, and inflation; Asian Development Bank, *Key Indicators of Developing Asian and Pacific Countries* for unemployment and poverty. Notes: a) Data from 1996 survey; b) Data from 1999 survey.

Table 10.4. Muslim South Asia—Population (2000–01)

	Population (mil.)	Pop. growth (2000)	Muslim share of pop. (%)	Muslim pop. (mil.)	Refugee pop. (000s)
Afghanistan	26.6	2.6	99	26.3	1,226.1[a]
Bangladesh	131.1	1.7	88	115.4	22.2
India	1,015.9	1.8	12	120.0	169.8
Pakistan	138.1	2.4	97	134.0	2,199.4

Sources: World Bank, *World Development Indicators 2002*, for population and population growth; Department of State, *Country Background Notes*, for Muslim share of population; Muslim population is calculated; UNHCR, *2001 Population Statistics* for refugee population. Note: a) 3.8 million refugees (14 percent of the total population) had fled Afghanistan as of 2001.

than 500,000. Some 35,000 people have died in the Kashmir conflict since 1990, the majority of them non-combatants.

The first generation of Kashmiri secessionists was ethno-nationalist rather than Islamist in orientation. The Jammu-Kashmir Liberation Front was the most prominent group, but its influence has declined since the early 1990s in favor of paramilitaries of a more Islamist cast. Even with these changes, however, not all supporters of secession are radical or violent. A separatist alliance tolerated by the Indian authorities, the All-Party Hurriyat Conference, includes organizations committed to a peaceful resolution of the Kashmir question. On May 22, 2002, however, its leader, Abdul Ghani Lone, was gunned down as he left a public rally in Srinagar.[49] No group claimed responsibility.

The extreme Islamists in Kashmir endorse a more-or-less conventional *jihadi* philosophy. They speak of an international conspiracy against Islam, decry India as infidel, and advocate the use of violence against civilians. One of the most famous of these latter groups is the Lashkar-e-Toiba ("Army of the Pure"). The Lashkar was founded in 1993 and currently has several hundred members. Most are Pakistani, not Kashmiri, and many are veterans of the Afghan war and Pakistani *madrassas*. The Lashkar has declared its ultimate aim is nothing less than the restoration of Islamic rule over the whole of India. The militia has sent squadrons of fighters on suicide missions against Indian bases in Kashmir and has attempted to assassinate hardline Hindu nationalist leaders in other Indian states. In 2000 it carried out an armed assault on the Red Fort in Delhi.

Another militant grouping, the Jaish-e-Mohammad (JM), was founded in 2000. It has several hundred fighters active in both Pakistan and Kashmir and operated training camps in Afghanistan prior to the fall of the Taliban.[50] The JM's leader, Maulana Masood Azhar, was imprisoned by Indian officials in 1994 but was freed in December 1999 as part of the demands of hijackers of an Indian Airlines flight to Kabul.[51] Since September 11, 2001, Azhar's organization has escalated its use of terror. Indian officials charge that JM was responsible for a bloody suicide attack on the Kashmir state assembly in October 2001 in which 40 people died. Although no group claimed responsibility for the action, Indian officials also blame JM and Lashkar-e-Toiba for an attack on the Indian parliament on December 13, 2001 in which 14 people died. On May 14, 2002, three suicide fighters clad in Indian army uniforms attacked an army camp in southwestern Kashmir, killing 31 people, including many women and children.[52] Indian officials blamed this attack on Lashkar-e-Toiba and JM. Pakistani authorities responded by re-arresting the founder of Lashkar-e-Toiba, who had earlier been detained but then released.

The brazenness of these attacks has led to speculation that elements of the Pakistani intelligence services, unhappy with President Pervez Musharraf's new relationship with the United States, may have played a role in sponsoring the attacks. Pakistan's armed forces have long provided assistance to the Kashmir rebels. The secretive ISI, the same intelligence body that coordinated Pakistan's support for the Afghan *mujahidin* and the Taliban, has provided the lion's share of training, tactical support, and supplies. However the influence of the violence in Kashmir now extends well beyond Kashmir and Pakistan. Since the mid-1990s, the conflict has become a *cause célèbre* in radical Islamist circles around the world, on par with the Chechen struggle against Russia. Militants from Central Asia, Chechnya, and Xinjiang have fought alongside the Kashmir guerillas.

Indian authorities continue to lay blame for the guerrilla attacks squarely on Pakistan's ISI. The allegation has placed President Musharraf in a quandary. Musharraf has gambled his presidency on forging a new alliance with the United States, ending his country's sponsorship of the Taliban, and reintegrating Pakistan into the global economy. Kashmir is the Achilles' heel in this bold experiment. For Musharraf to renounce his country's commitment to Kashmiri self-determination would be viewed by the political establishment as a betrayal of Pakistan's founding ambitions. But however limited his ability or complex his motives, Musharraf appears to want to curtail his country's support for extremism. In late December he launched a crackdown on Islamist extremists in Pakistan proper, directing his efforts against Sunni and Shi'a militants (from the Sipah-e-Sahaba and Tehrik-e-Jaffria, respectively) long involved in sectarian violence.[53] In January 2002 Musharraf banned two groups identified by Indian authorities as responsible for bloody attacks in India. Anxious not to wound nationalist pride, however, the president has refused to hand over militants whom Indian authorities consider responsible for the October attack on Kashmir's assembly. Many of the militants detained in the December and January crackdowns have also been released.

Whatever Musharraf's precise intentions, Kashmiri hardliners continue to defy his authority and launch violent attacks on Indian civilians. Many observers speculate that these attacks are intended to push India and Pakistan to the brink of war and, in so doing, destroy two of the most important links in the U.S. campaign against terrorism. It remains unclear to what degree the Kashmiri militants are acting on their own or in cooperation with actors in Pakistani intelligence. As Indian authorities charge, Al Qaeda operatives may also now be operating in Kashmir. Whatever its precise nature, the conflict in Kashmir represents the single most serious challenge to efforts to moderate Islamist politics in South Asia.

Muslim Southeast Asia

There are more than 200 million Muslims in Southeast Asia. Although resident in all the region's countries, Muslims are most numerous in Indonesia, Malaysia, Singapore, Brunei, the southern Philippines, and southern Thailand. Muslim culture in this region has long defied conventional stereotypes. From the earliest of times, Muslim women played prominent roles in the marketplace. In modern times they have moved with ease into higher education and the professions. In the 1960s and 1970s, Southeast Asian Muslims looked to the United States with a spirit of cooperation and friendship, supporting the American effort to contain communism. In the 1980s and 1990s, Muslim political leaders in Malaysia and Indonesia were at the forefront of those seeking to promote the integration of national businesses into the global economy. In the 1990s, Muslim leaders like Anwar Ibrahim of Malaysia and Abdurrahman Wahid of Indonesia received international acclaim for their efforts to promote pluralism, tolerance, and civil society. Southeast Asia has long seemed an almost textbook example of Muslim societies evolving toward democracy, prosperity, and tolerance.

Unfortunately, the situation in Muslim Southeast Asia was always more complicated than these hopeful observations imply, and it has become more

Table 10.5. Muslim Southeast Asia—Economy (2000–01)

	GDP ($ bn)	GDP growth (%)	Inflation (%)	Unemployment (%)	Poverty (%)
Brunei	5.7ª	1.0ª	...	...	...
Indonesia	209.1	4.8	3.7	6.1	27.1ᵇ
Malaysia	111.6	8.3	1.5	3.0	8.0
Philippines	88.2	4.0	4.4	10.1	39.0
Singapore	113.4	9.9	1.4	4.4	...
Thailand	170.3	4.3	1.6	2.4	15.9

Sources: World Bank, *World Development Indicators 2002*, for GDP, inflation, and unemployment; World Bank, *Country Notes* and Asian Development Bank, *Asian Development Outlook 2002* for poverty. Notes: a) Data for 1998; b) Data from 1999 survey.

so in recent years. Although mainstream groupings like Indonesia's Nahdlatul Ulama and Muhammadiyah (the first and second largest Muslim social organizations in the world, respectively) have long been forces for moderation, Indonesia has also always had a radical fringe. The 1950s saw rebellions aimed at establishing an Islamic state. Calls for jihad were also skillfully exploited by the leadership of the armed forces during 1965 and 1966 in an effort to mobilize Muslims against the Communist Party.[54]

Thailand

Since the 1960s, Thailand's three southern provinces (Pattani, Yala, and Narathiwat) have been plagued by low-intensity separatist violence. The provinces are 80 percent Malay Muslim, having been brought under Thai suzerainty only at the end of the eighteenth century. As the Thai government intensified its efforts at nation-building in the 1930s, it identified Thai nationalism with Buddhism and took measures to suppress Islam in the south. These efforts sparked widespread discontent and, in the 1960s, gave rise to a separatist movement. Today there are 20 separatist organizations, the most prominent of which are the National Revolutionary Front (BRN), the Pattani United Liberation Organization (PULO), and the New PULO.[55]

Founded in 1960, the BRN is the oldest of the secessionist organizations. Although established by Malay Muslims, the BRN is secular-socialist in orientation. After the Islamic resurgence of the 1970s and 1980s, the BRN's popularity declined, while that of Islamist groupings like PULO increased. The Islamist groups also tend to be more militant than their nationalist counterparts. Armed units associated with PULO have been involved in attacks on government offices, schools, Buddhist temples, and other symbols of Thai culture.[56] PULO escalated its armed campaign in the 1990s. It also became more active internationally, strengthening its ties to

Table 10.6. Muslim Southeast Asia—Population (2000–01)

	Population (mil.)	Pop. growth rate (%)	Muslim share of pop. (%)	Muslim pop. (mil.)	Refugee pop. (000s)
Brunei	0.3	2.4	67	0.2	...
Indonesia	210.4	1.6	87	183.0	74.4
Malaysia	23.3	2.4	53	12.3	50.7
Philippines	75.6	1.9	5	3.8	2.2
Singapore	4.0	1.7	16	0.6	neg.
Thailand	60.7	0.8	4	2.4	111.1

Sources: World Bank, *World Development Indicators 2002*, for population and population growth; *Department of State, Country Background Notes*, for Muslim share of population; Muslim population is calculated; UNHCR, *2001 Population Statistics* for refugee population.

extremists in the Middle East and South Asia. Thai authorities claim that in 1994 PULO played a key role in an attempted bombing of the Israeli embassy in Bangkok. The authorities claimed the effort had been organized by Hezbollah with the help of Iranian intelligence.[57]

Despite differences of leadership and ideology, PULO began to coordinate its attacks with the New PULO after 1997. Responding to appeals from Thai authorities, Prime Minister Mahathir Mohamad of Malaysia cracked down on militants' camps in northern Malaysia shortly thereafter. Attacks on Thai institutions continued nonetheless, though on a reduced scale. There was no notable escalation in violence after September 11. Individuals claiming to be linked to PULO did call for Muslims to unite against the U.S.-led campaign. For the time being, however, the situation in southern Thailand appears to have settled into a pattern of low-intensity sabotage and personal violence.

Philippines

Unlike southern Thailand, the situation among Muslims in the southern Philippines has become significantly more unsettled since September 11. Approximately six percent of the Philippine population is Muslim, with most of it concentrated in the south on the large island of Mindanao. Although the Spanish never obtained any more than a foothold in this region, the Muslim south was included in the 1898 transfer of sovereignty from Spain to the United States at the end of the Spanish-American War. It took 15 years and several thousand Muslim lives for American forces to pacify the territory.[58] In the aftermath of the military campaign, the United States encouraged immigration by Christian Filipinos to Mindanao. It was only in the 1960s and 1970s, however, that the Christian immigration grew to such proportions that it altered the island's ethnic and religious balance (by 1975,

60 percent of the population on once-Muslim Mindanao was Christian). These and other developments led to the formation in 1971 of the Moro National Liberation Front (MNLF).

From the beginning, the MNLF combined military operations with a relatively pragmatic attitude toward negotiations with the government. During the 1970s, the organization also demonstrated diplomatic skill, winning the recognition of the Organization of the Islamic Conference and securing steady increases in aid from the Middle East. Libya has been an especially generous donor, but Saudi and Pakistani foundations have also provided resources. In the early years, the Libyans helped arrange arms purchases. The Saudis have preferred to focus their aid on religious education (*da'wah*), using their funds to bolster groups like the Jamiat-ul Al Islamic Tabligh, a conservative organization dedicated to combating western influence.[59]

Even in its early years, the MNLF held talks with the Philippine authorities, and in September 1996 it signed an agreement (the Davao Consensus) with the government. In exchange for the establishment of a limited autonomous Muslim enclave in the south of Mindanao, the MNLF agreed to cease hostilities and integrate its forces into the Philippine security forces. The accord was rejected by two groups that had earlier split from the MNLF, the Moro Islamic Liberation Front (MILF) and the Abu Sayyaf group. These groups are more radically Islamist than the MNLF and include in their ranks veterans from the Afghan war. Both also call for the establishment of an Islamic state in which *shari'at* is fully implemented.

With some 11,000 armed supporters, the MILF is the larger of these two hardline groups. Although it has launched regular attacks on government institutions, the MILF has avoided targeting civilians. In 1997, however, Philippine authorities claim to have uncovered a secret MILF cell consisting of Pakistani and Saudi instructors who were training MILF cadres in assassination and suicide bombing techniques. The allegations, however, have never been confirmed.[60] The MILF did call for jihad against the United States in December 1998 after U.S. attacks on Baghdad and the Sudan. However, during this same period the organization's leadership continued to engage in behind-the-scenes negotiations with Philippine authorities. The two sides reached a tentative accord in November 1997, although fighting broke out again in 1998. Nonetheless, the MILF responded cautiously to the events of September 2001, taking care to distance itself from Abu Sayyaf.

The Abu Sayyaf group was formed in 1993 by militants who had fought in Afghanistan during the 1980s after being recruited by Muhammad Jamal Khalifa, Osama bin Laden's brother-in-law.[61] The Abu Sayyaf group calls for the establishment of a fully independent Islamic state and the expulsion of all Christians from Muslim territories in the southern Philippines. The organization's fighting strength is thought to have peaked in early 2001 at 1,200 fighters, up from just 200 in the mid-1990s, although it has plummeted since the arrival of U.S. military advisors in the Philippines. The Abu Sayyaf group has a tightly organized cell structure and a secretive leadership. It also regularly engages in acts of robbery, extortion, kidnapping, and beheading. Its successes during 2000 and 2001 allowed it to double the number of its fighters and upgrade their armaments. However, its reputation for criminal adventurism has irritated other Muslim rebels. A few weeks after the September 11 attacks, the MNLF agreed to cooperate with Philippine authorities in hunting down Abu Sayyaf operatives.

The Abu Sayyaf group has long had at least informal ties to Al Qaeda operatives. Searches of a Manila apartment rented to Ramzi Ahmed Yousef, the man convicted of the 1993 World Trade Center bombing in New York, revealed details of a planned joint operation between the Abu Sayyaf and Yousef scheduled for 1994 or 1995. The operation's objectives included plans to assassinate the Pope during his visit to the Philippines in 1995, launch suicide assaults on the FBI and CIA headquarters in the United States, and blow up 11 American passenger jets over the Pacific. The Abu Sayyaf was linked to the actual bombing of a Philippine Airlines jet in 1994, an act thought to have been a trial run for the planned 1995 hijackings.

Following the ouster of President Joseph Estrada from the Philippine presidency in early 2001, President Gloria Macapagal-Arroyo increased the government's efforts to extend the peace deal negotiated with the MNLF to the MILF. The president's efforts have not yet proven successful, but they do appear to have isolated the Abu Sayyaf group from other rebel groupings. Abu Sayyaf fighters have responded by intensifying their attacks on civilians in the south and unleashing a campaign of bombing in the Christian north. In May 2001, Abu Sayyaf militants abducted hostages from a resort on Palawan island and Lamitan, and in early August the fighters launched an attack on a Christian village.

At the end of January 2002, the United States initiated its first direct military intervention outside Afghanistan when it began joint anti-terror exercises with the Philippine military.[62] The operation involved 600 U.S. and 7,000 Philippines special forces. Its stated aim was to free U.S. and Philippine hostages and neutralize the Abu Sayyaf. Despite Philippine nationalists' reservations about the U.S. presence on Philippine soil, the public generally welcomed the U.S. assistance. A long-term U.S. presence, however, would likely increase these nationalist concerns. In spite of the campaign, however, the Abu Sayyaf has been able to carry out numerous acts of violence, including a bombing in April 2002 that killed 15 civilians. In contrast to the rapid advances of U.S. and Northern Alliance forces in Afghanistan, the campaign in the Philippines is moving slowly.

Indonesia

The activities of the Abu Sayyaf have raised questions about the extent to which there might be links between extremists in the southern Philippines and Indonesia. Although a few groups may have had contacts, there are great differences between them. After the collapse of the Suharto regime in May 1998, Indonesia saw a proliferation of hundreds of locally-based Islamist organizations.[63] However, a few groups, like the Laskar Jihad and the Islamic Defenders Front (Front Pembela Islam), were not purely parochial creations, but were organized by radical Islamists with secret ties to an Islamist faction in the armed forces. Since the mid-1990s, a small number of Indonesian military officers have sponsored Islamist paramilitaries to defend their business interests, attack members of the democracy movement and, more recently, contain regional unrest. Although its background is complex, the religious violence in the troubled provinces of Maluku and North Maluku in eastern Indonesia, where some 8,000 people have died in fighting between Christians and Muslims since 1999, has been exacerbated by this sponsorship of *jihadi* paramilitaries. (It should be noted that other security units have provided support to the Christian side.[64])

As the Maluku example illustrates, the armed forces are deeply divided on the question of Islam. Western intelligence reports and intra-service skirmishes suggest that many commanders disapprove of the support provided by some officers for Islamist paramilitaries. The Islamist paramilitaries also vary in their attitude toward the armed forces. Although the Laskar Jihad and Islamic Defenders' Front have close ties to certain military commanders, another group, the Majelis Mujahidin Indonesia (MMI—Indonesian Council of Jihad Fighters), has long had a hostile relationship with the army command. Founded in August 2000 with the aim of fighting for the implementation of Islamic law, the MMI includes among its senior leadership figures identified decades earlier with a Muslim rebel group called the Darul Islam.[65]

The MMI's spiritual leader, Abu Bakar Ba'asyir, previously had ties to the Darul Islam. Ba'asyir was sentenced to prison in the late 1970s for his opposition to Suharto. When, in the mid-1990s, some hardline Islamists reconciled with Suharto and backed his repression of the democracy movement (which they portrayed as Christian-secularist conspiracies to weaken Muslim Indonesia), Ba'asyir and his associates kept their distance. This legacy explains why Ba'asyir and the MMI have frosty ties with the armed forces.[66] In November 2001, Malaysian and Philippine authorities alleged that Ba'asyir was the leader of a pan-Southeast Asian terror organization with ties to Al Qaeda known as the Jemaah Islamiyah, but Indonesian authorities refused to arrest Ba'asyir, claiming that the evidence was weak.

Unlike the MMI, the Laskar Jihad has long enjoyed the patronage of a small but important faction in the armed forces.[67] The Laskar Jihad grew out of a conservative religious movement founded in the early 1990s by a young Arab Indonesian, Jafar Umar Thalib. Thalib studied in Saudi Arabia during 1986 and, under the auspices of the Saudi-sponsored Muslim World League, fought briefly in Afghanistan in 1988. He admits having met with Osama bin Laden while in Afghanistan, but insists (credibly) that he worked with a *mujahidin* faction closer to the Saudis than to bin Laden. In interviews, Thalib has admitted having uninvited contacts with Al Qaeda representatives as recently as May 2001. Thalib denies reports, however, that Al Qaeda fighters have assisted his forces in Maluku. In late September 2001, he also denied the allegation of a militant from a rival Islamist organization that bin Laden had given Thalib $240,000.

Nonetheless, in November 2001, western journalists traveling in Sulawesi reported seeing Afghan and Arab fighters, and on December 12, 2001, Indonesia's intelligence chief, Lieutenant General Abdullah Hendropriyono, confirmed these reports, commenting that Al Qaeda had established a training camp in Indonesia and was assisting jihad fighters in Maluku and central Sulawesi. The next day Minister of Defense Matori Abdul Djalil declared that he had "full confidence" in the validity of Hendropriyono's comments. Court documents provided by Spanish authorities after the arrest of Al Qaeda agents in Spain during November 2001 also spoke of an Islamist training camp in eastern Indonesia.[68] Indonesian observers expressed doubts about the quality of this evidence, however, and speculated that the intelligence chief may have made his charges in an effort to improve the military's relations with the United States, which have been strained since the early 1990s. With the exception of Matori, no cabinet officials backed Hendropriyono's charges, and three days later, faced with a barrage of criticism, Hendropriyono retracted his statement. In a widely publicized comment, he claimed he had been "misunderstood," and insisted he had never meant to say Al Qaeda had cells in Indonesia or ties to the Laskar Jihad.[69]

Although his lieutenants expressed enthusiasm for bin Laden in several interviews they gave in 2000, since September 11, Thalib has gone to great lengths to condemn the radical leader. Tellingly, however, Thalib did not condemn bin Laden because of the mass killing in the United States, but because of bin Laden's opposition to the government of Saudi Arabia.

Whatever his Middle Eastern contacts, there are sound domestic reasons for Thalib to keep his distance from Al Qaeda. The Laskar Jihad has been dependent on domestic backing from civilians linked to the former Suharto regime since its establishment in early 2000. These individuals have assisted the organization's military campaign. The influence of Suharto holdovers continues to complicate efforts to contain Islamist radicalism in Indonesia. Complicating matters further, President Megawati leads a fractious coalition government, and at the moment appears unable to move decisively. Vice President Hamzah Haz, moreover, has defied her and expressed sympathy for the Laskar Jihad.

The reluctance of Indonesian authorities to take action has been seen by some observers as proof that some in the government and military want to protect Muslim extremists. However, there has never been more than a small faction in the armed forces who support extremism of this sort. The greater obstacle to Indonesian cooperation with the U.S. campaign is the crisis of governance afflicting Indonesian society as a whole and the inability of any single faction in government to act decisively. Complicating the issue further is the military's resentment of U.S. criticism over its actions in East Timor and Aceh.

In early 2002, the Bush administration hinted that it was interested in renewing dialogue with the Indonesian armed forces. Shortly after this announcement, Indonesian authorities began to rein in Laskar Jihad activities in Maluku province. In early May, as U.S.-Indonesian relations thawed, the police arrested the leader of the Laskar Jihad after he gave a inflammatory speech opposing government efforts to bring peace to the troubled Malukus. Many analysts have applauded these actions as first steps toward halting the paramilitarist violence that plagues Indonesia. However, other observers warn bluntly that the warming of relations should not be presented to the Indonesian authorities as "rewarding the TNI [Indonesian armed forces] for progress in human rights accountability when there has been none."[70]

Malaysia

If Indonesian authorities have reacted hesitantly to the U.S.-led campaign against terrorism, Prime Minister Mahathir Mohamad of Malaysia has put his government squarely behind the effort. He has done so even while emphasizing that, on questions like the Israel-Palestine conflict, he continues to take exception to U.S. policy. Historically, mainstream Muslims in Malaysia have been more theologically conservative in their views than their counterparts in Indonesia. At the same time, however, Malaysia has seen little of the paramilitary violence that has plagued Indonesia. Even conservative Muslims in Malaysia show a willingness to play by the rules of constitutional politics. The main opposition party, the Pan-Malaysian Islamic Party (PAS), has long advocated Malaysia's transformation into an Islamic state, but it has been content to pursue this goal through the ballot box.[71] The party has governed the northern state of Kelantan for many years and has controlled the state government in neighboring Trengganu since 1999. In both states PAS has acquired a reputation for honest government, even while being deeply conservative in its interpretation of Islamic law. PAS's campaign to implement Islamic law at the state level has included advocating severe penalties for crimes of theft and adultery, but its efforts in this regard have been blocked by federal authorities.

With the arrest of Deputy Prime Minister Anwar Ibrahim in 1998 and his subsequent sentencing to 15 years in prison on sodomy and corruption charges, relations between Washington and Kuala Lumpur cooled. Mahathir's allegation the previous year that George Soros and the "Jews" may have had a role in the currency crisis savaging the Malaysian economy at that time had already contributed to U.S. displeasure. But whatever his reputation in international dialogue or the handling of dissidents, on matters of Islam Mahathir has long been known as a reform-minded modernizer. He has supported Muslim women's calls for equal rights and, while backing the Palestinian cause, has been a fierce critic of Islamist violence.

The post-September 11 campaign against terrorism offered the United States and Malaysia an opportunity to find new grounds for agreement on questions of Islam and the West. While continuing to emphasize his differences with U.S. policies in the Middle East, Mahathir made a series of bold speeches in late 2001 and early 2002 in which he appealed to Muslims around the world to condemn terrorism and take measures to modernize their societies.[72] His comments stood in stark contrast to those of the leaders of PAS. In late September 2001, as the United States prepared to take action against the Taliban, PAS spokespersons voiced their support for the Taliban regime and warned that if Washington attacked Afghanistan, Muslims everywhere would be obliged to wage jihad against the United States.

In the months following September 11, the Malaysian authorities arrested some 60 individuals on charges that they were associated with groups plotting to attack western targets. PAS officials dismissed the arrests as part of a general crackdown on the opposition.[73] However, the Malaysian charges were given a measure of credibility in December 2001, when Singaporean authorities arrested 14 Singaporeans and one Malaysian on grounds that they were plotting to attack western embassies and businesses in Singapore.[74]

Muslim politics in Southeast Asia is the most varied in all of Muslim Asia. On one hand, this region boasts some of the most outspoken moderate Muslim leaders, as well as the largest and best organized moderate organizations. Since September 11, however, it has also seen a serious escalation in radical Islamist agitation, some of it sponsored by groups suspected of having ties to Al Qaeda, through networks like the Jemaah Islamiyah. The complex balance of forces in the region will require an equally nuanced policy response.

Prospects and Policy

Three conclusions stand out from this survey of Muslim politics in Asia. The first is that in the late 1980s and throughout the 1990s, a new and more militant form of transnational Islam succeeded in establishing a loose network in parts of Asia. Relative to the mainstream Muslim community, the network is small, but it is capable of exercising an influence disproportionate to its representation in society. Although it may have the backing of some international funders, most of the network is not a centrally directed Islamist Internationale. Instead, it is a loosely structured array of affinity groups, among which only a few coordinate activities. Although some groups (the Islamic Movement of Uzbekistan, Abu Sayyaf in the Philippines, and Kashmir's Jaish-e-Muhammad, among others) have received support from Al Qaeda, most have not. Detailed information is lacking, but some groups have certainly received assistance from private foundations in Saudi Arabia and the Persian Gulf. However, this assistance has not led to the creation of a coordinated movement in any technical sense of this term. As with the Majelis Mujahidin and Laskar Jihad in Indonesia, groups that share certain general ideological values often become rivals.

A second point follows from this first and touches on the question of the radicals' future. Although surveys and ethnographic studies indicate that they represent but a small portion of the Muslim population, the radicals are likely to remain a destabilizing presence in Asian Muslim politics for some time to come. The reason for this has to do not with their numbers, but with the circumstances out of which they emerged. The radical Islamists are not merely an update of a traditional Muslim politics, and although they may claim that they model their actions on the life of the Prophet, they represent a politics as new to the Muslim world as fascism and Marxism-Leninism were to the modern West.

Sociologically speaking, the radicals originate at the confluence of two great currents of our age, the ethno-religious revival that occurred at the end of the twentieth century and the political and cultural globalization of the new millennium. The ethno-religious revival is not peculiar to the Muslim world, but has affected large portions of Asia, Africa, and the Americas. Its political impact has been greatest, however, where economic decline has combined with regime crises to place received ideas of nation and tradition in question. The Muslim world's revival occurred against the backdrop of the decline of Marxism (once popular in Muslim Asia) and the crisis of secular nationalism. Leaving aside backward countries like Afghanistan, the resurgence also occurred in a context of urbanization, mass education, and pluralization of religious authority.

Countries like Indonesia, Malaysia, the Philippines, and India saw the emergence of a moderate Islam that stressed the compatibility of the religion with modern pluralism and tolerance. A key theme stressed by this moderate Islam is the need to contextualize Islamic ideals by linking their emphasis on justice and equality to modern constitutional structures.[75] However, another branch of the Islamic resurgence, a radically conservative one, is anything but democratic. Rather than affirming the need to contextualize and renew, the radicals insist that Islam's meanings are the same for all ages. The radicals' effort to cloak themselves in the mantle of tradition, of course, ignores that, in their preoccupation with power and their reliance on Leninist models of organization, they are a thoroughly modern creation.

Cultural and economic globalization has been the second major influence on the rise of radical Islamism, and it is this influence more than any other that makes it likely that the radicals will be around for some years to come. With its pilgrimage sites, its great classical centers of religious learning, and its extensive involvement in international trade, historical Islam was from its beginnings transnational or globalizing. However, the globalization with which the new radicals are associated is of a different stripe than the old. In addition to its heightened mobility of people and goods, the new globalization is able to move ideas, images, and capital around the world faster than ever before. This accelerated circulation allows for the creation of specialized and "deterritorialized" communities. These are groups of people who are able to share ideas and resources even though they do not occupy contiguous territory. Far more than in the past, people today can create virtual communities that share a world-view without having physical proximity. Technologies like the Internet lower communication costs and allow a radical segmentation in the marketplace of Muslim ideas.

For ideas to have a practical impact, however, virtual connections must at some point be translated into concrete actions, organization, and power. Here too, the new radicals have been able to compensate for their disadvantage in numbers by taking advantage of the easy flow of people, ideas, and capital. The violence of September 11 required only inexpensive hardware and a small number of personnel. As long as radical groups are able to recruit a few true-believers and organize a strike force, this type of terrorism is, unfortunately, likely to continue. If this is true, the key policy question then becomes, "How great will the extremists' influence be?"

The ability to constitute a terror network is different, of course, from building a mass movement or controlling an entire country. The likelihood of a full-blown insurgency like that which brought the Taliban to power in Afghanistan appears remote in most of Muslim Asia. For the moment, even the Central Asian states are not experiencing economic depression, social dislocation, and destruction of the moderate center on a scale sufficient to create a full-scale revolution. If such a country-wide insurgency seems unlikely, there are nonetheless pockets in Muslim Asia where ethno-religious tensions have the potential for chronic instability. Xinjiang in China is one such locale. The conflict in this territory was primarily ethno-nationalist in origin, and today it still has less to do with radical Islamism than with the political and demographic displacement of the Uighurs indigenous to the region. Were Chinese authorities willing to extend autonomy and freedoms to the much marginalized Uighurs, this conflict could be easily contained, although it is likely to be dealt with on less civil terms.

The southern Philippines is another region where the political and demographic marginalization of indigenous Muslims has given rise to broad dissatisfaction and a smaller radical fringe. The Abu Sayyaf group's strange mixture of brutality and criminality has ensured that mainstream Muslim groupings, even rebel ones, have taken pains to distance themselves from this terrorist organization. Further complications include the presence of U.S. advisors, which will test Philippine nationalists' patience, and the failure of the Philippine government to fulfill all the terms of the earlier agreement with the MNLF. Ethno-religious tensions will remain a chronic feature of political life in the southern Philippines, but with a sustained government commitment to development and political autonomy in the Muslim south, this conflict may yet be resolved.

No country illustrates better the ability of small groups of radical Islamists to exercise an influence disproportionate with their numbers than Indonesia. Although tiny compared to moderate organizations like the Muhammadiyah and Nahdlatul Ulama, the radical extreme has set many of the terms of post-Suharto politics. The irony is that, in the 1990s, Indonesia developed the largest movement for a moderate Islam in the world. Rather than nurturing these civil Islamic seedlings, the Suharto regime tried to rip them out. However, to blame everything on Suharto or the pro-Islamist military would be to ignore the enormity of the crisis of governance and national identity Indonesia is experiencing. Rebuilding governance and civil society after the depredations of authoritarian rule will require that the armed forces agree to play a more restrained role in society than they did under Suharto. The military must do so if it is to develop the professionalism, discipline, and restraint this fractious country requires. If, somehow, this can be done, Indonesia's moderate majority may yet be able to renew its trek toward civil peace and democracy. As yet, however, it is unclear whether the effort to get the military on board the international campaign against terrorism will help or hinder this transition.

In Malaysia, a theologically conservative but politically unradical Islam linked to the opposition PAS party has long had the support of one-fifth to one-quarter of the population. Support for PAS increased after Mahathir Mohamad's heavy-handed treatment of his popular former deputy, Anwar Ibrahim, in 1998–99. However, in the fall of 2001, PAS seriously misperceived public opinion and called for jihad against the United States. The party then compounded its error by pressing forward with its campaign for the implementation of Islamic law. It simultaneously lashed out against liberal Muslims, such as the feminist Muslim organization Sisters in Islam. Mahathir's ruling United Malays National Organization (UMNO) has benefited from these actions. Over the long term, other moderate opposition groupings like the Justice Party may benefit as well. The most pressing question for Malaysian politics will be whether UMNO can finesse the post-Mahathir transition and reach some kind of reconciliation with the supporters of Anwar Ibrahim. However uncertain Malaysia's democratic transition, the long-term prospects for moderate Islam look good.

One territory in Muslim Asia stands alone in the severity of the threat to itself and the world: Kashmir. This state's majority Muslim population appears alienated from the Indian authorities who nominally control the state. Their disaffection has been compounded by the heavy-handedness of army units in dealing with Muslim civilians. In an all too familiar cycle of violence, however, the patience of the Indian armed forces has worn thin in the face of terrorist attacks. The situation has been further complicated by the role of the Pakistani intelligence services in sponsoring the rebels. The conflict in Kashmir shows a combustible mix of nuclear arms, terrorism, ethno-religious hatred, and international conflict. The United States' increased involvement in South Asia has offered the best hope in years for containing this incendiary conflict, although this is still a distant hope, one that will require enormous skill on the part of regional leaders and the major western powers if the threat of violence is to diminish.

Finally, if there is a general conclusion to be drawn from this survey, it is that U.S. policymakers should not allow the threat posed by Al Qaeda and Muslim terrorism to obscure the diversity and promise of Muslim Asia.

Terrorist violence demands vigorous action. Over the long run, however, the evolution of Muslim politics will depend upon the ability of local leaders and western nations to respond to mainstream Muslims' hopes for economic improvement and political participation. However much the Islamic resurgence of the 1980s and 1990s might look uniform from the outside, it was not. It gave rise to a fierce debate within Muslim society about the proper meanings of Islam and the proper forms for Islamic politics.

Radical Islamists are best able to move from the fringe to the center where there is a crisis of economy and legitimacy on a scale like that provoked by the Soviet invasion of Afghanistan, the conflict in Kashmir, the Israeli occupation of southern Lebanon, or fighting between Muslims and Christians in Indonesia's Maluku province. In less troubled settings, radical Islamists have difficulty achieving any more than a small following. It is this inability to mobilize followers using conventional methods that tempts many radicals to resort to violence. Moderate Muslims are the most common victims of these attacks, a fact that again should figure in western policymakers' reflections on what can be done to woo the majority.

The recent history of Muslim extremism in Asia illustrates how and why radicals inspire resentment among mainstream Muslims. The radicals are quick to accuse fellow Muslims of apostasy, a charge that carries a clear threat of violence. Most Muslims find the radicals' insistence on the exclusion of women from higher education and public life offensive. They chafe at the radicals' restrictions on popular entertainment. Afghanistan under the Taliban illustrated how ordinary Muslims even in a backward society resent restrictions on women, education, and entertainment. And although control of the state still lies in the hands of hardliners, Iran's recent elections also show how education, the desire for economic improvement, and global communications can work to deepen public support for more moderate Muslim politics.

The keys to stability in the Muslim world, then, are not all that different from those in the early twentieth century West: education, balanced development, participatory governance, and civil peace. The resolution of the Israel-Palestine conflict clearly is vital. But we should not allow that conflict to blind us to the broader currents of the Muslim world. We have seen in Afghanistan and Pakistan that, in times of state failure, radical Islamists turn religious schools into platforms for extremism. But these troubled examples must be seen in light of an even more pervasive cultural current. In most countries, the Muslim public's aspiration to economic and educational progress is forcing traditional schools to implement new programs of career training and education for women. Education remains an area where western aid can exercise a powerfully positive influence.

There is indeed a clash of cultures taking place in our world, but it is first of all a struggle among Muslims for the soul of Islam. It is only secondarily a conflict between radical Islamists and the West. The radicals' appeals run contrary to ordinary Muslims' thirst for economic improvement, educational enlightenment, and freedom from religious bullies. The hopes and dreams of the moderate majority are not so different from those of religious people in the West. The majority's desire for betterment, their anger at being labeled bad Muslims, and the utter unrealism of the radicals' plans for government and society, all present policy opportunities for western countries willing and able to support Muslim moderation.

Endnotes

1   See Ahmed Rashid, *Taliban: Militant Islam, Oil, and Fundamentalism in Central Asia*, New Haven: Yale University Press, 2000, pp. 128–40.

2   See Olivier Roy, *The New Central Asia: The Creation of Nations*, New York: New York University Press, 2000, pp. 143–60; and Roald Sagdeev and Susan Eisenhower, eds., *Islam and Central Asia: An Enduring Legacy or an Evolving Threat?* Washington, DC: Center for Political and Strategic Studies, 2000.

3   For an informed analysis of these concerns from the perspective of Muslim Southeast Asia, see Barry Desker and Kumar Ramakrishna, "Forging an Indirect Strategy in Southeast Asia," *The Washington Quarterly*, vol. 25, no. 2 (Spring 2002), pp. 17–45.

4   On the early diffusion and contemporary diversity of Asian Islam, see Bruce R. Lawrence, "The Eastward Journey of Muslim Kingship: Islam in South and Southeast Asia," and Dru C. Gladney, "Central Asia and China: Transnationalization, Islamization, and Ethnicization," in John L. Esposito, ed., *The Oxford History of Islam*, Oxford: Oxford University Press, 1999, pp. 395–431 and pp. 433–73, respectively.

5   See Patricia Crone, "The Rise of Islam in the World," in Francis Robinson, ed., *The Cambridge Illustrated History of the Islamic World*, Cambridge: Cambridge University Press, 1996, pp. 2–31.

6   On the role of Arab scholars in the Islamic revival in late nineteenth century Southeast Asia, see William R. Roff, *The Origins of Malay Nationalism*, Second Edition, Kuala Lumpur: Oxford University Press, 1994 (orig., 1967).

7   M.B. Hooker, "Introduction: The Translation of Islam into Southeast Asia," in M.B. Hooker, ed., *Islam in South-East Asia*, Leiden: E.J. Brill, 1983, pp. 1–22.

8   Peter van der Veer, *Religious Nationalism*, Berkeley: University of California Press, 1994, pp. 33–53; see also Asim Roy, *The Islamic Syncretistic Tradition in Bengal*, Princeton: Princeton University Press, 1983.

9   On Islam in the early modern history of Southeast Asia, see Anthony Reid, *Southeast Asia in the Age of Commerce, 1460–1680*, vol. 2, New Haven: Yale University Press, 1993, pp. 132–201.

10   Shi'ism was made the state religion of the Persian Safavid empire in 1500; the only Muslim state to have adopted Shi'ism in this way. Although there were

Persian-speaking communities across Central Asia, local rulers did not adopt Shi'ism, and the Safavids' shift to Shi'ism worked to diminish Persian influence in Central Asia while heightening Turkic. Today the only Persian-speaking majority in Central Asia are the Kyrgyz of Kyrgyzstan. Tensions between the Sunni majority and the Shi'i minority in Central Asia have continued to this day, limiting the spread of Iranian political ideas in Central Asia after the collapse of the Soviet Union.

[11] For an examination of the reform movement in Southeast Asia, see Roff, *The Origins of Malay Nationalism*; for the Indian subcontinent, see Barbara D. Metcalf, *Islamic Revival in British India: Deoband, 1860–1900*, Princeton: Princeton University Press, 1982.

[12] This discussion draws on, among other studies, Dale F. Eickelman and James Piscatori, *Muslim Politics*, Princeton: Princeton University Press, 1996; and Olivier Roy, *The Failure of Political Islam*, translated by Carol Volk, Cambridge, Mass.: Harvard University Press, 1994.

[13] Ahmed Rashid, *Jihad: The Rise of Militant Islam in Central Asia*, New Haven: Yale University Press, 2002, pp. 43–44.

[14] For Indonesia, see Robert W. Hefner, *Civil Islam: Muslims and Democratization in Indonesia*, Princeton: Princeton University Press, 2000.

[15] After the 1979 Islamic Revolution, Iranian authorities also provided direct assistance to Muslim organizations, giving the single largest share of their aid to Shi'a groups in Lebanon. In Muslim Asia, where the great majority of Muslims are Sunni, the Iranians found it difficult to work directly with societal groups in Asia, many of whom view Shi'ism as heretical. Rather than risk the ire of local religious leaders, the Iranians opted to channel their assistance through government-to-government ties. However, the burden of the Iran-Iraq war was such that the volume of Iranian aid to Muslim Asia remained small. Iran was more influential as an example to radical Muslim youths, many of whom saw the 1979 revolution as proof that Islam offered a third way between the perceived evils of western capitalism and a now discredited Marxist socialism. On Iranian efforts in post-Soviet Central Asia, see Shireen T. Hunter, "Iran, Central Asia and the Opening of the Islamic Iron Curtain," in Sagdeev and Eisenhower, *Islam and Central Asia*, pp. 171–91.

[16] On the balance between the political and non-political in the resurgence in Central Asia, see the studies in Jo-Ann Gross, ed., *Muslims in Central Asia: Expressions of Identity and Change*, Durham: Duke University Press, 1992. For a comparison from Southeast Asia, see Robert W. Hefner and Patricia Horvatich, eds., *Islam in an Era of Nation-States: Politics and Religious Renewal in Muslim Southeast Asia*, Honolulu: University of Hawaii Press, 1997.

[17] See Robert W. Hefner, ed., *The Politics of Multiculturalism: Pluralism and Citizenship in Malaysia, Singapore, and Indonesia*, Honolulu: University of Hawaii Press, 2002.

[18] For a sample of these democratic views, see John L. Esposito and John O. Voll, *Makers of Contemporary Islam*, Oxford: Oxford University Press, 2001; and Charles Kurzman, ed., *Liberal Islam: A Sourcebook*, Oxford: Oxford University Press, 1998.

[19] Larry P. Goodson, *Afghanistan's Endless War: State Failure, Regional Poli-*

tics, and the Rise of the Taliban, Seattle: University of Washington Press, 2001, p. 92.

[20] Goodson, *Afghanistan's Endless War*, p. 92.

[21] Rashid, *Taliban*, p. 82.

[22] David B. Edwards examines the modern history of this inclusive Islam, and the reasons for its demise in *Before Taliban: Genealogies of the Afghan Jihad*, Berkeley: University of California Press, 2002.

[23] Goodson, *Afghanistan's Endless War*, p. 97.

[24] See Paul Blustein, "In Pakistan's Squalor, Cradles of Terrorism," *The Washington Post*, March 14, 2002; and Rashid, *Taliban*, pp. 87–94.

[25] See Council of Foreign Relations, "Terrorism: Q & A—Harakat ul-Mujahedeen, Lashkar-e-Taiba, Jaish-e-Muhammad," May 2002, at <www.terrorism answers.com/groups/harakat.html>.

[26] An Iranian-style popular revolution is even less likely, since no Asian Muslim country has an Islamist movement even vaguely comparable to that of Iran at the end of the Pahlavi dynasty. Of greater concern is the possibility of a coup followed by a conservative military alliance with the radical Islamist fringe, as occurred in Pakistan under the rule of General Muhammad Zia ul-Haq.

[27] Kazakhstan's and Kyrgyzstan's populations are 35 and 22 percent Russian, respectively. Kazakhstan also has significant German (five percent) and Ukrainian (five percent) minorities, such that Muslims barely comprise a majority. Turkmenistan, Uzbekistan, and Tajikistan have seven, six, and two percent Russian minority populations, respectively. With the exception of Kazakhstan, the Russian population in all these states is unstable, as large numbers of Russians have emigrated as a result of ethnic tensions. See Goodson, *Afghanistan's Endless War*, p. 136.

[28] See International Crisis Group, *Recent Violence in Central Asia: Causes and Consequences*; and Rashid, *Jihad*, pp. 57–92.

[29] Asian Development Bank, *Asian Development Outlook 2002*, New York: Oxford University Press, pp. 111–25.

[30] For an overview of Islam and politics in Central Asia, see Rashid, *Jihad*, pp. 57–92. For analysis of more recent events, see International Crisis Group, *Central Asia: Drugs and Conflict*, Asia Report no. 25, Brussels: ICG, November 26 , 2001; and International Crisis Group, *The IMU and the Hizb-ut-Tahrir: Implications of the Afghanistan Campaign*, Central Asia Briefing, Brussels: ICG, January 30, 2002.

[31] See International Crisis Group, *The IMU and the Hizb-ut-Tahrir*, Central Asia Briefing, Brussels: ICG, 30 January 2002, pp. 6–10.

[32] International Crisis Group, *Uzbekistan at Ten – Repression and Instability*, Asia Report no. 21, Brussels: ICG, 21 August 2001; and Human Rights Watch, *Press Backgrounder: Human Rights Abuse in Uzbekistan*, World Report 2001, New York: September 26, 2001.

[33] Council on Foreign Relations, *Terrorism: Q & A – Uzbekistan*, New York: March 2002.

[34] See Rashid, *Jihad*, pp. 137–38.

[35] Rashid, *Jihad*, p. 141.

[36] ICG, *The IMU and the Hizb-ut-Tahrir*, p. 4–5.

[37] ICG, *The IMU and the Hizb-ut-Tahrir*, p. 11.

[38] There was a precedent for this behavior. Following the collapse of the Soviet Union, moderate Muslims in Tajikistan worked with the democratic opposition to oppose the neo-communists' grip on government. This did not prevent the country from sliding into a bloody civil war from 1992 to 1997. However, the Taliban capture of Kabul in 1996 prompted parties to the conflict in Tajikistan to put aside their differences, for fear that the Pushtun-dominated Taliban was about to strike at Tajiks in Afghanistan and Tajikistan.

[39] See Dru C. Gladney, *Muslim Chinese: Ethnic Nationalism in the People's Republic*, Harvard East Asian Monographs, no. 149, Cambridge, Mass.: Harvard University Press, 1991.

[40] See Ron Gluckman, "Uighurs: Strangers in Their Own Land," *Asia Week*, December 7, 2001.

[41] John Pomfret, "Muslim Chinese Fear for Rights," *Washington Post*, October 13, 2001.

[42] Erik Eckholm, "Official Praises China for its Cooperation in Rooting out bin Laden's Terror Network," *The New York Times*, December 7, 2001.

[43] See Jonathan N. Lipman, *Familiar Strangers: A History of Muslims in Northwest China*, Seattle: University of Washington Press, 1997, pp. 94–95.

[44] See Sean Yom, "Uighur Muslims and Separatism in China: A Looming Dilemma." *International Institute for Asian Studies Newsletter*, no. 27, March 2002, p. 6.

[45] Pomfret, "Muslim Chinese Fear for Rights," *Washington Post*.

[46] On the controversy surrounding the Ayodhya mosque, see van der Veer, *Religious Nationalism*, pp. 2–11. On the violence in Gujarat, in which hundreds died, most of them Muslim, died, see "India Violence Kills Nearly 500," BBC News Online, March 3, 2002.

[47] See Barbara D. Metcalf and Thomas R. Metcalf, *A Concise History of India*, Cambridge: Cambridge University Press, 2002, pp. 220–22.

[48] See "Who are the Kashmir militants?" BBC News online, August 10, 2000.

[49] Barry Bearak, "Kashmir Leader is Killed, Bringing Tensions to Boil," *The New York Times*, May 22, 2002.

[50] Council of Foreign Relations, *Terrorism: Q & A*.

[51] See "Profile: Maulana Masood Azhar." BBC News online, December 25, 1999.

[52] See "India weighs Kashmir response," BBC News online, May 16, 2002.

[53] See "Pakistan rounds up militants," BBC News online, January 4, 2002.

[54] One-half million people died in the subsequent violence. Indonesia's Hindu and Christian minority, it should be emphasized, also participated in the killing. See Robert Cribb, ed., *The Indonesian Killings 1965–66*, Clayton, Australia: Centre of Southeast Asian Studies, Monash University, 1990.

[55] See Omar Farouk, "The Historical and Transnational Dimensions of Malay-Muslim Separatism in Southern Thailand," in Jim Joo Jock and S. Vani, eds., *Armed Separatism in Southeast Asia*, Singapore: ISEAS, 1984, pp. 222–73; and Peter Chalk, "Militant Islamic Separatism in Southern Thailand," in Jason F. Isaacson and Colin Rubenstein, eds., *Islam in Asia: Changing Political Realities*, New Brunswick: Transaction Publishers, 2002, pp. 165–86.

[56] Farouk, "The Historical and Transnational Dimensions," p. 242.

[57] Chalk, "Militant Islamic Separatism," p. 172.

[58] See Peter G. Gowing, *Mandate in Moroland: The American Government of Muslim Filipinos*, 1899-1920, Quezon: New Day Publishers.

[59] Peter Chalk, "Militant Islamic Extremism in the Southern Philippines," in Isaacson and Rubenstein, eds., *Islam in Asia*, pp. 187–222.

[60] See Chalk, "Militant Extremism in the South Philippines," p. 198.

[61] See Council on Foreign Relations and International Policy Institute for Counterterrorism, "Terrorism: Q and A – Abu Sayyaf Group," March 2002, online at <www.terrorismanswers.com/groups/abusayyaf.html>.

[62] See Council on Foreign Relations and International Policy Institute for Counterterrorism, "Terrorism: Q & A – Philippines," March 2002, online at <www.terrorismanswers.com/havens/philippines.html>.

[63] On the Suharto and military support for extremist Islam in the late 1990s, see Hefner, *Civil Islam*, pp. 167–213. For an overview of the aftermath of September 11, see International Crisis Group, *Indonesia: Violence and Radical Muslims*, Indonesia Briefing, Brussels: 10 October 2001, pp. 12–13.

[64] See United States Commission on International Religious Freedom, "Report on Indonesia," Washington: USCIRF, May 2002; and International Crisis Group, *Indonesia: The Search for Peace in Maluku*, Asia Report No. 31, Brussels: ICG, 8 February 2002.

[65] The Darul Islam was an armed movement that declared an Islamic state and battled the Indonesian army, mostly in West Java, from 1948 to 1960.

[66] Robert W. Hefner, "Indonesian Islam at the Crossroads," *Van Zorge Report on Indonesia*, vol. 4, no. 3 (19 February 2002), pp. 12–20.

[67] See Reyko Huang, "In the Spotlight: Laskar Jihad," Washington, DC: Center for Defense Information, March 2002; and Hefner, "Indonesian Islam at the Crossroads."

[68] Richard C. Paddock, "Singapore's 'Osama' May Have Targeted U.S. Interests," *The Los Angeles Times*, February 5, 2002.

[69] See Hefner, "Indonesian Islam." A report issued by the Brussels-based International Crisis Group on August 8, 2002, shows that the question of Al Qaeda ties to groups in Southeast Asia is still very much alive. Based on an exhaustive field study, the ICG concludes that some individuals linked to the Majelis Mujahidin Indonesia do indeed have ties to international terror groups and have been engaged in violent activities. See International Crisis Group, "Al Qaeda in Southeast Asia: The Case of the 'Ngruki Network' in Indonesia," Brussels: ICG Indonesia Briefing, 8 August 2002.

[70] International Crisis Group, "Resuming U.S.-Indonesia Military Ties" Brussels: ICG Indonesia Briefing, 21 May 2002, p. 6.

[71] For an overview of Islamic movements in Malaysia, see K. S. Jomo and Ahmad Shabery Cheek, "Malaysia's Islamic Movements," in Joel S. Kahn and Francis Loh Kok Wah, eds., *Fragmented Vision: Culture and Politics in Contemporary Malaysia*, Honolulu: University of Hawaii Press, 1992, pp. 79–106.

[72] See Michael Richardson, "Mahathir Boosted by Terrorism Stance," CNN.com, October 31, 2001; and Shamsul A. B., "Beyond 11 September: A Malaysian Response," Nordic Institute of Asian Studies, November 2001, at <http://eurasia.nias.ku.dk/nytt/stories/storyreader$99>.

73 See "Malaysian Opposition Denounces Arrests," BBC News online, October 11, 2001.

74 See "Singapore terror suspects include military members," *South China Morning Post*, January 27, 2002.

75 Hefner, *Civil Islam*, pp. 3–20; Abdolkarim Soroush, *Reason, Freedom, and Democracy in Islam*, trans. by Mahmoud Sadri and Ahmad Sadri, Oxford: Oxford University Press, 2000.

STRATEGIC ASIA

INDICATORS

STRATEGIC ASIA
BY THE NUMBERS

The 20 pages that follow contain tables and figures generated from the Strategic Asia database and its sources. These data have been organized in five sections: one for the major Asian powers, and four subsequent regional sections for Northeast Asia, Central Asia, South Asia, and Southeast Asia. Each section is divided into two double-page spreads. The first contains data indicative of underlying trends in the major countries within each region. Specific indicators include economic growth, balance of trade, demographic change, and military strength. The second spread features more recent data on economic output, inflation, defense priorities, and trade and investment flows, and contains forward-looking estimates. Together, these data reveal some significant changes underway in the strategic environment in Asia—the rapid rise of China as an economic and military power, the much more modest increase in India's power and capabilities, Japan's decade-long stagnation, and the relative decline of Russia.

Further information and source details for each indicator shown in this appendix are listed in the endnotes on page 416. Additional information and data for all countries in Strategic Asia are available online in the Strategic Asia database at <http://strategicasia.nbr.org>. The purpose of this database is to provide in one place authoritative, up-to-date, and strategically significant data that until now has been widely dispersed. The Strategic Asia database gives users unprecedented access to this information and tools with which to manipulate, download, and tabulate it. In return for this access NBR asks that all sources, including The National Bureau of Asian Research, be cited. A fuller description of the database is contained in the preface on pages *xi–xii*.

A1. Major Asian Powers—Long-term Economic Trends[1]

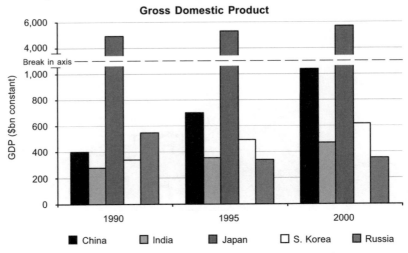

Gross Domestic Product

Source: World Bank, *World Development Indicators*.

A2. Major Asian Powers—Economic Growth and Output[2]

	GDP ($bn constant)			Avg. GDP growth (%)[a]		
	1990	1995	2000	1990–94	1995–99	2000
China	396.4	700.2	1,040.3	10.8	8.8	7.9
India	274.4	353.2	466.7	4.8	6.5	3.9
Japan	4,936.0	5,291.7	5,687.6	2.2	1.3	2.4
South Korea	341.6	489.3	617.5	7.5	5.0	8.8
Russia	543.7	337.7	357.3	-8.8	-1.2	8.3
United States	6,520.5	7,338.4	9,008.5	2.2	3.9	4.2

Source: World Bank, *World Development Indicators*. Note: a) Table shows average annual growth rate over period.

A3. Major Asian Powers—Exports and Trade Balance[3]

	Exports (share of GDP)[a]			Trade balance (share of GDP)[a]		
	1990–94	1995–99	2000	1990–94	1995–99	2000
China	19.8	22.4	25.9	1.7	3.3	2.7
India	9.1	11.3	14.0[b]	-1.8	-3.2	-2.6[b]
Japan	9.6	10.0	10.0	1.8	1.3	1.5
South Korea	27.9	37.3	45.0	-1.3	2.7	2.8
Russia	30.0	30.3	45.9[b]	2.7	6.2	21.1[b]
United States	10.1	11.2	10.7	-0.8	-1.6	-2.8

Source: World Bank, *World Development Indicators*. Notes: a) Tables show average annual percentage share over period; b) Data for 1999.

A4. Major Asian Powers—Military Balance[4]

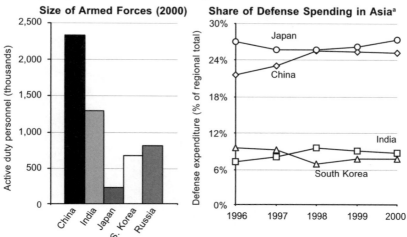

Source: International Institute for Strategic Studies, *The Military Balance*. Note: a) Figure shows defense spending as a share of total defense expenditures in Strategic Asia (excluding the United States, Canada, and Russia).

A5. Major Asian Powers—Armed Forces and Defense Spending[5]

| | Armed forces (thousands) | | | Def. exp. (share of GDP)[a] | | |
	1990	1995	2000	1990–94	1995–99	2000
China	3,030	2,930	2,340	5.2	5.6	5.3
India	1,262	1,145	1,303	2.8	3.0	3.1
Japan	219	240	235	1.2	1.0	1.0
South Korea	750	633	683	3.8	3.0	2.8
Russia	3,096[b]	1,339	817	8.0[c]	5.8	5.0
United States	2,118	1,547	1,366	4.6	3.4	3.0

Source: International Institute for Strategic Studies, *The Military Balance*. Notes: a) Table shows average annual percentage share over period; b) Data for Soviet Union; c) Data for 1994 only.

A6. Major Asian Powers—Population[6]

| | Total population (m) | | | Avg. population growth (%)[a] | | |
	1990	1995	2000	1990–94	1995–99	2000
China	1,135	1,205	1,262	1.3	1.0	0.9
India	850	929	1,016	1.9	1.8	1.8
Japan	124	125	127	0.3	0.3	0.2
South Korea	43[b]	45	47	1.0[c]	1.1	0.9
Russia	148	148	146	0.1	-0.3	-0.5
United States	249	265	282	1.1	1.2	1.2

Source: World Bank, *World Development Indicators*. Notes: a) Table shows average annual growth rate over period; b) Data for Russia as part of Soviet Union; c) Data excluding 1992.

A7. Major Asian Powers—Economic Indicators[7]

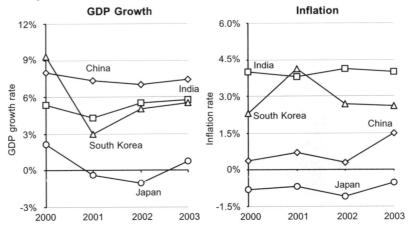

Sources: International Monetary Fund, *World Economic Outlook*; Asian Development Bank, *Asian Development Outlook*. Note: Data for 2002–03 are estimates.

A8. Major Asian Powers—Economic Outlook[8]

	GDP growth rate (%)			Inflation (%)		
	2001	2002	2003	2001	2002	2003
China	7.3	7.0	7.4	0.7	0.3	1.5
India	4.3	5.5	5.8	3.8	4.1	4.0
Japan	-0.4	-1.0	0.8	-0.7	-1.1	-0.5
South Korea	3.0	5.0	5.5	4.1	2.7	2.6
Russia	5.0	4.4	4.9	20.7	14.1	10.8
United States	1.2	2.3	3.4	2.8	1.4	2.4

Sources: International Monetary Fund, *World Economic Outlook*; Asian Development Bank, *Asian Development Outlook*. Note: Data for 2002–03 are estimates.

A9. Major Asian Powers—Defense Procurement Priorities[9]

	2001 def. bdgt ($bn)	Major planning, development, and delivery priorities in 2001	Major suppliers
China	17.0	Submarines, destroyers, fighters	Rus.
India	15.6	Aircraft carrier, frigate, tanks	Rus., Indig.
Japan	40.4	Helicopter carrier, minehunters	Indig., U.S.
South Korea	11.8	Fighters, helicopters, SAMs	U.S., Indig.
Russia	44.0	Fighters, cargo aircraft, tanks	Indig.
United States	310.5	Ballistic missile defense, fighters	Indig.

Source: International Institute for Strategic Studies, *The Military Balance*.

A10. Russia and United States—Major Trade Partners (2000)[10]

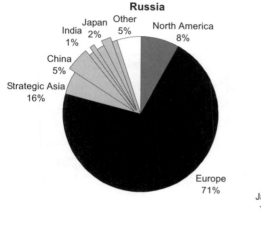

Russia

United States

Source: International Monetary Fund,
Direction of Trade Statistics.

A11. Major Asian Powers—Trade and Export Destinations[11]

	Trade (2000 – $bn)		Export Destinations
	Imports	Exports	(leading partners with share of export trade)
China	250.7	279.6	U.S. (21%); Hong Kong (18%); Japan (17%)
India	75.2	61.5	U.S. (22%); UK (6%); Germany (5%)[a]
Japan	459.7	528.8	U.S. (30%); Taiwan (7%) South Korea (6%)[b]
South Korea	192.5	206.5	U.S. (21%); Japan (11%); China (10%)[a]
Russia	62.5	115.5	U.S. (9%); Germany (9%); Ukraine (7%)[a]
United States	1,441.5	1,065.7	Canada (23%); Mexico (14%); Japan (8%)

Sources: International Monetary Fund, *International Financial Statistics*; Central Intelligence Agency, *World Factbook*. Notes: a) Data for 1999; b) Data is 2000 estimate.

A12. Major Asian Powers—Foreign Direct Investment[12]

	FDI inflows 2000		Origins of FDI
	$bn	% GDP	(leading partners with %)
China	38.4	3.6	Hong Kong (41%); EU (11%); U.S. (10%)
India	2.3	0.5	U.S. (8%); Japan (4%); UK (2%)
Japan	8.2	0.2	U.S. (32%); Germany (9%); Switzerland (7%)
South Korea	9.3	2.0	EU (29%); U.S. (19%); Japan (16%)
Russia	2.7	1.1	U.S. (28%); Neth. (14%); Germany (8%)
United States	287.7	2.9	-

Sources: International Monetary Fund, *International Financial Statistics*; U.S. Department of Commerce, *Country Commercial Guide.*

B1. Northeast Asia—Long-term Economic Trends[1]

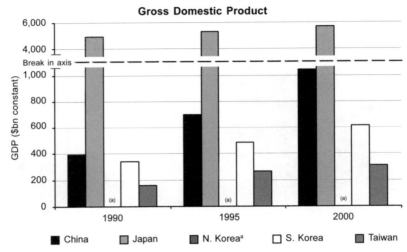

Gross Domestic Product

Source: World Bank, *World Development Indicators*; Central Bank of China (Taipei), *Financial Statistics*. Note: a) No reliable data for North Korea.

B2. Northeast Asia—Economic Growth and Output[2]

	GDP ($bn constant)			Avg. GDP growth (%)[a]		
	1990	1995	2000	1990–94	1995–99	2000
China	396.4	700.2	1,040.3	10.8	8.8	7.9
Hong Kong	107.3	139.2	164.6	5.3	2.2	10.5
Japan	4,936.0	5,291.7	5,687.6	2.2	1.3	2.4
North Korea[b]	-	-	-	-	-	-
South Korea	341.6	489.3	617.5	7.5	5.0	8.8
Taiwan	160.2	265.0	309.4	11.2	3.5	7.5

Sources: World Bank, *World Development Indicators*; Central Bank of China (Taipei), *Financial Statistics*. Notes: a) Table shows average annual growth rate over period. b) No data available.

B3. Northeast Asia—Exports and Trade Balance[3]

	Exports (share of GDP)[a]			Trade balance (share of GDP)[a]		
	1990–94	1995–99	2000	1990–94	1995–99	2000
China	19.8	22.4	25.9	1.7	3.3	2.7
Hong Kong	139.2	137.4	150.0	5.7	-0.5	4.7
Japan	9.6	10.0	10.0[c]	1.8	1.3	-
North Korea[b]	-	-	-	-	-	-
South Korea	27.9	37.3	45.0	-1.3	2.7	2.8
Taiwan	44.8	47.6	50.5	2.7	2.2	2.3

Sources: World Bank, *World Development Indicators*; Central Bank of China (Taipei), *Financial Statistics*. Note: a) Tables show average annual percentage share over period; b) No reliable data available; c) Data for 1999.

B4. Northeast Asia—Military Balance[4]

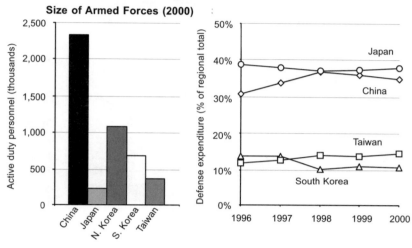

Source: International Institute for Strategic Studies, *The Military Balance*. Note: a) Figure shows defense spending as a share of total defense expenditures in Northeast Asia.

B5. Northeast Asia—Armed Forces and Defense Spending[5]

	Armed forces (thousands)			Def. exp. (share of GDP)[a]		
	1990	1995	2000	1990–94	1995–99	2000
China	3,030	2,930	2,340	5.2	5.6	5.3
Hong Kong[b]	-	-	-	-	-	-
Japan	219	240	235	1.2	1.0	1.0
North Korea	1,111	1,128	1,082	25.5[c]	26.0[d]	14.0
South Korea	750	633	683	3.8	3.0[d]	2.8
Taiwan	400	378	370	5.0	5.0	5.6

Source: International Institute for Strategic Studies, *The Military Balance*. Notes: a) Table shows average annual percentage share over period; b) United Kingdom (until 1997) and China responsible for Hong Kong's defense; c) Data for 1991–94 only; d) Data for 1995 only.

B6. Northeast Asia—Population[6]

	Total population (m)			Avg. population growth (%)[a]		
	1990	1995	2000	1990–94	1995–99	2000
China	1,135	1,205	1,262	1.3	1.0	0.7
Hong Kong	6	6	7	1.1	2.3	1.1
Japan	124	125	127	0.3	0.3	0.2
North Korea	20	22	22	1.4	1.0	0.4
South Korea	43	45	47	1.0	1.1	0.9
Taiwan[b]	20	21	22	1.1	0.8	0.9

Sources: World Bank, *World Development Indicators*; Central Bank of China (Taipei), *Financial Statistics*. Notes: a) Table shows average annual growth rate over period; b) Population growth rate for Taiwan calculated from population data.

B7. Northeast Asia—Economic Indicators[7]

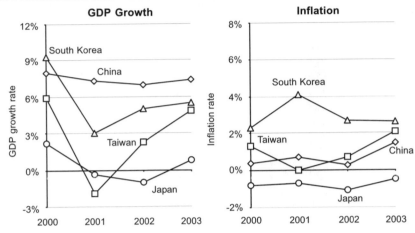

GDP Growth

Inflation

Sources: International Monetary Fund, *World Economic Outlook*; Asian Development Bank, *Asian Development Outlook*. Note: Data for 2002–03 are estimates.

B8. Northeast Asia—Economic Outlook[8]

	GDP growth (%)			Inflation (%)		
	2001	2002	2003	2001	2002	2003
China	7.3	7.0	7.4	0.7	0.3	1.5
Hong Kong	0.1	1.5	3.6	-1.6	-0.8	0.6
Japan	-0.4	-1.0	0.8	-0.7	-1.1	-0.5
North Korea[a]	-	-	-	-	-	-
South Korea	3.0	5.0	5.5	4.1	2.7	2.6
Taiwan	-1.9	2.3	4.8	0.0	0.7	2.1

Sources: International Monetary Fund, *World Economic Outlook*; Asian Development Bank, *Asian Development Outlook*. Notes: a) No reliable data available. Data for 2002–03 are estimates.

B9. Northeast Asia—Defense Procurment Priorities[9]

	2001 def. bdgt ($bn)	Major planning, development, and delivery priorities in 2001	Major suppliers
China	17.0	Submarines, destroyers, fighters	Rus.
Hong Kong[a]	-	-	-
Japan	40.4	Helicopter carrier, minehunters	Indig., U.S.
North Korea	1.3	Fighters	Rus.
South Korea	11.8	Fighters, helicopters, SAMs	U.S., Indig.
Taiwan	8.2	SAMs, destroyers, submarines	U.S.

Source: International Institute for Strategic Studies, *The Military Balance*. Note: a) China is responsible for Hong Kong's defense.

B10. China and Japan—Major Trade Partners (2000)[10]

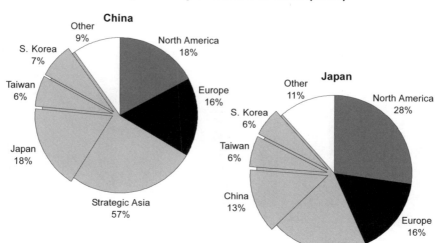

Source: International Monetary Fund,
Direction of Trade Statistics.

B11. Northeast Asia—Trade and Export Destinations[11]

	Trade (2000 – $bn)		Export Destinations
	Imports	Exports	(leading partners with share of export trade)
China	250.7	279.6	U.S. (21%); Hong Kong (18%); Japan (17%)
Hong Kong	236.5	244.2	China (33%); U.S. (24%); Japan (5%)[a]
Japan	459.7	528.8	U.S. (30%); Taiwan (7%); South Korea (6%)
North Korea	1.0[b]	0.5[c]	Japan (28%); South Korea (21%); China (5%)[d]
South Korea	192.5	206.5	U.S. (21%); Japan (11%); China (10%)[a]
Taiwan	160.5	167.5	U.S. (24%); Hong Kong (21%); Europe (16%)

Sources: International Monetary Fund, *International Financial Statistics*; Central Bank of China (Taipei), *Financial Statistics*; Central Intelligence Agency, *World Factbook*. Notes: a) Data for 1999; b) Data for 1999 c.i.f.; c) Data for 1999 f.o.b.; d) Data for 1995.

B12. Northeast Asia—Foreign Direct Investment[12]

	FDI inflows 2000		Origins of FDI
	$bn	% GDP	(leading partners with %)
China	38.4	3.6	Hong Kong (41%); EU (11%); U.S. (10%)[b]
Hong Kong	61.9	38.1	China (40%); Netherlands (10%); UK (10%)[b]
Japan	8.2	0.2	U.S. (32%); Germany (9%); Switzerland (7%)
North Korea[a]	-	-	-
South Korea	9.3	2.1	EU (29%); U.S. (19%); Japan (16%)
Taiwan	4.9	1.6	U.S. (18%); Europe (14%); Japan (10%)

Sources: International Monetary Fund, *International Financial Statistics*; Central Bank of China (Taipei); U.S. Department of Commerce, *Country Commercial Guide*. Notes: a) No reliable data availale; b) Data for 1999.

C1. Central Asia—Long-term Economic Trends[1]

Gross Domestic Product

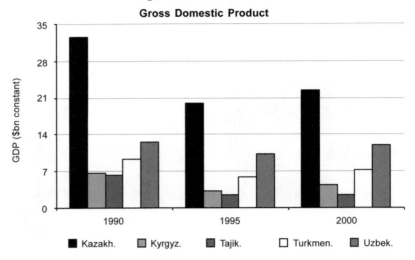

Source: World Bank, *World Development Indicators*.

C2. Central Asia—Economic Growth and Output[2]

	GDP ($bn constant)			GDP growth (%)[a]		
	1990	1995	2000	1990–94	1995–99	2000
Kazakhstan	32.5	19.9	22.5	-8.5	-1.0	9.6
Kyrgyzstan	6.6	3.3	4.4	-10.3	3.5	5.0
Russia	543.7	337.7	357.3	-8.8	-1.2	8.3
Tajikistan	6.3	2.4	2.4	-14.9	-3.7	8.3
Turkmenistan	9.4	5.9	7.2	-7.3	-0.2	17.6
Uzbekistan	12.5	10.2	12.0	-3.5	2.4	4.0

Source: World Bank, *World Development Indicators*. Note: a) Table shows average annual growth rate over period.

C3. Central Asia—Exports and Trade Balance[3]

	Exports (share of GDP)[a]			Trade balance (share of GDP)[a]		
	1990–94	1995–99	2000	1990–94	1995–99	2000
Kazakhstan	49.7[b]	36.4	58.9	-6.7[b]	-2.0	11.5
Kyrgyzstan	33.5	35.4	43.5	-9.5	-16.6	-11.7
Russia	30.0	30.3	45.9	2.7	6.2	21.1
Tajikistan	30.5[c]	63.3[d]	80.7	-5.6	-3.5	-3.9
Turkmenistan	52.4[e]	44.1	63.0	-2.4[f]	-15.9	9.6
Uzbekistan	29.7	33.8	44.1	-6.5	-3.9	5.5

Source: World Bank, *World Development Indicators*. Notes: a) Tables show average annual percentage share over period; b) Data for 1992–94 only; c) Data for 1990–91 only; d) Data for 1997–99 only; e) Data for 1993–94 only; f) Data for 1990–91 and 1993–94 only.

C4. Central Asia—Military Balance[4]

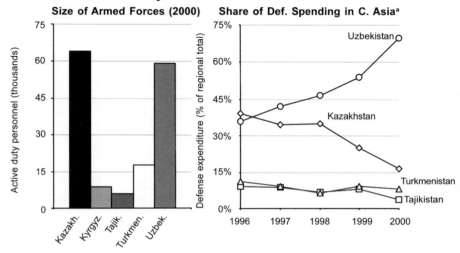

Size of Armed Forces (2000)   Share of Def. Spending in C. Asia[a]

Source: International Institute for Strategic Studies, *The Military Balance*. Note: a) Figure shows defense spending as a share of total defense expenditures in Central Asia (excluding Russia).

C5. Central Asia—Armed Forces and Defense Spending[5]

	Armed forces (thousands)			Def. exp. (share of GDP)[a]		
	1990	1995	2000	1990–94	1995–99	2000
Kazakhstan	-	40	64	26.0[c]	2.0	2.0
Kyrgyzstan	-	7	9	2.0[d]	3.6	2.4
Russia	3,096[b]	1,339	817	8.0[e]	5.8	5.0
Tajikistan	-	3	6	5.5[c]	9.6	6.3
Turkmenistan	-	11	18	2.0[c]	3.2	4.0
Uzbekistan	-	20	59	3.0	4.2	7.9

Source: International Institute for Strategic Studies, *The Military Balance*. Notes: a) Table shows annual average percentage share over period; b) Data for the Soviet Union; c) Data for 1992–94 only; c) Data for 1994 only; d) Data for 1993–94 only.

C6. Central Asia—Population[6]

	Total population (m)			Avg. population growth (%)[a]		
	1990[b]	1995	2000	1990–94	1995–99	2000
Kazakhstan	16	16	15	-0.4	-1.3	-0.4
Kyrgyzstan	4	5	5	0.7	1.7	1.0
Russia	148	148	146	0.1	-0.3	-0.5
Tajikistan	5	6	6	2.1	1.4	0.2
Turkmenistan	4	5	5	4.1	2.9	2.0
Uzbekistan	20	23	25	2.2	1.7	1.4

Source: World Bank, *World Development Indicators*. Notes: a) Table shows average annual growth rate over period; b) Data for countries when part of Soviet Union.

C7. Central Asia—Economic Indicators[7]

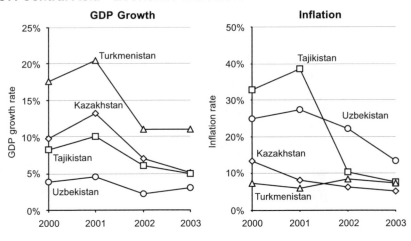

Sources: International Monetary Fund, *World Economic Outlook*; Asian Development Bank, *Asian Development Outlook*. Note: Data for 2002–03 are estimates.

C8. Central Asia—Economic Outlook[8]

	GDP growth rate (%)			Inflation (%)		
	2001	2002	2003	2001	2002	2003
Kazakhstan	13.2	7.0	5.1	8.3	6.4	5.1
Kyrgyzstan	5.0	4.5	4.5	7.0	6.1	5.5
Russia	5.0	4.4	4.9	20.7	14.1	10.8
Tajikistan	10.0	6.0	5.0	38.6[a]	10.5	7.6
Turkmenistan	20.5	11.0	11.0	6.0	8.5	7.5
Uzbekistan	4.5	2.2	3.0	27.2	22.2	13.5

Sources: International Monetary Fund, *World Economic Outlook*; Asian Development Bank, *Asian Development Outlook*. Note: a) Data for January to June. Data for 2002–03 are estimates.

C9. Central Asia—Defense Procurement Priorities[9]

	2001 def. bdgt ($bn)	Major planning, development, and delivery priorities in 2001	Major suppliers
Kazakhstan	0.2	Fighters, SAMs	Rus.
Kyrgyzstan	<0.1	-	-
Russia	44.0	Fighters, cargo aircraft, tanks	Indig.
Tajikistan	<0.1	-	-
Turkmenistan	0.2	-	-
Uzbekistan	0.3	-	-

Source: International Institute for Strategic Studies, *The Military Balance*.

C10. Kazakhstan and Uzbekistan—Major Trade Partners (2000)[10]

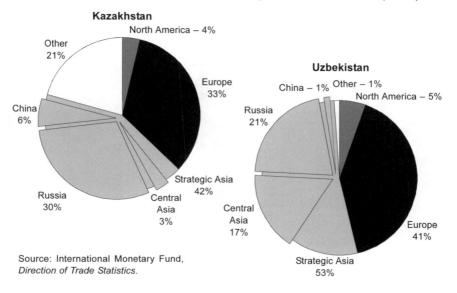

Kazakhstan

- North America – 4%
- Other 21%
- Europe 33%
- China 6%
- Russia 30%
- Central Asia 3%
- Strategic Asia 42%

Uzbekistan

- China – 1%
- Other – 1%
- North America – 5%
- Russia 21%
- Central Asia 17%
- Europe 41%
- Strategic Asia 53%

Source: International Monetary Fund, *Direction of Trade Statistics.*

C11. Central Asia—Trade and Export Destinations[11]

	Trade (2000 – $bn)		Export Destinations
	Imports	Exports	(leading partners with share of export trade)
Kazakhstan	9.0	10.4	EU (23%); Russia (20%); China (8%)[a]
Kyrgyzstan	0.7	0.6	Germany (33%); Russia (16%); Kazak (10%)[a]
Russia	62.5	115.5[b]	U.S. (9%); Germany (9%); Ukraine (7%)[a]
Tajikistan	-	0.8	Uzbekistan (20%); Russia (8%)[c]
Turkmenistan	-	-	Ukraine, Iran, Turkey[d]
Uzbekistan	-	-	Russia (13%); Switzerland (10%); UK (10%)[a]

Sources: International Monetary Fund, *International Financial Statistics*; International Monetary Fund, *Country Report*; Central Intelligence Agency, *World Factbook*. Notes: a) Data for 1999; b) Data for goods f.o.b.; c) Data for 1998; d) No percentages available.

C12. Central Asia—Foreign Direct Investment[12]

	FDI inflows 2000		Origins of FDI
	$bn	% GDP	(leading partners with %)
Kazakhstan	1.3	6.7	U.S. (36%); UK (17%); Italy (13%)
Kyrgyzstan	<-0.1	-	UK (28%); U.S. (18%); Turkey (10%)
Russia	2.7[a]	1.0	U.S. (28%); Neth. (14%); Germany (8%)
Tajikistan	<0.1	2.0	-
Turkmenistan	-	-	-
Uzbekistan	-	-	-

Sources: International Monetary Fund, *International Financial Statistics*; U.S. Department of Commerce, *Country Commercial Guide*. Note: a) Data from International Monetary Fund, *Country Report*, No. 01/169 May 2001.

D1. South Asia—Long-term Economic Trends[1]

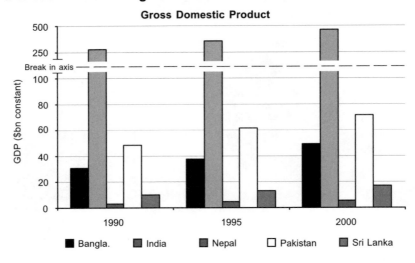

Gross Domestic Product

Source: World Bank, *World Development Indicators*.

D2. South Asia—Economic Growth and Output[2]

	GDP ($bn constant)			GDP growth (%)[a]		
	1990	1995	2000	1990–94	1995–99	2000
Afghanistan[b]	-	-	-	-	-	-
Bangladesh	30.6	37.9	48.9	4.7	5.0	5.9
India	274.4	353.2	466.7	4.8	6.5	3.9
Nepal	3.4	4.4	5.6	5.4	4.3	6.5
Pakistan	48.4	61.2	71.3	4.7	3.2	4.4
Sri Lanka	10.0	13.0	16.7	5.6	4.9	6.0

Source: World Bank, *World Development Indicators*. Note: a) Table shows average annual growth rate over period; b) No reliable data available.

D3. South Asia—Exports and Trade Balance[3]

	Exports (share of GDP)[a]			Trade balance (share of GDP)[a]		
	1990–94	1995–99	2000	1990–94	1995–99	2000
Afghanistan[b]	-	-	-	-	-	-
Bangladesh	7.8	12.2	14.0	-5.5	-6.1	-5.2
India	9.1	11.3	14.0	-1.8	-3.2	-2.6
Nepal	16.0	23.7	23.7	-9.9	-10.6	-8.3
Pakistan	16.2	15.7	15.5	-7.0	-6.0	-3.5
Sri Lanka	31.3	35.8	39.7	-9.7	-8.0	-10.8

Source: World Bank, *World Development Indicators*. Note: a) Tables show average annual percentage share over period; b) No reliable data available.

D4. South Asia—Military Balance[4]

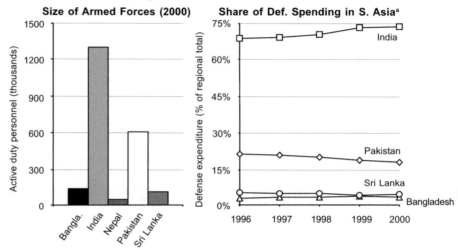

Source: International Institute for Strategic Studies, *The Military Balance*. Note: a) Figure shows defense spending as a share of total defense expenditures in South Asia.

D5. South Asia—Armed Forces and Defense Spending[5]

	Armed forces (thousands)			Def. exp. (share of GDP)[a]		
	1990	1995	2000	1990–94	1995–99	2000
Afghanistan[b]	58	-	-	-	-	-
Bangladesh	104	116	137	1.8	1.8	1.8
India	1,262	1,145	1,303	2.8	3.0	3.1
Nepal	35	35	46	1.0	1.0	0.9
Pakistan	550	587	612	7.2	6.4	4.8
Sri Lanka	65	125	113	5.0	5.6	5.3

Source: International Institute for Strategic Studies, *The Military Balance*. Note: a) Table shows average annual percentage share over period; b) No reliable data available.

D6. South Asia—Population[6]

	Total population (m)			Avg. population growth (%)[a]		
	1990	1995	2000	1990–94	1995–99	2000
Afghanistan	18	22	27	3.6	4.4	2.6
Bangladesh	110	120	131	1.9	1.7	1.7
India	850	929	1016	1.9	1.8	1.8
Nepal	18	21	23	2.4	2.4	2.4
Pakistan	108	122	138	2.5	2.4	2.4
Sri Lanka	17	18	19	1.3	1.2	1.6

Source: World Bank, *World Development Indicators*. Note: a) Table shows average annual growth rate over period.

D7. South Asia—Economic Indicators[7]

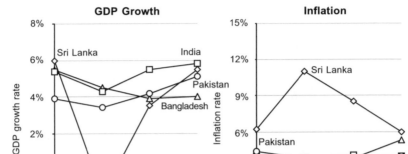

Sources: International Monetary Fund, *World Economic Outlook*; Asian Development Bank, *Asian Development Outlook*. Note: Data for 2002–03 are estimates.

D8. South Asia—Economic Outlook[8]

	GDP growth rate (%)			Inflation (%)		
	2001	2002	2003	2001	2002	2003
Afghanistan[a]	-	-	-	-	-	-
Bangladesh	4.5	3.9	4.0	1.8	3.8	5.3
India	4.3	5.5	5.8	3.8	4.1	4.0
Nepal	5.0	3.5	5.0	2.4	5.0	5.0
Pakistan	3.4	4.2	5.1	3.8	3.7	4.0
Sri Lanka	-1.3	3.5	5.5	11.0	8.5	6.0

Sources: International Monetary Fund, *World Economic Outlook*; Asian Development Bank, *Asian Development Outlook*. Note: a) No reliable data available. Data for 2002–03 are estimates.

D9. South Asia—Defense Procurement Priorities[9]

	2001 def. bdgt ($bn)	Major planning, development, and delivery priorities in 2001	Major suppliers
Afghanistan	-	-	-
Bangladesh	0.7	Frigate	S.Kor.
India	15.6	Aircraft carrier, frigate, tanks	Rus., Indig.
Nepal	<0.1[a]	Not reported	-
Pakistan	2.6	Ballistic missiles, submarines	Chi., Fr.
Sri Lanka	0.7[a]	Tanks, AIVFs	Rus.

Source: International Institute for Strategic Studies, *The Military Balance*. Note: a) 2000 data.

D10. India and Pakistan—Major Trade Partners (2000)[10]

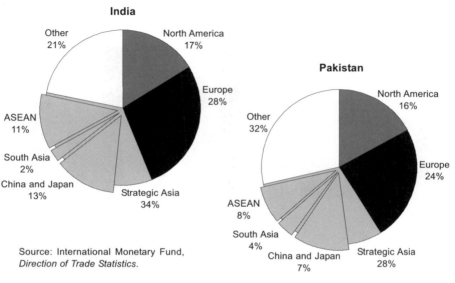

Source: International Monetary Fund,
Direction of Trade Statistics.

D11. South Asia—Trade and Export Destinations[11]

	Trade (2000 – $bn)		Export Destinations
	Imports	Exports	(leading partners with share of export trade)
Afghanistan	-	-	FSU countries; Pakistan; Iran[a]
Bangladesh	9.7	7.2	U.S. (31%); Germany (10%); UK (8%)[b]
India	75.2	61.5	U.S. (22%); UK (6%); Germany (5%)[b]
Nepal	1.8	1.3	India (33%); U.S. (26%); Germany (25%)[c]
Pakistan	12.2	10.1	U.S. (24%); Hong Kong (7%); UK (7%)
Sri Lanka	8.1	6.4	U.S. (39%); UK (13%); Middle East (8%)[b]

Sources: International Monetary Fund, *International Financial Statistics*; Central Intelligence Agency, *World Factbook*. Notes: a) No percentages available; b) Data for 1999; c) Data for FY 1997–98.

D12. South Asia—Foreign Direct Investment[12]

	FDI inflows 2000		Origins of FDI
	$bn	% GDP	(leading partners with %)
Afghanistan	-	-	-
Bangladesh	0.3	0.6	U.S.; Malaysia; Japan[a]
India	2.3	0.5	U.S. (8%); Japan (4%); UK (2%)
Nepal	-	-	-
Pakistan	0.3	0.5	UK (36%); U.S. (30%); Saudis Arabia (20%)
Sri Lanka	0.2	1.1	South Korea; Japan; U.S.[a]

Sources: International Monetary Fund, *International Financial Statistics*; U.S. Department of Commerce, *Country Commercial Guide*. Note: a) No percentages available.

E1. Southeast Asia—Long-term Economic Trends[1]

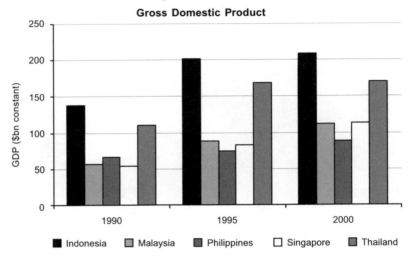

Gross Domestic Product

Source: World Bank, *World Development Indicators*.

E2. Southeast Asia—Economic Growth and Output[2]

	GDP ($bn constant)			Avg. GDP growth (%)[a]		
	1990	1995	2000	1990–94	1995–99	2000
Indonesia	138.4	202.1	209.1	8.0	1.7	4.8
Malaysia	56.5	88.8	111.6	9.3	5.2	8.3
Philippines	66.6	74.1	88.2	1.9	3.7	4.0
Singapore	53.9	83.4	113.4	9.3	6.0	9.9
Thailand	111.1	168.3	170.3	9.0	1.4	4.3
Vietnam	13.6	20.2	27.9	7.3	7.5	5.5

Source: World Bank, *World Development Indicators*. Note: a) Table shows average annual growth rate over period.

E3. Southeast Asia—Exports and Trade Balance[3]

	Exports (share of GDP)[a]			Trade balance (share of GDP)[a]		
	1990–94	1995–99	2000	1990–94	1995–99	2000
Indonesia	26.5	33.6	38.5	2.1	3.1	7.8
Malaysia	79.3	103.3	125.5	-0.4	9.1	21.1
Philippines	30.3	45.9	56.3	-5.7	-6.7	6.1
Singapore	186.9	167.4	179.9	10.1	16.3	18.5
Thailand	36.7	49.2	67.0	-5.3	3.4	8.1
Vietnam	30.8	41.0[b]	-	-3.0	-8.6	-2.3

Source: World Bank, *World Development Indicators*. Notes: a) Tables show average annual percentage share over period; b) Data for 1995–97.

E4. Southeast Asia—Military Balance[4]

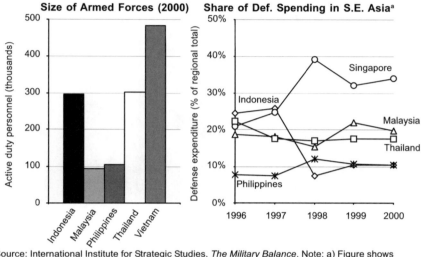

Source: International Institute for Strategic Studies, *The Military Balance*. Note: a) Figure shows defense spending as a share of total defense expenditures in Southeast Asia.

E5. Southeast Asia—Armed Forces and Defense Spending[5]

	Armed forces (thousands)			Def. exp. (share of GDP)[a]		
	1990	1995	2000	1990–94	1995–99	2000
Indonesia	283	275	297	1.4	1.6	0.9
Malaysia	130	115	96	4.2	3.8	3.2
Philippines	109	107	106	1.8	2.0	1.8
Singapore	76	56	61	4.8	5.6	4.9
Thailand	283	259	301	3.0	2.2	2.0
Vietnam	952	557	484	7.0	4.6	3.1

Source: International Institute for Strategic Studies, *The Military Balance*. Note: a) Table shows average annual percentage share over period.

E6. Southeast Asia—Population[6]

	Total population (m)			Avg. population growth (%)[a]		
	1990	1995	2000	1990–94	1995–99	2000
Indonesia	178	194	210	1.7	1.6	1.6
Malaysia	18	21	23	2.6	2.4	2.4
Philippines	61	68	76	2.3	2.1	1.8
Singapore	3	4	4	3.1	2.9	1.7
Thailand	56	59	61	1.3[b]	0.7	0.8
Vietnam	66	73	79	2.0	1.6	1.3

Source: World Bank, *World Development Indicators*. Note: a) Table shows annual average growth rate over period.

E7. Southeast Asia—Economic Indicators[7]

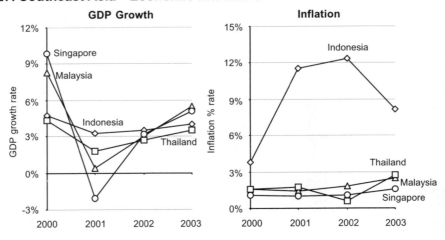

Sources: International Monetary Fund, *World Economic Outlook*; Asian Development Bank, *Asian Development Outlook*. Note: Data for 2002–03 are estimates.

E8. Southeast Asia—Economic Outlook[8]

	GDP growth rate (%)			Inflation (%)		
	2001	2002	2003	2001	2002	2003
Indonesia	3.3	3.5	4.0	11.5	12.4	8.2
Malaysia	0.4	3.0	5.5	1.4	1.8	2.5
Philippines	3.4	4.0	4.2	6.1	5.0	5.1
Singapore	-2.1	3.2	5.1	1.0	1.1	1.6
Thailand	1.8	2.7	3.5	1.7	0.6	2.7
Vietnam	4.7	5.3	7.0	0.1	4.9	3.7

Source: International Monetary Fund, *World Economic Outlook*. Note: Data for 2002–03 are estimates.

E9. Southeast Asia—Defense Procurement Priorities[9]

	2001 def. bdgt ($bn)	Major planning, development, and delivery priorities in 2001	Major suppliers
Indonesia	1.3	Helicopters, fighters	Rus.
Malaysia	1.9	Patrol craft, submarines, artillery	Ger., Tur.
Philippines	1.1	Fighters, patrol craft	Tai., U.S.
Singapore	4.3	Frigates, fighters, submarines	U.S., Fr.
Thailand	1.7[a]	Surface fleets, submarines	U.S., EU
Vietnam	1.8	SRBMs, Corvettes	N.Kor., Rus.

Source: International Institute for Strategic Studies, *The Military Balance*. Note: a) Estimate

E10. Thailand and Singapore—Major Trade Partners[10]

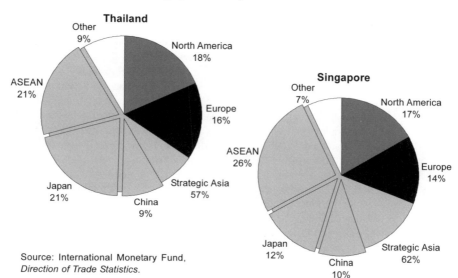

Source: International Monetary Fund, *Direction of Trade Statistics.*

E11. Southeast Asia—Trade and Export Destinations[11]

	Trade (2000 – $bn)		Export Destinations
	Imports	Exports	(leading partners with share of export trade)
Indonesia	55.4	70.6	Japan (21%); U.S. (14%); Singapore (10%)[a]
Malaysia	94.3	112.2	U.S. (21%); Singapore (18%); Japan (13%)[b]
Philippines	36.5	41.3	U.S. (34%); Japan (14%); Netherlands (8%)[c]
Singapore	148.9	166.0	U.S. (19%); Malaysia (17%); Hong Kong (8%)[d]
Thailand	71.7	81.8	U.S. (22%); Japan (14%); Singapore (9%)
Vietnam	17.3	17.2	China; Japan; Germany[e]

Sources: International Monetary Fund, *International Financial Statistics*; Central Intelligence Agency, *World Factbook*. Notes: a) Data is 1999 estimate; b) Data is 2000 estimate; c) Data for 1998; d) Data for 1999; e) No percentages available.

E12. Southeast Asia—Foreign Direct Investment[12]

	FDI Inflows 2000		Origins of FDI
	$bn	% GDP	(leading partners with %)
Indonesia	-4.5	3.0	Japan (20%); UK (17%); Singapore (9%)
Malaysia	3.8	4.2	U.S. (38%); Japan (15%); Netherlands (11%)
Philippines	1.2	1.7	U.S. (24%); Japan (20%); Netherlands (12%)
Singapore	6.4	6.9	U.S. (51%); EU (23%); Japan (21%)
Thailand	3.4	3.0	U.S. (35%); Japan (24%); UK (18%)
Vietnam	1.3	4.2	Netherlands (32%); UK (29%); Taiwan (13%)

Sources: International Monetary Fund, *International Financial Statistics*; U.S. Department of Commerce, *Country Commercial Guide*.

Endnotes

[1] Long-term economic trends—Figure shows comparative growth in GDP. Source: World Bank, *World Development Indicators*, CD-ROM, Washington, DC: World Bank, 2001 and 2002. GDP shown in 1995 constant dollars. Data for Taiwan from Central Bank of China (Taipei), *Financial Statistics*, Taipei: CBC, 1997, 2001, and 2002. GDP for Taiwan shown in 1990 constant dollars.

[2] Economic growth and output—Table shows GDP (constant 1995 dollars) and GDP growth (annual average percentage change). Source: World Bank, *World Development Indicators*. Data for Taiwan from CBC, *Financial Statistics*.

[3] Exports and trade balance—Table shows value of exports and trade balance as a percentage share of GDP. Source: World Bank, *World Development Indicators*. Data for Taiwan from CBC, *Financial Statistics*.

[4] Military balance—Figures show comparative size of armed forces (active duty personnel) and defense expenditures as percentage share of total regional defense spending. Source: International Institute of Strategic Studies, *The Military Balance*, London: IISS, various editions.

[5] Armed Forces and Defense Spending—Table shows size of armed forces (active duty personnel) and defense expenditures as percentage share of GDP. Source: IISS, *The Military Balance*.

[6] Population—Table shows size of population (millions) and population growth (annual average percentage change). Source: World Bank, *World Development Indicators*. Data for Taiwan from CBC, *Financial Statistics*.

[7] Economic Indicators—Figures show comparative GDP growth rates and inflation rates. Sources: International Monetary Fund, *World Economic Outlook*, Washington, DC: IMF, 2002; Asian Development Bank, *Asian Development Outlook*, New York: Oxford University Press, 2002.

[8] Economic Outlook—Table shows real and estimated GDP growth and inflation. Sources: IMF, *World Economic Outlook*; ADB, *Asian Development Outlook*.

[9] Defense Procurement Priorities—Table shows defense budget (billions of dollars), defense procurement priorities, and major suppliers. Source: IISS, *The Military Balance*.

[10] Major Trade Partners—Figures show leading partners with share of total trade. Source: IMF, *Direction of Trade Statistics*, Washington, DC: IMF, 2001.

[11] Trade and Export Destinations—Table shows imports and exports (billions of dollars) and leading export partners with percentage shares of total exports. Sources: IMF, *International Financial Statistics*, CD-ROM, Washington, DC: IMF-World Bank, 2002; Central Intelligence Agency, *World Factbook*, Washington, DC: CIA, 2001. Data for Taiwan from Central Bank of China, *Financial Statistics*. Data for Tajikistan from IMF, *Country Report No. 01/169 (May 2001)*, Washington, DC: IMF, 2001.

[12] Foreign Direct Investment—Table shows FDI inflows (millions of dollars) and origins of FDI with percentage shares. Sources: IMF, *International Financial Statistics*, Department of Commerce, *Country Commercial Guide FY 2002*, Washington, DC: Department of Commerce, 2001. Data for Taiwan from CBC, *Balance of Payments Quarterly*, Taipei: CBC, 2001.

INDEX

ABOUT THE AUTHORS

Thomas J. Christensen is Professor of Political Science at the Massachusetts Institute of Technology. He is author of *Useful Adversaries: Grand Strategy, Domestic Mobilization, and Sino-American Conflict, 1947–58* (Princeton University Press, 1996) and numerous articles, including "Posing Problems Without Catching Up," *International Security* (Spring 2001); "China: Getting the Questions Right," with Richard K. Betts, *The National Interest* (Winter 2000/01); and "Theater Missile Defense and Taiwan's Security," *Orbis* (Winter 2000). Professor Christensen is currently working on projects relating to the growth of Chinese power, China's contemporary military doctrine, and U.S. strategy toward East Asia.

Stephen P. Cohen is a Senior Fellow in the Foreign Policy Studies Program of the Brookings Institution and Adjunct Professor at Georgetown University. He taught for 34 years at the University of Illinois, and was the co-founder and director of the university's Program in Arms Control, Disarmament, and International Security (ACDIS). He has served as a consultant to the RAND Corporation and the Departments of State and Defense. Dr. Cohen has written or edited nine books, including *India: Emerging Power* (Brookings Institution Press, 2001) and *The Pakistan Army* (Oxford University Press, revised edition 1998). He is currently writing a book on the future of Pakistan.

Nicholas N. Eberstadt holds the Henry Wendt Chair at the American Enterprise Institute in Washington, DC, and serves on the Board of Advisors of The National Bureau of Asian Research. He often consults for the U.S. Government, and has frequently testified before Congress. He writes widely on issues of demography, development, and international security. His books on Korea include *Korea's Future and the Great Powers* (University of Washington Press, 2001, edited with Richard Ellings), *The End of North Korea* (American Enterprise Institute, 1999), *Korea Approaches Reunification* (M. E. Sharpe, 1995), and *The Population of North Korea* (University of California Press, 1992, with Judith Banister). His articles have appeared in the United States' leading foreign policy journals.

Richard J. Ellings is President and Cofounder of The National Bureau of Asian Research. He is the editor of *Strategic Asia 2001-02: Power and Purpose* (The National Bureau of Asian Research, 2001, with Aaron Friedberg), *Korea's Future and the Great Powers* (University of Washington Press, 2001, with Nicholas Eberstadt), and *Southeast Asian Security in the New Millennium* (M. E. Sharpe, 1996, with Sheldon Simon) and has authored *Private Property and National Security* (1991, with others) and *Embargoes and World Power* (Westview Press, 1985). He is also the founding editor of the *NBR Analysis* series. He frequently serves as a consultant to the U.S. Government, and worked as a legislative assistant in the U.S. Senate. He is also a former member of faculty of the University of Washington, where he received the Distinguished Teaching Award.

Aaron L. Friedberg is Professor of Politics and International Affairs and Director of the Center of International Studies and the Research Program in International Security at Princeton University. He was the inaugural Henry A. Kissinger Chair in Foreign Policy and International Relations at the Library of Congress in 2001/02. He is the editor of *Strategic Asia 2001-02: Power and Purpose* (The National Bureau of Asian Research, 2001, with Richard Ellings), and the author of two books. His articles on Asian strategic affairs have appeared in *Commentary*, *Harvard Journal of International Affairs*, *International Security*, and *Survival*. He has served as a consultant to the National Security Council, the Department of Defense, the Central Intelligence Agency, and Los Alamos National Laboratory. He has been a fellow at the Australian Strategic Policy Institute, the Norwegian Nobel Institute, Harvard's Center for International Affairs, and the Woodrow Wilson International Center for scholars.

Robert W. Hefner is Professor of Anthropology and Associate Director of the Institute for the Study of Economic Culture at Boston University, as well as a Research Associate on Religion and Democracy at the university's

Institute on Religion and World Affairs, where is currently directing a project for the Pew Charitable Trust on prospects and policies for the Muslim world. His most recent books include *Civil Islam: Muslims and Democratization in Indonesia* (Princeton University Press, 2000) and, as editor, *The Politics of Multiculturalism: Pluralism and Citizenship in Malaysia, Singapore, and Indonesia* (Hawaii University Press, 2001), and *Islam in an Era of Nation-States: Politics and Religious Renewal in Muslim Southeast Asia* (Hawaii University Press, 1998, with Patricia Horvatich).

Eric Heginbotham is a Senior Fellow at the Council on Foreign Relations and is completing his doctorate in political science at the Massachusetts Institute of Technology. He has been a visiting faculty member at Boston College and served as a Captain in the U.S. Army Reserve. Mr. Heginbotham has authored or coauthored a number of articles on East Asian security issues, including "The Fall and Rise of Navies in East Asia: Military Organizations, Domestic Politics, and Grand Strategy," *International Security* (forthcoming); "A New Asia Strategy: Strategic Engagement," *The National Interest* (forthcoming); "China's Coming Transformation," *Foreign Affairs* (July/August 2001); and "Mercantile Realism and Japanese Foreign Policy," *International Security* (Spring 1998).

Martha Brill Olcott is a Senior Associate at the Carnegie Endowment for International Peace. She is also an Adjunct Professor at Georgetown University. Prior to her work at the Carnegie Endowment, Dr. Olcott served as a consultant to former Secretary of State Lawrence Eagleburger. Dr. Olcott has written and edited numerous books, including *Kazakhstan: Unfulfilled Promise* (Carnegie Endowment for International Peace, 2002), *Getting it Wrong: Regional Cooperation and the CIS* (Brookings Institution Press, 1999, with Anders Aslund and Sherman Garnett), *The New States of Central Asia* (United States Institute of Peace, 1996), and *The Kazakhs* (Hoover Institution Press, expanded second edition 1995).

Richard J. Samuels is Ford International Professor of Political Science at the Massachusetts Institute of Technology, where he is Director of the Center for International Studies and Founding Director of the MIT Japan Program. In 2001 he became Chairman of the Japan-U.S. Friendship Commission. Professor Samuels has written or edited eight books, including *Rich Nation, Strong Army: National Security and the Technological Transformation of Japan* (Cornell University Press, 1994), and *The Business of the Japanese State: Energy Markets in Comparative and Historical Perspective* (Cornell University Press, 1988). His comparative history of political leadership, *Machiavelli's Children: Leaders and Their Legacies in Italy and Japan*, will be published by Cornell in the spring of 2003.

Sheldon W. Simon is Professor of Political Science and Faculty Associate of the Center for Asian Studies and Program in Southeast Asian Studies at Arizona State University, where he has been on the faculty since 1975. He has also served as Chair of Political Science and Director of Asian Studies at the university. Chairman of the Southeast Asian Studies Program at NBR and a member of the Executive Council of the U.S. Council on Security Cooperation in the Asia Pacific, Professor Simon is author or editor of nine books and over 100 scholarly articles and book chapters. His most recent book is an edited volume, *The Many Faces of Asian Security* (Rowman & Littlefield, 2001). He is a consultant to the U.S. Departments of State and Defense and visits Asia annually for research and lectures.

Michael Wills is Codirector of the Strategic Asia Program and Director of Southeast Asian Studies at The National Bureau of Asian Research. Before joining NBR, Mr. Wills was publications coordinator at the Cambodia Development Resource Institute in Phnom Penh. He has also worked for the international business risk consultancy Control Risks Group in London. Mr. Wills has served as technical editor for numerous books and articles, including most recently Richard Ellings and Aaron Friedberg, *Strategic Asia 2001–02: Power and Purpose* (The National Bureau of Asian Research, 2001), and Sheldon Simon, *The Many Faces of Asian Security* (Rowman & Littlefield, 2001).

William C. Wohlforth is Associate Professor of Government at Dartmouth College. He previously taught at Princeton and Georgetown Universities. He is author or editor of three books, including *Witnesses to the End of the Cold War* (Johns Hopkins University Press, 1996) and *The Elusive Balance: Power and Perceptions during the Cold War* (Cornell University Press, 1993). He is also author of numerous articles on Soviet and Russian foreign policy, as well as international relations theory and post-Cold War world politics, including most recently "American Primacy in Perspective," *Foreign Affairs* (July/August 2002). Professor Wohlforth has lived in Russia for extended periods, and is currently working on a study of Russia's adaptation to globalization and U.S. unipolarity.

ABOUT NBR

The National Bureau of Asian Research (NBR) is a nonprofit, nonpartisan institution devoted to bridging the policy, academic, and business communities with advanced, policy-relevant research on issues involving U.S. interests in Asia and the former Soviet Union. Through publications, conferences, television programs, email fora, and other projects, NBR serves as an international clearinghouse for information on a wide range of issues, from trade and investment to national security. NBR does not take policy positions, but rather sponsors studies by the world's leading specialists to promote the development of effective and far-sighted policy.

NBR's research agenda is developed and guided by a bipartisan Board of Advisors composed of individuals drawn from academia, business, and government, including 27 United States Senators and 53 Representatives. Its operations are overseen by a distinguished national Board of Directors. NBR was founded in 1989 with a major grant from the Henry M. Jackson Foundation.